psychology: an introduction

SECOND EDITION

psychology: AN INTRODUCTION

SECOND EDITION

JEROME KAGAN

Harvard University

ERNEST HAVEMANN

 HARCOURT BRACE JOVANOVICH, INC.
New York   Chicago   San Francisco   Atlanta

Cover and opening pages of the eight Parts by Corita Kent.

Illustrations on pages 77, 104, 127, 165, 171, 311, 313, and 405 by Benedict Umy. Figure illustrations by Eric Hieber, J & R Technical Services, Inc., and Andrew Mudryk.

Acknowledgments and copyrights for textual material
and for illustrations begin on page 600.

ISBN: 0-15-572609-9

Library of Congress Catalog Card Number: 70-181538

Printed in the United States of America

PREFACE

The second edition of *Psychology: An Introduction,* though significantly different from the first because of the rate at which psychological knowledge has advanced in the intervening four years, continues to have the same fundamental aims. We have kept the book to its original length, sixteen chapters of reasonable size, because it is especially intended for courses in which a brief book is most useful to instructors and students. Within this limit we have again attempted, through economy in organization and exposition, to cover all topics traditionally considered essential to a solid basic foundation in psychology, so that students who go on to advanced courses will have adequate preparation. But we have also continued to recognize that many students will have no further exposure to psychology and will therefore profit most from a book that applies psychological knowledge to their life situations. For both types of student, we have sought to present the materials clearly and simply, without becoming simplistic or compromising the integrity of the science.

In pursuing these aims in the second edition, we have been helped in many ways by the comments and advice of instructors who have taught from the first edition. In particular, the strong recommendations of users of the book have helped us avoid the temptation to let it grow in size. The problem in this connection was that many important and interesting new research studies and theoretical ideas published in the last four years simply had to be included. On the other hand, a textbook aiming at thoroughness can hardly omit the classical studies. The path of least resistance would have been a longer book—but we were deterred from this path by many comments best summarized by the words of one professor: "For my sake and the sake of my students, don't let the book get one word longer."

How we have tried to make the book contemporary without letting it become one word longer is best illustrated by the materials on learning. In this field, any modern textbook must discuss a number of topics not mentioned in the previous edition—such as operant conditioning of responses controlled by the autonomic nervous system (pages 62-66), new findings on the nature and role of reinforcement (pages 72-81), and the far-reaching implications of how we manage to retrieve (or fail to retrieve) the information stored in long-term memory (pages 96-108). Indeed a third of the bibliographical sources on which the learning chapters are now based did not exist at the time the first edition went to press. To make room for the new, we have condensed some of the materials in the first edition and have eliminated others that no longer seem of overriding importance.

The other changes that have been made in the second edition, largely because of new findings and trends in psychology or to better meet the needs of users of the book, can hardly be enumerated. To cite just a few examples, the section on the history of psychology in Chapter 1 has been expanded to include a discussion of the stimulus-response, humanistic, and cognitive schools of psychology as well as the approaches of Wundt, Galton, James, and Watson. The chapter also contains an expanded treatment of the experimental method—including, for the benefit of students who lack a scientific background, an insert on how to read graphs—and a new section on the relation of psychology to some of today's social problems. The final chapter, on social psychology, has been almost completely revised to reflect the contemporary interest in interpersonal attraction and group dynamics and decisions, including the phenomenon of "risky shift."

In these chapters, and those in between, our aim has been to present all important new findings without omitting any essential materials of the past.

The organization of the book has been changed so that the chapter on language, thinking, and problem solving immediately follows the learning chapters in Part 2; the senses and perception are presented together in Part 3; and the chapter on emotions precedes rather than follows the chapter on motives in Part 5. This is the chapter order for which a considerable majority of instructors expressed a preference.

Many characteristics of the first edition, however, have been retained. For example, there is an early and strong emphasis on learning, to which Chapters 2, 3, and 4 are again devoted. This emphasis reflects a belief that the acquisition of habits and changes in behavior and cognitive processes continue to be core issues in contemporary psychology. Moreover, the discussion of learning seems to provide the student with a strong foundation for the topics that follow; it helps explain and link such otherwise seemingly disparate topics as problem solving, perception, emotions, motives, frustration and conflict, personality, abnormal and developmental psychology, and social behavior.

To ensure full coverage, we have again included the biological correlates of behavior, discussed in the chapters called The Senses (now Chapter 6) and Heredity, Glands, and Nervous System (now Chapter 8). As in the previous edition, however, instructors who prefer to omit these chapters will find that students can skip them without jeopardizing their understanding of the rest of the book. In another chapter that is sometimes omitted (Chapter 13, Measurement), instructors again have the further option of assigning the first part, which explains the important implications of statistics for a general knowledge of psychology, without assigning the mathematical formulas, which have been reserved for the last part. Throughout the book, we have tried to recognize the diversity of today's students and classes in the introductory course by making each chapter a self-contained unit that can be studied and understood independently—so that instructors can assign the chapters in any order they choose and can omit those not pertinent to their needs.

To make the book easier to read and to study, we have again omitted bibliographical references from the body of the text and instead used numbers in parentheses keyed to a chapter-by-chapter bibliography at the end of the book. However, for the benefit of the instructor or student who finds it useful to have access to the number of the page on which a particular study is discussed, all sources mentioned in the bibliography are now listed in the index. The glossary has been expanded to include numerous terms that could not be presented in the text for lack of space but that may be useful to the student in understanding outside readings.

For those unfamiliar with the first edition, it should be added that *Psychology: An Introduction* is the result of a collaboration between an academic psychologist and a professional writer. Perhaps we can best describe our roles by stating that the psychologist has been primarily concerned with comprehensiveness of content, the writer with comprehensibility of style.

Jerome Kagan
Ernest Havemann

acknowledgments

A textbook is never a one-man job—or even a two-man job. This book could never have come into existence without the contributions to scientific knowledge provided by all the psychologists and other scholars cited in the bibliography plus many more who, though not mentioned by name, have advanced the thrust of the discipline. We are especially indebted to a number of psychologists who have greatly helped us as advisers and as critics of part or all of the first edition, the manuscript of the new edition, or both:

Carl W. Backman, University of Nevada
Ellen Berscheid, University of Minnesota
Dean Burchett, Orange Coast College
Thomas N. Cornsweet, Stanford Research Institute
James Croxton, Santa Monica City College
Elton Davis, Pasadena City College
James Deese, The Johns Hopkins University
Charles Dicken, San Diego State College
Peter Dodwell, Queen's University
Dan J. Ehrlich, La Guardia Community College
Donald W. Fiske, University of Chicago
Lois H. Flint, Glendale College
Wallace S. High, Glendale College
William A. Hunt, Loyola University, Chicago
Walter Kintsch, University of Colorado
Salvatore R. Maddi, University of Chicago

Glenn Martin, Santa Monica City College
Hyman Meltzer, Washington University
Allan F. Mirsky, Boston University Medical School
Edward J. Murray, University of Miami
Richard E. Nisbett, University of Michigan
Edward O'Day, San Diego State College
Jerrell Richards, Orange Coast College
Lillian Robbins, Rutgers University
Carol Roberts, Mesa College
Gloria M. Sanders, Clackamas Community College
Gerald Sjule, Orange Coast College
Norman J. Slamecka, University of Toronto
Donovan Swanson, El Camino College
William C. Ward, Educational Testing Service
Carl N. Zimet, University of Colorado Medical Center

We have also been assisted in invaluable ways by Ruth Havemann and Doris Simpson and by the following members of the staff of Harcourt Brace Jovanovich: Judith Aspinwall, Jane Bonnell, Judith Greissman, Alice Lundoff, Mary Monaco, William A. Pullin, Harry Rinehart, Alice Sanchez, Everett M. Sims, Patricia K. Stoltz, Meryl Sussman, and Thomas A. Williamson.

CONTENTS

part four
the body and brain

part five
feelings and motives

part six

the normal and abnormal personality

part seven

individual differences

part eight

the child, the adult, and society

psychology: an introduction

SECOND EDITION

... a new science

that deals with
age-old questions ...

PART ONE

Psychology is a relatively new science—founded less than a century ago—that deals with age-old questions. Its subject matter is something that has interested and puzzled mankind since the beginning of history—namely, the way human beings and other creatures behave and the reasons for their behavior. How do people learn all the complex skills required to get along in the world? How have they acquired the language that enables them to communicate with each other so richly and to pass along the accumulated knowledge of the centuries? What happens when they think? How do they manage to see, hear, and feel the objects in their environment and thus arrive at their perceptions of the world of reality? What are the motives that help shape one person into a world leader and another into an individual who would rather work as little as possible and spend his time listening to music and contemplating the beauties of nature? Why do some people appear to be "normal" and others to behave in ways that are labeled neurotic or even "crazy"?

All these are questions that psychology attempts to answer. However, it does so in ways that—because the subject matter is so old and the methods so new—are still widely misunderstood. An introductory textbook must begin, therefore, with a discussion of how the science began and how it now approaches the problems—in other words, an explanation of what the science is and what it is not.

Chapter 1, "The Scope and Goals of Psychology," suggests the wide range of the subject matter: the great variety of observable activity called *behavior* and also of the *mental activity* that goes on unseen and helps influence and explain behavior. The chapter describes the methods of psychology and includes a brief section on the history of the science and its founders. It also shows how the findings of psychology have been or could be applied to some of the practical problems of everyday life, including the social issues and conflicts that are so important in the United States and indeed around the world.

wHAt is psychology?

CHAPTER 1

THE SCOPE AND GOALS of psychology

Although the science of psychology is only about a century old, the word *psychology* has become one of the most popular in the English language. People often say they "use psychology" to get a job or a raise or to talk parents into a larger allowance. They talk about striking at the "psychological moment." When a friend starts behaving strangely, they say he has a "psychological problem." To judge by the number of times the word is used in everyday conversation, one might suppose that everybody who speaks English knows exactly what it means.

Yet, in actual fact, the science of psychology is quite different from what most people believe it to be, and often its findings are contrary to what people have generally taken for granted about human nature. Many people, for example, pride themselves on being "good psychologists" who can size up another man just by looking at him and can judge the other man's feelings by studying his facial expressions. Scientific investigation has proved that this is not easy at all. If you and your friends try to match the faces with the personalities of the people in Figure 1–1, you will probably find that none of you have much success. You

can you judge a person
by appearance?

1-1

All these people have figured in the news. They are a prominent scientist, professional athlete, author, policeman, political leader, and murderer. After trying to match the photos with these descriptions, turn to page 8 for the correct answers.

what emotions do these faces show?

1-2   These are unposed photographs of people expressing emotions. Of all the human emotions—such as joy, rage, fear, anger, grief, contentment—which are they? After you have made your guesses, check them against Figure 1-2a on page 10.

will probably have the same trouble guessing the emotions that are being expressed in Figure 1-2.

By the time a student arrives at college he has usually been tested and retested in numerous ways—for intelligence, mechanical skill, mathematical ability, and various kinds of vocational aptitude. He has also seen many other tests in newspapers and magazines; he has been invited to score himself as an introvert or an extrovert, an optimist or a pessimist, a good marriage prospect or a bad one. Thus many students think of psychology as being first of all the source for tests of all kinds of human traits and abilities. This is partly true, for tests have been devised that are good predictors of school grades, musical performance, and ability to work efficiently as an accountant or an electronics engineer or a hospital nurse. But testing is only one small part of psychology. And many of the tests seen in newspapers and magazines have no scientific value at all; they are merely parlor games. A psychologist would want to know a lot more than can be revealed by a few true-false questions before he would attempt to assess your personality or try to predict how you might succeed at such a complicated human relationship as marriage.

Many people believe that psychology provides some magic answers that will enable them to solve their own personal problems, advise others, and indeed manipulate the behavior of others to their own advantage. Again this is partly true, for psychologists have learned a great deal about the human personality and methods of relieving personality problems; they also have come to understand many of the factors that influence behavior and how behavior can often be changed by varying these factors. But even the best-trained psychologists, after many years of study and experience, do not claim to perform any magic. A psychologist who tries to help a person solve his personality difficulties knows that it may take a long time even to understand the problems, much less do anything to relieve them. Moreover, as the book will make clear, human behavior springs from so many complicated sources that it is very difficult for a person to understand why he himself behaves as he does, much less to understand and influence the behavior of someone else.

The people shown in Figure 1-1 are: **A,** murderer of fifteen people; **B,** political leader (United States Representative Shirley Chisholm); **C,** scientist (physicist Enrico Fermi); **D,** athlete (golfer Sandra Haynie); **E,** author (playwright Eugene O'Neill); and **F,** New York City policeman.

A. a definition of psychology   No

Some students are so surprised by the content of an introductory psychology course that they have a hard time getting the "feel" of the subject; they keep looking for what they had expected to find and fail to appreciate what is actually there. If you approach the subject with an open mind and are prepared to enjoy being surprised, you will have a much easier and more rewarding time.

What then is psychology really like? As the poet Alexander Pope wrote, "The proper study of mankind is man"—and one way to start trying to define psychology would be as the science that studies man. But this is only a partial definition. Psychology also studies lower animals; it is interested in the behavior of all living creatures, which it designates by the scientific term *organisms.* Indeed comparative psychology, which is the study of organisms other than man in an effort to find comparisons with human behavior, is a flourishing branch of the science—partly because the psychologist can perform experiments with lower animals that it would be unethical to attempt with human beings (for example, the removal of parts of the brain to discover what role these brain structures play in behavior). Moreover, in the case of human beings, psychology is interested not only in behavior but also in patterns of brain activity such as thinking and feelings.

DEFINITION

Perhaps the best possible definition of psychology is this: *Psychology is the science that systematically studies and attempts to explain observable behavior and its relationship to the unseen mental processes that go on inside the organism and to external events in the environment.*

No   *1.* the variety of human behavior

The definition covers an almost breathtaking range of subject matter. To demonstrate the great variety of human behavior and mental processes—and at the same time to introduce some of the major topics covered in this book—let us examine how a college woman might have started this day, from the time she woke up until the time she arrived at her first class.

She wakens quickly at the sound of the alarm, turns off the clock, and turns on the light in her room. Looking out a window for signs of the weather, she notes that the sky is cloudy. For further information she turns on the radio. But she has just missed the weather report, so she dials the telephone number of a friend who is always up early. The friend says there is only a 15 percent chance of rain, and she decides to ignore it when she chooses her clothes for the day.

She eats breakfast, gathers her notebooks, and goes to her car. As she starts the engine she sees that the gas is low and makes a note to stop at a filling station. Backing out of the driveway, she waits for two schoolchildren who are walking by, then for a mail truck. She stops for a traffic light, turns into the street she usually takes to school, finds it blocked off for repairs, and proceeds to an alternate

1-2 A All the faces shown in Figure 1-2 were those of students taking part— each in his own way—in a campus strike.

route. The lot in which she usually parks is filled; so she goes to a different one. Since she does not know the quickest route to her classroom from this lot, she asks another student who is getting out of a car. The directions are complicated—turn left after a block, then right, then cut across a corner of the campus—but she has no trouble following them and is in her usual seat when the class starts. As her instructor begins his lecture, she listens to the words and takes notes. An observer would see nothing but the movement of her pen, yet obviously a great deal of mental processing is going on as she decides which of the words are the key ideas and translates them into her own language.

And so the day begins. It is still very early in the morning of a more or less typical day in the life of a more or less typical student. Yet what a remarkable amount of activity has already occurred!

In this age of electronic computers it has become fashionable to admire the speed and precision of the computer and, conversely, to take a somewhat disparaging view of human capabilities. The computer can add and multiply faster than any human being; it can guide spaceships to the moon and to Mars. Why then should we not concede that the human being is a poor rival to the computer and rapidly becoming obsolete? Why should we bother studying the psychology of a human machine that is so overshadowed by the electronic machine?

10

The young woman, waking and going to school, gives us the answer. She demonstrates that <u>the electronic machine, for all its brilliant accomplishments, does not as yet begin to approach the skill and versatility of the human machine.</u>

Note all the very complicated "inputs" that our human machine has received in the course of the early morning: the sounds of the alarm clock, the radio, the telephone, the instructions on how to walk to the classroom, and the lecture; the sights of the sky, the traffic and traffic signals, and the blocked roadway. Note all the "data processing" she has done: making the decisions on what to wear, to take an alternate route to the campus, to park in an alternate lot. And note how many complicated actions she performed: dressing, eating, driving a car, asking directions, walking to the classroom, taking lecture notes. The human organism is still the most remarkable "machine" ever created. The more one studies it, the more one is forced to marvel at its intricate workings.

2. how psychology views behavior

To the psychologist, the young woman's activities on this early morning fall into several categories that form prominent divisions of the subject matter of the science and of this book. For example, her movements while dressing and driving her car represented skills she did not have when she was born but instead acquired through learning; this important process and the rules it follows are the subject of Chapters 2, 3, and 4. Finding her usual route to the campus blocked presented her with a problem that she immediately surmounted by taking an alternate street—but though her decision seemed easy and indeed almost automatic, it actually required a great deal of complicated mental activity of the kind described in Chapter 5 ("Language, Thinking, and Problem Solving").

Her inputs of sounds and sights depended on her sense organs, in this case her ears and eyes, and the way they respond to the environment and send messages to her brain, as will be explained in Chapter 6 ("The Senses"). Out of the messages from her sense organs she organized meaningful patterns of what was happening in the world around her, as will be explained in Chapter 7 ("Perception"). Her sleeping and eating were responses to biological drives, representing a combination of physiological needs and brain activity, that demanded satisfaction; the drives and how they influence behavior are discussed in Chapter 10 ("Drives and Motives").

3. some other influences on behavior

Even if the topics mentioned up to now were the only forms of behavior and mental activity, psychology would constitute a rich field of study. But there is a good deal more, as can be seen if we compare this young woman with another woman in her class. Let us say that both student A and student B are the same age. They come from much the same kinds of families and went to the very same high school. On their College Boards, which are a kind of intelligence test that measures ability to succeed in college, they made about the same scores (see Figure 1-3).

two students—alike yet different

1-3 In age, background, and College Board scores, these two students are very much alike; in their present behavior in college, they are very different. Why? For a possible answer, see the text.

Miss A.	BACKGROUND	Miss B.
18	Age	18
Excellent	Health	Excellent
None	Physical defects	None
Mechanic	Father	T.V. repairman
Nurse	Mother	Store clerk
San Pedro H.S.	High school	San Pedro H.S.
	COLLEGE BOARD SCORES	
542	Verbal	545
521	Math	519
	RECORD IN COLLEGE	
C's	Grades	A's and B's
Marriage	Ambition	Career
Few, but close	Friends	Many
Yes	Seeks advice?	No
Apologetic	Usual response to criticism	Angry

There the resemblance ends. Student A is content to get C's in her courses; her special ambition is to become a wife and mother; she likes to spend her spare time reading or in the quiet company of a few close friends; she often seeks advice; she seldom says an unkind word about anyone; if she is criticized, she tends to become flustered and to apologize. Student B, on the other hand, studies hard and usually makes A's and B's; her ambition is to be a lawyer; she is usually surrounded by friends; she shuns advice; she is frequently sarcastic and insulting; if she is criticized she strikes back.

These two young women have the same biological drives and have had very similar opportunities for learning; they have an approximately equal capacity for thinking and problem solving; their sense organs operate in much the same ways. Why, then, are they so different?

One reason is that human beings vary in the kinds of events that trigger emotions such as fear and anger and in the way they display their emotions, as will be explained in Chapter 9. Moreover, human behavior springs from a variety of motives. As will be discussed in Chapter 10, all of us as we grow up acquire through the learning process a number of motives or desires that we attempt to fulfill. The pattern of motives—among others, whether we lean more strongly to achievement or affiliation, to independence or dependence—can create innumerable individual differences. Emotions, motives, and many other factors go to make up different kinds of personality and cause some people to engage in what is called abnormal behavior (the subjects of Chapters 11 and 12).

→ *4.* the goals of psychology

GOALS

Thus the scope of psychology is very wide indeed; the subject matter of the science covers all the *overt* or observable behavior that human beings and other organisms exhibit and also the *covert* or hidden mental processes that go on inside the organism and often affect overt behavior. *The goals of psychology,* it can now be added, *are to understand and predict behavior.*

To put this another way, the goal of psychology, as in every science, is to create satisfactory theories—in this case, statements of general principles that provide a plausible explanation for the phenomena of behavior and mental life observed in the past and that, if sufficiently accurate, will be borne out by future phenomena. In the field of learning in particular, as will be seen in the next three chapters, we already have some fairly powerful theories, derived from the evidence of the past, that enable us to predict when and how learning is most likely to take place.

B. the history of psychology

Mankind's efforts to understand and to predict human behavior go back, presumably, to the very origins of the human race. We can assume from what is known about some of the primitive tribes that exist today in isolation from modern civilization that men have always been mystified by their dreams. A man goes to sleep and in his dreams seems to travel. He goes fishing on a distant river; he goes hunting on a distant plain; he meets his friends; he even meets and converses with people who are long since dead. When he wakes up, anyone can tell him that his body has not moved at all from his bed. What could be more natural than to suppose that the human body is also inhabited by a human soul, which can leave and reenter the body at will and survives after death? The ancient Greek philosophers were also fascinated by this apparent division of human existence into body and soul. And they speculated endlessly on the nature of the human mind, which they conceived to be a part of the soul, or perhaps the same thing. This was the age in which the science of mathematics was reaching great heights, and the Greek philosophers marveled that the human mind could create the world of mathematics—a world, though purely imaginary and theoretical, that was much more logical and "pure" than the real world of sleeping and eating and physical illness and death.

As for attempts to predict behavior, the Greeks had their oracles, notably the Delphic Oracle, who were supposed to bring them messages from the gods. Presumably all civilizations, and even the generations that preceded civilization, have had soothsayers, witch doctors, and wise men to whom they looked for

guidance about the future. We still have them today, even in our modern scientific America. Almost every city has its fortune tellers, and the newspapers print columns in which astrologers predict what will happen to us today.

In recent years there seems to have been an increased popular interest among Americans, and especially young people, in such occult matters as astrology and fortune telling with tarot cards; and some students are attracted to the introductory psychology course because they expect it to deal with extrasensory perception, mental telepathy, and clairvoyant insights into the future. The student who has such expectations is likely to be disappointed.

True, some psychologists have made studies of extrasensory perception (or ESP for short), which means the ability to receive information about the environment through some rather mysterious means existing outside the channels of the known human senses of vision, hearing, taste, smell, and touch—for example, the ability to make better than chance judgments of how cards are arranged in a shuffled deck or to perform mental telepathy, which means the ability of one mind to perceive what is going on in another mind without any known means of communication, as if somehow one brain could send invisible signals to another. A few psychologists have decided on the basis of experiments that there is firm evidence that some people are gifted with ESP (1, 2).* However, the great majority of psychologists remain unconvinced and believe that the whole weight of scientific knowledge and everyday observation rules against any such possibilities. (If there were such a thing as ESP and it were actually possible to sense the arrangement of cards in a deck, then it would seem that the Nevada gambling houses would be consistent losers and would have to go out of business.) Though a minority claim to have found evidence supporting the existence of ESP, most psychologists believe that the evidence is at best highly controversial and the whole idea rather implausible.

Indeed what distinguishes the mainstream of psychological investigation from many previous attempts to understand and predict human behavior is that psychology refuses to regard man as the possessor or creature of unproved forces. Although a few of its practitioners may hold to the contrary, psychology does not believe that a man's life is affected by the position of the stars at the moment of his birth. Moreover, it does not seek divine revelations from some Delphic Oracle and is not content to describe man as some past philosopher, however brilliant, may have imagined him to be. It does not accept the adages of previous generations, no matter how common-sensical those adages may seem to be. (Many of the adages, as a matter of fact, are mutually contradictory. Is it true that "a bird in the hand is worth two in the bush," or do we do better to believe "nothing ventured, nothing gained"?)

Instead, the science of psychology is *empirical*—that is, it is based on controlled experiments and on observations made with the greatest possible precision and objectivity. This is the quality it shares with other natural sciences, such as physics and chemistry; this, indeed, is what makes it a science.

*The numbers in parentheses, which will be found throughout the book, are keyed to references and source materials (concerning both text and illustrations) that are listed at the end of the volume.

/. Wilhelm Wundt and his laboratory

Like other sciences, psychology evolved slowly and was the result of many contributions by many men. The philosophers of the seventeenth and eighteenth centuries helped create the realistically inquiring attitude of mind that made the science possible. The physiologists of the nineteenth century did their part by making numerous discoveries about the human nervous system and the human brain. The year in which all these factors came together and psychology emerged as a science in its own right is usually put at 1879, when Wilhelm Wundt established the first psychology laboratory at Germany's University of Leipzig.

Wilhelm Wundt, shown at left, was a solemn, hard-working, and tireless man who devoted himself to scholarship from the time he was a boy until he died at the age of eighty-eight. A preacher's son, he first became a physician, but instead of practicing medicine he taught physiology. He soon lost interest in the physical aspects of human behavior, for he was much more concerned with consciousness. His laboratory was the first place in the world where a serious and organized attempt was made to analyze and explain human consciousness.

Wundt was the University of Leipzig's most popular lecturer; no classroom there was big enough to hold all the students who wanted to listen. And his laboratory attracted scholars from all over the world, including a number from the United States, who absorbed the notion of experimental psychology and returned to their homelands to introduce the work to others. Wundt and his followers belonged to what is known as the *structural* school of psychology, so named because its members concentrated on the structure or contents of conscious experience, such as sensations, images, and feelings. Their method was introspection, or inward examination of mental processes.

Compared with some of the modern experiments that will be discussed later in the chapter, Wundt's work may seem rather unexciting. For example, he was interested in the human reaction to the sounds of a metronome, and he and his students spent hours in the laboratory listening to the click of a metronome set at low speeds and high speeds, sometimes sounding only a few clicks at a time, sometimes sounding many. As they listened, they tried to analyze their conscious experiences. Wundt decided that listening to some kinds of clicks was more pleasant than listening to others. He noticed that he had a feeling of slight tension before each click and a feeling of relief afterward. He also concluded that a rapid series of beats made him conscious of excitement and that a slow series made him relaxed. Wundt and his students listened to the same kinds of clicks, then carefully reported their conscious experiences and compared notes. They may not have produced powerful laws about behavior, but they did establish a systematic method of study.

→ 2. Francis Galton and measurement

Wilhelm Wundt and his followers were interested mostly in discovering in what ways human beings are alike—in particular, whether they had the same

Wundt

STRUCTURAL
PSYCHOLOGY

Galton

INDIVIDUAL

DIFFERENCES

Individual differences
in children's play

kinds of conscious experiences in response to the same kinds of events, such as the clicks of a metronome. To this day, the sameness of human behavior is one of the chief interests of psychology; it still seeks laws governing the kinds of behavior that all people have in common.

Another of its modern interests, however, is the study of *individual differences,* a phrase you will find used time and again in this book and in any future psychology courses you may take. Psychology tries to learn, for example, why the young woman discussed earlier in this chapter is so different from the other woman in her class. No two human beings, not even identical twins, are exactly alike; they differ physically, and their behavior is different. Psychologists want to know why and how they got this way.

In this area the pioneer was Francis Galton, an Englishman whose most important work was done in the 1880's, shortly after Wilhelm Wundt's laboratory first opened its doors. By coincidence, Galton was also a physician by early training, but there the resemblance to Wundt ends—proof that even two of the founding fathers of the same science are likely to display enormous individual differences.

As can be seen on page 15, the two men were quite unlike in physical appearance. And where Wundt was solemn and studious, Galton was quick and restless. Before he began concentrating on the work that made him famous in psychology, he was at various times an inventor, world traveler, geographer, and meteorologist.

Galton began his psychological studies because of an interest in heredity. He made a study that showed that men who had achieved unusual success in life had sired a greater number of successful sons than less eminent fathers. He also discovered that when a tall man married a tall woman, their children were usually taller than average. This seemed to him to be another proof of the importance of heredity, although he was baffled by the fact that the children, though taller than average, were usually not so tall as the parents. From these studies and observations he moved on to attempt measurements of human size, strength, and abilities. He invented devices to test people's hearing, sense of smell, color vision, and ability to judge weights and used them on thousands of people. At one time he set up his equipment at an International Health Exhibition in London. So great was popular interest in the emerging science of psychology that people actually paid an entrance fee to visit his laboratory and contribute their measurements to his growing array of statistics.

No matter what Galton measured, he always found wide individual differences. Galton established the principle that all human traits vary over a wide range from small to large, weak to strong, slow to fast; this is true of height, weight, physical strength, and various kinds of abilities, including, as we now know, the ability to learn, which is commonly called intelligence. There can be no further doubt, after Galton's discoveries, that the men who drew up the Declaration of Independence were only partly right when they wrote, "All men are created equal." Men may be equal in the eyes of God or at the bar of justice, but in other respects they are not identical.

3. William James's "science of mental life"

James

FUNCTIONAL
PSYCHOLOGY

The most prominent of the early American psychologists was William James, whose photograph is shown at left. James was another man who studied medicine but never practiced. Like Galton, he possessed many talents and had a difficult time finding his true vocation. At one time he wanted to be an artist, then a chemist, and once he joined a zoological expedition to Brazil. In his late twenties he suffered a severe mental breakdown and went through a long period of depression in which he seriously thought of committing suicide. But he recovered—largely, he believed, through what he called "an achievement of the will"—and went on to become a Harvard professor and a prolific writer on psychology and philosophy.

James firmly believed in experimentation, and there is some evidence that he established a laboratory of sorts at Harvard even before the more famous Wundt laboratory opened in Leipzig. But James himself never conducted any experiments; he was much more interested in observing the workings of his own mind and the behavior of other people in real-life situations. He differed from Wundt in that he took a much broader view of human consciousness; he was less interested in its structure or contents than in how it helps men adjust to their environments. He and his followers developed the *functional* school of psychology, so named because it emphasized the functions of mental processes, especially as related to behavior, rather than their structure.

A textbook written by James began with the words, "Psychology is the study of mental life." But the distinguishing feature of mental life, he felt, was that human beings constantly seek certain end results and must constantly choose among various means of achieving them. The study of the long-term and short-term goals men seek and the actions they take or abandon in pursuing these goals was the core of James's work. In one passage he wrote:

> I would . . . if I could, be both handsome and fat and well-dressed, and a great athlete, and make a million a year, be a wit, a *bon-vivant,* and a lady-killer, as well as a philosopher; a philanthropist, statesman, warrior, and African explorer, as well as a "tone-poet" and saint. But the thing is simply impossible. The millionaire's work would run counter to the saint's; the *bon-vivant* and the philanthropist would trip each other up; the philosopher and the lady-killer could not well keep house in the same tenement of clay. Such different characters may conceivably at the outset of life be possible to a man. But to make any of them actual, the rest must more or less be suppressed. . . . This is as strong an example as there is of . . . selective industry of the mind. (3)

James contributed some valuable observations on specific aspects of human experience, such as habits, emotions, religious feelings, and mental disturbances. But mostly he was interested in the broad pattern of human strivings—the cradle-to-grave progress of human beings as thinking organisms who adopt certain goals and ambitions, including spiritual ones, and struggle by various means to attain the goals or become reconciled to failure.

4. John Watson, behaviorist

Watson

BEHAVIORISM

Was William James perhaps more a philosopher than a scientist? One American who thought so was John Watson, who about the year 1913 founded the movement known as *behaviorism*. He declared that "mental life" was something that cannot be seen or measured and thus cannot be studied scientifically. Instead of trying to examine any such vague thing as "mental life" or consciousness, he concluded, psychologists should concentrate on overt behavior—the kinds of actions that are plainly visible.

There was no room in Watson's theories for anything like James's "achievement of the will." He believed that everything we do is predetermined by our past experiences; to him all human behavior was a series of events in which a *stimulus*, that is, an event in the environment, produces a *response*, that is, an observable muscular movement or some physiological reaction, such as increased heart rate or glandular secretion, that can also be observed and measured with the proper instruments. (For example, shining a bright light into the eye of a person or other organism is a stimulus that causes an immediate response in which the pupil of the eye contracts; a loud and unexpected noise is a stimulus that usually causes the response of muscular contraction or "jumping" and increased heart rate.) Watson believed that through *conditioning*, a type of learning that will be discussed in Chapter 2, almost any kind of stimulus could be made to produce almost any kind of response; indeed he once said that he could take any dozen babies at birth and, by conditioning them in various ways, turn them into anything he wished—doctor, lawyer, beggar, or thief.

Watson was inclined to doubt that there was any such thing as a human mind. He conceded that human beings had thoughts, but he believed that these were simply a form of talking to oneself, by making tiny movements of the vocal cords. He also conceded that people have what they call feelings, but he believed that these were only some form of conditioned glandular response to a stimulus in the environment.

Watson's theories burst upon the world at a time when many psychologists were dissatisfied with the progress of their science. The attempts to examine man's consciousness—his "mental life," to use the James terminology—had not been very fruitful; there was some question whether looking inward into the human mind was really scientific at all. The notion that it is better to examine and measure overt behavior than to try to study the invisible mind was very appealing, and for many years Watson was the most influential of American psychologists.

5. S-R psychology and B. F. Skinner

One school of psychological thought that grew out of Watson's theories is known as *stimulus-response psychology*, or S-R psychology for short. The S-R psychologists emphasize study of the stimuli that produce behavioral responses, the rewards and punishments that help establish and maintain these responses, and the modification of behavior through changes in the patterns of rewards and punishments. The leader of the S-R school has been B. F. Skinner, who ranks as another of the most prominent American psychologists of the past half-century. Skinner has been chiefly interested in the learning process and has revised and expanded Watson's ideas into a theory of learning that continues to influence much psychological thinking. He has made many important contributions to our knowledge of how patterns of rewards and punishments produce and modify connections between a stimulus and a response and thus help control the organism's behavior—often in the most complex ways.

6. some new schools of psychology

Skinner

S-R PSYCHOLOGY

There is no doubt that Watson and his successors among the S-R psychologists did a great deal to advance the science. They emphasized that psychology should be empirical and based as much as possible on controlled experiments and measurements of behavior and that too much introspection (that is, examination of a "mental life" that nobody but its possessor can observe in operation) can lead to chaos. But for many years Watson's insistence on behaviorism put psychology into a straitjacket. There is a good deal more to human life and behavior than a series of conditioned responses or other responses following one after another in a pattern over which we have no control. Human beings are by no means pieces of machinery that automatically perform in a certain way every time a certain button is pushed. We do make choices, as William James pointed out. We have complicated thoughts, feelings, emotions, and attitudes that cannot possibly be explained by a simple pushbutton theory.

All these aspects of "mental life," once ruled out of bounds by the behaviorists, have now been drawn back into the field of study and have led to the development of a number of new schools of psychology.

One of the new schools is known as *cognitive psychology;* its followers maintain that human behavior cannot be explained in full by stimulus-response connections and indeed that the human mind is not just a reflection of the stimuli that its possessor has encountered; instead the mind actively processes the information it receives into new forms and categories. The cognitive psychologists tend to think of the mind as a sort of "mental executive" that actively makes comparisons and decisions. A simple example sometimes cited is this: if you say a string of digits to another person, such as 5, 9, 3, 2, 8, 6, then repeat the same string with one digit missing, or 5, 9, 3, 8, 6, your listener will have no trouble stating immediately that the missing number is 2. What has happened, as the cognitive psychologists interpret it, is that he is not just making a specific response dictated by a specific stimulus but instead has engaged in some sort of decision-making process that scans the two strings of digits, compares them, and notes the difference. What is most important about human mental activity, the cognitive psychologists believe, is that it includes such comparisons and understandings, as well as the discovery of meanings and the use of knowledge to find new principles that aid in constructive thinking and problem solving.

Perhaps the leading figure of the cognitive school is the Swiss psychologist Jean Piaget, who has extensively investigated the manner in which the mental

Piaget

COGNITIVE
PSYCHOLOGY

Rogers   Maslow

CLIENT- CENTERED THERAPY   SELF-ACTUALIZATION

skills of children develop as they grow older. Piaget's observations of the stage-by-stage process through which children become increasingly able to understand and think about new situations (pages 530–32) are among the outstanding psychological contributions of recent years.

NO

Another new school with a quite different approach is called *humanistic psychology;* this school, as its name implies, is especially interested in the qualities that distinguish human beings from other animals. Among the leaders of humanistic psychology have been the American psychologists Carl Rogers, who invented the optimistic form of treatment of emotional disturbances called *client-centered therapy* (pages 415-16), and Abraham Maslow, who introduced the theory that human beings possess a motive called *self-actualization* (pages 356-57), which makes them strive to realize fully their potential for creativity, dignity, and self-worth.

7. Sigmund Freud and psychoanalysis

Another movement that originated apart from psychology but has had a profound influence on psychological thinking is the school of *psychoanalysis,* which was founded around the turn of the century by Sigmund Freud. Freud began his career in Vienna in the 1880's as a physician and neurologist. He became interested in psychological processes as the result of his experiences with patients who were suffering from hysteria—that is, from paralysis of the legs or arms that seemed to have no physical cause. His final theories represent a lifetime of observing and treating many kinds of neurotic patients and also of attempting to analyze his own personality.

Freud himself was rather neurotic in his youth, suffering from feelings of anxiety and deep depression. He retained some neurotic symptoms all his life; he was a compulsive smoker of as many as twenty cigars a day, was nervous about

Freud

traveling, and was given to what were probably hypochondriacal complaints about poor digestion, constipation, and heart palpitation. However, he managed to overcome his early inclinations toward depression and lived a rich professional, family, and social life—an indication that in his case the physician had managed to heal himself, at least in large part.

One of Freud's great insights into the human personality was the discovery of how it is influenced by *unconscious processes,* especially motives of which we are unaware. At first his ideas were bitterly attacked; many people were repelled by his notion that man, far from being a rational animal, is largely at the mercy of his irrational unconscious thoughts. Many were shocked by his emphasis on the role of sexual motives (which were prominent among those that the society of that period preferred to deny) and particularly by his insistence that even young children have intense sexual desires. Over the years, however, the furor has died out. There is considerable controversy over the value of psychoanalytic methods in treating neurotic patients, but even those who criticize psychoanalysis as a form of therapy accept some of Freud's basic notions about personality and its formation. His theories will be discussed in detail on pages 404-08.

NINE PSYCHOLOGISTS

1. WUNDT (STRUC.)
2. GALTON (DIFFER.)
3. JAMES (FUNC.)
4. WATSON (BEHAV.)
5. SKINNER (S-R)
6. PIAGET (COG)
7. ROGERS }
NO *8. MASLOW* } *(HUM.)*
9. FREUD (ANAL.)

All the various strands of psychological thinking that have been described here are now being drawn together, and it appears likely that the science is entering its richest and most rewarding period—in which it will manage to combine all the best features of Wundt's structuralism, Galton's interest in individual differences and statistical methods, James's concern with the functionalism of man's will and spiritual aspirations, Watson's warning that science must be kept empirical, the importance of learning as emphasized by the S-R psychologists, the cognitive psychologists' view of mental activity as a processing of information, the humanists' concern for man's dignity and worth, and Freud's insights into some of the more baffling aspects of human personality. Although followers of the various schools often disagree sharply with one another, all have made contributions that may someday be synthesized into general theories that will greatly expand man's knowledge of his behavior and his mental processes and suggest ways to alleviate emotional disturbances and better understand human nature.

*c.*the methods of psychology

Each school of psychology has tended to emphasize one aspect of behavior or mental processes, and each has developed its own preferred methods for studying the phenomena in which it has been most interested. As has already been stated, the structuralists concentrated on introspective reports on the elements of consciousness, the functionalists on the relationship between introspective reports of consciousness and adjustment to the environment. The behaviorists and S-R psychologists have taken the more mechanical view that psychology is essentially a study of what the organism does, and that what the organism does can in turn be explained as a series of stimulus-response connections.

In general, because human behavior and mental processes take such a wide variety of forms, psychology has had to adopt a number of different ways of studying them and is constantly seeking new ways. Among the most prominent methods of study now in use are the following.

→ 1. the experiment

The most powerful tool of psychology, as of all sciences, is the study method known as the *experiment*—in which the psychologist, usually in his laboratory, makes a careful and rigidly controlled examination of cause and effect. Just as the chemist can determine that combining hydrogen and oxygen will produce water, the psychologist can determine that certain conditions will result in certain measurable changes in the behavior of his subjects, either human or animal.

For example, one psychologist was interested in this question: If a person is suffering from anxiety—that is, if he is worried and fearful about what might be about to happen to him—is he more likely than usual to seek the company of other people? This is an important question because it concerns the effects of anxiety, which as will be seen in Chapter 9 is one of the most influential of human emotions, and also the operation of the affiliation motive, which will be discussed in detail in Chapter 10. In everyday terms, the question gets to the core of whether it is true, as is generally believed, that "misery loves company."

To answer the question, the psychologist devised an experiment in which women students at a university, when they arrived at his laboratory to take part in the study, found a frightening looking piece of apparatus and were told that it was designed to deliver severe electric shocks. After being thus made anxious about the nature of the experiment, they were told that they had their choice of waiting their turn alone or in the company of other subjects; and the experimenter carefully noted their decisions. It turned out that only 9 percent preferred to wait alone and fully 63 percent preferred company, while 28 percent said that company or lack of it made no difference to them.

The Independent and Dependent Variables. Every experiment is an attempt to discover relationships among certain conditions or events that can be changed or that result from changes; these are called *variables*. The experimenter sets up some of the conditions; he controls and manipulates them. Any condition controlled by the experimenter, because it is set up independently of anything the subject does or does not do, is called an *independent variable.* The change in the subject's behavior that results from a change in an independent variable is called the *dependent variable.* In the experiment with what the university women believed was a shock machine, the subjects' degree of anxiety was the *independent variable.* Their behavior in response to the independent variable—that is, their decision whether to wait alone or in company—was the *dependent variable.*

In most human situations, in and out of the laboratory, there are many variables. Ordinarily, however, the experimenter wants to study the effect of only one independent variable; therefore he tries to hold all other variables constant.

In this case, for example, he did not want his results to be confused by any differences between women and men (the sex variable); therefore he studied only female subjects. He was not interested in the effect of any age variable; therefore he chose subjects who were all of college age rather than a mixed group of adults, teenagers, and elementary school pupils. He manipulated only one independent variable, degree of anxiety, and measured its effect on one dependent variable, the tendency to prefer company.

The Control Group.   As has been said, measurements of the dependent variable in this experiment showed 9 percent of subjects preferring to wait alone, 63 percent preferring company, and 28 percent in the "don't care" category. As you doubtless have already decided, however, these results are strangely unsatisfactory; it is impossible to figure out, from these figures alone, what if anything the experiment proves. The natural questions to ask are: What would have happened if the subjects had *not* been made anxious? What kind of preferences would they then have displayed toward waiting alone or in company?

To answer these questions, the psychologist used another important experimental tool known as a *control group*. He selected an approximately equal number of women students from the same university, asked them to report to the same laboratory, gave them the same choice of waiting alone or in company—but did not make them anxious. Instead of seeing and being told about a "shock machine," they were told that the experiment would not be at all unpleasant. Of these nonanxious subjects in the control group, it turned out, 7 percent preferred to wait alone, 33 percent preferred company, and 60 percent were in the "don't care" category. As you can see, this information about the control group enables us to interpret the results for the anxious women. The total design of the experiment included manipulation of an *independent variable* (anxiety) and measurement of the resulting changes in a *dependent variable* (preference for company, or what is called affiliative behavior), for both an *experimental group* (the subjects made anxious) and a *control group* (the nonanxious subjects). The results, which are presented in several forms in Figure 1-4, show clearly that at least under these particular experimental circumstances, college women suffering from anxiety are much more likely to display affiliative behavior than women who are free from anxiety (4).

Control groups are essential to many psychological experiments, and their selection demands considerable care. In dealing with human subjects, the ideal method would be to find many pairs of identical twins, who, as will be seen in Chapter 8, are as nearly alike as any two people can possibly be, and assign one member of each pair to the experimental group and the other to the control group. Since this is usually impossible, experimenters take many other precautions to ensure that their experimental and control groups are similar in all important respects. In most experiments on learning, for example, a psychologist would want to make sure that his experimental and control groups were approximately equal at least in average age and average number of grades or years of college completed—as well as, if at all possible, in average scores on intelligence tests and average grades obtained in their classes.

1-4

The graphs used to report the results of psychological experiments are simply a convenient way of enabling the reader to grasp the results very quickly, often at a single glance. As is explained in the text, most psychological experiments measure what happens to a dependent variable when an independent variable is changed. The measurements can usually be expressed in figures—such as the percentages of subjects in the "shock machine" experiment who preferred to wait alone, preferred company, or were in the "don't care" category. These figures can be shown in a table, as in illustration A. Or the figures can be converted into a bar graph (B) or a line graph (C).

In this bar graph, as in most, measurements made by the experimenter—the dependent variable—are plotted along the vertical axis at the left, called the ordinate. Other conditions of the experiment are plotted along the horizontal axis or abscissa. The percentages of subjects who preferred each type of waiting condition are shown by the height of the bars—colored bars for those in the experimental group (made anxious), shaded bars for those in the control group (nonanxious). By laying a ruler across the top of each bar to the figures on the ordinate, as indicated by the dashed lines, you can determine that the height of the bars represents exactly the same figures shown in table A—for example, 9 percent of the experimental group and 7 percent of the control group preferring to be alone, 63 percent of the experimental group and only 33 percent of the control group preferring company. The striking difference in the heights of the colored and shaded bars showing percentages preferring company makes the meaning of the experiment quite evident.

In the line graph, dots are put down in their proper place in relation to the ordinate and abscissa and then connected by lines—a colored line for the experimental group, a black line for the control group. Again, the exact percentages can be determined by running a ruler from the line to the figures on the ordinate, as indicated by the dashed lines.

Single Blind and Double Blind. In many experiments, another precaution is necessary. For example, one way of studying the effect of marijuana on a person's ability to drive an automobile would be to recruit an experimental group who would receive a known dosage of the drug and a control group who would not receive the drug, then measure their performance on a test simulating driving performance. But obviously their performance might be affected by their knowledge of whether they had taken the drug and their expectations of what it might do to them. To avoid this possibility, it would be important to keep them from knowing whether they had received the drug; this could be done by giving half the subjects an injection of the drug and the other half an injection of a salt solution that would have no effect, without telling them which was which. This experimental method, in which subjects are prevented from knowing whether they belong to the experimental or the control group, is called the *single blind technique.*

Not even the single blind technique, however, would ensure valid results, for if the experimenter knew which of his subjects had or had not taken the drug, his judgment of their driving performance might be affected by this knowledge. To make the experiment foolproof, the drug or salt solution would have to be injected by a third party so that the experimenter himself would have no way

TABLE

A		Subjects' preferences while waiting	
	ALONE	COMPANY	"DON'T CARE"
Anxious subjects (experimental group)	9%	63%	28%
Nonanxious subjects (control group)	7%	33%	60%

BAR GRAPH

LINE GRAPH

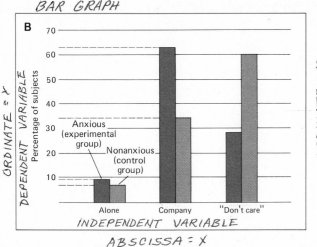

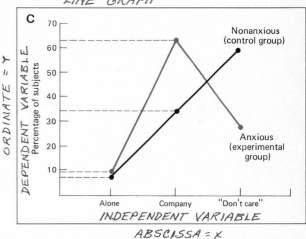

of knowing which subjects had received which kind of injection. This method, in which neither the subject nor the experimenter knows who is in the experimental group and who is in the control group, is the *double blind technique*. It is particularly valuable in studying the effects of all kinds of drugs—for example, the adrenalin that has been used in studies of emotions (pages 311–12) and the various tranquilizers and antidepressants used in the treatment of emotional disturbances (page 424). It is also used in other experiments where knowledge of the experimental conditions might affect the performance of the subjects or the judgment of the experimenter.

The Virtues of the Experiment. As developed and refined over the years, and with the checks provided by such methods as use of a control group and the double blind technique, the experiment is indeed psychology's most powerful tool. For one thing, an experiment can be repeated by another experimenter at another time and in another place, ruling out the possibility that the results were accidental or influenced by the first experimenter's personality or preconceived notions of what would happen. (In this connection, a word frequently found in psychological literature is *replicate;* to replicate an experiment is to perform it again in the same manner and obtain the same results.) When facts have been established by the experimental method and verified time and again by other experimenters, we can have great faith in their validity.

→ 2. naturalistic observation

In many cases, unfortunately, experiments are impossible. This is true not only in psychology but in other sciences as well; astronomers cannot manipulate the planets and stars but can only watch their behavior. Psychologists work under a special handicap, however, because it would be highly unethical to perform many experiments that might result in important additions to our store of knowledge. For example, we cannot deliberately rear a group of children under conditions of brutal deprivation and punishment and then compare their behavior with a control group brought up under more humane conditions.

One thing the psychologist can do, however, is what the astronomer does— observe events pertinent to his science with extreme care and precision and with an open and unprejudiced mind. Thus some of our most valuable knowledge of the behavior of infants and how they develop has come from science-oriented observers who actually went into the homes where babies were growing up. Or sometimes young children have been brought into nurseries where they could be watched at play and in contact with other children, often by observers looking through a one-way mirror so that they could see the children without themselves being seen, as shown in Figure 1-5. This is the study method known as *naturalistic observation.*

Unlike the experimenter, the investigator who is using the method of naturalistic observation does not manipulate the situation and cannot control all

a hidden observer studies child behavior

1-5   Unseen behind a one-way mirror, an investigator uses the method of naturalistic observation to study a child at play. From the outside the panel looks like a sheet of clear glass. From the inside it looks like a mirror.

the variables. Indeed he tries to remain unseen, as behind the one-way mirror, or at least as inconspicuous as possible, lest his very presence affect the behavior that he is trying to study. This method has been especially useful in adding to our knowledge not only of children but also of animals and the people of other societies.

In a sense all human beings constantly use the technique of observation; everybody observes the behavior of other people and draws some conclusions from this behavior. If we note that a woman student dislikes speaking up in a classroom and blushes easily in social situations, we conclude that she is shy, and we treat her accordingly. (We may try to put her at her ease, or if we feel so inclined, we may enjoy embarrassing her and making her squirm.) Scientific observations are much more rigorously disciplined than those ordinarily made in everyday life. The observer sticks to the facts. He tries to describe behavior objectively and exactly, and he is loath to jump to conclusions about the motives behind it.

3. tests

The pioneer work done by Francis Galton on tests of human abilities has already been mentioned. Since Galton's time, many more tests have been devised, measuring not only abilities but feelings, motives, attitudes, and opinions; and the tests have been tried on enough persons to determine exactly what they measure and how well. As will be seen in Chapter 14, a carefully designed test—which itself has been tested by repeated use and by analysis of the results—is a valuable tool for exploring human behavior and especially for comparing one human being with another.

4. interviews

Kinsey

One of the best-known studies using the interview method was the work of Alfred Kinsey, who became interested in human sexual behavior when some of his students at Indiana University asked him for sexual advice. When he went to the university library for information, he found many books of opinion about sexual behavior but almost none that cast any light on what kind of sexual experiences men and women actually had in real life or how often. So Kinsey determined to find out, and the only possible way seemed to be to interview as many men and women as he could and ask them about their sexual feelings and experiences from childhood until the present time, as he is shown doing at the left. His well-known reports on male and female sexual behavior were the result.

5. questionnaires

Closely related to the interview is the *questionnaire*, which is especially useful in gathering information quickly from large numbers of people. A questionnaire is a set of written questions that can be answered easily, usually by putting a checkmark in the appropriate place. In order to obtain accurate results, a questionnaire must be carefully worded. For example, an investigator interested in crime might want to know whether the inmates of a state penitentiary had fathers who tended to be very lenient or very strict. But if he simply asked, "Was your father very lenient toward you?" he might not get accurate answers. For one thing, many convicts would not know the meaning of the word *lenient*. For another, many people tend to answer *yes* to any question just to be agreeable. So he would probably put the question like this:

When you did something that your father did not like, did he

- ☐ always spank you?
- ☐ sometimes spank you?
- ☐ bawl you out?

- ☐ tell you you were a bad boy and let it go at that?
- ☐ laugh and forget it?

Interviews and questionnaires are sometimes challenged by critics who think that the people who are asked the questions may not tell the truth. Kinsey's work, for example, has been attacked on the ground that nobody would be likely to be honest about his sexual behavior. But an investigator who is experienced in interviewing or in making up questionnaires and checking them against the facts that he can obtain in other ways knows how to recognize people who are not telling the truth or who are exaggerating. Interviews and questionnaires do not always reveal the complete truth, but when carefully planned and executed, they can be extremely useful.

To summarize this section on the methods of psychological investigation, it should be pointed out again that human behavior is considerably more complex than the behavior of even the most remarkable computer ever invented. It is certainly much harder to study than is the behavior of two chemicals in a test tube or gas in a pressure chamber. Moreover, human beings cannot be manipulated the way the chemist can manipulate chemicals. If we want to find out whether very lenient or very harsh treatment by parents inclines a child toward being a criminal, we cannot deliberately indulge a thousand selected children and subject another thousand to brutal discipline. We have to study human behavior as best we can, by any humane method that seems scientifically promising.

No D. applications of psychology

All our modern sciences were founded by men whose chief motive was simply to satisfy their own curiosity about the mysteries of the universe. The first physicists were curious about the nature of light and the behavior of falling objects, the first chemists about the nature of matter. These pioneers sought knowledge for the sake of knowledge; they were interested in *pure science;* they did not know or especially care whether their discoveries would ever serve any useful purpose.

Yet the discoveries of the pure scientists have of course been put to practical use, and in our modern world we are surrounded on all sides by *applied science.* The physicist's knowledge of electricity has been put to work in lighting and air conditioning the buildings in which we live and work. The automobile is also a product of applied physics, as are radios, television sets, and spaceships. Applied chemistry has produced medicines, plastics, and synthetic fabrics.

Psychology, too, is a pure science that has already had many practical applications, even though it is much younger than physics or chemistry. In today's world, many psychologists are busy studying the pure science; they are interested solely in increasing our knowledge of human behavior. Many other psychologists, however, are engaged in the practice of applied science and are using the knowledge we now have in many practical ways. This work has changed our world more than most people realize.

1. clinical psychology and counseling

Clinical psychology is the diagnosis and treatment of behavior problems. *Counseling* is a closely related field that offers assistance to people who need temporary guidance on problems such as school difficulties, vocational choices, or marriage conflicts. More psychologists today specialize in these two fields than in any other branch of the science; the number has been variously estimated at somewhere between 39 percent (5) and 48 percent (6).

In diagnosing problems, clinical and counseling psychologists often use the kinds of tests of personality, abilities, vocational aptitudes, and interests that will be described in Chapter 14. In the treatment of behavior disorders, clinical psychologists use the method called *psychotherapy* (Chapter 12), which generally takes the form of getting the troubled person to talk about his fears and conflicts and perhaps, with the psychologist's help, to see them in a new and more constructive light. In general, clinical psychologists believe that mental and emotional disorders that have no obvious physical basis are the result of an unfortunate form of learning; it is the patient's prior experiences, the attitudes he has developed toward them, and the emotions they now arouse that account for his present troubles.

Many clinical psychologists practice *group therapy,* which is the treatment of a number of people at the same time—partly to save time and money and partly because groups often seem to be more helpful than individual therapy. One such method is the recently well-publicized *encounter group,* which will be discussed further in Chapter 12.

2. psychology in schools and industry

Some clinical psychologists and counselors work in schools, where they not only attempt to diagnose the cause of students' problems but also consult with teachers and families in an attempt to change the conditions that have caused the problems. Others work in industrial firms, where it has been found that many employees fail at the job not because of lack of skill but because of bad personal relations with their fellow workers or bosses. In addition, psychology has found many other applications in the schools and in industry.

In the schools, psychology's best-known contribution has been its standardized tests. Intelligence tests offer a reasonably good prediction of how well a student can be expected to perform—although, as will be discussed in Chapter 14, they have certain weaknesses and are more successful in rating students from middle-income homes than students from low-income homes. Standardized achievement tests are a generally accurate measure of how well an individual student is progressing year by year in various skills, such as reading and arithmetic, or of how one school compares with others in the nation.

Psychology has also influenced teaching methods, the organization of the curriculum, and the preparation of textbooks and educational films. Indeed most of the principles of learning that will be discussed in Part 2 of this book can be applied to schoolwork. Some colleges have a special course in the applied psychology of learning designed to help students do better in their classes.

In industry, psychologists have discovered many facts about worker fatigue, working hours, rest periods, and employee morale. They have also created many training devices that make it easier to learn particular skills and contributed to *human engineering,* which is the design of equipment and machinery that will be more efficient and easier to use because they fit the actual size, strength, and capabilities of the human beings who will use them.

3. public opinion surveys

The Gallup Poll is one well-known example of the application of psychological techniques to the examination of public opinion, which has disclosed many previously unknown facts about how people feel about all kinds of public issues, including military expenditures, welfare programs, racial tensions, sexual behavior, birth control and abortion, marriage and divorce, and many others. Thanks to public opinion surveys, it is now possible to acquire much more information than ever before on what our society is really like and how opinion actually divides on important social issues.

Public opinion surveys depend for their accuracy on two techniques that will be discussed in Chapter 13. Careful *sampling,* that is, selecting a group of people who are representative of the entire population in regard to education, income, religion, place of residence, and political affiliation, makes it possible to determine the attitudes of the nation as a whole by surveying a relatively small number of people. *Statistical analysis* makes it possible to interpret the validity and significance of the results. Public opinion surveys have been used to predict election results and by businessmen to measure the reaction to various types of products and sales and advertising campaigns. Probably their greatest value, however, is the information they help provide on social problems—a topic that deserves discussion of its own.

NO E. psychology and social problems

As anyone who reads a newspaper or watches a television news program is well aware, hardly a day goes by without some important and often disquieting new development in the pattern of modern American society. The years since the end

BASIC QUESTION OF MODERN SOCIETY —

of the Second World War have produced rapid and sometimes bewildering social change. The population has grown swiftly and the cities have become more and more crowded; at the same time there has been an education boom that has given more and more young people high school and college degrees. Technology has sent men to the moon and produced an "affluent society" in which more people enjoy more material goods than ever before in history—yet it also has resulted in widespread pollution, concern about the ecology, numerous large pockets of poverty, and uncertainty about the ability of material prosperity to satisfy human yearnings. Issues of race relations and school integration are constantly in the news. The divorce rate has risen, and the women's liberation movement has raised some profound questions about the whole institution of marriage and the family and the relationships between men and women.

Of all the problems of modern society, perhaps the basic one is this: How, in this new world of rapid and tumultuous change, can man get along satisfactorily with himself and with his fellows? It is a question to which many psychologists have devoted themselves in many various ways. One must not expect too much of the science, of course—for the psychologist, as a human being, is just as baffled by the upheavals in his society as anyone else. However, the psychologist can at least investigate and analyze some of the facts; and factual information, rather than mere guess or prejudice, is the great need of the modern world.

It would be impossible to list all the social problems to which psychology has contributed insights. Some of them, however, deserve special mention here.

1, the "generation gap"

One of the most widely discussed and controversial problems of recent years has centered around what has come to be called the "generation gap." Because of differences in dress, life styles, and attitudes, many young people have decided that adults represent an "establishment" that they are prepared to reject or perhaps even tear down; many adults have decided that young people are self-indulgent, mindlessly rebellious, and dangerous to the American society.

This is a problem that public opinion polls and psychological analysis of trends in American society can at least put into perspective. The surveys show that there are indeed a number of sharp differences of opinion between many young people and many older people, on all kinds of topics ranging from military policies to issues of race and poverty and the nature of the college curriculum. But the evidence seems to indicate that these differences represent more of an "education gap" than a "generation gap." As a 1971 report of the Census Bureau made clear, there has been a tremendous boom in education in the United States. In a mere three decades beginning in 1940, the number of young Americans with college degrees almost tripled, going from 6 to 16 percent; the number with at least a year of college more than doubled, going from 13 to 31 percent; the number with high school diplomas rose from 38 to 75 percent (7).

These figures mean that today's young people, on the average, have had far more formal education than their parents. In fact nearly two-thirds of today's college students have fathers who never went to college. And many research studies have shown that people who have attended college tend to have different opinions from noncollege people on such questions as politics, sexual behavior, child-rearing practices, religion, and relations among ethnic and racial groups (8); they also tend to be more concerned about the general welfare of society than about their own personal advancement. In the opinion of some psychologists who have studied the so-called generation gap, today's young people often seem threatening to their elders in part because they have more education and have developed the kinds of attitudes that increased education generally fosters.

Surveys have also shown that the "gap," whatever its cause, is not nearly so large as some of the militant young people and more conservative adults often assume—or as even an objective observer might gather from some of the news events reported on television and in the newspapers. Careful psychological surveys made in 1965 and 1968 showed that only about 2 to 10 percent of all college students took active part in the various campus protests of those years, with the lower figure holding for such abstract issues as educational reform and the higher figure for more personal issues such as dormitory rules and standards of dress (9). A public opinion survey of Americans aged fifteen to twenty-one, made at the end of 1970, showed that 66 percent did not have trouble communicating with their parents, 73 percent agreed with their parents' values and ideals, and 84 percent were satisfied with the kind of education they had received up to that point (10). Quite clearly, the American youth movement, if thought of as a highly militant attack on the Establishment and its ideas, is not nearly so large as its own leaders and the adults who oppose it often believe. Moreover, a study of history and of current trends in other nations shows that differences between young people and their elders have existed many times before and exist today in many other parts of the world, including Mexico, France, Japan, and the Soviet Union.

"What are you worried about? The youth movement is basically healthy. The really alienated dropouts like me are only a small, though vocal minority."

2. drugs

One thorny aspect of the "generation gap" has centered around the use of drugs, notably marijuana. Many adults are convinced that marijuana is a dangerous drug that leads to antisocial behavior and probably to addiction to even more dangerous drugs such as heroin. Indeed possession of marijuana is a crime throughout the United States and in many places is punishable by long prison sentences. Many young people, however, use marijuana despite the fact that it is illegal and consider it no more dangerous than alcohol. A large-scale survey of freshmen entering college in 1970 showed that 38 percent favored legalizing the use of marijuana—almost double the number who had favored legalization only two years earlier (11).

Research into the actual effects of marijuana poses some extremely difficult problems. Even if a psychologist set up a careful double blind experiment to inquire into its effect on automobile driving, as described on page 24, the results would have little real value. They would show only what happens when a known amount of the active chemical in marijuana is administered under laboratory conditions and the subject then tested on a machine that simulates the driving experience (see Figure 1-6). They would not necessarily predict what might

1-6

Subjects "drive" stationary automobiles through the traffic hazards shown on a movie screen. Their responses—steering, braking, or speeding up—are recorded and analyzed. As discussed in the text, this type of device has been used in an attempt to discover the effects of marijuana on driving ability.

happen when many different kinds of drivers, in many different kinds of automobiles under different road conditions, smoke varying quantities of marijuana (12). This is especially true because researchers have found that there are probably more than 100 different varieties of the marijuana plant, some of which may be 400 times as strong as others (13). Moreover, marijuana users often combine the drug with varying amounts of alcohol, thus further complicating the problem of studying its effects.

Thus all experimental evidence on marijuana has to be viewed with reservations. Insofar as can be judged from laboratory experiments, marijuana raises the pulse rate and causes reddening of the eyes and dryness of the mouth and throat; it does not produce any other very marked physical effects. As for the psychological effects, laboratory subjects often report that they get feelings of happiness and elation, become more friendly for a time and then tend to withdraw, become less aggressive, have trouble concentrating, tend to get dizzy and feel as if they were dreaming, and eventually become sleepy. On a simulated test of driving skill they make more speedometer errors, as if they were not watching the speedometer as much as they normally would (14). Tests of ability to think through a series of logical steps have suggested that the drug reduces short-term memory (see pages 99–101) and the ability to make decisions rapidly (15). In one experiment a control group received marijuana from which the active ingredients had been removed, while other groups received various strengths of the drug. The subjects then were asked to start with a number such as 114, subtract 7, then add either 1, 2, or 3, and repeat the process until they reached another number, such as 54. The combined score for speed and accuracy was highest for the control group, which did about 50 percent better than subjects who had received a small dose of marijuana and more than 100 percent better than subjects who had received a large dose (16).

Studies of people who use the drug outside the laboratory have suggested that they probably have different reasons and obtain different kinds of reactions. One investigator, after interviewing a large group of college students and "street people" who were regular users, concluded that they fell into three categories: 1) "insight users," who believed the drug gave them an expanded awareness and made them more creative; 2) "social users," who took the drug mostly

for enjoyment and a feeling of warmth and togetherness with their friends; and 3) "release users," who found that it lowered their inhibitions and gave them a feeling of escape from reality (17). This study may explain why there are so many conflicting reports about the kinds of effects that users experience.

Some observers have concluded that the regular use of marijuana produces long-term personality changes, notably loss of motivation, ambition, and judgment (18). Other observers, however, have concluded that it is less likely that the drug causes loss of motivation than that people who have low motivation to begin with are more inclined than others to use it heavily (19).

So far as is known, marijuana does not produce any physical dependence that makes its users crave the drug and suffer withdrawal symptoms in its absence, as do users of a "hard" drug such as heroin. However, it does seem to produce a psychological dependence. In Egypt, where marijuana can be obtained easily despite laws against it, a study of people who use it five to fifty times a month showed that two-thirds wanted to stop—yet continued because of its soothing and mood-elevating effects as well as the fact that they were used to smoking it in social situations (20). Whether the use of marijuana tends to lead to addiction to heroin is not known. Many heroin addicts began with marijuana (21)—but obviously only a small number of marijuana users go on to hard drugs (14).

As for statistics on the number of young people who use marijuana, the National Institute of Mental Health estimated in 1969 that between 2 and 4 percent of students in high schools and colleges across the nation used it regularly, between 5 and 10 percent used it socially on occasions when it was readily available, and between 13 and 26 percent had used it anywhere from one to ten times and then had given it up. This means that the total number of students who had ever used the drug ran between 20 and 40 percent, depending on the school (22). However, the statistics seem to change rapidly. A public opinion poll in early 1971 indicated that 42 percent of students in college at that time had tried marijuana at least once (23). There is some indication that marijuana use has some of the aspects of a fad—that it may become widespread on a particular campus for a time, then drop off (19).

There is no question at all about the extreme danger of "hard" drugs. Heroin is highly addictive, and anyone who thinks he can get away with trying it for a few times is likely to become dependent on it before he is ever aware that he is "hooked." The addict needs more and more of the drug as time goes on, not only to achieve the feeling the drug produces but also to avoid extremely painful withdrawal symptoms, and his habit may eventually cost as much as $125 a day—a fact that leads many addicts to turn to crime. Overdose frequently kills addicts; indeed in New York City heroin addiction is the leading cause of death among people between the ages of fifteen and thirty-five (24). As for the amphetamines, sometimes known as "pep pills," "meth," and "speed," these too are addictive in that users build up a tolerance and must use more and more to achieve the same effect. The "high" created by amphetamines, especially when injected into the blood stream, may be accompanied by severe feelings of anxiety and irrational thinking leading to violent behavior, followed by a depression in which the user becomes suicidal. The drug can cause psychological disturbances that make it

impossible for the user to keep attending college or work at a job (25), and prolonged abuse of the drug has been found to produce brain damage (26).

3. the population explosion

Another serious social problem of recent years has been the population explosion that has occurred throughout the world, chiefly because improved sanitation methods and medical techniques have greatly increased the average life span. In the underdeveloped nations, population has been increasing so rapidly as to threaten to outstrip the food supply and to result in widespread starvation. In the United States, where a careful census is taken every ten years, total population increased from 76 million at the beginning of this century to 203.2 million at the time of the 1970 census. Moreover, there has been a vast migration of Americans from rural areas and small towns to big cities. In 1900, as is shown in Figure 1-7, more than half of all Americans lived in areas described as rural; by 1970, almost 75 percent of them lived in urban areas. The combination of population growth and the move to the cities has produced many new problems of crowding, housing, personal relationships, pollution of the environment, and violence and crime.

Although statistics on crime leave much to be desired—because many crimes are never reported and because different law enforcement agencies have different ways of tabulating those that are reported—there seems to be little doubt that crimes of all sorts have been increasing rather rapidly in the United States. And although crime and violence are certainly not confined to the cities, there appears to be something about the big-city environment that fosters them. In one experiment, for example, a psychologist arranged to have an automobile abandoned in the streets of New York City, with its license plates removed and the hood up.

"When will it ever end, Miss Hartley? When will it ever end?"

Drawing by Peter Arno, © 1936, 1964, The New Yorker Magazine, Inc.

our more crowded nation

1-7

The United States has grown rapidly in recent years to a population of 203.2 million at the time of the 1970 census. Most of the growth has been in urban areas, defined as cities of 2500 population or more—and much of it has been in very crowded metropolitan areas, such as those in and around New York, Los Angeles, and Chicago. (27)

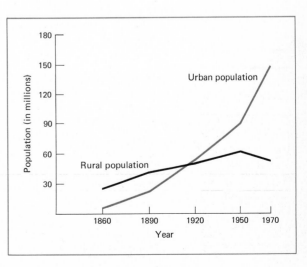

Within ten minutes, a respectable looking family composed of a father, mother, and young son emptied the trunk and glove compartment and removed the radiator and battery. Within three days the car was a pile of junk, stripped of all useful parts, its windows broken, and its body and fenders battered. The same psychologist similarly abandoned another automobile in the city of Palo Alto, California, which had a population of about 55,000 at the time. This car remained undamaged and unlooted for a full week; in fact one man who walked past it while rain was falling tried to protect it by lowering the hood (28).

Violence, Anonymity, and "Bystander Apathy." One factor that appears to encourage crime and violence is the anonymity of big-city life. In New York a person can walk for blocks without meeting anyone he knows; he is simply a face in the crowd. And there is experimental evidence that people are more likely to behave aggressively when their identities are not known than when they could be held responsible for their actions (29).

Along somewhat similar lines, psychologists have been interested in what has become known as "bystander apathy"—a term that grew out of a well-publicized 1964 incident in New York City in which a young woman named Kitty Genovese was murdered on the street one early morning in full view of thirty-eight neighbors who heard her cries and ran to their apartment windows. Although the assault went on for a half-hour and many of the spectators watched for the entire time, no one called the police or took any other action. When confronted with such a remarkable incident, any psychologist interested in social problems—indeed in the whole large field known as *social psychology* (the subject of Chapter 16)—naturally must ask, "Why?"

helpfulness to strangers:
big city versus small town

1-8

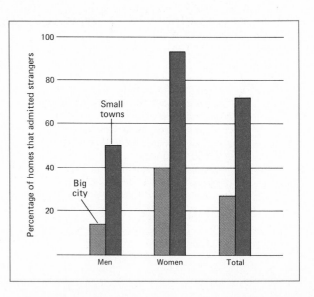

The "strangers" were investigators who rang doorbells, pretended to be lost, and asked to use the phone. The people they asked for help were inclined to admit women investigators to their homes, more inclined to turn men investigators away. But to both sexes, people in small towns were much more helpful than big-city residents.

In one study inspired by the Genovese case, investigators rang doorbells, explained that they had mislaid the address of a friend in the neighborhood, and asked to use the phone. Half the investigators were men and half were women, and they went to homes in both a large city (middle-income housing developments in New York) and small towns. The results are shown in Figure 1-8. In both the big city and the small towns, the women investigators were admitted to more homes than the men—but both women and men investigators received much more help in the small towns than in the city (30). The psychologists who conducted the experiment believe that one explanation for the results is that big-city residents have a greater suspicion and fear of strangers.

Further light on bystander apathy comes from experiments that have explored the relationship between the number of people who witness an incident—such as a fire, a theft, or a call for help—and the likelihood that anyone will take any action. In a typical experiment of this kind, men students at a university who arrived at a psychology laboratory were asked to sit in a small waiting room until they could be interviewed. Some of the subjects waited alone, others in groups of three, and still others in groups of three that contained only one actual subject and two confederates of the experimenter. Soon smoke began to seep into the room through a ventilator in the wall; the smoke continued until someone took steps to report a fire, or if no one did, for six minutes. As is shown in Figure 1-9, most of the subjects who were alone took action to report the smoke, usually rather quickly. But when three subjects were waiting together, only 13 percent ever reported the smoke. Of the subjects who were sitting with two of the

bystander apathy and number of spectators

1-9

How many students, sitting in the waiting room of a psychology laboratory, would report the presence of smoke that seemed to indicate a fire? The answer seems to depend on how many people are present. In group 1, there were three people in the room—one actual subject and two confederates of the experimenter who were instructed to ignore the smoke. In group 2, three actual subjects were waiting in company. In group 3—the only one in which a majority took action—the subject was alone in the room and presumably felt a greater sense of personal responsibility. (31)

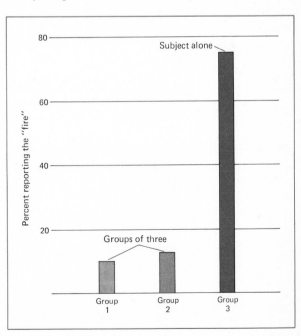

experimenter's confederates—who were of course instructed to pay no attention to the smoke—only 10 percent took action.

Similar experiments also have shown that a person is much more likely to do something about an apparent emergency if he is the only witness, much more likely to display bystander apathy if he is only one of several or many witnesses, especially if the others seem indifferent to what is happening. The psychologist who designed the experiments believes that two factors may be at work: 1) the presence of others may relieve the individual of feelings of personal responsibility, and 2) any apparent indifference on the part of the others may cause him to downgrade the seriousness of the situation. At any rate, a person who needs help is hardly likely to find safety in numbers; the fewer people present the greater are his chances of getting assistance.

Apathy and the Big-City Rush.   Another possible explanation for bystander apathy comes from an experiment in which the subjects were students at a theological seminary—and therefore men who might be expected to lend a helping hand to anyone in trouble. The subjects had volunteered to record a brief talk; when they arrived at the experimenter's office they received some printed material that was to be the basis of the talk, studied it, and then were directed to proceed to a recording studio in a nearby building. The route, as shown on a map each received, took them through an alley in which they passed a confederate of the experimenter who was lying in a doorway, coughing and groaning as if in pain. The question, of course, was how many of them would stop to assist the man in trouble—as did the subject shown in Figure 1-10.

In an attempt to study some of the factors that might influence the subjects, the experimenter gave half of them a discussion of job opportunities for seminary

a "Good Samaritan" offers help

1-10

One of the subjects in an experiment on bystander apathy stops to offer help to a man lying in an alley doorway. Was he really a "Good Samaritan"—or did he just stop because he was in no special hurry to get anywhere? For the answer, see the text.

graduates to use as the basis for their talk; he gave the other half the story of the Good Samaritan, which, it seemed, might remind them of man's duty to help his fellow man. Moreover, the experimenter tried to measure whether they would be influenced by how much of a hurry they were in to reach the recording studio; he told some of them that they were early and should take their time, others that they were just about on schedule, and still others that they were late and should rush to the studio as fast as possible. In other words, the experimenter put a third of his subjects in what he termed a "low hurry" situation, a third in an "intermediate hurry," and another third in a "high hurry" situation.

Which subjects offered help to the man in pain and which did not? It turned out that it made no significant difference whether a subject had just read the Good Samaritan parable or the material on job opportunities. What did make a difference was how much of a hurry he was in. Of the "low hurry" subjects, 63 percent offered help; of the "intermediate hurry" subjects, 45 percent; and of the "high hurry" subjects, only 10 percent (32). The study would seem to indicate that bystander apathy is encouraged not only by the crowding in today's world but also by the rush of big-city life as contrasted with the more leisurely pace of smaller towns.

Some Conflicting Evidence on Bystander Apathy.   Before leaving the subject of bystander apathy, it must be pointed out that not all experiments have produced uniform results. For example, in one study investigators pretended to collapse on the floor of a New York City subway car. In some cases they smelled of alcohol and carried a whisky bottle in a paper bag; it was logical for people riding in the car to assume that they were drunk. In other cases they showed no signs of having been drinking but instead carried a cane; it was logical to assume that their collapse was due to illness. Over a large number of trials, someone in the car went to the assistance of the "drunk" half the time, to the assistance of the "sick man" 95 percent of the time (33). In this experiment the "bystanders"— actually by-sitters—may have been more inclined to help because they were in a face-to-face situation with the "victim" and in a confined space where they could not just ignore him and walk past. At any rate, the various experiments on bystander apathy indicate that it is a rather complex phenomenon that depends on many factors and takes varied forms under different circumstances.

4. other social problems

There are many other social problems for which the findings of psychology have provided, if not the answers, at least some solid and objective information. Some of the information has already been put to work by our society. For example, research by clinical psychologists into the problem of abnormal behavior has helped bring about vast changes in the treatment of the mentally disturbed, who are no longer subjected to such barbarous practices as having holes bored into their skulls to let out evil spirits or being dosed with nauseating chemicals to purge them of their ailments. Disturbed children are no longer all classified alike and thrown together into institutions for the hopeless. Research has made it possible to distinguish among those who are mentally retarded for organic reasons or through faulty heredity, those who have been held back by bad environments, those who suffer from the psychosis called schizophrenia, and those who are delinquents; these various groups now receive different and often more successful treatment.

Research also has dispelled the old pessimistic notion that many people are destined from birth to be stupid or psychotic; it has shown that environment as well as heredity plays an important part in creating these problems. In particular, psychologists have learned the importance of the early years of childhood in establishing personality and have pointed the way toward more favorable methods of dealing with the child in the family, nursery schools, and day-care centers. They are investigating whether violence on TV can be harmful to children and have helped in the creation of shows that have a proven educational value. They also have provided valuable information about teaching in the schools, the problems of adolescents, sexual behavior and homosexuality, tensions in marriage, and the problems of divorce.

summary
1. Psychology is the science that systematically studies and attempts to explain observable behavior and its relationship to the unseen mental processes that go on inside the organism and to external events in the environment.

2. The subject matter of psychology includes learning, thinking, problem solving, the senses, perception, emotions, motives, personality, and abnormal behavior.

3. The goals of psychology are to understand and predict behavior.

4. The science of psychology is empirical, which means that it is based on studies made with the greatest possible precision and objectivity.

5. Psychology began as a science when Wilhelm Wundt opened the first psychology laboratory in 1879.

6. Other important early psychologists were Francis Galton, who was interested in measuring individual differences; William James, who believed psychology to be "the science of mental life"; and John Watson, the founder of behaviorism.

7. Other important names in the history of psychology are B. F. Skinner, of the school of stimulus-response psychology; Jean Piaget, of the cognitive school; Carl Rogers and Abraham Maslow, of the humanistic school; and Sigmund Freud, the founder of psychoanalysis.

8. The methods of psychology include the experiment, naturalistic observation, tests, interviews, and questionnaires.

9. In an experiment, the experimenter controls the independent variable, which is set up independently of anything his subject does or does not do, and then studies the dependent variable, which is a change in the subject's behavior resulting from a change in the independent variable.

10. Although psychology is a pure science, interested in knowledge for the sake of knowledge, many of its findings have had a practical application in modern life. Examples of applied psychology include:

   a. Clinical and counseling psychology, or the diagnosis and treatment of behavior problems.

   b. The use of standardized tests and of the principles of learning.

   c. The use by industry of studies of the effects of fatigue, working hours, and employee morale; also of human engineering, which is the design of equipment and machinery that fit the actual size, strength, and capabilities of the human beings who will use them.

   d. Public opinion surveys.

11. Psychology has contributed insights into many social problems, including the generation gap, the use of drugs, and the results of the population explosion (including violence, crime, and "bystander apathy").

recommended reading

Barker, R. G. *Ecological psychology*. Stanford, Calif.: Stanford University Press, 1968.

Boring, E. G. *History of experimental psychology*, 2nd ed. New York: Appleton-Century-Crofts, 1950.

Coopersmith, S., ed. *Frontiers of psychological research*. San Francisco: W. H. Freeman, 1964.

Freeman, H. E., and Jones, W. C. *Social problems: causes and controls*. Chicago: Rand McNally, 1970.

Murphy, G., and Kovach, J. K. *Historical introduction to modern psychology*, 3rd ed. New York: Harcourt Brace Jovanovich, 1972.

Postman, L., ed. *Psychology in the making: histories of selected research problems*. New York: Knopf, 1962.

Scott, W. A., and Wertheimer, M. *Introduction to psychological research*. New York: Wiley, 1962.

Truzzi, M. *Sociology and everyday life*. Englewood Cliffs, N.J.: Prentice-Hall, 1968.

Watson, R. I. *The great psychologists: from Aristotle to Freud*, 2nd ed. Philadelphia: Lippincott, 1968.

How do we change
from helpless baby
to competent adult?

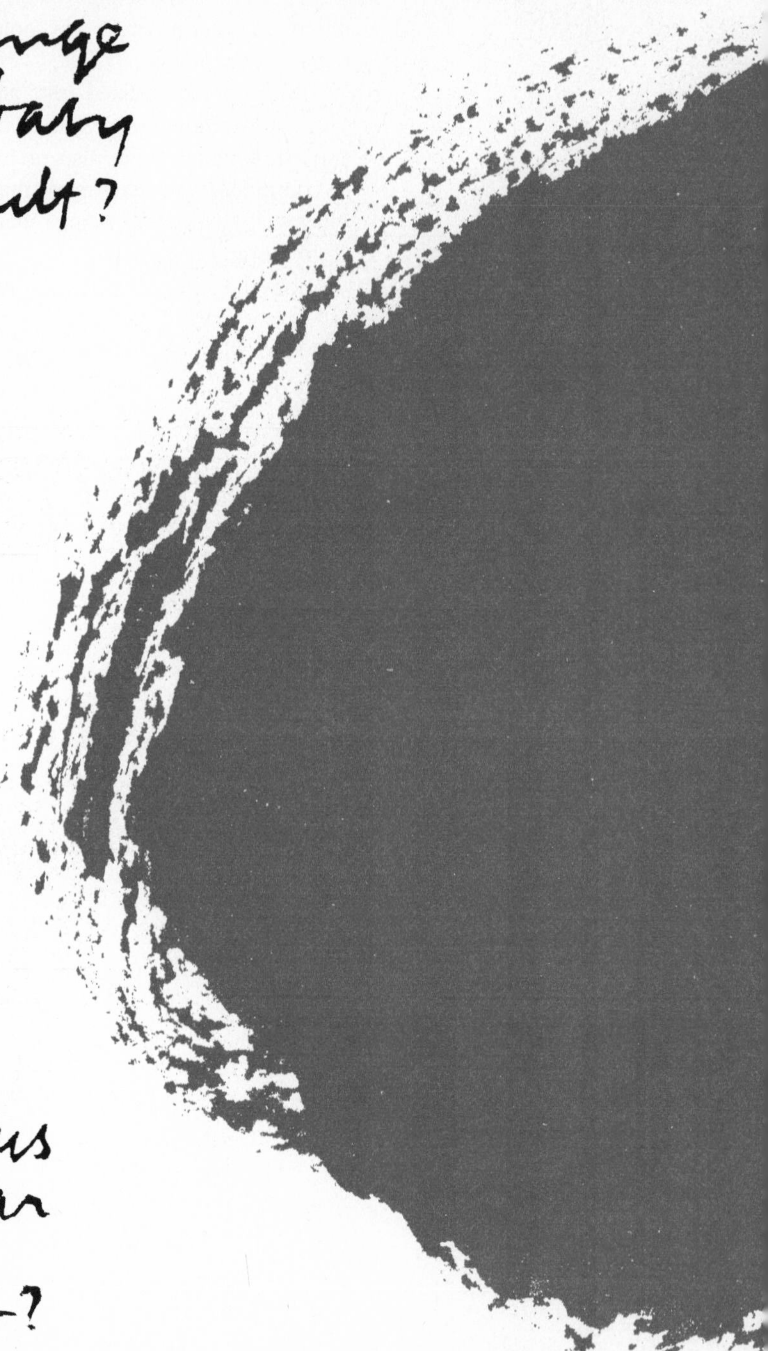

How can two of us
with such similar
potentialities
be so different?

One answer is that we learn.

PART TWO

Part 1 described some of the responses to biological drives and some of the motor activity, thinking, and problem solving that constituted a college woman's behavior and mental activity on a typical morning. It also described some of the many striking ways in which she was different from another young woman in her class, largely because of differences in motives and emotions.

All these matters, from biological drives to emotions, are important fields of study; and later in the book you will find more complete discussions of what is known about them. The key problem of psychology, however, is this:

At birth the college woman was incapable of all the many kinds of activity in which she engaged on that typical morning. She did possess the biological drives of hunger and thirst, but all she could do about them was cry and make sucking movements with her lips. Her motor behavior was limited to some simple and un-coordinated movements of the muscles of her arms, legs, and body. She had no motives or emotions, at least not like an adult's.

How did the young woman become capable of the many kinds of behavior and mental activity that she now engages in?

How did the other woman in her class, who also started as a helpless baby, become capable of the kinds of behavior *she* exhibits today—and why is she so different?

The answer is that the two young women *learned.*

Almost all the behavior and mental activity that we exhibit as adults has been learned. Thus learning is a central concern of psychology and a logical place to start studying the science. This second part of the book, therefore, contains three chapters on various aspects of the learning process and a fourth on the closely related topics of language, thinking, and problem solving.

LEARNING AND PROBLEM SOLVING

CHAPTER 2

THE PRINCIPLES OF LEARNING

Two baby robins, pecking their way out of the eggs, are destined to lead much the same kind of lives; both of them will exhibit much the same kind of behavior from birth to death. Two human babies, lying in adjoining cribs in a hospital, are not set in any such pattern. They will behave very differently as children and still more differently as adults.

Much of the behavior of birds, insects, and fish is regulated by *instincts, which are elaborate inborn patterns of activity, occurring automatically and without prior learning.* The robin, even if it never sees another robin build a nest, will instinctively build the round and shallow nest characteristic of the species. The spider will weave its characteristic web. The salmon will migrate from its birthplace in a river to the depths of the ocean, then return to the shallows of the river to spawn.

This is not true of human behavior. If there are any human instincts, they play an insignificant part in our behavior, and some psychologists believe that there are no human instincts at all. Certainly most of the popular talk about human instincts is in error. People often say that human beings have an "instinctive fear" of snakes, but this is incorrect. A child who has not learned to fear snakes may eagerly try to play with one, just as he might play with a cat. People also talk of an "acquisitive instinct," as if all human beings liked to accumulate money and possessions. But there are many societies in which human beings never learn to show interest in acquiring property.

A, the "nature versus nurture" argument

The plasticity of human behavior—the fact that it can be molded in ways that the more rigid and predetermined behavior of lower organisms cannot be molded—has always impressed observant men and has been the center of one of the important philosophic arguments of history, the "nature versus nurture" argument. The argument revolves around this question: To what extent is human behavior determined by factors present at birth, and to what extent is it molded through experience and learning? Sometimes the question is put another way: To what extent does human behavior depend on heredity and to what extent on environment (or the total of all the influences exerted by family and society)?

John Locke, the seventeenth-century philosopher, popularized the idea that the mind of the human baby is what has been called a *tabula rasa,* a "blank tablet" on which anything can be written through experience and learning. This idea greatly influenced other philosophers who helped create the intellectual climate in which psychology was born as a science, and it was also attractive to many of the early psychologists. Note that it is a very optimistic idea. If the mind of the human baby is indeed a "blank tablet," then human history has unlimited possibilities. All the evils that have plagued humanity—jealousy, emotional conflicts, crime, even war—are not inevitable but are the result of the wrong kind of learning. By discovering the principles of learning we can point the way toward a brighter future for mankind.

Many thinkers of the past, however, rejected the idea of the *tabula rasa*. They argued that every human being was born, if not with instincts that would unfold as detailed patterns of behavior, at least with strong predispositions toward certain kinds of behavior. They believed that one baby inherited the tendency to be happy, another to be melancholy; one baby was born to be a leader, another to be a timid follower, another to be a troublemaker or even a criminal. Carried far enough, this becomes a rather fatalistic view of human behavior, containing little hope for any improvement. If the future of the human being is laid down at birth to any substantial degree, then there is not much point in parents' attempting to find better ways of bringing up their children or in the schools' attempting to find better ways of educating them.

1. nativists and empiricists

DEFINITION:
1. NATIVISTS
2. EMPIRICISTS

The argument between these two very different points of view still continues, and there are influential thinkers on both sides. Those who believe that many of the important factors that determine behavior are present at birth are

instinctive versus learned home building

2-1 The row of photographs below shows three bird species—from left, penguin, vireo, and robin—and their distinctive nests. At right are some of the many kinds of houses human beings have learned to build: igloo, hut, and apartment building.

often called *nativists;* those who believe that learning and experience are most important are known as *empiricists.*

NATIVIST

On the nativist side of the argument, there is the obvious fact that nature sets certain limits on human behavior. All human babies are more or less alike at birth in many respects; all of them, whether born to a woman in a jungle tribe or to a college-educated mother in Denver, have much the same kind of bones, muscles, sense organs, nervous systems, and glands. It is unlikely that any human being will ever learn to run 100 yards in eight seconds flat, and it is certainly impossible for any human being to learn to fly like a bird or to live underwater like a fish (although we have learned to build mechanical devices that enable us to imitate these feats). Moreover, it has been established that babies are born with some innate preferences in how they use their sense organs; they will spend more time watching a moving light than a stationary light and looking at patterns rather than plain surfaces (1)—tendencies that help them absorb such important information about the environment as the appearance of the mother's face and of the objects they must avoid once they start to crawl or walk. It is also known that many of the individual differences that interested Sir Francis Galton—ranging from potential size to potential learning ability—are present at birth, controlled by patterns of inheritance in the mother's egg cell and the father's sperm cell. Indeed even very young babies show noticeable differences; some are much more active than others, some more irritable, some more easily "bored" (2, 3).

EMPIRICIST

Most psychologists, however, lean toward the empiricist side of the argument; while acknowledging that we have some inborn traits, they believe that this inborn equipment appears to set only the limits and the broad tendencies of behavior, leaving room for a wide range of possibilities. Hence the importance of the learning process. The human baby, newborn and lying helpless in his crib, will not lead his life—at least not to any appreciable degree—as the slave to any instincts laid down at his birth. One of the great contrasts between instinctive behavior and learned behavior is illustrated in Figure 2-1. Human babies are not predestined to build a single type of house, or court their mates in any specific

way, or travel to a certain part of the world to live their maturing years and then return to their birthplace to produce their children.

By and large and within our inherited limitations, we human beings become what we are through the process of learning. One man learns to become an Adolf Hitler. Another man, not very different at birth, learns to become a benefactor of humanity. One woman learns to become a notorious poisoner of six husbands. Another woman, not much different at birth, learns to become an outstanding schoolteacher and the successful mother of happy children.

Let us examine the elements of learning, starting with the simplest of them and proceeding to the more complex and noting, as we go, how each of the elements forms the firm foundation for the next.

B. the reflex response

DEFINITION:
REFLEXES

All human babies exhibit the same form of behavior in response to certain events. If you brush a baby's lips, he makes a sucking motion. If you stroke a baby's cheek at the left side of his mouth, he turns his head to the left. If you stroke the right cheek, he turns his head to the right. If you tickle the sole of his foot, he lifts and spreads his toes. If you clap your hands and make a loud noise, he raises his arms and legs, as if in fear. When an object is placed in the palm of his hand, he closes his fingers around it.

These actions are called *reflexes*. They are automatic responses to something that happens to the organism. They come naturally. They are not learned. They take place without any conscious effort. Like the instincts of lower organisms, they are inborn. But they are not elaborate processes such as the building of the robin's nest or the migration of the salmon. Instead they are merely one particular action or group of actions—usually an action that protects the organism from damage or harm or that in some way helps the organism adjust to changes in the environment.

If you touch a hot piece of metal, for example, you immediately pull your hand away. This is a reflex response. You do not have to stop and think. As a matter of fact, you seem to pull your hand away before you actually become aware that the metal is hot. The reflex action protects you from being burned.

If you walk into a dark room, the pupils of your eyes automatically grow larger. If a bright light strikes your eyes, the pupils automatically and very quickly grow smaller. These are reflex responses that help your eyes adjust to the condition of the environment—that is to say, to the amount of light that is present.

1. the reflex mechanism

What causes a reflex? How does a reflex operate? The answers to these questions lie in the fact that in some ways the human organism can be roughly compared to a house that is wired in a certain way for electricity. If you press a button inside the front door, the outside entrance light goes on. You can press other buttons that will turn on the television set, a fan, or an air conditioner. Similarly, the "wiring" of the human organism—which is of course the network of nerves inside our bodies—is so constructed that the touch of hot metal makes our fingers draw away; a beam of light makes our pupils smaller, and so on.

REFLEX PROCESS

The human body is liberally supplied with nerves sensitive to temperature, touch, light, sound, and so on. These nerves run to the central nervous system, which consists of the spinal cord and brain; there they connect, sometimes directly and sometimes indirectly, with other nerves that send out messages that activate our muscles (causing movement), our internal organs (causing our hearts to beat faster or our digestive systems to operate or cease operating), and our glands (resulting, for example, in the secretion of saliva from our salivary glands or perspiration from our sweat glands).

Every reflex starts with a *stimulus,* which can be defined as any form of energy capable of exciting the nervous system. In the case of the hot metal, the stimulus is the energy of heat. This stimulus excites nerves in the skin and sets off nervous impulses that travel to the central nervous system, where, in accordance with a built-in pattern, they in turn set off other nervous impulses that travel back to the muscles of the hand and arm and result in the response of pulling the finger away. All this happens automatically, because of the way we are "wired"; it does not have to be learned. But the human nervous system is far more complicated than the electrical system inside a house. Thus reflexes, though not themselves learned, can be modified by learning—a fact that constitutes the second element of learning.

c. the conditioned response

Perhaps the best-known single experiment in the history of psychology was performed in the early years of this century by the Russian scientist Ivan Pavlov, a man whose name and work will certainly survive as long as the science itself. Pavlov began his experiment, which is illustrated in Figure 2-2 on the following page, by making a sound, such as the beat of a metronome, that the dog in the harness could hear. The dog made a few restless movements, but no saliva flowed from the glands of its mouth. This was what Pavlov had expected. The stimulus for reflex action of the salivary glands is the presence of food in the mouth—not the sound of a metronome. As far as the salivary reflex is concerned, sound is a neutral stimulus that has no effect one way or the other. When food was delivered and the dog took it into its mouth, saliva of course flowed in quantity.

Now Pavlov set about trying to connect the neutral stimulus of the sound with the reflex action of the salivary glands. While the metronome was clicking he delivered food to the dog, setting off the salivary reflex. After a time he did the same thing again—sounded the metronome and delivered food. After he had done this many times, he tried something new. He sounded the metronome but

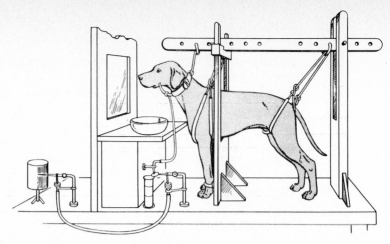

Pavlov's dog

2-2 The dog is strapped into a harness in which it has grown used to standing. A tube attached to the dog's salivary gland collects any saliva secreted by the gland, and the number of drops from the tube is recorded on a revolving drum outside the chamber. The experimenter can watch the dog through a one-way mirror and can deliver food to the dog's feed pan by remote control. Thus there is nothing in the chamber to distract the dog's attention except the food, when it is delivered, and any other stimulus that the experimenter wishes to present, such as the sound of a metronome. For the discoveries Pavlov made with this apparatus, see the text. (4)

Pavlov (right), dog,
and assistants

DEFINITIONS:

1. CONDITIONED RESPONSE
2. CLASSICAL CONDITIONING
3. UNCONDITIONED STIM-
    ULUS
4. CONDITIONED STIMULUS
5. UNCONDITIONED RE-
    SPONSE
6. CONDITIONED RESPONSE

did not deliver any food. Saliva flowed anyway. The sound alone was a sufficient stimulus to set off the salivary reflex (5).

The response of the glands to the sound is called a *conditioned response*. The dog had been conditioned, through a very simple form of learning, to associate the sound with the response of salivating. In this form of learning, which is called *classical conditioning*, the food is the *unconditioned stimulus*—the stimulus that naturally and automatically produces the salivary reflex, without any learning. The sound is the *conditioned stimulus*, which is neutral at the start but eventually produces a similar response. The reflex action of the salivary glands when food is placed in the dog's mouth is the *unconditioned response*, the one that is naturally built into the animal's "wiring" and takes place automatically, without any kind of learning. The response of the glands to the sound is the *conditioned response*, resulting from some kind of change in the "wiring" that is caused by pairing the conditioned stimulus with the unconditioned stimulus and therefore with the salivary reflex.

1. reinforcement in classical conditioning

Once Pavlov had established the conditioned salivary reflex, he was interested in learning how long and under what circumstances it would persist. When he merely sounded the metronome without ever again presenting food, he

2-3

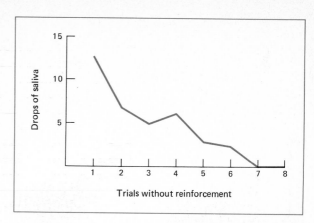

This graph shows what happened to Pavlov's dog when the conditioned stimulus of sound was no longer reinforced by the unconditioned stimulus of food. The conditioned salivary response, very strong at first, gradually grew weaker. By the seventh time the metronome was sounded the conditioned response had disappeared. Extinction of the response was complete.

found that in a very short time the flow of saliva in response to the sound began to decrease, and soon it stopped altogether, as shown in Figure 2-3. But if he occasionally followed the sound with food—not every time but sometimes—the conditioned response could be made to continue indefinitely. Since pairing the food with the sound not only established the conditioned response but also strengthened it and kept it alive, Pavlov called this process *reinforcement*.

DEFINITION:
REINFORCEMENT

2. extinction and spontaneous recovery

Pavlov's experiments demonstrated many of the rules and provided much of the terminology of learning. The process through which the conditioned response (or any other learned behavior) tends to disappear if reinforcement is withdrawn is called *extinction*. But Pavlov also discovered that even after extinction the conditioned response tends to operate again after a rest. This phenomenon is called *spontaneous recovery*.

DEFINITIONS:

1. EXTINCTION
2. SPONTANEOUS
   RECOVERY

Pavlov found that he could just as easily condition the dog's salivary reflex to the sound of a bell or to a flash of light as to the metronome. Subsequent experimenters have shown that apparently almost any kind of reflex can be conditioned and that almost any kind of previously neutral stimulus can be used as the conditioned stimulus. If the conditioned response is reinforced by occasional pairings of the conditioned stimulus and the unconditioned stimulus, it continues to operate. If not, it undergoes extinction.

3. stimulus generalization and stimulus discrimination

Another important fact about learning demonstrated in the Pavlov experiments was this: once the dog had been conditioned to salivate to the sound of a bell, it would also salivate to the sound of a different bell or of a buzzer. If the sound was very similar to that of the original bell, the dog salivated in quantity. As the sound became more and more different from the original bell, the amount of salivation decreased, and sometimes no salivation occurred at all.

This phenomenon is called *stimulus generalization*—which means that once the organism has learned to associate a stimulus with a certain kind of behavior, it tends to display this behavior toward similar stimuli.

After Pavlov had established the principle of stimulus generalization in the dog, he went on to demonstrate its counterpart, which is called *stimulus discrimination*. He continued to reinforce salivation to the bell by presenting food. But, when a different bell or a buzzer was sounded, no reinforcement was presented. Soon the dog learned to salivate only to the sound of the original bell, not to the other sounds; the animal had learned to discriminate between the stimulus of the bell and the other stimuli. If the experiment is carried far enough, it can be shown that a dog is capable of quite delicate stimulus discrimination; it can learn to respond to the tone of middle C, yet not to respond to tones that are only a little higher or a little lower.

DEFINITION:
STIMULUS
DISCRIMINATION

4. conditioned responses in life situations

The conditioned response is far more than just a strange phenomenon that can be made to happen in a specially constructed laboratory. As a matter of fact, Pavlov began his laboratory experiments because he had already noticed something about dogs that aroused his curiosity. In studying the digestive system of dogs he had noticed that their saliva and other digestive juices began to flow not only when they actually had food in their mouths but also when they merely saw the food—or even the man who usually fed them. In other words, the salivary reflex of the dogs had already been conditioned to the stimulus provided by the sight of food or of the man who was the customary source of food. In his laboratory experiments Pavlov showed how this kind of conditioning takes place.

Nor is classical conditioning something that happens only to animals. Many kinds of human reflexes have also been conditioned to many kinds of stimuli. For example, the sound of the first note of Beethoven's Fifth Symphony has no effect on the human eyelid. A puff of air directed at the eye, however, produces a reflex action in which the eyelid blinks shut. If you sit in a laboratory long enough while an experimenter sounds the musical note and then quickly directs a puff of air toward your eye, eventually the first note of the symphony will produce the reflex of blinking.

5. conditioning and emotions

Some far-reaching effects of classical conditioning among human beings were discovered by John Watson, who was mentioned in Chapter 1 as the founder of behaviorism. One study that Watson helped conduct is known as the "Albert experiment"—referring to the first name of the eleven-month-old boy who was the subject. A child, as has been noted, automatically responds to an unexpected loud noise with signs of fear. Watson was interested in learning whether this reflex response could be conditioned to other stimuli. He therefore showed Albert a rat. Displaying no signs whatever of fear, Albert tried to play with the rat. Then the rat was shown again, and a loud noise was sounded. As

ALBERT EXPERIMENT

illustrated in Figure 2-4, Albert showed signs of fear and shrank back. After this was repeated several times, Albert showed signs of fear whenever he saw the rat, even when the noise was not sounded. The unconditioned response associated with the emotion of fear, set off automatically by the unconditioned stimulus of a loud noise, had now been conditioned to occur to the conditioned stimulus of the rat. In fact Albert, in accordance with the law of stimulus generalization, now showed signs of fear when he saw anything that was furry like a rat, including a rabbit or a man with a beard.

Something very similar to the Albert experiment often happens to children in real-life situations. For example, another unconditioned stimulus that automatically sets off the responses associated with fear is the sensation of falling. Now suppose that a dog—even a dog that the child has previously known and liked—suddenly jumps on him and knocks him down. In the future the child will probably show signs of fear at the very sight of the dog, which after a single pairing has become a conditioned stimulus setting off a conditioned response.

<u>If unreasonable fears or other unpleasant or disruptive emotions can be established by classical conditioning, then presumably they can also be removed by going through some sort of reconditioning process.</u> For example, Albert's fear

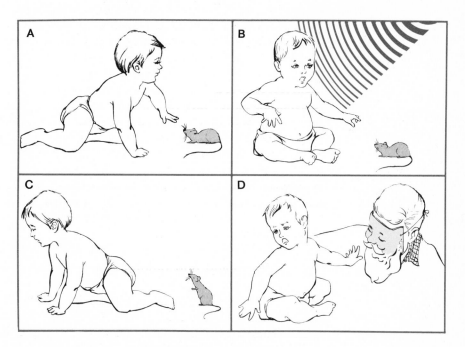

conditioning the fear response

2-4   The unconditioned baby reaches eagerly toward a rat (A). Then a loud noise is presented at the same time as the rat (B). After this conditioning, the baby fears the rat (C) and even a man whose beard resembles the furry animal (D). (6)

of furry objects might be overcome through the process of extinction if conditions could somehow be arranged in which a furry stimulus could be presented without arousing the fear response. Or, more likely, the stimulus might be attached through new conditioning to a more pleasant response, such as relaxation or active delight. This technique of reconditioning a stimulus-response relationship established through classical conditioning has actually been used with considerable success in a form of treatment known as behavior therapy, as will be explained in detail in Chapter 12.

6. conditioned responses and illness

Other experiments in classical conditioning have raised the possibility that the conditioned response may also be a direct source of psychosomatic illnesses—that is, illnesses in which the physical symptoms seem to have mental and emotional causes. (Some examples of psychosomatic illnesses might be abdominal pains, fainting spells, ulcer, and asthma.) In one experiment, rats were dosed with the drug insulin, which caused a rapid drop in the level of blood sugar and put them into a state of shock. The unconditioned stimulus of insulin was paired with a bright flash of light and of course with the slight pain of the hypodermic needle used to inject the insulin. After a number of pairings the light flash and needle without the insulin put the animals into shock; these had become a conditioned stimulus that was now sufficient to produce the conditioned response of a drop in blood sugar and the resulting state of shock (7).

If a bodily reaction as dramatic as the state of shock can be conditioned to a previously neutral stimulus, then presumably many other bodily reflexes can also be conditioned, and perhaps many psychosomatic pains and disorders are simply the result of unfortunate pairings of reflexes and some kind of external events, such as job difficulties or social stresses. Reports by Russian scientists raise the further possibility that the conditioned stimulus may sometimes come from inside the body rather than from the outside. These scientists say that they have managed to condition the salivary reflex of a dog to pressure on the intestinal wall (8)—which would indicate that the organism can learn to respond to one kind of bodily change with other kinds of changes that would otherwise be inexplicable.

John Watson, impressed by the many ways in which classical conditioning can be shown to modify behavior, decided that the conditioned response was the basic unit of behavior. Depending on how a person's responses had been conditioned, he believed, a given stimulus would always produce the same response—almost as automatically as the unconditioned stimulus of food produces the unconditioned response of salivation.

Certainly the classical conditioning of responses constitutes one of the important ways in which behavior is modified by learning. And the laws that Pavlov discovered by studying classical conditioning—the principles of reinforcement, extinction, spontaneous recovery, stimulus generalization, and stimulus discrimination—are keys that have unlocked some of the mysteries of learning.

ⅅ. operant behavior

Not all behavior, however, represents a reflex response to a particular stimulus. For example, if a rat is placed in a cage, it behaves in many ways that seem to be quite spontaneous. It may sniff at the cage, stand up to get a better look, scratch itself, wash itself, and touch various parts of the cage. Similarly, a baby in his crib makes many spontaneous actions; he may move his arms and legs, try to turn over or to grasp his blanket or the bars of the crib, turn his head and eyes to look at various objects, and make sounds with his vocal cords.

None of these actions, on the part of either the animal or the baby, is an automatic reflex or even a conditioned response to some specific outside stimulus. The actions are initiated by the organism; it is the organism itself that puts them in motion. Instead of having something in the outside environment produce a reflex response, we have here just the opposite; the animal or the baby is acting on the environment. The organism is "operating" on the world around it, so to speak—often with the result of bringing about some change in the environment. Hence this type of activity is called *operant behavior*.

Like the inborn reflexes, operant behavior can also be modified through learning. One of the ways is through a form of learning that, since it resembles classical conditioning in many respects, is known as *operant conditioning*.

DEFINITIONS:

1. OPERANT BEHAVIOR

2. OPERANT CONDITIONING

ⅇ. operant conditioning

The classic example of how operant conditioning may take place was demonstrated by B. F. Skinner through the use of the kind of cage shown in Figure 2-5. When a rat was first placed in the cage it engaged in many kinds of spontaneous operant

the Skinner box

2-5

With this simple but ingenious invention, a box in which pressing the bar automatically releases a pellet of food or a drop of water, B. F. Skinner demonstrated many of the rules of operant behavior. For what happens to a rat in the box, see the text.

behavior. Eventually it pressed the bar, and, automatically, a pellet of food dropped into the feeding tray beneath the bar. Still no learning took place; in human terms, we might say that the animal did not even "notice" the food but continued its random movements as before. Eventually it pressed the bar again, and another pellet dropped. This time the animal "noticed" the food and a connection was established between pressing the bar and the reward of eating; the rat began pressing the bar as fast as it could eat one pellet and get back to the bar to produce another (9).

In other words, what happened was that the rat placed in the cage (now famous as the "Skinner box") operated on it in various ways. One particular kind of operant behavior, pressing the bar, had a satisfying result; it produced food. Therefore it was repeated. Using the same language that is applied to classical conditioning, we say that the presentation of the food constituted a reinforcement of the bar-pressing behavior. The law of operant conditioning is that operant behavior that is reinforced tends to be repeated, while operant behavior that is not reinforced takes place only at random intervals or is abandoned.

LAW OF OPERANT CONDITIONING

1. operant escape and avoidance

ESCAPE

One of the things that the organism can find rewarding and that can thus provide reinforcement for operant conditioning is the escape from an unpleasant situation. Again we are indebted to the Skinner box for the simplest and most convincing demonstration.

This time let us arrange the box so that the rat is standing on an electric grill. When current flows through the grill, it produces a mild but thoroughly unpleasant shock. We place the rat in the box and turn on the current. The rat makes its random movements—now much more rapidly because of its discomfort—and happens to press the bar. The result, instead of a food pellet, is an end to the shock. Under these circumstances the rat soon learns to press the bar to escape from the shock.

AVOIDANCE

Avoidance of as well as escape from an unpleasant situation can provide reinforcement, as was demonstrated in an experiment in which a dog was placed in a box that had two compartments, separated by a hurdle. A light was turned on, and ten seconds later an electric shock was administered. By jumping over the hurdle into the other compartment, the dog could get away from the shock. After a few trials the animal learned to avoid the shock by leaping the hurdle when the light went on. This conditioned operant behavior was remarkably resistant to extinction. Even though the dog never again felt a shock, it would continue day after day to leap into the other compartment when the light went on (10).

A great deal of human behavior seems to represent some learned form of operant escape and avoidance. For example, consider the case of a young child who finds the presence of a stranger in the home distasteful and wants to escape. He may make a series of random movements and eventually hide his head in his mother's lap, thus shutting out the sight and sound of the stranger. Having once found hiding from an unpleasant situation to be rewarding, he conceivably may be operantly conditioned to withdraw from all unpleasant situations—and may turn into the kind of adult who stays away from social functions and remains as inconspicuous as possible at the most inconspicuous possible kind of job.

Many defenses against anxiety appear to be a common form of operant escape or avoidance. For example, many people who are made anxious by criticism become overly apologetic. This apologetic behavior is perhaps a form of conditioned operant behavior that in some way served as a successful escape from anxiety in the past—perhaps with a mother who stopped criticizing and instead showed affection when her child apologized.

2. operant extinction, recovery, generalization, and discrimination

In many ways, operant conditioning follows the same laws that Pavlov discovered for classical conditioning. If reinforcement is withdrawn, the conditioned operant behavior tends to go through the process of extinction; if we stop rewarding the rat with food when it presses the bar, it probably will eventually stop pressing. After a rest period away from the Skinner box, however, it will again start pressing the bar, demonstrating that conditioned operant behavior, like the conditioned response, obeys the law of spontaneous recovery.

The manner in which operant conditioning follows the laws of stimulus generalization and stimulus discrimination has been best shown in experiments with pigeons placed in a variation of the Skinner box. Once a pigeon has learned to obtain food by pecking at a white button, it will also peck at a red or green button. But, if only the operant behavior toward the white button is reinforced, the pigeon will quickly learn to discriminate among the three stimuli, pecking at the white button and ignoring the red and green.

3. the shaping of operant behavior

Operant conditioning begins with behavior that seems to serve no special purpose in producing an effect on the environment. In the conditioning process a particular kind of behavior is reinforced and becomes a *conditioned operant*—a form of behavior with which the organism operates on its environment to produce a desired result.

In the Skinner box the situation is simple. Pressing the bar is random behavior through which the rat more or less stumbles upon the secret of obtaining food. The manner in which animals and human beings learn to perform more complicated actions through operant conditioning involves the principle known as *shaping*, which can best be explained by describing another experiment performed with a somewhat different kind of Skinner box. In this case a pigeon was the subject, and an attempt was made to condition the pigeon to peck at a black dot inside a white circle on one wall of the box, as shown in Figure 2-6. Left to its own devices, the pigeon might never have stumbled upon the action. But its operant behavior was shaped into the desired form step by step.

Making its random movements, the pigeon moved about and eventually faced the white circle. This behavior was reinforced by the presentation of food. When the pigeon again faced the circle, reinforcement was repeated. The next time this

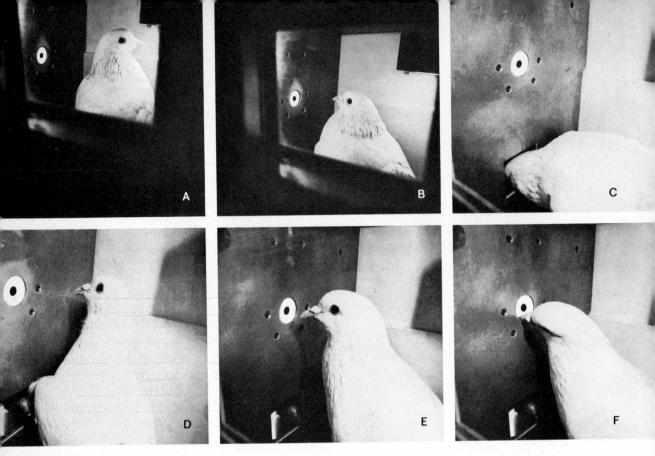

shaping a pigeon's behavior

2-6 At first the pigeon merely looks about the box at random (A). When it faces the circle (B), it receives the reinforcing stimulus of food in the tray below (C). The next time the pigeon approaches the circle (D), it is again rewarded with food. Later the pigeon is not rewarded until it approaches closer to the circle (E), and still later it is not rewarded until it pecks at the circle (F). The next step, not illustrated here, will be to withhold reward until the pigeon pecks at the small black dot inside the circle.

happened, however, reinforcement was withheld. Not until the pigeon happened to take a step toward the circle while facing it was the behavior reinforced. Later reinforcement was withheld until the pigeon pecked at the white circle, and finally it was withheld until the pigeon pecked at the black dot. Thus the pigeon was led to the end result. A simple free operant—facing by chance toward the white circle—was "shaped" into a conditioned operant that for a pigeon is extremely complicated and difficult.

Anyone who tries to teach a dog to carry a newspaper from the front door to its master is engaged in the process of shaping. You start with the fact that the dog sometimes grasps objects in its mouth and shape this one rather simple form of operant behavior into a much more complicated process. As shown in Figure 2-7, animal trainers achieve some striking results with shaping; they have taught bears to play musical instruments and rabbits to deposit coins in a piggy bank. People who watch trained animals sometimes feel sorry for them, imagining that they must have been subjected to brutal punishment to force them to learn their stunts. But the fact is that most animal training is done with shaping, based on the principle of operant conditioning and with food as the reinforcing stimulus. The animals' only discomfort lies in the fact that they have to be kept hungry during the training and at the time of their performance so that the food will actually serve as a reinforcing stimulus.

some results of shaping

2-7

Among the accomplishments of animal trainers, using the technique of shaping and the reward of food, are elephants and bears that play musical instruments, a rabbit that hoards its money in a piggy bank, and a dolphin that leaps through a hoop.

4. shaping human behavior

A dramatic example of how shaping can change human behavior has been reported by therapists who treated a woman who was suffering from depression and refused to eat; when the treatment began she weighed only 47 pounds. Although she would not eat, the therapists found that she seemed to take considerable pleasure from the comforts of her hospital room—including a TV set, radio, record player, and books and magazines from which visitors would read to her, as well as the pictures and flowers in the room and the pleasant view from the window. Since she would probably soon have died unless induced to take food, the therapists decided to use these comforts as reinforcements in a drastic but potentially life-saving attempt at shaping her behavior.

The woman was moved to another room, completely barren except for a bed, nightstand, and chair. Meals—as light and tempting as possible—were set in front of her as before. If she ate nothing, the therapists did nothing. If she ate anything at all, her behavior was reinforced by providing one of the comforts of which she had been deprived—for example, her radio. Gradually the therapists withheld the reinforcement unless she ate more and more, until the point was reached where reinforcement depended upon eating everything on the plate. Then the size of the meals and their nutritional value were gradually increased.

Under this program of shaping, with such rewards as radio, television, and visitors as the reinforcements, the woman gained 17 pounds within two months and could be released from the hospital. A follow-up eighteen months later showed that she had continued to gain weight and was leading a fully active life (11).

5. operant conditioning of "involuntary" bodily activities

One of the most important advances in the field of learning in recent years has been the discovery that operant conditioning can have a significant effect on bodily activities that had heretofore been considered "involuntary" and impossible to control through any such learning. In order to explain this new development, it must be pointed out that we ordinarily do not have much if any control over many of the processes that go on inside our bodies. The internal responses that regulate blood pressure, rate of heartbeat, contraction or relaxation of the muscles of the stomach and intestines, and the glandular activity affecting many bodily states (including, as will be seen in Chapter 9, those associated with such emotions as fear and anger) are not under the direct control of the central nervous system. Instead they are regulated by another network called the autonomic nervous system, which, as its name implies, seems to operate independently and in disregard of any commands we may try to give it.*

As was stated in the section on the conditioned response, it has been known for some time that classical conditioning can affect responses controlled by the

---

*Further information about the autonomic nervous system, the glands, and the difference between "voluntarily" controlled or striped muscles and "involuntarily" controlled or smooth muscles will be found in Chapter 8.

autonomic nervous system. In the Pavlov experiment, the response of the salivary glands became attached to the previously neutral stimulus of sound; in the Albert experiment, the bodily states associated with fear became attached to the previously neutral stimulus of furry objects. However, responses of this kind did not seem to be capable of being altered in any way by operant conditioning.

Recently Neal Miller and his associates at Rockefeller University have performed an ingenious series of experiments that seem to establish beyond doubt that responses under the control of the autonomic nervous system can indeed be modified through operant conditioning. In the first of these experiments, an attempt was made to change the rate of activity of the salivary glands of two groups of dogs. Both groups were kept somewhat thirsty at the time of the experiment and for both the reinforcement was water, which does not in itself have any effect on the activity of the salivary glands. The dogs in one group were rewarded with water every time their glands produced a burst of spontaneous salivation, as they ordinarily do from time to time without any stimulation. The dogs in the other group were rewarded under exactly the opposite circumstances—that is, when activity of the glands decreased and they went long intervals without producing saliva. The results of the test, shown in Figure 2–8, show quite clearly that the dogs in the first group learned to increase the rate of activity of their salivary glands, those in the second group to decrease it (12).

Next an attempt was made to change the rate of heartbeat. For this experiment, rats were used. In order to ensure that the animals learned to control the heart muscle itself, rather than "voluntary" muscles that might indirectly affect the rate, their "voluntary" muscles were paralyzed through injections of a drug called curare. (Since the muscles of breathing were among those paralyzed, the animals were kept alive through artificial respiration.) Through the use of shaping—first rewarding small changes with a pleasant form of brain stimulation, then rewarding only successively larger changes—some rather rapid and substantial learning

SALIVARY GLANDS

HEARTBEAT

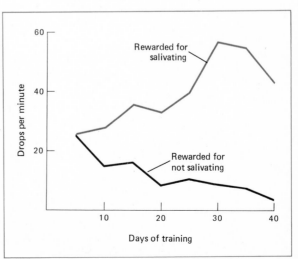

conditioning the salivary glands

2-8

One group of dogs was rewarded, in the manner explained in the text, when the rate of activity of their salivary glands increased. Another was rewarded when the rate decreased. Daily forty-five-minute training periods produced substantial differences between the two groups after about ten days, and the differences became even more evident as additional days passed. (12)

was produced. Within ninety minutes of training, animals rewarded for increasing the heart rate averaged a 20 percent jump, and those rewarded for decreasing the rate averaged a 20 percent slowing of the rate (13).

INTESTINAL CONTRACTIONS

Using similar techniques, Miller and his associates found that rats could also learn rather quickly to increase or decrease the number of intestinal contractions, as shown in Figure 2-9. They could also learn to change their blood pressure, increase or decrease stomach contractions, produce a larger or smaller flow of blood to the stomach or to the kidneys, and even to increase the amount of blood flowing through one ear while the flow through the other ear remained unchanged (15). Figure 2-10 shows Neal Miller and an associate preparing a rat for one of their experiments.

BLOOD PRESSURE

Another group of experimenters has succeeded in using operant conditioning to reduce blood pressure in human subjects. The subjects, all men, were hooked up to an apparatus that constantly measured their blood pressure after each heartbeat and signaled a decrease by sounding a tone and flashing a light. The subjects did not know what kind of bodily activity was being measured but were asked to try to make the light flash as often as possible; their reward, after every twenty flashes, was to look at a slide projection of a pleasant photograph, as shown in Figure 2-11. After a little more than twenty-five minutes of training, interrupted by rest periods, the average blood pressure of the subjects dropped from 120 to less than 116 (16).

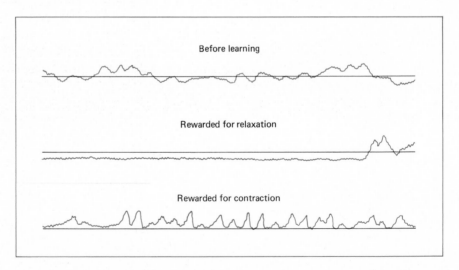

conditioning the digestive muscles

2-9 The top curve shows the typical pattern of intestinal contractions of a rat, with each jump in the curve recording a contraction. If the rat is rewarded for relaxing the muscles of the intestines, the number of contractions decreases as shown by the middle curve. If the conditions of the experiment are reversed and the animal is rewarded for contracting the muscles, the curve changes to the form shown at the bottom. (14)

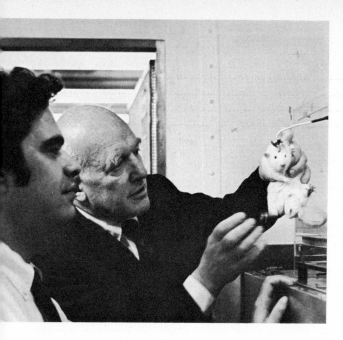

2-10 A rat is prepared by Neal Miller (right) and his associate Leo DiCara for one of their experiments in operant conditioning of responses controlled by the autonomic nervous system—experiments that have opened up many exciting new possibilities in the field of learning.

learning to control blood pressure

2-11

For the reward of looking at a pleasing photograph, a subject learns to reduce his blood pressure.

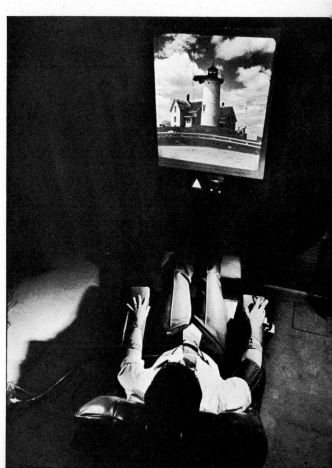

Can Operant Conditioning Cure Psychosomatic Illnesses? On the basis of the experimental findings, Miller has suggested that many psychosomatic symptoms, which have proved resistant to change through classical conditioning, may possibly be relieved through new techniques of operant conditioning. Perhaps people who suffer from psychosomatically induced high blood pressure may learn to keep the pressure down; those who have an abnormally fast or irregular heartbeat may learn to control it; those who have asthma attacks without any apparent physical cause may learn to prevent them; and those who suffer from "nervous" stomachs or intestines may learn to relax these organs. It even seems possible that people who have insomnia may learn to produce the particular kind of brain waves that are associated with going to sleep. Experiments are now being conducted along these lines.

Miller has also theorized that many psychosomatic symptoms are perhaps acquired in the first place through operant conditioning. For example, he suggests the case of a young child who is afraid to go to school in the morning because he is unprepared for a test. His fear may produce several different kinds of bodily states regulated by the autonomic nervous system—on one occasion, perhaps changes in heart rate and blood pressure that make him pale and faint, on another occasion a queasy stomach. If his mother is especially concerned about his being pale and faint, she may keep him home from school—and the reward of having his fears relieved may reinforce the tendency to respond with circulatory symptoms. If she is especially concerned about digestive upsets and keeps him home for this reason, his tendency toward this kind of bodily response may be reinforced. Certainly the new studies have opened up a promising field for further investigation.

F. learning through observation

Up to this point, four of the elements of learning have been discussed—the reflex response and the conditioned response, operant behavior and operant conditioning. Now a fifth must be added. This is *learning through observation*, or, as some psychologists prefer, *learning through modeling* or *learning by imitation*. All three terms are more or less self-explanatory. Many lower animals, and more especially human beings, often learn new behavior simply by observing the behavior of another organism; the other organism's behavior serves as a model that is then imitated. This kind of learning is so common that it is recognized in the well-known saying, "Monkey see, monkey do"—one popular adage that is based on solid evidence.

1. animal learning through observation

One of the most impressive demonstrations of observation learning in animals was conducted in a variation of a Skinner box designed for cats. Pressing the bar did not ordinarily result in the reward of food. If the bar was pressed within fifteen seconds after a light went on inside the box, however, food automatically dropped into a feeding tray. Two cats learned through operant conditioning to press the bar when the light went on. Then other cats were permitted to watch them obtain food in this manner. The cats that observed the trained animals were then tested, and they proved to learn very quickly to press the bar when the light went on—much more quickly than other cats who had to learn through operant conditioning without any opportunity for advance observation.

Similar results were obtained in an experiment on operant avoidance. This time cats were placed in a cage that had two compartments separated by a hurdle. A buzzer was sounded, and after it had been on for fifteen seconds the animal received an electric shock unless it jumped into the other compartment. Cats placed in the cage, as might be expected from experiments described earlier, learned through operant conditioning to make the jump and avoid the shock. Other cats that had an opportunity to observe them making the avoidance response, however, proved to learn much faster than animals that started from scratch without having watched this kind of behavior (17).

2. human learning through observation

One well-known demonstration of observation learning in human beings, illustrated in Figure 2-12, was recorded on film by Albert Bandura. Children watched a movie showing an adult playing with a large doll in a highly aggressive manner, striking it with a hammer. Given an opportunity to play with the doll themselves, as is shown in the photographs, the children displayed remarkably similar behavior.

imitation of aggression

2-12   Why are the boy and girl at the left acting so aggressively toward the toy? And why does their aggressive behavior take such a remarkably similar form? The answer is that they were imitating the behavior of a model—the woman at the right, who had behaved in exactly this fashion in a movie they had watched.

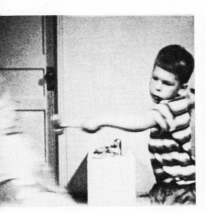

One need hardly go to the laboratory, however, for examples of human learning through observation. Obviously we learn many things in this manner. Children imitate the play of other children. As we grow up we learn through observation how to start an automobile; we imitate some of the mannerisms of our parents and other adults. The learning we do in school is largely the result of observation and imitation; even learning from books is a sort of indirect and symbolic version of this kind of learning.

It has been suggested that learning through observation is the primary method by which human beings acquire language, ideas, and social habits (17). Therefore learning through observation occupies an important place in the study of psychology, especially in such fields as development, personality, and social behavior. Since we learn so many things by observation and imitation, a significant question becomes: Whom do we imitate, and why? For example, clinical psychologists who work in schools and communities are well aware that the delinquent underachiever is imitating the conduct of one kind of model and the well-behaved and ambitious student the conduct of quite a different model.

The fact that observation learning can also be used successfully as a form of psychotherapy has been demonstrated in a more recent series of experiments by Bandura. As will be explained in more detail on pages 419–20, the experiments have indicated that many kinds of abnormal fears, for example, can be relieved through therapy in which the psychologist gives his client an opportunity to imitate more desirable behavior (18).

G. the question of <u>what</u> is learned

The basic elements of learning have now been described: 1) the simple and unlearned reflex, built into the organism's "wiring"; 2) the process through which the unconditioned reflex can be modified and turned into a conditioned response; 3) operant behavior; 4) the way operant behavior can be modified and shaped

68

through operant conditioning; and 5) the process, perhaps most important of all in human beings, of learning through observation and imitation. Now the question must be asked: When we learn, *what* do we learn?

At first thought, this seems like a simple question with an obvious answer. You may be inclined to say, "That's easy; we learn to *do* something." Pavlov's dog learns to salivate to the sound of a metronome; the rat in the Skinner box learns to press the bar to get food; a student learns to speak French by observing and imitating the sounds made by his instructor.

But this answer, though it is true as far as it goes, does not explain the entire learning process. To show why, let us begin with another experiment in simple classical conditioning. Suppose that we put a dog in a harness like Pavlov's, arranged so that one paw rests on a metal plate. We pass an electric current through the plate, and the dog responds by pulling its paw away. Now we do the same thing with another dog, only this time we paralyze its leg with curare, so that it cannot pull away. While the leg is immobilized, we pair a high-pitched sound with a shock and present a low-pitched sound without administering a shock. The dog hears the tones and sometimes feels the shock but *cannot pull its paw away*. It makes no movement in response to either the shock or the high-pitched sound. Nothing has happened, so far as we can see. Under these circumstances, does any conditioning take place? Does the dog learn that the high-pitched tone is associated with shock?

If we go on the theory that learning is always a matter of doing something, we would have to say no. But, when we let the curare wear off and then sound the tones, we are in for a surprise. When the dog hears the high tone it pulls its paw away; when it hears the low tone it does not. The behavior of pulling the paw away has been conditioned to the high tone even though the action was never taken during the conditioning process (19).

The experiment is an indication that <u>even in the simplest form of conditioning, the actual physical response is not always essential to learning.</u> What the dog seems to have learned is not the overt action but some kind of invisible connection between the conditioned stimulus of the high-pitched tone and the unconditioned but previously unpracticed response of pulling the paw away.

1. learning without overt action

There is a possible objection to the experiment with the paralyzed dog; it may be that the pairing of the high-pitched tone and the shock has conditioned the animal to respond with the bodily states of fear—and that fear then makes the dog pull its paw away when it can. But it can easily and convincingly be demonstrated that <u>human beings often learn without any kind of overt action.</u> Indeed you can try your own experiment. Use a word such as *syzygy*, an unusual word that has never been heard or spoken by the average person. (It is pronounced siz-i-jee, with the *siz* as in *scissors*, the *i* as in *it*, and the *jee* as in *jeep*; it means "a joining together.") As your experiment, say to a friend, "Don't say anything. Just listen. The word is *syzygy*. Don't say anything." Then change the subject. A half-hour later, ask your friend, "What word did I say a while ago?" Almost surely, he will answer correctly, "Syzygy."

Even though he had never heard the word before and took no overt action when you first said the word to him, he managed to learn it. Again, as in the case of the dog with the paralyzed leg, some kind of connection was set up inside him. It was this connection, not an overt response, that was learned.

You may recall a related experiment discussed earlier in which cats learned through observation something about pressing a bar for food or avoiding a shock even though they took no overt action during the period of observation. And it is easy to think of many real-life examples. For instance, a small child learns the meaning of words long before he learns to speak them; he can point to his nose or his mouth while still unable to say either of those words. An older child watches a movie or a television program and several days later, at play, acts out one of the scenes. An adult watches a plumber repair a leaky faucet, does nothing at the time, but weeks later can fix the faucet himself. All of us, if we keep an observant eye on our behavior, will find ourselves doing things that we saw one of our parents do years ago. We did not repeat our parent's behavior at the time; we took no overt action at all; but some sort of lasting connection was formed inside us, and we act that way now.

2. the learning connection

What is the nature of the learning connection? Almost surely, it represents some kind of change in the nervous system and especially the brain, which is an enormously complicated switchboard of nerve fibers. As will be seen in Chapter 8, certain tiny but probably significant chemical and electrical changes seem to take place in or between nerve fibers when learning occurs. These changes seem to lay down a more or less permanent pathway or pattern, so that once the nervous system has learned to operate in a certain way it is likely to operate the same way again in response to the same kind of stimulus. The exact nature of the changes is not known and is a matter of controversy. Some psychologists believe that they are of such a nature that they can be facilitated by some yet undiscovered drug—in other words, that we may someday have a "learning pill" that will help us acquire and remember new knowledge (20). Indeed some psychologists have reported that animals sometimes seem to acquire a new skill if they are injected with brain tissue from other animals that had learned the skill (21), although attempts to repeat their experiments have been generally unsuccessful (22). About all that can be said at the moment is that we must be content to describe the way in which learning connections operate and wait for future investigations to tell us exactly why and how.

3. the mediational unit

As to how the learning connections operate, there is a great deal of experimental evidence, some of which has already been discussed and more of which will be described in the following pages. There is considerable disagreement among psychologists, however, over the interpretation of the evidence. The viewpoints range from those generally held by the S-R school of psychology (page 17) to those of the cognitive school (page 18).

The S-R psychologists tend to regard the learning connection as a rather direct association between a stimulus and a behavioral response. The cognitive psychologists tend to regard it as the acquisition of information and of the ability to remember this information and manipulate it in useful and sometimes even creative ways. These different viewpoints probably result in part from the different kinds of experiments that members of the two schools have performed. The S-R psychologists have chiefly studied lower animals, such as rats and pigeons, where the results of learning can be observed only in the form of overt behavior. The cognitive psychologists have chiefly studied human beings, from whom it is possible to obtain reports of the unseen mental processes that go on inside the organism. Indeed the differences in viewpoints may someday be found to have merely reflected the fact that the learning process itself takes a number of different forms, ranging from the establishment of rather direct associations between a stimulus and a behavioral response to the acquisition of very complex forms of information and rules for using it.

Pending a final resolution of the debate, an increasingly popular and relatively noncontroversial term to describe an association established by learning is *mediational unit*. The term is derived from the fact that whatever happens in the nervous system as a result of learning serves as an intermediary between environment and behavior. An event in the world, a stimulus, excites the nervous system. Somehow the result is to set up a mediational unit, a go-between, that becomes a more or less permanent part of the organism. At any time, immediately or in the future, the mediational unit when again aroused can go to work and produce behavior. The chain of events is *stimulus* to *mediational unit* to *behavior*.

One can think of the chain as being either relatively simple and direct (as the S-R psychologists view the learning process) or quite complex and self-directed (as the cognitive psychologists prefer). Therefore the term mediational unit is a useful one and will appear frequently throughout the book. The description of the term must be somewhat long-winded: *A mediational unit is some sort of more or less permanent nerve pathway or pattern established inside the organism through learning. It serves to connect a stimulus, on the one hand, and on the other hand, other mediational units or actions; it serves as an intermediary between the stimulus and immediate or future behavior or mental activity.*

4. psychology as the study of mediational units

There are many kinds of mediational units. Among them are *images* or recollections of sensory experiences; we can close our eyes and "see" the face of someone we know well and we can imagine the taste of a hamburger or the smell of an onion. The knowledge of words in our memories is made up of mediational units; we can respond as readily to the sound of the word *fire* as to the actual sight or feel of fire and to the word *food* as to the sight of food.

Indeed learning is the very core of psychology, and the mediational units that we acquire through learning constitute the great part of psychology's subject matter. Nearly everything discussed in the later chapters of this book is a mediational unit—for example, the words, concepts, and other elements of thinking (Chapter 5, "Language, Thinking, and Problem Solving"); the learned associations

MEDIATIONAL UNIT
CHAIN OF EVENTS

1. STIMULUS
↓
2. MEDIATIONAL UNIT
↓
3. BEHAVIOR

DEFINITION:
MEDIATIONAL UNIT

that influence the way we perceive the world (Chapter 7, "Perception"); our emotions (Chapter 9); our motives (Chapter 10); our normal and abnormal personality traits (Chapters 11 and 12); and the attitudes toward other people that influence the way we behave in our society (Chapter 16, "Social Psychology").

H. the role of reinforcement

Before the discussion of the elements and principles of learning can be considered complete, it must be directed to the subject of reinforcement, a process that has traditionally been considered a key to learning. The word has already been used a number of times in the chapter. For example, it was pointed out that the classical conditioning of Pavlov's dog depended on reinforcement by food that actually produced the salivary response—and that, if the reinforcement of food was withheld long enough, the conditioned response underwent extinction. On the matter of operant conditioning, it was stated that the general rule is that behavior that is reinforced tends to be repeated, while behavior that is not reinforced tends to be abandoned. To these general rules, there must now be added some important specific findings on the role of reinforcement—as well as a warning that new work in this field has shown that the entire idea of reinforcement is quite tricky and controversial.

1. secondary reinforcement

In most of the experiments cited thus far, the reinforcement was something that quite obviously constituted a direct reward—food for the hungry animal, water for the thirsty animal. A stimulus such as food or water, something in itself rewarding to the organism, is known as a *primary reinforcing stimulus.* But this is not the only kind of reinforcement that will help the organism learn, as can be demonstrated in another kind of experiment with a rat and the Skinner box.

DEFINITION:
PRIMARY REINFORCING
STIMULUS

In this experiment, before being put into the box, the rat is kept in an ordinary cage and is fed food one pellet at a time. Each time it gets a pellet of food a buzzer sounds. This situation, you will note, is much like the Pavlov experiment in conditioning the salivary reflex to a conditioned stimulus. But in this case we are not interested in whether the rat will begin to salivate to the sound of the buzzer alone. We are interested only in what will happen when it is put into the Skinner box, which is now rearranged so that pressing the bar does not release a pellet of food but instead sounds a buzzer.

DEFINITION:
SECONDARY REINFORCING
STIMULUS

What happens is that, as before, the rat makes its free operant movements, eventually presses the bar, and hears the buzzer. And now it turns out that the buzzer serves as a very effective reinforcing stimulus. The rat is quickly conditioned to press the bar by the reward of hearing the buzzer—which now serves as a *secondary reinforcing stimulus,* or something that has become rewarding through association with a primary reinforcement.

Many experiments have been performed in which animals have been oper-antly conditioned through secondary reinforcement. Chimpanzees, for example, have been conditioned not only with primary reinforcement provided by food but also with secondary reinforcement provided by poker chips that they can put into a sort of vending machine that delivers food when a chip is dropped into a slot, as shown in Figure 2-13.

The human parallel, of course, is that for a child jelly beans may provide strong reinforcement, and money, at the beginning, no reinforcement at all. But, since money can buy jelly beans, it becomes a secondary reinforcing stimulus. One of the problems in studying and attempting to assist in human learning is that almost anything apparently can become a secondary reinforcing stimulus—and that something that operates as a strong secondary reinforcing stimulus for one person may have no effect at all on another person.

secondary reinforcement of a chimpanzee

2-13

The chimpanzee has been operantly conditioned by the secondary rein-forcement of a poker chip, which it now drops into a vending machine to obtain the primary reinforcement of food.

2-14

The steep drop in the curve shows how rapidly learning fell off when reinforcement—in this case food obtained when rats pressed a bar in a Skinner box—was delayed for intervals varying from a few seconds to about two minutes. Note that no learning at all took place when reinforcement was delayed for slightly more than 100 seconds. (23)

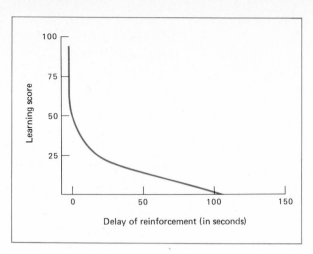

2. delay of reinforcement

Many experiments in operant conditioning have studied the effects of the timing of reinforcement. For example, in the case of the Skinner box, experimenters have arranged to present food immediately after the bar is pressed, a few seconds afterward, or many seconds afterward. The results of one such experiment are shown in Figure 2-14. Note that the animals learned by far the fastest when the reinforcement was presented immediately. When reinforcement was delayed even for a few seconds, learning fell off rapidly—and with a delay of slightly more than 100 seconds there appeared to be no learning at all.

Similar results have been found in many other operant learning situations. The general principle, which is that immediate reinforcement produces the most learning and that delay of reinforcement reduces the amount of learning, has many implications. If you want to teach a dog a trick, you will have much more success if you reward the animal immediately after its successful attempts rather than five minutes later.

PRINCIPLE OF REIN-
FORCEMENT TIMING
IN OPERANT LEARNING

3. partial reinforcement

Another fact about reinforcement in operant learning can be demonstrated by placing two rats in Skinner boxes and rewarding them on different schedules. One rat receives a food pellet every time it presses the bar. The other rat receives food every fourth time. The second rat is thus on a schedule of what is called *partial reinforcement* or *intermittent reinforcement*—receiving a reward not every time but only sometimes. Which kind of reinforcement is more effective, constant or partial?

DEFINITION:

PARTIAL REINFORCEMENT
OR
INTERMITTENT REINFORCE-
MENT

One way to answer this question is to stop giving the two rats any reinforcement at all and observe how long it takes before they stop pressing the bar.

74

When this is done, it is found that extinction is much faster for the animal that was on a schedule of constant reinforcement than for the animal that was on a schedule of partial reinforcement.

One convincing experiment of this type has measured an animal's ability to learn to run a maze, another device frequently used in studies of learning. (An example of a more or less typical maze is illustrated in Figure 2-15.) Some of the animals that ran the maze successfully and reached the goal found food there 100 percent of the time, others 80 percent, others 50 percent, and still others only 30 percent. Then the reinforcement of food was withdrawn entirely to determine how fast extinction of the maze-running response would occur. The results of the experiment are shown in Figure 2-16—a clear-cut demonstration that operant behavior conditioned by partial reinforcement persists longer than behavior conditioned by constant reinforcement.

PRINCIPLE OF PAR-TIAL REINFORCEMENT IN OPERANT LEARNING

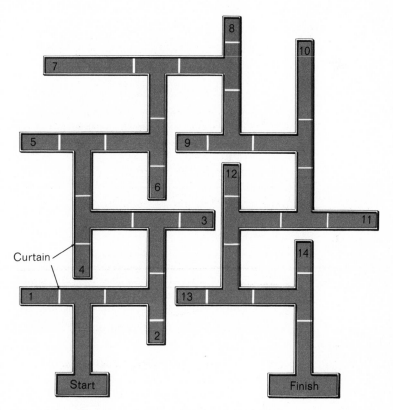

a maze used in learning experiments

2-15 This is one type of maze frequently used in animal learning experiments. The animal's progress at learning the maze can be measured by the time it takes to get from start to finish, by the number of errors made by entering the fourteen blind alleys, or by both.

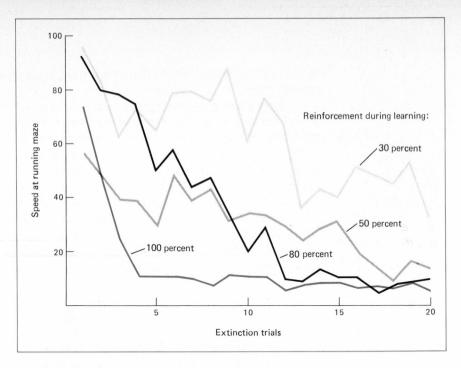

partial versus constant reinforcement

2-16　In this experiment in maze running by rats, some of the animals were on a schedule of constant reinforcement (100 percent). Others received partial reinforcement—after 30, 50, or 80 percent of their successful trials. Once they had learned to run the maze quickly, they were given twenty trials without any reinforcement at all. Note that the process of extinction during these twenty trials was fastest for the animals that had received constant reinforcement and that the animals on a 30 percent schedule of partial reinforcement resisted extinction the most. (24)

In real-life situations, partial reinforcement is the rule rather than the exception. The rat that has learned to seek food in certain ways will not succeed every time. Among human beings, the persistence of behavior learned through partial reinforcement helps explain why a man who once won a daily double at the race track keeps trying again despite a long succession of losing days.

4. reinforcement and "superstition"

Perhaps closely related to partial reinforcement are the findings obtained in the following experiment. Pigeons were placed in a Skinner box in which pecking at a lighted key caused food to drop into a feeder. After they had pecked at the key only three times and obtained food as a result, the key was entirely disconnected from the feeding mechanism and food dropped into the feeder at irregular intervals on a varying schedule set up arbitrarily by the experimenter. Pecking the key did not produce food, but food did appear from time to time. Under these circumstances, would you expect the pigeons to continue pecking at the key—or to learn that the key had nothing to do with whether or not they received food?

Rather strangely, the pigeons kept pecking away. They were returned to the box for twenty sessions of slightly more than twenty minutes each, and during these periods they pecked at the key for an average of 2700 times each. Even in the final session, they were still pecking at the key on the average of three times a minute (25). In human terms, we might say that the pigeons had acquired a superstition; they "believed" that pecking somehow produced food, even though in fact their behavior had nothing to do with when or whether the food appeared.

It is interesting to note how quickly the "superstition" was established—that is, within three pairings of key pecking and food. Indeed there is evidence that this kind of "superstitious" behavior may be established by a single pairing (26). It is also interesting that the key-pecking behavior persisted at such a high level of strength over so long a period. The psychologist who performed the experiment has suggested that "superstitions" probably play a far larger role in animal behavior than has heretofore been suspected. He reasons that every animal is capable of a wide variety of operant behaviors. Any one of its responses can be operantly conditioned through reinforcement—certainly by three pairings of response and reinforcement, possibly by only a single pairing. And nature provides many kinds of reinforcement that occur independently of any response the animal makes, for example, rain that falls when the animal is thirsty, fruit that drops off a tree when the animal is hungry. If the environment just happens to provide food immediately after the animal has scratched its ear, and since food will appear again as a result of events over which the animal has no control, the animal may very well acquire a lasting "superstition" that will make it scratch its ear regularly.

Although there is no experimental evidence, we are probably entitled to assume that many human superstitions have a similar kind of origin. One widely held superstition may have been started by a small boy who fell into a mud puddle and remembered that he had just walked under a ladder, another by a little girl who found a penny just after she had seen a clover with one too many leaves. Once such a superstition has been established, it would be kept alive by the fact that events may prove unlucky or lucky through no doing of our own.

5. reinforcement and behavior

Some other recent experiments have also resulted in rather strange findings that are well worth our attention. In one of them, pigeons were again taught to press a lighted key to obtain food from a feeding cup. There was also another feeding cup in the Skinner box; but during their training, which lasted seven days, this cup was always empty. After the seventh day the second cup was kept constantly filled; it provided a constant source of "free food" for which no work had to be done. One might think that the pigeons would now eat the free food and that the response of pecking at the key would become extinct. However, quite the opposite happened. It turned out that the pigeons, though they ate some of the "free food," continued to get most of their food by pecking

2-17

The bars show the number of times a pigeon in a Skinner box pecked at a lighted key that opened a feeding cup. After seven days in which the pigeon could get food only by pecking at the key, "free food" was placed in a second cup and was available at all times for the next eleven days. The pigeon continued to peck at the key, however, and in fact made more responses than before. Then the food cup operated by the key was covered, and for the next eleven days the pigeon could eat only from the "free" cup; under these conditions it pecked at the key only occasionally. Finally the food cup operated by the key was uncovered again and the pigeon went back to a high rate of key pecking. For the probable explanation, see the text. (27)

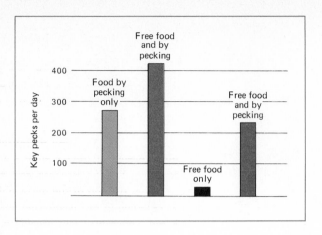

at the key. When the food cup operated by the key was covered, so that they could get no food from this source, they did almost abandon pecking at the key; but when the cup was uncovered again, they went back to key pecking as their preferred method of obtaining food. The results for one pigeon are illustrated in Figure 2-17.

Similar results were obtained for rats that had their choice of eating free food or pressing a bar to get it. One can only assume that the animals found that the act of producing their own food, by pecking at the key or pressing the bar, served as its own reward. Once established, the behavior persisted as if it had a life of its own.

Another experiment, however, has shown that this kind of behavior has limitations. In this case, rats also learned to press a bar to obtain food. But in some of their learning trials they received food every time they pressed the bar, in other trials only after every second press, and in still others only after every ten presses. When these rats had their choice of pressing the bar to get food or eating from a dish of free food, they continued to press the bar if they were rewarded for every press or every second press. If they had to press ten times, however, they changed their preference and ate more free food than food produced by pressing the bar (28). In human terms, they seemed to prefer working for their own food when the work was relatively easy—but, when the work grew too hard, they preferred free food. You may draw your own conclusions about the relation of this experiment to human behavior.

6. latent learning

Let us now consider another experiment in reinforcement that raises some important questions. In this experiment three groups of rats were placed in a maze exactly like the one that was illustrated in Figure 2-15. Group 1 always found food at the end of the maze. For this group the reinforcing stimulus was obvious. The operant behavior to which the rats were conditioned was running a direct route from the start of the maze to the finish. Their progress in learning was measured by counting the number of errors they made by going into blind alleys. As might be expected, group 1 did better every day. In the original experiment of this type, the group 1 rats made about ten errors the first day but only about four errors on the tenth day.

Group 2 never found food at the end of the maze. These rats were simply placed in the maze and permitted to move around in any way they chose for a given period of time. Group 3 was treated the same way as group 2 for the first ten days. On the eleventh day, however, and on every day thereafter, food was placed at the end of the maze. The results of the experiment are shown in Figure 2-18. Even in just wandering around the maze, without reinforcement, the group 3 rats apparently had learned a great deal about the correct path. As soon as reinforcement was provided, they began to demonstrate their knowledge.

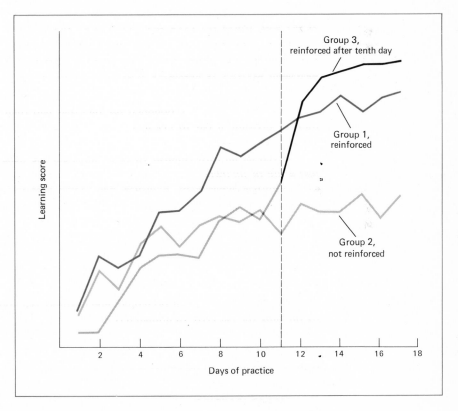

maze learning with and without reinforcement

2-18   The graph shows the progress at learning the maze in Figure 2–15 made by three groups of rats under different conditions of reinforcement. For the meaning of these results, see the text. (29)

DEFINITION :
LATENT LEARNING
OR
INCIDENTAL LEARNING

The kind of learning that the group 3 rats did on the first ten days is called *latent learning*—that is, learning that takes place but lies latent, not being put into overt performance until reinforcement is provided. It is also called *incidental learning,* meaning that it takes place casually, almost as if by accident. The rats received no apparent reinforcement, but they learned anyway.

In everyday human affairs there are many examples of latent or incidental learning. A friend takes you by car to the nearby city of Smithville. You have no intention of ever returning to Smithville. You make no effort to learn the route. Still, if the occasion ever arises when you yourself have to drive to Smithville, you find that you remember the way, at least to some extent. Wandering through the downtown district of the city in which you live, you pass a shop that has pipes and smoking tobacco in the window. As a nonsmoker, you take no interest in the shop. Later, when you decide to become a pipe smoker, you find that you remember the location of the shop. Why? What was the reinforcement for learning?

7. theories of reinforcement

As the questions raised by latent learning indicate, the nature of reinforcement has always been a puzzle. Even today psychologists are hard-pressed to describe what it is or how it operates. The only completely accurate definition that can be offered is this: *A reinforcing stimulus or event is anything that strengthens and induces repetitions of behavior.* And indeed some psychologists believe that reinforcement is not really essential to learning (30).

At one time it was generally thought that all primary reinforcing stimuli were those that satisfied or at least reduced biological drives—for example, food to satisfy the hunger drive, water to satisfy the thirst drive. This theory, however, though by no means abandoned by all psychologists, was dealt a severe blow by the discovery that an animal that is hungry but not thirsty will learn to press a bar for reinforcement by water sweetened with saccharine, which has no food value and therefore cannot satisfy the hunger drive (30).

There seems to be a possibility that saccharine water serves as a reinforcing stimulus because of the sheer pleasure—unrelated to the biological drives—of tasting something sweet. There is evidence, indeed, that there may be some kind of "pleasure center" deep in the brain. When an electrode is placed in this center and hooked up to the bar in a Skinner box, an animal will learn to press the bar for the reward of this particular kind of brain stimulation; indeed, when a choice is permitted, a hungry animal sometimes prefers the brain stimulation to food (31). It is interesting to note that the stimulation makes the animal more active; it seems to "excite" the animal and cause moving around and exploration of the environment, as if the stimulation had aroused the motive to engage in some kind of behavior (32).

Partly because of the findings concerning the "pleasure center," there has been a growing interest among many psychologists in a possible connection between reinforcement, arousal of the organism, and the motivation to engage

DEFINITION:
REINFORCING STIMULUS

in behavior. It has been noted that a rat, when it has been placed in a Skinner box, has pressed the bar, and has received the reinforcement of a food pellet, seems to be in a special state of arousal when it eats—also that it behaves as if motivated to return to the bar as quickly as possible. A child who has just held his fork correctly and has received reinforcement in the form of a kiss from his mother seems to be similarly aroused and motivated.

One possibility is that the chief effect of a reinforcing stimulus is, by arousing and motivating the organism, to attract the organism's *attention.* In the Skinner box, for example, the arrival of the food pellet may make the rat sit up and take notice, so to speak; it tunes the rat in to the general situation and to what has just occurred, namely the pressing of the bar. In the case of human learning, the idea that reinforcement may be closely related to attention fits in neatly with something that the history of mankind seems to show: that human beings are lively and curious animals who constantly exhibit a keen interest in their world and their fellows. If a reinforcing stimulus is thought of as anything that can attract a person's attention long enough for some new item of information to be stored in memory, then the latent learning that takes place on the road to Smithville or in passing the tobacco shop seems less of a mystery.

summary
1. Much of the behavior of lower organisms represents the operation of *instincts,* which are inborn patterns of activity. Most human behavior, however, is learned.

2. One basic element in learning is the *reflex,* an unlearned and inborn *response* to a *stimulus* (which is defined as any form of energy capable of exciting the nervous system).

3. Through learning, a reflex can become attached to a stimulus that did not originally cause the reflex. This process, first demonstrated when Pavlov "taught" a dog to respond to a sound with the salivary reflex originally caused by the presence of food in the mouth, is called *classical conditioning.*

4. In classical conditioning, the stimulus that naturally causes the reflex is called the *unconditioned stimulus.* The previously neutral stimulus to which the reflex becomes attached is called the *conditioned stimulus.* The original reflex is called the *unconditioned response,* and the response to the conditioned stimulus is called the *conditioned response.*

5. The pairing of the unconditioned stimulus and the conditioned stimulus is called *reinforcement.* When reinforcement is withdrawn, the conditioned response tends to disappear—a process called *extinction.* After a rest period, however, it tends to reappear—a process called *spontaneous recovery.*

6. When a response has been conditioned to one stimulus, it is also likely to be aroused by similar stimuli—a process called *stimulus generalization.* Through further training, however, the organism can learn to respond to a particular conditioned stimulus but not to other stimuli even when they are very similar—a process called *stimulus discrimination.*

7. Another basic element in learning is *operant behavior,* such as the random actions of a rat in its cage or a human baby in his crib.

8. Through learning, operant behavior can become attached to a specific stimulus. This process is called *operant conditioning.* The learned behavior is called a *conditioned operant,* meaning a form of behavior with which the organism "operates" on its environment to obtain a desired result.

9. *Operant escape* and *avoidance* are behavior, learned through operant conditioning, whereby the organism seeks to escape or avoid an unpleasant stimulus such as an electric shock or criticism or rejection by other persons.

10. The learning of complicated tasks through operant conditioning is called *shaping,* a process by which complex actions are built up step by step by rewarding simpler actions that lead to the final behavior.

11. An important new finding is that operant conditioning can modify "involuntary" bodily activities controlled by the autonomic nervous system—such as heart rate, blood pressure, and contractions of the digestive muscles. The discovery raises the possibility that operant conditioning may help relieve psychosomatic illnesses associated with these bodily activities.

12. In *learning through observation* (also called *learning through modeling* or *learning by imitation*), the organism learns by copying the behavior of another organism (the model). It is especially important among human beings.

13. The physiological explanation of learning seems to be some kind of chemical and electrical changes that take place in or between nerve fibers, especially in the brain.

14. What is learned is best described as a *mediational unit*—that is, some sort of more or less permanent nerve pathway or pattern that serves as an intermediary between a stimulus and immediate or future behavior or mental activity.

15. Psychology is largely the study of such mediational units as images, words, concepts, perceptions, emotions, motives, and attitudes.

16. *Reinforcement* has traditionally been considered a key to learning. A reinforcing stimulus or event can be defined as *anything that strengthens and induces repetitions of behavior.*

17. A *primary reinforcing stimulus* is something that is in itself rewarding to the organism, such as food to satisfy hunger or water to satisfy thirst.

18. A *secondary reinforcing stimulus* is anything that has become rewarding through association with a primary reinforcing stimulus.

19. In general, a reinforcing stimulus is most effective when presented immediately. Any delay in reinforcement usually reduces the amount of learning.

20. *Partial reinforcement* takes place when conditioned operant behavior is rewarded on only some occasions, not all occasions. Behavior learned through partial reinforcement, which is common in real-life situations, tends to be especially persistent.

21. Many psychologists now believe there is a close connection between reinforcement, arousal of the organism, and the establishment of motivation to engage in behavior. One possibility is that the chief effect of a reinforcing stimulus may be, by arousing and motivating the organism, to attract the organism's *attention.*

recommended reading

Ayllon, T., and Azrin, N. H. *The token economy: a motivational system for therapy and rehabilitation.* New York: Appleton-Century-Crofts, 1968.

Bandura, A. *Principles of behavior modification.* New York: Holt, Rinehart and Winston, 1969.

Gagné, R. M. *The conditions of learning,* 2nd ed. New York: Holt, Rinehart and Winston, 1970.

Glaser, R., ed. *The nature of reinforcement.* Columbus, Ohio: Merrill, 1971.

Hilgard, E. R., and Bower, G. H. *Theories of learning,* 3rd ed. New York: Appleton-Century-Crofts, 1966.

Kimble, G. A., ed. *Foundations of conditioning and learning.* New York: Appleton-Century-Crofts, 1967.

Pavlov, I. P. *Conditioned reflexes: an investigation of the physiological activity of the cerebral cortex.* London: Oxford University Press, 1927 [reprinted by Dover, New York, 1960].

Skinner, B. F. *The behavior of organisms: an experimental analysis.* New York: Appleton-Century-Crofts, 1938.

CHAPTER 3

REMEMBERING ANd FORGETTING

We learn. Some kind of new mediational unit is formed inside us. Sometimes the mediational unit persists; it continues to exist and to be available—and we say that we remember. Sometimes it seems to disappear or to become somehow beyond our ability to recapture it—and we say that we have forgotten.

At one time you learned the name of your first-grade teacher. Do you remember it now, or have you forgotten? If you have forgotten the name, do you still remember the face? And could you perhaps remember the name if something happened to "jog your memory," as people say?

What we have learned is of no value to us unless we can remember it, and thus it is of the utmost importance to inquire: Why do we remember some things and forget others? Is there any way we can improve our ability to remember?

The principles of learning described in Chapter 2 were derived largely from the study of hungry animals that learned to perform a motor response, such as pressing a bar or running a maze, to obtain the reward of food. Most human learning takes place under quite different circumstances. Usually we are not hungry; we learn verbal rather than motor responses; our reward is not food but some token of approval from another person or the kind of self-approval that accompanies success. The principles of learning that apply to other animals are of course important in human learning as well—but in this chapter there will be less emphasis on learning mediational units that are tied to motor responses (such as learning how to operate a typewriter) and much more emphasis on how we learn, remember, and forget such mediational units as words, facts, and the rules for manipulating our knowledge.

A. curves of forgetting

A classic experiment on remembering and forgetting was performed in the nineteenth century by a German named Hermann Ebbinghaus, the first influential student of memory. Ebbinghaus wanted to study remembering and forgetting in the purest possible form, unaffected by any emotional factors or any other aspects of personality or past experience. He sought to have his subjects learn something that had no meaning to them—and no possible connection with their feelings or with anything they had learned in the past—and then to find how much of it

MEMORY —   Ebbinghaus

MESSAGE OF GRAPH

they remembered for how long. He therefore <u>used nonsense syllables,</u> which experimenters have been using ever since. He drew up lists of thirteen syllables each, like the two shown in Figure 3-1. Using himself as a subject, he memorized the lists until he could repeat them twice without error, keeping track of the amount of time this took him. Then, after an interval in which forgetting naturally took place, he set about relearning them, again keeping track of how long this took. <u>The difference between the amount of time it took to learn the lists originally and the amount of time it took to relearn them was a good measure of how much he remembered.</u>

Using many different lists and varying the time between original learning and relearning, <u>Ebbinghaus came up with the graph</u> shown in Figure 3-1. This is the typical *curve of forgetting* for many kinds of learning. It does not always apply, because we learn some things so thoroughly that we never seem to forget anything about them. However, it tells a great deal about the forgetting of such varied kinds of learning as motor skills, poems we have memorized, and college courses we have taken; and its message is this: *When we learn something new, often we quickly forget much of what we have learned, but we remember at least some of it for a long time.*

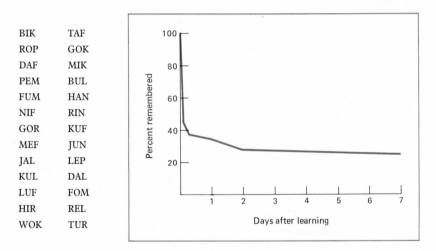

BIK	TAF
ROP	GOK
DAF	MIK
PEM	BUL
FUM	HAN
NIF	RIN
GOR	KUF
MEF	JUN
JAL	LEP
KUL	DAL
LUF	FOM
HIR	REL
WOK	TUR

a study of forgetting

3-1   In his classic study of forgetting Ebbinghaus memorized lists of thirteen nonsense syllables similar to those shown here, then measured his memory for the lists by noting how long it took him to relearn them perfectly. The graph he constructed from his study showed very rapid forgetting immediately after the learning. After twenty minutes, he remembered only 58 percent and after about an hour only 44 percent. After the initial sharp dip, however, the curve flattened out. After one day he remembered about 34 percent and after two days about 28 percent. Although the graph line does not extend that far, he still remembered 21 percent after a month. (1)

GENERAL PRINCIPLE
OF FORGETTING

Two other curves of forgetting are shown in Figure 3-2. These illustrate another general principle, which is that we tend to remember what we have learned about motor skills considerably better than we remember such verbal learning as nonsense syllables. Both curves resemble the classic Ebbinghaus curve, but the one for motor learning declines much more slowly than the one for verbal learning. Thus we tend to retain a good deal of the skill we once acquired as children at such motor tasks as swimming, riding a bicycle, roller skating, or sewing with a needle and thread. On the other hand we tend to forget many of the childhood jingles and poems that we once knew so well that we could recite them forward or backward.

The sharp rise at the start of the curve of motor forgetting in Figure 3-2 illustrates a phenomenon that has often been observed but is still not completely understood. In this case the subjects learned to keep a pointer on a rotating target to a degree of skill that was arbitrarily called 100 percent, then stopped practicing. The first time they were tested afterward, it turned out that they had not forgotten any of their skill but on the contrary had improved; they actually did much better than before. This often happens in the learning of motor skills; a common example if the golfer who takes a lesson, learns to hit the ball pretty well by the end of the lesson, then does even better the first time he picks up the club the next day. It also happens at times in verbal learning that has not been carried to completion. For example, you may try to memorize a poem and quit after you seem to have learned about 75 percent of it. The next time you try to recite it, you may find that you can recall more than 75 percent.

This phenomenon is called *reminiscence*. One possible explanation for reminiscence is that we get tired at the end of a learning period and cannot perform as well as we can later, after a rest.

DEFINITION:
REMINISCENCE

verbal and motor forgetting

3-2

In the experiment illustrated by this graph the same subjects learned a rather simple motor skill (holding a pointer on a circle that was rotating as on a record player) and a list of nonsense syllables. The curves of forgetting show that the subjects remembered the motor skill much better than they remembered the nonsense syllables. For an explanation of the strange jump at the beginning of the curve for the motor skill, see the text. (2)

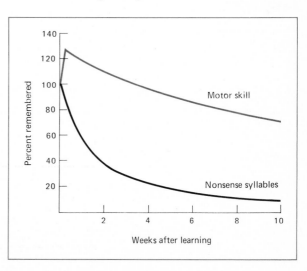

1. how remembering and forgetting are measured

After we have learned something, there are three standard methods of measuring how much of it we remember and how much we have forgotten.

Recall. One way to prove you have learned the Gettysburg Address is to recite it—which means to demonstrate that you can *recall* it, that you can retrieve it intact from wherever it is stored in memory. In school, a common use of recall as a measurement of learning is in the essay type of examination. When a teacher asks a question such as "What is classical conditioning?" he is asking you to recall and write down what you have learned.

Recognition. There are many situations in which we cannot recall what we have learned, at least not completely, but can prove that we have learned something about it by being able to recognize it. For example, if you ask a schoolchild to recall the Gettysburg Address, he may prove unable to do so. But if you show him the words "Fourscore and seven years ago our fathers brought forth on this continent" and ask him what begins with these words, he may immediately recognize the Gettysburg Address, thus demonstrating that he has certainly learned something about the speech.

You can probably think of many examples from your own experience. Someone asks, "Do you remember the name of the textbook we used in high school algebra?" and you reply, "No, but I'd recognize it if I saw it." You might give the same reply to questions such as, "Do you remember what dress Mary Smith wore to the dance last year?" or "Do you remember the number of the house we used to live in?"

Multiple-choice examinations are a test of recognition; you are asked to choose the right answer from among several possible answers and thus to prove that you recognize it. Because recognition is easier than recall, many students would rather take a multiple-choice test than an essay examination.

Indeed our ability at recognition is remarkably high. One experimenter showed college students a deck of more than 600 index cards, on each one of which a different sentence was typed (for example, "A dead dog is of no use for hunting ducks"). After the subjects had gone through the deck, they then looked at sixty-eight other index cards on which two sentences were typed—one a sentence that they had already seen, the other a new one. Asked to recognize which sentence was familiar, they proved to be extremely accurate; half of them correctly pointed to the familiar sentence 88 percent of the time or more. When single words were presented instead of sentences, the comparable score was 90 percent; for pictures it was 98 percent (3).

Relearning. The most sensitive method of measuring learning is one that is seldom used. This is the method of *relearning,* which is accurate but cumbersome. All of us once learned the Gettysburg Address, or, if not that, then some other well-known piece of writing such as the funeral oration in Shakespeare's

Julius Caesar. We may not be able to recall them now. Our ability to recognize them proves that we learned and remember something but is not a very precise measure of how much. <u>If we set about relearning them, however, the length of time this takes us will serve as a quite accurate measure.</u> (Note that this was the method Ebbinghaus chose.)

Figure 3–3 shows the results of an experiment that measured the same kind of learning by each of the three methods just discussed. The subjects made the highest scores—in other words, showed the least forgetting—when tested for recognition. The next highest scores were made for relearning and the lowest scores for recall.

Note, however, that in Figure 3–3 the curves for recognition and relearning are beginning to approach each other at the end of the two-day period. The curve for recognition is still declining noticeably, though slowly, while the curve for relearning is flattening out. If the experiment had been continued for a longer period of time, it can be assumed that the curve for recognition would eventually have dipped below the curve for relearning. Indeed there is some evidence from experiments in relearning that by this measure there may be at least some cases in which we do not ever completely forget what we have learned. Ebbinghaus, for example, once memorized some of the stanzas of Byron's poem *Don Juan.* After a lapse of twenty-two years he could not recall anything about these stanzas. But, when he set about relearning them, he found that this took him less time than it took him to learn some stanzas that he had never memorized before. As measured by relearning, the curve of forgetting had not dropped to zero even after all those years. This is an important point to which the discussion will return later, when theories of forgetting are considered.

the three measures of learning

3-3

The three forgetting curves were obtained by using all three measures of learning to test a group of subjects who had learned lists of nonsense syllables. (4)

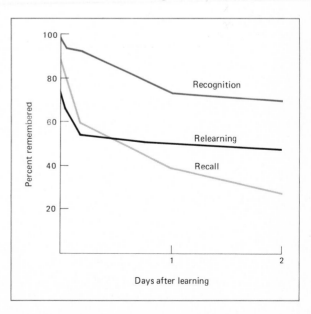

2. the measurements and performance

MEASUREMENT OF
PERFORMANCE

On the matter of measuring how much has been remembered and how much has been forgotten, one word of caution must be introduced. In actual fact, we cannot directly measure these matters. All we can really measure is the subject's *performance* when he is asked to recall, recognize, or relearn—and his performance may not be an entirely accurate reflection of what he has remembered.

For example, let us say that two girls in elementary school are taking the same arithmetic course. They listen to the same explanations by their teacher and study the same textbooks. Now one day the teacher gives a written examination. Girl A gets 90. Girl B gets 70. The logical conclusion is that girl A learned her arithmetic very well and remembered it and that girl B either learned it rather badly or quickly forgot it.

The truth, however, is that we do not really know. All we are actually justified in saying is that girl A *performed* much better on the examination than did girl B. It may very well be that girl B had learned addition, subtraction, and the multiplication tables backward and forward and did badly on the examination because these subjects were so old hat to her that she was bored when asked to show how well she could perform.

MOTIVATION

Performance on a test of remembering can be influenced by many factors. Prominent among them is motivation. One person, with strong motives to compete and to excel, makes the most of what he has learned and remembered; he gets good grades, wins athletic contests, and gets ahead in his job and in his community. Another person may actually learn and remember more, yet, because of strong motives to remain inconspicuous and to avoid the envy or hostility of others, get poorer grades, lose at games and contests, and never rise to a position of prominence or power.

CONFLICTING BEHAVIOR

Performance is also strongly influenced by the presence or absence of conflicting behavior. An actor may know his lines perfectly but get them confused because of stage fright. Many students, because of anxiety, consistently do badly on examinations even though they remember the contents of the course. And no one can do his best under circumstances in which he cannot help thinking about the fact that he is getting hungry and wishes it were lunchtime or about a vacation that is soon to begin. Tests of remembering and forgetting are always subject to this kind of error.

B. why we forget

Obviously, however, studies of forgetting are at least a reasonably close approximation of the facts about memory. We do forget some things rather quickly and remember others for a long time, perhaps forever. We can usually recognize far more than we can recall. The question is: *Why* do we forget—and why is forgetting such a selective process? The answer to the question, it must be admitted at the outset, is not yet fully known. But there are a number of theories well worth considering—especially since some of the most exciting experimental work of recent years has been directed toward reexamining the old theories and formulating new ones.

1. theory 1: fading of the "memory trace"

At one time the most generally accepted theory of remembering and forgetting centered around the phrase *memory trace*. According to this theory, the nerve pattern or "trace" set up in the organism through learning resembled the marks of a pencil or a path worn into a plot of grass. It could be kept functioning through use, as a pencil mark can be emphasized by tracing and retracing and a pathway can be kept clear by continuing to walk over it. Without use, the memory trace tended to fade away, as a pencil mark fades with time and a pathway becomes overgrown when abandoned.

The theory that the memory trace can decay has a certain common-sensical appeal. The nerve cells in the brain, like all cells, are living bits of protoplasm that take in oxygen and food from the blood stream, create energy, and throw off waste products. In this process, it seems quite possible that they might undergo important changes. Moreover, brain cells die and are forever lost; indeed after a person has reached maturity, many thousands of cells die each day (5). However, there is no real evidence for the theory of decay of the memory trace; and there is considerable evidence that argues against it.

One argument against the decay theory has already been cited; this is Ebbinghaus's finding that even after twenty-two years he remembered something of the stanzas he had once memorized from *Don Juan.* Another important piece of evidence comes from the work of a brain surgeon, who, in the course of operations performed under local anesthetic, has found that electrical stimulation of certain parts of the brain often results in the vivid, intense, and detailed recapture of events thought long since forgotten; the patient seems to be actually listening to a piece of music heard long ago or to a telephone conversation that he once took part in, almost as if a tape recording of it were being played (6). Old memories also are sometimes recalled by people under hypnosis, a rather strange and not entirely understood state of consciousness in which the hypnotized person seems to become oblivious to his present surroundings and to be capable of intense concentration on whatever is suggested to him. These findings indicate that at least many cases of forgetting are the result not of memory trace decay but of an inability, under ordinary circumstances, to reactivate the trace.

2. theory 2: distortion of the "memory trace"

One thing that goes wrong with memory at times was pointed out by experimenters nearly a half-century ago. One psychologist presented brief stories to his subjects, then, later on, asked them to reproduce the stories. He

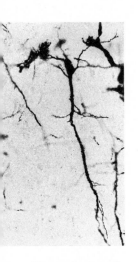

Human brain cells

found many distortions. The subjects usually remembered the general outline of each story, but they changed the names of the characters and many other details. Another psychologist showed his subjects a picture such as A, at left. To some of his subjects, he said, "This resembles a bottle"; to others he said, "This resembles a stirrup." Later, when he asked his subjects to draw the picture they had seen, they tended to distort the original in the direction of what he had told them. Subjects who had been told the picture resembled a bottle tended to reproduce it as in B. Those who had been told it resembled a stirrup tended to draw it as in C. Some of the other distortions found in the experiment are shown in Figure 3-4.

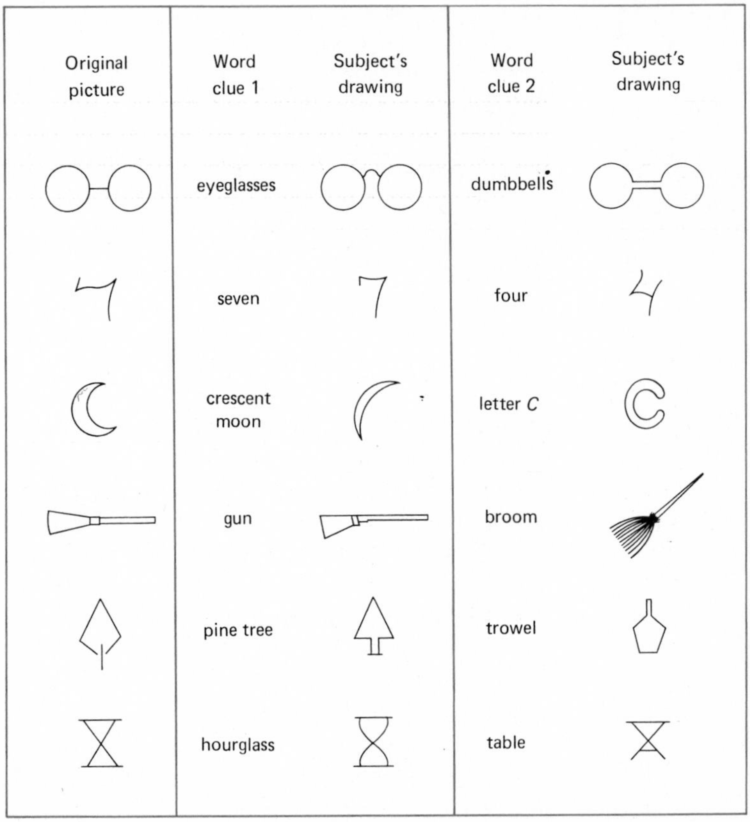

Original picture	Word clue 1	Subject's drawing	Word clue 2	Subject's drawing
	eyeglasses		dumbbells	
	seven		four	
	crescent moon		letter C	
	gun		broom	
	pine tree		trowel	
	hourglass		table	

memory distortions

3-4   An experimenter showed the drawings in the left-hand column to two groups of subjects. One group was told that the drawings looked like the objects listed under word clue 1, the other that the drawings looked like the objects listed under word clue 2. The use of different word clues sometimes produced distortions as extreme as those shown in the third and fifth columns. (7)

These experiments indicate that we remember the theme of a story or the general idea of a picture, but the details are forgotten and we try to reconstruct them the best we can (8). But whether this means that the memory trace has been distorted or points to some other kind of process is a matter of controversy.

3. theory 3: motivated forgetting

Another theory is that we often forget simply because we want to forget. For example, we forget the name of a person we dislike, or we forget the problems we had at a certain stage of life and look back to that period as a time when we were ideally happy. People who gamble are notoriously prone to remember the times they won and to forget the times they lost, often leading them to a totally false impression of how well they have done over the years.

The theory of motivated forgetting is based in large part on psychoanalytical studies of repression, which seem to show that we push many unpleasant memories into our unconscious minds as a way of getting rid of them; the mediational units that make up these memories are still present, but they are carefully blocked from our thinking. There is also some experimental data in support of the theory (9). There seems to be no doubt that motivated forgetting takes place, but it is probably a rather special kind of forgetting that accounts for only a rather small part of our failure to remember.

4. theory 4: interference

Another theory of forgetting centers around the word *interference;* it holds that, when we learn something, our ability to remember it is interfered with by things we have learned previously and also by things we learn in the future. To use a figure of speech, this theory assumes that the mediational units set up by learning are not traces that are prone to fade with the passage of time but instead are more like iron filings clustered in a magnetic field. Like iron filings, they are virtually indestructible—but the patterns in which they cluster can be pulled apart and rearranged when other filings are introduced into the field. The pattern of old filings—the mediational units we have learned in the past—helps determine where the new ones will cluster. But new filings may also influence and shift the old patterns.

The interference theory of forgetting is based largely on a considerable body of experimental evidence demonstrating two related processes that are called *retroactive inhibition* and *proactive inhibition.*

Retroactive Inhibition.   Many laboratory experiments, in which the task was learning and remembering such things as nonsense syllables or lists of words, have demonstrated how new learning can and does interfere with the ability to remember the old. When the learning of task 1 is followed by the learning of task 2, memory for task 1 is less than it would otherwise be—and, the more similar task 2 is to task 1, the greater is the amount of interference. A typical laboratory demonstration of this fact is illustrated in Figure 3-5.

"I joined the Legion two or three weeks ago to try to forget a girl called Elsie or something."

3-5

The recall scores were obtained ten minutes after the subjects had learned a list of adjectives. During those ten minutes most of the subjects were kept busy at new learning tasks, but one group merely rested by reading jokes. The difference between this last group's high scores and the other groups' lower scores demonstrates the effect of retroactive inhibition. Note that the more similar the new learning is to the original, the greater the amount of retroactive inhibition. (10)

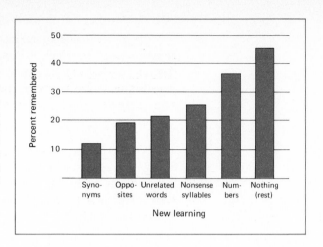

The interference of new learning with old is called *retroactive inhibition*. Retroactive means affecting something that occurred in the past. Inhibition means the act of restraining or stopping. Thus *retroactive inhibition is the partial or complete blacking out of old memories by new learning*.

It has been found that not only new learning but any kind of activity can cause retroactive inhibition, as shown in Figure 3-6. The person who is asleep, and thus as near to a state of suspended animation as possible, forgets less rapidly than the person who is awake and active.

forgetting curves when asleep and awake

3-6

The black forgetting curve was obtained from a subject who learned lists of ten nonsense syllables immediately before going to bed and was wakened for testing at various times of the night. The color curve is for the same subject, but in this case he learned the lists in the morning, went about his usual waking activities, and was tested at various times of the day. Question: Why does the curve drop so much more sharply during waking hours than during sleep? For the answer, see the text. (11)

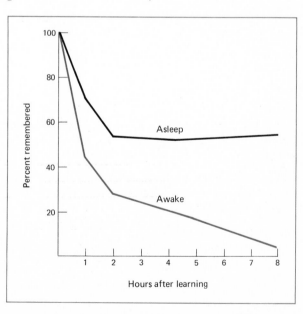

However, some kinds of memory are less subject than others to the effect of retroactive inhibition, as has been demonstrated in a later refinement of the sleeping-waking experiment. In this case, subjects were asked to memorize not just lists of words but some meaningful material—some short stories that had been carefully constructed so that each one contained twelve elements that were essential to the plot of the story and twelve elements that were not essential. The subjects were then tested eight hours later for their recall of the stories, sometimes after sleeping and sometimes after going about their usual daytime activities.

As far as the nonessential elements of the stories were concerned, the results were much the same as in the earlier experiment with nonsense syllables. The subjects who had slept for the eight hours recalled 47 percent of these nonessential elements. Those who had been awake for the eight hours recalled only 23 percent. But the results for the essential elements of the plots were strikingly different. The sleepers recalled 87 percent, the others 86 percent—scores that are virtually identical (12). Other studies have also shown that retroactive inhibition has a greater effect on the meaningless, the nonessential, and the specific detail than on the more basic elements that underlie meaningful learning. To return again to the figure of speech used earlier, the iron filings that cluster together in the firm associations formed around logic and understanding tend to stick together. It is the less tightly bound filings—the mediational units learned by rote, the unimportant, the details—that are likely to be shaken loose by later learning.

DEFINITION :

PROACTIVE INHIBITION

Proactive Inhibition. In retroactive inhibition, as we have seen, the new interferes with memory for the old. When the opposite happens and the old interferes with memory for the new, the process is called *proactive inhibition.*

Proactive inhibition is demonstrated by the experiment illustrated in Figure 3–7, where the learning of previous word lists was found to interfere sharply with

proactive inhibition

3-7

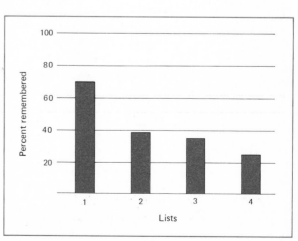

The subjects learned a list of paired adjectives. Two days after learning they were tested for their recall of list 1 and asked to learn list 2. After a similar interval they were tested on list 2 and learned list 3. Two days later they were tested on list 3 and learned list 4. Finally, after another two-day interval, they were tested on list 4 and the experiment ended. The recall scores, which decline with each list, show the effect of proactive inhibition resulting from the learning of the prior lists. (13)

the ability to remember new lists. Like retroactive inhibition, proactive inhibition interferes more with the remembering of meaningless materials such as word lists and nonsense syllables than with the remembering of meaningful material and general principles.

There is no doubt that retroactive and proactive inhibition take place and have a considerable effect on our ability to remember. There is some doubt, however, as to whether they operate by interfering with the mediational units set up by learning or in some other way—a point that will become clear as the discussion progresses.

5. theory 5: forgetting as a failure in retrieval

DEFINITION:
RETRIEVAL

Because the old theories of forgetting did not seem to account for all the facts, a great deal of new experimentation has been performed in recent years—and out of it has emerged a word that is of increasing interest to students of learning and forgetting. The word is *retrieval;* it means the process by which we somehow manage to sort through all the mediational units stored somewhere in memory and find those that are appropriate to the present situation. A considerable number of psychologists have concluded that retrieval is the key process in remembering and forgetting. If we succeed in finding the right mediational units, we remember. If we fail to find them, we say we have forgotten. Thus forgetting, according to the new theory, is the result of a failure in retrieval.

One of the most interesting experiments in retrieval is illustrated in Figure 3-8. A picture was flashed on a screen for a very brief time, a tenth of a second. Then the subjects, who were university students, were asked to describe what they had seen in as much detail as possible and at the same time to make a drawing of the picture, with labels for the various details they included. Typically, their drawings were rather meager, as can be seen from the first drawing (A) of one subject illustrated in Figure 3-8.

After making the drawing, the subjects were asked to look again at the screen on which the picture had been flashed, to concentrate as hard as possible on what they had seen, and to say out loud any words that happened to come to mind, regardless of whether they had any apparent connection with the picture. That is to say, they were asked to free-associate to their memory of the picture—to blurt out any associations that occurred to them. The first twelve words they came up with were put on index cards, and these words were used to evoke some further free associations; the subjects were asked to look at each of the twelve words, one at a time, and to say out loud any words that these suggested. They were permitted to look at each of the twelve words until it had suggested ten additional words. Finally, after they had finished going through the twelve words and had come up with a total of 120 associations, they were asked to try to draw the picture again. This time, as can be seen from drawing B in Figure 3-8, they came much closer to the original, including many details that they had been unable to remember while making their first drawing. By one kind of scoring, the average improvement by the subjects was about 44 percent (14).

3-8

When the picture at the top was flashed on a screen for a tenth of a second and a student was asked to reproduce what he had seen, he could do no better than drawing A. After the experimenter helped his retrieval process through methods described in the text, however, the student produced the much more detailed drawing B.

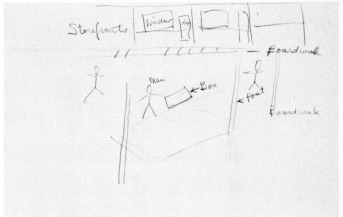

A

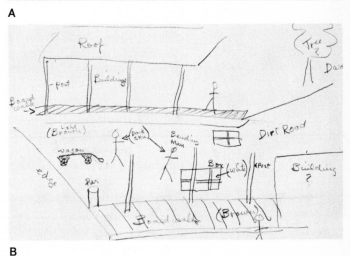

B

The experiment seems to show that the subjects learned and stored in memory considerably more information about the picture than they were able to retrieve when they made their first drawings. Free association, however, provided new clues that aided the retrieval process—and thus enabled them to remember more about the picture when they made their second drawings.

Retrieval is obviously an important process, and much more must be said about it. Further discussion will be more understandable, however, if we digress at this point to consider some other recent findings that shed new light on the nature of memory—and especially on the differences between what are called sensory memory, short-term memory, and long-term memory.

c. the three kinds of memory

One of the most interesting aspects of memory can be illustrated by the following example. A student is driving across the country to college. He expected to arrive at about 5 o'clock in St. Louis, where he has been invited by a friend to spend the night. On the outskirts of the city, however, his automobile develops engine trouble, and a mechanic at a roadside garage tells him the repairs will take an hour or two. He goes to a phone booth to call his friend and explain that he will be late.

In the phone book, he looks up his friend's number, 624-1954. But at that moment there is a loud squeal of brakes out on the highway. Startled, he looks up and sees that there has been a near collision. Turning back to the phone, he finds that he has completely forgotten the number; indeed it seems that the number never registered at all in his memory. He looks it up again and this time starts silently repeating it to himself—*six, two, four, one, nine, five, four*—as he turns from the book and drops a dime into the phone. He dials the number correctly but gets a busy signal. By the time he has fished his dime out of the coin return slot, dropped it back into the phone, and waited for a dial tone, he finds that he has forgotten the number again. He remembered it longer this time—but not long enough.

He looks up the number again, and now, while repeating it to himself, he notices a peculiarity. The number is exactly the same as his birth date, for he was born on June 24, or 6/24, in 1954. Now he remembers the number no matter how many times he gets a busy signal and has to try again. In fact he may remember it the rest of his life.

In the opinion of a growing number of psychologists, this sort of incident demonstrates that there are three kinds or systems of memory, as illustrated in Figure 3-9.

1. sensory memory

The first system, activated by stimuli from the outside world, is *sensory memory;* it is just the lingering traces of information sent to the brain by the senses—for example, an image of the numbers 624-1954 as seen in the phone book. (For this reason it is sometimes called the *sensory register.*) Information that reaches the sensory memory (or sensory register) fades rapidly unless it is transferred to the next kind of memory; under some experimental conditions it has been shown to deteriorate substantially within a few tenths of a second and to

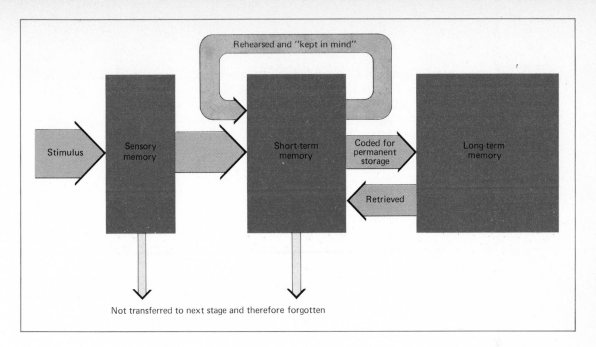

Not transferred to next stage and therefore forgotten

how we remember

3-9

The three systems of human memory appear to operate as shown here. Stimuli from the outside world register briefly in the *sensory memory;* some are promptly lost but others are transferred to *short-term memory.* There again some are lost, but others are rehearsed and "kept in mind" long enough to be coded for permanent storage in *long-term memory,* from which they can later be retrieved. The process is described in further detail in the text. (15)

have vanished by the end of a full second (16). In the case of the student in the phone booth, the squeal of brakes prevented transfer from the sensory memory and therefore the number was quickly lost.

2. short-term memory

The second system, into which some but not all the information that arrives in the sensory memory is transferred, is short-term memory. To use a very loose figure of speech, we might compare short-term memory to a small in-basket for the mail arriving in a large business office. Since the basket has a limited capacity, it must be emptied out frequently to make room for new arrivals. The important mail is transferred to permanent filing cabinets; the unimportant is thrown out. Like the in-basket, the short-term memory has a limited capacity and rapid turnover. Indeed information stored in it ordinarily gets "thrown out"—or forgotten—within about thirty seconds (17). Some of the information, however, gets transferred to permanent storage in the long-term memory.

In the case of the student at the telephone, his second look at the phone book resulted in transfer of the number to short-term memory. There it remained long enough for him to dial it once—but, when he tried to dial again after getting a busy signal, it had already been "thrown out."

Similarly, the cashier in a supermarket remembers only briefly that she must give the customer $3.76 change from a ten-dollar bill; by the time she starts checking out the next customer, the figure $3.76 has already vanished from her memory. When we add a column of figures such as

$$37$$
$$49$$
$$65$$
$$\underline{22}$$

we say to ourselves (adding the right-hand digits from the top down) 16, 21, 23; then write down the 3 and start over on the left-hand numbers, 5, 9, 15, 17; thus we get the answer 173. All the intermediary numbers that flash through our consciousness—the 16, 21, 23, 5, 9, and 15—disappear almost as rapidly as they are formed.

Because so much information is lost in this way, one psychologist has aptly described the short-term memory as a "leaky bucket" (18). It must be pointed out, however, that the rapidity with which we forget in short-term memory is often a valuable asset. The supermarket cashier would be hopelessly confused by the end of the day if she recalled every transaction starting with the first one of early morning. The addition of long columns of figures would be impossible if we recalled every step of the process; the numbers would get hopelessly in one another's way.

Processes in Short-Term Memory. It is impossible to say what kind of nervous activity takes place in short-term memory. However, the kinds of processes that must go on in the system can be described in a general way, and among them the following have been suggested (19). First, the short-term memory must engage in *scanning* of the information in sensory memory. It must then set up some sort of *rehearsal system,* in the process of which it often transforms visual information into the sound of words. (As the student in the phone booth did when he began saying the numbers to himself.) It must then engage in the actual *rehearsal,* a process through which information can be kept in short-term memory as long as desired. It must also, through some sort of interaction with the long-term memory, retrieve information from long-term storage and compare it to the new information, some of which will then be coded into long-term memory—that is to say, associated with mediational units already in long-term memory and added to them. Information that is not coded into long-term memory becomes lost as new information arrives in short-term memory, via sensory memory, and displaces the old because of the limited capacity of the short-term memory.

In the case of the student at the telephone, on one occasion he held the number in short-term memory, through rehearsal, long enough to dial it once; it was then lost as he did the dialing, listened to the busy signal, and reached to get back his dime. On the next occasion, while he was rehearsing the number, an interaction between short-term and long-term memory produced the association

PROCESSES IN
SHORT-TERM MEMORY

1, SCANNING

2, REHEARSAL SYSTEM

3, REHEARSAL

between the number and his birth date; the number was then coded into long-term memory.

The coding process takes time, and this fact sets a limit on how much information can be learned—that is, transferred to long-term memory—within a given period. For example, one experimenter presented lists of words to his subjects at the rate of one word a second for 120 seconds, or two minutes. For some subjects, the list contained 120 words, each presented once; for others the list contained 60 words each presented twice, or 40 words each presented three times, or 30 words each presented four times, or 24 words each presented five times. If one tried to guess the results, common sense would seem to indicate that the subjects who saw just 24 words would remember more than the subjects who saw 120 words. However, it turned out that the number of words made no difference. All the groups, regardless of whether they saw 24, 30, 40, 60, or 120 words, remembered an average of 12 of them (20). For the average subject in this kind of learning task, apparently twelve words is the limit of what can be coded into long-term memory in two minutes.

3. long-term memory

Once information has been coded into long-term memory, it may of course still be lost because of such factors as brain injury or the inevitable loss of nerve cells in the brain that occurs with aging (see page 91), especially in very old people whose blood vessels are no longer able to supply sufficient nourishment to the brain (17). However, most students of short-term and long-term memory now assume that these are minor causes of forgetting, that the long-term memory is a permanent storehouse of information, and that forgetting is caused chiefly by a failure in retrieval (21). This belief is based on experimental work that is somewhat too complex to be covered in an introductory course.

An interesting aspect of the difference between long-term memory and short-term memory has been demonstrated by the case of a man who had a particular kind of brain operation at the age of twenty-nine. Afterward, his long-term memory remained intact. Indeed his scores on intelligence tests, which measure one's ability to recall and apply old information, were if anything somewhat higher than before. Moreover, his short-term memory still appeared to operate; he was capable of holding new information in short-term memory by rehearsing it. However, the connecting link between short-term and long-term memory seemed to have been broken, and he was no longer able to code new information into long-term storage. In other words, he was incapable of learning anything new. He could not learn the address of the new house to which his family had moved. Nor could he remember where the family lawn mower was kept, even a single day after he had used the mower. He read the same magazines over and over again, and worked the same jigsaw puzzles, without ever realizing that he had seen them before (22).

This case, and others like it, suggest strongly that the nerve changes that take place in learning and remembering are quite different for short-term memory and long-term memory (23) and indeed probably occur in different parts of the brain. The connecting link between short-term and long-term memory appears to be a part of the brain called the *hippocampus,* which was the area cut in the young man's brain surgery. When the link provided by the hippocampus is severed, information previously coded into long-term memory remains intact and short-term memory continues to operate, but the coding of new information from short-term to long-term memory becomes impossible.

D. coding and retrieval

As to how information is coded into long-term memory and later retrieved, you can observe a few elementary principles by trying an experiment of your own. Ask several of your friends to try to remember as many names as they can of cities in the United States. As you listen to them start reciting a list, you will find that many of them—and particularly those who can quickly name a considerable number of cities—are making some sort of systematic search of memory. One person may go through the alphabet, starting with cities that begin with *A* (Atlanta, Albany, Altoona), then, after he can think of no more, moving on to *B* (Boston, Birmingham, Boise). Another may proceed state by state; for example, he may start with California and call out San Francisco, Los Angeles, San Diego. Another may start with the city in which he was born and the towns around it. Someone who has enjoyed the study of geography may begin by listing all the state capitals, and a baseball fan may begin by listing the cities in the major leagues.

As this informal experiment shows, there are many possible ways that information can be coded into memory and retrieved, and different people tend to use different methods. Moreover, information seems to be stored in what have been called "chunks"; if the letter *A* is used as a cue to retrieval, it pulls out a whole group of cities that begin with *A*.

1. the "tip of the tongue" phenomenon

As a very rough analogy, we might say that the information stored in long-term memory is something like the definitions in a dictionary. If the words in the dictionary were listed totally at random rather than in alphabetical order—in other words, if *aardvark, metaphysics,* and *zoology* were all on the same page—the book would have little value; we would never be able to find what we were looking for. Similarly, the information stored in memory has to be organized and "chunked" in some way that makes it easy to find.

The human memory, however, is a good deal more complicated than a dictionary. Suppose, for example, that we ask someone to tell us the word that is defined "A navigational instrument used in measuring angular distances, especially the altitude of sun, moon, and stars at sea." Knowing the definition would not help him find the word (which is *sextant*) in the dictionary; the dictionary is not organized in a way that makes it possible to work backward from definition to word. But, if a person has the word *sextant* successfully coded into long-term memory, the definition may well provide sufficient cues for him to call it out.

The definition of *sextant* was one definition used in a study that has quickly become famous among psychologists who specialize in learning. The subjects were university students, and they were asked to recall, from hearing the definitions, such words as *sextant, sampan, nepotism,* and *ambergris*—all being fairly unusual words that they probably once had an opportunity to learn but would not have had many occasions to use. As was expected, it turned out that often they could not remember the word but felt that they had it "on the tip of the tongue." The study is important for what it has demonstrated about the nature of the "tip of the tongue" phenomenon and the light this sheds on the processes of coding and retrieval.

Often students who had the word "on the tip of the tongue" but could not actually recall it thought of words that had a similar sound. When trying to remember *sampan,* for example, they thought of such words as *Saipan, Siam, Cheyenne,* and *sarong,* and even such made-up words as *sanching* and *sympoon.* Often they thought of words that had not a similar sound but a similar meaning; for example, in the case of *sampan,* which is defined as a small Chinese boat, they thought of *barge, houseboat,* and *junk.*

The students could often—indeed in 57 percent of the cases—guess the first letter of the word they were seeking. They also seemed to have considerable recall for the last letter of the word. Moreover, as is shown in Figure 3-10, they were quite accurate in guessing how many syllables were in the word—at least if the number of syllables, as in the great majority of English words, was no more than three. There was even some indication that they knew which syllable of the word the accent was on (24).

The study indicates that coding and retrieval are extremely complex processes. Information in the human memory is organized in a way far more sophisticated and efficient than any dictionary. Obviously words are stored in auditory terms (that is, how many syllables they have and how they are pronounced), in visual terms (the letters with which they begin and end), and in terms of meaning (so that they are "chunked" with other words that mean more or less the same thing).

"tip of the tongue" results

3-10

In the experiment described in the text, students who had a word "on the tip of the tongue" but could not quite recall it were asked to guess how many syllables it had. The figures in the color band show the number of students who correctly guessed the number of syllables in each word. Their guesses were more often right than wrong unless the word had more than three syllables.

		Number of syllables guessed by subjects			
		1	2	3	4	5
Actual number of syllables	1	9	7	1	0	0
	2	2	55	22	2	1
	3	3	19	61	10	1
	4	0	2	12	6	2
	5	0	0	3	0	1

2. made-up stories as an aid to coding and retrieval

Many other experiments have been devised in recent years to explore, for both theoretical and practical reasons, the nature of the processes of coding and retrieval. In one of the experiments, a list of ten words was handed to a university student, who was asked to try to memorize the words in their correct order by making up a little story using them. The length of time it took him to study the words and make up his story, usually between one and two minutes, was recorded and then another list was handed to him, until he had studied and made up stories about twelve lists in all. (Examples of the kinds of lists used in the experiment and the kinds of stories made up around them are shown in Figure 3–11.) Then another student was asked to study each of the lists for exactly as long as the first student had taken, but without receiving any instructions about how to try to remember them.

an experiment in memorizing word lists

3–11   These are two of the twelve word lists used in the experiment described above, along with examples of the kinds of stories made up by the subjects to help them remember the words.

Word Lists

1. LUMBERJACK	6. DUCK	1. VEGETABLE	6. BASIN
2. DART	7. FURNITURE	2. INSTRUMENT	7. MERCHANT
3. SKATE	8. STOCKING	3. COLLEGE	8. QUEEN
4. HEDGE	9. PILLOW	4. NAIL	9. SCALE
5. COLONY	10. MISTRESS	5. FENCE	10. GOAT

Stories Built Around Them

A LUMBERJACK DARTed out of a forest, SKATEd around a HEDGE past a COLONY of DUCKs. He tripped on some FURNITURE, tearing his STOCKING while hastening toward the PILLOW where his MISTRESS lay.

A VEGETABLE can be a useful INSTRUMENT for a COLLEGE student. A carrot can be a NAIL for your FENCE or BASIN. But a MERCHANT of the QUEEN would SCALE that fence and feed the carrot to a GOAT.

This process was repeated with twenty-four students in all, half of them with instructions to make up stories, the other half with no instructions. Both groups then were permitted to look at the first word in each list and asked to recall the other words in order. When tested immediately after studying the lists, both groups remembered the lists almost perfectly. When they were tested some time later, however, a remarkable difference was found, as shown in Figure 3-12. The students who had made up stories still remembered almost all the words in the lists; the students who had not made up stories had forgotten most of the words. In fact the students who had made up stories remembered about six or seven times as much about the lists as the other students (25).

What does this study tell us about coding and retrieval? In the opinion of the experimenters, the students told to make up stories found some sort of theme—meaningful to them if not necessarily to anyone else—into which the ten words in each list could be integrated. (To put this in terms already used in the chapter, they found a central theme that aided in bringing the words together into "chunks.") The stories often made a liberal use of *imagery,* or mental pictures; for example, the student whose story is shown in the left-hand column of Figure 3-11 apparently coded into long-term memory a sort of picture of a lumberjack darting out of a forest, skating around a hedge, and so on. (The formation of such images, as other studies have shown, is of considerable help in coding and retrieval (26).) On the basis of the cue of the first word in each list, the students

results of the word-list experiment

3-12

As the graph lines show, the subjects who made up stories to help them remember the twelve word lists remembered far more of the words in their correct order than did the control subjects, who tried to memorize the lists by rote. In fact the subjects who made up stories showed almost perfect memory for the fourth through the twelfth lists.

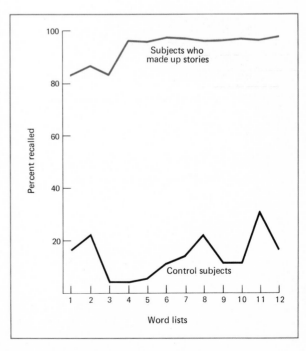

seemed to recall the theme, reconstruct the stories they had made up, and pull out the significant words. The same complex sort of process may occur when you take an examination on a college course; the question may serve as a cue that helps you retrieve what you know about the general principles that form the theme on which the course was organized, and this theme may then help you pull out of long-term memory the details called for by the question.

3. categories as an aid to retrieval

In another important experiment, lists of words were drawn up that could be organized into logical patterns. In the list shown in Figure 3–13, for example, the words all fell into the general category of minerals; the general category could be broken down into the subcategories of metals and stones; and these subcategories could again be divided into different kinds of metals (rare, common, and alloys) and different kinds of stones (precious stones and stones used in masonry). The experimenters prepared four such categorized lists, including 112 words in all. An experimental group of students was asked to try to learn the words in four learning trials. For a control group, which also had four trials, the words were not presented by category; they were simply jumbled up and presented at random. As is shown in Figure 3–14, the students who had been helped to organize the words into categories proved far superior; indeed they remembered all 112 words perfectly on the third and fourth trials (27). Obviously

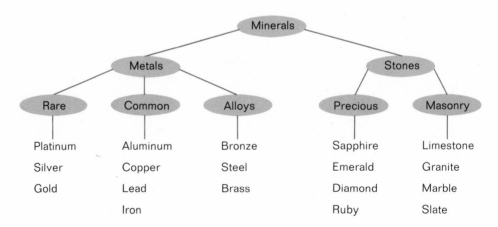

learning by category

3-13   This is one of the word lists used in the learning experiment described above. The treelike organization of the list helped subjects organize the words into a general category (minerals), and two subcategories (metals and stones), with the two subcategories then broken down into lesser subcategories (for metals, rare, common, and alloys; and for stones, precious and masonry). For an explanation of how this organization helped subjects learn the words, see the text and Figure 3–14.

3-14

The graph lines show how much more rapidly word lists were learned by students who saw them arranged by category, as in Figure 3–13, than by students who saw them in random order.

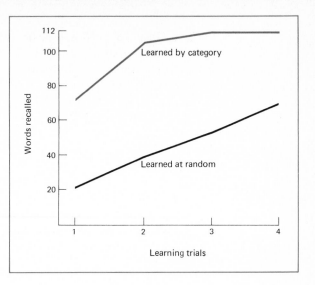

the processes of coding and retrieval are helped considerably when we possess category labels into which new items of information can be logically fitted or "chunked."

4. how cues help retrieval

Another experiment on learning by categories sheds particular light on the retrieval process. In this experiment, high school students listened over a tape recorder to a word or phrase naming a category, followed by one or more words that fitted into the category. For example, at one point they heard the phrase "four-footed animals" followed by *cow* and *rat*, and "forms of entertainment" followed by *radio* and *music*. They were told that they did not have to remember the category labels but should try to remember as many as possible of the words that followed the labels. Afterward, they were asked to write down, in booklets supplied by the experimenters, as many of the words as they could recall. Half the students received booklets that simply contained as many lines as the number of words they had heard. The other half received booklets that listed all the category names that had been heard over the tape recorder, followed by as many lines as the number of words that had been presented in each of the categories.

As a moment's analysis of the experiment will show, it was extremely ingenious. Both groups of students had exactly the same opportunity to learn under exactly the same conditions; in trying to code the words into long-term memory, they both had the help of ready-made categories supplied by the experimenters. Presumably both groups had succeeded equally in the coding process and had stored an equal number of words in long-term memory. Only the retrieval process was different; one group received no help at all, while the other group had the category labels to do what is known in everyday language as "jog their memories."

The recall scores of the two groups are shown in Figure 3–15. The scores make it quite clear that the cues provided by the category labels were of consid-

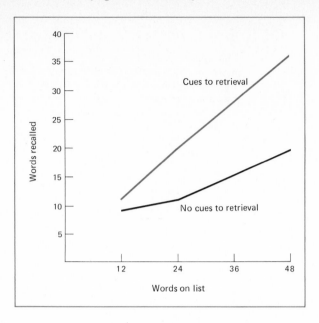

3-15

The graph shows how retrieval cues, presented as explained in the text, enabled one group of high school students to recall more words from a list than students who did not have the cues available. The scores shown here were made on lists that contained two items in each category—for example, the category "four-footed animals" followed by *cow* and *rat*. (Adapted from 28)

erable help in the retrieval process; they were quite successful indeed in "jogging memory." The students who had the benefit of the help were able to recall substantially more words than the other students—who presumably had just as much information stored in long-term memory but were unable to retrieve all of it (28). The experiment is another strong argument for the theory that forgetting represents a failure in retrieval rather than a fading of the memory trace.

However, cues to retrieval aid in the recall of information only when they are associated with the information at the time it is coded into long-term memory. Other experiments have shown that it would have been of no help to the students if the category labels had appeared in their test booklets without having been presented over the tape recorder along with the words to be remembered (29). Thus coding and retrieval must be considered as a sort of two-way street. When information is well coded into long-term memory, it seems to get "chunked" with other similar kinds of information in the brain's equivalent of some kind of elaborate system of cataloguing and cross-indexing. The more ways in which it is catalogued and cross-indexed, the more likely it is to be available when we have occasion to look for it—and the more different cues that can help us retrieve it.

E. the requirements for learning

Although the experimental evidence is perhaps too new to evaluate fully, more and more psychologists are proceeding on the assumption that memory is indeed a three-part system (sensory, short-term, and long-term)—and that the key processes in determining whether we remember or forget are the coding of information

108

into the long-term memory and retrieval from the storehouse of mediational units thus set up in the long-term memory. This model of how memory operates, even if it will have to be revised after further study, fits in neatly with much of what has been known for a long time about learning, remembering, and forgetting. In particular, it offers a ready explanation for the fact that learning does not take place unless certain requirements are met—a fact that has considerable practical as well as theoretical importance.

For all of us, as we go about our daily lives, learning often takes on rather puzzling aspects, some with pleasant results, some that are highly frustrating. Sometimes learning seems to occur spontaneously, without any effort and almost by accident. Such is the case in latent or incidental learning, which was discussed on page 80. (The example given was this: A friend drives you to Smithville in his car. You have no intention of ever returning to Smithville and make no effort to learn the route. Yet, if for some reason you have to drive to Smithville at some time in the future, you may find that you learned a good deal about the route and the landmarks.)

At other times, learning does not take place no matter how hard we try—or think we try. A person may attempt to become a good bridge player and fail utterly. Another may try hard to learn some elementary words of Spanish, in preparation for a trip to Mexico, and have no success whatever. There probably are many reasons for failures of this kind, not all of which are as yet understood. But at any rate we can be sure, from both everyday observations and laboratory experiments, that learning does not take place unless certain requirements are met. In our lifetimes we see millions of sights and hear millions of sounds; we read innumerable pages of books, magazines, and newspapers; we look at many road maps and street signs. We remember only a very small percentage of all these things.

Perhaps many requirements must be met if learning is to take place—that is, if we are to acquire more or less permanent mediational units that can later be reactivated and thus remembered. But three of them seem to be basic. From laboratory experiments and everyday observation, it appears that *learning is most likely to take place when there are 1) a distinctive stimulus, 2) attention to the stimulus, and 3) a unit of innate or previously learned behavior to which the stimulus can be attached.* All three requirements, as will now be seen, can be viewed as essential for a stimulus to register in sensory memory, then to be transferred to short-term memory and held there long enough to be successfully coded into long-term memory.

1. requirement 1: the distinctive stimulus

Unless a stimulus is *distinctive*—that is, unless it is somehow prominent and stands out—it is hardly likely to result in any learning. In terms of the theories just discussed, it may not even register in sensory memory, or it may fade out without being transferred to short-term memory and thus be forever lost.

All of us have listened to a lecturer from whom we learned absolutely nothing, because he spoke in such a monotonous voice and with so little emphasis on the points he was trying to make that there seemed to be no distinctive stimuli at all in his talk. As we often state, "the words all ran together." Equally ineffective is the kind of fire-and-brimstone lecturer who shouts every word at us, never once lowering his voice. The best lecturer is the one who places sharp emphasis on the points he wants to make—that is, the special stimuli to which he wants to attract our attention. He makes these stimuli distinctive by using a different tone of voice and perhaps by gestures or by writing his main points on a blackboard, and often he repeats them for added emphasis. A stimulus can of course be distinctive for psychological as well as physical reasons; each of us has his own pattern of things that interest him (and therefore stand out) a great deal, somewhat, or not at all.

Closely related to the requirement that the stimulus be distinctive is the fact that learning takes place most effectively in the absence of distraction. When Pavlov set about conditioning his dog, he attempted to eliminate all sights and sounds except the unconditioned stimulus of food and the conditioned stimulus of sound. One reason he did this was to make sure that no other factor would influence the learning process. But he also eliminated distractions. If at the same time he presented the sound of the metronome he had also sounded a bell and a whistle, flashed a red light and a green light, sprayed perfume into the cage, shaken the dog's platform, and hit the dog's flanks with a paddle, the dog would have had a difficult time learning to respond to the metronome alone. In terms of the three-system theory of memory discussed earlier, the distractions would have overtaxed the limited capacity of the short-term memory.

2. requirement 2: attention to the stimulus

The second of the three requirements for learning is that the stimulus, besides being distinctive, must also be attended to. For example, one cannot learn the contents of a classroom lecture if he is not paying attention, if he is thinking about something else. Under these circumstances, however skillful the speaker may be at presenting a distinctive stimulus, the lecture will "go in one ear and out the other." It may never be transferred from sensory memory to short-term memory—or if it is transferred, it will not be rehearsed and held in short-term memory long enough to be successfully coded into long-term memory.

Although attention is obviously essential if learning is to take place, it operates in ways that have thus far resisted analysis. In the latent learning that takes place on the trip to Smithville, why does one pay attention to some of the things he sees, apparently without any effort, and not to others? Why did we pay so much attention to the many insignificant and useless pieces of information that stick in our memories—while failing, presumably, to pay attention to many others of more importance?

It has been discovered that paying attention has an effect on the brain's activity, at least under certain circumstances. For example, if a subject is told that a flash of light will alert him to the fact that a tone will soon be sounded, and that he should be prepared to press a key the instant he hears the tone, the pattern of electrical waves produced by his brain changes in the marked fashion

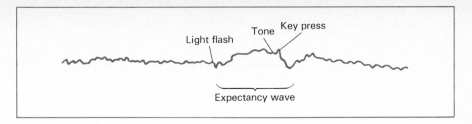

Light flash

Tone Key press

Expectancy wave

3-16   As the tracing clearly shows, the electrical waves produced by the brain often change sharply during states of expectancy—in this case, after a flash of light signaled the subject that he would soon hear a tone. The tracing was made by an electroencephalograph, a device that will be described in more detail on pages 290–91. (30)

illustrated in Figure 3-16. As soon as the light flashes, there is a buildup of what has been called an "expectancy wave" that continues until the tone sounds and the key is pressed (30, 31). The same sort of wave appears if a subject is told that a light or tone will signal the fact that he is about to do something interesting, such as view a photograph. These findings suggest that attention may in some way put the brain in a state of readiness that would be conducive to learning. Yet, aside from having discovered the "expectancy wave," psychologists have no more real knowledge than the average person—who, though he has a working knowledge of what it means to "pay attention," would have a hard time defining the phrase.

Perhaps attention, as was mentioned on page 81, is related to reinforcement. And certainly it is closely related to motivation; the person who has a strong motive to learn is much more likely to pay attention to the stimulus—and to do the work that is required to code information from the short-term memory into the long-term memory. Indeed, as was stated on pages 80-81, one theory holds that reinforcement aids learning precisely by setting up a motivational state conducive to learning.

3. requirement 3: a unit to which the stimulus can become attached

In the last analysis, all learning is a matter of establishing new connections between previously unconnected items. One of these items, the stimulus, often comes from outside the organism. The other item or items must exist inside the organism. Pavlov's dog could not have learned to salivate to the sound of the metronome, for example, had it not had the innate capacity to salivate. The inner unit to which the outside stimulus becomes attached can be actual physical behavior, as in the case of Pavlov's dog, or it can be a mediational unit that has previously been learned. In human learning, especially when language is involved, the presence of previously learned mediational units to which new stimuli can become attached is particularly important. They constitute a kind of cataloguing system that helps code new information into the long-term memory and also makes subsequent retrieval easier.

111

How Component Parts Aid Learning.   One way in which previously learned mediational units assist in learning is well illustrated by *syzygy*, that unusual word mentioned in Chapter 2. Although *syzygy* is hardly worth remembering, the chances are that you remember it very well. If you tried the experiment that was suggested and presented *syzygy* without warning to a friend, in all probability he also remembers it. Why should this strange word be learned so quickly—in one trial and without any further practice—and remembered so well?

Before the answer is presented, it should be pointed out that the results would almost surely have been far different if we had tried the experiment with the French word *aujourd'hui* (which is roughly pronounced oh-zhoor-dwee) or the German word *Schneeglöckchen* (the pronunciation of which can hardly be rendered into English letters at all). Or, to make the point even more clearly, suppose we had used a Chinese or Japanese word. In that case it is highly unlikely that the friend, after hearing it only once, would have been able to repeat it a half-hour later, much less now.

Why should this be? The answer is that all the component parts of the word *syzygy* are already familiar to any American adult. All of us have often used the sounds *syz*, as in *scissors; i*, as in *it;* and *jee*, as in *jeep.* They are a part of the repertory of language sounds we have already learned. They are mediational units that we already carry around in our heads. To form them into the new word *syzygy,* all we have to do is build one new mediational unit—an association among the three familiar syllables. When we deal with foreign words made up of unfamiliar sounds and syllables, we cannot learn so quickly, because we do not have the same kind of building blocks for learning already present in the form of previously learned mediational units.

Another example is the way we build our vocabularies. Take, for instance, the word *horizon.* If you try to teach the meaning of this word to a four-year-old child, you will find the task impossible. But the average ten-year-old child who has never heard the word before needs only one explanation to grasp the meaning and add the word to his vocabulary. By the age of ten, he has learned the various mediational units—concepts of space, earth, and sky—that are component parts of the meaning of *horizon.* All he needs to do is form one more mediational unit—a bond between these previously learned units and the word *horizon.* He can form this new mediational unit, the bond, in a single trial.

Even in learning that cannot be accomplished in a single trial, component parts are significant. For a young child, learning to ride a bicycle is difficult because he has not yet mastered any of the component parts; he has to learn how to balance himself, how to steer, and how to pedal. If that same boy later buys a motorcycle, however, he quickly learns to ride the new machine. He already knows how to balance and steer; all he now needs to learn is the mechanical operation.

A young man from Africa who has never thrown a baseball would have a hard time learning to be a big-league pitcher. But the minor leaguer who aspires to the big leagues already knows how to hold the ball, release it as a fast ball or a curve, and aim it over the plate; he already knows many of the component parts of throwing a slider and a change of pace.

Memorizing the Gettysburg Address would be a difficult task for a child in the lower grades; he would first have to learn to recognize and pronounce words such as *conceived, dedicated,* and *consecrated.* The older child, already familiar with the words, finds it much easier to link them together. When we possess the component parts, learning comes easy.

The role of component parts in learning explains what would otherwise be a rather baffling fact about schoolwork. Insofar as can be measured, a fourteen-year-old in the eighth grade has matured to the point where he seems to have all the nervous and physical equipment that makes learning possible. His innate capacity for learning will not increase very much; he is already just about as smart, to use the popular term, as he will ever be. Yet everybody knows that high school freshmen can learn things that would be beyond an eighth-grader; high school seniors can learn even more difficult things; and college students can go a long step beyond. The reason is that each year the student acquires more of the component parts of higher learning—a bigger vocabulary, more concepts, more mathematical symbols.

Other Attachment Units. The learned mediational unit to which a new stimulus can become attached need not, however, be a component part. It can be any kind of mediational unit to which the stimulus can readily be associated—in other words, any mediational unit that makes it easy for the stimulus to be coded into the long-term memory. To illustrate, let us consider the following incident.

A kindergarten teacher who has gone to Europe for the summer takes two coins to her class. "This one," she says, passing it around to her pupils, "is an English shilling." Then she passes the other around and says, "This is a French franc."

Now there is nothing very complicated about learning the words *shilling* and *franc.* As far as knowing the necessary components is concerned, every pupil in the class starts on equal terms.

Let us further suppose, however, that there is one pupil in the class whose family has frequently gone traveling in Europe. This boy has often heard his parents talk about England and France and about exchanging American dollars for foreign money. In addition he has been entrusted with sums of money that he has been permitted to spend for himself; he knows the difference between a United States nickel and a United States quarter or half dollar. On the other hand, there is a little girl in the class who has never heard the words *England* and *France* mentioned in her home. She does not know that there is any nation in the world except the United States, and she has never had any money of her own to spend, so that she has only a vague notion of what a coin is.

Which of these two pupils is likely to remember, on the following day, which of the two coins the teacher holds up is the shilling and which is the franc? Naturally the boy is more likely to learn and remember; he possesses mediational units to which the words *shilling* and *franc* can be attached. With the girl, the words tend to fall on deaf ears. She simply has nothing inside her to which the words can readily be attached.

For another example of the importance of this kind of attachment unit, consider the case of a college student of a generation ago who happened to read a newspaper story about some event in Southeast Asia. He would probably not have had any previously learned mediational units—any knowledge about South-

REQUIREMENTS
FOR LEARNING

1. DISTINCTIVE STIMULUS
2. ATTENTION TO STIMULUS
3. UNIT OF PREVIOUSLY
    LEARNED BEHAVIOR

east Asia or its role in world affairs—to which the news story could readily be attached and thus coded into long-term memory. Thus he probably would not have learned very much. More recent students, however, are likely to know a great deal about Southeast Asia's geography, people, politics, armies, and world importance. They can readily remember the contents of a new article about Southeast Asia because they possess many mediational units to which the new article can become attached.

4. how learning builds on learning

The ultimate message of the third requirement for learning—the presence of a unit to which the stimulus can become attached—is that learning builds on learning. Perhaps this point can best be made by an analogy.

Let us suppose that we are facing a cork wall that is almost completely covered by small squares of hard tile, with only a few gaps of cork showing between the tiles. At this wall we start throwing darts. When the dart hits cork, it naturally sticks to the wall. When it strikes a tile, it does not stick, but let us say that it does knock the tile away, exposing another area of cork. At first, not many of our darts will stick to the wall. Later, as more and more tiles are knocked away and more and more gaps of cork appear, more and more of our darts will sink home.

This is the way learning takes place. Just as the dart sinks home only when it hits an area of cork to which it can stick, so the new stimulus is learned only when it gets attached to some unit already present inside the organism. The larger the area of cork, the more likely that any given dart will stick; similarly, the more units already present inside the organism, the greater the chance that the new stimulus will be coded into long-term memory and thus learned.

The possession of component parts makes learning easier and faster. So does the possession of other kinds of mediational units to which a new stimulus can be attached—as the word *shilling* can be attached to words and concepts such as *England, travel, money, coin,* and so forth. Each new unit we learn helps us in turn to learn others.

This is one reason children from low-income families often have a difficult time in school, thus continuing a vicious circle that leads one generation after another to have trouble getting along. A child whose parents had very little formal education and use a limited vocabulary starts school with a severe handicap. There are hundreds and perhaps even thousands of words and concepts that he has never heard of but that are already familiar to children his age whose parents are better educated and more affluent. He simply does not have the mediational units required for the attachments between new and old that come easy to children whose parents speak a richer language. School would be easier for these children if teachers could develop some technique of building on the mediational units that the children actually do possess—that is, on the kind of previous knowledge that the children take to school from their own families, rather than on the kind of previous knowledge acquired in a middle-class home and taken for granted by a teacher who has himself had a middle-class background. As it is, many children from low-income families give up and eventually drop out of school, even though they may have a great deal of inborn learning ability and, if they once started building a vocabulary, might quickly acquire a storehouse of mediational units and catch up by leaps and bounds.

William James on Attachment Units. Although William James lived and wrote many years before the discovery of most of what is now known about the processes of coding into long-term memory and retrieval, he sensed the importance of mediational units to which new stimuli can become attached and summarized the entire matter quite beautifully:

> *The more other facts a fact is associated with in the mind, the better possession of it our memory retains.* Each of its associates becomes a hook to which it hangs, a means to fish it up by when sunk beneath the surface. Together, they form a network of attachments by which it is woven into the entire tissue of our thought. The "secret of a good memory" is thus the secret of forming diverse and multiple associations with every fact we care to retain. . . . Most men have a good memory for facts connected with their own pursuits. The college athlete who remains a dunce at his books will astonish you by his knowledge of men's records in various feats and games, and will be a walking dictionary of sporting statistics. The reason is that he is constantly going over these things in his mind, and comparing and making series of them. They form for him not so many odd facts but a concept-system—so they stick. So the merchant remembers prices, the politician other politicians' speeches and votes, with a copiousness which amazes outsiders, but which the amount of thinking they bestow on these subjects easily explains. The great memory for facts which a Darwin and a Spencer reveal in their books is not incompatible with the possession on their part of a brain with only a middling degree of physiological retentiveness [by which James means inborn ability for remembering]. Let a man early in life set himself the task of verifying such a theory as that of evolution, and facts will soon cluster and cling to him like grapes to their stem. Their relations to the theory will hold them fast; and the more of these the mind is able to discern, the greater the erudition will become (32).

The following chapter will discuss *management of learning,* the term used to describe the various ways in which learning can be made more efficient. All the aspects of management of learning are important and have considerable practical value, but no other has such a basic and all-pervasive significance as the one described in these words of William James. It is our storehouse of mediational units—those areas of receptive cork to which a new stimulus can stick like a dart sinking home—that determines more than anything else how well we will learn and remember.

summary 1. *Curves of forgetting* show that when we learn something new we very quickly forget much of what we have learned but remember at least some of it for a long time.

2. Since it is impossible to measure learning and remembering directly, we are forced to use the best available substitute, which is performance. Since performance requires not only learning but also a) a motive to perform and

b) the absence of conflicting behavior, it does not always accurately reflect how much has been learned and remembered.

3. Three measures of learning and remembering (as reflected by performance) are *recall, recognition,* and *relearning.* Recognition is usually easier than recall.

4. Theories of why we forget include a) fading of the "memory trace," b) distortion of the "memory trace," c) motivated forgetting, d) interference by prior or subsequent learning, and e) failure in retrieval.

5. There is a growing belief among psychologists that there are three kinds or systems of memory: a) *sensory memory,* b) *short-term memory,* and c) *long-term memory.*

6. Stimuli that register in sensory memory appear to be forgotten within a second at most unless transferred to short-term memory.

7. Information held in short-term memory is forgotten within about thirty seconds unless held there through the processes of *scanning* and *rehearsal* long enough to be coded into long-term memory.

8. In the coding of information into long-term memory, the new information becomes associated with older mediational units to form "chunks" of information that can later be pulled out of memory (or *retrieved*) more or less as a whole.

9. Many psychologists now believe that long-term memory constitutes a permanent storehouse of information, and that forgetting represents a failure of the retrieval process. (The information is there but we "can't get at it.")

10. The "tip of the tongue" phenomenon indicates that the coding of words into long-term memory and their subsequent retrieval are complex processes that involve storage in auditory terms (how words sound and how many syllables they have), visual terms (the letters with which they begin and end), and terms of meaning (so that they are "chunked" with other words that mean more or less the same thing).

11. Anything that aids "chunking" (that is, the association of new information with old) aids in coding and retrieval. Among methods that have proved successful are making up stories that use the words in a word list and learning by categories.

12. Learning is most likely to take place when three requirements are met: a) a distinctive stimulus, b) attention to the stimulus, and c) a unit of innate or previously learned behavior or information to which the new stimulus can become attached (an *attachment unit*).

13. Because of the importance of attachment units, learning and remembering depend to a great extent on the number of previously learned mediational units to which a new stimulus can be attached. What this means in practical terms is that learning builds on learning. The more we know, the more we are likely to learn.

recommended reading

Adams, J. A. *Human memory.* New York: McGraw-Hill, 1967.

Bartlett, F. C. *Remembering: a study in experimental and social psychology.* New York: Cambridge University Press, 1932.

Broadbent, D. E. *Perception and communication.* Elmsford, N.Y.: Pergamon Press, 1958.

Cowan, J. L., ed. *Studies in thought and language.* Tucson: University of Arizona Press, 1969.

Deese, J. E., and Hulse, S. *The psychology of learning,* 3rd ed. New York: McGraw-Hill, 1967.

Dixon, T. R., and Horton, D. L., eds. *Verbal behavior and general behavior theory.* Englewood Cliffs, N.J.: Prentice-Hall, 1968.

Hilgard, E. R., and Bower, G. H. *Theories of learning,* 3rd ed. New York: Appleton-Century-Crofts, 1966.

James, W. *Principles of psychology,* vol. 1. New York: Holt, 1890 [reprinted by Dover, New York, 1950]. Chapter 16.

Kintsch, W. *Learning, memory and conceptual processes.* New York: Wiley, 1970.

Neisser, U. *Cognitive psychology.* New York: Appleton-Century-Crofts, 1967.

Norman, D. A. *Memory and attention: an introduction to human information processing.* New York: Wiley, 1969.

Norman, D. A. *Models of memory.* New York: Academic Press, 1970.

CHAPTER 4

efficiency in Learning

Let us suppose that you have volunteered to campaign for a political candidate. You have written a speech explaining why you think he should be elected. Now you want to memorize the speech so that you can deliver it without notes.

Will you be better off trying to learn the speech a paragraph at a time and then putting the paragraphs together—or learning the whole thing as a unit?

Will you learn more quickly if you read the speech a few times and then attempt to recite it—or if you just keep rereading?

Is it more efficient to keep studying without any breaks—or to study for a number of short periods, with rests in between?

The answers to questions such as these have been sought in the interests of pure science—but the findings have also been put to immediate practical use and now constitute one of the largest fields of applied psychology. Since the findings are used mostly by teachers and in classroom situations, they are called by the term *management of learning,* which means the attempt to arrange the most favorable possible conditions for learning to take place.

Discussion of favorable conditions for learning is bound to revolve around the three requirements for learning: 1) a distinctive stimulus, 2) attention to the stimulus, and 3) some unit of innate behavior or a previously learned mediational unit to which the stimulus can be attached. It is only by manipulating these three requirements that learning can be managed and made more efficient. The first part of this chapter on efficiency or management of learning, therefore, can best be organized around the requirements for learning—taken up, for reasons of convenience, in reverse order.

the importance of attachment units

As William James realized long ago and as new knowledge of one-trial learning and component parts has again emphasized, nothing is so vital to the learning process as the storehouse of information we already possess, into which we can integrate the new. That general principle has already been discussed in some detail. Some specific ways in which the principle has been shown to work can now be added.

119

4-1 A group of rats was raised from birth in a cage that had circles and triangles on the walls. The geometric figures had no relation to the rats' feeding or other activity; they were simply present as a sort of decoration, like the pictures hanging on a living room wall. After the rats had grown up, they were asked to learn, as one is shown doing in the drawing, that food would always be found behind the circle but not behind the triangle, or vice versa; in other words, they were asked to learn to discriminate between the two geometric forms. The same task was also given to another group of rats that had grown up under the same conditions in a cage exactly the same except that the walls were blank. Question: Which group learned faster? For the answer, see Figure 4-2.

1. familiarity with the stimulus

The purpose of the experiment shown in Figure 4-1 was to discover whether familiarity can help learning. The finding, shown in Figure 4-2, was that it most certainly can. Just being around the two stimuli while growing up helped the rats learn to discriminate between them later.

results of the familiarity experiment

4-2

The graph charts the results of the experiment shown in Figure 4-1. The rats that had grown up in the cage with circles and triangles on the walls learned much faster and much better than the other rats. (1)

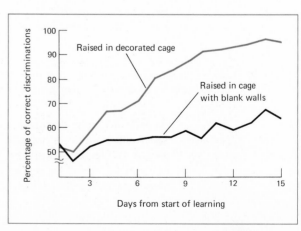

When the automobile was first introduced, many people had difficulty learning to drive. Today's generations, familiar with the automobile from childhood, have far less trouble. Children who grow up in houses that contain musical instruments seem to learn to play them more easily than other children, and children who have watched their parents read newspapers and magazines and books seem to learn to read more easily. Americans, living in a nation full of all kinds of machinery, can usually learn to operate a new factory machine or military vehicle more easily than can the native of a South Pacific island who has never seen any machinery more complicated than a water wheel.

In school, the best teacher is generally the one who can relate new and unfamiliar material to the things his students already know and who explains it in the most familiar language possible.

2. meaningfulness

Figure 4–3 illustrates an experiment that you can try for yourself by following the instructions given in the caption. If you do this, the scores you make on each of the four lists will probably be quite similar to the results found in the original experiment, which are shown in Figure 4–4.

It should come as no surprise that list 1, composed of actual three-letter words, should be the easiest of all the lists to learn. But why is list 2 easier to learn than list 3, and list 3 in turn easier than list 4? The answer is that the lists were drawn up in an attempt to discover how the degree of *meaningfulness* influences learning. Each of the nonsense syllables in list 2 is meaningful in the sense that it tends to remind almost everyone of some actual word—that is to say, all of us already have some word in our vocabulary with which the nonsense syllables of list 2 can easily be associated. In list 3, about half the words have this sort of meaningfulness. In list 4, none of the syllables do; in this list, all the syllables are truly "nonsense" in that they do not suggest associations with

which list is easiest to learn?

4-3

These are the kinds of lists used in a well-known learning experiment, which you can repeat for yourself. Study list 1 for two minutes, then test yourself to see how many of the ten items you remember. Now do the same for each of the other three lists. To find how your scores compare with those obtained in the original experiment, see Figure 4–4. (Nonsense syllables, 2)

List 1	List 2	List 3	List 4
SIT	DOZ	SIQ	ZOJ
HAT	RAV	CUK	JYQ
BIN	ROV	BYS	XUY
COW	SOF	NOK	QOV
RIM	HOL	GEV	GIW
RAN	SUR	RYS	VAF
MET	LIF	CYP	CEF
POT	GYM	FYS	XYH
HUG	RUF	JAL	VYQ
FIG	BEV	QAT	ZYT

4-4

These are the scores made by the subjects in the original experiment. For an explanation of why there was such a large variation in how much was learned from the four different lists, see the text. (3)

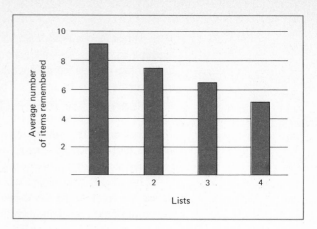

actual words. Thus the results shown in Figure 4-4—and probably your own results if you tried the experiment—demonstrate how the meaningfulness of the material to be learned affects ease of learning.

Many other experiments have produced similar results. In one of the earliest experiments, subjects were asked to memorize a list of 200 nonsense syllables, a list of 200 digits in random order, a 200-word passage of prose writing, and 200 words of poetry. The results are shown in Figure 4-5. Note how much longer it took to learn the nonsense syllables and the nonsense arrangement of digits than to learn the passages of prose and poetry. Poetry—which has not only meaningfulness but also a sort of internal logic and organization provided by the cadence and rhymes—proved easiest of all to learn.

The more meaningful the material we try to learn, the more readily it can be associated with something that we already know. To go back to the analogy of the darts and the wall that was used in the previous chapter, we might say that a meaningful stimulus is like a well-aimed dart directed toward an area of

meaningful versus meaningless material

4-5

The height of the bars demonstrates how much more easily subjects in one experiment learned meaningful writing than lists of random digits and nonsense syllables. (4)

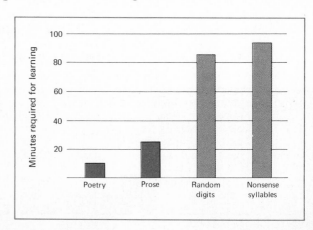

cork where it can sink home. If in addition the material has some organization and logic of its own—that is, if it tends to form its own internal associations and "hang together" as does poetry—the job of learning becomes easier still.

3. learning by rote versus learning by rule

Closely related to the matter of meaningfulness is another well-established fact about learning: we learn more easily and remember longer if we learn by rule—or, as some might prefer to say, by logic—than if we learn by rote. An experiment that neatly demonstrates this is illustrated in Figure 4-6. Most of the students who tried to learn the numbers shown in the right-hand photograph, it should be mentioned, managed to discover the principle that lay behind the arrangement. You may want to try to discover it also before reading on to the next paragraph.

As you may have figured out for yourself, the numbers following the first number 5 are obtained by regularly adding 3-4-3-4-3-4-3-4 to the preceding number. Thus 5 is followed by 8 (which is 5 plus 3); 8 is followed by 12 (which is 8 plus 4); 12 is followed by 15 (which is 12 plus 3); and so on. Number 26 at the end of the first line is followed by 29 (26 plus 3) to start the second line, and 29 is then followed by 33 (29 plus 4).

As the experiment was set up, the first class was in effect asked to learn the numbers by rote—that is to say, by sheer repetition, mechanically, without any regard to meaning. The second class learned by rule—with an understanding

rote versus rule

4-6

In both these classes the students have been asked to memorize the numbers on the blackboard. In the class at left the instructor suggests that the easiest way to remember them is in groups of three, as he has arranged them. In the class at right the instructor points out that the two lines of numbers are not arranged in random order but according to a definite and logical pattern, with the pattern the same for both lines. The students are left to find the pattern for themselves (as you may also want to try to do). The experiment was designed to see which class would learn the numbers more easily. For an explanation of the pattern of the numbers and the results of the experiment, see the text.

of the meaningfulness and logic of the pattern. The two classes, as it happened, learned about equally well. When tested a half-hour later, 33 percent of the students in the first class and 38 percent of the students in the second class recalled the numbers perfectly, exactly as shown on the blackboards. But their ability to remember the numbers for a period of time was sharply different. Three weeks later, not one of the students who had learned the numbers by rote remembered them correctly. Of the students who had learned by a logical rule, 23 percent still knew the numbers perfectly (5).

Most of the learning we do in school is a combination of rote and logical rule. There is no easy way for the elementary school pupil to learn his multiplication tables; he has to memorize them one step at a time, by rote. But he learns long division by grasping the rules that govern it. When we learn a foreign language, we have to acquire the vocabulary largely by rote—though, as we learn more and more words, we see certain patterns and sometimes figure out the meaning of a word that we hear or see for the first time. For conjugating the verbs and declining the nouns we can learn some logical rules.

Although the multiplication tables are an exception, for a special reason that will be explained later, we tend to forget rather quickly the things we learn in school by rote. The logical rules that we have grasped tend to stay in our memories. Five years from now, for example, you may very well have forgotten words from this course such as operant and reinforcement. But the general rules of how learning takes place and modifies behavior will probably have stuck with you. A study that demonstrates what college students tend to remember from a course is shown in Figure 4–7.

The term *chunking* is a useful description of the process of learning by rule. Material that has a logical set of principles tends to hang together like a chunk of wood or stone, in a tightly bound mass that resists the erosion of forgetting.

DEFINITION:

CHUNKING

what college students remember

4-7

These scores were obtained by testing college zoology students, first at the end of their course and again more than a year later. They show that the students had forgotten about half the terminology they had learned for animal structures and many specific facts. But they still knew the principles as well as ever and could apply them to new situations. On the matter of interpreting experiments that they had never heard of before, they were actually better than at the end of the course. This improvement was probably due to the greater general knowledge and maturity acquired in an additional year of college. (6)

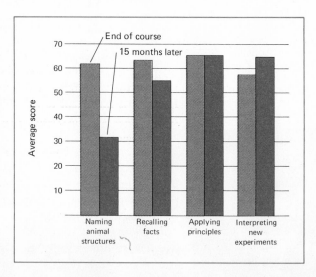

4. the role of guidance

From everything that has been said in the past few pages it follows that learning can be made easier by anything that helps us find elements of familiarity and meaningfulness in new material and learn it by logic and rule rather than by rote. Hence *guidance* plays an important role in the management of learning.

A textbook is one form of guidance. An enterprising student could find every fact and every theory in this book somewhere else in a library; he would find all the experiments reported in some psychological journal, and he could read the original books by the pioneers who have been mentioned here, such as Wundt, Galton, James, and Watson. But this would be the hard way to read about the science of psychology. The student who tried it would probably have considerable difficulty in relating Pavlov's experiments on conditioned responses to Skinner's experiments on operant conditioning. He might not see any connection between the learning of nonsense syllables and actual learning in the classroom or the learning of such aspects of personality as motives and anxieties. Many of the words he found in the literature would be completely unfamiliar. Much of the material would at first glance seem meaningless. The underlying principles would not be apparent for a long time, and he would therefore have to make a dogged attempt to memorize many things by rote that proper guidance would have enabled him to learn by logical rule.

Also helpful to the learner is the special kind of guidance that can be provided in person, by a good teacher. The art of teaching revolves largely around the manipulation of familiarity, meaningfulness, and learning by rules and logic—in other words, around the formation of associations between the new and the old that constitutes the third requirement of learning.

5. a special note on rote learning

Most learning done in school, as has been mentioned, is a combination of rote and rule. The same thing is true in many situations outside the classroom—in everything from learning football plays to breaking in at a new job. Hence it is important to ask: What are some of the ways in which learning by rote, which is a necessary evil in so many life circumstances, can best be accomplished?

One well-established fact is that rote learning takes time. The processes of holding materials in short-term memory and somehow coding them into long-term memory require a good deal of work, and the work cannot be done unless sufficient time is devoted to it. By and large, the more time that is spent at learning, the more that will be learned.

In one study of rote learning, the experimenter asked his subjects to study two lists of fifteen words each, presented by a voice on a tape recorder at the rate of one word every 1.5 seconds. The words in the two lists were presented

4-8

The two bars at the left show what happened when subjects listened to the words in two lists, presented in random order, and had 4.5 seconds to study those in list 1 and only 1.5 seconds to study those in list 2. The two bars at the right show what happened when another group of subjects again had 4.5 seconds to study the words in list 1 but had 7.5 seconds to study those in list 2. Note especially that the percentage of words remembered from list 1 dropped even though the words were studied for just as long a time. (7)

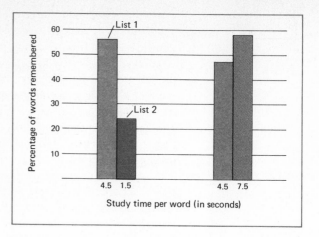

in random order, but those in list 1 were repeated three times in the course of the recording, while those in list 2 were spoken only once. Thus the subjects had a total of 4.5 seconds to study each of the words in list 1 but only 1.5 seconds to study each of the words in list 2. The results of the experiment provided a clear-cut and convincing demonstration of the fact that <u>additional time produces additional learning</u>. As is shown in Figure 4-8, the subjects remembered fully 56 percent of the words in list 1 but only 24 percent of the words in list 2.

The experimenter then went on to demonstrate another important fact about the effect of time on rote learning. To another group of subjects, he presented the same two lists of words. The words in list 1 were again repeated three times, or for the same total of 4.5 seconds each. But the words in list 2 were presented not just once but five times, or for a total of 7.5 seconds each. Note that the total amount of time that the subjects had to learn the words in list 1 did not change—but the proportional amount of time devoted to these words, as compared with the amount of time devoted to the words in list 2, did change and was substantially lower. The number of words remembered from list 1 also was substantially lower; it fell to 47 percent, while the number remembered from list 2 rose all the way to 58 percent.

The psychologist who conducted the experiment has concluded, on the basis of this and other evidence, that <u>the amount of learning depends on both the total or *absolute* time spent in study and also the *proportional* time in relation to other materials that are being studied during the same period</u> (7). Taking into account this view of the importance of both absolute and proportional time seems to explain many phenomena that have been observed in the learning of materials such as word lists and nonsense syllables, as well as in many everyday situations where learning is a combination of rote and rule. For example, every student knows that it is easier to study for final examinations that are spaced out over a period of days; under these circumstances each subject can be tackled separately and given full attention, so that the proportional amount of time devoted to it is very high.

ABSOLUTE AND PROPORTIONAL TIME

126

Mnemonic Devices. Countless beginning sailors have been faced with a rote learning problem in remembering the confusing and easily forgotten difference between port (the left side of the ship) and starboard (the right side). Many of them have solved the problem by learning the simple sentence, "I left port." Similarly, many generations of English-speaking people have remembered how many days there are in the various months of the year because they learned the jingle that begins "Thirty days hath September."

A crutch of this kind is called a *mnemonic device,* after the Greek word for remembering. Indeed the idea of using such memory crutches may have originated with the Greeks, whose orators used an ingenious system to help them remember the order of the various points they wanted to make in their speeches. They imagined themselves walking through a familiar temple, moving in the usual order past one after another of its familiar statues. With the first statue they associated the first topic or paragraph of the speech, with the second statue the second topic, and so on. To avoid omitting any topic, all they had to do was recall each of the statues encountered in walking through the temple (8).

You can develop your own mnemonic system, useful in helping learn short lists of words or objects, by memorizing an easily remembered jingle that has been used in a number of psychological experiments:

One is a bun; two is a shoe;
Three is a tree; four is a door;
Five is a hive; six is sticks;
Seven is heaven; eight is a gate;
Nine is wine; ten is a hen.

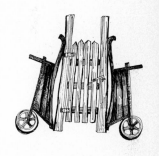

Let us say that the jingle is to be used to help remember, in order, the following list of words: 1) pencil, 2) knife, 3) horse, 4) battleship, 5) briefcase, 6) newspaper, 7) apple, 8) wheelbarrow, 9) table, 10) lightbulb. The trick is to form some kind of mental image, like those shown in the margins, connecting the words to be remembered with the words that rhyme with the numbers.

In one experiment, subjects who did not know the jingle were first asked to learn a list of ten words without any help. Then half of them were given an opportunity to memorize the jingle and use it to help them learn a second list of ten words. The other half, used as a control group, were not told about the jingle and had to learn

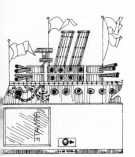

127

4-9

The experimental group studied the words in list 1 without help, then tried to learn the words in list 2 with the aid of a mnemonic jingle, as explained in the text. The control group learned both lists without the help of the jingle. Note the superior performance of the experimental group on list 2 when the study time per word was four seconds or more. When allowed eight seconds of study time, with the aid of the mnemonic device, the experimental group almost reached the perfect learning score of 20. (9)

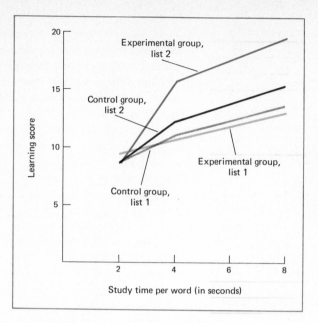

list 2 without any help. Some subjects were permitted to study each word in both lists for two seconds; others studied each word for four seconds and still others for eight seconds. The results of the experiment are shown in Figure 4-9. Note that the subjects who used the jingle as a mnemonic device remembered list 2 much better than the control subjects who did not use the jingle, provided that they had at least four seconds to form some kind of mental image related to the jingle. Indeed those who had eight seconds to form an image made an almost perfect score. Two seconds, however, proved insufficient for most subjects to make a connection between the words in list 2 and the words in the jingle (9).

The experimenters found that the subjects who used the jingle liked the idea and "felt genuinely indebted for being let in on a 'valuable' secret." Similar systems, more elaborate in that they often provide memory hooks for as many as 100 items, are the secret of the "memory experts" in show business who perform such seemingly incredible feats as quickly learning long lists of objects or of people's names. For rote learning of things that would ordinarily be difficult to remember, mnemonic devices are unquestionably useful. The reason is that they provide a ready-made system of attachment units for new stimuli that could not otherwise readily be attached to existing units through logical rule or chunking.

3. attention to the stimulus

When we pay attention—eagerly and single-mindedly—learning tends to be easy. When we do not pay close attention, learning tends to be difficult or even impossible. But, as every student knows, these simple facts are not in themselves very

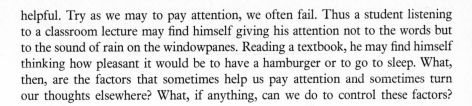

helpful. Try as we may to pay attention, we often fail. Thus a student listening to a classroom lecture may find himself giving his attention not to the words but to the sound of rain on the windowpanes. Reading a textbook, he may find himself thinking how pleasant it would be to have a hamburger or to go to sleep. What, then, are the factors that sometimes help us pay attention and sometimes turn our thoughts elsewhere? What, if anything, can we do to control these factors?

1. motives

One powerful aid to paying attention is motivation. Some people seem to have an almost insatiable thirst for knowledge—any kind of knowledge. They find it easy to pay attention regardless of the subject matter. Some students who are motivated mostly by the desire for good grades also pay close attention regardless of whether they are studying psychology, philosophy, or ancient history. Most of us, however, are somewhat more selective; we are strongly motivated to learn some things, less strongly motivated to learn others. We are most likely to pay attention when the learning stimulus seems to satisfy our own particular and rather specialized motives.

If the subject matter can somehow be related to a person's motives, attention can be sharpened. Thus the study of Spanish becomes easier if the student keeps reminding himself that he may be traveling or even working someday in a Spanish-speaking country. The most successful teachers are those who manage to relate their subjects to the hopes and ambitions of their students.

2. feedback

It has been observed for some time that *feedback*—a term borrowed from the field of automation—plays an important role in learning. Feedback means information on how well the learning process is going, that is, how the learner is progressing, how much he has learned, how many mistakes he is making, and what kind of mistakes.

One reason feedback helps the learning process is that it enables the learner to correct his mistakes quickly. This is especially important in motor learning. For example, a student trying to learn typing on a dummy keyboard might be hitting the wrong keys without ever knowing it; on an actual typewriter, feedback from the printed page tells him at once when he makes a mistake. Another reason—perhaps even more important—is that feedback helps capture and hold attention. Whatever the motives for paying attention and learning, they are generally best satisfied by some kind of evidence that learning is actually taking place. Thus feedback serves as a sort of reinforcing stimulus that encourages learning.

In some situations, immediate feedback seems to be the most effective; for example, it has been found that classroom examinations are sometimes most helpful if they are scored and given back to students right then and there (10). In other situations, delay seems to be better; in one study feedback of examination results was found to be most effective when delayed for a day, and even a four-day delay was found to produce better results than immediate feedback (11). In general, young children appear to profit most from immediate feedback. Older children and adults, especially if they are highly motivated to spend time after the examination thinking about their answers, often do better when feedback is delayed.

3. rewards

Perhaps the most frequently used tool in the management of learning is a reward. Laboratory rats are rewarded with food pellets for learning to press the bar in a Skinner box, trained whales with pieces of fish for learning to jump out of water. Babies are rewarded for each new accomplishment with a smile and a pat. Older children are rewarded with gold stars, candy, and trips to the movies. Even college students are rewarded for learning—with good grades and eventually diplomas, and sometimes with increased allowances or automobiles from their parents.

All these tokens of success, from food pellets to college diplomas, are *external rewards* (also sometimes called *extrinsic rewards*). They are in a sense merely bribes provided by another person, but they can be effective and useful. Many an adult has been happier and more successful because of knowledge originally acquired mostly for the external reward of good grades and praise from a parent. Many a man is glad that he learned to play the piano as a boy—something he would never have done without the external reward of a new bicycle or a fishing trip.

A second group of rewards, more difficult to control, is *internal rewards* (also sometimes called *intrinsic rewards*). Internal rewards are feelings of satisfaction. An example is a boy learning to ride a bicycle. In part his attention may be drawn by external rewards, such as the respect of his friends. But the rewards are primarily internal—pleasant feelings arising from the satisfaction of his desire to prove his ability and from the sense of power derived from traveling faster on wheels than he can travel on foot. Other examples are adults who try very hard to learn to dance, to play a musical instrument, or to take beautiful photographs. Their attention is absolutely riveted on the learning situation—not because they seek any external reward but because they want the internal reward of learning a new skill, the reward that comes from meeting an internal standard of perfection.

In many learning situations, both internal and external rewards help recruit attention. The musician may learn both for his own pleasure and for praise from his friends. The mechanic may learn more about automobiles partly because of the inner satisfactions of his job and partly because he wants more pay. Of the two kinds of rewards, the internal seem to be the more effective and lasting aid to attention. In the management of learning, the teacher who can make his students eager to know for the inner satisfaction of knowing wields a powerful tool.

It has been found, however, that external rewards can be a valuable tool in starting the learning process. In one recent study, a psychologist worked over a period of years with about 400 boys between the ages of thirteen and eighteen who had done so badly in school that they were considered "uneducable." To give them an incentive to learn, he first paid them small sums of money, then later rewarded them for successes by permitting them to study subjects that they

DEFINITIONS:

1. INTERNAL OR INTRINSIC REWARD

2. EXTERNAL OR EXTRINSIC REWARD

especially liked. On the average these boys managed to cover between two and three years of schoolwork in a single year, and even their scores on intelligence tests improved substantially. The psychologist has concluded that the external rewards of money and permission to study favored subjects served to get the boys going—and finally to reach the point where they studied for the intrinsic reward of learning for the sake of learning (12).

4. punishment

Another frequently used tool is punishment. Just as we are rewarded for our successes from the early days of childhood, so are we punished for our failures. Babies are punished by a slap on the hand if they threaten to knock over a lamp and sometimes by a slap on the bottom if they seem to cry too much. Older children are punished if they are "sassy," get into fights or the cookie jar, or make poor grades at school. The punishment comes in a wide range of severity—from a mere "No!" stated in a firm tone of voice to a harsh spanking.

In elementary school, teachers punish pupils by keeping them after hours, by making them write essays on the evils of laziness, and by sending them to the principal's office for a stern lecture. In college, the punishment is more subtle. Poor grades are in themselves a kind of punishment and being flunked out is the ultimate.

Animal Experiments.   Because ethical considerations prevent most kinds of experiments with human beings, psychological knowledge about the effectiveness of punishment comes almost entirely from studies of animals. Many of the studies have shown that in the case of animals—though not necessarily in the case of people—punishment often results in rather rapid and long-lasting learning (13).

Some of the factors that influence the effectiveness of punishment in animal learning have been demonstrated in experiments in which rats were placed in a Skinner box with a grid floor through which an electrical shock could be administered. After the animals had learned to press the bar for food, they were divided into a control group and several experimental groups. The control animals continued to receive food as before. But, when the experimental groups pressed the bar, they received not only food but also a shock of varying intensity and duration; and the shock made them tend to avoid the bar. The intensity of punishment had a substantial effect; the more severe the shock, the less likely the rat was to press the bar. The duration of punishment also was found to have a marked effect; the longer the shock lasted, the less likely the rat was to press the bar.

As might be expected from the findings on delay of reinforcement discussed in Chapter 2 (page 74), the timing of the shock also proved important. If the punishment followed immediately after the animal pressed the bar, the animal tended to stop pressing. But even a very short delay reduced the effectiveness of the punishment. In one of the experiments the grid was set to administer a shock thirty seconds after the bar was pressed. In many cases the animal pressed the bar again in the meantime, so that often the delay between bar pressing and punishment was not even as much as thirty seconds. Yet the effect of the punishment dropped substantially and often to zero (14).

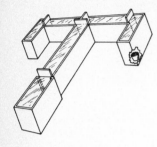

Other experiments with animals have shown that punishment is most effective of all when combined with reward—that is to say, when the "wrong" response is punished and the "correct" response is rewarded. For example, if a rat is placed at the entrance of a T-shaped maze, in which the "correct" response is to turn right, it will learn this response very quickly if rewarded with food when it turns right and punished with shock when it turns left. A real-life demonstration of the same principle is provided by the house-breaking of a young puppy, which, as countless dog owners have discovered, is best accomplished by punishing the animal immediately with a slap with a rolled-up newspaper when it wets a rug but giving clear indications to the animal that the same act is acceptable and even praiseworthy outdoors.

Adverse Effects of Punishment.   Even in the case of animals, however, there is experimental evidence that punishment, though often effective, must be used with considerable caution. To explain this point, it is necessary to lapse into some rather unscientific language and speak of animals as being able to "know" things in the way that human beings know them. In these terms, if an animal does not "know" why it is being punished or how to avoid or escape the punishment, learning does not take place and in fact there may be some very drastic and undesirable effects.

In one experiment, for example, dogs were strapped into a type of harness similar to the one used by Pavlov (page 52). While thus immobilized, they received a series of sixty-four electrical shocks, each lasting five seconds, delivered at random intervals. There was no way that they could avoid the shocks or escape from them; they were helpless to prevent the shocks or cut them off before the five seconds were up. Next day the dogs were placed in the kind of hurdle or shuttle box described on page 58—a box with two compartments separated by a shoulder-high barrier. From time to time the light inside the box was dimmed, and ten seconds later a shock was administered through the floor of the compartment in which the dog had been placed. The animal could avoid the shock altogether by jumping over the barrier into the other compartment before the ten seconds were up, or it could escape the shock by jumping after the electricity was turned on. If the dog did not jump into the other compartment, the shock continued for a full fifty seconds.

The results of the experiment, shown in Figure 4-10, were quite dramatic. The dogs had ten trials in which they could learn to avoid or escape the shock, but the amount of learning that took place was very small. In most cases the dogs simply accepted the shock for the full fifty seconds, making no attempt to leap over the barrier. By contrast, a control group of dogs that had not previously received inescapable shocks learned very quickly to jump the barrier in time to avoid the shock or to escape in a hurry once the shock had begun.

LEARNED
HELPLESSNESS

How are we to account for the failure of the experimental dogs to learn—for their passive acceptance of a severe and long-lasting shock? The experimenters attribute it to what they have called *learned helplessness.* While in the Pavlov harness, the dogs learned that nothing they could do had any effect on whether they received a shock or for how long. To speak about animals in human terms

4-10

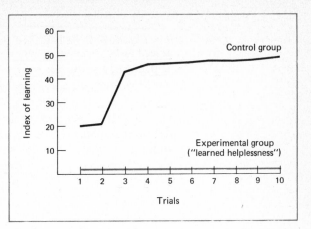

The graph lines show the results of the experiment, described in the text, in which a group of dogs acquired "learned helplessness" because of receiving unavoidable punishment. When these dogs were later placed in a hurdle box from which they could easily avoid or escape a shock, they showed very little learning; indeed most of them took no action and endured the shock for its full duration (colored line). Animals that had not previously received unavoidable punishment, on the other hand, were very quick to learn to avoid the shock or escape from it after it began (black line).

again, they carried this knowledge over to the situation in the hurdle box; they had no "expectation" that they could do anything about the shock and therefore no "incentive" to try to escape (15).

Punishment in Human Education. The experiment on "learned helplessness" suggests some of the dangers of the use of punishment in human situations. Many parents who believe in the old adage "Spare the rod and spoil the child" are quick to punish almost any kind of activity, often with the same degree of verbal or physical intensity regardless of how major or minor the child's transgressions may be. Some parents, indeed, seem to operate by whim; depending on their moods, they may at times severely punish exactly the same kind of behavior that they ignore at other times. There may be long intervals between the time a child's misbehavior takes place and the time it is discovered and punished; indeed, it is still common in some households for spankings to be delayed until the father gets home from work.

It seems reasonable to assume that when a child is continually "bawled out" or spanked—especially if the punishment is often inconsistent or long-delayed—he may very well acquire a "learned helplessness" of his own; he may decide that he has no control over when, how, or why he is punished. Like the dogs that never learned to escape the shock in the hurdle box, he may give up trying to learn what his parents are trying to teach him, in which case his parents' attempts to punish him into learning the difference between good behavior and bad become self-defeating. He may even become what the experimental dogs would have to be called in human terms—that is, seriously neurotic. The same serious results may occur when an elementary school teacher who is "down" on the slow learners in her class constantly berates them for their stupidity.

Direct experimental studies of the effect of punishment on human learning are of course impossible. But observation of children who received a considerable amount of verbal or physical punishment has shown that they tend to acquire a considerable dislike for the people who punish them, for example their parents or teachers, and also for any activities that have led to punishment, for example, schoolwork (16). It has also been found that children who are frequently criticized

133

tend to develop an expectation of failure and soon may stop working at their school tasks. It appears, too, that children who are harshly punished tend to be aggressive and punishing toward other children—perhaps as a result of learning through observation, perhaps in an attempt to take out their own sufferings on others.

Most psychologists have rejected the adage about sparing the rod and believe instead in the opposite old saying that "you can catch more flies with honey than with vinegar." In other words, they believe that rewards are a more useful and far less dangerous tool than punishment in the management of learning. Even the Army, which used to believe in letting drill sergeants harass new soldiers into proper behavior during basic training, is studying the opposite method of rewarding good performance with movie privileges and overnight passes (17).

5. novelty

Figure 4-11 illustrates one professor's somewhat unorthodox efforts at management of learning. Certainly students are not likely to fall asleep in a classroom where such things are known to happen, and, if they should fall asleep, they will soon be jolted back to consciousness. The professor's methods represent an attempt to capture attention through *novelty*. The new and unexpected always contains a certain amount of built-in capacity to attract attention. People used to run outside their houses to watch an automobile drive by or to watch that curious new invention known as the airplane pass overhead. When television was new a few decades ago, people stared for minutes on end at the test patterns. Children in southern California are excited by rain, and children from the northern states are fascinated when they first see a palm tree. The unexpected and surprising

novelty in the classroom

4-11

Puffed rice goes flying in a physics class at El Camino College as Professor Julius Sumner Miller, an advocate of dramatizing the subject, demonstrates the Principle of Bernoulli.

seems to recharge the attentional system, and <u>thus novelty is another useful tool in the management of learning</u>.

The tool must be used with caution. <u>If wielded too flamboyantly or too often, it may do the opposite of what is intended—it may *dis*tract attention from the real business of learning at hand</u>. Even when carefully used it has only a temporary effect, for <u>novelty soon wears off</u>. But the teacher who employs it skillfully is like a long ball hitter who can also bunt; the students, like the infielders in the ball game, are likely to stay on their toes.

2. the distinctive stimulus

In this discussion of the management of learning, organized around the three requirements for learning, one more requirement remains—the need for a distinctive stimulus. The question that must now be asked is: How can the learning stimulus be made more distinctive and helped to sink home like a dart in a cork wall?

Although the answer depends in large part on how distinctive the stimulus can be made, it also depends on avoiding interference between the particular learning stimulus and other learning. Thus here we get into such problems as whether it is better to try to learn a speech as a whole or by paragraphs, whether it is better to read only or to read and recite, and whether it is better to study for one long, unbroken period or for a series of shorter periods. In other words, we must consider techniques of study—for all techniques of study are in essence an attempt to manipulate the stimulus and present it in the most efficient way and on the most efficient time schedule.

Before we get into specifics, let us consider two findings that have a bearing on this problem. One of them is another of the contributions made by Ebbinghaus, illustrated in Figure 4-12. As the curve shows, <u>doubling the amount to be learned</u>

the more to learn, the harder the task

4-12

The way in which learning becomes progressively more difficult as the amount of material increases is demonstrated by this curve, constructed from another of the experiments with nonsense syllables performed by Ebbinghaus. Note the steep rise in the curve from the time it took Ebbinghaus to learn each of the syllables in a list of seven (a mere 0.4 second) to the time it took him for each syllable in a list of thirty-six (22 seconds).

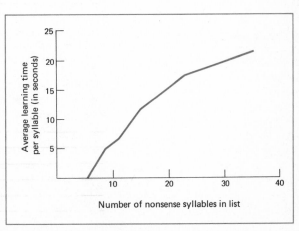

Average learning time per syllable (in seconds)

Number of nonsense syllables in list

does not just double the time required for learning but increases the time by much more than double. When Ebbinghaus increased the length of his list of nonsense syllables from seven to thirty-six, or to slightly more than five times the original length, the time required for learning per syllable increased by fifty-five times!

The other finding is shown in Figure 4-13, which is an experimental demonstration of a fact you may have noticed in your own studies and classroom work. We usually remember the first part of a lecture very well and also, although slightly less well, the last part. The middle is much harder to remember. The same thing happens in many other situations. If we listen to a fifteen-minute news broadcast and someone asks us afterward to tell about the news, we tend to remember the first items and the last ones but to forget the ones in the middle. If we make out a shopping list and lose it, we are more likely to remember the first and last items than the middle ones. In any series of stimuli, *serial position* helps determine which are learned best.

LAW OF PRIMACY AND RECENCY

SERIAL POSITION

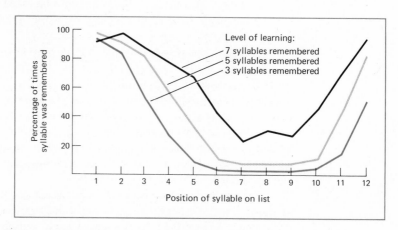

the law of primacy and recency

4-13   The graph shows what happened when subjects were asked to study a list of twelve nonsense syllables and were tested at various stages of the learning process to see how many syllables they remembered— especially *which* ones they remembered. To interpret the graph, note first the bottom line, which shows what had happened by the time the subjects had reached the level of learning where they knew three of the twelve syllables. In almost all cases the subjects were successful at remembering the first syllable on the list; well over 80 percent of the time they remembered the second syllable. The third syllable on the list was remembered about half the time, as was the last syllable on the list. Very few of the subjects remembered the fifth through the tenth syllables on the list. By the time the subjects had learned seven of the twelve syllables they still favored the ones at the beginning of the list and to a lesser extent those at the end. The seventh, eighth, and ninth syllables stuck in their memories least of all. The findings demonstrate the *law of primacy and recency*, which is explained further in the text. (18)

*LAW OF PRIMACY
AND RECENCY*

The *law of primacy and recency* states that out of a series of stimuli we find it easiest to remember the ones that came first (which had primacy) and the ones we encountered last (which had recency)—because these are the most distinctive of the stimuli. This law, of course, holds only when the stimuli in the series are of approximately equal familiarity and meaningfulness.

2. whole versus part learning

We are back now to the question of whether it is better to learn a speech as a whole or in parts. As a start toward answering it, let us see if we can apply what has just been said.

a. If you try to learn a speech as a whole, it follows from the law of primacy and recency that you will learn the beginning and the end of it first; you will know these parts by heart long before you master the middle. Score one point for the part method—for it seems a waste of time to keep working on the beginning and end of the speech long after you have mastered them.

b. As is apparent from the fact that difficulty of learning increases disproportionately with the amount of material, it will take you much longer to learn a ten-paragraph speech than it would take to learn ten separate paragraphs. Score another point for the part method.

PART LEARNING

c. Going back to what was said in the preceding section of this chapter, it is also known that feedback and reward are important in preserving attention. If you learn the speech a paragraph at a time, you will get more feedback; you will be able to notice the results more quickly. As you learn each paragraph the knowledge that you have accomplished something will serve as a reward to keep you going. Score another point for the part method.

However . . .

a. Also to be considered are the role of meaningfulness and the importance of learning by logical rule versus rote learning. Does the speech as a whole tend to hang together? Does it have more meaning as a whole than when broken up into individual paragraphs? If so, score a point for the whole method.

b. Similarly, the problem of transitions must be considered. If you learn the speech a paragraph at a time, studying each paragraph over and over until you know it, the last words of each paragraph tend to become associated with the first words of the same paragraph. To avoid repeating yourself when you deliver the speech, like a record player with a stuck needle, you must break these associations and establish new associations between the end of each paragraph and the start of the following paragraph. This is not always easy—so score another point for the whole method.

WHOLE LEARNING

How does the score add up? It all depends. Generally speaking, the whole method seems to be indicated when the material to be learned is relatively brief and has a logical theme that ties it into a meaningful unit. The question of who is doing the learning must also be taken into account. In general, the whole method works best for people who have had considerable practice with it and who are above average in their interest and experience in learning similar materials—factors that help in making new material more meaningful.

2. combination methods

Often a combination of the two methods seems most efficient. In studying a chapter in a textbook, for example, one good system is to begin by skimming through it quickly, trying to grasp the general pattern and logic without paying very much attention to the details. Usually the introductory paragraphs and the summary are especially helpful. Sometimes, indeed, it is possible to get a good idea of the sense of a chapter simply by reading the first few paragraphs, glancing at the various headings and the words and ideas emphasized by italics or heavy type, and then reading the summary. Once this feel for the chapter as a whole has been acquired, a slower and more detailed study of the individual parts is in order—with particular attention to the parts that seem difficult to remember.

In learning a speech or any other material that has to be remembered word for word, there often seem to be definite advantages to the *progressive part method,* as it was termed by the psychologist who first suggested it (19). In this method, you learn the first paragraph (or first stanza or whatever unit seems natural). Then you learn the second. Next you learn to put the first and second together. Once you have these two down pat, you put them aside and learn the third, then combine the first, second, and third into a unit—and so on to the end. This method seems to combine many of the virtues of both whole and part learning and to minimize some of the disadvantages.

One of the troubles, of course, is that you still spend more time than is necessary on the early paragraphs or stanzas, particularly the first one. You *overlearn* these parts. But overlearning, it should now be pointed out, is not necessarily bad.

3. overlearning

Adults are often surprised by how well they remember something they learned as children but have never practiced in the meantime. A man who has not had a chance to go swimming for years can still swim as well as ever when he gets back in the water. He can get on a bicycle after several decades and still ride away. He can play catch and swing a baseball bat as well as his son. A mother who has not thought about the words for years can teach her daughter the poem that begins "Twinkle, twinkle, little star" or recite the story of Cinderella or Goldilocks and the three bears.

One explanation is the *law of overlearning,* which can be stated as follows: Once we have learned something, additional learning trials increase the length of time we will remember it. A laboratory demonstration of this law is shown in Figure 4-14.

In childhood we usually continue to practice such skills as swimming, bicycle riding, and playing baseball long after we have learned them. We continue to listen to and remind ourselves of jingles such as "Twinkle, twinkle, little star"

LAW OF OVERLEARNING

4-14

These are the results of an experiment in which subjects learned a list of twelve single-syllable nouns. Sometimes they stopped studying the list as soon as they were able to recall it without error—in the words used in the chart, as soon as they had "barely learned" the words. At other times they were asked to continue studying the list for half again as many trials as bare learning required (50 percent overlearned) or to continue studying for the same number of extra trials as the original learning had required (100 percent overlearned). Whether measured after a day or at later intervals, the subjects who had over-learned by 50 percent remembered considerably more than those who had barely learned, and the subjects who had overlearned by 100 percent remembered most of all. (20)

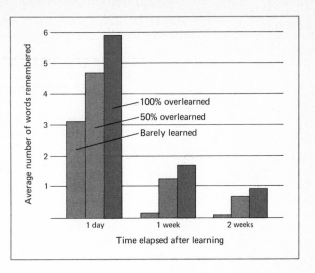

and childhood tales such as Cinderella and Goldilocks. We not only learn but overlearn.

Earlier in the chapter, it was mentioned that the multiplication tables are an exception to the general rule that we tend to forget rather quickly the things that we learn in school by rote. An explanation was promised later—and now, of course, you have it, for the multiplication tables are another of the things we overlearn in childhood.

The law of overlearning explains why cramming for an examination, though it may result in a passing grade, is not a satisfactory way to learn a college course. By cramming, a student may learn the subject well enough to get by on the examination, but he is likely soon to forget almost everything he learned. A little overlearning, on the other hand, is usually a good investment toward the future.

4, distribution of practice

Another argument against cramming is that it represents an attempt to learn through what is called *massed practice*—that is, a single long learning session. Studies of a wide range of situations involving both human and animal learning have indicated that massed practice is generally less efficient than *distributed practice*—that is, a series of shorter learning periods. As Figure 4-15 shows, the same total amount of time spent in learning is often strikingly more efficient when invested in short, separated periods than all at once.

Three possible explanations have been suggested for the superiority of distributed practice:

1. Distributed practice reduces the fatigue that often accompanies massed practice in motor learning and the boredom that often occurs in massed practice in verbal learning.

4-15

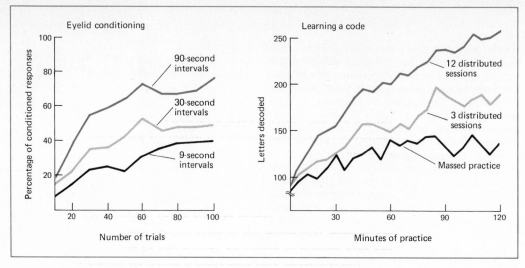

This graph shows the results of an experiment in which the eyelid-blinking reflex, produced by a puff of air directed at the eye, was conditioned to a light. More conditioned responses were obtained when there were 90-second intervals between trials than when the intervals were shorter—that is, when the practice was more massed. (21)

This graph shows the results of an experiment in which the subjects learned to substitute numbers for letters. Progress was slowest in a single massed session of 120 minutes of practice, higher when the subjects worked in three 40-minute sessions spread over six days, and highest of all when twelve 10-minute sessions were spread over six days. (22)

COVERT REHEARSAL
CONSOLIDATION

2. In the intervals between distributed practice sessions the learner may continue to mull over the material he has learned, even without knowing that he is doing so. This process is called *covert rehearsal* and results in what is called *consolidation* of what has been learned.

3. In many kinds of learning it seems likely that we learn not only what we want to learn but a number of useless and irrelevant habits that may actually interfere. A student learning to type, for example, might at the same time learn to grit his teeth, squint, and blink his eyes—habits that do not help his skill but hurt it. During the intervals between distributed practice sessions these extraneous habits may be forgotten more quickly than the basic subject matter of the learning. The process is called *differential forgetting*.

DIFFERENTIAL
FORGETTING

It must be added, however, that distributed practice does not always give such spectacular results as those shown in Figure 4-15. It seems less helpful in learning by logical rule than in learning by rote, possibly because rule learning involves less boredom. In learning situations that require a lot of "cranking up" time—getting out several books and notebooks, finding some reference works on the library shelves, and finding a comfortable and well-lighted place to work—short practice periods may be less efficient than long ones. Moreover, distributed

140

*SUPERIORITY OF
DISTRIBUTED LEARNING*

*REDUCES FATIGUE &
BOREDOM*

*COVERT REHEARSAL
→ CONSOLIDATION*

*DIFFERENTIAL
FORGETTING*

practice does not appear to have much effect if any on how well the learning is remembered; even when it results in substantial savings of the time required for learning, it does not seem to improve retention. But the general idea of distributed practice is a useful tool in the management of learning. Probably all learning tasks can be best accomplished through some pattern of distributed practice—in some cases many short periods separated by long intervals, in some cases fewer and longer periods separated by shorter intervals, and in some cases perhaps a combination. The trick is to find the pattern that best suits the particular situation.

5. recitation

We come now to the last of the questions posed at the beginning of the chapter: Is it better just to keep reading when you study or to read a while and then attempt to recite? An answer will be found in Figure 4-16.

Experimenters have found that it makes no difference whether the subjects are children or adults or whether the material being learned is nonsense syllables, spelling, mathematics, or a foreign vocabulary. In every case it is more efficient to read and recite than to read alone.

Let us say that you have eight hours to devote to learning this chapter and that reading through the chapter takes you two hours. The least efficient way to spend your study time would be to read through the chapter four times. You would do much better to spend more time in trying to recite what you have learned than in reading—for, as Figure 4-16 shows, devoting as much as 80 percent of study time to recitation may be more efficient by far than mere reading.

Recitation seems to assist learning in a number of ways. It certainly helps make the stimulus more distinctive; it casts a telling searchlight on what you have grasped quickly and what you have not, on what you understand and what you still find obscure. It provides a form of feedback that sharpens your attention.

the value of recitation

4-16

The subjects were elementary school pupils and university students who studied a list of sixteen nonsense syllables. The total time spent in study was the same for all the subjects. Some subjects, however, spent the entire time reading the material, while others spent 20 to 80 percent of the time reciting. When the various groups were tested immediately and four hours later, the results were as shown here. (23)

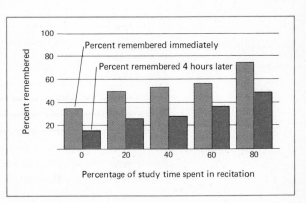

It helps you find meaningfulness and logical principles in the material. Of all study techniques, recitation is the one of most clearly proved value.

Recitation is the heart of a widely recommended study method called the SQ3R system (24), which holds that the most efficient way to study a chapter is to approach it through five steps:

SQ3R SYSTEM
1. SURVEY
2. QUESTION
3. READING
4. RECITATION
5. REVIEWING

1. *Survey.* That is, study the outline at the beginning of the chapter (if there is one, as in this book) and then glance through the chapter to get a general idea of how much attention is devoted to each point in the outline and to the sub-headings.

2. *Question.* Look through the chapter again in a more inquisitive fashion, asking yourself questions that the headings and subheadings suggest; let the topics you find there whet your curiosity.

3. *Reading.* Now read the chapter straight through, without taking notes.

4. *Recitation.* You have made a survey of the chapter, asked some questions about it, and read it. Now see how much of the chapter you can recite, either silently to yourself or out loud to a cooperative friend.

5. *Reviewing.* Go through the chapter again, making another survey of its topics and noting how much of it you were able to recite and what points you left out. The reviewing process will show you where you must devote further study.

2. transfer of learning

Most educators once believed firmly that learning Latin and ancient Greek would exercise and discipline the mind. The beneficial effects, it was thought, would *transfer* to other kinds of learning: once a person had studied Latin and Greek, he would be that much better at learning anything from basket weaving to higher mathematics. A large-scale survey reported in the early 1920's demolished this theory of general transfer. In the survey, 13,000 high school students were tested for learning ability, then tested again a year later. Careful records were kept of the subjects they studied in the meantime. For example, some of the students took algebra, history, English, chemistry, and French, while some took algebra, history, English, chemistry, and Latin. If the second group had shown a substantially higher increase in learning ability than the first group, it would have seemed reasonable to attribute the improvement to the superiority of Latin to French. In the same way, using different groups from the big sample, it was possible to study the effects of all kinds of different subjects. Most closely connected with an increase in learning ability, it turned out, were the high school courses in mathematics (algebra, geometry, and trigonometry), with the social sciences and psychology not far behind. Latin was well down the list, nowhere near the top. At the bottom were biology and dramatic art (25).

All the differences from the very top of the list to the bottom were quite small; the students who took mathematics improved somewhat more in learning ability than students who took biology and dramatic art but hardly enough to be worth mentioning. <u>Much more significant in determining how much the students improved was the amount of learning ability they started with</u>. The students who were brightest to begin with improved the most; the students at the bottom improved the least. <u>The investigators who conducted the survey concluded that the chief reason mathematics stood at the top of the list was simply that it tended to attract the ablest learners</u>. In the days when the transfer theory was popular, it can be assumed, the best students were attracted to Latin or Greek (or persuaded by their teachers to take these subjects); it was the quality of the students, not the subject matter, that made Latin and Greek seem so stimulating to the mind.

Although the old general theory of transfer has been disproved, nonetheless it is true that <u>certain specific kinds of transfer do take place, sometimes making new learning easier and sometimes making it more difficult.</u>

1. positive transfer

One significant experiment in transfer is illustrated in Figure 4-17. The results of the experiment can be predicted from what has already been said about learning. List 1 is a clear case of forming simple connections between a stimulus, namely the first of each pair of syllables, and a response, namely the second syllable. In list 2, the responses remain exactly the same, and the stimuli are only slightly different from those in list 1. From what we know about stimulus generalization (page 53), we would expect anyone who had learned list 1 to do very well on list 2. This indeed proved to be the case. It took the subjects only 44 percent as many trials to learn list 2 perfectly as it took subjects who had not learned list 1, which means that the *positive transfer* of learning from list 1 to list 2 was 56 percent—a very substantial amount.

But what about list 3? Here, though the responses remain the same, the stimuli are totally different. Stimulus generalization cannot operate. What can operate, however, is something else that has been discussed at considerable

an experiment in transfer

4-17

Subjects first learned the pairings in list 1, so that when presented with the stimulus of REQ they responded with KIY and when presented with TAW they responded with RIF. Some of them then learned list 2, in which the responses are the same and the first syllables in the list are quite similar to those in list 1. Others learned list 3, in which the responses are the same but the first syllables are totally different. Question: Did learning list 1 help in learning lists 2 and 3, and, if so, which did it help more? For the answer, see the text. (26)

List 1		List 2		List 3	
REQ	KIY	REF	KIY	FIZ	KIY
TAW	RIF	TAS	RIF	MIP	RIF
QIX	LEP	QIL	LEP	BUL	LEP
WAM	BOS	WAP	BOS	NIC	BOS
ZED	DIB	ZEL	DIB	CAJ	DIB

length—that very important role played in learning by previously learned mediational units to which a new stimulus can become attached. All the responses required by list 3, being the same as those in list 1, have already been learned. To learn list 3, the responses need merely become associated with new stimuli. It should come as no surprise, therefore, that the amount of positive transfer from list 1 to list 3, though smaller than to list 2, was also substantial—37 percent.

POSITIVE TRANSFER

As a sort of shorthand helpful in discussing matters such as these, the symbol S_1 is often used for the original learning stimulus and R_1 for the original learning response. Learning ordinarily consists in forming the association S_1-R_1. When a new learning situation calls for the same response to become associated with a new stimulus, as in the experiment in Figure 4-17, the formula becomes S_2-R_1. Learning S_1-R_1 generally makes it easier to learn S_2-R_1—in other words, results in positive transfer—and the more similar S_2 is to S_1, the greater is the amount of transfer likely to be.

There are many everyday examples. Early in life we learn to turn on a water faucet. Later on, we encounter faucets of all sizes, shapes, and colors but have no trouble adjusting to them. Learning to use the handlebars of a tricycle helps us later to use the handlebars of a bicycle and still later the steering wheel of an automobile.

The principle of positive transfer has been of great practical value in the construction of relatively inexpensive training aids that teach people to operate the most complicated and expensive kinds of machinery. Commercial pilots, for example, learn almost everything they have to know about flying new planes without ever leaving the ground. And astronauts are similarly trained for space flight and work on the moon.

2. negative transfer

Figure 4-17 was a classic demonstration of what happens when S_1-R_1 is followed by S_2-R_1. What happens, however, when S_1-R_1 is followed by S_1-R_2—in other words, when the learning task calls for the same stimulus to become associated with a new response?

NEGATIVE TRANSFER .

The same investigator responsible for the experiment in Figure 4-17 went on to study the S_1-R_2 situation as illustrated in Figure 4-18. This time, it

a demonstration of negative transfer

4-18

Again, as in Figure 4-17, the subjects first learned the pairings in list 1. Then they learned list 2, in which the first syllables remain the same but call for totally new responses. For an explanation of how learning list 1 affected learning list 2 in this case, see the text. (27)

List 1		List 2	
REQ	KIY	REQ	SEJ
TAW	RIF	TAW	BOC
QIX	LEP	QIX	PUW
WAM	BOS	WAM	GIT
ZED	DIB	ZED	LIM

developed, learning list 1 did not help the new learning but actually hindered it. There was a *negative transfer* amounting to 9 percent.

In another experiment with the S_1-R_2 situation, rats were placed in a simple T-maze. They started at the bottom of the T. At the point where they had to turn to either the right or the left, a light gave them the clue. If the light was on, they found food to the right. If the light was off, they found food to the left. They learned this, on the average, in 286 trials. Once they had thoroughly acquired this S_1-R_1 pattern, the task was reversed; when the light was on, the food was to the left, and, when the light was off, the food was to the right. In the new S_1-R_2 pattern, R_2 was exactly the opposite of R_1. The result was so much negative transfer that the rats required 603 trials to master the new S_1-R_2 situation (27).

Negative transfer causes considerable trouble in everyday situations. Having grown up with faucets that we turned, we may have trouble with some of the new faucets that must be pressed. Being used to faucets that we turn to the left, we run the risk of scalding or freezing ourselves in some of the new showers where the cold water faucet has to be turned in one direction and the hot water faucet in the other. Knowing how to steer a bicycle and an automobile only confuses us when we first try to operate the tiller of a boat.

3. learning sets

When we learn, it has been discovered, we learn not only specific behaviors or items of information but also something that is often equally important: we learn how to learn. We tend to develop what are called *learning sets*—that is, attitudes and strategies that help us in similar learning situations in the future.

The classic experiment on learning sets is illustrated in Figure 4-19. The monkey in this experiment, asked to perform a long series of learning tasks that

a monkey "learns to learn"

4-19

A monkey in a cage learns to discriminate between two objects, one of which has food beneath it. Sometimes, as in this photo, the food was always under the funnel and never under the cylinder. Sometimes it was under a circle but not a rectangle, a cube but not a sphere, or a black object but not a white object. In all, the monkey was asked to learn to discriminate between more than 300 different pairs of objects. Question: Did the animal learn faster toward the end of the series than at the beginning? For the answer, see Figure 4-20.

4-20

On each of the learning problems the monkey had a 50–50 chance of finding the food on the first trial, and its score on this trial averaged 50 percent. On the first eight problems the animal made rather slow progress and still was averaging less than 80 percent correct on the sixth trial. Note, however, how much more rapidly it learned on problems 25–32 and especially on problems 257–312. (28)

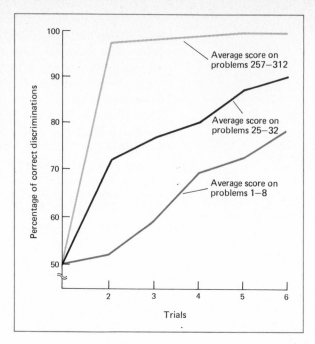

were similar in general but different in detail, got better and better at learning as the series went on. As is shown in Figure 4-20, toward the end the animal was able to master each new problem in a single trial. Whether or not it found the food on the first trial, it went almost unerringly to the correct object on the second and subsequent trials. In most convincing fashion, it had learned to learn.

In an experiment with human beings, using a similar but more difficult series of problems, the results were much the same. It was found in addition, as might be expected, that college students were quicker to develop effective learning sets than fifth-graders, and the fifth-graders in turn were considerably quicker than preschool children (29). It is the development of various kinds of learning sets that helps make students far more efficient learners in high school than they were in elementary school and even more efficient in college than they were in high school.

E, management of learning and the schools

In recent years many psychologists (and also sociologists) have become concerned about the learning process as it takes place in the American school system. Numerous large-scale studies have demonstrated that elementary and secondary schools are failing to provide many of their students with adequate preparation either to go on to college or to hold any but the most unskilled kinds of jobs (30). This is particularly true of children whose parents rank low in education and income. Indeed the contrast in scholastic achievement between these children and others has been found to be quite startling. By the sixth grade the average child from a low-income home has dropped about two years behind the average child from a middle-income home; by the eighth grade the difference has grown to three years. Children from low-income homes are much more likely to drop out before finishing high school and much less likely to go to college even if they finish high school and have the ability to go on (31).

The danger is obvious, because the schools' failure to reach and educate so many young people is likely to result in large numbers forced to spend their adulthoods in marginal jobs or on public assistance—and at a poverty level that probably destines their own children to repeat the cycle. One of the most pressing social problems of our day, therefore, is to answer the questions: Why are the schools failing? How can the failure be remedied?

1, middle-income versus poverty-area schools

In the past, it was generally believed that schools in places such as wealthy suburbs did a better job than schools in the slums or in poor rural areas because they could afford superior facilities. This notion was disproved, however, by a now well-known study called the Coleman Report, prepared by a sociologist in 1966 for the United States Department of Health, Education, and Welfare (32). The study found very little relation between pupils' achievement and such facilities as modern buildings, libraries, and laboratories, or between achievement and the kinds of salaries paid teachers or the presence or absence of guidance counselors.

More important than a school's physical facilities, according to the Coleman Report, is what might be called its psychological atmosphere. By and large, it was found, a pupil tends to learn more if he is surrounded by other children who come from families that encourage learning and who themselves are ambitious to do well in school—a situation much more likely to prevail in schools in middle- or upper-income areas than in schools in poverty areas. But most important of all in determining how well a pupil is likely to do are his own feelings about himself and his environment. If he has what the report terms a good "self-concept" (meaning confidence in his own ability) and a sense of control over his environment (that is, a belief that he can control his destiny through his own efforts and is not just a helpless pawn of other people and the world in general), he is likely to do well in school. But these are exactly the attitudes that children from low-income homes have been found to lack to a conspicuous degree (33)—and that the schools have apparently failed to encourage.

2, an experiment on class attitudes toward school

An experiment that seems to have an important bearing on social class and the school system was performed as follows. From among first-grade pupils, a psychologist selected twenty-four boys from white middle-class homes, twenty-four from white lower-class homes, and twenty-four more from black lower-class homes. The boys were asked one at a time to play a "game" with a box that had two switch buttons, one on the left and one on the right. The object of the game, they were told, was to guess which button should be pushed on each occasion over a series of forty chances. To half the boys from each group, the experimenter said, "Each time you press the wrong button, I will say *wrong*"—thus establishing a situation in which they were punished with disapproval for failure. To the other half, he said, "Each time you press the right button, I will say *right*"—thus rewarding them with approval for success.

Once the game began, the experimenter simply decided at random which button was correct, but always in such a way that the left-hand button was declared correct 70 percent of the time, the right-hand button only 30 percent of the time. The experimenter was interested in three questions: 1) How quickly would these young boys catch on that they could make more correct responses by choosing the left-hand button most of the time? 2) Would they do better if rewarded with approval or punished with disapproval? 3) What relation if any would their family background have to their performance?

The results, shown in Figure 4-21, were extremely interesting. Approval or disapproval made little difference to the middle-class boys; they did about equally well either way. With the lower-class boys, both white and black, the story was strikingly different. The lower-class boys who were subjected to disapproval did quite poorly. Those who were rewarded with approval, however, did extremely well—in fact better than either group of middle-class boys.

social class and effect of punishment

4-21

The graph shows the results of an experiment in which boys from different social classes were either rewarded for the correct responses by approval (colored lines) or punished for incorrect responses by disapproval (black lines). The lower-class boys did much better when rewarded than when punished. The middle-class boys made about the same scores regardless of whether they were rewarded or punished. For a possible explanation of the results, see the text. (34)

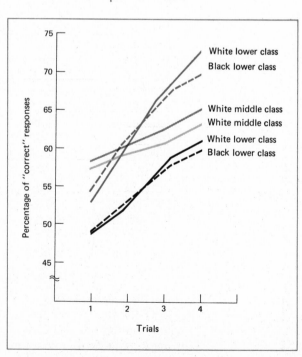

The psychologist who performed the experiment has offered the following possible interpretation of the results. As compared with middle-class children, those from lower-class homes are likely to feel more ill-at-ease in school, because their backgrounds have not led them to consider it a very pleasant or important experience. They are likely to be particularly uncomfortable and anxious around middle-class adults such as the usual schoolteacher (or in this case the experimenter). Therefore they are especially vulnerable to any disapproval, which may lead them to perform far below their real abilities. On the other hand, the experiment may offer the hope that a long-term program of encouragement by their teachers could raise their level of performance (34). Perhaps the crucial factor here is that children from low-income homes do not expect approval from strangers, are surprised by it, and therefore tend to respond to it as an important kind of positive reinforcement.

3. programed learning and the teaching machine

One approach to improving efficiency in the classroom has been the development of *programed learning,* in which the contents of a course are broken down into a series of very small steps. At each step a single new term or new idea is introduced or material that has been covered previously is reviewed. When programed learning is offered in printed form, as shown in Figure 4–22, the student ordinarily fills in a blank or sometimes several blanks at each step. He

a programed psychology book

4-22

Frames from a programed textbook in psychology discuss classical conditioning. The student fills in the blank in each frame at left, then looks at the correct answer (right) before going on to the next frame. (From *The analysis of behavior* by James G. Holland and B. F. Skinner. Copyright © 1961. Used with permission of McGraw-Hill Book Company.)

When a man's hand is touched by a hot surface or receives an electric shock, the hand is immediately withdrawn. Since this reflex was not established by previous conditioning, it is a(n) ____ ____ . 2-24	unconditioned reflex 2-24
In this unconditioned hand-withdrawal reflex, heat is the ____ ____ . 2-25	unconditioned stimulus 2-25
In the unconditioned hand-withdrawal reflex, the movement of the arm is the ____ ____ . 2-26	unconditioned response 2-26
If a bell sounds 30 seconds before a hot object touches the hand (and the procedure is repeated several times), ____ will take place. 2-27	conditioning 2-27

then can uncover the answer and see immediately if his response was correct before going on to the next step.

Programed instruction has in recent years often been presented through a *teaching machine,* an example of which is shown at the left. The machine displays one step (or *frame*) at a time. Again the student writes in his answer and the machine shows him whether he was right or wrong before he turns a knob that moves the program along to the next frame. Programed learning can also be presented through a computer. The student may sit at a terminal like a typewriter that types out the program a step at a time; he then types his answer and the computer tells him in type whether he was right or wrong. Or the program may be presented on a sort of television screen on which the student indicates his answer with a light-pen that sends a signal back to the computer through the screen. Some of the systems—called computer-assisted instruction or CAI for short—have been developed to the point where they can virtually hold a dialogue with the student about his progress and, if he continues to make mistakes, can switch him to remedial steps that will lead him to the right answer.

Whether presented in print, by machine, or by computer, the success of programed learning depends in large part on how carefully the program is drawn up; it also seems to depend at least in part on the student's own personal characteristics and attitudes. For example, one study has shown that college students who have a high degree of anxiety about tests and a low degree of sociability do better when they work alone at a computer terminal, while those who are low in anxiety and high in sociability do better when they work in pairs (35).

Two of the most ambitious and successful attempts at presenting programed instruction have been developed at Stanford University, where central computers have served a network of terminals in elementary school rooms in many parts

results of computer-assisted instruction

4-23

The bars show the results of an experiment in teaching arithmetic by computer-assisted instruction in a group of schools where achievement levels were below average. A standard test of level of achievement was given the pupils at the beginning of the school year, then some were taught with the help of programed instruction presented by computer and others by the standard classroom methods. When the pupils were tested again at the end of the year, those taught with the help of the computer were found to have made significantly more progress than the others. Similar results were found in grades four through six. (36)

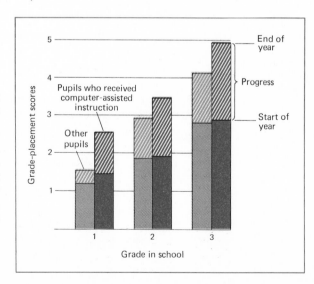

METHODS OF PRO-
GRAMED LEARNING

1. PRINT
2. MACHINE
3. COMPUTER

ADVANTAGES OF
PROGRAMED LEARNING

. OWN PACE
. INDIVIDUALIZED
  INSTRUCTION
. IMMEDIATE FEED-
  BACK

of the nation. By 1971 the computers were providing daily instruction in reading and arithmetic for several thousands of pupils, all the way from California to Washington, D.C. The instruction has proved generally successful—particularly for pupils whose skill at reading and arithmetic was below the national average. Figure 4-23 shows the progress made by one group of below-average pupils in learning arithmetic through computer-assisted instruction.

Computer-assisted instruction and less complex teaching machines have several advantages, especially for young children of below-average achievement in overcrowded classrooms. They enable the pupil to proceed at his own pace, without regard to the learning speed of his classmates. They provide a sort of individualized instruction that teachers with large classes cannot always offer. And they provide immediate feedback, which, as has been said, appears to be particularly effective for young children and for others without high general motivation to learn.

summary 1. The attempt to arrange the most favorable possible conditions for learning to take place is called *management of learning*.

2. It is easiest to make new learning associations when the stimulus is *familiar, meaningful,* and can be *learned by logical rule rather than by rote*.

3. *Guidance*—as furnished by a textbook or preferably in person by a teacher—is the most effective form of management of learning because it points out the elements in the learning situation that are familiar, meaningful, and possible to learn by principle.

4. In the learning of materials by rote, the amount of learning depends on both the *absolute* time spent in study and the *proportional* time in relation to other materials that are being studied during the same period.

5. Rote learning can often be facilitated by the use of a *mnemonic device,* such as a jingle, that provides a ready-made system of attachment units for new stimuli that could not otherwise readily be attached to existing units through logical rule or chunking.

6. In attracting attention to the learning stimulus, one important factor is *motivation*. Attention is sharpened when the subject matter can be related to the individual's motives, whatever these may be.

7. *Feedback,* or knowledge of the results of learning, is important because it helps the learner correct his mistakes and also helps capture and hold attention.

8. *Rewards* also capture attention and are effective in the management of learning. *External rewards* (also called *extrinsic rewards*) are those provided by another person, such as praise, good grades, or cash payments. *Internal rewards* (also called *intrinsic rewards*) are the learner's own feelings of satisfaction resulting from successful learning.

9. *Punishment,* another tool frequently used in management of learning, appears to be effective in some situations and ineffective in others. Its usefulness depends on many factors and is a subject of controversy.

10. *Novelty* helps attract attention and is a useful tool in management of learning.

11. Two characteristics of the learning stimulus that have an important effect on the learning process are the following:

   a. *Amount.* As the amount to be learned increases, the difficulty of learning it increases disproportionately, so that doubling the amount more than doubles the difficulty.

   b. *Serial position.* In any series of learning stimuli the first ones are most easily learned, the last ones next most easily; the ones in the middle are learned last. This is called the *law of primacy and recency.*

12. Study techniques are attempts to manipulate the learning stimulus so as to present it in the most efficient way on the most efficient time schedule. Among the findings about study techniques are the following:

   a. Learning something *as a whole* has certain advantages, such as making the material more meaningful and more susceptible to learning by logical principle. *Part learning* provides more rapid feedback and avoids the overlearning of portions of the material. Often a combination of the two methods is most efficient.

   b. The more trials on which we continue to learn beyond the point where we can barely achieve recall, the longer we tend to remember. This is called *overlearning.*

   c. *Distributed practice,* in which the learning process is broken up into separated periods, is generally more efficient than *massed practice.*

   d. *Recitation* has been demonstrated to be the most effective of all study techniques. It is far better to spend as much as 80 percent of the study period in an active attempt to recite than to spend the entire period reading the material.

13. The old theory of general transfer of learning, which held that studying Latin and Greek "improved the mind" and made future learning easier, has been somewhat discredited.

14. In many cases, however, learning task 1 makes it easier to learn task 2. This is called *positive transfer.* It occurs most often in situations where task 2 calls for making the same response to a different stimulus (the S_1-R_1/S_2-R_1 situation).

15. In other cases learning task 1 makes it more difficult to learn task 2, and this is called *negative transfer.* It occurs most prominently in situations where a new response must be made to an old stimulus (S_1-R_1/S_1-R_2).

16. When we learn, we also develop *learning sets*—or attitudes and strategies that help us in similar learning situations in the future.

17. The Coleman Report has pointed out that a pupil's achievement in school depends less on such factors as modern buildings and salaries paid teachers than on a) the pupil's "self-concept" or confidence in his own ability and b) the educational ambitions of the other children in his school.

18. *Programed learning* is an attempt to improve classroom efficiency by breaking down the contents of a course into brief steps that can be taken one at a time. Programed instruction is often presented through *teaching machines,* including computers.

recommended reading

Bower, G. H. Analysis of a mnemonic device. *American Scientist,* 1970, **58**, 496–510.

Broadbent, D. E. *Perception and communication.* Elmsford, N.Y.: Pergamon Press, 1958.

Bruner, J. S. *Toward a theory of instruction.* Cambridge, Mass.: Harvard University Press, 1966.

Hilgard, E. R., ed. *Theories of learning and instruction.* 63rd Yearbook, Part I, National Society for the Study of Education. Chicago: University of Chicago Press, 1964.

Kintsch, W. *Learning, memory and conceptual processes.* New York: Wiley, 1970.

Klausmeier, H. J., and Harris, C. W., eds. *Analysis of concept learning: proceedings.* New York: Academic Press, 1966.

Morgan, C. T., and Deese, J. *How to study,* 2nd ed. New York: McGraw-Hill, 1969.

Riessman, F. *The culturally deprived child.* New York: Harper & Row, 1962.

Rosenthal, R., and Jacobson, L. *Pygmalion in the classroom: teacher expectation and pupil's intellectual ability.* New York: Holt, Rinehart and Winston, 1968.

Schulman, L. S., and Keislar, E. R., eds. *Learning by discovery: a critical appraisal.* Chicago: Rand McNally, 1966.

CHAPTER 5

LANGUAGE, THINKING, AND PROBLEM SOLVING

Until recently, it was believed that the use of language was the one form of behavior above all that distinguished man from other organisms. This belief was based in part on the fact that every human society ever studied, no matter how remote and isolated from other societies, has been found to have a language, whereas no animal society has ever been known to develop one. It was also based on the failure of many attempts to teach the use of language to animals. Experimenters have raised chimpanzees in their homes just like their own children; the chimps learned such human habits as eating with a spoon and brushing their teeth but never learned to speak more than a few simple words (1). Dolphins, which seemed promising subjects because they have brains that closely resemble the human brain, also proved unable to learn. As for birds that "speak," such as parrots and parakeets, they simply imitate the sound of the human voice but show no evidence of attaching any meaning to the sounds.

More recently, man's uniqueness as a user of language has been challenged by two experiments. In one, an attempt was made to teach a chimpanzee named Washoe to learn one of the sign languages used by the deaf; the experimenters believed that the use of hand signals might come more naturally to the animal than the use of the vocal cords. By the time the animal had three years of training, she seemed to have learned a vocabulary of eighty-five signals (see Figure 5-1) and to be able to string as many as three or four of them together

a chimpanzee "talks"

5-1

At the age of two and a half, the chimpanzee named Washoe makes the sign language signal for "drink."

into sentences such as "Hurry gimme toothbrush" and "Please tickle more" (2). In another experiment a chimpanzee named Sarah was taught to construct sentences such as "Sarah insert banana in pail" by stringing together blocks marked with colored symbols for words (3).

When deliberately taught and urged by human beings, it now appears, chimpanzees can acquire at least a childlike ability to manipulate the symbols of language. And many animals in the wild state communicate with one another even though they do not engage in the creative manipulation of symbols that is the essence of human language. Bees that have found a new food supply go back to the hive and perform a dance, the nature and speed of which "tell" the other bees where the food supply is (4). Birds sing their characteristic songs to attract mates and to discourage interlopers. Dolphins make sounds to one another. Wild chimpanzees use sounds and gestures to alert their friends to danger and to threaten their enemies. But these other organisms seem to possess only a limited "vocabulary" of sounds and gestures and to use them rather infrequently. Wild chimpanzees, for example, usually make calls to one another only when excited, as in case of danger; under ordinary circumstances they are generally silent (2).

The fact remains that man alone of all organisms is the spontaneous creator and user of highly sophisticated languages that permit the communication of a wide range of knowledge and ideas. His ability does not depend primarily on the structure of his vocal cords, for other mammals also have vocal cords and even birds can make many of the sounds of human language. It probably depends instead on the structure and dynamics of the human brain. As far as is known, man is the only organism in which one particular part of the left half of the brain is larger than the corresponding part of the right half—and it has been found that the ability to understand and speak language depends primarily on this part of the left half of the brain (5).

A. the importance of man's language

Man's special ability to use language enables him to learn many things that are beyond the capacity of other organisms—and to think and solve problems in ways that presumably no other animal can even begin to approach. For a simple example, consider the part that language plays in the learning of stimulus generalization and discrimination.

1. language and learning

To the lower animals, stimulus generalization and stimulus discrimination are based on physical characteristics—on the similarities or differences among sounds, shapes, brightnesses, sometimes colors. As shown in Figure 5-2, a duck can learn that food is always found beneath a three-sided figure and never under a figure with four or more sides, regardless of the exact shape of the figures. But for a duck or a rat this is a slow and laborious process. The animal eventually

5-2

After many trials the duck has learned that food is always found underneath some kind of three-sided figure. It can now generalize all triangles and discriminate between triangles and other geometrical figures.

learns to discriminate between a three-sided figure and a four-sided figure, but the process takes a long time.

Now let us suppose that we tried to teach a duck or a rat that it would find food behind any of the objects in the left-hand column below but not behind any of the objects similar in appearance listed in the right-hand column:

Cap pistol	Revolver
Building block	Brick
Small rubber ball	Orange
Basketball	Cantaloupe
Tricycle	Motorcycle
Drum	Barrel
Doll	Child
Paintbox	Cigarette case

In this case the animal is really in trouble. It can learn only by trial and error. Even if it manages to learn, one by one, that food is found behind the objects listed on the left, it will again be baffled if we introduce a miniature xylophone or piano, a rag doll, a stuffed tiger, a rattle, or a toy train.

To the animal, a cap pistol is not a very different stimulus from a revolver, but it is far different from a red rubber ball, a shiny tricycle, and a plastic doll. To the child, however, as soon as he has learned the meaning of the word *toy*—on the average, at the age of three or four—all toys have something in common. Thus does language facilitate stimulus generalization between objects as vastly different in physical size, shape, color, and texture as a little black stub of crayon and a giant stuffed tiger. The process is called *mediated generalization*—because it depends on the mediational units of language, resulting in the association of objects that do not of themselves possess any physical similarities.

Language is also the basis of most stimulus discrimination. To a baby an orange looks like a rubber ball, and if he has learned to play with a ball, he will also try to play with the orange. It is mostly on the basis of language that he learns to discriminate between a spherical object that is a toy and a spherical object that is food.

Applying language labels to objects and events in the world enables man to understand his environment infinitely better than any other organism can.

DEFINITION:
MEDIATED
GENERALIZATION

Language is the basis of all scientific knowledge—and of such abstract ideas as justice, law, and democracy. Moreover, it enables man to draw on all the learning of the past. Language—and especially written language—makes available to us the philosophies of the ancient Greeks, the mathematical systems of the ancient Arabs, the scientific discoveries of Galileo. Thanks to language, each of us knows more than any one person, starting from scratch, could discover in a thousand lifetimes.

2. the structure of language

One of the interesting facts about language is that all its richness—for example, all the words found in an unabridged English dictionary—is based on a rather simple foundation. All language depends on the number of sounds that can be produced by the human vocal cords, and the number is quite limited. This may seem hard to believe, in view of the apparent complexity and variety of all the sentences that can be heard in the halls of the United Nations Building— English, French, Spanish, German, Russian, and all the languages of Asia and Africa—but it is true. No language contains more than eighty-five different basic sounds. English has forty-five, and the simplest language known has fifteen. These basic sounds are called *phonemes* and are the building blocks of language. In English they include such sounds as the vowel *e*, pronounced as in *be*, the consonant *t* at the beginning of *tack*, the *ch* in *chip*, the *th* in *the*, and the *sh* in *shop*.

By themselves, the phonemes have no meaning. But two or more of them can be put together to form a combination of sounds that does have meaning. For example, we can start with the phoneme *t*, add the phoneme pronounced as *ee*, then add the phoneme *ch*, and arrive at the combination *teach*. The combination is called a *morpheme*—a combination of phonemes that possesses meaning in and of itself. Like *teach*, many morphemes are words. Others are prefixes or suffixes, which can in turn be combined with other morphemes to form words. For example, we can combine the three morphemes *un-* (a prefix), *teach* (a word in itself), and *-able* (a suffix) to form the word *unteachable*.

Thus from the forty-five English phonemes is built a language capable of a tremendous variety of expression. The phonemes are combined in various ways to produce more than 100,000 morphemes or basic units of meaning, and the morphemes are in turn combined with one another to produce the approximately 600,000 words found in the largest dictionaries.

3. the rules of language

The most important feature of language, however, is the manner in which the phonemes and morphemes are put together into meaningful utterances. This is accomplished by virtue of the fact that every language is in essence a set of rules for combining meaningful sounds into an almost infinite number of sentences conveying an almost infinite variety of meaning. These are the rules of *grammar*. Some of them are rather simple, such as the one in the English

DEFINITION:
PHONEMES

language dictating that a singular noun can be turned into a plural by adding an *s*. Others are more complex and regulate the combination of nouns, verbs, and adjectives into phrases and sentences that convey a meaning readily understood by anyone else who speaks the language. For example, every child knows the individual words *cat, to, runs, yellow, milk, now,* and *drink*—but the words when presented in that order do not convey any message. When rearranged according to the rules of grammar into *yellow cat runs to drink milk now,* the words immediately become a meaningful sentence.

In learning a language, one acquires these rules; the rules enable him to recognize another person's meaning even if he has never heard the same words in the same order before and to generate meaningful sentences of his own, including new sentences that he himself has never before uttered. Children and even adults usually are not aware of all the rules. But we use them even if we cannot explain what they are—and they are the magic key to human communication.

One of the interesting things about the rules is that, with various minor variations, they are pretty much the same in all the several thousands of different languages spoken in the world today and were probably similar in the now dead languages spoken in the past. This fact suggests that human beings may have an inherited tendency to use and understand language according to rules that are somehow biologically determined by the structure and dynamics of the human brain (6). To put this another way, language may be a species-specific behavior dictated by man's biological inheritance; just as fish are born to swim and moles to burrow, men are born to speak.

4. how language is learned

Even if language and its rules indeed spring from man's innate nature, they must of course still be learned; the American child is not born knowing the meaning of the word *house* and may never discover that the French word meaning the same thing is *maison*. Acquiring a knowledge of all the many words and the rules for stringing them together seems an almost awesome accomplishment—yet children learn very quickly. By the age of two, they are already speaking such simple sentences as "Baby drink milk." By the age of five, they understand the meaning of about 2000 words (7). By about the age of six, they have learned all the basic rules of grammar. How do young children accomplish all this so quickly?

It is well established that the baby does not have to learn to make the sounds of the phonemes. He utters the sounds spontaneously, presumably because of movements of the mouth, throat, and vocal cords associated with breathing, swallowing, and hiccoughing. The fact that all normal babies "babble" and produce the phoneme sounds spontaneously—rather than by imitating anything they hear—has been demonstrated by observations of a deaf baby both of whose parents were deaf and mute. During the first two months of life this baby who never heard a sound did substantially the same kind of babbling as any other (8). Indeed it appears that children of all nationalities make the same sounds in their earliest babbling; American infants, for example, have been observed to utter phonemes that are not used by English-speaking adults but only by the French or Germans (9). <u>Soon, however, the baby begins to concentrate on the sounds appropriate to his own language and to eliminate the others.</u> (Rather sadly for those who attempt to learn foreign languages, these other sounds are eliminated quite thoroughly; many adult Americans who try to speak French or German are never able to pronounce some of the phonemes properly, even though they did it naturally when they were babies.)

Acquiring the Rules. <u>Although uttering the phonemes comes naturally, obviously something more is required if the child is ever to turn the simple building blocks provided by the phonemes into meaningful language. The crucial factor appears to be exposure to the sounds of languages as used by older people.</u> For example, a six-year-old girl was found years ago in a secluded home in Ohio where she had been brought up by a deaf-mute mother and had never been around another human being. This girl, who had never heard another person speak, could not talk and in fact made no sounds at all except croaking noises. But after a week of being around people who used language she began to imitate their voices, and in two years her speech and her use of language were normal (10).

Given exposure to language, the child rapidly begins to use words and to string them together into meaningful utterances; he begins to acquire some kind of knowledge of the rules of language. At first his words may seem to be thrown together haphazardly and his meaning unclear; for example, a child of about two may say "Put suitcase for?" when an adult would say "What did you put it in the suitcase for?" or "Who dat . . . somebody pencil?" when an adult would say "Whose pencils are they?" (11). But even then his speech is organized on definite principles, though not the same kind as he will adopt later, and there is meaningful content to his utterances. <u>The young child's speech has been called *telegraphic,* meaning that it is condensed and abbreviated; he uses only words most important to his meaning and omits the articles, adjectives, and often even verbs. It is also *holophrastic,* meaning that the child uses a single word to stand for an entire idea or a complicated sentence;</u> he may, for example, simply say "ball" to convey the thought that he wants a ball or wants to play ball with his mother. Later he becomes more sophisticated about the rules and begins to add plurals, negatives, and the passive tenses of verbs, as well as the voice inflections appropriate to a question such as "That's a flower, isn't it?" There appears to be an orderly progression to his growing skill—indeed a continual increase in the average length of his utterances month by month.

Theories of Language Learning. <u>Just how the learning process takes place is a matter of debate. Some theorists believe that language is learned chiefly through a rather simple form of operant conditioning and shaping (12).</u> According to this school of thought, <u>some of the sounds made by the baby in his early babbling are reinforced by the mother's smile or fondling or other behavior, and these sounds tend to be repeated. Other sounds, not appropriate to the language, are not reinforced and tend to disappear.</u> Later the child learns that he can operate on the environment by using language; just as the rat in the Skinner box can

DEFINITIONS:

1. TELEGRAPHIC SPEECH

2. HOLOPHRASTIC SPEECH

get food by pressing the bar, the baby can get food simply by saying such magic words as *milk, cookie,* or *eat.* When the child pronounces a word incorrectly, his parents encourage him to shape the word into its correct form.

Other theorists have stressed the role of observation learning (13); these theorists maintain that the stringing together of phonemes into words and words into sentences is more a matter of direct imitation of the parents than of operant conditioning.

A newer theory that appears to be gaining increasing acceptance is based on the importance of the rules of grammar and the evidence that the use of language and its rules may be a species-specific behavior dictated by man's inherited biological equipment. The theory maintains that neither operant conditioning nor observation learning can possibly explain how the child comes to understand the meaning of sentences he has never heard before or to put words together into original sentences of his own. It is learning the rules, according to this theory, that enables the child to understand speech at such an early age and to "generate" new and original utterances of his own (14). The theory has received considerable support from experiments indicating that subjects are quick to learn the logical rules of artificial languages known as "miniature linguistic systems" (15).

According to this theory, there is an analogy between human language and the songs of birds. A tendency to sing appears to be a built-in part of the biological equipment of the bird; a bird reared in isolation, where it can never hear the characteristic song of its species, will sing something that resembles the song as soon as it has grown large enough to have the necessary physical equipment for producing the sounds. But at least some species of birds, if reared in isolation, do not sing the song in its full richness and variety; their version is by contrast quite simple and undeveloped (16). Although these birds have an inborn tendency to sing a particular kind of song, they apparently can acquire the total pattern only through exposure to the song as performed by adults of their species. But if the bird is exposed to the song when too young to make the sounds, and is later kept in isolation, it will render the song faithfully as soon as physically mature enough. In other words, the bird does not have to make any actual response at the time of exposure to the song; the exposure itself is sufficient. It may be that the child's exposure to the language of his parents is a similar case in which events in the environment make it possible for an inherited capacity to be displayed (17)—through a form of learning that cannot be categorized as either operant or observation.

LANGUAGE
THEORIES

1. OPERANT CON-
DITIONING

2. OBSERVATION
LEARNING

3. SPECIES - SPECIFIC
BEHAVIOR

language and concepts

All words are *symbols*—that is to say, they are learned mediational units that stand for or represent something. Thus *water* is a symbol for the colorless fluid that we drink; *fire* is a symbol for the process of burning. Because we have acquired and know the meaning of such symbols, we can respond as readily to a shout of

"*Fire!*" as to the actual sight of flames. Using words as symbols, we can communicate our need for water (or food or an aspirin tablet) without the actual presence of these objects. Imagine the difficulties you would encounter if you were in a strange country where you did not know a single word of the native language and none of the inhabitants knew a word of English. You would be able to shop only in stores that had the goods on display, so that you could point. And how would you go about ordering even as much as a piece of bread and an egg in a restaurant?

In every language, however, only a few words are symbols for specific, one-of-a-kind objects—in the English language, for example, the names of the planets Mars and Jupiter. All other words are symbols for entire groups of objects, events, actions, and ideas. Even a word of such apparent simplicity as *water* is a symbol not only for the colorless fluid in the glass we may be holding in our hands but for any somewhat similar fluid anywhere, including the salty contents of the oceans and the drops that fall from the sky as rain. The word *justice* is a symbol for many different abstract ideas held by men around the world at various times in history and embodied in many forms of legal codes and practices. Thus most words constitute a complicated form of symbol called a *concept*, which can best be defined as a *symbol that stands for a common characteristic or relationship shared by objects or events that are otherwise different.*

DEFINITION: CONCEPT

Concepts can be formed without the use of language; for example, the duck in Figure 5-2 must have some sort of primitive concept of triangle and quadrangle and the difference between them. But language enables human beings to develop concept systems of tremendous variety, richness, and value. We do not have to deal with every new object or experience that we encounter as a unique event; we can fit it into an already existing concept (18). Think how complicated life would be if we had to have a separate word for every object and event in the world—or had to learn anew how to behave every time we encountered a new stimulus!

1. some kinds of concepts

One investigation into the way concepts are formed is illustrated in Figure 5-3. In this experiment the subjects were asked to learn the meanings of the concepts that the experimenter had arbitrarily assigned to nonsense words. If you try the experiment yourself, you will probably learn the definitions of a LING, FARD, and so on just from studying the information available in the figure. (If not, you may want to try again with the additional clue that the drawings in column three are, from top to bottom, a LETH, MANK, FARD, LING, STOD, PILT, MOLP, RELF, and PRAN.)

The subjects in the experiment tended to be quickest at learning that a RELF was a face, a LETH a building, and a MOLP a tree. Next they learned that FARD meant circular, PRAN meant two diagonals crossed by another diagonal, and STOD meant a loop. The fact that LING was two, PILT five, and MANK six was usually most difficult to learn. In other words, the subjects first learned the concepts of definite objects, then of shapes, and last the more abstract concepts of numbers.

an experiment in concept formation

5-3 These drawings were shown one at a time on a revolving drum, starting from the top to the bottom of the first column, then from the top to the bottom of the second column, and so on. After the final drawing in the last column the entire series of drawings was shown again. For each picture the experimenter spoke a nonsense word, as shown in the boxes in the first two columns. The subjects were asked to learn the name of each drawing and, as soon as they had learned it, to say it before the experimenter spoke. They were told that the experiment was merely a study of memory, and they did not know that any concept formation was involved. At some time in the course of showing the second column of drawings, however, most subjects noticed that the nonsense words were being repeated and caught on that there must be some general rule for naming the drawings. You may try the experiment yourself; fill in the empty boxes, then turn to the text to check the answers. (19)

It appears that children—like subjects confronted with these nonsense words—first learn concepts of concrete objects and of shape and only later learn more abstract concepts such as mathematical relationships. But this may be because they encounter more concrete stimuli than abstract concepts; they constantly respond to such objects as clothing, food, toys, furniture, human faces, and buildings and less frequently to abstract ideas.

2. the concepts of adults

By the time we have reached adulthood so many factors have gone into our building of concepts that it is impossible to trace or even to list them. Indeed most of the words we use as adults involve concepts within concepts. What, for example, do we mean by *man*? To a certain extent, we still think of man in the kinds of terms children use to form their first concepts—such characteristics as his physical attributes and what he does. But we also tend to have a concept of man as the highest (another concept) of all mammals (still another concept!) —a mammal being a particular kind of organism (another concept!) that produces its young inside the body of the mother (another!), which nurses (another!) the baby (another!) after birth (another!).

As a figure of speech, it might be said that the adult's concepts are like the catalogue file of a library, indexed and cross-indexed so that a search starting with a word such as *man* can lead almost anywhere. One card lists man's functions; it leads in turn to other cards that list the details of all his past and present activities. Another lists the places where he is found; it leads in turn to detailed lists of the characteristics of the continents, cities, and physical circumstances in which man dwells. Another lists his component parts and another his physical attributes. Beyond these four cards there are innumerable others that list more abstract and sophisticated attributes of man—that talk about him in terms of history, philosophy, and science and include his aspirations, triumphs, doubts, and failures.

One of the measures of how much a person has learned is how many cards there are under each concept in this mental filing system. A child, for example, makes no connection between the concept *man* and the concept *whale*, but the educated adult knows that these two very dissimilar organisms are related in that both are mammals. To the young child, the concept *man* never calls up an association with an ancient Egyptian Pharaoh or with the lamas of Tibet; to an adult, it may very well do so. The richness of our adult concepts depends on how many similarities we have found to exist among all the apparently diverse elements in our environment and our history.

3. the "salient characteristic" of concepts

We can follow the trail of cross-indexed concept cards almost any-where. In our thinking and problem solving we often rummage through them at length and in depth. Most of the time, however, we tend to ignore the great bulk of the cards and to think of a particular concept in terms of what we consider its one outstanding feature. To a theologian, for example, the word *man* might ordinarily call up the concept of a creature of God, possessing a soul. To a physician, *man* might ordinarily mean a functioning collection of physiological apparatus, all subject to various diseases. To the zoologist, it might mean simply another kind of animal; to the policeman, an adult as opposed to a juvenile; to the military officer, a soldier; to a romantic young woman, a person whom one might marry.

Thus each of us has his own primary definition of each particular concept he uses, based on what to him is the *salient characteristic* of the various objects, events, or ideas that are included in the concept. A group of adults may be well aware that *salt* is a concept that means a certain kind of chemical compound, found in various forms in nature, in the laboratory, and in the human body. But to a cook in the group the salient characteristic of salt is that it is a seasoning used on food. The chemist usually thinks of it as a compound in which the hydrogen of an acid has been replaced by a metal. The physician thinks of it as a component of the human body. This tendency to concentrate on the salient characteristic and ignore other aspects depends in part on a feature of concept formation that is called *concept hierarchies.*

4. concept hierarchies

In any list, one item must be at the top and the others must then follow in order to the bottom. So it is with the various lists in our filing system of concepts. This can best be illustrated in the case of a concept such as *vegetable.* Most of us, asked to draw up a list of vegetables, would think first of the very familiar ones such as tomato and potato. Only much later, if at all, would we think of such seldom encountered ones as artichoke or kale. Asked to draw up a list of animals, most of us would not think immediately that man is the most familiar animal of all; we might head our list with dog or cat, or, if we happened to come from ranch country, horse. Way down toward the bottom of the list would come such unfamiliar animals as aardvark and lynx. Asked to list colors, most of us would start with red and take a long time to get to puce and cerise.

The term used to describe this fact is *concept hierarchies*—a hierarchy being a power structure in which the rank of each individual is clearly defined, from bottom to top, and each individual is subordinate to the one above him. In concept hierarchies the links between the concept and the associations at the top of the list are very powerful; the links between the concept and the associations toward the bottom of the list are weaker.

5. systems of concept hierarchies

One of the interesting facts about concept hierarchies is that they tend to vary depending on the situation and the subject. When we talk about inanimate objects such as buildings, for example, concepts based on physical attributes are usually well up in the hierarchy. When we talk about a person, however, our concept is based mostly on what might be called his personality characteristics;

we tend to think of him as aggressive or meek, ambitious or easygoing, hostile or friendly.

We build these concepts of a person just as we develop our other concepts—by noticing similarities. For example, we notice over a period of time that a person on one occasion argues over who has the right to a parking space, on another occasion pushes his way to a crowded store counter, and on still another occasion dominates the conversation at a party. These are all different kinds of behavior, taking place in different situations, but they all have a common thread that fits into the concept *aggressive*. We note that another man seems a little shy in company, prefers to stay home and read rather than go to a football game, and spends a good deal of his time alone. In these different forms of behavior we find a similarity, and we call him an introvert.

Our concepts of our own selves form a still different hierarchy. We tend to use evaluative concepts; we think of ourselves as good or bad, smart or stupid, popular or unpopular. Thus do our concept hierarchies vary according to the subject at hand. We use one system of hierarchies for inanimate objects, another for people, and still another for ourselves.

6. concepts and connotations

In the system of concept hierarchies that we apply to ourselves, as has just been stated, we make evaluations. But, even in situations where we think we are being objective and using neutral concepts, we are also making evaluations of a sort. This is because most words—and particularly the words used as concepts—not only have the meaning that is apparent on the surface but also carry other implied meanings known as *connotations*. That is to say, they connote (or imply or suggest) certain qualities and values. A good example is the concept word *landlord*. Its dictionary definition is "a person who owns property and rents it to others." That is its plain and simple meaning. But the word also has some highly unpleasant connotations; one may think of a landlord as grasping, unkind, and miserly.

The importance of connotations in the concepts we use has been studied by C. E. Osgood, who devised the type of scale shown in Figure 5-4. Each line of the scale, you will note, contains seven steps from an adjective such as *weak* at one end to its opposite such as *strong* at the other. To large groups of subjects, Osgood presented a wide variety of words, which they were asked to rate somewhere along each of the lines on his scale, only ten of which are included in Figure 5-4. As it turned out, there were considerable individual differences in the way people rated each word, but the average ratings made by one group were remarkably similar to the average ratings made by another group at a different time and place.

The scale is what Osgood called the *semantic differential*. It measures difference in meaning—not in the dictionary sense of meaning but in terms of the patterns of qualities and values that words connote. To a majority of people, for example, the word *success* proved to have connotations of being strong, large, active, good, hot, healthy, and happy. To a somewhat lesser extent, it suggested

5-4

The lines show the ratings given by one subject for three different words on ten lines of the Osgood *semantic differential*. For an explanation of what the ratings indicate, see the text. (20)

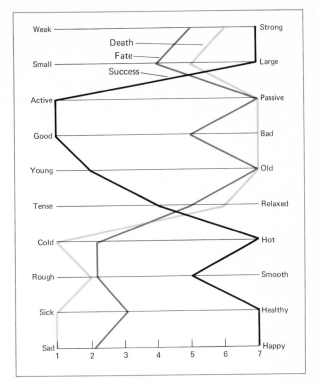

young and smooth. Other words turned out to have quite different patterns on the semantic differential, as can be seen for *death* in Figure 5-4.

Osgood found that the most important dimension of all on his scale was good-bad; a very large number of words carry strong connotations of goodness or badness. To enlarge upon the figure of speech used earlier, one might say that our catalogue file of concepts, with its cross-indexed hierarchies, is also organized in another way—as if the "good" concepts were printed in black ink on white paper, the "bad" concepts in white ink on black paper. Our tendency to think in terms of good and bad starts in childhood: among the "good" concepts are mother, father, friend, day, obedience, present, warmth; among the "bad" ones are stranger, night, disobedience, spanking, cold. As adults, we still think of a common thread of goodness running through such different concepts as health, angels, cleanliness, food, bed, work, Sunday, peace, freedom, wealth. We find a common thread of badness running through such varied concepts as sickness, devil, hunger, fatigue, idleness, war, slavery, poverty.

The second most important dimension on the scale, Osgood found, was strong-weak; this line accounted for the second largest number of significant connotations. Success is strong; so are concepts such as father, war, and devil. Mother is weak; so are such varied concepts as poem and illness. The third most important dimension was active-passive: many concepts have connotations of activity (such as success, social, and play), and many others have connotations of passivity (such as fate, death, introvert, and water).

167

A great majority of all words and concepts have significant connotations on one or more of the top three dimensions. This has proved true not only for Americans but for peoples of other nationalities. Different cultures may disagree as to what particular things are good or bad—for example, a Polynesian would regard work as "bad" and idleness as "good," in contrast to many Americans. In some societies the father is "weak" and the mother is "strong." But all people everywhere seem to use goodness, strength, and activity as important dimensions along which to organize most of their concepts.

7. concepts and personality

Although Osgood's work shows some significant similarities in the way all human beings organize their concepts and concept hierarchies, it must also be pointed out that there are many individual differences. As was mentioned earlier, we form our concepts on the basis of our experiences. The similarities to which we are exposed most often are the ones that we notice first; they are also the ones that tend to be bound together by the most powerful associations and to occupy a high place in our concept hierarchies. The mechanic's son builds strong and persistent concepts of a mechanical nature; to him an automobile and a boat powered by the same kind of engine may seem more alike than two automobiles with different engines. The philosophy professor's daughter tends to form highly abstract concepts; her concept of an automobile may involve close associations with Phoebus' chariot in Greek mythology.

In one experiment, subjects were asked which word did not belong among the following four:

prayer, skyscraper, temple, cathedral

As you will note, this is an ingenious grouping of words. A person who has a tendency to respond to religious concepts can argue that *skyscraper* is different from the other words. A person who responds to the words as belonging to a hierarchy of architectural concepts can argue that *prayer* is out of place. As it happened, 70 percent of the subjects in the experiment chose *skyscraper* as being the word that did not belong. Then the same words were presented to another group but in different order:

skyscraper, prayer, temple, cathedral

This time the number who chose *skyscraper* dropped to 40 percent (21). Obviously the decrease was caused by the set created by the first word in the series. When *prayer* was the first word, most subjects were set for religious concepts; when *skyscraper* was the first word, most were set for concepts involving buildings. But even the effect of *skyscraper* in creating a set did not influence all the subjects. Many subjects' own concept hierarchies, with religious concepts occupying a prominent place, still led them to associate *prayer, temple,* and *cathedral* and to consider *skyscraper* the wrong word in the series.

As this fact indicates, each of us has his own catalogue file—to use that figure of speech again—with its own system of lists and cross-indexing. The same stimulus—the same word, the same action by another person, the same event taking place—may set off in different people entirely different lines of search through the files, leading each of them eventually to take down a different book from the shelves—that is, leading them to engage in very different kinds of behavior.

To put it another way, the concepts we have learned and the way we have built them into hierarchies and have related and interlocked them one with another constitute our own personal system of organizing our environments. They influence what we select to pay attention to in our environments and how we organize what we see and hear. Moreover, most of our concepts carry connotations of goodness and badness, strength and weakness, activity and passivity. We use our system of concepts to label and understand ourselves, our fellow men, and the objects and events in our environments; the labels themselves help determine whether we approve or disapprove, admire or deplore. In our development from infant to adult we have learned not only concepts but ways of responding to these concepts.

c. thinking

The most important of all covert behavior is *thinking,* a word that all of us understand but that is difficult to define precisely. Perhaps it can best be described as *the mental manipulation of images, symbols, concepts, rules, and other mediational units.* Sometimes thinking manipulates objects that are physically present in the environment, as does the thinking of a carpenter while he is working with tools and lumber to build a cabinet. But note that the carpenter does not just move these objects about; he thinks about their uses and measurements in relation to the as yet unfinished product he is building. In other cases, thinking is entirely independent of physical objects; we can think about objects that are not present, about events that occurred in the distant past, or about abstract concepts that have no physical reality at all. Thinking is man's most useful tool precisely because it can range so widely and is so free from restrictions imposed by the immediate environment. In the process of thinking we can manipulate any or all of the mediational units acquired in our lifetimes.

1. some tools of thinking

One of the kinds of mediational units manipulated in thinking, as has been stated, is the *image*—or the recollection of a sensory experience. Dreaming is this type of thinking. When we dream, we seem to see a series of events happening much as if we were watching a movie. Besides the visual images, our dreams also contain images of sounds; we often seem to speak or be spoken to. Certain kinds of thinking of a high level of complexity and discipline are also possible through the manipulation of images. Mathematicians often think in "pictures" of space and of intersecting planes. Some musicians can compose or

orchestrate by manipulating the images of sounds that they "hear" only inside themselves; Beethoven, for example, wrote many of his greatest works after he became deaf and could not actually hear tones at all.

We also manipulate various kinds of *nonverbal symbols.* The musician may manipulate symbols standing for notes and keys; the scientist may think in terms of mathematical formulas. The most commonly used tools of thinking, however, are *words* and *concepts.* Words, as has been said, enable us to label the objects and events in our environment and thus to manipulate them without seeing or touching them. Concepts enable us to treat them as groups containing various similarities and relationships.

Among the concepts of particular importance in thinking are *facts* and *premises*—or the things we have learned to know or believe are true about the objects and events of our environment. We have discovered, for example, that holding a finger in a flame causes pain and if continued long enough causes physical damage. We know from experience that if we slip off an edge we will fall. In thinking about fire and about mountain climbing, these facts are among the elements we manipulate.

When we have great faith in a relationship, we call it a *fact.* Thus we consider it a fact that fire burns flesh or that gravity causes falls. Many of what we accept as facts come from our own observations. Others represent the pooled observations of many people in our society—the kind of pieces of information found in various handbooks of fact in our libraries. Our thinking about the desirability of various cities as places to live, for example, might take into account the following: New York City is the largest in the United States; the average annual rainfall in Oregon is high; the sun shines in Miami, Florida, on most days of the year. We may base our thinking about automobiles on various facts about the horsepower and miles per gallon of different models.

Other facts come from the empirical observations of science. When we think about the sky and the solar system, we take for granted the astronomer's observation that the moon revolves around the earth and that the earth and the other planets revolve around the sun. We accept the physiologist's observation that the blood stream carries oxygen from the lungs to the cells of the body, the finding of medical science that surgery is the best cure for appendicitis, the chemist's finding that an alkali neutralizes an acid.

A *premise* is a basic belief that we accept even though it cannot be demonstrated so convincingly as the relationships we call facts. The line between premise and fact is often hazy and difficult to draw, for many of the beliefs generally accepted as fact cannot actually be proved and are in truth merely premises. In science, for example, such ideas as the theory of evolution and many advanced mathematical theories are really still only premises, though they are in accord with the best observations currently possible and have at least a certain claim to factual validity.

Many premises are the result of individual experiences and learning. They are not necessarily based on objective observation, and they may vary greatly from one person to another. One person, from what he has heard and observed, believes that most people are honest; much of his thinking about other people includes this firmly held premise. Another person holds just as firmly to the premise that most people are dishonest. One person bases much of his thinking (and overt behavior) on the premise that it is wise to keep one's nose to the grindstone, another on the premise that all work and no play makes Jack a dull boy. The importance of individual differences in premises as an element in thinking will become apparent in a moment.

2. thinking as a process

In our thinking, we build images, symbols, words, rules, and concepts—especially those concepts of relationship called facts and premises—into mental associations of varying length and complexity. The associations take two forms, each of which deserves discussion. They are 1) thinking by means of *logical rules* and 2) a far less precise, more personal kind of thought process that can best be described by the term *mediational clustering*. Let us start with the more formal of the two.

Logical Rules.   All of us know, at least in a general way, what it means to think logically. It means to be sensible and reasonable and to draw conclusions that are justified by the evidence. In logical thinking we add up the facts and conclude that two plus two equals four, not three or five.

The application of mathematical rules is one of the best examples of logical thinking. The circumference of a circle is always $2\pi r$, and π is defined as 3.1416. Therefore, if r (the radius) is 5 feet, the circumference has to be 31.416 feet. To reach any other conclusion would be totally illogical.

Outside the field of mathematics, a well-known example of logic is the *syllogism*, a three-step kind of thinking that goes as follows:

1. All men are mortal.
2. I am a man.
3. Therefore I am mortal.

In the syllogism, statement 1 is known as the major premise, statement 2 as the minor premise, and statement 3 as the conclusion. If the major premise and the minor premise are taken for granted, the conclusion follows inescapably.

Note that the syllogism is an argument from the general to the particular. It is logical to think:

All mammals nurse their young.
A whale is a mammal.
Therefore a whale nurses its young.

It would not be logical to think:

Some mammals live on land.
All whales are mammals.
Therefore some whales live on land.

People often fall into errors of logic. A young woman may decide to become a schoolteacher as a result of this line of thought: "My mother says she was extremely happy when she was teaching school; therefore I will be happy teaching school." The fallacies here are that the young woman may have very different tastes and that schoolteaching may have changed as a profession in the meantime. A man with a stomach ache takes a pill that was once prescribed for a friend on the ground that "the pill helped him; therefore it will help me." But his stomach ache may be of an entirely different kind and may only be aggravated by the medicine.

Often when we accuse people of being illogical, however, we are wrong. Their logic is sound, granted their premises, and it is the premises that we disagree with. For example, the navigators of the Middle Ages were quite logical in believing that anybody who kept sailing due west from Europe would eventually fall off the earth. Their reasoning was as follows:

> All flat surfaces have edges.
> The earth is flat.
> Therefore the earth has edges and anyone who sails that far will fall off.

The logic was sound, but the minor premise was wrong: the earth is not flat.

Many arguments and misunderstandings, among statesmen and nations as well as between husbands and wives, are caused not so much by fallacies of logic as by belief in different premises. One government economist, using faultless logic, may reach the conclusion that taxes should be raised this year. An equally brilliant economist, using equally flawless logic, may conclude that taxes should be lowered. One person decides, after much reasonable thought, that capital punishment should be abolished. Another person decides that it is essential. Which economist and which of the two opinions on capital punishment is right, and which is wrong? We cannot really say, because we have no way of establishing the validity of most of the premises that various people hold. We cannot be sure that a premise is wrong unless it clearly violates proved fact, and this is seldom the case. We know now for a fact, as the navigators of the Middle Ages did not know, that the earth is spherical rather than flat. And, if a man claims to be Napoleon, we know that he is definitely and unquestionably wrong, and we label him a psychotic. Mostly, however, we hold our premises more or less on faith; we can agree or disagree with another person's premises but cannot usually prove them right or wrong. Thus, even though rules of logic such as the syllogism are formal and well disciplined, people adhering to the rules can reach very different conclusions.

Mediational Clusters.   In sharp contrast to logical reasoning is the other kind of thinking process—the kind best described by the term *mediational cluster-ing.* This is dependent upon all the various kinds of associations mentioned earlier in the discussions of language and particularly of concepts. We carry around with us, as has been said, elaborate systems of concepts arranged in hierarchies and connected to one another by a sort of cross-indexing; moreover, the concepts carry powerful connotations of such qualities as goodness, strength, and activity. When we tap any part of this store of knowledge, we in effect tend to tap all of it. To go back to a figure of speech that was used earlier in the book, the learning process is like a cork wall in which new stimuli—new words, new ideas—sink home and become attached, like darts. Now, when we try to pull out one of the darts, a whole section of the wall, containing a cluster of other darts, comes away.

Let us say that we ask a college student to think of the word *angel* and to report every word and idea that it suggests. As the student digs out the dart for *angel,* all kinds of associated words and thoughts pull loose. The student may start by describing the attributes of an angel (the white robe, the benign expression), then functions (playing a harp), location (in heaven), and connotations (good, weak, passive). The student may then move on to the concept of religion and the concepts that this word arouses in turn and at last to the opposites that *angel* suggests, such as the word *devil* and all its evil associations and connotations.

This kind of thinking is simply based on the clustering together of mediational units and the connections between clusters such as angel-good and their opposites such as devil-bad. It is the kind of thinking that is often called free association or stream of consciousness. Yet the associations are not altogether "free." The way each person has organized his concepts into hierarchies and systems of hierarchies, with some associations powerful and others weak, helps dictate each new link in his chain of thinking. A priest, starting with the word *angel,* might forge a chain of thought directly to the philosophical implications of the newest papal encyclical. A musician might make a chain of associations from angel to harp to his own special musical interests. An athlete might link angel-fly-fly ball-baseball.

Most chains of thinking involve associations dictated by mediational clusters rather than by logic. Indeed mediational clusters play a dual role in that they are the source of most of the premises upon which we base even our logical thinking. Premises such as those mentioned earlier—that most people are honest or that most people are dishonest, that hard and unremitting work is the source of success or of dullness—are not so much the result of objective observation as of the clustering of mediational units and their connotations.

3. undirected versus directed thinking

The discussion has proceeded from the elements of thinking to the two methods by which associations are made and linked together into chains of thinking. Now it must be pointed out that there are two very different kinds of thinking: 1) *undirected thinking,* which takes place spontaneously and with no goal in view, and 2) *directed thinking,* in which we try to forge a chain of associations that will reach a definite goal.

One example of *undirected thinking* is dreams, where we have no conscious control whatever over the chain of associations. The psychoanalysts maintain that dreams have an unconscious goal of some kind and represent the acting out of wishes we are afraid to express openly. But on the conscious level, at least, dreams seem to occur whether we want them or not and to proceed without rhyme or reason. Even in our waking moments a somewhat similar kind of thinking takes place. We look out the window and see a dog trotting across the yard. Immediately a long chain of images and thoughts occurs to us. The chain is undirected and uncontrolled. The sight of the dog seems to set it off almost automatically, much as the physician's hammer sets off the knee reflex. We start thinking because we cannot help it, along lines of associations that seem to proceed of their own accord.

Directed thinking, on the other hand, is something that we deliberately set into motion and that we discipline toward a goal. Directed thinking is aimed at 1) finding a solution and 2) recognizing the correct solution once it has been found. This is the kind of thinking we do when we try to answer questions such as "Shall I go to college?" "Which college?" "What courses shall I take?" "What kind of job do I want?" And, later on in life, "Shall I buy or rent a house?" "What kind of insurance should I buy?" Or, on a more philosophical plane, "What political candidate shall I vote for?" "What is my obligation to the community?" "What are my ultimate aims in life?" "What values do I want to try to instill in my children?"

Much directed thinking takes the form of *problem solving,* which can be considered now as a topic of its own.

D. problem solving

Many years ago an experimenter put cats into a number of "puzzle boxes"—little cages from which the cats could escape only by lifting a latch or pulling a loop of string. Outside each box he placed food. The cats had a goal—namely, to get out of the box and get the food. But how? This was the problem.

It developed that the cats could solve the problem only through the method called *trial and error.* They made all kinds of movements; they stretched, bit, and scratched. Eventually, by chance, they stumbled on the solution and made their escape (22).

The chimpanzee shown in Figure 5-5 is also faced with a problem. High above its head hangs a bunch of bananas. Its goal is to reach them. But how? The solution to the problem, as the chimp has just discovered, is to pile the boxes one atop another and climb up. In this case the animal caught on; it got the idea; the solution came to it not after long and laborious trial and error but in a sudden flash of what is called *insight.*

The chimpanzee in Figure 5-6 has solved a different kind of problem through insight. In both cases there may have been some trial and error in the sense that the chimps thought of other possible ways to try to solve the problems and had to discard these methods as impracticable. But, if there was trial and error, it took place covertly, through the manipulation of symbols. In a way that is beyond the capacity of lower animals the chimpanzees solved their problems by thinking. Exactly how they did it—what kind of symbols they used and how these symbols were linked—we of course cannot know.

a chimp does some thinking

5-5 The chimpanzee is in a cage with a bunch of bananas hanging high above its reach and with three boxes, none of which is high enough in itself to enable the chimp to climb up and reach the bananas. After looking the situation over for some time, it starts to pile one box atop another for additional height and thus manages to reach the bananas.

another example of insight

5-6

This chimpanzee was confronted with some sticks that posed a problem. The very short stick was within reach but was too short to pull in the piece of fruit. The very long stick that would pull in the fruit was well out of reach. At last the animal has caught on and is using the shorter sticks to reach the longer ones; it will have the fruit in a moment.

7. steps in problem solving

The process of problem solving in human beings has been studied in detail. It appears to require seven separate steps for maximum efficiency.

Step 1: Defining the Problem. Sometimes, especially in school situations, this is done for us. For example, a question on an examination may pose a definite problem: "If a circular lake is ten miles across and a man walks at the rate of four miles an hour, how long will it take him to walk around the lake?" Other examination questions, however, may require that we define a large part of the problem ourselves. We may be asked an extremely abstruse question such as, "How do the aphorisms of Sartre derive from the metaphysics of Hume and Nietzsche?" Here we have to break down the problem into units we can comprehend; we must ask ourselves the meanings of the words *aphorism* and *metaphysics* and what we know about the writings of the men mentioned in the question. Outside the classroom the problem may be something like, "How can I feel happier?" Here we must decide: What is happiness? What is there about my present situation that dissatisfies me and how can I change it? Not until we have a grasp of the problem can we start to solve it.

Step 2: Evaluating the Definition. Once the problem has been defined, the proper next step is to pause and ask: Have I defined it correctly? Failure to make this check may make all the rest of the problem-solving process a waste of time, for many of us have a tendency to jump to the wrong conclusions about the nature of the problem.

Step 3: Holding the Problem in Memory. We cannot solve the problem unless we remember it—and remember it accurately. This seems obvious, but failure to take this step is very common. Many students come up with the wrong answers on examinations because somewhere along the line they forget exactly what the question was. For example, a student cannot correctly solve the problem of the man and the lake if he forgets that the man was walking at the rate of four miles an hour and uses five miles an hour instead.

Step 4: Searching for Hypotheses. A hypothesis is a theory—in problem solving, a theory as to how the problem might be solved. In step 4, the object is to search for all possible theories of solution. A person who poses the problem, "How can I feel happier?" might come up with many hypotheses: Change my college or my courses. Break off some friendships that have become burdensome. Find a new life style. And so on.

Step 5: Choosing the Best Hypothesis. In the case just mentioned, the person seeking to be happier might decide that several of his theories would help solve the problem. In most cases, however, one hypothesis is clearly best, and sometimes only one hypothesis will work at all. There is usually only one correct answer, for example, to a mathematical problem or a multiple-choice question. There was only one way for the chimpanzees in Figures 5-5 and 5-6 to reach the food.

Step 6: Evaluating the Hypothesis.   Once a hypothesis has been chosen, another check is in order. The problem solver must pause and ask if he has considered all the possibilities and is really sure, on second thought, that the hypothesis will work. Many of us tend to be impulsive and to favor the first hypothesis that comes to mind. Or we may choose an unsatisfactory hypothesis simply because we are loath to do the additional work that is involved in searching for additional theories. Thus, before we commit ourselves, we had better take another look.

Step 7: Implementing the Hypothesis.   This is the final and critical step. On an examination we work out the arithmetic that is required by a mathematical problem and write down the answer. In situations outside the classroom we undertake the actions that we have decided will make us happier or will enable us to reach whatever other goal we are seeking.

2. failures in problem solving

In actual practice, few people follow these seven steps in problem solving. Even successful thinkers often seem to reach the solution through some kind of process of mediational clustering, then work backward to make sure the solution is correct. Often, however, a failure to follow all the steps leads to an incorrect solution. By and large, most of us are not nearly so good at problem solving as we like to think we are. One ingenious demonstration is shown in Figure 5-7, which you should examine before going on to the next paragraph.

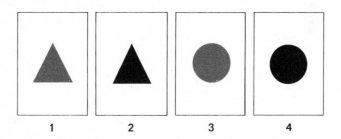

a test in problem solving

5-7   Shown here are four cards that have symbols on both sides. Each card has on one side a triangle, which may be either colored or black, and on the other side a circle, which also may be either colored or black. You are asked to prove or disprove the following statement about the cards: *Every card that has a colored triangle on one side has a black circle on the other side.* How many cards—and which ones—would you have to turn over to find out whether the statement is true or false? For the answer, see the text. (23)

The problem presented in Figure 5–7 is really quite simple—yet few people manage to solve it. The answer is that you must turn over cards 1 and 3. If card 1 has a colored circle on the back, or if card 3 has a colored triangle on the back, then the statement you are asked to prove or disprove is false. But if card 1 has a black circle on the back, and card 3 has a black triangle on the back, then the statement is true.

Most people insist that the cards to turn over are 1 and 4. But in fact card 4 has no bearing on the problem. Regardless of whether the triangle on the back is colored or black, this card cannot prove or disprove the statement. The only kind of card that could disprove the statement is one with a colored triangle on one side and a colored circle on the other. If there is no such card—and the only possible cards of this kind are 1 and 3—then the statement is true.

If you do not believe the solution even after reading it, you are by no means alone; many people refuse to believe the answer. But it is absolutely correct. In the opinion of the psychologist who designed the problem, the failure to reach or believe the answer demonstrates that most of us have a strong tendency to look for evidence that will support our hypotheses or guesses—and also a strong tendency to ignore any line of thinking that might prove our first hunches wrong.

Individual personality traits also affect and sometimes get in the way of successful problem solving, as was demonstrated by two psychologists who presented their students with a rather simple problem of a different kind. Each student received a piece of paper on which was written the question: "A man bought a horse for $60 and sold it for $70. Then he bought it back again for $80 and sold it for $90. How much money did he make in the horse business?" The students were asked to check one of five possible answers: lost $10, broke even, made $10, made $20, or made $30.

It turned out that men students and women students reacted quite differently to the problem. As is shown in Figure 5–8, considerably more women than men checked "broke even." Considerably more men than women got the correct answer,

male-female differences in problem solving

5-8

The bars show the percentages of men and women college students who selected the various possible answers to the horse-trading problem described in the text. Note how many more women than men selected "broke even" and how many more men than women selected the correct answer, "made $20."

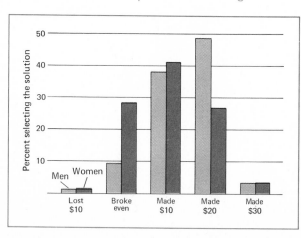

which is "made $20." The psychologists who conducted the experiment concluded that women tend to favor the "broke even" answer because they are more conservative and less aggressive than men; they prefer to think of people as breaking even in financial transactions rather than as taking risks and winding up with a large profit (24).

3. barriers to problem solving

Experiments with children have shown that their failures at problem solving result from many factors. One experiment with six-year-olds has shown that even though they possess the knowledge required to solve a problem, they may not retrieve this knowledge when seeking a solution (25). Another with children of ten and eleven has shown that they may fail because they 1) do not understand the problem, 2) cannot remember the elements of the problem even if they do understand it, 3) reach an arbitrary and impulsive solution, or 4) do not check and evaluate their solution (26).

Efficiency at problem solving can be improved through practice, and one can learn to become a better problem solver just as one can learn anything else. To adults it often seems most difficult to improve at step 4, searching for good hypotheses. At this point, the problem solver frequently runs into two barriers that may frustrate all his efforts. One is *persistence of set,* the other a special form of set called *functional fixedness.*

Persistence of Set.   One of the best-known experiments on the difficulties caused by persistence of set is shown in Figure 5-9. Before going on to the next paragraph, try the problems in Figure 5-9 for yourself, keeping track of your solutions in any way you choose.

the water jar problem

5-9

The problem is to measure out the number of quarts of water in the final column, using jars of the sizes shown in columns A, B, and C. In problem 1 the solution is to fill jar A, then remove nine quarts from it by filling jar B three times. (27)

Problem	Size of jars (*in quarts*) A	B	C	Quarts of water needed
1	29	3	—	20
2	21	127	3	100
3	14	163	25	99
4	18	43	10	5
5	9	42	6	21
6	20	59	4	31
7	23	49	3	20
8	15	39	3	18
9	28	76	3	25
10	18	48	4	22
11	14	36	8	6

In working out the problems, you will doubtless have discovered that numbers 1 through 6 are solved by filling the largest of the water jars first, then measuring off some of this water by pouring it into the smaller jars. Problems 2 through 6 can all be solved B − A − 2C—in other words, by filling jar B, then from this jar filling jar A once and jar C twice, leaving just the number of quarts you want. The interesting question about the problems, however, is how you approached numbers 7 through 11. Most people, having found the B − A − 2C formula, continue to apply it to number 7, even though this problem can be solved much more directly simply by filling jar A and from this jar filling jar C (A − C), and also to problem 8, though this problem can most easily be solved by adding the contents of jars A and C (A + C). Most people, indeed, continue to try the B − A − 2C formula on problem 9 and therefore fail to solve it at all, although there is an easy solution, A − C. Even after this failure they continue to apply their method to problem 10, most easily solved by A + C, and to 11, most easily solved by A − C. Having discovered a successful method for solving 1 through 6, they seem to stick with the method through thick and thin.

Most of us have this strong tendency toward *persistence of set*. We learn to apply certain hypotheses to the solving of problems; these hypotheses work for us; and we build up the habit of continuing to apply them—often overlooking hypotheses that would be much more efficient. It is persistence of set that makes it so difficult for most of us to solve brain-teasers that require a fresh new approach to familiar situations. For example, there is the old puzzle about the man who lived on the top floor of a nine-story apartment building. Every morning, when he went to work, he got on the elevator at the ninth floor. But in the evening, returning home, he got off at the eighth floor and walked up the remaining flight. Why? A somewhat similar puzzle concerns the man, bitter about life, who planned one last grim joke on humanity; his body was found hanging, with his feet a good 24 inches from the floor, in an otherwise empty closet. How did he manage to hang himself? Only by a determined effort to avoid persistence of set can we come to the answers.*

Functional Fixedness.   A special form of set called *functional fixedness* is a tendency to think of objects as functioning only in one certain way and to ignore their other possible uses. A demonstration of how functional fixedness can interfere with problem solving is illustrated in Figure 5-10. Test your own skills on the problem presented in Figure 5-10 before going on to the next paragraph or turning the page to Figure 5-11, which shows the solution.

As can be seen in Figure 5-11, the key to solving the problem is to forget about the ordinary uses of a pair of pliers and to turn the pliers instead into a support for the flower stand. In an experiment in which subjects were asked to solve the problem by actually manipulating the objects, it was found that their

---

*The man in the elevator was a midget who could reach only as high as the button for the eighth floor. The man who hanged himself stood on a cake of ice that had melted by the time his body was discovered.

attempts were hampered if they had to begin by using the pliers to loosen the wire; this seemed to serve as a reminder that the usual function of pliers is to loosen or tighten wires, turn bolts, or pull nails—not to serve as the legs of a flower stand. Subjects for whom the wooden bar was merely tied to the board and could be removed by simply untying a knot—and who therefore did not have to use the pliers to loosen a wire—were considerably more successful at finding the solution (28).

The flower stand was one of several similar problems devised by the same experimenter; some of the other solutions required using a box as a platform instead of a container or bending a paper clip and using it as a hook. The subjects who had to begin by using the objects in the normal way—the pliers to untwist wire, the box to hold things, the paper clip to fasten papers together—managed to solve 61 percent of the problems. The subjects who did not start this way and thus had less functional fixedness to overcome solved 98 percent.

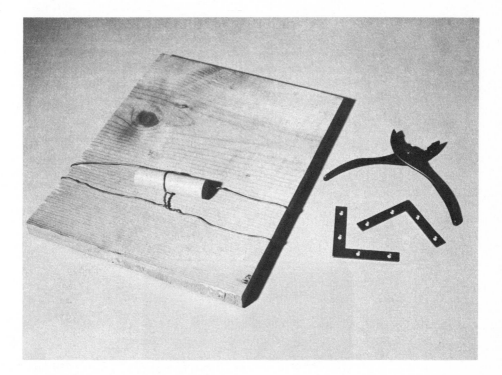

the flower stand problem

5-10 Subjects were asked to arrange any or all of these objects so that the board would stand firmly on supports and could serve as a stand for a vase of flowers. The problem is particularly difficult to solve from a photograph, without actually manipulating the objects, but you may be able to visualize the solution before turning to Figure 5-11, which demonstrates how the job can be done. The first step, of course, is to use the pliers to loosen the wire and detach the wooden bar.

the solution to the flower stand problem

5-11   The problem posed in Figure 5–10 can be solved only by using the pliers in an unusual way, as two "legs" for the flower stand. The metal joints go unused.

Another example of functional fixedness is shown in Figure 5–12. The problem illustrated in the photograph was preceded by what the subjects were told were speed tests; the experimenter gave them the diagrams and parts for an electric circuit and asked them to build it as fast as possible. One group of subjects built a circuit containing the microswitch shown in the photograph. The other group's circuit contained the relay. When the two groups moved on to the problem of tying the strings together, a significant number of the subjects who had just

the string problem and functional fixedness

5-12   The problem is to tie the two strings together. It can be solved by attaching an object to one of the strings and setting it swinging so it comes into reach while you are holding the other string. Only two of the objects—the microswitch (A) and the electric relay (B)—are heavy enough to do the job. For an explanation of which subjects chose the microswitch and which chose the relay and the light this casts on functional fixedness, see the text.

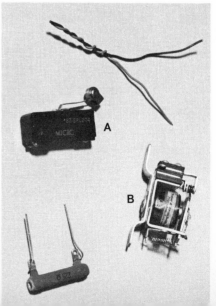

used the microswitch as part of an electric circuit passed it by and chose the relay as the weight for the string. The subjects who had just used the relay in a circuit did the opposite (29).

Functional fixedness is of course a type of negative transfer—a classic case of S_1-R_1 followed by S_1-R_2. Having learned to use the pliers or the microswitch in one way, we find it difficult to cast aside the S_1-R_1 association and use them in an entirely different S_1-R_2 fashion. The old associations keep cropping up and interfering with the establishment of the new.

In many real-life situations, functional fixedness reduces our efficiency at solving problems. A nail file is for filing nails; we may overlook entirely the fact that it might help us tighten a screw and thus repair a broken lamp. A goldfish bowl is for fish; the first person who used one as a terrarium for growing house plants had to break some powerful old associations. Similarly, we have a tendency to think that things that perform the same functions should look alike. As old photographs show, the first automobiles strongly resembled buggies.

4, persistence of set, daily living, and creativity

Although persistence of set and functional fixedness often interfere with problem solving, nonetheless they have certain important advantages in meeting the routine problems of daily living. We are set to use many of the articles around us in certain ways—the soap and toothbrush in the bathroom, our clothing, the knives and forks on the table. These sets help us bathe, dress, and eat breakfast almost without thinking about what we are doing. We are set to start an automobile in the routine way, to stop at red lights and start at green lights, to step on the brake when something gets in our path. Sets are particularly valuable when we must react quickly, as when avoiding another automobile or a pedestrian, and do not have time to ponder all the possible hypotheses of what action might be best.

On the other hand, it is persistence of set and functional fixedness that account for the fact that truly creative thinking is so rare. For example, early attempts to teach language to chimpanzees failed because the experimenters were set to think of language in terms of speech; it was not until this set was broken by the brilliant idea of using sign language that the attempts began to be more successful. Historians of science have made a good case that the theory of relativity should have been discovered by a French mathematician named Poincaré, who had all the factual and theoretical background required for putting the theory together. But for all his genius Poincaré was temperamentally not prepared to synthesize this creative idea, and the theory remained for Einstein to discover.

Studies of creative people have disclosed that they tend to have a number of traits in common that are not shared by most other people. Generally speaking, they were lone wolves in childhood; they either were spurned and rejected by other children or sought solitude themselves. If being different from other children caused them anxiety, they eventually overcame it; they grew up with no need to conform to the people and the ways of life around them. In fact creative people tend to *want* to be different and original and to produce new things. They are

not afraid of having irrational or bizarre thoughts, are willing to examine even the most foolish-seeming ideas, and are not worried about success or failure. Many of them are aggressive and hostile, not at all the kind of people who win popularity contests or elections (30).

Creativity of any kind—the invention of a new mechanical device such as the airplane, the discovery of a new scientific principle, the writing of a great and original poem or novel—demands superior intelligence. But of the people who have the required intelligence perhaps not even as many as 1 percent are in fact creative. Even more than intelligence, creativity demands the kind of personality that scorns the tried and true, does not get imprisoned by persistence of set, but on the contrary seeks out new and unusual hypotheses even in the face of failure and ridicule.

Attempts have been made to devise tests that would spot creative people early in their school careers so that they might receive special treatment that would encourage their talents. Two such tests are shown in Figure 5-13 and Figure 5-14. Unfortunately, it is easier to test and study sheer originality of response than other qualities that are also necessary for true creativity. Mere novelty is not enough. Besides being new and unusual, a creative hypothesis must also be *appropriate*. A new scientific theory must, like Einstein's, be in accord with the known facts. The person who looks at a creative painting or hears creative music must have some kind of perception of aptness, of a disciplined relationship to the world as he knows it, if he is to consider the work of art esthetically pleasing. Hence the

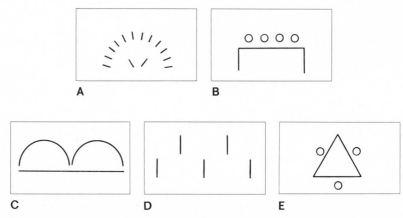

a test of creativity

5-13 These drawings are shown to fifth-grade children, who are asked to try to imagine what they might look like when completed. Most children make routine responses, but a few come up with original and creative ideas. The usual responses are: (A) the sun, (B) table with glasses on it, (C) two igloos, (D) raindrops, and (E) three people sitting at a table. Unusual responses would be: (A) a lollipop bursting into pieces, (B) a foot and toes, (C) two haystacks on a flying carpet, (D) worms hanging, and (E) three mice eating a piece of cheese. (31)

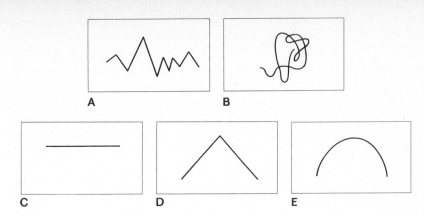

A   B

C   D   E

a variation of the creativity test

5-14   In this variation of the creativity test, children are asked what these lines suggest to them—the lines as a whole, not just in part. Ordinary responses would be: (A) mountains, (B) string, (C) stick, (D) arrow, and (E) rising sun. Unusual and original responses would be: (A) squashed piece of paper, (B) squeezing paint out of a tube, (C) stream of ants, (D) alligator's open mouth, and (E) fishing rod bending with a fish. (31)

critical debate over modern abstract art and modern music that uses dissonances and unusual sources of sound such as whistles and electronic devices. These types of art and music are undoubtedly novel. But many critics believe that they are merely bizarre and fantastic rather than truly creative. In art, music, literature, and sometimes even science, the final verdict may have to await the test of history. Some allegedly creative innovations are rejected by future generations as mere fads; other innovations, though ridiculed at first, turn out to have been ahead of their time and eventually are recognized as genuinely creative achievements.

summary 1. The ability to use language probably depends on the structure of the human brain and the dynamics of how the brain operates. It enables men to communicate, learn, think, and solve problems in ways that presumably no other animal can even approach.

2. The building blocks of language are the basic sounds called *phonemes*. English uses forty-five phonemes, and no language uses more than eighty-five. The phonemes are combined into meaningful units known as *morphemes*, which may be words themselves or may be combined with one another to produce words.

3. The most important feature of language is that it is in essence a set of rules, notably the rules called *grammar*, for combining morphemes into words and words into an almost infinite number of sentences conveying an almost infinite variety of meaning.

4. The rules are quite similar in all the thousands of languages of the world, both present and past—a fact suggesting that human beings may have an

inherited tendency to use and understand language in a manner somehow biologically determined by the structure and dynamics of the human brain.

5. Some theorists believe that the child learns language through operant conditioning. Others consider observation learning more important. A new and increasingly popular theory stresses the learning not of specific words or phrases but of the rules of grammar; this theory offers a new explanation for the fact that the child comes to understand the meaning of sentences he has never heard before and to "generate" new and original sentences of his own.

6. Some words are used as symbols for a specific object, such as the names of the planets Mars and Jupiter.

7. Most words, however, are *concepts*. A concept is a *symbol that stands for a common characteristic or relationship shared by objects or events that are otherwise different.* Thus the word *water* is a symbol that stands not only for the fluid that comes out of a faucet but for any somewhat similar fluid anywhere, including the salty contents of the oceans and the drops that fall as rain.

8. The concepts used by adults represent many kinds of shared similarities and relationships that have been found to exist among all the apparently diverse elements in the environment and in human history. Ordinarily each person's primary definition of a concept is based on what is to him the *salient characteristic* of the various objects, events, or ideas that are included in the concept.

9. The associations that make up concepts are arranged in *concept hierarchies,* meaning that some of the associations are very strong and likely to be thought of immediately, whereas others are weaker and less likely to come to mind.

10. Besides their surface or dictionary meanings, most words and concepts also have implied meanings called *connotations.* A great many words carry connotations of goodness or badness, strength or weakness, and activity or passivity.

11. There are many individual differences in the way people learn concepts, build them into hierarchies, and relate and interlock them. Thus each individual has his own personal system of organizing his environment and responding to it.

12. Thinking is *the mental manipulation of images, symbols, concepts, rules, and other mediational units.*

13. The thinking process makes associations in two ways: a) by means of *logical rules* and b) through *mediational clustering.*

14. Two types of thinking are *undirected thinking,* which takes place spontaneously and with no goal in view, and *directed thinking,* the most important form of which is *problem solving.*

15. Human problem solving is most efficient when performed in seven steps: a) defining the problem, b) evaluating the definition, c) holding the problem in memory, d) searching for hypotheses, e) choosing the best hypothesis, f) evaluating the hypothesis, and g) implementing the hypothesis.

16. A common barrier to problem solving is *persistence of set,* including a special type of set called *functional fixedness.*

recommended reading

Blumenthal, A. L. *Language and psychology: historical aspects of psycholinguistics.* New York: Wiley, 1970.

Brown, R. W. *Words and things.* New York: Free Press, 1958.

Bruner, J. S., and Olver, R. R. *Studies in cognitive growth.* New York: Wiley, 1966.

Chomsky, N. *Language and mind,* enl. ed. New York: Harcourt Brace Jovanovich, 1972.

Deese, J. E. *Psycholinguistics.* Boston: Allyn and Bacon, 1970.

Furth, H. G. *Piaget and knowledge: theoretical foundations.* Englewood Cliffs, N.J.: Prentice-Hall, 1969.

Kintsch, W. *Learning, memory and conceptual processes.* New York: Wiley, 1970.

Klausmeier, H. J., and Harris, C. W., eds. *Analysis of concept learning: proceedings.* New York: Academic Press, 1966.

Mandler, G., and Mandler, J. M., eds. *Thinking: from association to gestalt.* New York: Wiley, 1964.

Singer, J. L. *Daydreaming: an introduction to the experimental study of inner experience.* New York: Random House, 1966.

Wallach, M. A., and Kogan, N. *Modes of thinking in young children: a study of the creativity-intelligence distinction.* New York: Holt, Rinehart and Winston, 1965.

Witkin, H. A., and Lewis, H. B., eds. *Experimental studies of dreaming.* New York: Random House, 1967.

The senses
provide
the raw information.
Perception
gives meaning
to what
we see,
hear,
taste,
and smell.

PART THREE

The computer is totally dependent on its inputs—that is, on the kind of information that is fed into it. Rather similarly, the organism is dependent on the kind of information it receives from its environment and the manner in which it is able to organize this information into patterns of meaning.

Hence the importance of the human senses, which will now be discussed in Chapter 6. Note the difference, for example, between the kind of information a human being receives through such sense organs as the eyes and ears and the information on which a paramecium must rely. The paramecium is sensitive in a general way to light and dark and to heat and cold, and it can move toward or away from them. But it is not at all influenced by many of the things that influence human beings; it is unaware of the existence in the environment of colors and the rise of the sun, of sounds and words, of newspapers and books. Its behavior is limited to a few simple functions, such as moving, feeding, and its own primitive kind of reproduction.

As important as the raw information provided by our senses is the manner in which we organize and interpret the information—the processes described in Chapter 7, on perception. For example, your own behavior and thinking at this moment depend not so much on the fact that you can see the book as on the fact that you regard it—or perceive it—as a particular kind of object called a college textbook. A child, though seeing the book exactly as you see it, might interpret it as something to draw on or to build into piles like blocks.

The senses provide the raw information that enables us to behave and think like human beings. The process of perception gives meaning to what we see, hear, feel, taste, and smell. Together, they enable us to understand the objects and events in our environment and to start dealing with them successfully.

pERCEiviNq THE woRld

CHAPTER 6

THE SENSES

our ancestors who thought about the matter, the human senses
most puzzling mysteries. Here you stand, and out there, many
y unconnected in any apparent way with your body or your
w are you able to see that tree? Why does its trunk look brown
en? Why are the roses near it red and the marigolds yellow?
nding near the tree opens his mouth, and you hear words. What
d why does his voice sound different from the voice of anyone
Vhy does a piano sound different from a violin, and a violin

you see out in the yard smell entirely different from the
does not taste at all like lemon juice or quinine. Some objects
em cold; some seem warm and some so hot that you have to
way in pain. Why?
s nobody knew the answers to these questions. Even the best
could only guess. Some of the guesses, as we now know, came
truth. For example, one Greek philosopher who lived around
d that all objects gave off some kind of invisible substance that
s or the pores of our skin and then traveled to our brains. Not
there any better explanation.

this book you are demonstrating the two basic principles now
lved in the operation of our senses.
must be a *stimulus.* As the Greek philosopher rightly guessed,
tually impinge upon our bodies. In this case it is the light waves
book. Turn out the light and darken the room, thus removing
d you can no longer see the book, even though it is still there.
re must be *receptors* that are sensitive to the stimulus. The
rong in thinking that anything could enter our pores and then
What happens is that the stimulus activates the receptors—in
sensitive nerve endings in your eyes—which then send nervous
ain, where they are translated into conscious sensations. Block
y closing your eyelids, and again you cannot see the book. You

DEFINITIONS:
1. STIMULUS
2. RECEPTOR

cannot see with your skin or your ears, because they do not possess any receptors that respond to the stimulus of light.

A *stimulus* has already been defined as any form of energy capable of exciting the nervous system; among the sensory stimuli are light waves, sound waves, the chemical energy that causes the sensations of taste and smell, and the mechanical energy that we feel through the skin as pressure and pain. A *receptor* can be defined as a specialized nerve ending capable of responding to energy.

If we regard the human organism as a sort of computer, then our senses provide our inputs. They tell us what kind of world we are living in and how the world is changing from moment to moment. Without the evidence provided by our senses, all the rest of our complicated physical and nervous equipment would be useless—just as a modern heating system would be useless without the sensitive element in the thermostat that says the building is now warm and the heat must be turned off, or the building is getting cold and the heat must be turned on. Our sensory receptors relay the fact that the traffic light up ahead has turned red, and by a complicated process of mental and motor activity we step on the brake and stop the automobile. Our sensory receptors inform us that the weather has turned cold, and we put on more clothing lest we freeze to death.

↙ the range and limits of the human senses

The receptors in the human eye are so sensitive that on a night when the air is clear but the moon and stars are blacked out by an overcast, a man sitting on a mountain can see a match struck fifty miles away. Our noses can detect the odor of artificial musk, a perfume base, in as weak a concentration as one part musk to thirty-two billion parts of air.

Even so, our senses are by no means perfect. Owls can see far better in the near-dark than we can. Hawks soaring high in the air can see mice that we would never be able to distinguish at such a distance. Bees can see ultraviolet light (the rays that produce sunburn), which we cannot see at all. Dogs and porpoises hear tones that go unheard by the human ear. (You can buy whistles that will call your dog without disturbing your neighbors.) The minnow, which has taste receptors all over its body, has a far sharper sense of taste than we do. Bloodhounds are used to track down criminals because they have a far sharper sense of smell.

ELECTROMAGNETIC
RADIATION

In some ways the deficiencies of our sense organs are a blessing. Light waves, as the physicists have shown, are one form of electromagnetic radiation. So are many other things, such as cosmic rays, X-rays, radio and television signals, and the electric currents passing through the wires of our houses. The length of the wave determines which of these forms the radiation takes. Light waves, the only wave lengths to which our eyes are sensitive, are a tiny fraction of the entire range. If we could see all the wave lengths—everything from cosmic rays to the radio and television signals passing through the air and the flow of electricity—we would surely be completely confused. Our eyes would give us a hopeless jumble of impressions.

2. the absolute threshold

With the help of a friend, you can make a simple test of your own hearing that points to one of the important facts about the senses. Have your friend hold a watch somewhere in the vicinity of one ear, moving it closer and farther away. The watch is constantly ticking, sending out sound waves. But sound waves decrease in volume as they travel through the air, and if the watch is too far away, you cannot hear it at all. As it is moved closer, eventually there comes a spot at which you can hear it quite clearly. At one distance the sound waves are too weak to make the receptors in your ear respond. A little closer the waves are strong enough; the receptors send signals to your brain and you can hear the watch. The test is a crude measurement of the *absolute threshold* of hearing in that ear—in other words, the minimum amount of stimulus energy to which the receptors will respond. By comparing your threshold with that of other people, you can get a rough idea of whether your sense of hearing is average, sharper than average, or below average.

Measurements establishing the precise absolute thresholds for the various senses under various conditions have been made with procedures known as *psychophysical methods*—techniques of measuring the psychological equivalents of changes in the physical strength of a stimulus. In a typical psychophysical experiment a subject is placed in a dark room and brief flashes of light are presented, with the exact intensity of the light controlled down to the tiniest fraction. Some flashes are so weak in intensity that the subject never sees them. Other, stronger flashes are seen every time. In between, there is a sort of twilight zone of intensities at which the subject sometimes sees the flash and sometimes does not.

There are many reasons for this "sometimes" factor. The human body is constantly at work: the heart is beating, the lungs inhaling or exhaling air. Each cell of the body, including the sensory receptors, is being fed by the blood stream and is throwing off waste materials. All sorts of spontaneous nervous activity are constantly going on in the brain. Sometimes all these conditions work together in favor of detecting a weak stimulus; sometimes they work against it. So the absolute threshold is not really "absolute." It is arbitrarily considered to be the intensity at which the subject sees the flash half the time.

A synonym for threshold is the word *limen*; a *subliminal* stimulus is below the threshold, a *supraliminal* stimulus above it.

3. the difference threshold

Let us return for a moment to the psychophysical method of measuring a subject's absolute intensity threshold for a brief flash of light. This time let us change the experiment and present two lights to the subject, side by side. We start with two lights of exactly equal intensity; and the subject, as we would expect, sees them as exactly the same. We show him the two lights again, but this time we have increased the intensity of the light on the right by a tiny fraction. If

DEFINITION:
ABSOLUTE
THRESHOLD

DEFINITION:
PSYCHOPHYSICAL
METHODS

DEFINITIONS:
1. LIMEN
2. SUBLIMINAL
3. SUPRALIMINAL

we continue the experiment long enough, keeping the left-hand light at the same intensity and varying the intensity of the right-hand light, eventually we will discover the smallest possible difference that his eyes are capable of recognizing 50 percent of the time. This is the *difference threshold,* or *difference limen,* an important concept in sensory psychology.

DEFINITION:

DIFFERENCE
THRESHOLD

The difference threshold—often called the *just noticeable difference* or j.n.d. for short—is a measurement of our basic capacity to discriminate among different stimuli. Psychophysical measurements have shown that if the left-hand light in our experiment has an intensity of 1, the right-hand light must have an intensity of 1.016 to be recognized as different. If the left-hand light is 10, the right-hand light must be 10.16. If the left-hand light is 100, the right-hand light must be 101.6. In other words, the difference in intensity between two lights must be 1.6 percent before it can be recognized. For sound, the just noticeable difference is about 10 percent.

DEFINITION:

WEBER'S LAW

This rule that the difference threshold is a fixed percentage of the original stimulus is called *Weber's Law* in honor of the physiologist who discovered it more than a century ago. The law does not apply at very low intensities or at very high intensities, but it holds generally over the greater part of the range of stimulation. In practical terms, it means this: the more sensory stimulation to which the human organism is being subjected, the more additional stimulation must be piled on top of this to produce a recognizable difference. In a room where there is no sound except that of a mosquito buzzing, you can hear a pin drop. On a noisy city street you can hear the honk of an automobile horn but may be completely unaware of the fact that a friend is shouting to you from down the block. At an airport where jet planes are warming up, a small cannon could go off close beside you without making you jump.

4. sensory adaptation

At this moment, unless you happen to be sitting in a draft or in an unusually hot room, you almost surely are not conscious of feeling either hot or cold. And you probably feel the same all over; you are not conscious that your feet are cooler or warmer than your hands or that the skin on the calves of your legs is any cooler or warmer than the skin on the small of your back. Yet careful measurements of your skin temperature would probably show small but significant differences for your feet, which are encased in socks or stockings and shoes; your uncovered hands; your calves, covered by a pair of trousers or by nylon stockings; and the small of your back, covered by several layers of clothing and a belt.

Nor are you conscious of any special pressures against your skin. But wherever your clothing touches your skin, there certainly is pressure; and at some places the pressure is made so intense by a wristwatch band or by a belt that you may find marks on your skin tonight when you undress.

DEFINITION:

SENSORY
ADAPTATION

Why do you not feel these stimuli? The answer lies in the principle of *sensory adaptation,* which means that after a time the sensory receptors adjust to a stimulus—they "get used to it," so to speak—and stop responding.

The classic example of sensory adaptation is this simple experiment. Fill a bowl with water of just about skin temperature—water that feels neither hot nor cold to your hand, water that we may say has a neutral temperature. Fill a second bowl with cold water and a third bowl with water that feels quite warm to the touch. Now put your left hand in the bowl of cold water and your right hand in the bowl of hot water. After a minute or two, put both hands in the bowl that contains water at the neutral temperature. Even though you know perfectly well that both hands are in the same water, your left hand will feel warm, your right hand cool. The receptors in your left hand have become adapted to cold water, and water of neutral temperature now seems warm. The receptors in your right hand have adapted to warm water, and water of neutral temperature now seems cold.

In some ways, the tendency of our senses to adapt to stimuli makes them less accurate than they would otherwise be. The human skin would make a poor thermostat for a heating system; what we want in a heating system is a thermostat that will invariably turn the heat on when the room temperature drops to 69 degrees and turn the heat off as soon as the temperature rises to 71 degrees. But in everyday living, sensory adaptation is generally an advantage. It would be distracting indeed if we were conscious all day of the pressure of every garment we wear and of every slight temperature change from one patch of our skin to another. If our noses did not gradually get used to the odors about us and stop sending signals to our brains, the people who work in fish markets and gas plants would be a lot less happy than they are.

Because of the principle of sensory adaptation, some scientists like to define a stimulus as a *change in energy* capable of exciting the sense organs. Such a definition is not literally correct, because we never adapt completely to a pressure strong enough to cause severe pain, and we continue to feel uncomfortably warm in a 110-degree room no matter how long we stay there. But the definition is nonetheless useful to keep in mind, because it emphasizes the fact that our sensory apparatus is best equipped to inform us of changes in our environment, and it is awareness of change in the environment that is most valuable to us.

With these general principles of the operation of the senses in mind, let us now examine our senses separately and in detail. It is popularly assumed that we are gifted with five senses; the best order in which to explore the five is to start with the simplest and least efficient one, which is *taste*, and proceed to *smell*, the *skin senses, hearing, and vision*. Even after we have examined the so-called five senses, however, it will be necessary to add two more—*bodily movement* and *equilibrium*—to explain the full range of human sensory apparatus.

SENSES:

1. TASTE
2. SMELL
3. SKIN SENSES
4. HEARING
5. VISION
6. BODILY MOVE-
    MENT
7. EQUILIBRIUM

taste

In view of the variety of foods we recognize and either enjoy or reject, it may seem strange to call the sense of taste our simplest and least efficient. What is generally called the "taste" of food, however, turns out to depend only in small

DEFINITION:
TASTE BUDS

part on our sensory receptors for taste. Much of the sensation depends on other factors—on warmth, cold, the consistency of the food, the mild pain caused by certain spices, and above all on smell. When our noses are stuffed up by a cold, food seems almost tasteless.

If you examine your tongue in a mirror, you will note that it is covered with little bumps, some very tiny, others a bit larger. Inside these bumps, a few of which are also found at the back of the mouth and in the throat, are the *taste buds,* which are the receptors for the sense of taste. Each bump contains about 245 taste buds, and each taste bud in turn contains about twenty receptors sensitive to chemical stimulation by food molecules. Food in solution spreads over the tongue, enters small pores in the surface of the bumps, and sets off chemical changes that depolarize the receptors and thus set off nervous impulses that are sent to the brain. Apparently the receptors respond to four basic qualities: *sweet, salty, sour,* and *bitter.* Some of the taste buds respond to only one of these qualities, others to two or three of them, and some to all four.

Our knowledge of the taste receptors explains why people who quit smoking often find that food tastes better and why older people often find they have to use much more salt and spice to make food taste as good as it did in their youth. Tobacco smoke temporarily reduces the sensitivity of the taste receptors (and also of the receptors for smell). In people past middle age the number of sensitive taste buds begins to decline, so that older people simply do not have as many taste receptors capable of responding. People who live to extremely advanced ages sometimes lose the sense of taste entirely.

Animals—at least some of them—apparently have a very different sense of taste from the human kind. Cats do not seem to be sensitive to sweetness; they show no fondness for candy. Dogs usually like candy and horses seem to prefer a lump of sugar to any other kind of taste.

c. smell

DEFINITION: OLFACTORY EPITHELIUM

At the very top of the nasal passages leading from the nostrils to the throat, as can be seen in Figure 6-1, lies the *olfactory epithelium,* the membrane that contains the receptors sensitive to smells. As we breathe normally, the flow of air from nostrils to throat takes a direct route, as the drawing indicates, but a certain amount rises gently to touch the olfactory epithelium. The receptors for smell are sensitive only to gases and to volatile substances that become dissolved in the air much as sugar dissolves in water. An actual molecule of the substance must touch the smell receptors; this is the stimulus that causes the receptors to "fire" and send nervous impulses to the brain.

It has been known for a long time that substances with a very small molecular size have very little odor and that very large molecules are not volatile and therefore have no odor at all, while the molecules of in-between size have the strongest odor. Recent studies seem to indicate that not only the size but also the shape of the molecule may determine how a substance smells. According to

6-1

A cross section of the human head shows the position of the *olfactory epithelium,* containing the receptors for the sense of smell. The normal passage of air through the nasal passages is indicated by the arrows.

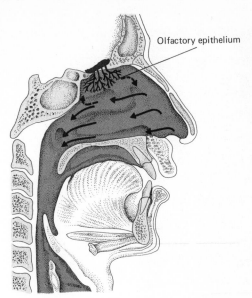

Olfactory epithelium

THEORY OF SMELL one theory, the smell receptors have very tiny slots or hollows of varying shapes, into which molecules of different shapes fit like a plug into an electric socket or a jigsaw piece into a puzzle; when a receptor is "filled" by the appropriate kind of molecule, it fires and sends its message to the brain. Proponents of the theory have suggested that there appear to be seven basic classes of molecules producing seven basic odors: camphorlike, musky, flowery, pepperminty, etherlike, pungent, and putrid. Some molecules apparently fit into more than one kind of receptor and thus produce the more complex sensations that result from combinations of the seven basic odors (1).

the skin senses

One of the tools developed for studying the sensitivity of the human skin is the *esthesiometer,* shown in use in Figure 6-2. If the two points of the esthesiometer are close together, they feel like the touch of a single object. If they are far enough

two sensations or one?

6-2

With an instrument developed for this special purpose, an experimenter determines how far apart two pressure stimuli must be before the subject can feel them as two separate sensations instead of as one.

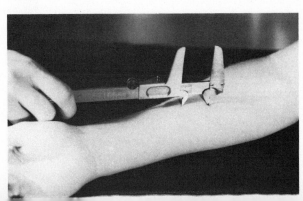

apart, they feel like the two separate objects that they in fact are. In other words, the esthesiometer measures what is called the *two-point threshold* for the sense of pressure.

Experiments with the esthesiometer make it immediately apparent that the two-point threshold differs widely for various parts of the body. To be felt as two objects, the points have to be thirty-four times as far apart on the middle of the back as on the fingertips and twice as far apart on the fingertips as on the tip of the tongue.

From what has already been said about stimuli and sensory receptors, we know what the esthesiometer is telling us. In the first place, there must be receptors capable of responding to the stimulus of pressure in the skin of each part of the body. In the second place, the receptors in parts of the body such as the fingertips and tongue must be more numerous, more sensitive, or both than the receptors in places such as the middle of the back.

But which is it? Are the pressure receptors at the tip of the tongue and in the fingertips more numerous, or are they more sensitive? Or are they both?

One way of answering these questions is to try to map the surface of the skin, searching point by point for spots that are sensitive to pressure and using different degrees of pressure to measure the absolute threshold at these points. The technique is shown in Figure 6-3.

When the skin is mapped in this fashion, it turns out that there are more spots sensitive to pressure at the tip of the tongue and in the fingertips than on the back. Moreover, the absolute threshold at these spots is far lower at the tip of the tongue and at the fingertips. We have our answer: in the regions of the body where the two-point threshold is lowest, the pressure receptors are *both* more numerous and more sensitive.

mapping skin sensitivity

6-3

A grid is printed on the skin, and the experimenter goes over the grid searching for spots sensitive to the pressure of human and animal hairs of different thicknesses. These are pressed against the skin just hard enough to make them bend, and the exact pressure exerted by each thickness of hair can be measured by pressing it in similar fashion against a delicate weighing balance. Sensitive spots are recorded on a copy of the grid. The same area can also be mapped for spots sensitive to pain, warmth, and cold—often giving results as shown in Figure 6-4.

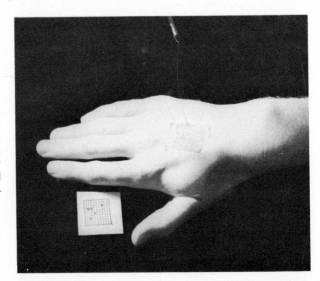

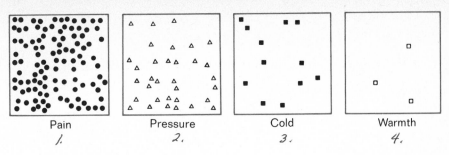

Pain	Pressure	Cold	Warmth
1.	*2.*	*3.*	*4.*

the results of skin mapping:

6-4 The drawings show the typical results when the same small area of skin is mapped for sensitivity to pain, pressure, cold, and warmth.

The number of sensitive spots usually found per square centimeter varies considerably depending on the part of the body mapped.

	Spots per square centimeter			
	PAIN	PRESSURE	COLD	WARMTH
Tip of nose	44	100	13	1.0
Forehead	184	50	8	0.6
Chest	196	29	9	0.3
Back of hand	188	14	7	0.5

If we continue to explore the skin with other stimuli, we make a further discovery. The stimulus of pressure has given us one kind of map. A warm stimulus shows a very different kind of map for the spots sensitive to warmth. A cold stimulus gives a third kind of map, and a needle used to elicit pain gives a fourth pattern. The four different kinds of maps are illustrated in Figure 6-4. As the figure shows, the number of sensitive spots varies greatly from one part of the body to another for pain, cold, and warmth as well as for pressure; but in any single area there are usually more pain spots than pressure spots, always more pressure spots than cold spots, and always more cold spots than warmth spots.

A strange thing about the cold spots is that they respond not only to a stimulus colder than skin temperature but to a very warm stimulus. When one of these spots is touched by a rod heated to 110 degrees Fahrenheit or more, we actually feel a strong sensation of cold at that point. This phenomenon is known as *paradoxical cold*—and it seems to explain how we distinguish a hot stimulus from a merely warm stimulus. When we touch a surface heated to more than 110 degrees Fahrenheit, both the warmth receptors and the cold receptors respond and send their nervous impulses to the brain, and it is this mingling of both that results in the sensation of heat. This can be demonstrated by the dual coils shown in Figure 6-5. When cool water is passed through both coils, the device naturally feels cool to the touch. When warm water is passed through both coils, it feels warm. But when one coil is warm and the other cool, the device suddenly—and to the amazement of anyone who touches it—feels hot.

From the various experiments we know that the skin really has four separate senses—pain, pressure, cold, and warmth, with a combination of the last two

DEFINITION:
PARADOXICAL
COLD

SKIN SENSES
PAIN
PRESSURE
COLD
WARMTH
HEAT = COLD
+ WARMTH

201

6-5

Warm water can be passed through both coils, or cool water can be passed through both, or warm water can be passed through one coil and cool water through the other. For a description of the unexpected result of passing warm water through one coil and cool water through the other, see the text.

producing the sensation of heat. As it happens, the nerve endings in the skin come in four general forms—some in little branches (called free-ending nerves), some in globular bulbs, some in egg-shaped corpuscles, and some in the form of "baskets" surrounding the roots of the hairs. This fact naturally has suggested the possibility that each type of nerve ending might be a receptor for each of the four sensory stimuli, and a great deal of experimental work has been done in an attempt to establish a connection. The efforts have thus far failed.

As for pain receptors, these are found in all our muscles and internal organs as well as in our skin, and some of the most excruciating pains come from cramps or from distension of the intestines by gas. Yet most of the internal organs do not respond to the ordinary stimuli for skin pain. The intestines, for example, can be cut or even burned without arousing any sensation of pain.

Although pain seems to be one of the crosses that we must bear, it actually serves a purpose. Without the warning given us by pain we might hold our hands in a flame until the tissues were destroyed or cut off a finger while peeling an apple. Even the pain of headache, which cannot be attributed to any specific outside stimulus, is probably a warning that we have subjected ourselves to too much physical or psychological stress; by forcing us to slow down or even take a day off, the headache takes us away from a situation that, if continued, might cause some serious damage to the tissues of our bodies or to our mental stability.

E. hearing

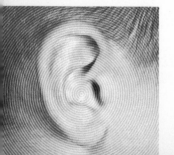

When you hit the key for middle C on a piano, a hammer strikes the string for middle C, the string vibrates, and you hear a sound. Not just any sound, but a very definite sound. You can distinguish it from other notes on the piano; it seems higher than the B just below it and lower than the D just above it. It also sounds different from the middle C on other musical instruments; if someone in the room were playing the same note on a clarinet, you would recognize at once that the sounds were alike yet somehow different.

If you hit the key a little harder, the sound, though remaining the same in every other respect, is louder. Hit the key a little more gently, and the sound is softer.

Striking the piano key is a start toward exploring some of the basic facts about the sense of hearing. Sound is an extremely complicated stimulus, ranging from the lowest notes of a tuba to the highest tones of a shrill whistle, changing in volume from the merest hint of a whisper to the most deafening clap of thunder, taking such diverse and varied forms as the click of two coins in a pocket, the human voice, and the blended richness of a hundred different instruments in a symphony orchestra. The receptors in the human ear have to be very sensitive indeed to respond to such a wide range of stimuli.

1. the physical nature of sound

The stimulus for sound is sound waves, rippling unseen through the air. Sound waves are roughly analogous to waves on water. If you throw a stone into a quiet pond, waves start to radiate out. It looks as if the surface of the water is moving away from the stone, forming circles of ever increasing size. Actually, as you can tell if there are some twigs or fishing corks floating on the surface, this is not true. The twigs and corks stay in the same spot and merely bob up and down.

What happens when the stone hits the surface of the pond is that it puts pressure on the water. The surface is pushed up, then falls, and in so doing passes the pressure along to the adjoining water. The rising and falling motions continue outward in ever widening circles, with the ripples getting smaller and smaller as the pressure of the stone's impact is absorbed.

When you hit that middle C on the piano, something very similar happens in the air. The piano string starts to vibrate. As it vibrates in one direction, it compresses the air, just as an accordion player compresses the air inside the instrument by pushing the ends together. As the string vibrates in the other direction, it expands the air and creates a partial vacuum, as the accordion player does when he pulls the ends of the instrument apart. These alternations of compression and expansion are passed along through the air, growing weaker in volume as they go, until at last the energy from the string's vibration is used up and the waves disappear. The sound waves, then, are ripples of compression and expansion of the air. Regardless of how loud or soft they may be or whether they are high sounds or low sounds, they travel through the air at a standard rate of speed; the speed of sound is around 750 miles an hour, or 1100 feet per second.

Frequency = Pitch. Fortunately for our study of sound waves, it is possible to turn these unseen air ripples into pictures that tell us a great deal about them. This is done with a device called a cathode-ray oscilloscope, as shown in Fig-

DEFINITION:
OUND WAVES

PEED OF SOUND

CATHODE - RAY
OSCILLOSCOPE

6-6

Sound waves picked up by a micro-phone are converted into electric currents and fed into an *oscilloscope*, which has a screen similar to a tele-vision screen, where "pictures" of the waves can be studied.

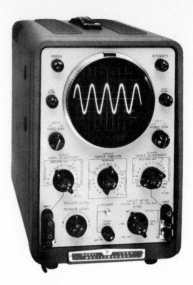

ure 6-6. The wavy lines that flicker across the screen of the oscilloscope are one of our most useful tools for exploring the varied nature of sound waves.

The kind of picture we see on the oscilloscope screen is shown in Fig-ure 6-7. Note how the characteristic called *frequency,* meaning the number of waves per second, determines the *tone* or *pitch* that we hear.

DEFINITION:

FREQUENCY

DEFINITION:

AMPLITUDE

Amplitude = Loudness. The drawings in Figure 6-8 illustrate the second important characteristic of sound waves, called *amplitude,* that is, the height of the waves, which determines the *loudness* that we hear. It has to be pointed out,

how sound varies in frequency

6-7

The tone of middle C would look like this on the oscilloscope screen. As the air is compressed the line rises; then the line drops back to the base line and continues downward as the air expands. A single cycle of the curve is shown in color on the graph. For middle C, 256 of these cycles flash across the oscilloscope screen every second; in other words the *frequency* of the sound wave for middle C is 256 cycles per second.

The C above middle C, sounded at exactly the same degree of loudness, would look like this. Here the waves flash across the screen exactly twice as fast, for the frequency of the C above middle C is 512 cycles per second. Thus the oscil-loscope screen demonstrates that the higher the frequency of the sound waves, the higher the pitch we hear. The height of the waves, however, remains the same.

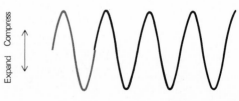

6-8

Here again is the oscilloscope picture of middle C, sounded as before in Figure 6–7. A single cycle is shown in color.

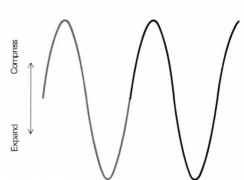

Here the same tone is sounded with double the force. The frequency of the wave remains the same, but the wave is now twice as high as before. The height of the waves is called their *amplitude,* and the oscilloscope screen demonstrates that it is the amplitude of the waves that determines how loud they sound to our ears.

however, that amplitude and loudness are not entirely synonymous. If tones of 100 cycles, 1000 cycles, and 10,000 cycles are sounded at exactly the same amplitude and therefore seem exactly the same in volume to the oscilloscope, to our ears the middle tone sounds much louder than the high tone, and the high tone sounds louder than the low tone. The absolute threshold of hearing follows the same pattern. We can hear small amplitudes at 1000 cycles that we could not hear at 10,000 cycles and can hear amplitudes at 10,000 cycles that we could not hear at 100 cycles.

These last facts raise an interesting question. If our sense of hearing is least sensitive of all to very low tones, why is such a low tone used for foghorns? The answer is that sound waves of low frequency travel much farther than waves of high frequency. High-frequency waves are absorbed much faster by the air through which they travel and by any objects that get in their way, while low-frequency waves travel on and on. The next time you hear a band playing in the distance—as when a parade is approaching or when you are driving toward a football stadium—notice that it is the tubas you hear rather than the flutes.

DEFINITION :

DECIBEL

A familiar measure of amplitude is the *decibel;* the decibel scale is shown in Figure 6–9. You will note, of course, that this is not an absolute scale; a clap of thunder at 120 decibels is far more than twice as loud as conversation at 60 decibels. But it is an ingenious scale (of the type mathematicians call logarithmic) that condenses the entire range of possible amplitudes of sound into meaningful numbers. Sound-sensitive devices that give readings expressed in decibels can be used to measure everything from the applause at television shows to the effectiveness of a sound-absorbent ceiling in reducing the noise level in a business office. An absolute scale of amplitude would have to use numbers going all the way up to 500,000, for the smallest amplitude we can hear is just about 1/500,000 as great as the largest amplitude.

6-9

The zero point on the decibel scale is set at the absolute threshold of hearing, and from there the readings go up to the neighborhood of 60 decibels for the sound of ordinary conversation, around 120 for a clap of thunder, and 150 for a jet airplane engine. (3, 4)

ING SOUNDS

NATURE OF SOUND

1. FREQUENCY = PITCH
2. AMPLITUDE = LOUDNESS
3. COMPLEXITY = TIMBRE

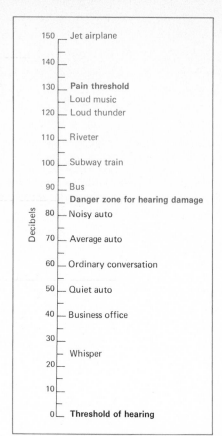

Decibels

150	Jet airplane
140	
130	**Pain threshold**
	Loud music
120	Loud thunder
110	Riveter
100	Subway train
90	Bus
	Danger zone for hearing damage
80	Noisy auto
70	Average auto
60	Ordinary conversation
50	Quiet auto
40	Business office
30	
20	Whisper
10	
0	**Threshold of hearing**

Prolonged exposure to sounds above about 85 decibels can cause hearing damage—a fact of considerable importance because the noise level in city streets often goes above that figure. Moreover, many people like to have the sound level very high when listening to modern music; in a small and crowded hall the decibel reading on electric guitars and amplified drums is often around 125. Tests of college freshmen who have listened to a great deal of rock music have shown that many of them can hear no better than the average person aged sixty-five (5). At extremely high levels, about 130 decibels or more, sounds reach the point where they actually cause pain.

Complexity = Timbre. In the previous diagrams of sound waves as they are seen on the oscilloscope screen, we have been showing pure tones. In fact, however, pure tones do not exist outside sound laboratories; the closest thing to a pure tone in real-life situations is the sound made by that very simple musical instrument, the flute.

The sound waves that actually reach our ears have a third characteristic, in addition to frequency and amplitude, that is called *complexity*. When you strike middle C on the piano, as has been mentioned, the string vibrates at a frequency of 256 cycles a second, creating its characteristic pitch. However, it also vibrates

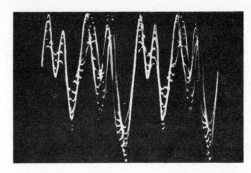

a complex sound wave

6-10

A trumpet note takes a much more complex form than the "pure" tones that were shown in Figures 6-7 and 6-8. This is the oscilloscope pattern of A above middle C as altered by the characteristic overtones of the trumpet.

DEFINITIONS:

OVERTONES

. TIMBRE

in other and more complicated ways. Each half of the string vibrates separately, at a rate of 512 cycles a second. Each third of the string vibrates, at a rate of 768 cycles a second. And each quarter of the string also vibrates, at a rate of 1024 cycles a second. These additional vibrations are called *overtones*. They have less amplitude than the fundamental tone, but they play an important role in changing the shape of the sound wave that comes from the piano.

The complexity of the sound wave (see Figure 6-10) determines what is called its *timbre*. Each musical instrument has its characteristic pattern of overtones, and the note of middle C struck on a piano therefore has a noticeably different timbre from the middle C of a violin or a clarinet. Timbre, as well as pitch, helps account for the ease with which we distinguish one voice from another.

2. locating sounds

You are walking across the campus and someone behind you, where you cannot see him, calls to you. You know immediately that he is toward your left or toward your right; you turn in that direction without even thinking. Or you are sitting in a room, not looking out the window. An automobile passes by and you know without thinking that it is moving from left to right. Something about the sound waves gives the receptors in the ears some important clues about the direction from which the sound is coming and the direction in which it is moving. What are the clues?

The answer has been provided by experiments with the pseudophone (see Figure 6-11), a set of earphones that capture the sound waves at the right ear

DEFINITION:

SEUDOPHONE

a device to fool the ear

6-11

The young woman wears a pseudophone, a laboratory device that carries the sounds that would ordinarily reach her right ear to her left ear instead and the sounds that would ordinarily reach her left ear to her right ear. As explained in the text, experiments with the pseudophone have revealed how we locate sounds.

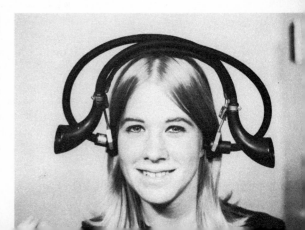

and transfer them over to the left ear and send the sound waves that would ordinarily reach the left ear to the right ear. When a person wears the pseudophone and keeps his eyes closed, the automobile that goes past from left to right sounds as if it were moving in the opposite direction, from right to left.

Obviously the stimulus that arrives at one ear is not the same as the stimulus that arrives at the other ear. Under ordinary circumstances, a sound wave from the left reaches the left ear a tiny fraction of a second before it reaches the right ear. It is in an earlier phase of the curve from compression to expansion of the air. It is also a tiny bit louder than after it has passed around the head to the right ear. And its overtones are slightly different. The clues to locating sounds thus are *timing, phase, amplitude,* and *timbre.*

LOCATING SOUNDS

1. TIMING

2. PHASE

3. AMPLITUDE

4. TIMBRE

3, the ear and its receptors

The structure of the ear is shown in Figure 6–12. Sound waves enter the outer ear and set up vibrations in the eardrum. These vibrations then pass through the middle ear, which is an air-filled cavity containing three small bones

HEARING PROCESS

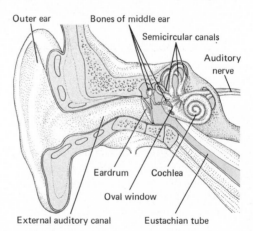

the structure of the ear

6-12 Sound waves reaching the outer ear pass through a short canal across the end of which the eardrum is stretched. Vibrations of the eardrum are then conducted and amplified by the three bones of the middle ear, the last of which connects to the *oval window* of the *cochlea* in the inner ear. The receptors for hearing lie in the cochlea. The *Eustachian tube* connects with the air passages of the mouth and nose and keeps the air pressure in the middle ear the same as the pressure outside. (When this tube is temporarily blocked, as it often is when we have a cold or when we go up or down in an elevator, we feel a sense of pressure against the eardrum.) The *semicircular canals* of the inner ear play no part in hearing but will be discussed later for their role in the sense of equilibrium. (6)

that conduct and amplify the vibrations, and finally to the inner ear. Here they reach the *cochlea,* a bony structure shaped like a snail's shell, which contains the receptors for hearing.

The cochlea is filled with fluid, and stretched across it, dividing it more or less in half, is a piece of tissue called the *basilar membrane.* Sound waves are transmitted to the *oval window* of the cochlea, where they set up motions of the fluid that bend the basilar membrane. Lying on the membrane is the *organ of Corti,* a collection of hair cells that are the receptors for hearing. The cells are bent as the membrane bends and are thus stimulated to fire.

4. how the hearing receptors work

When sound waves are transmitted to the cochlea through the oval window, the entire basilar membrane responds with complicated wavelike motions that move along its length and breadth (7). These motions sometimes reach their greatest intensity at one part of the basilar membrane and sometimes at another. Apparently the frequency of the sound waves determines which part of the membrane moves the most, and it seems quite possible that our sensation of pitch depends on which particular part of the membrane receives the most stimulation. This is called the *traveling wave theory* of hearing. There is some evidence that the sensation of pitch also depends, at least at times, on the number of receptors stimulated and on the combined frequency of the nervous impulses that they send to the brain (8).

TRAVELING WAVE THEORY

vision

A boat whistles in the distance, and we see the blast of steam before we hear the sound. We see the lightning flash before we hear the thunder. From these observations we realize that light travels much faster than sound.

Sound waves, as has been mentioned, are alternations of compression and expansion of the air; they travel at a speed of around 750 miles an hour. Light waves, on the other hand, are pulsations of electromagnetic energy, closely related to such other wavelike forms of energy as cosmic rays, X-rays, radio waves, and electricity. They do not create any motion of the air and indeed can travel through a total vacuum, as they do when light reaches us across the vast expanses of empty space from a star. If you could arrange to make two coins hit together inside a vacuum tube, you would hear no click, because sound waves cannot be formed in a vacuum. But the light waves from a filament inside a vacuum tube shine brightly. They travel at a speed of 186,000 miles a second, the fastest speed known and presumably the fastest possible. (If a light wave could be reflected around the world, it would get back to the starting point in less than one-seventh of a second.)

In the daytime, light waves intense enough to illuminate our entire landscape reach us from the burning fires and explosions of the sun. At night, they reach us by reflection from the moon and, at much lower intensities, from the more distant suns that we call stars. Light waves can be produced by burning a candle or by using electricity to heat a lightbulb's filament.

1. the physical nature of light

Although light waves are very different from sound waves, there is a close parallel in the way the two kinds of waves produce sensations. Sound waves, it will be remembered, vary only in frequency, amplitude, and complexity, yet variations in these three characteristics produce a wide range of pitch, loudness, and timbre. Light waves also have three variables. They vary in *wave length*, which is the distance between the peaks of the waves. (The shortest light waves are about 16/1,000,000 inch long; the longest are about twice that length.) They vary in *intensity*, which is the amount of energy they possess. And they vary in *complexity*—that is to say, the light that reaches our eyes may be composed of waves of only a few different lengths or it may be composed of many lengths. As in the case of sound, these three differences account for the range of sensations produced by light waves.

LIGHT WAVE VARIABLES

1. WAVE LENGTH (HUE)

2. INTENSITY (BRIGHTNESS)

3. COMPLEXITY (SATURATION)

Wave Length = Hue.   Just as the frequency of the sound wave determines its pitch, so does the wave length of the light wave determine its *hue*—the scientific name for the characteristic usually called color. The hues range from violet, for the shortest of light waves, to red, for the longest. They include what are ordinarily called "all the colors of the rainbow." But hue is the proper term for them because many of the sensations ordinarily described as colors depend on other factors than wave length, as will be noted a little later.

As is indicated in Plate I,* light that appears white to us is actually a mixture of the wave lengths of all the hues. When a white light such as a sunbeam is broken down into its components, as by the prism in Plate I, the wave lengths are separated and the result is a *spectrum* of all the wave lengths and corresponding hues from shortest to longest.

Intensity = Brightness.   The harder we strike a piano key, the more amplitude we produce in the sound wave and the louder the sound we hear. In vision, the strength of the light wave is called the intensity, and the sensation that the intensity produces is called *brightness*. A 100-watt electric lightbulb produces light waves of stronger intensity than does a 50-watt bulb and thus looks brighter. Or, much as a band sounds louder when it is close than when it is far away, the light from the sun looks much brighter than the light from other, more distant stars, even though some are much bigger.

Just as was noted for hearing, however, the intensity of light waves does not fully account for all the degrees of brightness we see. Our eyes are most

*The color plates can be found between pages 212 and 213 in this chapter.

sensitive to the green and yellow at the middle of the spectrum, and under good illumination these hues look brighter than violets or reds of equal intensity.

Complexity = Saturation.   The third way in which light waves vary is illustrated in Plate II. In the squares of Plate II the hue of red does not change. Nor does the brightness. But as more and more gray is added—thus mixing in wave lengths of all the other hues—the red that we see becomes what might be called "less red," or "duller," or "muddier."

This characteristic of the visual stimulus is called *saturation,* which can be defined as the degree to which one particular hue is "pure" or unmixed with other wave lengths. You will note that again there is a parallel of sorts with hearing. In hearing, the complexity of the sound wave determines timbre. In vision, the complexity of the mixture of light waves determines saturation.

2. mixing the hues

Every schoolchild who owns a paint set knows that if you have no green, you can produce it by combining blue and yellow, but every schoolchild is wrong. If you combine the wave length of blue with the wave length of yellow, you do not get green at all. Until fairly recently, as a matter of fact, nobody had ever combined any of the various hues. You cannot do this with paint, for the following reason.

As was demonstrated in Plate I, the white light from the sun, which illuminates our world by day, is a combination of all the wave lengths of the spectrum. So is the artificial light by which we see at night, though in an imperfect way. (Candlelight and electric light are both yellowish.) The reason that black paint looks black is that it absorbs nearly all the waves, of all lengths, and reflects almost no waves at all back to our eyes. Blue paint looks blue because it absorbs most of the wave lengths except those in and around the blue portion of the spectrum, including, since no paint is a pure blue, some of the green waves. Yellow paint absorbs most of the waves except those in and around the yellow part of the spectrum, including some of the green waves. When you add blue and yellow paint together, you get a mixture that absorbs all the wave lengths of the spectrum except the greenish ones that both the paints happen to reflect. But this is not *adding* light waves; it is more like *subtracting* them.

WAVE LENGTHS
VS.
PIGMENTS

It was not until the invention of some modern devices that the addition of one light wave to another became possible. One of these devices is the color filter, which permits only waves of a certain length to get through. With two slide projectors equipped with two different kinds of filters, hues of two wave lengths can be thrown on the same white screen and thus mixed, as shown in Plate III. Another device is the color wheel, on which papers of different hue can be rotated so fast that they are seen as a single image.

Starting at the top of Plate III, note what happens when the wave length of violet, taken from the shortest end of the spectrum, is mixed with the wave length of red, taken from the longest end of the spectrum. The result is a purple.

For some unknown reason, it looks like a hue in its own right, even though it can be produced only by a mixture of wave lengths.

Mixing blue and green gives a result that seems to have some of the characteristics of each. (The same is true for a mixture of green and yellow.)

When red and green are mixed, the result is yellow.

When blue-violet is mixed with yellow, the result is not the green that the schoolchild with his paint set would expect—but a hueless and neutral gray.

Let us now try to find a hue that we can combine with green to produce a gray. Search where we will among the wave lengths of the spectrum, we cannot find such a hue. The only way we can neutralize green into gray is shown by the final example in Plate III. It must be combined with the purple produced by combining violet and red.

These observations are summarized in Plate IV. From this circle, composed partly from nature's own spectrum of wave lengths and hues and partly from the man-made purples, we can predict what will happen when any two hues are mixed. Hues opposite each other on the circle combine into a neutral gray and are known as *complementary hues.* Any two hues not opposite each other will mix into the hue that is midway between them on the circle.

But the circular guide is just another of the discoveries that raise more questions than they answer. When we mix a violet wave length with a green wave length, we do not fool the prism, which can still separate the two wave lengths. But our eyes see the combination as a greenish-bluish hue that looks exactly the same as a certain wave length of light lying midway between the two hues we have mixed.

COMPLEMENTARY
HUES

3. the structure of the eye

The receptors for the sense of vision lie in a small patch of tissue at the back of each eyeball, called the *retina.* Each retina, if flattened out, would appear as an irregular circle with a diameter of a little less than an inch and a total area of only about three-fourths of a square inch—about the size of a quarter. Yet with these two very small pieces of sensory apparatus we can clearly see the much larger pages of a book such as this and indeed an entire room; from an airplane we can see thousands of square miles of the landscape.

RETINA

This would be impossible unless the eye, in addition to its receptors, had some sort of equipment for bending light waves and focusing them sharply on the retina, much as a fine camera takes a sharp photograph of a wide sweep of landscape by focusing the light waves on a small piece of film. The structure of the human eye, indeed, greatly resembles a camera. If you have ever taken photographs, particularly with one of the more complicated cameras that must be focused and set before each picture, you will feel right at home with the diagram of the eyeball in Figure 6-13, which should now be studied carefully.

The iris and pupil of the eye resemble the diaphragm at the front of a camera; when the pupil is opened to its maximum size, it admits about seventeen times as much light as when it is contracted to its smallest size. The lens of the eye

Plate I THE HUES OF THE SPECTRUM

A beam of white light passing through a prism is turned into a *spectrum*. The explanation is that sunlight is a mixture of all the wave lengths to which our eyes are sensitive; the prism, bending each wave length at a slightly different angle, separates the mixture into all the component wave lengths, each of which has its own color or, to use the more scientific term, *hue*. The violets are the shortest wave lengths to which our eyes are sensitive, the reds the longest.

HUES OF THE SPECTRUM

YELLOW-GREEN

YELLOW

YELLOW-RED

GREEN

RED

BLUE-GREEN

PURPLE

BLUE

VIOLET

BLUE-VIOLET

Plate II SATURATED VERSUS UNSATURATED COLOR

This series of colors shows what happens if we start with the purest possible red wave length and then gradually add more and more gray of equal brightness. The square at the extreme left is said to be completely saturated. The square at the extreme right is the least saturated red that can be distinguished from pure gray.

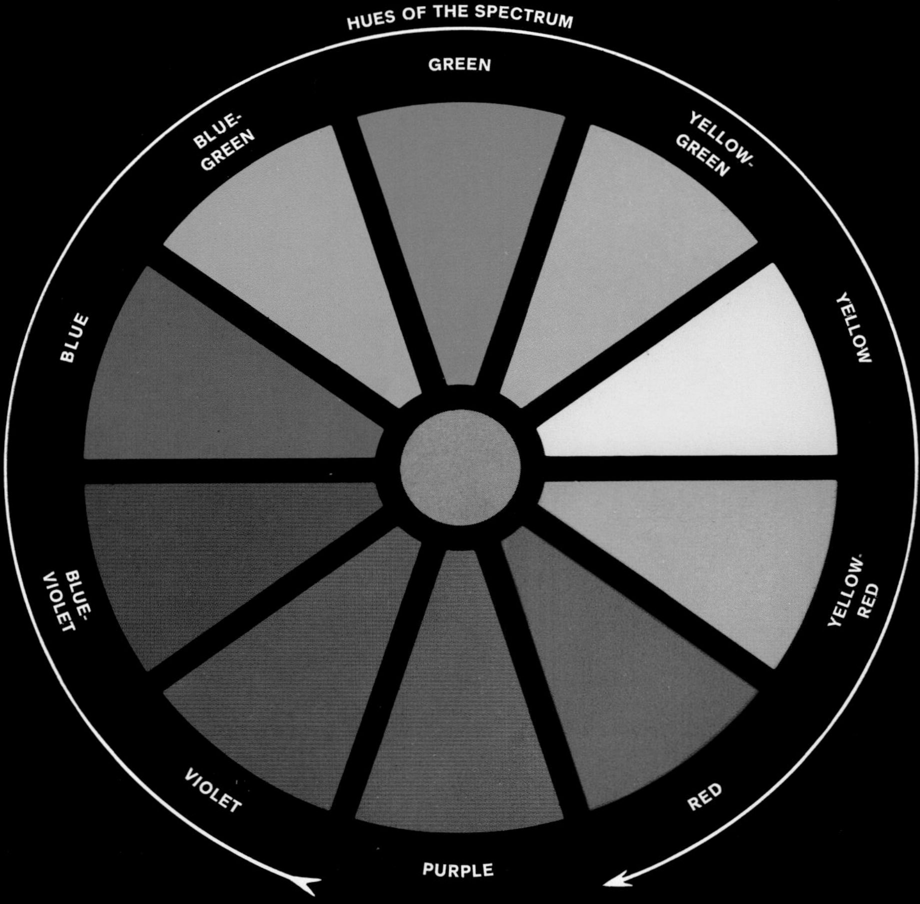

Plate III COLOR MIXTURE

When light waves are combined by projecting filtered light waves onto a screen, some of the results are these. One projector provides the hue at left, the other the hue at right. The mixture of the two hues is in the center. For an explanation, see Plate IV and the text.

Plate IV A CIRCULAR GUIDE TO THE HUES

The laws of color mixture can be summarized by bending the spectrum into an incomplete circle, as shown here, and filling in the gap with the purple that is also seen as a very distinct hue. (Purple is a combination of the wave lengths at the red end of the spectrum and the wave lengths at the violet end.) To find what hue a mixture of any two colors will produce, draw a line between them. If the line passes through the center of the circle, the result will be gray. If not, the result will be the hue midway between the two hues being mixed.

Plate V A TEST OF COLOR BLINDNESS

In the circle at left, people with normal color vision see the number 92; in the circle at right, they see a 23. Totally color-blind people see no number at all in either circle. These are two of the ingenious combinations of hues and brightnesses that make up the Dvorine Pseudo-Isochromatic series of color-blindness tests.

(Reproduced by permission of the author of the Dvorine Pseudo-Isochromatic Plates, published by the Scientific Publishing Co., Baltimore, Md.)

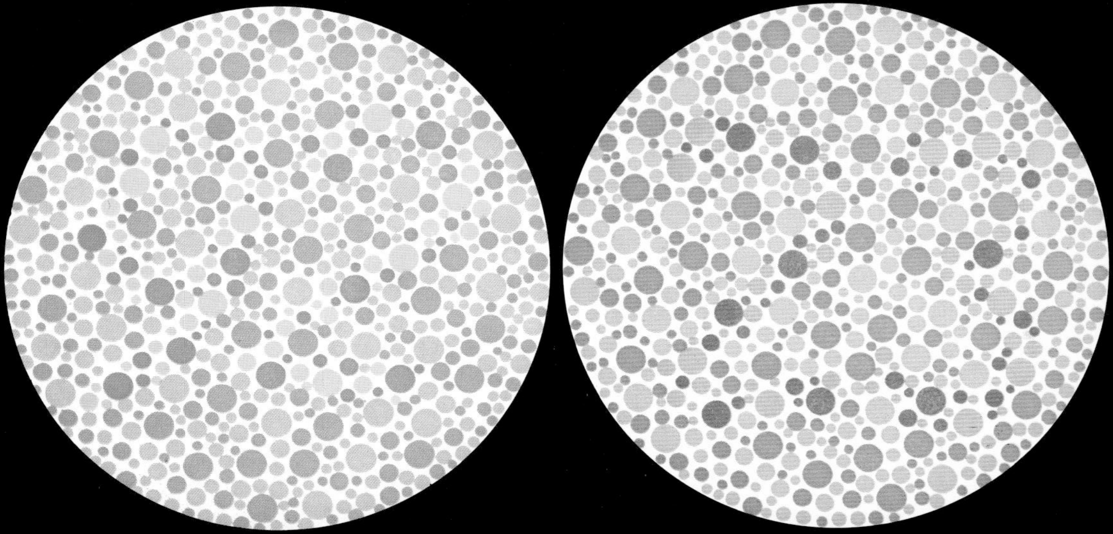

Plate VI THE VISUAL AFTERIMAGE

The principle of the afterimage produces a startling effect in this modern paint-ing. Look at the top rectangle for about half a minute, fixing your gaze on the white spot in the center. Then shift your eyes quickly to concentrate on the dark spot in the lower rectangle. (This painting, "Flags," is by Jasper Johns. Oil on canvas with raised canvas, 1965. Collection: the artist.)

serves the same purpose as the lens of a camera but in a way that would not be possible with even the most carefully designed piece of glass. The lens of a camera has to be moved forward and backward to focus on nearby or faraway objects. The lens of the eye remains stationary but changes shape. The ciliary muscles flatten it out to bring faraway objects into focus and squeeze it into a thicker shape to focus on nearby objects.

As we grow older, the lens of the eye starts to harden gradually; the process

PROCESS OF VISION

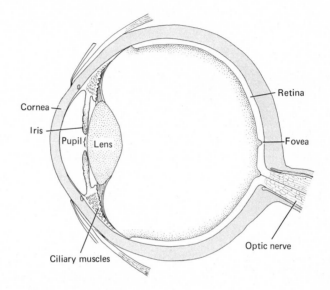

a cross section of the eye

6-13   Light waves first strike the *cornea,* a transparent bulge in the outer layer of the eyeball. The cornea serves as a sort of preliminary lens, gathering light waves from a much wider field of vision than would be possible if the eyeball merely had a perfectly flat window at the front. The waves then pass through the *pupil,* which is an opening in the *iris,* a circular arrangement of muscles that contract and expand to make the opening smaller in bright light and larger in dim light. (When you look at your eyes in a mirror, the pupil is seen as the dark, almost black circle at the center; the iris is the larger circle around it and contains the pigments that determine eye color.) Behind the pupil lies the transparent *lens,* the shape of which is controlled by the *ciliary muscles.* The lens focuses the light rays on the *retina,* which contains the light-sensitive receptors of the eye; the most sensitive part of the retina is the *fovea.* Messages from the receptors are transmitted to the brain by way of the *optic nerve,* which exits from the back of the eyeball, a little off center. Attached to the eyeball are muscles that enable us to look up, down, and sideways. The space inside the eyeball is filled with a transparent substance, as is the space between the cornea and the iris. (9)

6-14 Hold the book about a foot in front of you, close your right eye, and look at the face on the right. Now move the book slowly closer. When the image of the cat at the left falls on the blind spot of your left eye, it will disappear. To demonstrate the blind spot of the right eye, repeat with the left eye closed and your gaze concentrated on the cat at the left.

begins almost at birth and continues constantly throughout life. Therefore most people over the age of forty-five have to wear glasses for reading. By the mid-forties the lens has grown so hard that the ciliary muscles can no longer squeeze it into as large a bulge as is required for sharp focusing on a nearby object such as a book.

At the point where the optic nerve exits from the eyeball it creates a small gap in the retina; there are no receptors for vision at this point. The area is almost insensitive to light and is therefore known as the *blind spot*. We are never aware of this blind spot in ordinary life, but you can discover it by examining Figure 6-14.

BLIND SPOT

4. the receptors of the eye

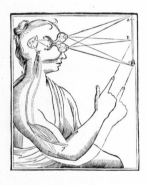

A seventeenth-century concept of vision

RODS
CONES

Any experienced photographer would tell you that the lens of an expensive camera is sharper than the lens of the human eye and that the camera diaphragm has a much wider range than the iris. But a comparison of the very best camera film to the retina is something else again. It takes two different kinds of camera film to take pictures in color and in black and white. The retina, however, does both jobs at once; it is sensitive both to colors and to black and white. Moreover, the retina is sensitive to very low intensities of light that would not register at all on photographic film and at the same time it can function under very high intensities of light that would completely burn out a photographic film. Most important of all, it responds continuously, without any winding from one frame to the next. At this instant you see these words on the page; if you raise your eyes slightly, you immediately see the wall of the room; if you shift your eyes again, you look out the window and see the landscape—all in one continuous and uninterrupted series of visual sensations. In photographic terms, the retina is a highly versatile "film" capable of constantly renewing itself.

Packed into the small area of each retina are about 125,000,000 receptors. Most of them are rather long and narrow in shape, a fact that has given them the name *rods*. About 5 percent of the receptors are somewhat thicker and are tapered; these are called *cones*. The rods function chiefly under conditions of low illumination and send information to the brain about movement and about whites, grays, and blacks but not about color. The cones function in bright light and provide information not only about movement and about the black-white dimension but also about color. The cones are most numerous toward the center of the retina; indeed there is one small but important area at the very center, called the *fovea*, that contains only cones, packed together more tightly than anywhere else.

The manner in which light waves stimulate the receptors of the retina was discovered many years ago when physiologists managed to extract a substance known as *visual purple* from the rods. Visual purple is highly sensitive to light, which bleaches it at a rate depending on the intensity and wave length. Thus light waves striking the retina produce chemical changes in the visual purple, and these chemical changes cause the rods to fire (10).

More recently, it has been found that the cones also contain substances somewhat akin to visual purple. There are three kinds of cones. All three show chemical changes, and therefore fire off their messages, in response to a broad range of wave lengths—but one is most sensitive to the wave lengths at the red end of the color spectrum, another to the middle wave lengths of green and yellow, and the third to the wave lengths at the blue-violet end (11, 12).

One of the remarkable things about the receptors for vision is that although the chemical changes in response to light constantly break down and destroy the visual purple of the rods and the similar substances in the three kinds of cones, the receptors last a lifetime. They do this by constantly manufacturing a new supply of their light-sensitive substances to replace the old and exhausted (13). Once a photographic film has been exposed to light, its chemical qualities are forever changed and it can never take a picture again. The retina keeps renewing itself and "takes pictures" as long as we can hold our eyes open.

5. from receptor to brain

When the receptors fire, they discharge their messages into a highly elaborate network of very short nerve fibers at the back of the retina, as shown in Figure 6-15. This network, which is extremely important in vision, acts as a sort of funnel between the retina, with its 125,000,000 rods and cones, and the ganglion cells of the optic nerve, which has only about 1,000,000 fibers over which messages are finally transmitted to the brain.

Ganglion cells serving the outer part of the retina, composed mostly of rods, get messages from as many as several thousand receptors. But ganglion cells serving the densely packed cones in the fovea get messages through the network from only a relatively few receptors. Moreover, each cone in the fovea sends its messages to several different ganglion cells, each of which compares the information coming from this and other cones and thus extracts different kinds of information from the different patterns of messages it receives. Thus our vision is sharpest—in scientific language, has the most *acuity*—at the fovea; therefore when we read or do anything else that requires a very sharp image, we keep the object in the center of our field of vision so that its light waves fall on the fovea. Because fewer receptors feed into each ganglion cell—and because each ganglion cell is capable of distinguishing among many possible patterns of messages—the ganglion

FOVEA

ISUAL PURPLE

ACUITY

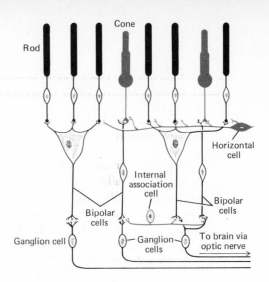

Rod
Cone
Horizontal cell
Internal association cell
Bipolar cells
Bipolar cells
Ganglion cell
Ganglion cells
To brain via optic nerve

the retina's rich network of nerves

6-15 This is a simplified diagram of the elaborate network of nerves through which messages from the rods and cones of the retina are transmitted to the optic nerve and thence to the brain. Messages from a number of individual receptors are picked up by tiny nerves known as *horizontal cells, bipolar cells,* and *internal association cells* and eventually are transmitted to the *ganglion cells.* A single ganglion cell may receive messages from only a few receptors, as do those serving the cones in the fovea, or from several thousand receptors, as do those serving the rods in the outer part of the retina. Moreover, messages from the cones are routed through the network to not just one but several ganglion cells. When you remember that there are about 125,000,000 rods and cones in the retina, constantly being fired by light waves and discharging their messages into this network, you can appreciate the very complicated nature of the patterns of nervous activity that go on at the back of the retina and the wide variety of messages that can then be transmitted to the brain through the fibers of the optic nerve. (14)

cells serving the fovea can send along rather precise information on the exact part of the retina that has been stimulated and by what kind of object.

On the other hand, the outer part of the retina is most sensitive to low intensities of light. This can be noted by finding a very dim star in the skies at night. If you look directly at the star, so that its light waves fall on the fovea, it disappears. But if you glance at it from the side, so that its waves fall on the outer part of the retina, it reappears. One or more ganglion cells, picking up messages from many thousands of receptors, has gathered in enough stimulation through the network to fire off its own message to the brain. The greater sensitivity to light of the outer part of the retina, however, is accompanied by a considerable loss of acuity. The message sent to the brain by the ganglion cell could have originated in the stimulation of any one of the many thousands of receptors it serves; therefore the exact spot at which the retina was stimulated and the exact nature of the stimulus cannot be specified (12).

6. color vision

Color vision depends not only on the fact that there are three kinds of cones, differentially sensitive to different wave lengths of light, but also on the processing of information from the receptors of the retina that goes on in the nerves that carry the cones' messages to the brain. Studies of animals whose color vision is similar to man's have shown that there are six different kinds of nerve cells that pass along messages to the brain from the color-sensitive fovea. Two of them detect whether the stimulus is white or black; they do this by comparing the total amount of light striking one part of the retina with the amount hitting adjacent parts. The other four detect colors by comparing the extent to which the different kinds of cones have been activated. One of the four, for example, detects a red stimulus by comparing the activity of cones sensitive to wave lengths at the red end of the spectrum to the activity of cones sensitive to the green-yellow wave lengths. The other three, by making different types of comparisons, signal green, yellow, and blue (15).

7. color blindness

Poor color vision can of course be caused by an inherited lack of one or another of the three types of cones. However, it may also be caused by deficiencies in the nerves that relay messages from the cones to their eventual destination in the brain; animals that have poor color vision have been found to possess, among the nerves responsible for relaying the messages, a low proportion of cells able to detect color relative to those that detect black and white. More men than women have defects of these kinds. Only about one woman in a thousand suffers from color blindness, but about seven men in a hundred have some form of it.

Total color blindness, in which the whole world is seen only in shades of gray, like a black-and-white photograph, is extremely rare. In the United States, with a population of around 200,000,000 there are probably no more than 5000 people in all who are totally color blind. The most common forms of partial color blindness involve difficulties in distinguishing between reds and greens.

For a good test of color blindness, turn to Plate V. Take a quick look at the two circles. Note the numbers you see in them, if any. Then read the caption.

If you pass the test, try showing it to some of your friends—especially male friends. You should soon come to one who fails; and if so, you will have an experience that is worth going to some trouble to obtain. It seems almost unbelievable that you can look at the circle and clearly see one number, while someone else clearly sees another number or is absolutely sure that there is no number at all.

8. visual adaptation

Everybody knows, from everyday experience, that the eyes can function under an extremely wide range of illumination. For example, you are walking down a street in the glare of the summer sun; then you enter a movie theater where there is hardly any light at all. At first the inside of the theater seems pitch-black, and you have trouble finding your way down the aisle and into an empty seat. But after a while, as your eyes get used to the dark, you find that you can clearly see the aisles, the seats, and the people around you—so well that if you happen to have sat down near a friend, you will easily recognize him.

Full adjustment to dark conditions takes about an hour, and at this point the eyes are about 100,000 times more sensitive to light than they were in the bright sunlight. Note that we do not see colors in a dimly lighted place such as a theater—nothing but shades of gray. This is because our vision then depends on the rods.

As was mentioned earlier, all sensory receptors adapt to a steady intensity of stimulation and eventually stop responding. Yet, no matter how hard we stare at something, it never disappears from view. While our eyes are open our field of vision never goes blank. Does this mean that the rods and cones are an exception to the rule and never stop responding to a stimulus?

No, the rods and cones are not an exception. They do adapt and stop firing. The reason we are not aware of the fact is that our eyes are constantly moving. As you read this book, for example, you gaze first at a word or two at the beginning of the line; then your eyes "jump" to the next word or words and so on until you have reached the end of the line, when they jump to the start of the next line. In a line of print the width of this one, your eyes make five to fifteen jumps and stops. When you look at a landscape or even a fairly simple photograph, your eyes jump from point to point, as shown in Figure 6–16, at the rate of three to four jumps a second. Besides these jumps, the eyes also make tiny but rapid movements, like very fast pendulum swings, at the rate of 30 to 100 per second.

These eye movements constantly shift the incoming light waves from one part of the retina to another, so that the stimulus for each rod and cone does not long remain the same. Moreover, each time you blink your eyelids you give the entire retina a brief rest.

With laboratory equipment using an arrangement of mirrors and lenses, experimenters have managed to keep an image falling on exactly the same group of rods and cones despite eye movements; the equipment is so designed that every time the eyeball moves the image moves with it. These experiments have demonstrated that the receptors of the eye adapt and stop firing rather quickly. A fine line viewed through such an apparatus, for example, seems to disappear within a few seconds (16). Another investigator has obtained the same results with a sort of "slide projector" so tiny that it can be mounted directly on the cornea, where it throws its picture on the same part of the retina no matter how much the subject moves his eyes (17).

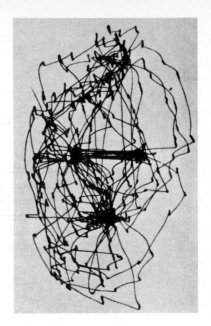

a pattern of eye movements

6-16 The pattern of lines was made by bouncing a light beam off the white of a man's eye as he looked at the photograph of the girl, thus recording his eye movements. Note how many movements took place and how they trace all the important elements of the photograph.

9. eye movements

The pattern of eye movements shown in Figure 6-16 demonstrates one very important way in which the human eye differs completely from a camera. You can point a camera at a landscape and within a fraction of a second make a photographic record of everything that is in that landscape; you can study it later and count how many horses and cows are in the picture, how many trees shade the farmhouse, how many windows the house has. If one thinks of the film in terms of human attributes, it "remembers" everything.

The next time somebody is driving you through the countryside, close your eyes as the automobile goes over the top of a hill, open them, take a quick look at the new landscape that spreads out in front of you, close them again—and discover for yourself how little your eyes have really told you about that landscape. Perhaps you know that you saw some horses and cows—but how many? Were they moving or grazing? How many houses did you see? What color were they? Did the road ahead of you curve to the right or to the left?

You will probably be surprised to realize how few such questions you can answer; you thought you saw the landscape, but you actually saw very little of it. This is because your eyes did not have time to make the kind of movements shown in Figure 6-16.

219

Our eyes never give us a single, unified, complete picture, as does a photographic film. As Figure 6-16 indicates, they receive an impression of one part of the scene in front of us, then another, and another, on and on until we have seen the whole as a succession of many different parts. We might compare the process to the creation of a mosaic. The receptors in the retina fire off a message about one small piece of the mosaic, then another. The visual centers of the brain, probably with the help of the network of nerves at the back of the retina, then put the pieces together into a unity. Study of the structure of the eyeball and of the rods and cones of the retina tells us many interesting and important things, but in the last analysis these represent only the mechanics of vision. The ultimate nature of the seeing process, like life itself, is still a mystery about which we can only speculate and marvel.

10 afterimages

There is one way in which our visual sense seems to differ from all the other senses. This is illustrated in Plate VI, and you should experiment with this figure, according to the instructions, before you continue to the next paragraph.

What Plate VI demonstrates is the phenomenon known as the *afterimage.* As you stare fixedly at the pattern of colors, you provide a prolonged stimulus to the retina. When the stimulus is then withdrawn (as you withdrew it by transferring your gaze to another part of the page), you see an afterimage that is in complementary colors to the original stimulus. If you follow the instructions carefully, the afterimage should be so vivid as to startle you—if not on the first try, at least after a little practice.

Presumably various parts of the retina are constantly sending afterimages to the brain, but ordinarily they are so faint and fleeting that we do not notice them. The experiment in Plate VI provides a stronger afterimage than usual, because you fix your gaze on the color pattern rather than making your usual constant eye movements. The experiment also enables you to see the afterimage more clearly, because you then transfer your gaze to an empty space rather than to a space already filled with other patterned stimuli. You can get the same effect anywhere by staring fixedly at a color or a pattern of colors and then quickly transferring your gaze to a blank surface such as a ceiling or a plain wall.

In actual fact, although this is difficult to show except under laboratory conditions, there are two afterimages. Immediately after the stimulus is withdrawn you see a *positive afterimage,* in the same color as before. But this quickly vanishes and is replaced by a *negative afterimage,* in which the complementary colors appear. The generally accepted explanation is based on the action of visual purple and the substances sensitive to hue that are believed to be present in the retina. The chemical changes produced in these substances by the light stimulus would presumably continue briefly even after the stimulus is removed. Then an opposite chemical change would occur as the substances "return to normal," so to speak. This change in the opposite direction could serve as the stimulus for sensations of the complementary color.

POSITIVE AFTER-
IMAGE

NEGATIVE AFTER-
IMAGE

G. bodily movement

Exploration of the "five senses" has now been completed, but, as was pointed out earlier, there are two other senses that are less prominent and less obvious but equally important in enabling us to function.

Perhaps the most vital of the senses is our sense of bodily movement—a sense that most people never even realize they possess. One way of demonstrating the existence and importance of this sense is as follows. Close your eyes and then point a finger straight up toward the ceiling, down toward the floor, off to your due left, and then to your due right; stand up; raise your left knee and touch it with your right hand.

What you have just done may not seem very remarkable; it is something that we take for granted. But think about it for a moment. How did you know where your arm was to begin with, and how did you know when you had moved it so that your finger was pointing up, down, or to the sides? How did you know where your left knee was and how to move your right hand to touch it?

None of your "five senses" helped you do this; they had no way of telling you about the position of your arms and legs and could only verify the fact, through the pressure receptors of the skin, that you had actually succeeded in finding and touching your knee. You could never have done what you did without the sense of bodily movement, which keeps us constantly informed of the position and movement of our muscles and bones.

The receptors for the sense of bodily movement are nerve endings found in three parts of the body. The first are in the muscles, and they are stimulated when the muscle stretches. The second are in the tendons that connect our muscles to our bones; they are stimulated when the muscle contracts, putting pressure on the tendon. The third, and apparently most important, are in the linings of the joints between our bones, and they are stimulated by movement of the joint.

Without these receptors we would not be able to walk without great difficulty; we would have to keep constant watch with our eyes to help guide the motions of our legs and feet. Even with the help of our eyes we could never perform the rapid and closely coordinated movements required to dance or to play baseball.

H. equilibrium

When we walk, we walk erect, not at an angle to the ground; when we lose our footing and start to fall, we catch our balance through reflex action, without even thinking about it. Standing in a closed elevator and unable to see any motion, we nonetheless know when we start to move and whether we are moving up or down; and we also know when we stop. If we sat blindfolded in a totally silent swivel chair, we would know immediately when someone began to rotate the chair.

All these facts depend on our sense of equilibrium, the receptors for which are in the inner ear. If you look back at Figure 6-12, you will note that the cochlea, containing the receptors for hearing, is only one part of the inner ear. The rest of the inner ear is made up of three *semicircular canals,* extending out from a *vestibule.* The canals are filled with liquid, and the liquid in one or more of the canals is set into motion any time we move in any direction whatever. The movement of the liquid stimulates hairlike receptors with which the canals are equipped. In the vestibule, which is also filled with liquid, the hairlike receptors are matted together and tiny pieces of stonelike crystal are embedded in the mattings. The little crystals put pressure on the receptor cells in the direction of the force of gravity and keep us oriented to an upright position even when we are not moving. Between them, the receptors of the canals and the receptors of the vestibule are constantly aware of the position of the head and any change in position, thus providing the messages needed to keep us in balance and oriented to the force of gravity. The messages operate by reflex action to produce the muscular movements required to preserve our equilibrium.

Perhaps the most dramatic evidence of how the sense of equilibrium operates is an old experiment involving a lobster—chosen because its equivalent of the human inner ear is readily accessible when the lobster sheds its shell. For the stones that are the lobster's equivalent of the crystals in the human vestibule the experimenters substituted iron filings. These worked just as well as the stones, and the lobster had no problem of equilibrium. But when a magnet was placed above the lobster, exerting a stronger upward force on the iron filings than the downward force of gravity, the lobster turned right over on its back.

SEMICIRCULAR CANALS

VESTIBULE

summary
1. The role of the senses in human behavior is to keep us informed about the kind of world we live in and especially about how the world around us is changing from moment to moment.

2. The two essentials of sensation are a *stimulus,* any form of energy capable of exciting the nervous system, and a *receptor,* a nerve ending capable of responding to a particular stimulus.

3. To cause a receptor to fire, a stimulus must be of an energy above the *absolute threshold* of the receptor, and a change in stimulus must be above the *difference threshold.* The thresholds are affected by *adaptation,* the tendency of all receptors to stop responding to a continued level of stimulation.

4. Taste receptors are sensitive to only four qualities: sweet, salty, sour, and bitter. Most of what we call "taste" depends on the sense of smell.

5. The receptors for smell appear, according to some recent investigators, to be sensitive to seven basic classes of molecules producing seven basic odors, which are then combined into all our various sensations of smell.

6. The skin has patterns of four kinds of spots—presumably related to nerve endings immediately beneath or near the spots—sensitive to pressure, pain,

warmth, and cold. A temperature over 110 degrees Fahrenheit stimulates both warmth and cold spots and produces the sensation of heat.

7. The stimulus for hearing is sound waves, which are alternations of compression and expansion of the air. Sound waves vary in *frequency, amplitude,* and *complexity.* The frequency determines the *pitch* we hear; the amplitude determines the *loudness* (although not entirely), and the complexity determines the *timbre.*

8. Our ability to tell whether a sound is coming from the left or right is based on the fact that the sound wave arrives at one ear before the other ear. When it arrives at the second ear, the wave is slightly different in *timing, phase, amplitude,* and *timbre.*

9. Sound waves strike the eardrum and are amplified and conducted by the bones of the middle ear to the *cochlea* of the inner ear, where they set up complicated wavelike motions of the *basilar membrane.* The receptors for hearing are the hairlike cells of the *organ of Corti,* lying on the basilar membrane; these cells are stimulated by motion of the membrane.

10. The stimulus for vision is light waves, a pulsating form of electromagnetic energy closely related to cosmic rays, X-rays, radio waves, and electricity. Light waves vary in *wave length, intensity,* and *complexity.* Wave length determines *hue;* intensity determines *brightness* (although not entirely); and the complexity of the mixture of waves determines *saturation.* White light is a mixture of all the wave lengths, as can be demonstrated by passing it through a prism and obtaining a *spectrum* of the hues.

11. Light waves enter the eyeball through the transparent *cornea* and the *pupil,* which is an opening in the *iris,* and then pass through a transparent *lens,* which is changed in shape by the *ciliary muscles* to focus the waves sharply on the *retina* at the back of the eyeball. The receptors for vision are nerve endings in the retina called *rods* and *cones.*

12. The rods function chiefly under conditions of low illumination and send information to the brain about movement and about whites, grays, and blacks but not about color. The rods contain *visual purple,* a substance that is bleached by light; presumably it is the chemical reaction of the visual purple to light that causes the rods to fire.

13. The cones function in bright light and provide information not only about movement and about the black-white dimension but also about color. There are three kinds of cones; one contains a chemical particularly sensitive to the wave lengths at the red end of the color spectrum, another to the middle wave lengths of green and yellow, and the third to the wave lengths at the blue-violet end.

14. Considerable processing of information from the receptors of the eye takes place in a complicated network of nerves behind the retina, especially by *ganglion cells* that compare the relative activity of the receptors that feed into them.

15. Color blindness is caused by an inherited lack of one or another of the three types of cones or by a deficiency of cells able to detect color among the nerves that relay the messages to the brain. Total color blindness is very

rare; partial color blindness, usually involving difficulties in distinguishing between red and green, is suffered by about 7 percent of men but much less frequently by women.

16. One outstanding quality of the human eye is the wide range of intensities to which it is sensitive. When the eye is completely adjusted to the dark, its absolute threshold declines to the point where it will respond to a stimulus with only 1/100,000 of the intensity required to cause a response under sunlight conditions. At low intensities only the rods function, and color vision is absent. The cones have a much higher absolute threshold.

17. Under ordinary circumstances, our eyes make a rapid and constant series of movements, focusing on one part of the field of vision, then jumping to another. These fragmentary "pictures" or pieces of mosaic are then put together, by the brain and presumably also by the elaborate network of connecting nerves at the back of the retina, into a unified pattern, so that we seem to be seeing the entire field of vision as a single whole.

18. In addition to the "five senses" we ordinarily think of—*taste, smell,* the *skin senses, hearing,* and *vision*—we have two other important senses. The sense of *bodily movement,* the receptors for which are nerve endings in the muscles, tendons, and joints, keeps us informed of the position of our muscles and bones and is essential for the coordination of such complex movements as walking. The sense of *equilibrium,* the receptors for which are hair cells in the inner ear, keeps us in balance and oriented to such forces as movement and gravity.

19. The stimuli and receptors of the human senses are as follows:

Sense	*Stimulus*	*Receptor*	*Sensation*
Taste	Molecules of soluble substances	Taste buds of tongue	Flavors (sweet, salty, sour, bitter)
Smell	Molecules of volatile substances	Nerve endings in olfactory epithelium	Odors (camphorlike, musky, flowery, pepperminty, and so on)
Skin senses	Mechanical energy, heat	Nerve endings in skin	Pressure, warmth, cold, pain
Hearing	Sound waves	Hair cells of organ of Corti	Sounds, tones
Vision	Light waves	Rods and cones of retina	Colors, movement, patterns
Bodily movement	Mechanical energy	Nerve endings in muscles, tendons, joints	Position and movement of muscles and bones
Equilibrium	Mechanical energy and gravity	Hair cells of semicircular canals and vestibule	Movement in space, pull of gravity

recommended reading

Békésy, G. v. *Experiments in hearing.* New York: McGraw-Hill, 1960.

Békésy, G. v. *Sensory inhibition.* Princeton, N.J.: Princeton University Press, 1967.

Geldard, F. A. *The human senses.* New York: Wiley, 1953.

Gibson, J. J. *The senses considered as perceptual systems.* Boston: Houghton Mifflin, 1966.

Gregory, R. L. *Eye and brain: the psychology of seeing.* New York: McGraw-Hill, 1966.

Helson, H. *Adaptation-level theory.* New York: Harper & Row, 1964.

Mueller, C. G. *Sensory psychology.* Englewood Cliffs, N.J.: Prentice-Hall, 1965.

Mueller, C. G., and Rudolph, M. *Light and vision.* New York: Time-Life Books, 1966.

Stevens, S. S., and Warshofsky, F. *Sound and hearing.* New York: Time-Life Books, 1965.

CHAPTER 7

PERCEPTION

beings move around the world confidently, secure in the belief
nd the nature of our environment. When we look out a window,
thinking that it is a rectangular pane of transparent glass and
e see a long stretch of grass, a roadway, and other houses down
now that the houses are three-dimensional and that behind their
We know which is farthest from us and which is closest. If there
in sight, it does not matter whether we see a motionless hood
a motionless rear window and rear bumper, or a silhouette
our field of vision. We know what we are looking at; if it is
w in what direction and approximately how fast. A sound comes
we know that it is an ambulance siren. Another sound comes
we know that it is a voice; the sounds form a natural pattern
ning without any effort on our part. We notice a smell and know
e is baking and that dinnertime is near.

e take for granted. Actually, it represents a quite remarkable
as can be realized if we think for a moment of how the world
d to us when we were babies.

can see and hear; he can smell and taste food; his skin is sensitive
, warmth, and cold; he receives sensations from his own body
uch states as hunger and thirst. In other words, he has all the
e senses; and his senses operate, if not nearly so efficiently as they
r, at least well enough to bring him many sensations from the
rom inside himself. The main difference between the baby's world
world is not so much that the baby's sensations lack clarity
ot yet learned to interpret the meaning of what he sees, hears,

aby's mother approaches, the image of her face that reaches his
r. But quite possibly he is not aware that this means she is moving;
erely seem to be expanding, like a balloon being inflated. When
away, she may seem to disappear and to be replaced by another
image, that of her back, which the baby has not as yet discovered
nection at all with her face. When he looks at his own hand and
it under a blanket, quite possibly the hand no longer seems to

has no idea, at first, that the palm of his hand also has a back;

227

he does not know that the bars of his crib have an opposite side or that beyond the walls of his room lie other rooms. The window must seem like a sort of painting drawn on the wall, for the baby can have no idea that beyond the window is a three-dimensional world full of trees and grass and other houses down the block. To him the world is a strange panorama in which objects appear and disappear, grow smaller and larger, and vanish entirely when he closes his eyes. He is unaware of any connection between the movement of his mother's lips and the sounds that simultaneously reach his ears; even when he himself cries, as a reflex response to hunger sensations, he does not recognize that he is the source of the sounds he then hears.

The baby grows up and becomes a mature human being who sees the world and interprets its sights, sounds, and other sensations much as all of us do, yet also in a way that is probably individual and unique. His adult impressions of the world around him are determined by the important psychological process called *perception.*

Perception is a rather difficult term to define; in making the attempt, we can best start with an example that most of us have experienced. We are riding along a highway. Ahead of us, at the side of the road, we see a dead dog. Then, as we draw closer, we find that we do not see a dead dog at all. It is a piece of rumpled cloth. At one moment there is no doubt in our minds that we are looking at a dog. The next instant we know that we are looking at a piece of cloth. The fact is that we did not see a dog. We did, however, *perceive* a dog. In perception, we scan the stimuli in our world much as an electronic computer in a bank might scan the face of a check, looking for the numbers that will identify it (1). We seek to identify and "make sense" out of the objects in the environment. The process is rapid and more or less automatic; we seem to leap to our conclusions. Sometimes our interpretations, when based on insufficient evidence as in the case of the nonexistent dog at the side of the road, are incorrect. Usually, however, they give us an accurate picture of what is going on around us—and thus help us take appropriate action.

Perception, then, is *the process through which we become aware of our environment by organizing and interpreting the evidence of our senses.* Our perceptions are usually immediate and made without any apparent effort or deliberate thought. We perceive the mythical dog, for example, without trying, in fact almost in spite of ourselves, for perception is often a process over which we have little or no conscious control.

Perception influences our entire impression of the world around us, including all the sights and sounds that the world presents to us. As one psychologist has said, "Perception is extracting information from stimulation" (2). Perception also influences our impressions of other people and their behavior. For example, at the end of a day you might think, "My professor sneered at me today." Did the professor really sneer, or did you merely perceive his facial expression that way? Or a friend might say, "My girlfriend was delighted with the present I bought for her birthday." Was she really delighted, or did he merely perceive her behavior that way?

DEFINITION:

PERCEPTION

perception versus sensation

As strange as it may seem at first thought, many of the things we seem to see and hear in the world are not really there, or at least not there in exactly the form we believe them to be. The "dog" at the side of the road is by no means unusual in human experience. Many of the illustrations in this chapter will show how easily the perception of an event can be in error. Identical objects seem to be of different size; stationary objects seem to be moving. Many of the ways other people apparently behave toward us—the affection or dislike that they seem to show or the criticism, anger, envy, disapproval, approval, warmth, or praise that they seem to express—are not realities but merely our own biased and incorrect perceptions.

Our senses of vision, hearing, touch, smell, and taste are constantly being bombarded by many kinds of stimuli from the outside world—by light waves, sound waves, the mechanical energy of pressure, and the chemical energy of the things we smell and taste. Out of these stimuli we organize our impressions of an endlessly varied yet stable and consistent world of space and time and three dimensions. To realize how perception modifies the evidence of the senses, you need only glance at a tree. Look first to the left of the tree, then move your gaze slowly to the right. As you do this, the image of the tree that reaches your eyes definitely moves; the stimuli coming from the tree fall first on one part of your eyes, then cross over to another part. As far as the evidence reaching your sense of vision is concerned, that tree has moved just as surely as if it were an automobile passing across your field of vision as you held your eyes stationary. But the tree does not seem to move. It stays in place. Your perceptual organization of the world says that a tree is a stationary and motionless object, and this is the way you perceive it. This is something that you have learned, as you can tell if you look at the tree again through a pair of binoculars. Since you have never had the opportunity or necessity to build up a perceptual organization of the world as seen through binoculars, the images seen through the lenses catch you by surprise. As you swing the binoculars from left to right, the tree seems to move.

real versus perceived movement

Motion pictures do not really move; they are simply a series of still pictures like snapshots, flashed on the screen at the rate of about twenty per second. When we think we see an automobile crossing a movie screen, we actually see it for about one-twentieth of a second at one spot on the screen, then for one-twentieth of a second a little farther along, and so on. We ourselves "fill in" the gaps and seem to see a continuous movement. Our eyes are the victims—or perhaps one should say the beneficiaries—of the phenomenon called *stroboscopic motion,* meaning apparent motion produced by a rapid succession of images that

DEFINITION:
STROBOSCOPIC
MOTION

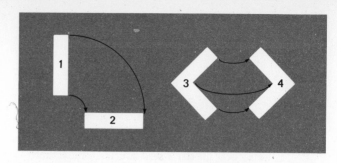

7-1

When a light is flashed behind opening 1 in a screen and an instant later behind opening 2, the bar of light seems to move as shown by the arrows; we perceive light moving across the screen between the two openings even though no light is actually there. When a light at opening 3 is quickly followed by a light at opening 4, the light seems to flip over and move in three dimensions, as if the page of a book were being turned. These are two examples of the apparent motion called the *phi phenomenon*.

DEFINITION:

PHI PHENOMENON

are actually stationary. The simplest form of stroboscopic motion, called the *phi phenomenon*, is illustrated in Figure 7-1. Another example is shown in Figure 7-2; the flashing of four stationary lights in quick succession apparently results in a moving circle.

A different kind of apparent movement takes place when a light, seen at some distance in a dark room, is made brighter, then dimmed to its original brightness. As it gets brighter, it seems to grow larger and to move closer. As it dims, it seems to grow smaller and to move away. This apparent movement is called the *gamma phenomenon*. It can sometimes be observed on the roads at night, if you come across a light that is blinking on and off to warn of a barricade. As the light goes off and its brightness drops to zero, it seems to move away. As it flashes on again, it seems to approach.

DEFINITION:

GAMMA
PHENOMENON

7-2

Lights 1, 2, 3, and 4, mounted on a stand, are flashed on in rapid succession. A person watching them in a dark room seems to see a band of light traveling in a circle.

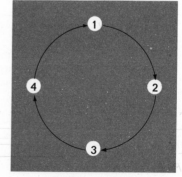

2. the autokinetic illusion

Ask a person to enter a dark room. Then turn on a pinpoint of light somewhere in the room, instruct him to stare at the light as steadily as he can, and ask him if he sees any movement. Although the light is in fact motionless, he will soon perceive it as making all kinds of movements—large and small, up, down, and sideways. If he is a suggestible person, and you tell him that the light is going to trace a word, he may actually perceive the motions of handwriting. This phenomenon is called the *autokinetic illusion,* meaning the illusion of self-generated movement that a stationary object sometimes creates.

Other kinds of autokinetic illusions have been produced by modern artists who are practitioners of what is often called "op (optical) art." Two examples are shown in Figures 7–3 and 7–4. The illusory motion in such paintings is obvious even in the small reproductions shown here and is quite startling when they are seen in full size. The explanation is not fully understood. You will probably note, however, that though the effect is striking when you look with both eyes, it is reduced and perhaps even eliminated when you look with one eye only.

DEFINITION:
AUTOKINETIC
ILLUSION

an artist's illusion of motion

7-3   Note the illusory movement at the center of the circles. This modern art work, by Wolfgang Ludwig, is titled "Cinematic Painting."

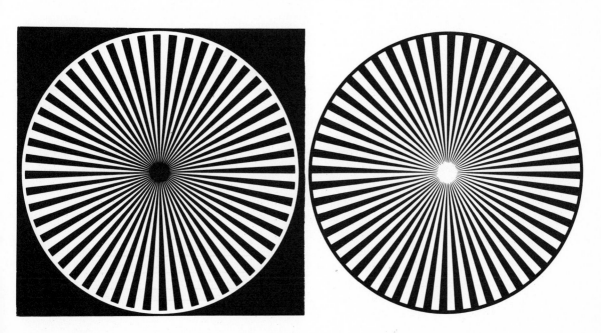

7-4

The illusory movement in this modern painting takes the form of strange pulsations and flickers. This is "Current," by Bridget Riley.

3. other sensory illusions

If you ever had to sit toward the very side of a movie theater, down front close to the screen, you no doubt noticed that the men and women on the screen seemed distorted—very tall and thin, like figures seen in an amusement park mirror. This is indeed the pattern of visual stimuli reaching your eyes at that unusual angle. After a time, however, the distortion probably disappeared; the people on the screen began to look normal again, as if you were sitting in a better seat. The visual stimuli had not changed: what you saw halfway through the picture was distorted just as at the beginning. But somehow your perception of the stimuli had changed. You had made allowance for the distortion and now saw the people on the screen as having the normal shape that you know people to have. Much the same thing happens when you watch television. A television picture ordinarily contains considerable distortion; the lines forming the edges of buildings and doors are not quite straight, and the faces are somewhat lopsided. You perceive the picture, however, as perfectly symmetrical.

In perception we not only seem to see, hear, and feel what is not there or something different from what is actually there but also sometimes add up our sensations in rather strange and unpredictable ways. As is demonstrated by the experiment illustrated in Figure 7-5, in perception two plus two does not always equal four!

7-5

One light is attached to the rim of a wheel, a second light to the hub. With the rim light on (A), the wheel is rolled along a table in a room that is otherwise totally dark. A person looking at the light perceives it as moving in the pattern shown by the dotted line, which is in truth the path followed by the light. Now the rim light is turned off and the hub light turned on (B). When the wheel moves, the light is seen as moving in a straight line. Finally, both lights are turned on, and the wheel is rolled along the table again. Theoretically, the observer should see a combination of the two sensations (C). Actually, he perceives what is shown in the bottom drawing: one light rotating around another light that moves in a straight line (D). This perception can hardly be called an illusion, because it represents what is actually happening, but it certainly is not the sum of the eyes' sensations. (3)

A. Rim light

B. Hub light

C. Theoretical combination

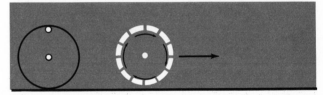

D. Actual perception

PERCEPTION:

SELECTION

ORGANIZATION

There is by no means a perfect correspondence between the evidence of the world that reaches our senses and our perception of the world. Perception is an active process in which we greatly modify the evidence of our senses and manipulate it in various ways. In perception, we select which sensory stimuli to consider and then organize those selected stimuli into our own patterns of meaning. These two processes, *selection* and *organization,* are the key factors in perception.

selection as an element of perception

During every waking moment our senses are bombarded with a barrage of miscellaneous stimuli. At this instant, for example, your eyes are receiving stimuli not only from this page of the book but also from many other objects that are within your field of vision—the light by which you are reading, the walls of the room, many objects of furniture, perhaps the outdoors as seen through a window. To

233

your ears come many sounds—the crackle of a page as you turn it, someone talking, an automobile going past, perhaps a radio playing softly in the distance. The smell of food cooking may be reaching your nostrils, and on your tongue may linger the taste of a salted peanut. Your skin senses feel many things—the pressure of clothing, the warmth of a sweater, the coolness of a draft blowing across the back of your neck.

You cannot pay attention to all these stimuli at once. You have to select some to which you will give your attention and thrust the rest into a sort of neutral gray background of which you are only dimly aware or perhaps not aware at all. As long as you attend to the words on the page you do not perceive all the other visual stimuli that strike your eyes. You do not perceive the voice talking, the automobile going by, or the radio playing unless you shift your attention. You are not aware of smells or of the pressure of your clothing unless you deliberately choose to pay attention to them.

Driving an automobile often furnishes striking examples of the selective nature of perception. As you drive along a highway where the traffic is light, you are listening to a football game on the radio. It is an interesting game and you are paying close attention, following every word and every play. Then suddenly an intersection looms ahead. Other cars are moving into the intersection; the lights are changing; you have to slow down, veer into a different lane, watch out for a car that has moved slowly into your path. When the traffic crisis is over, you start listening to the game again and find to your surprise that the score has changed. While your attention was directed elsewhere, a touchdown was scored without your ever knowing it. The radio was on just as loud as before, but you did not seem to hear it.

1. stimulus characteristics and selection

Some of the factors that determine whether we will select one particular stimulus, out of all the many around us, appear to be tendencies, either inborn or learned very early in life, to be attracted to certain stimulus characteristics. Among them are the following.

Change. This is the most compelling stimulus characteristic of all. As was explained in Chapter 6, our sense organs adapt rather rapidly to any steady and continued level of stimulation and quit responding. They are alert, however, to a change in stimulus. For example, when a radio is playing softly in the next room, we soon adapt to the sound and no longer hear it, but we notice at once if the sound stops. We are instantly aware of the change when a light dims because a filament has burned out or when it becomes brighter because of a sudden surge of electricity.

INTENSITY
AND
QUALITY

Besides being attracted to a change in the intensity of a stimulus, we are attracted to any change in its quality. For example, we are in a restaurant where a number of people are talking at once, all around us. After a while we hear only the conversation at our table; the rest is just background noise to which we have adapted and stopped responding. But now a baby cries in the room. The cry does not make the background noise any louder or softer than before, but we are immediately aware of it.

One attention-compelling form of change is *movement*. Even very young babies try their best to follow with their eyes any kind of moving object. If we adults look at a pasture full of horses, those that are running about attract our attention more than those that are quietly grazing. An advertising sign that uses stroboscopic motion is a better attention-getter than a sign whose message remains stationary.

Another important form of change is *contrast*—that is, a sharp difference between two stimuli. If a black triangle is placed in the field of vision of a baby only two days old and a photographic record is kept of his eye movements, it turns out that he spends most of his time focusing on a point or apex of the triangle—the spot where there is the sharpest contrast between the black of the triangle and the light background (4). Indeed the baby's early interest in the human face, especially the face of his mother, is dictated largely by the strong effect of contrast as an attention-getter. What he notices particularly in the human face is the high degree of contrast between a light face and dark eyes or between a dark face and the whites of the eyes and the teeth.

Some other examples of the role of contrast are these. One mountain among many does not necessarily attract our attention; the same mountain on an otherwise level plain would attract us at once. A six-foot man stands out in a room full of smaller men because he is so tall and at a meeting of basketball players because he is so short. A sports jacket with black and white checks is far more conspicuous than a jacket with checks in two shades of blue.

Even *repetition* can serve as change and thus attract attention. For example, suppose that you are in a football stadium, which in itself constitutes a sort of sea of change—a football game unfolding play by play on the field, the loudspeaker following the progress of the game, the crowd moving and shouting in reaction. Now a friend of yours is paged over the loudspeaker. You may not notice his name the first time or two—but, if it is repeated often enough, you eventually will.

Size.　Another factor in attracting attention is *size;* in general, a large object is more likely to be noticed than a small object. A mountain that looms on the horizon is a more compelling stimulus than a hill. When we look at the front page of a newspaper, we are attracted to the biggest headlines first.

Intensity.　All other things being equal, it is the brightest or loudest stimulus that is likely to attract our attention. If we are driving at night through a downtown street where all the advertising signs are by some coincidence of equal size, the brightest of them seems the most compelling. The blasting noise of a sound truck passing by is likely to draw our attention away from the softer sounds of conversation or of a radio. Similarly, we are more likely to pay attention to a sharp poke in the shoulder than to a gentle tug at the elbow.

STIMULUS
SELECTION

CHANGE
  MOVEMENT
  CONTRAST
  REPETITION
. SIZE
. INTENSITY

All these factors are important of their own accord; there is something about them that is basically appealing to the attention of the human organism (and in many cases apparently to lower animals as well). We naturally and automatically select stimuli that display these characteristics. These rules of perception either are learned very early or are somehow built into the organism, like the reflexes.

2. the perceiver and selection

There are other important factors influencing selection that are not so automatic and that have little to do with the characteristics of the stimulus itself. To a considerable extent, what is selected for attention depends on which individual is doing the perceiving and on what he has learned in the past and what his physical condition and emotional state are at the moment.

It is a well-known fact, which you doubtless have observed yourself, that people who go through the same situation often perceive different things. A family goes out for an automobile ride. The husband, who is thinking about trading in his automobile, concentrates his attention on the new cars on the highway. The wife is hardly aware of the other cars but keenly aware of all the details of a new shopping center. A son who wants a bicycle perceives the afternoon as a succession of children riding various types of bicycles.

Two sisters, living at college, go home for a weekend visit. After an evening of talking with their mother, one sister has noticed that the mother smiled on several occasions, which she takes to mean that the mother is in a happy mood. The other sister has noticed several frowns, which she takes to mean that something is troubling the mother. Thus does perceptual selection depend on the perceiver.

c. organization as an element of perception

The "dog" at the side of the road mentioned earlier in the chapter is eloquent proof of how, in the process of perception, we organize the evidence of our senses into patterns. We do not perceive the world as the chaotic and miscellaneous collection of stimuli that reaches our senses. On the contrary, the perceptual process organizes these stimuli into meaningful objects. We perceive not mere patches of light but houses, people, trees, and roadways. (And sometimes, because an error has been made in organizing the pattern, we perceive a nonexistent dog lying at the side of the road.) We hear not miscellaneous sound waves but voices, musical tunes, and doorbells.

GOAL OF
PERCEPTION

Indeed the whole goal of perception is to make sense of what we see, hear, touch, taste, and smell. In a way it is a process of finding meaningful relationships among the events in our environment—relationships that are partly dictated by the physical attributes of objects in the environment and partly manufactured by our mental activity. Note, for example, the picture in Figure 7-6. The sharp contrast between the roof and the sky—or between the trees and the rock—forces

perception of hidden figures

7-6   The drawing contains a number of hidden objects that you are not likely to see at first glance. After you look long enough, however, you will perceive the objects so clearly that they will almost seem to leap out at you.

us to see these objects as separate; in this case our perceptual process is automatic and unlearned. However, there is no pronounced physical separation between the horse and the rider; it is our knowledge of horses and men that makes us perceive them as separate objects. The building and the water wheel *are* separated physically, yet we perceive them as a unit because we know that water wheels are attached to buildings.

It should be added that in looking at such a picture we usually select a point of focus or reference, without realizing it, and organize the other information around this focal point. Most people would describe this picture as "A man on a horse passing a house," indicating that they have chosen the rider and horse as their point of reference, probably because a human being is a more compelling stimulus than an inanimate object. It would be very unusual for a viewer to describe it as "A house and some trees with a rider approaching."

Note also that on more careful examination the picture turns out to contain some hidden objects, such as a large cat in the upper left corner. These hidden objects may go unnoticed at first, but once you have become aware that some of the visual stimuli are organized in this manner, it is almost impossible *not* to see them.

For a further demonstration of the part organization plays in perception, you can try an old experiment that requires no more equipment than a few headlines cut from a newspaper. All must be of the same size, and you must not have seen any of them before. Have a friend determine the farthest distance at

237

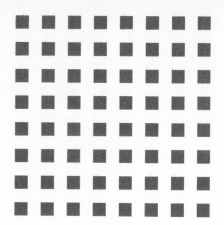

As you look at this collection of colored squares of uniform size and spacing, what do you see? Look at it closely for a time, letting your eyes shift from one part of it to another if you are so inclined, and compare your perceptions with those described in the text.

which you can read the type by testing you with a new headline each time he moves back. Once he has reached a spot just beyond your range of vision, so that you cannot make out the words, have him read the headline out loud and then show it to you again. After you have heard the words, you will find you can read them so easily that you will wonder why you ever had any trouble with them. Here knowledge of the stimulus received through the sense of hearing has helped you organize the visual stimulus into a pattern, and your perception, at first a blur, is now sharp and meaningful.

WUNDT: STUDIED ORGANIZATION OF PERCEPTION

Study of the organization of perceptions began with Wilhelm Wundt. In his experiments with the sensations aroused by the sound of a metronome, Wundt noted that the clicks were always perceived in some kind of pattern, even though each of them was of exactly the same loudness and presented after exactly the same time interval. One person might perceive them in march time: *click*-click, *click*-click, *click*-click. Another might perceive them in waltz time: *click*-click-click, *click*-click-click, *click*-click-click. Or the sounds might be perceived in more complicated patterns such as CLICK-click-*click*-click, CLICK-click-*click*-click. At any rate, some kind of pattern was always perceived in sounds that of themselves had no pattern.

An early experimental tool in the study of visual organization was the checkerboard shown in Figure 7-7. Here, much as in the case of the metronome, all the colored squares are of equal size and are equidistant from one another. There is no inherent pattern in the drawing. As we look at it, however, we tend to perceive various kinds of patterns, which shift as we continue to stare at it and move our eyes from one point to another. We may perceive horizontal lines, vertical lines, or diagonals. Or we may perceive various patterns in which the individual squares seem to be arranged in pairs or in groups shaped like rectangles or squares.

factors in organization

In one way or another, then, we organize our sensory stimuli, often imposing a pattern where in fact none exists. Like the way we select, the way we organize is partly a matter of inborn tendencies, partly a matter of learning, though it is difficult to say where one leaves off and the other begins.

Figure and Ground.   One of the ways we organize our sensory stimuli is demonstrated by what you perceive as you read this paragraph. In terms of light waves it is composed of many irregularly shaped splotches of white and of black. But you do not perceive a mere jumble of white and black. You perceive letters and words of black, against a background of white. You organize the stimuli into figures that are seen against a ground.

This tendency to organize visual stimuli into *figure and ground* is one of the basic rules in perception. A picture on the wall is perceived as a figure against a ground. So is a chair, or a person, or the moon seen in the sky. The figure hangs together; it has shape; it is an object. The ground is primarily a neutral and formless setting for the figure. What separates the two and sets the figure off from the ground is a dividing line called a *contour*.

One interesting example of how we organize visual stimuli into figure and ground is shown in Figure 7-8, where the contours can be interpreted in two different ways. In the drawing at the right you can perceive a white figure against a dark ground, the goblet, or a dark figure against a white ground, the faces. But you cannot perceive both at once. When you perceive the goblet, the faces recede into a formless background. When you perceive the faces, the goblet fades. In the drawing at the bottom of the page the stimuli are meaningless until you organize them into figure and ground; then you clearly see *TIE*.

CONTOUR

the figure-ground phenomenon

7-8

Most people first perceive the drawing at right as a white goblet against a dark background. It can also be perceived, however, as two dark faces in profile against a white sheet. The drawing below is usually perceived as a series of rather strange black figures against a white ground. If you look at it long enough, however, the figure and ground shift into something quite different.

 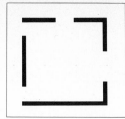 

7 - 9   Though the figures are incomplete in one way or another, we perceive them at once for what they are. (Drawing of cat, 5)

Closure. To perceive a figure, we do not need a complete and uninterrupted contour. If part of the contour is missing, our perceptual process fills it in. Indeed we tend to fill in any of the gaps that might interfere with our perceiving an object. This perceptual process, called *closure,* is illustrated in Figure 7-9. An interesting example of the effect of closure in combination with our tendency to perceive contours separating figure and ground is shown in Figure 7-10.

Continuity. Closely related to closure is *continuity,* which is illustrated in Figure 7-11. We tend to perceive continuous lines and patterns, and in any complex visual field we tend to perceive the organization that hangs together with the greatest continuity. The two lines shown at the left of Figure 7-11 have their own kind of continuity, but when they are put together a more compelling kind of continuity makes us perceive them quite differently.

Every beginning photographer has had the embarrassing experience of taking what he thought was a fine snapshot of a friend, only to discover, when the film was developed, that a tree could be seen growing out of the friend's head. At the time the picture was taken the photographer was completely unaware of the tree. This is partly the effect of figure and ground, for a photographer perceiving his friend as figure tends to ignore the rest of the visual field as merely a neutral ground. But it is also partly the result of the continuity factor. When we look at a person's head, we perceive a continuous curved line and are not aware that—seen another way—the curved line merges into the spreading foliage of a tree.

7-10

Between the two semicircular patterns we perceive a white stripe. It seems to have contours—straight lines that separate it from the two patterns—though in fact no such contours exist. The drawing is another early contribution to the study of perception made by Friedrich Schumann, the inventor of the checkerboard that was shown in Figure 7-7.

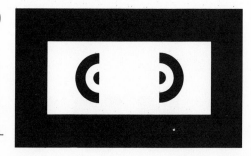

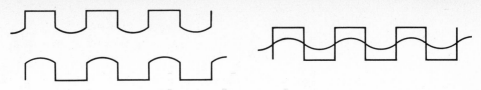

7-11 At the left we clearly perceive two continuous lines that are combinations of straight and curved segments. When the two lines are put together as at the right, however, we find it difficult to perceive the original pattern. Instead we perceive a continuous wavy line running through another continuous line of straight horizontal and vertical segments.

Proximity. If Wundt had used not a metronome giving out a steady series of clicks but a device that varied the intervals between the clicks, his results would have been somewhat different. When we hear click-click . . . click-click . . . click-click (with the dots indicating a pause), we organize the sounds into pairs. When we hear click-click-click . . . click-click-click, we perceive patterns of threes. Indeed, several quite different sounds presented this way, such as click-buzz-ring . . . click-buzz-ring . . . click-buzz-ring, would still be perceived in groups of three.

Such is the effect of *proximity;* we tend to make patterns of stimuli that are close together. This is true not only of sounds presented close together in time but also of visual stimuli that are close together in space, as can be seen in Figure 7–12.

the effect of proximity

7-12

Checkerboard A is a repetition of Figure 7–7. Note what happens to our perception of it when some of the squares are moved closer together as in B, C, and D.

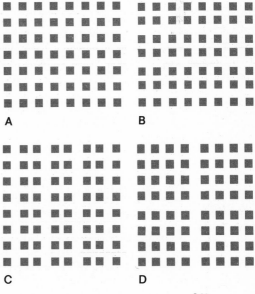

A

B

C

D

7-13

Here the checkerboard squares are equidistant from one another, as they were in Figure 7-7, but some have been changed to white squares or white circles. The similar stimuli hang together, and we perceive lines and patterns dictated by the similarity.

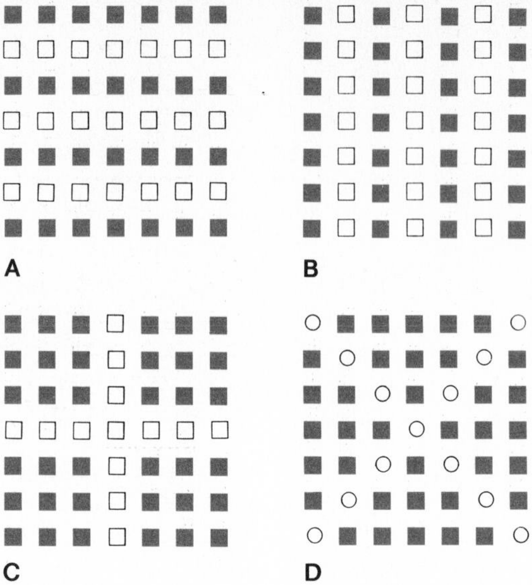

A

B

C

D

Similarity. Much in the same way that we make patterns of stimuli that have proximity, we make patterns of those that have *similarity*. This is demonstrated by the checkerboard variation in Figure 7-13. Except that some of the colored squares have been changed to white squares or white circles, the checkerboard is the same as in Figure 7-7. Theoretically it is still possible to perceive many kinds of patterns. But in fact it is very difficult to perceive anything except the lines and groupings dictated by similarity. The white cross in Figure 7-13C, for example, fairly leaps from the page at us.

Common Movement. Let us try to imagine ourselves in a clearing in an Indian jungle, looking toward a dense growth of trees and foliage. Somewhere in our field of vision is a tiger, poised motionless. Try as we will, we cannot see it. Its stripes blend in so perfectly with the jungle pattern that it is totally camouflaged. Then it moves. Immediately the stimuli become a pattern of their own. The tiger is now an object, and we perceive it clearly. This is the result of the perceptual factor called *common movement*—the fact that when stimuli move together, we tend to organize them into a pattern of their own.

2. perceptual constancy

Several other factors that play a large part in determining how we organize the evidence of our senses can be grouped together under the term *perceptual constancy*—the fact that we tend to perceive a stable and consistent world even though the stimuli that reach our senses are inconsistent and potentially confusing.

Consider, for example, a simple dinner plate. Unless we deliberately pick up the plate and hold it in a vertical position in front of our eyes, we almost

242

never see it as a circle. <u>Ordinarily the image of the plate reaches our eyes at an angle; the image is not a circle but an ellipse. Yet we perceive it, whatever the circumstances, as a round plate.</u>

We may see the Empire State Building from the sidewalk right in front of it, looking up, or from a very different angle when we are in an airplane. We may see it as a tower in the distance or even as a tiny photographic image on a printed page. Yet we perceive it as constant and unchanging. When a friend extends his hand toward us, the image of his hand on our eyes is far bigger than the image cast by his entire body when he is a half block away from us, yet we perceive him as of constant size and proportion. <u>The camera, which does not possess the perceptual process, "sees" all kinds of distorted images, as is shown</u> in Figure 7-14. <u>We</u> *see* <u>the same kind of images, but we</u> *perceive* <u>them without the distortion.</u>

<u>To add to the complications, many of the stimuli that reach our eyes are moving or changing.</u> Our friend is walking toward us across a room or past us on the sidewalk, or he is riding by in a rapidly moving automobile. Often we ourselves are moving and thus altering our relation to all the stimuli in our field of vision. Part of the visual field is in brightness; part is covered by shadows. The illumination changes from the bright sunshine of noon to dim twilight. <u>All this makes very little difference to us.</u> We perceive our friend as the same person despite all the confusions of motion or lighting. The snow seems just as white in the shadow of the house as in the open.

what we really see

7-14

To the human eye, as to the camera, a close view of the horse presents an enormous muzzle, an elongated head, giant eyes and ears, and legs that are tiny by comparison. But we *perceive* the horse in proper proportion, without the distortion that the camera records.

Once we have learned about the objects in our world, we perceive them as constant and unchanging—in shape, brightness, color, location, and size.

Shape Constancy.   We perceive the dinner plate as round even though its image seldom reaches our eyes as a circle. Similarly, we perceive a door as a rectangle not only when we are directly facing it but also while it is swinging open toward us and its image is continually changing. In other words, we perceive objects as retaining their shape regardless of the true nature of the image that reaches our eyes—a fact that is called _shape constancy_.

Brightness Constancy.   The light reflected from a black shoe in the sunshine may be as bright as the light reflected from a patch of snow in the deep shade. A photographic light meter would "see" them as the same and give them the same reading. But to us the shoe looks definitely black and the snow definitely white. Our perceptions of the shoe and the snow are influenced by what is called _brightness constancy_.

A rather startling demonstration of how brightness constancy operates is provided by the experimental setup shown in Figure 7-15. The spotlight is focused

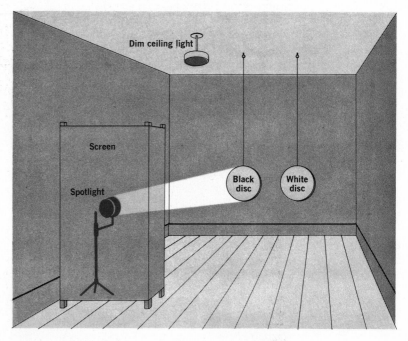

an experiment with brightness

7-15   A concealed spotlight and two cardboard circles suspended from the ceiling, one black and one white, provide the tools for an experiment that often startles the subjects. For an explanation, see the text. (6)

on the black circle so that the entire circle is illuminated but no light spills over to the background. The ceiling light and any others in the room are then dimmed until the two circles are of exactly equal brightness. The amount of light reflected from each circle is now the same, and they would register as equal on a light meter. Moreover, to a person who walks into the room and cannot see the concealed spotlight, they actually look the same under these circumstances; they are seen as two dimly lighted white surfaces. But the instant the observer becomes aware of the spotlight—for example, if a puff of smoke is blown into its beam or a hand moved into the beam—he suddenly sees that one circle is black. It looks completely and strikingly different the instant he receives a clue that permits brightness constancy to operate.

Color Constancy. Just as we tend to perceive objects to be of the same brightness regardless of the amount of light they actually reflect, so do we tend to perceive colored objects as displaying *color constancy.* One of the best demonstrations of this fact was an experiment in which small pieces of gray paper were cut in the shapes of familiar objects such as a banana, a lemon, a carrot, and a tangerine. The papers were then mounted on blue-green backgrounds and covered with screens of finely ground glass. Because of the principles of color contrast, the gray figures against the blue-green background looked brownish orange. All should have seemed to be the same color. But when subjects were shown the banana-shaped paper and told that it was a banana, they tended to perceive it as yellowish; and when shown the tangerine-shaped paper and told that it was a tangerine, they tended to perceive it as reddish orange. Similarly, they perceived the lemon as yellowish and the carrot as orange (7).

Location Constancy. As was explained in Chapter 6, our sense of direction for sounds depends on the fact that sound waves coming from the left strike the left ear a tiny fraction of a second before they strike the right ear, while sound waves from the right strike the right ear first. This has been demonstrated, it was pointed out, by experiments with a laboratory device called the pseudophone, a set of earphones that pick up sound waves that would ordinarily reach the left ear and transfer them to the right ear, while also transferring sounds that would ordinarily reach the right ear to the left ear instead. When a person puts on a pseudophone, sounds get completely turned around; he may see an automobile traveling from left to right, but he hears it as moving from right to left. After a few days, it should now be pointed out, this changes. The wearer adjusts his perceptual processes and perceives the sounds to be in the proper location.

A similar experiment with vision was performed many years ago by an investigator who built an unusual and elaborate pair of "eyeglasses" that turned the world he saw upside down and reversed right and left. The glasses were a bulky and heavy device, but he persisted in wearing them during his waking hours for eight days. At first he was confused and helpless. Every time he moved his head the world swam about (a fact we might expect from what happens when we look at a tree through binoculars). He had trouble recognizing even the most familiar surroundings and found it almost impossible to feed himself. Gradually, however, the world began to straighten out. Toward the end he was able to function quite well; he could avoid bumping into objects and could perform acts such as eating almost without thinking about them. The world no longer moved when he moved his head. Most of it still looked upside down, but he had adjusted his perceptual processes and perceived the location and movement of objects more or less automatically. Indeed he had established new perceptual patterns so thoroughly that when at last he took off the glasses, he again was confused and disoriented for a time (8).

The pseudophone and the inverted glasses demonstrate that even under the most difficult circumstances we manage to establish *location constancy,* which enables us to perceive objects as being in their rightful and accustomed place and as remaining there even when we move.

A more recent experiment with a different kind of eyeglasses sheds some additional light on location constancy. In this experiment the glasses shifted the visual field to the right. A person wearing them would reach out to touch a doorknob, for instance, and miss it by nearly a foot. When two students, a man and woman, put on the glasses, both were equally inaccurate when they tried to touch objects, always erring on the right. Then the woman, still wearing the glasses, stepped into a wheelchair. The man, still wearing the glasses, began pushing her around the campus. After this had gone on for a time, they were again tested for accuracy at reaching toward objects. The woman still missed as before. The man touched them unerringly (9). This would indicate that location constancy is developed at least in part by moving around in the world and learning to combine perception and motor coordination, just as the pseudophone indicates that it is also partly a result of cooperation among the senses.

Size Constancy.   The final type of perceptual constancy can be demonstrated by an experiment that requires no more equipment than a full-sized dinner plate and a salad plate of the same pattern, the same in every respect except that it is much smaller. Put the dinner plate on a table, trying not to look at it. Now stand above it, hold the salad plate in front of your face, and look down toward the table. Keeping one eye closed, move the salad plate away from you until it just blots out the dinner plate—in other words, to the point where, if you moved it any farther away from your eye, you would begin to see an outline of the dinner plate.

What you have done, as is shown in Figure 7-16, is set up a situation where the visual images of the two plates are exactly the same size. Now move the salad plate to one side and open both eyes. What you perceive, without question or doubt, is a small plate fairly close to you and a large plate on a table. The dinner plate looks big; the salad plate looks small. You cannot perceive them any other way.

This simple but convincing experiment demonstrates *size constancy*—the fact that we tend to perceive objects in their correct size regardless of the size of the actual images they cast on our eyes. The experiment also shows that perceived size depends to an important extent on perceived distance. When we have good

7-16 Both plates cast images of exactly equal size on the young woman's eye. When she moves the plate she is holding so that she can see both, do they look the same size or does one look larger? You can try the experiment yourself or find the answer in the text.

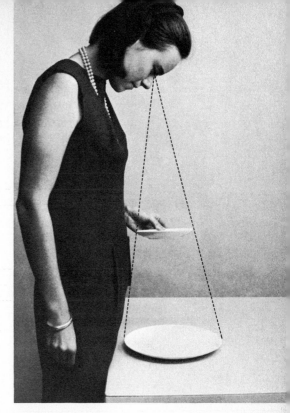

PERCEPTUAL CONSTANCY

1. SHAPE CONSTANCY

2. BRIGHTNESS CONSTANCY

3. COLOR CONSTANCY

4. LOCATION CONSTANCY

5. SIZE CONSTANCY

clues as to how far away an object is, we can estimate its size with considerable accuracy. For example, the Air Force once made tests of how well pilots could judge the height of stakes planted in a field—and found that, even when a stake about 6 feet high was nearly a half mile away, the subjects erred by an average of less than 4 inches (10). In experiments where subjects are deprived of clues to distance, however, their accuracy is substantially reduced (11).

Perceived size also depends on prior knowledge of how big an object actually is, and on other factors that are less well understood. You can observe one unexplained fact about size perception for yourself the next time you are watching television. Note that a face seen in close-up on the screen or a person seen full-length looks quite large. But make a loose fist and look through it, holding the circle formed by your thumb and forefinger against your eye and making as small a peephole as possible with the curve of your little finger. (Close the other eye, of course.) You probably will be startled to discover how small the face or figure on the screen suddenly becomes. Similarly, the full moon looks quite large when it is just coming up over the horizon—but quite small when it is high above you.

Experimenters have devised numerous optical illusions that fool the tendency toward size constancy. The one shown in Figure 7-17 is an interesting manipulation of the relationship between perceived size and perceived distance. The illusion seems to depend for its effect at least in part on special kinds of prior experience with visual stimuli.

247

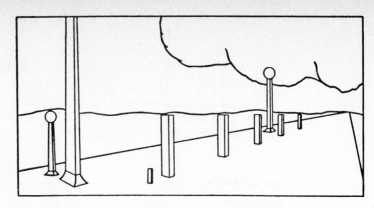

perceived size as a function of perceived distance

7-17　The lamppost and block of wood at the far right look much bigger than the lamppost at the far left and the block of wood in the foreground. We perceive them as larger because we perceive them as farther away. Actually—as measurement with a ruler will show—the two lampposts and blocks of wood are exactly the same size. (12)

3. perception of distance

In our three-dimensional world, the ability to perceive distance is extremely useful. Merely to walk through the world without bumping into doors, furniture, trees, and other people, we must not only perceive these things as objects but also know how far away they are. Our skill at distance perception, which is usually quite accurate, seems to depend on the following clues.

Perceived Size.　Just as perceived size depends in considerable part on perceived distance, so does perceived distance depend on perceived size. To a large extent, we judge how far away the Empire State Building is—or a basketball being thrown down the court—by how large it seems in relation to other objects in our visual field. Our perception of distance can be thrown off badly if we misjudge size. For example, experiments have been conducted with playing cards much larger or much smaller than the kind people ordinarily use for playing bridge or poker. When seen in a room that affords no other visual clues, the oversized cards always seem closer than they really are, the undersized cards farther away.

Binocular Vision.　Since our eyes are about $2\frac{1}{2}$ inches apart, they receive different images—a fact that you can demonstrate for yourself by looking at some object in the distance while holding a finger a foot or so in front of your nose. If you close first your left eye and then your right, your finger seems to move, because the image it casts on one eye is in a noticeably different part of the visual field from the image it casts on the other eye.

Ordinarily we focus both eyes on the same object, and the two images are somehow put together in the brain. (Although sometimes, if we are ill or have had too many drinks, this process is disturbed and we "see double.") The slight difference between the two images greatly assists our perception of distance. This fact is the secret of the three-dimensional or stereoscopic camera, which simultaneously takes two pictures through two different lenses and on two different pieces of film that are about as far apart as the human eyes. When the two pieces of film are seen through a viewer that presents one to the left eye and one to the right, we perceive a vivid and unmistakable three-dimensional effect.

Focusing our eyes also requires movements of the muscles that control the position of the eyeballs and the shape of the lens of the eye. It is believed that the sensations produced by these movements may also provide clues to distance perception.

Interposition. This is the term used for the fact that nearer objects interpose themselves between our eyes and more distant objects, blocking off part of the image. The manner in which interposition serves as a clue to distance—such an important clue that when manipulated in the laboratory it can completely fool the eye—is illustrated in Figure 7-18.

Perspective. Artists learned many centuries ago that they could convey the impression of distance and three dimensions on a flat piece of canvas by following the rules of *perspective*, which all of us use in real life as clues to distance.

Artists speak of two kinds of perspective. One, *linear perspective,* refers to the fact that parallel lines seem to draw closer together as they recede into the

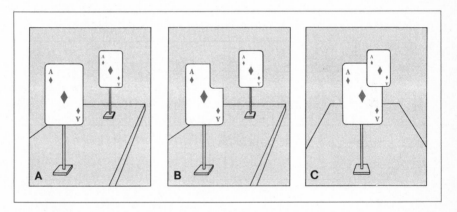

interposition and distance perception

7-18   Two playing cards are arranged as shown in A and are the only objects visible in an otherwise dark room. An observer looking at them through one eye has visual images as illustrated—one large card and one small card. The relative size tells him clearly that the smaller card is farther away. Now a corner is clipped from the near card, as shown in B, and the stand holding this card is moved to the right, so that the images are seen as in C. The cue of interposition now makes the observer think that he is looking at a small card, close to him, and a larger card farther away. (3)

7-19 Serving as clues to distance in this single photograph are all three kinds of perspective—linear, aerial, and gradient of texture.

distance. A good example is railroad tracks or the edges of a highway seen on a level stretch of ground. *Aerial perspective* refers to the fact that distant objects, because they are seen through air that is usually somewhat hazy, appear less distinct and less brilliant in color than nearby objects. If you have lived within sighting distance of mountains or the skyscrapers of a large city, you may have noticed that the mountains or buildings seem much closer on days when the air is unusually clear.

Another factor in perspective is *gradient of texture,* which you can best observe by looking at a large expanse of lawn. The grass nearby can be seen so well that every blade is distinct, and therefore its texture looks quite coarse. Farther away, the individual blades seem to merge, and the texture becomes much finer. This and the other aspects of perspective as a clue to distance are illustrated in Figure 7-19.

how shadows create the third dimension

7-20

The mere addition of shadowing turns the flat circle into a three-dimensional ball. (10)

7-21 The road seems to be winding down a long hill. But turn the page upside down to see what this really is.

PERCEPTION OF DISTANCE

1. PERCEIVED SIZE
2. BINOCULAR VISION
3. INTERPOSITION
4. PERSPECTIVE
      LINEAR
      AERIAL
      TEXTURE
      SHADOWING

Shadowing. The pattern of light and shadow on an object often offers clues that aid in perception of three-dimensional quality. Figure 7-20 illustrates how the addition of shadowing turns what we perceive as a circle on the printed page into a ball. Figure 7-21 demonstrates how an unexpected pattern of shadows can mislead our perception.

4. perception of height and depth

One special kind of distance perception concerns the vertical dimension of our world. Imagine yourself standing on a high diving board. At what height are you? Or, to put it another way, how deep is the space beneath you? And how do you know?

Some interesting facts about the perception of height and depth have been disclosed by experiments with the apparatus shown in Figure 7-22. This device, which its inventor has termed a "visual cliff," is a piece of heavy glass suspended above the floor. Across the middle of the glass is a board covered with checkered cloth. On one side of the board the same kind of cloth is attached to the bottom of the glass, making this look like the solid or shallow side of the cliff. On the other side the cloth is laid on the floor, and to all appearances there is a drop at that side.

As is shown in Figure 7-22 a six-month-old baby crawls without hesitation over the shallow-looking side but hesitates to crawl to the deep side. Animals

251

a baby and the "visual cliff"

7-22 At left, a six-month-old baby fearlessly crawls toward his mother on the glass covering the shallow-looking side of the visual cliff. But, at right, he appears afraid to cross over the glass covering the "deep" side. (13)

also show this tendency. A baby chick less than twenty-four hours old avoids the deep side. So do baby lambs and goats tested as soon as they are able to walk.

DEFINITION:
MOTION PARALLAX

By manipulating the various clues on which depth perception on the visual cliff might be based, it has been found that the essential one is *motion parallax.* This refers to the fact that when we move our heads, near objects move across our field of vision more rapidly than objects that are farther away. You may have noticed this when on a moving train: the telephone poles along the tracks seem to race past the window, while buildings in the distance do not. When the baby or animal on the visual cliff moves its head, the checks on the cloth at the shallow side move rapidly across its field of vision; the checks on the deep side do not. This clue to depth perception appears to be the secret of how animals—particularly those like goats that are born into an environment full of mountains and sharp drops—manage to avoid falls.

5. perceptual conflicts

One more experiment on the organization of perceptions deserves mention. Subjects were asked to look at a small square of white plastic through what looked like an ordinary pane of glass but was actually a lens that made the plastic square look like a rectangle, twice as high as it was wide. While they looked, they were also asked to reach behind the "glass" and feel the plastic square; they did this through a piece of black cloth that prevented them from seeing any distortion of their hand. Thus they did not catch on that the "glass" was really a lens.

252

Here was a situation in which two different senses brought two different kinds of evidence. The subjects saw a rectangle. At the same time they *felt* a square. How did they actually perceive the piece of plastic?

The answer is that they perceived the plastic as a rectangle. Most of them were not even aware that there was any conflict between the appearance and the actual feel of the plastic (14). The sense of vision was dominant—an indication that whoever coined the phrase "seeing is believing" was more correct than he probably ever realized.

the perceiver and perception

The factors discussed up to now operate in very much the same manner for everyone. All of us seem to have our attention attracted to stimuli by change (including movement, contrast, and sometimes repetition), size, and intensity. All of us seem to organize the stimuli in accordance with the rules of figure-ground, closure, continuity, proximity, similarity, and common movement. We all perceive objects as having constancy of shape, brightness, color, location, and size. Except when it is affected by some kind of physical handicap, one person's accuracy at distance perception is pretty much like another's and apparently based on the same kind of clues afforded by perceived size, binocular vision, interposition, perspective, and shadowing.

There are also many factors in perception that depend on who is doing the perceiving and on his prior experience, learning, and physical and emotional state at the moment. These factors can vary greatly from one person to another, so that two people exposed to exactly the same stimuli may perceive them in entirely different ways.

1 early experience

A chimpanzee named Kora, born in the late 1940's, is well known among psychologists for her contribution to knowledge of the importance of early experience to visual perception. For the first seven months of her life Kora was raised in darkness, with the exception of an hour and a half a day of vague illumination. (This was necessary to prevent actual degeneration of the nerve tissue of the eyes.) At no time in these seven months did she have an opportunity to see any kind of patterns in her visual field. At the end of that period she was tested for perception of visual patterns.

Compared with other chimpanzees of that age, she proved to be severely retarded. She did not blink when a moving object approached her eyes. She could not fix her gaze on a stationary person or a moving person or even follow the movements of a feeding bottle. It took her six days to learn to blink, thirteen days to fix her gaze on a stationary person or follow a moving person, and twenty days to follow the movements of the bottle. She had considerable trouble learning to avoid a mild electric shock that was paired with the presentation of a large disc prominently striped in yellow and black. Most chimpanzees learn this in one or two pairings, but Kora required two pairings a day for thirteen days (15).

Another chimpanzee, named Rob, was deprived of experience with the sense of touch: his forearms, hands, lower legs, and feet were covered, first with bandages and later with cardboard tubes. When Rob reached the age of thirty-one months, the experimenters removed the covers and tried to teach him to distinguish his right hand from his left. When his right index finger was squeezed, he was rewarded if he turned his head to the right; when his left index finger was squeezed, he was rewarded if he turned his head to the left. Another thirty-one-month-old chimpanzee, raised normally, learned this in about 200 trials. Rob showed very little sign of learning it even after 2000 trials. He performed normally, however, on learning tasks based on visual perception (16).

This and other evidence indicates strongly that human beings and higher animals require a considerable amount of early sensory experience if they are to show normal ability at making even the simplest kind of perceptual discriminations and performing tasks based on these discriminations.* In particular, they appear to need experience with stimuli showing a high degree of contrast. Fortunately, most of them receive this experience, and it is only under unusual circumstances that the retarding effect of early sensory deprivation can be observed.

For lower animals early sensory deprivation does not seem to be so damaging. Rats raised in darkness, for example, demonstrate normal size and distance perception as soon as they are moved into light and catch up quickly with other rats on tests involving the discrimination of visual patterns. You will recall, however, what happened when rats were raised in cages with circles and triangles on the walls (page 120). These rats performed better than others on tests requiring discrimination between circles and triangles. In another experiment, newly born rats were divided into three groups. One group was raised in regular wire cages, from which they could observe all the angles of the walls and doors in the laboratory room. The other two groups were raised in cages entirely enclosed by milk glass, which admitted light but did not permit them to see out. For one group the milk-glass walls were decorated with curved lines and for the other group with lines meeting at angles. When the groups were tested for discrimination between triangles and squares, the group raised inside milk-glass walls with curves did poorly. But the group raised inside milk-glass walls with angles did just as well as the group raised in normal cages. Experience with angles—of whatever nature—seemed to be the key factor (17).

In the experiment in sensory deprivation shown in Figure 7–23, note that the two kittens had an equal amount of exposure for three hours a day to the

---

*For the benefit of students who will go on to take advanced courses, it should be pointed out that perception is the subject of one of the liveliest and most fascinating of scientific debates. It can be argued that the cases just cited do not prove anything about the subjects' perception but only about their inability to coordinate other behavior with their perceptions. Perhaps Kora had no trouble perceiving the yellow-and-black disc and Rob no trouble perceiving which finger was squeezed. It may have been only their learning of suitable responses to these perceptions that was retarded. There are many such subtle and controversial problems, making the study of the finer points of perception much more complicated than the broad general outline presented in this chapter.

7-23 Two kittens were raised in darkness except for three hours a day in this apparatus. One kitten always did the walking; the other always got a ride. But note that the harness and the gondola are connected in such a way that the kitten that rides faces the striped walls at exactly the same angle as the kitten that walks. For a comparison of the perceptual abilities of the two kittens after ten days of using the apparatus, see the text.

visual contrast and patterns provided by the striped walls. At the end of the experiment the kitten that had done the walking showed normal perception; for example, it blinked at approaching objects and put up its paws to avoid collisions. The kitten that rode in the gondola was perceptually retarded. This experiment is somewhat reminiscent of the one mentioned earlier in which two students wore lenses that shifted their visual fields toward the right. In that case, you will recall, the student who rode around the campus in a wheelchair did not adjust to the lenses, but the one who pushed the wheelchair was able to reach accurately toward objects. Perhaps the experiment with the kittens is further indication that the development of normal behavior depends on moving around in the world and learning to combine perception and motor coordination; many psychologists have so concluded.

Just as sensory deprivation can cause retardation, so enriched sensory experience can help the organism improve the perceptual process. It has been found, for example, that most babies start reaching for objects when they are about five and a half months old. But when babies are surrounded from birth by large numbers of interesting visual objects, such as mobile toys of various shapes and colors hanging in their cribs, they tend to reach for objects sooner than usual (18). It appears that enriched experience is more effective very early in life than if it comes later.

2, perceptual expectations

One other important influence on perception remains to be discussed. All other things being equal, we tend to perceive at any given moment what we expect to perceive. To put this another way, perception depends to a considerable degree on our *perceptual expectations.* You can demonstrate this fact for yourself by trying the simple experiments suggested in Figures 7-24 and 7-25.

255

the effect of expectation on figure-ground

7-24 To demonstrate how the organization of figure and ground is affected by perceptual expectations, show drawing A to a friend, keeping the other two covered. Then let him look at drawing B. Almost surely, he will perceive drawing B as the face of the pretty young woman in A. To another friend, show drawing C before you let him look at B. This friend will probably perceive drawing B as the face of the old hag in C. (19)

man or rat?

7-25 Cover the bottom row of pictures, then show those at the top to a friend, one at a time, beginning at the left. The chances are that he will perceive the final picture as the face of a man. Then cover the top row and show the bottom row to another friend in the same manner. The chances are that he will perceive the final picture as a rat. The psychologists who devised this experiment found that 85 to 95 percent of their subjects could be induced to see the final picture as a man if they saw pictures of other human heads first, as a rat if they saw the animals first. (20)

DEFINITION:
TACHISTOSCOPE

Other impressive demonstrations have been made with a laboratory tool called the tachistoscope, a device with which words or pictures can be shown to a subject for very brief exposure times, as small a fraction of a second as the experimenter desires. Many experiments with the tachistoscope have shown that a subject who knows in general what to expect can recognize words and objects much faster than a subject who has no idea what is coming. If a subject is told that he will be shown the names of fruits or vegetables, for example, he perceives them much more readily than does a subject who has no clue about the nature of the words.

In one of the early experiments with the tachistoscope, one group of subjects was told to expect words dealing with birds or animals and another group to expect words dealing with transportation and travel. Among the words that were then shown, each for a mere one-tenth of a second, the experimenter slipped in some combinations of letters that were not words at all, though they resembled real words. The first group has a strong tendency to perceive them one way, the second group a very different way. *Pasrort* was often seen as parrot by members of the first group and passport by members of the second group; *dack* as duck and deck; *wharl* as whale and wharf; and *sael* as seal and sail (21). Thus did perceptual expectations influence what the subjects perceived.

Perceptual expectations play an important role in many of the interpretations we make of the environment. When we are around a relative who has a reputation for being cranky and critical, we notice his more acid remarks and may not even be aware that a good deal of his conversation is just as pleasant as that of anyone else. Indeed we may interpret as sarcastic many remarks that, said in exactly the same words and tone by someone else, would probably strike us as harmless or perhaps even good-natured. When we are around someone we know likes us and from whom we expect warmth and acceptance, we may be totally unaware of a momentary outburst of anger or hostility.

3. influences on perceptual expectations

Many different factors inside the organism can affect perceptual expectations and therefore what is actually perceived. Among them are hunger and thirst, motives such as a desire for achievement or acceptance, emotions such as anger and fear, and interests and values. Presumably all these factors operate by the same process. We tend to be preoccupied with them; we *think* about them; and our thoughts create a form of mental set.

A number of experiments have demonstrated the effect of these various influences on perception. In one of them, three groups of people were asked to describe "pictures" that they were told they would see dimly on a screen. Actually there were no pictures, merely blurs or smudges, but the subjects did their best to perceive some sort of pattern. One group had gone only an hour since eating, another group four hours, and the third group sixteen hours. It turned out that the subjects who had gone four hours without eating thought they saw more objects related to food than did those who had gone merely an hour and that the subjects who had gone sixteen hours without eating "saw" the most food-related objects of all (22).

In another experiment, two groups of subjects were used—one group highly motivated for achievement, the other group with low motivation for achievement. Both groups were tested on words shown with a tachistoscope, some of which, such as *strive* and *perfect,* were related to achievement and others of which were not. It was found that the subjects who had high achievement motivation could recognize the words related to achievement more rapidly than could the other subjects (23).

Another experiment using the tachistoscope was performed with six groups of people who had a high level of interest in religion, politics, economics, society, the arts, or theory. It was found that most of them were quicker to recognize words relating to these special fields than other words. The subjects interested in religion were quick to recognize *sacred,* for example, and those interested in economics were quick to recognize *income* (24).

As has been said, we tend to perceive what we expect to perceive, and the experiments just cited demonstrate that we tend to expect to perceive what we would like to perceive at the moment or what in general we value most highly. In everyday terminology, our perceptual expectations depend on our state of mind, and our state of mind, in turn, depends on the situation of the moment and on all kinds of prior experience and learning.

summary 1. Perception is the process through which we become aware of our environment by organizing and interpreting the evidence of our senses.

2. Our perceptions often differ from the actual sensory stimuli on which they are based. For example, we sometimes perceive motion when the stimuli are in fact stationary—as in the *phi phenomenon,* the *gamma phenomenon,* and the *autokinetic illusion.*

3. The key factors in perception are *selection* and *organization.* We pay attention to only some of the stimuli that reach our senses, and we organize these selected stimuli into our own patterns of meaning.

4. The organism has a tendency to select certain stimuli in preference to others. Among the stimulus characteristics that automatically affect selection are *change* (including movement, contrast, and sometimes repetition), *size,* and *intensity.*

5. The tendency to organize sensory stimuli is so compelling that we tend to perceive patterns in stimuli that do not of themselves possess a pattern—in the steady clicks of a metronome, for example, or a uniform mass of checkerboard squares.

6. One of the strongest influences in perceptual organization is *figure-ground.* We tend to perceive an object as a figure set off from a neutral ground by a dividing line called a *contour.*

7. Other factors that influence organization are *closure, continuity, proximity, similarity,* and *common movement.*

8. An important learned factor in organization is *perceptual constancy,* which refers to the fact that we tend to perceive objects as constant and unchanging even though the image of them that reaches our senses varies because of changing angle and distance.

9. Perceptual constancy includes *shape constancy, brightness constancy, color constancy, location constancy,* and *size constancy.*

10. Size constancy plays a significant role in perception of distance, because perceived distance varies with perceived size.

11. Other perceptual clues to distance and depth are *binocular vision* (the slightly different images received by the two eyes), *interposition, perspective,* and shadowing.

12. Human beings and higher animals seem to require a considerable amount of early experience with sensory stimuli if they are to acquire normal perception (or at least the normal responses to what they perceive).

13. The *perceptual expectations* (a form of set) that have been learned are a strong influence on perception. All other things being equal, we tend to perceive what we expect to perceive.

14. Among the factors that help create perceptual expectations are drives, emotions, motives, interests, and values.

recommended reading

Broadbent, D. E. *Perception and communication.* Elmsford, N.Y.: Pergamon Press, 1958.

Epstein, W. *Varieties of perceptual learning.* New York: McGraw-Hill, 1967.

Forgus, R. H. *Perception: the basic process in cognitive development.* New York: McGraw-Hill, 1966.

Gibson, E. J. *Principles of perceptual learning and development.* New York: Appleton-Century-Crofts, 1969.

Gregory, R. L. *Eye and brain: the psychology of seeing.* New York: McGraw-Hill, 1966.

Gregory, R. L. *The intelligent eye.* New York: McGraw-Hill, 1970.

Kidd, A. H., and Rivoire, J. L., eds. *Perceptual development in children.* New York: International Universities Press, 1966.

Neisser, U. *Cognitive psychology.* New York: Appleton-Century-Crofts, 1967.

Rock, I. *The nature of perceptual adaptation.* New York: Basic Books, 1966.

Segall, M. H., Campbell, D. T., and Herskovits, M. J. *The influence of culture on visual perception.* New York: Bobbs-Merrill, 1966.

We cannot rise
above
our physical limitations;
we are born to behave
and think
in ways dictated
by the kinds
of muscles,
glands,
and nervous systems
we have inherited.

PART FOUR

It is impossible to understand many aspects of human behavior and mental processes without knowing something about the human body and brain. For example, our ability to learn, think, and solve problems (discussed in Part 2) depends on the kind of nervous system we possess and especially on the structure and dynamics of the brain. Our information about our environments (as was explained in Part 3) depends on the ability of our sense organs to detect stimuli in the world around us and the manner in which our brains select and organize messages from the sense organs into our perceptions.

Many of the topics that still remain to be discussed also are closely related to physical and biological characteristics. Our emotions are closely tied to the activity of the glands inside our bodies. We are driven by such physical states as hunger, thirst, and sleepiness, and we must work in various ways to protect ourselves from heat, cold, and pain; thus there is a physical basis for the drives and motives that help determine much of our behavior. Biological characteristics help determine our personalities and can be responsible in part for abnormal behavior.

Thus we must now make a sort of detour into a subject that at first glance may seem more appropriate to physiology but that is nonetheless basic to psychology. The subject will be treated in a single chapter that covers three main topics. The first part of the chapter discusses the process of *heredity* and how it determines both the similarities and individual differences we display in size, physical strength, learning ability, eye and skin color, and many other characteristics. The second part discusses the functions of those rather small but extremely important structures called the *endocrine glands*. The final part describes the *nervous system*—particularly that remarkable coordinating, learning, and thinking device called the brain.

One reason these three topics are important is that we cannot rise above our physical limitations; we are born to behave and think in ways dictated by the kinds of muscles, glands, and nervous systems we have inherited from our ancestors. No human being can swim like a fish, fly like a bird, or run as fast as a race horse. Nor can any human being perform arithmetical calculations as fast as a computer—though, as will be seen, the human brain performs marvels of its own.

THE body ANd bRAiN

CHAPTER 8

HEREdiTy, GLANds, ANd NERVOUS SYSTEM

In the physical equipment they possess, all organisms are more or less like the others of their species. The rats studied in the laboratory may differ somewhat in size, color, and such characteristics as excitability and ability to learn, but by and large they are more alike than different. Human beings, since they are more complicated and highly developed than other organisms, show a wider range of differences than do the members of other species; they vary considerably in size, strength, color of skin, facial characteristics, and intelligence. Nonetheless, human beings vary only within limits. As a poet once said, we are all brothers and sisters under the skin. The surgeon and the witch doctor, the dwarf and the giant, the Einstein and the high school dropout, all have more in common than they have in contrast.

Why are we all alike, yet each one different? This is a question that must be answered before any attempt is made to describe the physical basis for behavior.

the genes: key to heredity

Human life starts, of course, when the egg cell of the mother is penetrated and fertilized by the sperm cell of the father. In this process the two join into a single cell—and this single cell eventually grows into a human baby. It does so by a process of division; the single cell splits and becomes two living cells, then each of these in turn splits to make four, and so on.

Thus the original fertilized egg cell must somehow contain the whole key of life. Something inside it must direct the entire development from single cell to the baby at birth (whose body contains about 200 billion cells organized into the various specialized parts of the body) and beyond that from infant to fully matured adult. Something in it must also determine the inherited characteristics of the individual to be born—the color of the eyes, the shape of the facial features, the potential size, the learning capacity.

CHROMOSOMES

This "something" is the *chromosomes*—the tiny structures shown in Figure 8-1 as seen under a powerful microscope. The original fertilized cell contains forty-six chromosomes. When the cell splits, the chromosomes also divide. Thus each cell of the newborn baby—and indeed of the fully grown human body— contains exactly the same forty-six chromosomes that were present in the fertilized egg with which life began. The chromosomes are the key to the development of the human adult and are the carriers of heredity.

265

8-1

When enlarged 750 times, the human chromosomes look like this. These are from a man's skin cell, broken down and spread out into a single layer under the microscope. The labels point out the X- and Y-chromosomes, the importance of which is discussed on page 268.

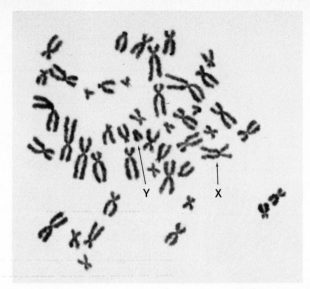

GENES

DNA

Each chromosome, though tiny in itself, is composed of hundreds of even smaller structures called *genes,* each of which is a molecule of a complex chemical called *DNA* (deoxyribonucleic acid). Recently scientists managed to extract a single gene from a chromosome of one of the lower organisms and, through a microscope, take the photograph of it shown in Figure 8-2.

Human genes have not yet been isolated, examined, or counted. But it is believed that there are at least 20,000 of them in each human cell and perhaps as many as 125,000. Each gene is believed to be responsible—sometimes by itself

a single gene

8-2

The first gene ever isolated and photographed under high magnification was this twisted strand taken from one of the bacteria frequently found in the human intestinal tract. It is fifty-five millionths of an inch long. (1)

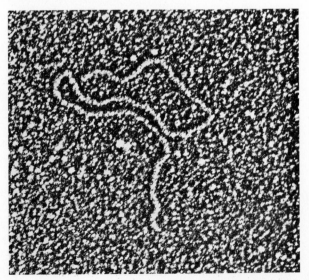

but more often in combination with other genes—for some particular phase of development. The genes direct the process by which some cells of the body grow into skin and others grow into nerves or muscles and also the process by which cells become grouped into organs such as the heart, the stomach, and the liver. They control such aspects of development as the color of the eyes and the length of the bones.

Our heredity depends on those many thousands of genes, organized into our forty-six chromosomes. It is the particular kinds of genes present in the original fertilized egg that make us develop into human beings and into the individual kind of human being that each of us is.

1. where we get our genes

In the living cell, it must now be emphasized, the chromosomes are not arranged as in Figure 8–1, where they were deliberately separated and spread out to pose for their microscopic portrait. Instead they are arranged in pairs—twenty-three pairs of chromosomes. In each pair the two chromosomes are similar in structure and function and are composed of genes of similar structure and function. For purposes of exposition, we can think of them as pairs A_1-A_2, B_1-B_2, C_1-C_2, D_1-D_2, and so on.

In growth, the twenty-three pairs of chromosomes with their matched genes duplicate themselves exactly, so that each new cell also has pairs A_1-A_2, B_1-B_2, C_1-C_2, D_1-D_2, and so on. But the cells of reproduction—the mother's egg cell and the sperm cell of the father—are formed in very different fashion. Here the pairs split up. Half of each pair goes into one egg or sperm cell, the other half into another cell. Thus each egg or sperm cell has only twenty-three chromosomes, not twenty-three pairs.

When two cells of reproduction are formed by this process, it is a matter of chance whether cell 1 will receive A_1 or A_2, B_1 or B_2, C_1 or C_2, and so on. Cell 1 may receive A_1, B_2, and C_1, in which case cell 2 will receive A_2, B_1, and C_2. Or cell 1 may receive A_2, B_2, and C_1, in which case cell 2 will receive A_1, B_1, and C_2. This random splitting of the twenty-three pairs can itself result in 8,388,608 different possible reproductive cells with different combinations of the two halves of the original pairs. Moreover, the splitting has a further complication. Sometimes A_1, in breaking away from A_2, leaves some of its own genes behind and pulls away some of the A_2 genes. Any of the twenty-three chromosomes can and often does behave in this way, with anywhere from one to several hundred genes from its paired chromosomes. All in all, there are many billions of possible combinations of the original pairs of chromosomes and genes.

An egg cell containing one of these combinations of the chromosomes and genes present in the mother is fertilized by a sperm cell containing one of the combinations of the chromosomes and genes present in the father. The chromosomes and genes pair up, and life begins for another unique human being. Never before, unless by a chance so mathematically remote as to be almost impossible, did the same combination of genes ever exist. Never again is it likely to be repeated.

The one exception to the fact that each human being is unique is in the case of identical twins. Here a single egg cell, fertilized by a single sperm cell, develops into two individuals. They have the same chromosomes and genes in the same combination, and, as all of us have noted, they tend to be very much alike in every basic respect. Their differences are due to events that occurred after conception—possibly starting with different positions in the womb and slight variations in the food supply they received there and certainly including their varied learning experiences, food intake, and chance encounters with disease germs or physical accident after birth.

2. how sex is determined

One of the twenty-three pairs of chromosomes present in the fertilized egg cell plays a particularly important role in development: It determines whether the fertilized egg will develop into a boy or a girl. In Figure 8-1 you will note that two chromosomes are pointed out by arrows. One of them, as the caption states, is called an X-chromosome, the other a Y-chromosome. Despite their different appearances, they constitute a pair—the only exception to the rule that paired chromosomes are similar in structure. You will also note that the chromosomes in Figure 8-1 are from a cell taken from a male. The X-Y pairing always produces a male. When there is an X-X pair, the result is always a female.

This, then, is how sex is determined. When the mother's X-X pair of chromosomes splits to form an egg cell, the result is always a cell containing an X-chromosome. When the father's X-Y pair splits to form two sperm cells, however, the X-chromosome goes to one of the cells, the Y-chromosome to the other. If the sperm cell with the X-chromosome fertilizes the egg, the result is an X-X pairing and a girl. If the sperm cell with the Y-chromosome fertilizes the egg, the result is an X-Y pairing and a boy.

Recently there has been considerable interest in the discovery of a rather rare abnormality in men, the presence of an extra chromosome—an X-Y-Y combination. Only about one man in 2000 is believed to have this abnormality. Among men in prisons and hospitals for mentally disturbed criminals, however, the proportion has been found to be considerably higher—somewhere around two to four in 100 (2, 3). There has been speculation that the X-Y-Y pattern may result in a tendency to be less intelligent than average but taller and inclined toward aggressive and antisocial behavior. Some psychologists who have studied the evidence, however, believe that there is as yet no firmly established link between the X-Y-Y pattern and criminal tendencies (4, 5).

3. dominant and recessive genes

If a man with blue eyes marries a woman with blue eyes, we can predict with absolute certainty that all their children will also have blue eyes. When a man with brown eyes marries a woman with brown eyes, we can never be sure. All we can say is that their children have a greater chance of being brown-eyed than blue-eyed. The fact that we cannot rule out the possibility of a blue-eyed child has some important implications for our study of heredity.

Eye color is determined by one particular pair of genes or perhaps by a particular group of paired genes. For convenience, let us assume that a single pair is involved, and let us call the pair GEC_1–GEC_2—meaning that gene for eye color 1 was inherited from the father and gene for eye color 2 from the mother. If GEC_1 and GEC_2 are both for brown eyes, the eyes will be brown. If GEC_1 and GEC_2 are both for blue eyes, the eyes will be blue. Sometimes, however, GEC_1 is for brown and GEC_2 for blue, or vice versa. What happens when the genes for blue and for brown compete? The answer is that the gene for brown eyes always prevails; it is a *dominant gene*. The gene for blue eyes is a *recessive gene,* and its effects are always suppressed by the dominant gene. Any person with one GEC for brown and one GEC for blue will have brown eyes. But when his chromosome and gene pairs split to form reproductive cells, half the reproductive cells will carry the GEC for brown, the other half the GEC for blue. If one of the reproductive cells containing the GEC for blue happens to fertilize or to be fertilized by another reproductive cell containing the GEC for blue, the result will be a blue-eyed child. Thus can a person pass along a trait that he himself does not possess. The mechanics of the process are illustrated in Figure 8–3.

Among the genes known to be dominant in producing physical characteristics, besides those for brown eyes, are those that cause baldness in men,

DOMINANT GENE

RECESSIVE GENE

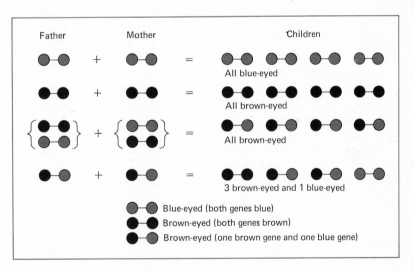

Father	Mother	Children
●─● +	●─● =	●─● ●─● ●─● ●─●
		All blue-eyed
●─● +	●─● =	●─● ●─● ●─● ●─●
		All brown-eyed
{ ●─● ●─● } +	{ ●─● ●─● } =	●─● ●─● ●─● ●─●
		All brown-eyed
●─● +	●─● =	●─● ●─● ●─● ●─●
		3 brown-eyed and 1 blue-eyed

●─● Blue-eyed (both genes blue)
●─● Brown-eyed (both genes brown)
●─● Brown-eyed (one brown gene and one blue gene)

how eye color is inherited

8-3 All blue-eyed people have inherited a gene for blue from each parent; a blue-eyed man and a blue-eyed woman will have only blue-eyed children. Some brown-eyed people have inherited a gene for brown from each parent; all their children will have brown eyes. If one parent has two genes for brown and the other has two genes for blue, their children inherit one brown gene and one blue gene; since the brown gene is dominant, they will have brown eyes. If both parents have one gene for brown and one gene for blue, the probability is that three of their children will have brown eyes and one will have blue eyes.

dwarfism, and cataracts of the eye. Certain recessive genes carry color blindness and some rather rare forms of hearing defects and mental retardation.

Most of the characteristics of the organism—human or animal—are determined not by a single pair of genes but by two or more pairs, often many. Human skin color and height, for example, are believed to be controlled by several pairs of genes. Many other physical traits, such as facial characteristics, muscular strength, and speed of reactions, as well as psychological traits such as intelligence and emotional tendencies, are also controlled by many genes—a fact that helps account for the wide range of human physical appearance and personality.

4. some experiments in heredity

An experiment on the effect of heredity was once conducted with a group of laboratory rats of mixed ancestry. From this random group the experimenters undertook to breed a "bright" strain of rats, as measured by ability to learn a maze, and a "dull" strain. The rats that made the best maze scores were interbred, as were those with poorer scores. This selective mating of "bright" with "bright" and "dull" with "dull" was continued for many generations with the quite remarkable results illustrated in Figure 8-4.

Many similar experiments have been performed. Rats have been selectively bred to produce one group that was extremely active and another group that was lethargic and to produce one group that was much more emotional (in popular

an experiment in selective breeding

8-4

These graphs illustrate the results of an experiment that started with 142 laboratory rats that, as the top graph shows, made a wide range of scores in a maze-learning task. The rats with the best scores were then mated, as were those with poorer scores. This interbreeding of "bright" with "bright" and "dull" with "dull" continued in successive generations. As the middle graph shows, two very different groups had begun to emerge by the second generation. By the seventh generation (bottom graph) the "bright" and "dull" groups were quite distinct, and the average score of the "dull" group was only a fourth as good as the average score of the "bright" group. The effect of the selective breeding was about as strong by the seventh generation as it ever became; graphs for the eighth through eighteenth generations looked much the same. (6)

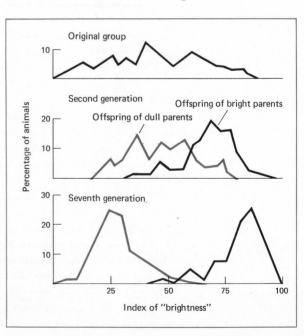

language, "nervous") than another (7). Fruit flies have been selectively bred to produce one group that was strongly attracted to bright lights and another group that was not (8).

What selective breeding does, of course, is increase the chance that the newer generations will receive genes that act to produce such traits as brightness in learning a maze, emotionality, and a tendency to move toward light. The result is a greater percentage of individuals that show the trait to a pronounced degree. Note, however, that selective breeding has its limits. In the experiment illustrated in Figure 8-4, the "bright" group showed no further improvement when interbreeding was continued after the seventh generation. Moreover, no individual in the "bright" group ever greatly surpassed the performance of the brightest member of the original group of rats. Selective breeding did not produce superindividuals, but only a greater percentage of individuals that performed close to the upper limits for the trait.

5, the implications of heredity

Men are born, live their lives, and die. But the chromosomes and the genes are passed on from generation to generation, from parent to child. All of us carry around, in every cell of our bodies, the genes that have influenced human development and behavior since man's appearance on earth. They guarantee that we will grow up in the image of our ancestors rather than into apes or fish. Yet the particular combination of genes that each of us carries is unique, coming from a grandfather here, a great-grandmother there, and so on back through countless individuals in countless generations.

So complicated is our inheritance of genes, so vast the possible combinations, that it would have been impossible to predict at the moment of conception what any of us would be like. Two parents who are below average in intelligence can produce a genius. A brilliant husband and brilliant wife may have a mentally retarded child. In a family of twelve children no two may look at all alike.

From what has been said here about heredity, it should now be clear what was meant by the statement that psychology, although it tends to lean toward the notion that the mind of the human baby is a *tabula rasa* or "blank tablet," does so with reservations. The particular combination of chromosomes and genes that comes together at the moment of conception constitutes a master key for the development of the new individual's body—his potential size, his appearance, his internal organs, his nervous system, his glands.

Recent studies indicate that many characteristics that can broadly be characterized as personality traits also are controlled by the genes at least in part, although environment is always a factor. For example, the severe form of mental disturbance called *schizophrenia*, which occurs in only about one person in a hundred, is much more common among people who have a parent or a brother or sister who suffers from the disturbance. This fact cannot be attributed entirely to the environmental effect of living around someone who is schizophrenic; a study of children reared away from their own families in foster homes has shown that of fifty children of normal mothers not one developed schizophrenia, but of forty-seven children born to schizophrenic mothers, five became schizophrenic (9). <u>There is some evidence that heredity also plays a large part in determining whether an individual will be</u> *extroverted,* <u>that is, inclined to be sociable and outgoing, or</u> *introverted,* <u>that is, inclined to be withdrawn and preoccupied with himself</u> (10).

B. how the glands affect behavior

Among the specialized anatomical structures in the body, as has been mentioned, are the <u>glands.</u> Some of them are of little interest to psychologists; <u>they simply produce substances that aid the bodily processes in routine ways.</u> For example, the salivary glands deliver saliva to the mouth and thus aid the digestive process; the tear glands keep the surface of the eyeball clean and moist; the sweat glands help keep the temperature of the body constant. <u>There is another group of glands, however, that have a pronounced effect on behavior.</u> All of them have a common characteristic; unlike the salivary, tear, and sweat glands, they possess no ducts for delivery of the substances they produce. Instead they discharge their substances directly into the blood stream, which then carries them to all parts of the body. For this reason, they are <u>sometimes called the *ductless glands.*</u> <u>They are also known as *endocrine glands,*</u> which means glands of internal secretion. The positions of the important endocrine glands in the body are illustrated in Figure 8-5.

ENDOCRINE GLANDS

the human endocrine glands

8 - 5

These are the endocrine glands most important to human behavior. For their functions, see the text.

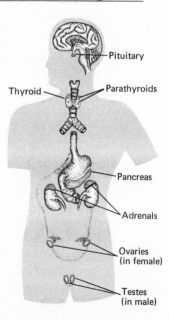

Pituitary

Thyroid

Parathyroids

Pancreas

Adrenals

Ovaries (in female)

Testes (in male)

1. functions of the endocrine glands

HORMONES

The substances produced by the endocrine glands and released into the blood stream are called *hormones,* meaning activators. The hormones are complicated chemicals that trigger and control many kinds of bodily activities and behavior, as can be seen from the following list of functions performed by the various glands.

PITUITARY

Pituitary. This is the master gland, secreting a number of different hormones that have a profound effect on the life process. In the early years the pituitary secretes a growth hormone that regulates the development of the body. As is illustrated in Figure 8-6, if the gland produces too little of this hormone, development is arrested and the child becomes a dwarf, while too much of the hormone causes the child to grow into a giant. At the time of puberty the pituitary secretes another hormone, which activates the sex glands, which in turn take over and control the change from child into man or woman. The pituitary also produces hormones that speed up or inhibit the activity of the other endocrine glands.

effects of the pituitary gland

8-6

The result of defects of the pituitary is dramatically illustrated in this photograph from Britain of a dwarf (underactivity of the gland) and a giant (overactivity).

THYROID

METABOLISM

Thyroid. This gland, a double-lobed mass of tissue lying at the sides of the windpipe, secretes a substance that controls the rate of *metabolism*—the never-ending process by which the cells inside the body convert food into energy or into new living protoplasm. When the thyroid manufactures too little of its chemical, the metabolic process is slowed down; a person with an underactive thyroid tends to be sluggish and to tire easily. If the thyroid is overactive, a person is likely to be excitable and "keyed up" and to have trouble sleeping.

PARATHYROIDS

Parathyroids. These glands, lying around the larger thyroid gland, help maintain a normal state of excitability of the nervous system by regulating the balance of calcium and phosphorus in the blood.

PANCREAS

INSULIN

Pancreas. This large gland, lying below the stomach, secretes hormones that are essential in maintaining the proper level of blood sugar and in the metabolism of blood sugar to provide energy, especially for the brain. One of them is the well-known hormone called *insulin.* An underactive pancreas results in the disease called diabetes, which was invariably fatal before the discovery that injections of insulin from animals could be used as a substitute for the body's own hormone.

ADRENALS

ADRENAL ME-
DULLA

ADRENALIN

NORADRENALIN

ADRENAL CORTEX

STEROIDS

CORTISOL

Adrenals. These two glands lie atop the kidneys. Each of them has two parts with quite different functions. The inner part, or *adrenal medulla,* secretes powerful stimulants called *adrenalin* and *noradrenalin.* These two hormones tend to affect the rate of heartbeat, raise the blood pressure, and cause the liver to release increased quantities of sugar into the blood to provide additional energy. They also tend to relax the muscles of the digestive system, tense the muscles of movement, shift the flow of blood away from the digestive organs and toward the muscles, and act as a clotting agent that makes the blood coagulate more quickly if exposed to air, as in case of injury. The outer part of the glands, or *adrenal cortex,* produces a number of hormones called *steroids,* which are so essential to the body's functions that a lack of them would quickly cause death. Among the important functions of the steroids are maintaining a suitable salt balance in the body and turning the body's proteins into sugar for a readily available supply of energy. One of the steroids is called *cortisol*—a name you may recognize as being similar to cortisone, the synthetic drug used widely in the treatment of such diseases as rheumatism and arthritis.

OVARIES

Ovaries. In addition to producing the egg cells, the ovaries are glands of internal secretion. When activated by the pituitary gland, they secrete hormones that bring about the bodily changes known as secondary sex characteristics—for example, the development of the breasts. Their hormones also control menstruation, the production of egg cells, and the course of pregnancy after an egg cell is fertilized.

TESTES

Testes. In addition to producing the sperm cells, the testes are also glands of internal secretion. Hormones from the testes bring about such secondary male sex characteristics as the growth of facial hair and change of voice and also play a part in male sexual arousal.

2. the glands as an integrating system

Taken together, the endocrine glands constitute an elaborate and efficient system for integrating many bodily activities. The hormones they produce travel to all parts of the body via the blood stream. They regulate growth and sexual development. They help keep the rate of heartbeat and blood pressure at suitable levels. They control the metabolic process and thus the rate of bodily activity.

Of particular interest is the role the endocrine glands play in regulating behavior in times of emergency. When danger threatens, they rapidly secrete hormones that make the heart pound, raise the blood pressure, lift the level of blood sugar, and in many other ways prepare the body to take drastic action.

As will be seen in Chapter 9, these internal bodily changes are closely related to the emotions of fear and anger but in rather complex ways that need not concern us just now. For the moment, let us merely point out that the man in the grip of fear or anger is a man whose endocrine system is working at top speed and who is therefore capable of extraordinary levels of physical activity. The endocrine glands constitute an integrating mechanism that quickly mobilizes all our physical resources for "fight or flight." They enable us to fight for our lives harder and longer than would otherwise be possible or to run away from danger faster and farther. Indeed they go into action to counteract any kind of stress—a fact that in modern life constitutes a rather mixed blessing, as will be seen in the discussion of the relation of emotion to psychosomatic illnesses in Chapter 9.

ENDOCRINE
GLANDS

1. PITUITARY
2. THYROID
3. PARATHYROIDS
4. PANCREAS
5. ADRENALS
　ADRENAL ME-
　　DULLA
　ADRENAL CORTEX
6. OVARIES
7. TESTES

.the nervous system

A one-celled animal does not, of course, possess a nervous system. The entire "body" of the paramecium, for example, is somehow sensitive to light and heat and capable of initiating its own movements. All the more complicated animals, however, do possess specialized nerve cells—fibers that convey messages from one part of the body to another. In the lowly little sea creature called the coral, there is simply a network of nerves, with no particular central point. The nerves and the various parts of the body work together much like the government of a loose federation of states, each preserving considerable independence. Higher up in the scale of evolution, the network of nerves becomes more complicated, and the beginnings of a central nervous system appear. The organism, it might be said, now has the beginnings of a strong central government, exercising control over all its parts. In man, the central nervous system has reached its peak of development: a large and enormously complex brain serves as a center of power and decision that regulates the behavior of all parts of the body in the most complicated and delicate fashion.

NERVE CELL

Unlike the paramecium, we would be helpless without a nervous system. We would be unable to react to stimuli from the outside world. We would not even be able to move our muscles. Indeed we could not live at all, for our hearts would not beat and our lungs would not breathe.

1, the nerve cell

The basic unit of the nervous system is the individual nerve cell, technically called *neuron,* an example of which is shown in Figure 8-7. Some of these fiber-shaped neurons are quite long; for example, the motor neurons that enable us to wiggle our toes extend all the way from the lower part of the spinal column to the muscles of the toes. Others, particularly in the brain, are only the tiniest fraction of an inch in length.

The neuron's *cell body,* which contains the chromosomes and genes that caused it to grow into a nerve cell in the first place, performs the work of metabolism. The *dendrites* are the neuron's "receivers"; when they are stimulated, they start a nervous impulse that travels the length of the fiber to the end of the *axon.* The speed at which the impulse travels depends partly on the size of the neuron; the greater the diameter of the fiber, the greater the speed. It also depends, to a much greater extent, on whether the neuron possesses a *myelin sheath,* as does the one shown in the figure. In neurons that have the sheath, the impulse often travels slightly faster than 300 feet a second, compared with a typical speed of only a little more than 3 feet a second in neurons without the sheath.

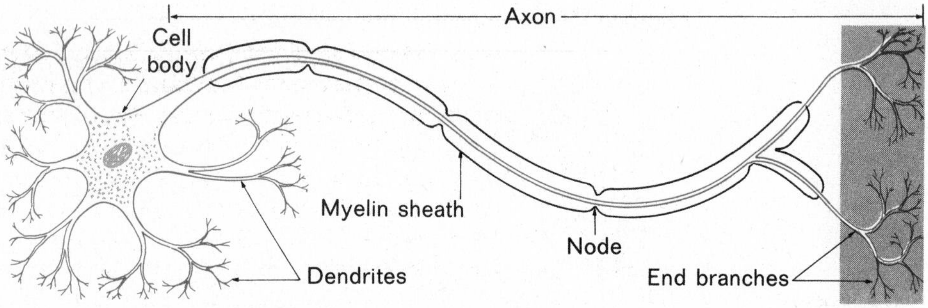

NEURON

CELL BODY

DENDRITES

AXON

MYELIN SHEATH

a nerve cell (neuron)

8-7 Like this motor neuron, all neurons are fiber-shaped cells with a *dendrite* or *dendrites* at one end, an *axon* at the other end, and a *cell body* somewhere in between. Stimulation of the dendrites sets up a nervous impulse that travels the length of the neuron to the end of the axon. In the case of this motor neuron, the *end branches* of the axon would be embedded in a muscle fiber, and the nervous impulse would make the muscle contract. The *myelin sheath* is a whitish coating that protects many neurons but not all. The *nodes* are constrictions of the sheath that act as relay stations to improve transmission of the nervous impulse. (11)

NODES

2. the nervous impulse

The nature of the nervous impulse is so foreign to anything else in our ordinary experience that it is somewhat difficult to describe or to comprehend at first. It is a tiny charge of electricity passing from one end of the fiber to the other, but it does not travel like the electricity in the wires of a house—as might be guessed from the fact that electricity travels not at a mere 3 to 300 feet a second but at 186,000 miles a second. The charge can be compared to the glowing band of fire that passes along a lighted fuse, except that no combustion takes place in the neuron and that the neuron, far from being destroyed by the nervous impulse, quickly returns to its normal state and is ready to fire off another impulse.

ALL OR NOTHING PRINCIPLE

The neuron ordinarily operates on what is called the *all or none principle.* That is to say, if it fires at all, it fires as hard as it can. Too weak a stimulus will not set off the nervous impulse at all. All stimuli of sufficient power set off the same kind of impulse, of approximately the same strength in every case.

RECOVERY

Once the neuron has fired, it requires a brief recovery period before it can fire again. This recovery period has two phases. During the first phase the neuron is incapable of responding at all. During the second phase it is still incapable of responding to all the stimuli that would ordinarily make it fire, but it can respond if the stimulus is powerful enough. Some neurons have a fast recovery rate and can fire, when sufficiently stimulated, as often as 1000 times a second. Others recover much more slowly and have a top limit of only a few firings per second.

Figure 8-8 shows the actual sequence of nervous impulses in a neuron over a period of several tenths of a second. Note that each impulse was of approximately equal intensity, as measured by the height of the jump it made in the lines. Stronger stimuli made the neuron fire more often but not with greater intensity.

As remarkable as it may seem, those little jumps in the lines in Figure 8-8

records of a neuron's activity

8-8

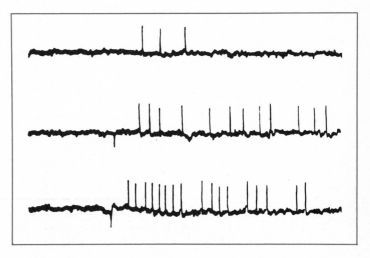

These are tracings from an electrode that was placed on the neuron of a rat. Each upward jump of the lines shows a separate impulse. The neuron was from the rat's tongue, and the stimulus was salt solution in varying strengths. The response of the neuron to the weakest salt solution is shown in the top line. In the center line the stimulus was ten times stronger and in the bottom line a hundred times stronger. (12)

are much of the story of what goes on inside the human nervous system. The neurons fire off their tiny waves of electricity, barely enough to jolt the needle of the most sensitive recording device. For each neuron, each wave is of similar intensity; the major difference is in the number and rapidity of the impulses. Yet somehow these impulses—by the way they are routed through the nervous system and the patterns they form—manage to tell us what our eyes see and our ears hear; they enable us to learn and to think; they direct our glands and our internal organs to function; they direct our muscles to perform such intricate and delicate feats as driving an automobile or playing a violin.

How they do all this is still something of a mystery. There are, however, some important clues to the process, which will be the subject matter of the rest of this chapter.

3. the synapse

NEURON CONNECTIONS
SYNAPSE

The way one neuron connects with another is shown in Figure 8-9. The junction point, or *synapse*, marks the end of one nervous impulse and the start of a new one. The impulse of the first neuron cannot leap across the synapse; it can go only as far as the end of the axon and no farther. For many years, scientists were unable to explain how the axon of the first neuron could stimulate the dendrite of the second neuron and cause the second neuron to fire. It is now known, however, that either of two things can happen at the synapse. In some cases, transmission across the synapse is purely electrical; the electrical charge delivered by the axon of the first neuron changes the electrical potential at the synapse enough to make the second neuron fire (13). In most cases, however, a chemical change takes place at the synapse. When the first neuron fires and its "message" reaches the end of its axon, the axon releases any one of several chemicals. One of them is noradrenalin—the same chemical produced by the adrenal glands. Another is an important substance called *acetylcholine*. These chemicals act on the dendrite of the second neuron and cause it to fire (14). What

NORADRENALIN
ACETYLCHOLINE

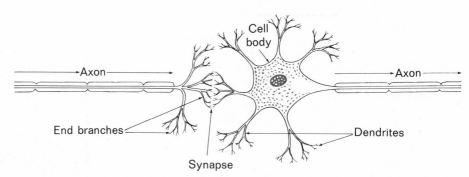

the synapse

8-9   The junction between the axon of one neuron and the dendrites of another neuron is called a *synapse*. For an explanation of what happens at the synapse, see the text.

is now known about transmission at the synapse, as will be explained a little later, offers a plausible explanation of what happens when we learn.

4. the three kinds of neurons

The neurons of the human body, which are believed to number more than ten billion, come in many different lengths, diameters, and shapes. They can, however, be divided into three classes.

1. *Afferent neurons.* These are the neurons of the senses. The word *afferent* is derived from the Latin words *ad,* which means to or toward, and *ferre,* which means to bear or to carry. The afferent neurons carry messages toward the central nervous system—from our eyes, ears, and other sense organs.

2. *Efferent neurons.* These carry messages *from* the central nervous system. Their axons end in either muscles or glands. Their impulses make the muscles contract or activate the glands.

3. *Connecting neurons.* These are middlemen between other neurons. They are stimulated only by the axon of another neuron. They do not end in muscle or gland tissue but only in other synapses where they stimulate other neurons to fire. Most of them, though not all, are found within the central nervous system.

A simple example of how these three kinds of neurons work together is provided by the infant's grasping reflex, illustrated in Figure 8-10. As will be

KINDS OF NEURONS

1. AFFERENT
NEURON

2. EFFERENT
NEURON

3. CONNECTING
NEURON

connections for the grasping reflex

8-10

Stroking the palm of the baby's hand stimulates an afferent neuron whose axon ends inside the spinal cord at a synapse with a connecting neuron. This connecting neuron, in turn, ends at a synapse with an efferent neuron. The impulses from the afferent neuron stimulate the connecting neuron, which in turn stimulates the efferent neuron, which makes the muscle of the hand contract. Note that the afferent neuron enters the spinal cord from the back, and the efferent neuron leaves from the front. This is always the case.

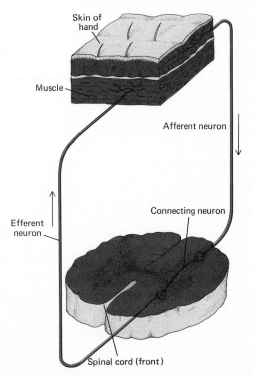

seen, the nervous messages that produce the reflex begin with the stimulation of an afferent neuron, which in turn stimulates a connecting neuron, which in turn stimulates an efferent neuron—whose impulses cause the muscle to contract.

5 multiple nerve connections

Most synaptic connections between neurons, especially the connecting or "middleman" neurons, are far more complicated than the diagrams would suggest. Indeed the synapses can best be thought of as complicated switching points where one large group of neurons ends and another begins. The axon of each "incoming" neuron that delivers messages at the synapses has many branches, each terminating in a *synaptic knob* (see Figure 8-11). These branches are in contact with the dendrites and the cell bodies, which are also sensitive to stimulation, of a large number of "outgoing" neurons. Thus each incoming neuron delivers its messages to scores or perhaps even hundreds of outgoing neurons, and each outgoing neuron can be stimulated by scores or hundreds of incoming neurons.

Ordinarily an outgoing neuron is not stimulated to fire by a single nervous impulse arriving at one of its many dendrites or its cell body. The firing process requires multiple stimulation—a group of nervous impulses arriving at once or in quick succession from several or perhaps even a great many of the incoming neurons. Moreover, the outgoing neurons differ in the ways they respond to multiple stimulation.

Thus the multiple connections at the synapses provide an almost astronomical number of possible pathways. The nervous impulses arriving from the incoming neurons may not "get through" at all; they may be too few in number

the synaptic knobs

8-11   This photograph, shown at a magnification of about 2000 times life size, is the first ever made of the synaptic knobs of a neuron. Presumably these knobs play an important part in the transmission of impulses from one neuron to another. The photograph is of the neuron connections in a snail. (15)

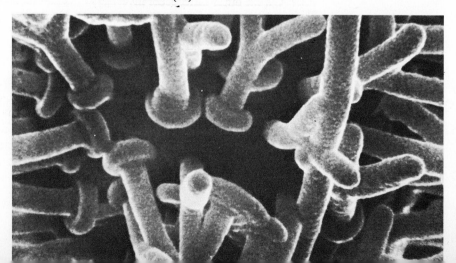

or too far apart in time to fire any of the outgoing neurons, or incoming impulses tending to fire the outgoing neurons may be canceled out by impulses tending to inhibit firing. At times the incoming nervous impulses may be of such a number and such a pattern as to fire one of the outgoing neurons but no more. At other times several outgoing neurons may be fired. The particular ones that are stimulated into activity may vary. The number of impulses they fire and the rate at which they fire may also vary.

All this means that no new impulses at all may be set up at the synapse, or that new impulses may travel in any one of many directions or in several directions at once. The new impulses that go along to the next switching point or points in the nervous system may be few or many, slow or rapid. Small wonder that the human nervous system is capable of so many accomplishments. By comparison, the nation's telephone network is just a child's toy.

6, the nerve paths and learning

The multiple connections at the synapses and the new discoveries about transmission across the synapse offer a plausible theory of how learning takes place. When we learn, we obviously route nervous impulses over a particular pathway, going through a number of synapse switching points in a particular pattern. The pattern can later be reactivated—and we remember.

Studies of lower animals have suggested that at synapses where the axon of one neuron stimulates the dendrite of another neuron to fire by releasing such chemicals as noradrenalin and acetylcholine, the chemicals produce a long-lasting change in the efficiency of the synapse (16). That is to say, the second neuron becomes more likely to fire again in the future. The change makes it easier for nervous impulses to follow the same route again. The pathway set up by learning becomes, so to speak, a path of least resistance.

The theory is supported by what is known about acetylcholine. In one study, a group of rats was raised from birth under conditions where they were more or less constantly occupied with learning tasks. Another group of similar rats did no learning at all except what came naturally in their lives in a cage. An analysis of their tissues indicated that there had been considerably more acetylcholine in the brains of the rats that had done the learning (17).

On the other hand, some investigators believe that learning is coded inside nerve cells by changes in a chemical called RNA, which is similar to DNA and, like DNA, is present in all cells. This suggestion was first made by a scientist in Sweden who reported that learning appeared to cause permanent changes of the RNA molecules in the neurons of mice (18); and subsequent experimenters have trained certain kinds of organisms to perform a task, extracted RNA from their brains, injected it into untrained organisms, and found that the untrained organisms then behaved as if they too had learned the task (19, 20). These experiments raise the question of whether it might someday be possible for a student to acquire knowledge of a difficult subject without studying it, merely through an injection of RNA from the brain of an expert. However, there is also much contradictory evidence (21) and the issue remains in doubt.

One interesting fact about the human brain is that all its nerve cells are present at birth; the number never increases. Yet the brain grows substantially, from about 11 ounces at birth to over 2 pounds in adulthood. Part of the added weight is caused by the fact that the nerve cells of the brain grow in size and develop additional dendrites much as a young tree develops new branches. This growth process appears to be stimulated by learning, as has been demonstrated in experiments with animals. For example, if one group of rats is raised in ordinary cages and another group in an enriched environment containing numerous visual stimuli and toys, examination after death shows that the animals from the enriched environments have substantially larger and heavier brains (17). Stimulation also has been shown to cause an increase in the development of dendrites in the brain cells of rats (22).

TYPES OF NERVOUS SYSTEMS
1. PERIPHERAL NERVOUS SYSTEM
2. CENTRAL NERVOUS SYSTEM
*   SPINAL CORD*
*   BRAIN*

D. the central nervous system

As indicated in Figure 8–12, the neuron fibers of the human nervous system extend to all parts of the body. Arranged in groups of fibers called *nerves,* they carry messages to and from the face, the arms, the entire trunk and the digestive organs, the legs, and the feet. The outlying nerves and the individual neurons that make up these nerves are called the *peripheral nervous system.* All of them eventually connect with that versatile coordinating device known as the *central nervous system—*the *spinal cord* and the *brain.* The afferent neurons and nerves of the peripheral system carry their impulses inward to the central nervous system, where they account for what we call our sensations, such as hearing and the feeling of pain. The efferent nerves, originating in the central nervous system, deliver their impulses outward and thus control the glands of the body and muscles as far away as the fingers and toes.

As was noted earlier, the spinal cord itself provides the connections for simple reflexes. Mostly, however, it is a sort of central transmission channel, with

the human nervous system

CRANIAL NERVES

SPINAL NERVES

8-12 Like the tributaries that form a river, individual neuron fibers at all the far reaches of the body join together to form small *nerves,* which is the name for bundles of neuron fibers. The small nerves join with others to form larger nerves, at last becoming the very large ones that join with the central nervous system—the brain and the spinal cord. Twelve *cranial nerves,* in pairs going to the left and right sides of the head, connect directly with the brain. There are also thirty-one pairs of large *spinal nerves,* connected with the spinal cord at the spaces between the bones of the spine. Many of these nerves are made up of both afferent and efferent neurons. The spinal nerves, however, are divided into two just outside the spinal cord. The afferent fibers (as was pointed out in Figure 8–10) enter the spinal cord from the back, while the efferent fibers leave from the front.

a vast number of connecting neurons that carry nervous impulses to and from the brain, the master control center of the nervous system.

1. functions of the brain

The brain is a truly remarkable part of the human body. As one psychologist has written:

> The brain is the source of emotions, such as love, fear, and rage. . . . The brain organizes information from our sense organs to provide an orderly basis for our perception of the world about us. It achieves the marvelous coordination of our motor movements. It learns from our experience and stores our memories. It retrieves appropriate memories, plans for the future, thinks, and reasons creatively. Since the brain is the supreme organ of integration, there are many beautiful interrelationships among these apparently diverse functions (23).

A seventeenth-century theory of the mind

One of the characteristics of the brain is its great versatility. Some of its cells function much like sense organs; some are alert to changes in the composition of the blood and other bodily fluids and recognize when the body needs food or water; some are alert to temperature changes in the blood stream and send off messages that cause the body to take steps to warm or cool itself. Some of the cells act like glands and secrete hormones. For example, one part of the brain recently has been found to produce a hormone that acts directly on the pituitary and causes the pituitary in turn to release a hormone that controls the activity of the thyroid (24). Other cells of the brain, of course, perform a purely nervous function; they serve as an elaborate network of communication among the messages received by the sense organs, the efferent neurons that activate our muscles of movement, and other neurons that control the activity of our internal organs.

2. the structure of the brain

Figure 8–13, a diagram of the human brain as it would appear if divided down the middle, shows the structures of most interest. At the bottom, connecting with the spinal cord, is a group of structures collectively called the *brain stem.* Atop this lies a much larger mass of structures collectively known as the *forebrain.*

BRAIN STEM

The Brain Stem. In the brain stem, four structures are of particular importance.

MEDULLA

The *medulla* is the connection between the spinal cord and the brain. Nervous impulses travel through it to and from the higher parts of the brain. It also contains centers that help regulate heartbeat, blood pressure, and especially breathing. These centers, though they play no part in what are usually thought of as mental processes, are so essential that damage to them causes death.

CEREBELLUM

The *cerebellum* controls body balance; it is the part of the brain that keeps us right side up. It also assists in coordinating our bodily movements and keeping them rhythmic and accurate.

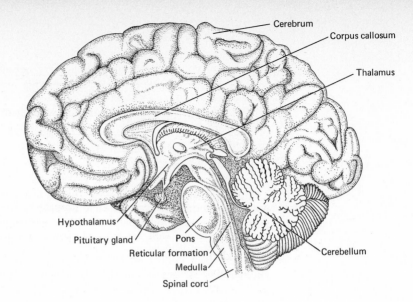

a sectional view of the brain

8-13　The functions of the brain structures shown in this drawing are discussed in the text. (25)

PONS

The *pons* is a group of nerve fibers lying under and in front of the cerebellum and connecting the two sides of the cerebellum, as well as the cerebellum and the cerebral cortex. Until recently, the functions of the pons were not known. New experiments indicate that the pons helps to regulate breathing (26) and is responsible in part for the nervous impulses that cause the rapid eye movements of a person who dreams during sleep.

RETICULAR FORMATION

The *reticular formation* gets its name from the fact that under a microscope it appears as a criss-crossed (or reticulated) network of rather short neurons connecting with other neurons in the brain stem and the hypothalamus. The afferent pathways carrying nervous impulses from the senses to the cerebral cortex—the extreme importance of which will soon be explained—have side branches that enter the reticular formation. Nervous impulses originating in the sensory receptors and traveling through these side branches appear to stimulate the reticular formation to send impulses of its own to all parts of the cortex, keeping the cortex in a general state of arousal and activity. When an electrode is placed in the reticular formation of an animal, the animal can be abruptly awakened from deep sleep by a mild electrical stimulus (27).

FOREBRAIN

The Forebrain. The forebrain, or highest part of the brain, also contains four structures of special interest.

CEREBRUM

The *cerebrum* is the largest part of the human brain—of such importance in so many different ways that it deserves discussion of its own a little later.

CORPUS CALLOSUM

The *corpus callosum* is a large nerve bundle, lying beneath the cerebrum, which transmits messages between the left side of the cerebrum and the right side.

THALAMUS

The *thalamus* is the brain's major relay station, connecting the lower struc-

284

tures of the brain and the spinal cord with the cerebrum. In the thalamus lie the cell bodies of important connecting neurons for the various senses; these neurons receive messages from the sense organs and send them on to the cerebrum.

HYPOTHALAMUS

The *hypothalamus* has connections with both the higher and lower parts of the brain and with the pituitary gland; it is also an important link with the other endocrine glands and plays a significant role in emotions, the drives of hunger and thirst, sexual behavior, metabolism, and the preservation of a constant body temperature. It is also an important terminal for the reticular activating system and as such helps direct sleeping and wakefulness.

LIMBIC SYSTEM

Another important part of the forebrain, not shown in the diagram because of its complexity, is the *limbic system*, which includes the hypothalamus and other structures and circuits carrying messages between lower and higher parts of the brain. The limbic system performs many functions. It receives sensory messages from the visceral organs and helps control their activities. It also plays a role in emotions and memory. It seems to be particularly important in controlling adaptive behavior such as eating, escaping from danger, and mating, which require the performance of a series of actions undertaken in sequence (28).

3. functional organization of the brain

One way of viewing the functional organization of the brain is by regarding it as composed of three "blocks" as illustrated in Figure 8-14.

FIRST BLOCK (A)

The first block is composed of the brain stem, particularly the reticular formation, and the thalamus and hypothalamus. This part of the brain controls wakefulness and the general level of activity in the cerebrum; it sends impulses up to the cerebrum that keep it functioning efficiently and able to discriminate among the stimuli it receives. When this part of the brain is damaged—or indeed even when a person is sleepy, which means that this part of the brain is not doing

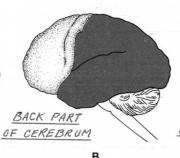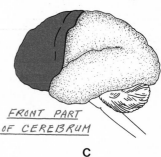

BRAIN STEM
RETICULAR FORM.
THALMUS
HYPOTHALAMUS   **A**

BACK PART
OF CEREBRUM   **B**

FRONT PART
OF CEREBRUM   **C**

a functional map of the brain

8-14   From the functional point of view, the brain can be divided into three "blocks." Block A controls wakefulness and the general level of activity in the highest part of the brain. Block B analyzes information received from the sense organs, codes it, and stores it. Block C is the brain's "organizer." For further discussion, see the text.

its job as well as usual—thoughts and impressions of the world received through the sense organs become disorganized.

The second block, which is the back part of the cerebrum, analyzes information received from the sense organs, codes it, and stores it.

The third block, which is the front part of the cerebrum, is the brain's "organizer." It regulates attention and concentration and plays a part in every kind of complex behavior; it decides what we are going to do and formulates plans and programs (29).

4. the cerebrum and cerebral cortex

If we could look down through the top of a transparent skull, we would see the human brain as shown in Figure 8-15. We would be looking at only a single one of its many parts—but, as it happens, the very part that most distinguishes man from the lower animals. This is the extremely large, highly developed *cerebral cortex,* the surface of the cerebrum. The cerebral cortex can best be

described as a sort of carpet of densely packed neurons, with cell bodies, dendrites, and axons forming a closely knit fabric with innumerable connections and interconnections. This "carpet" contains so many nerve cells and is so big in area that it could not find room within the skull were it not for the fact that it is elaborately folded and refolded, or convoluted. We can see only about a third of the cortex; the rest is hidden because of the convolutions.

In appearance, the outstanding features of the cerebral cortex are these convolutions, the fact that it is divided into two separate halves called the *left*

hemisphere and the *right hemisphere,* and its color. Because it is made up mostly

a top view of the brain

8-15

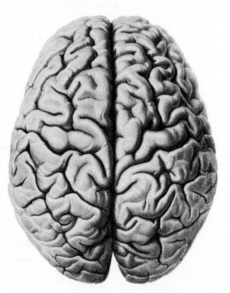

This is the human *cerebral cortex,* the surface of the *cerebrum,* as seen from above. Note how it is divided into two hemispheres of similar size and appearance. Note also the many folds and fissures that add to its area. No other organism except the porpoise has such a large, intricately convoluted, and highly developed cerebral cortex. (25)

8-16

On this side view of the cerebral cortex the areas that are known to have special functions have been mapped. (25)

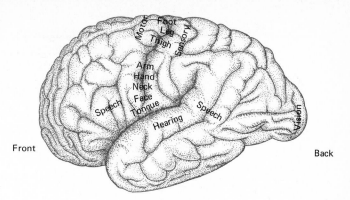

Front

Back

of neuron cell bodies and dendrites, the cerebral cortex is gray, the color of unsheathed neuron tissue. It is the color of the cortex that has made "gray matter" a popular synonym for intelligence.

A side view of the cerebral cortex is shown in Figure 8-16. Note that there is a particularly prominent fissure extending downward from almost the very top of the cortex. At the sides of this fissure lies the *sensory-motor strip,* the control point for our sensory impressions of the body and the body's motor movements.

The sensory-motor strip has been mapped through electrical stimulation of this area in human patients during brain surgery under local anesthetic. When various parts of this area are stimulated, the patients report sensations of pressure or movement in various parts of the body. As the figure shows, the body is represented in the sensory-motor area in upside-down position—with the feet and legs at the top of the area and the head at the bottom.

The *visual area,* as Figure 8-16 shows, is at the very rear of the cortex. Stimulation of this area produces various kinds of visual sensations, and destruction of the area seems to destroy the ability to perceive visual patterns. When the visual area is surgically removed from a monkey or a rat, the animal cannot distinguish a circle from a triangle.

The *auditory area* lies just below another prominent fissure, which curves diagonally upward from the bottom left of the cortex toward the upper right. The two areas marked *Speech* in Figure 8-16, though rather widely separated, both seem to be essential to speaking and to understanding the speech of others.

In general, the left hemisphere of the cerebral cortex receives sensory impressions from and controls movement in the right side of the body, while the right hemisphere deals with the left side of the body. Almost invariably, one of the two hemispheres is dominant—that is, it plays the greater part in controlling such activities as physical skills, reading, writing, and speech. Usually the dominant hemisphere is the left. This is almost always true of right-handed people, as might be expected, but it also seems to be true of most left-handed people. The two hemispheres cooperate closely, however, through the corpus callosum.

When the corpus callosum connecting the two hemispheres is cut, as must sometimes be done for medical reasons, some rather strange results occur. One case has been reported of a 49-year-old man whose intelligence, personality, and

SENSORY-MOTOR STRIP

VISUAL AREA

AUDITORY AREA

287

general behavior appeared to remain almost entirely unaffected by the operation. However, careful testing showed that in some ways he acted almost as if he possessed two separate brains that functioned independently. He was unable to read words that fell on the left half of his field of vision and were therefore transmitted to the right hemisphere of the brain—not to the left hemisphere, which is responsible for language. When he performed a motor task with his left hand, which is controlled by the right hemisphere, and then was questioned, he could not recall what he had done—an indication that the dominant left hemisphere of his brain did not know or remember anything about the activities of the right hemisphere. When touched on one side of the body, he could point to the spot only with the hand on that side, not with the other hand (30).

5. the brain and behavior

Knowledge of how the various parts of the normal brain perform different functions—and also of how they cooperate—has been growing at a rapid pace. In cases of brain damage through accident or illness, psychologists and physicians can now make a fairly accurate judgment of where the damage has occurred simply by observing the patient's behavior.

Studies of the brain have included some rather remarkable experiments in controlling the behavior of animals through electrical or chemical stimulation of various parts of the brain or through surgery that destroys some of the brain tissue. For example, when a particular small part of the hypothalamus is destroyed in experimental surgery, animals stay awake until they die of exhaustion. When another small part of the hypothalamus is destroyed, the animals spend most of their time sleeping (31). Injecting different kinds of chemicals into the hypothalamus has been found to make a rat stop eating, even if hungry, or to make it eat, even if already gorged on food (32).

Other experiments have resulted in the control of emotional behavior—one might almost say the personality. As shown in Figure 8-17, stimulation of one part of the brain makes an animal unusually docile, while stimulation of another spot makes the animal hostile and aggressive. Indeed electrical stimulation of the brain can result in the complex pattern of behavior illustrated in Figure 8-18.

The most valuable thing we know about the brain, however, goes far beyond this knowledge of the functions of its various specific parts. In a normal organism, with an intact and undamaged brain and with no artificial stimulation coming from electrodes, the brain acts as a unit; it works as an entity to integrate behavior and especially as the instrument through which behavior is modified by learning. We know that the pathways of learning laid down in the brain are the real controllers of behavior; they influence how we will interpret and respond to the stimuli that reach our senses; they influence what we find pleasant and what we find unpleasant; they determine what we find psychologically stressful and what we will react to emotionally; they, even more than real physical needs, influence our habits of sleep, hunger, thirst, and sexual behavior.

In the day-to-day life of the normal organism the pathways of learning act very much as do the electrodes or the surgical knife that, in experiments, can

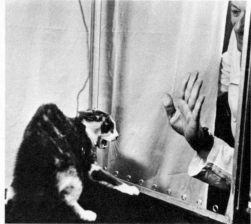

electrical control of behavior

8-17   The cat in the photograph at left is made so friendly and docile by an electrical stimulus applied deep in the front part of its cerebrum that it happily ignores its traditional prey. The cat at right, electrically stimulated in the region of the hypothalamus, is enraged by the very presence of a laboratory assistant whose attentions, were it not for the stimulation, would be most welcome.

"fighting" a bull by radio

8-18   In the photo at left, a wild bull charges Dr. José M. R. Delgado of the Yale University School of Medicine, who is armed only with a cape and a radio transmitter. At right, Dr. Delgado presses a button on the transmitter and the bull stops short, raising clouds of dust. The radio transmitter sends a mild current to electrodes that have been carefully planted in particular spots in the bull's brain.

make the organism move muscles, sleep, wake, act hungry or thirsty, and behave docilely or aggressively. It is as the instrument of learning that the brain is most important in psychology.

6. some electroencephalograph studies

ELECTROENCEPHALOGRAPH   One laboratory device that has been used to study the activity of the intact brain is the electroencephalograph, or EEG for short, which has electrodes that can be placed on the outside of the skull at any desired spot. The EEG is sensitive enough to produce tracings of the electrical activity in those parts of the brain lying below the electrodes.

Some typical EEG tracings are shown in Figure 8-19. As they indicate, some form of electrical activity goes on constantly in the brain, even when a person is sound asleep. The activity changes in nature, however, in many interesting ways. The brain "at rest," when the eyes are closed, characteristically shows a pattern

ALPHA WAVES   of steady waves of about ten per second, called *alpha waves*. These are replaced by faster waves of lower amplitude when the brain receives sensory stimuli, as when the eyes are open. In deep sleep, the alpha waves are replaced by a slower rhythm, which is broken up during periods of dreaming. When a person knows that he is about to do something interesting, such as look at a picture, another distinctive kind of wave appears (the "expectancy wave," described on page 111).

It has been found that through operant conditioning, a person can learn to keep the brain producing alpha waves even when the eyes are open. An EEG that signals when these waves appear by sounding a tone serves as a reinforcement for learning (35). Subjects who have learned to do this report that it produces

some EEG tracings

8-19

These are reproductions of actual EEG tracings made under various circumstances. (Tracings for eyes closed and eyes open, 33; deep sleep and dreaming, 34)

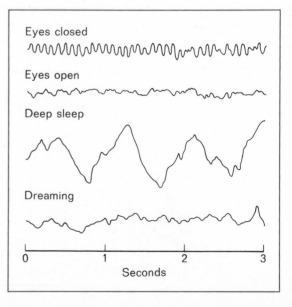

Eyes closed

Eyes open

Deep sleep

Dreaming

0   1   2   3

Seconds

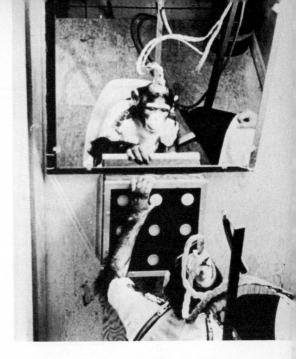

8-20 This chimpanzee was trained at UCLA to play ticktacktoe. The wires carry EEG readings of its brain activity to a computer that analyzes them instantly and finds patterns that would not be apparent in visual examination of the tracings. As explained in the text, the computer can predict the animal's next move. (37)

an extremely pleasant frame of mind, probably akin to the relaxed and blissful states achieved in yoga and Zen meditation (36).

In recent years computer analysis of EEG tracings has revealed some additional facts that had previously not been apparent from the tracings themselves. For example, the brain waves of the chimpanzee shown in Figure 8-20, which has been taught to play ticktacktoe, are constantly being fed into and monitored by a computer—and the computer is able to detect whether the animal's next move will be right or wrong. When analysis of the waves indicates a state of brain activity that the experimenters have called "trained attentiveness," the chimpanzee is always right; otherwise it makes a mistake. The same experimenters have tried a similar experiment with human volunteers whose brain waves were monitored while they were asked a series of questions; computer analysis revealed which of the questions produced embarrassment or stress (38). The possible implications for further study of the brain's activity—and application of the knowledge to learning situations and emotional problems—seem rather breathtaking.

the autonomic nervous system

Closely allied with the central nervous system is another network called the autonomic nervous system, which connects the central nervous system with the glands, the heart muscles, and the so-called smooth muscles. (The heart muscles are of a special type found nowhere else in the body. The *smooth muscles* are found in the blood vessels, stomach and intestines, and other internal organs; they are different in appearance and function from the *striped muscles*, which account for motor behavior such as moving the arms and legs.)

The word *autonomic* means independent or self-sufficient, and the autonomic nervous system gets its name from the fact that in many ways it operates like

A sixteenth-century drawing of the sympathetic nervous system

GANGLIA

SYMPATHETIC DIVISION

PARASYMPATHETIC DIVISION

a completely independent integrating system, regulating many bodily activities over which we have very little conscious control. For example, we cannot ordinarily will our adrenal glands to secrete their hormones or our hearts to beat faster; we cannot order our stomach muscles to digest food or to stop the process of digestion so that the flow of blood can be directed away from the stomach and toward other parts of the body. The nervous impulses that give the body such commands are distributed by the autonomic nervous system—a process that goes on constantly, even during periods when we are asleep or in the deep coma caused by an anesthetic or a brain injury. Only recently has it been discovered that activities controlled by the autonomic nervous system can sometimes be modified through operant conditioning, as was explained on pages 62–66.

The autonomic nervous system is composed of centers called *ganglia,* which are masses of nerve cells and synapses forming complex and multiple connections, just as in the brain itself though on a much smaller scale. Some of the neurons originating in these ganglia have dendrites that receive messages from the central nervous system. Other neurons send messages via their axons to the glands and the smooth muscles, as shown in Figure 8–21.

There are two parts of the autonomic system, and they are quite different in structure. In the *sympathetic division* the ganglia lie in long chains extending down either side of the spinal cord, all connected and interconnected. Many of the axons extending outward from these chains of ganglia meet again in additional ganglia, where they form complicated interconnections with the neurons that at last carry the messages of the sympathetic division to the glands and smooth muscles.

The ganglia of the *parasympathetic division* are more scattered; most of them lie near the glands or muscles to which they deliver their messages. For this reason the parasympathetic division tends to act in piecemeal fashion, delivering its impulses to one or several parts of the body but not necessarily to all. The sympathetic division, with its more central connections and interconnections, tends to act as a unit, delivering its impulses simultaneously to all the glands and smooth muscles.

1. functions of the sympathetic system

When the sympathetic division of the autonomic nervous system goes into action, as in fight or flight situations, it does many things all at once. It stimulates the adrenal glands and pancreas, resulting in increases in the level of blood sugar and the rate of metabolism. It also stimulates the liver to release sugar into the blood. It causes the spleen, a glandlike organ in which red corpuscles are stored, to release more of them into the blood stream, thus enabling the blood to carry more oxygen to the body's tissues. It changes the size of the blood vessels, enlarging those of the heart and striped muscles and constricting those of the smooth muscles such as the stomach and intestines. It causes the lungs to breathe harder. It enlarges the pupils of the eyes, which are also smooth muscles, and slows the activity of the salivary glands. ("Wide eyes" and a dry mouth are characteristic of strong emotion.) It also activates the sweat glands and contracts the muscles

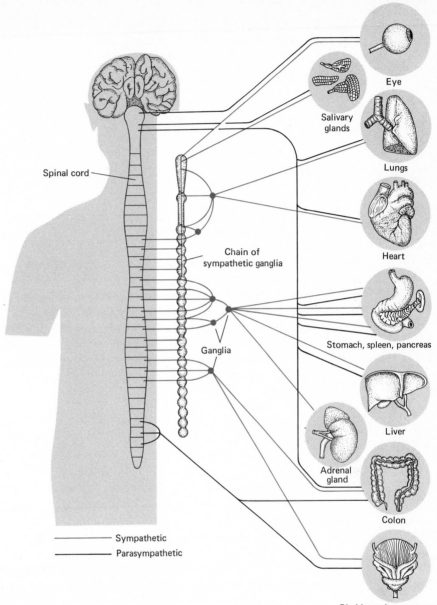

Spinal cord

Eye

Salivary glands

Lungs

Chain of sympathetic ganglia

Heart

Stomach, spleen, pancreas

Ganglia

Liver

Adrenal gland

Colon

——— Sympathetic
——— Parasympathetic

Bladder and sex organs

the autonomic nervous system

8-21 The *parasympathetic division* of the autonomic nervous system connects with the brain and with the lower part of the spinal cord. The *sympathetic division* is composed of long chains of ganglia, one on either side of the spinal column, which connect with the spinal cord in the region of the trunk and the small of the back. Both divisions have fibers extending to the smooth muscles and glands of the body as shown. (39, 40) at the base of the hairs on the body, causing the hair to rise on animals and producing gooseflesh in human beings.

2. functions of the parasympathetic system

The parasympathetic division is also active at times in situations of emergency, although in ways that are not yet entirely clear. In general, it seems to play its most important role as a regulator of bodily functions during those frequent periods when no danger threatens and the body can relax and go about the ordinary business of living. Impulses from the parasympathetic division constrict the pupil of the eye, stimulate the salivary glands, and lower the blood pressure. They also activate the stomach and intestines, thus setting into motion the normal processes of digestion, and they facilitate the functions of elimination from the intestines and bladder.

Considered as a whole, the autonomic nervous system is a valuable adjunct to the central nervous system. More or less independently and automatically, it directs many of the body's functions while we are asleep as well as while we are awake, and it moves quickly to help mobilize the body's resources of emergency. It relieves the central nervous system from the necessity of issuing all the continuing demands necessary to keep the body functioning at an optimum level. As will be seen in the next chapter, it is also an important part of the physical basis for that rich, colorful, and sometimes exasperating form of behavior called emotion.

summary 1. The mechanisms of human heredity are the twenty-three pairs of *chromosomes*, forty-six in all, found in the fertilized egg cell and repeated through the process of division in every cell of the body that grows from this cell.
2. The chromosomes are made up of a large number of *genes*, which are composed of a chemical called DNA. The genes direct the growth of cells into parts of the body and also account for the individual differences we inherit.
3. Egg and sperm cells are created through a splitting process that sends half of each pair of chromosomes and genes to one cell and the other half to another cell in a random manner that makes each egg and sperm cell different, permits billions of variations, and virtually guarantees that every individual will be unique (except for identical twins, who develop from the same fertilized egg cell).
4. A *recessive gene*, such as that for blue eyes, inherited from one parent will be suppressed by a *dominant gene*, such as that for brown eyes, inherited from the other parent. But a recessive gene can be passed along to the next generation.

5.   The *endocrine glands,* or *ductless glands,* influence behavior by secreting chemical substances called *hormones* into the blood stream. A list of important endocrine glands and their functions follows:
   a. The *pituitary* is a master gland that secretes hormones that control growth, cause sexual development at puberty, and regulate other endocrine glands.
   b. The *thyroid* regulates the rate of metabolism and affects the body's activity level.
   c. The *parathyroids* regulate the balance of calcium and phosphorus in the blood, an important factor in maintaining a normal state of excitability of the nervous system.
   d. The *pancreas* secretes *insulin,* which burns up blood sugar to provide energy.
   e. The *adrenals* are composed of an *adrenal medulla,* which secretes the powerful stimulants *adrenalin* and *noradrenalin,* and an *adrenal cortex,* which secretes *steroids* that are essential to many bodily processes.
   f. The *ovaries* control the development of secondary female sexual characteristics.
   g. The *testes* control the development of secondary male sexual characteristics.

6.   The nervous system is made up of fiberlike cells called *neurons,* which are stimulated through their *dendrites* and pass along a nervous impulse to the end of their *axons.* The nervous impulse is a tiny wave of electricity traveling at 3 to 300 feet a second.

7.   The junction point between the axon of one neuron and the dendrite of another neuron is a *synapse.* Most synapses, especially in the central nervous system, are multiple connection points where arriving impulses may not get through at all or may set off few or many impulses traveling in any one (or more) of many different directions.

8.   *Afferent* neurons carry impulses from the sense organs to the central nervous system. *Efferent* neurons carry messages from the central nervous system to the glands and muscles. *Connecting* neurons are the middlemen between other neurons.

9.   Some investigators believe that the passage of nervous impulses across the synapses produces a long-lasting chemical change in the efficiency of the synapse and that this change accounts for learning. Other investigators believe that learning is coded inside nerve cells by a change in a chemical called RNA, similar to DNA.

10.   The central nervous system is made up of the *brain* and the *spinal cord.*

11.   The spinal cord provides the connections for simple reflexes but is mostly a central transmission channel carrying nervous impulses to and from the brain.

12.   Important parts of the *brain stem* are:
   a. The *medulla,* the connection between the spinal cord and the brain. It is vital to life because it helps regulate heartbeat, blood pressure, and breathing.

b. The *cerebellum,* which controls body balance and helps coordinate bodily movements.

c. The *pons,* a structure of neurons connecting the opposite sides of the cerebellum and the cerebellum with the cerebral cortex. The pons helps regulate breathing and is apparently responsible in part for the nervous impulses that cause rapid eye movements during dreaming.

d. The *reticular formation,* a way station through which messages from the nerves of the senses pass, setting up nervous impulses that are sent to the cerebral cortex and keep the cortex in a general state of arousal and activity.

13. Important parts of the *forebrain* are:

a. The *cerebral cortex,* highly developed in the human being, a dense and highly interconnected mass of neurons and their cell bodies. It contains areas that seem to account for our sensory impressions and to initiate movements and speech.

b. The *cerebrum,* the large brain mass of which the cerebral cortex is the surface.

c. The *corpus callosum,* a large nerve tract connecting the *left hemisphere* and the *right hemisphere* of the cerebrum and enabling the two hemispheres to cooperate and share in duties.

d. The *thalamus,* the way station connecting the lower structures of the brain and the spinal cord with the cerebrum.

e. The *hypothalamus,* which serves as a sort of mediator between the brain and the body, helping control sleep, hunger, thirst, metabolism, body temperature, and sexual behavior, and is also concerned with emotions.

f. The *limbic system,* which includes the hypothalamus and other structures and circuits carrying messages between higher and lower parts of the brain. It plays important roles in controlling the visceral organs, in emotions and memory, and in adaptive behavior that requires the performance of a series of actions taken in sequence.

14. In terms of functions, the brain can be thought of as composed of three "blocks." The first block (brain stem, thalamus, and hypothalamus) controls wakefulness and the general level of activity in the cerebrum. The second block (back part of the cerebrum) analyzes information received from the sense organs, codes it, and stores it. The third block (front part of the cerebrum) regulates attention and concentration and is responsible for decisions, plans, and programs.

15. Electrical stimulation of various parts of the brain has been shown to affect behavior in many ways, such as by causing rage, docility, sexual arousal, hunger, thirst, pleasure, and pain.

16. The *autonomic nervous system* connects the central nervous system with the glands, the heart muscles, and the smooth muscles of the body. Acting more or less independently and automatically, it helps regulate such activities as breathing, heart rate, blood pressure, and digestion; and in times of emergency it works in conjunction with the endocrine glands, mobilizing the body's resources for drastic action by speeding up the heartbeat, directing

the flow of blood away from the digestive organs and toward the muscles of movement, and stimulating the liver to provide additional blood sugar for quick energy.

17. The autonomic nervous system is composed of two parts: a) the *sympathetic division,* which tends to be active in case of emergency, and b) the *parasympathetic division,* which is most active under ordinary circumstances. Both divisions are made up of *ganglia,* or masses of neuron cell bodies, that have dendrites coming from the central nervous system and axons traveling out to the glands and smooth muscles. The ganglia of the sympathetic division lie in long chains along both sides of the spinal column. The ganglia of the parasympathetic division are more scattered, lying near the glands and muscles they affect.

recommended reading

Fraser, A. S. *Heredity, genes and chromosomes.* New York: McGraw-Hill, 1966.

Fuller, J. L. *Motivation: a biological perspective.* New York: Random House, 1962.

Glass, D. C., ed. *Neurophysiology and emotion.* New York: Rockefeller University Press, 1967.

Landauer, T. K., ed. *Readings in physiological psychology: the bodily basis of behavior.* New York: McGraw-Hill, 1967.

Morgan, C. T. *Physiological psychology,* 3rd ed. New York: McGraw-Hill, 1965.

Rosenthal, D. *Genetic theory and abnormal behavior.* New York: McGraw-Hill, 1970.

Thompson, R. F. *Foundations of physiological psychology.* New York: Harper & Row, 1967.

All of us
experience
swings of mood
and spend our energies
pursuing
some kind of goal...
simple or complex,
selfish
or humanitarian

part five

The human brain, described in Part 4, can in some ways be compared to a computer, with network upon network of complicated circuits and switching points. As was discussed in Part 3, it receives the equivalent of the computer's inputs through the sense organs and the process of perception. As was discussed in Part 2, it has its own kind of memory bank, laid down in the pathways of learning, and does its own kind of data processing in the form of thinking and problem solving.

In the remaining chapters of the book, however, we come to a series of topics where any comparison between the human being and the computer breaks down. For example, no human being goes through life as mechanically and dispassionately as the computer. All of us experience swings of mood. Depending on how things are going at the moment, we may feel mildly confident, buoyant, or even elated; on the contrary, we may feel "blue," grief-stricken, or panicky. We experience anger, fear, and anxiety. Moreover, most of us spend a great deal of our energies pursuing some kind of goal. The goal may be a simple one, such as passing a college course or finding time to watch a favorite television show every week. It may be a complicated and long-term goal, such as becoming a nurse or a successful musician. It may be an abstract goal, such as helping humanity and making the world a better place to live. Indeed we usually have many goals, some simple and immediate and others complex and long-range, some of them selfish and some of them humanitarian.

In the following part of the book, Chapter 9 discusses the origins and consequences of emotions, and Chapter 10 ("Drives and Motives") discusses the search for goals. Between them, emotions and motives go far to account for and clarify the variety and richness of human personality and behavior—and to start demonstrating the contrast between man and machine.

FEELINGS AND MOTIVES

CHAPTER 9

EMOTIONS

Series game, a dignified and usually soft-spoken judge jumps
e umpires, moans when the other team scores a run, and sheds
his own team comes from behind in the ninth inning. In battle,
cautious and timid in civilian life performs the most daring
n an emergency involving a sick child, a mother who had always
physically fragile finds that she can stay awake and alert for

me of the more striking examples of how emotions influence
is the kind of human drama in which men in the grip of rage
or men in panic push women aside to get to the lifeboats of
liner. In more ordinary situations, emotions involving mild
rness often help us learn faster or get a job done more efficiently.
lving fear and anxiety can make us forget everything we knew
g an important examination or strike us dumb when we get
e a speech.

e among the most powerful of the forces that influence behavior.
g, we do not seem to have much control over them. They seem
own accord; even in situations where we have determined in
calm, we find ourselves unaccountably angry, frightened, or
tions command our attention and we cannot ignore them. <u>When
motional, we cannot concentrate on performing our jobs as we</u>
<u>g our words carefully, or even listening to music or reading.</u>
ions—of the kind that made Oedipus gouge out his eyes, Juliet
ily for Romeo, and Hamlet kill his uncle the king—have been
of the world's literature, in all nations throughout history.
always tried to understand them, and they have been an impor-
ological investigation ever since the earliest studies of Wilhelm

are riding in a bus, minding your own business. The man next
gently on the arm, politely begs your pardon for interrupting
a perfectly calm tone of voice and with a noncommittal facial

expression that shows no sign that he is in any way upset or angry, "I don't like you." Then he turns away and quietly resumes reading his newspaper. If you were asked afterward whether he had displayed emotion (not just signs of eccentricity), what would you say?

Now suppose that you carelessly drive through a stop sign, run into another automobile, and badly damage the whole side of it. The other driver gets out and says, "It's all right; don't worry about it; everybody makes mistakes; anyway, I'm insured." You note, however, that his voice is quivering, his facial muscles are twitching, and his hands are trembling. Is he emotional or is he not?

To the first question most people would answer *no,* even though the kind of aggressive behavior involved in a remark such as "I don't like you" ordinarily is highly emotional. To the second question most people would answer *yes,* even though a matter-of-fact remark such as "It's all right" is usually considered to show the absence of emotion. Most scientific investigators of emotion would agree about the driver of the automobile. Before agreeing about the man on the bus they would want to make sure that he was really as calm inwardly as he appeared on the surface.

Both scientists and laymen reserve the words *emotion* and *emotional* for cases in which physiological changes accompany mental activity. The easiest cases to recognize are those in which the organism is quite obviously "stirred up." We assume that another person is emotional when we note that his voice is unusually high-pitched, when he blushes or gets pale, when his muscles grow tense or tremble. We know that we are ourselves emotional—even if we manage to conceal all outward signs—when we can feel that we are inwardly shaking or are "hot under the collar" or that our mouths are dry, our pulses racing, or our stomachs "full of butterflies." But there are also quieter emotions in which the body almost seems to be "toned down." Such are the calm, peaceful, and contented feelings of a mother nursing a child or of a person enjoying a sun bath, a beautiful piece of music, or a cup of coffee after a satisfying meal. In these cases too, however, the physiological processes are affected in some manner.

The relationship between mind and body in emotion seems to work both ways. Think about something very pleasant, such as inheriting a million dollars from an unknown relative or anything else that appeals to you. Quite possibly you will soon *feel* pleasant. Think of something that angers you, such as a bad grade, a social snub, being blamed for someone else's mistake. Soon you may *feel* angry. Or try the opposite. Make a smile, hold it, and see if you do not begin to feel happy and have pleasant thoughts. Clench your fist, keep clenching it, and see if you do not begin to feel angry and have aggressive thoughts.

What does it mean to be "stirred up"? In search of the answer, investigators have used laboratory apparatus of many kinds, such as the device shown in Figure 9–1. Their measurements have shown that a wide variety of changes take place in the body in states of emotion (1).

measuring the "stirred-up" state of emotion

9-1 This machine makes a continuous record of four physiological processes. The tube around the young woman's body measures her *rate of breathing*, the electrodes attached to her hand her *galvanic skin reflex* (or change in the electrical conductivity of the skin caused by sweating), and the band around her upper arm her *heart rate* and *blood pressure*. These physiological processes and many others that can be measured by more complicated apparatus may be affected in states of emotion. This particular machine is a so-called lie detector.

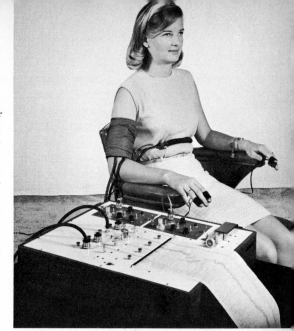

1, the nature of the changes

STRIPED MUSCLE MOVEMENT

Some of the bodily changes in emotion represent activity of the striped muscles of movement. One of them is *muscle tension,* as when the teeth are clenched in anger. Another, *tremor,* occurs when two sets of muscles work against each other. Many people, when emotionally excited, have a tendency toward *eye blinking* and other *nervous movements,* such as brushing back their hair and drumming their fingers on a desk. And many emotions result in *facial expressions,* such as frowns, grimaces, and smiles, or *vocal expressions,* such as laughter, snarls, moans, and screams. All these activities are normally under conscious control but in emotional states they do not appear to be voluntary; they "just happen" as part of the general pattern of change that accompanies emotion.

AUTONOMIC NERVOUS SYSTEM

Other changes are controlled by the autonomic nervous system (pages 291-94) and by the endocrine glands (pages 272-75), over which we have little conscious control even under ordinary circumstances. In many emotional states the rate of heartbeat jumps, sometimes from the normal of 72 per minute to as high as 180. Blood pressure may also rise sharply, and blood is often diverted from the digestive organs to the striped muscles and to the surface of the body, resulting in flushed cheeks and the sensation of being "hot under the collar." The composition of the blood changes. The number of red corpuscles, which carry oxygen, increases markedly, and the secretion of hormones by the endocrine glands produces changes in the level of blood sugar, acidity of the blood, and the amount of adrenalin and noradrenalin (powerful stimulants secreted by the adrenal glands) in the blood stream.

The normal movements of the stomach and intestines, associated with the digestion and absorption of food, usually stop during anger and rage; in other emotional states they may show changes resulting in nausea or diarrhea. The body's

305

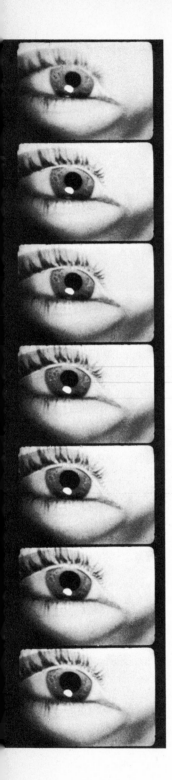

metabolic rate tends to go up; food in the blood stream and the body tissues themselves are burned off at a faster rate, creating additional energy. Breathing may change in rate, depth, and ratio between time spent breathing in and time spent breathing out; we may gasp or pant. The salivary glands may stop working, causing the feeling of dryness in the mouth that is often associated with fear and anger. The sweat glands, on the other hand, may become overactive, as shown by the dripping forehead that may accompany embarrassment or the "cold sweat" that sometimes accompanies fear. The muscles at the base of the hairs may contract and raise gooseflesh. Finally, the pupils of the eyes may enlarge, causing the wide-eyed look that is characteristic of rage, excitement, and pain.

2. pupil size as a measure of emotion

Indeed studies have indicated that changes in the size of the pupil may be an extremely sensitive measure of emotion, including active interest. In the experiment illustrated in Figure 9–2 a camera photographed the eye twice a second. As is shown in the figure, the diameter of one male subject's pupil increased 30 percent in four seconds while he was looking at a picture of a woman's face. In general, male subjects showed significant increases in pupil size when looking at pictures of women, especially pin-up pictures; female subjects showed pronounced increases when looking at pictures of a baby and especially of a mother with a baby. When the subjects looked at pictures they found unpleasant, as when women looked at pictures of sharks, the pupil size did not increase (2).

As part of the same study, men were shown the two photos in Figure 9–3, with the intriguing results that are described in the caption. Before reading on, study the photos and the caption and try to figure out why the photo at left produced a stronger reaction than the photo at right.

The only difference between the two photos, as you may have discovered, is that the one at left has been retouched to make the young woman's pupils seem larger. This very slight change presumably was the cause of the greater response. The difference between the photos was not noted consciously by the subjects in the experiment—a fact that may indicate that changes in our pupil size can reveal reactions of which we ourselves are not even aware.

Pupil size has been found to increase reliably when a person is engaged in mental activity such as solving mathematical problems or trying to remember a telephone number, and the more difficult the problem is the larger the pupil becomes.

a photographic record of pupil response

9-2   The subject was a man. The photographs of his eye were taken as he looked at a picture of a woman's face. Note the rather rapid increase in pupil size from the normal, at top, to the bottom, where the diameter is about 30 percent greater.

why do these photos produce different reactions?

9-3 These were two of the pictures shown to male subjects while a camera recorded any changes in their pupil size, as in Figure 9–2. Both pictures produced increases in pupil size, and afterward the subjects said that the two pictures were exactly alike. For some reason, however, the picture at left produced twice as large an average increase in pupil size as did the picture at right. See if you can figure out why before turning to the text for the explanation.

development of theories of emotion

As has been noted, the stirred-up bodily states that are a part of emotion are highly diffuse. They include various kinds of tension, tremor, and other movements of the striped muscles controlled by the central nervous system, as well as many changes regulated by the autonomic nervous system that affect the endocrine glands, blood chemistry, and the smooth muscles of the visceral organs, the blood vessels, and the iris of the eye. When we are emotional, it might be said, we tend to be emotional all over. In the adult human being, who has learned to hide many of the outward signs of emotion, this fact may be apparent only to the delicate

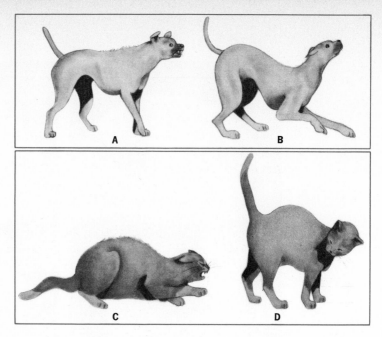

emotional postures in dog and cat

9-4 The dog approaching an enemy exhibits many signs of stirred-up bodily state (A). The bristling hair and the wide and staring eyes are evidence of activity of the autonomic nervous system. The dog's entire posture has been affected: it walks stiffly, holds its tail high and pricks its ears forward, and growls. If it discovers that it is approaching not a hostile stranger but its own friendly master, the pattern immediately changes (B). The hair and pupils return to normal, and the dog may begin salivating. The muscles of its body relax; it lays back its ears and wags its tail. The cat's display of emotion is somewhat different—it crouches toward an enemy (C) and arches its back and purrs for its master (D)—but equally diffuse. (3)

measuring apparatus of the laboratory. It is much more obvious in the case of animals, as is shown in Figure 9-4.

the James-Lange theory

In the long history of scientific investigation of the emotions, these widespread and often dramatic forms of bodily activity have naturally received a great deal of attention. They were the basis of an influential theory of emotion proposed by William James, a theory that has particular interest because it completely reversed all previous thinking about emotions. Common sense says that we cry because we are sad, strike out because we are angry, tremble and run because we are afraid. James made the suggestion—startling to the scientific world of his day and even now to the person who hears it for the first time—that things were exactly the opposite.

James said that emotion occurs in this fashion. Certain stimuli in the environment set off the physiological changes. These changes in turn stimulate the various sensory nerves leading from the visceral organs and other parts of the body to the brain. It is these sensory messages from our aroused bodies that we then perceive as emotion. In other words, we do not cry because we are sad; on the contrary, we feel sad because we are crying. Similarly, we do not tremble because we are afraid but feel afraid because we are trembling (4).

This notion that the physiological changes come first and that the perceived emotion is a feedback from the changes and comes afterward was also proposed at about the same time by the Danish scientist Carl Lange and persisted more or less unchallenged for many years as the *James-Lange theory of emotion.*

The Body in Anger and Fear.   If perceived emotion is strictly a matter of feedback from aroused bodily states, then it follows that there should be a different pattern of bodily activity for each emotion, resulting in a distinctive and recognizable pattern of sensory feedback. Many studies have been made, therefore, of the physiological activities that accompany the various emotions.

For anger and fear, the findings have been along lines that the James-Lange theory would predict. In one study, subjects were placed in an apparatus similar to the one shown in Figure 9-1. Laboratory technicians then behaved in ways that angered or frightened the subjects, without disclosing that the actions were deliberate and a part of the experiment. Each subject was made angry on one occasion and fearful on another, and the combined results of the physiological measurements showed some significant differences. In anger there was a tendency for the heart rate to go down, blood pressure to go up, and muscular tension to increase. In fear there was a tendency toward faster breathing and a more spasmodic activity of the muscles. There was also a pronounced difference in the electrical conductivity of the skin (5).

The physiological changes found in this study to be characteristic of anger are the kind known to be produced by the hormone noradrenalin, and the changes found characteristic of fear are known to be produced by the hormone adrenalin. Thus it would appear that the adrenal glands are unusually active in secreting one hormone in anger and a different one in fear—a notion for which additional evidence has been found. In one study, a chemical analysis was made of the urine of players on a professional hockey team to learn how much noradrenalin and adrenalin they were secreting before and after a game. It turned out that the players actively taking part in the game, fighting to win, showed about six times as much noradrenalin after the game as beforehand. But two players who were injured, unable to play, and worried about their future with the team showed increased amounts of adrenalin. The coach sometimes showed more noradrenalin and at other times more adrenalin, depending on how well his team had done in the game (6).

Along the same line, it has been found that animals such as lions, which survive by fighting and killing their prey, have large quantities of noradrenalin in their systems, while rabbits, which survive by running away, have large quantities of adrenalin (7). Thus it appears that anger and "fight" are associated with the physiological effects of noradrenalin and fear and "flight" with the effects of adrenalin.

The Body in Other Emotional States.   Aside from the findings about fear and anger, however, there is not much evidence to support the view that each different emotion depends on a unique pattern of bodily sensations. Certainly no experimenter has ever been able to find a hundred different physiological states to match the hundred different kinds of emotional experience described by our language. In general, the bodily changes in emotion are what recent investigators have called "rather diffuse and global in character" (8). It has proved very difficult to determine, from physiological measurements alone, what kind of emotion a person is experiencing. Indeed the same person, on two separate occasions when he says he feels joyous, may show different bodily changes. And different people may show quite different patterns when experiencing the same emotion. Among students anxious over an examination, one may tend to perspire a great deal, another to show muscle tension, another to have a rapid pulse (9).

In addition, the visceral organs, which James considered to be especially important in emotion, tend to respond rather slowly to impulses from the autonomic nervous system or to stimulation by the hormones. As was noted in Figure 9-4, a dog or cat sometimes changes almost instantly from a posture of rage to a posture of friendliness when it sees that what it thought was a hostile stranger is really its master; the pattern of sensations from the animal's visceral organs could not change that rapidly.

For these reasons and others, the James-Lange theory began to fall into disfavor, and around 1930 a different kind of theory was proposed, based on the rapidly expanding knowledge of how the brain works.

2. the Cannon-Bard theory

Behavior that appears to be emotional can be triggered by electrical stimulation of the brain: if an electrode is planted in one area of the hypothalamus of a cat, for example, the animal can be made to behave as if enraged by the presence of an enemy. Other studies have also pointed to the importance of the hypothalamus in emotion. Even when the entire cerebral cortex of a dog is removed, the animal still displays most of its typical rage pattern; in fact the "rage" is produced by mild forms of stimulation that would not disturb a normal dog. The pattern persists in the absence of some other brain structures as well as the cerebral cortex. But it does not occur unless the hypothalamus is intact (10).

It appears that the hypothalamus, with its close relationship to the autonomic nervous system and to the pituitary gland, plays a special role in emotion. This fact led to the formulation of theories of emotion based on brain activity, one of the oldest and best known of which is the *Cannon-Bard theory.* According to this theory, certain stimuli in the environment cause the hypothalamus to fire off patterns of nervous activity that arouse the autonomic nervous system and thus trigger the physiological changes that are associated with emotion. At the same time, the hypothalamus fires off patterns of messages to the cerebral cortex that result in the feelings of emotion. The Cannon-Bard theory, it will be noted, attaches no importance to the feedback of bodily sensations, which is the basic element of the James-Lange theory.

the cognitive theory of emotion

Some newer studies raise the interesting possibility that both the James-Lange and the Cannon-Bard theories of emotion were partially right but that neither offered the full explanation. Modern thinking about emotions has been greatly influenced by experiments performed by Stanley Schachter at Columbia University, which are so important that they deserve discussion here in some detail.

1. the "happy stooge" and the "angry stooge"

In one experiment Schachter used a volunteer subject, a university student, who agreed to submit to an injection of what he was told was a harmless drug whose effect on vision was being studied. The drug, so the subject was told, would produce certain physical effects—numbness of the feet, itching of the skin, and a slight headache. In truth the subject received an injection of that powerful stimulant adrenalin, in an amount sufficient to produce many of the stirred-up physiological changes that accompany strong emotion.

The subject was asked to sit in a waiting room for a time. In the room was another student, a "stooge" who had specific instructions from Schachter. The stooge began behaving quite strangely. He wadded up paper and used it like a basketball, with a wastebasket as his target. He found a hoop in the room and used it like a hula hoop, dancing around with gay abandon. He folded pieces of paper into toy airplanes and sailed them in all directions. In other words, he acted like a person who was a little out of his head with high spirits. When he invited the subject to join in the fun, the subject found himself unable to resist. Soon he too was gripped by a feeling of excitement and happiness and was sailing paper airplanes even more boisterously than the stooge.

Another of Schachter's subjects received the same kind of injection and the same story about its effects and also found another student in the waiting room. This time the stooge behaved differently. Instead of acting happy he pretended to be angry; he was bitter and aggressive. Soon the subject, too, found himself feeling angry and behaving in an angry fashion.

The experiment with the two kinds of stooges was performed with a number of subjects. In general, the subjects whose bodies were stirred up with adrenalin felt happy and behaved in a giddy fashion when they were exposed to the happy stooge, and they felt angry and behaved aggressively when exposed to the angry stooge. In each case, presumably, the physiological effects of the adrenalin were more or less the same. The accompanying emotion depended on what was happening around them—the context in which they found themselves.

In another part of the experiment the subjects were treated in exactly the same fashion except that they were told the truth about what kind of physiological reactions to expect from the injections; they were correctly informed that they would experience a fast pulse, hand tremors, and a flushed feeling in the face. These subjects were much less inclined to be influenced by the mood of the stooge; they tended to hold themselves aloof from his high spirits or his anger. A control group of subjects who received a salt water injection also tended to resist the stooge (11).

2. making a funny movie funnier

In another experiment, Schachter had three groups of subjects watch a slapstick movie. Before the movie was shown, group 1 received an injection of adrenalin, and group 2 received an injection of a tranquilizer that suppresses activity of the sympathetic nervous system and therefore has physiological effects that are generally the opposite of those produced by adrenalin. Group 3, the control group, received an injection of salt water. The subjects whose bodies were stirred up by the adrenalin showed the greatest signs of amusement while watching the movie and afterward gave it the highest rating for being funny. The subjects whose physiological activity was suppressed by the tranquilizer showed the least amusement and gave the movie the lowest rating. The control group's reactions were in the middle (12).

3. implications of the Schachter experiments

One conclusion toward which the Schachter studies seem to point is that changed bodily states are indeed an essential element in producing feelings of emotion and not just a side effect as the Cannon-Bard theory assumed. It was the subjects stirred up by adrenalin who reacted emotionally to the happy stooge and the angry stooge. It was the subjects injected with adrenalin who found the movie the most hilarious.

The James-Lange version of *why* feedback from bodily sensations is important, however, appears to be contradicted by the studies. The stirred-up bodily activity produced by the adrenalin injections did not by itself result in a specific emotion or even in any emotion at all. The subjects who had been correctly informed about what kind of bodily sensations to expect did not become giddy when exposed to the happy stooge or angry when exposed to the belligerent stooge. Those who had been misinformed became giddy in one context and angry in another context, even though, presumably, their bodily states were generally alike.

Schachter and his colleagues have concluded that emotions depend on two factors: 1) physiological arousal and 2) a mental process by which the subject interprets or labels his physiological sensations. Thus a subject aroused by adrenalin may interpret his sensations as merely being the physical symptoms of rapid heartbeat and tremor that he was told to expect, and he may therefore experience no emotion at all. The subject aroused by adrenalin and aware of physiological sensations that he does not understand may interpret these sensations as a giddy happiness in one context and as anger in another. Or he may have exaggerated feelings of amusement and joy when he sees a funny movie.

Since the Schachter findings emphasize the mental processes of interpretation

and labeling, they are consistent with the position of the cognitive school of psychology (pages 19–20). This view of emotions has been colorfully named the "juke box" theory of emotion (8). This is because the stimulus that causes physiological arousal—in normal situations some stimulus in the environment rather than an injection of adrenalin—can be compared to the dime placed in a juke box. It presumably sets off patterns of brain activity, especially in the hypothalamus, that in turn activate the autonomic nervous system and the endocrine glands, causing a general state of physiological arousal. Sensory receptors in the body report these physiological changes to the brain. But the sensations are vague and can be labeled in many different ways, just as the juke box activated by the dime can be made to play any one of a number of different records depending on which button is pushed. We label the sensations on the basis of the environmental context and what we are thinking about at the moment. If they are caused by the sight of a snake, we feel afraid; if they are caused by a slap in the face, we feel angry.

In the juke box, we start the mechanism by inserting the dime and select the record by pushing a button. In emotion, a stimulus gets physiological changes started, and we ourselves decide what emotion these changes represent.

4. a tentative definition of emotion

The Schachter findings lead to a definition of emotion that, though it must be advanced with caution, seems to cover many of the known facts: *An emotion is the interpretation of a change in level and quality of internal sensations in a particular context.* The internal sensations result from physiological changes caused by patterns of brain activity, especially in the hypothalamus and limbic system, that act chiefly through the autonomic nervous system. The interpretation is a psychological process that seeks to determine the relationship between the sensations and the environmental context and that accounts for our subjective feelings.

There is an interesting parallel between the psychological process involved in emotion and another process discussed earlier in the book. In Chapter 7, you will recall, perception was defined as the process through which we become aware of our environment by organizing and interpreting the evidence of our senses. In emotion, we organize and interpret the sensations from within our bodies. Just as perceptions are the patterns of meaning we find in external stimuli, so our emotional feelings are the patterns of meaning we find in internal stimuli—influenced, however, by our perception of the environmental context of the moment.

Note that the definition speaks of a *change* in internal sensations, not an absolute level of sensation. Just as our sense organs are most sensitive to a change in environmental stimuli, so the sensory nerves inside the body are most sensitive to a change in internal conditions. Some emotions are based on a stirred-up condition of the body. Others, such as sadness and loneliness, may involve a level of activity lower than normal, reduced heart rate and blood pressure, and a lack of muscle tone rather than tremor. A hard-driving executive may be more or less

DEFINITION:
EMOTION

stirred up at all times yet unaware of any emotion except when his high rate of physiological activity decreases for some reason.

As for the interpretation we make of the changes in our internal sensations, it is sometimes immediate and automatic. If we find a snake in our path, for example, everything seems to happen at once: our hearts jump, we feel afraid, and we exhibit fearful behavior by leaping back. At other times the interpretation takes longer and is less clear-cut. A student who has a changed pattern of visceral sensations while sitting alone in his room at night may decide that he is lonely. Another student whose best friend recently died may interpret the same pattern of sensations as grief. A student who has a difficult examination coming up may interpret it as fear or anxiety, and another who has put in an unusually hard day's work may decide that he is merely tired.

Typically, the person who becomes aware of changed internal sensations attempts to explain and understand them. He scans the environment and reaches a decision. Sometimes his decision is immediate and often it is reached unconsciously. At other times it involves a longer and more deliberate search that is akin to problem solving; the person may select one hypothesis, test it, and discard it in favor of another. At the end of the search he applies an emotionally toned label to his feelings; he decides that he is happy or sad or angry.

The behavior that is undertaken depends largely on how the emotion is labeled. Moreover, the labeling process itself appears in many cases to produce further bodily changes and intensified feelings. Once a person has decided that he is afraid, he is likely to experience additional activity of the autonomic nervous system, intensified physiological changes, and greater feedback, all of which add to his feelings of fear.

The behavior that may result from emotion also depends on learning, a fact that has been made quite clear from studies of the differences in expressions of emotion in different cultures. When a Chinese schoolboy is scolded, he shows sorrow and shame not by hanging his head but by grinning; when a Navajo or Apache Indian is angry, he does not raise his voice but lowers it; when an inhabitant of the Andaman Islands wants to show his joy at greeting a visiting relative, he sits down in the visitor's lap and weeps (13).

5. other studies on emotion and interpretation

In one of the many interesting experiments inspired by the work of Schachter and his colleagues, college men were told that they would listen to the amplified sounds of their own heartbeats while looking at photographs of women taken from *Playboy* magazine and flashed on a screen. The photographs were shown for fifteen seconds each at one-minute intervals and the men were asked to rate the women on a scale ranging from 0 (for not at all attractive) to 100 (for extremely attractive).

If the conditions had really been as the subjects were told, this would have been a simple experiment in determining whether the subjects' rate of heartbeat rose noticeably when they looked at a seminude woman whom they considered especially attractive. But the sounds to which the subjects listened were not really their own heartbeats but some others previously recorded on a tape. The recordings were deliberately manipulated so that the rate of heartbeat remained more or less constant while the subjects were looking at half the photographs and rose quite markedly when they looked at the other half. Thus the real question the experiment was designed to test was this: If a man *thinks* his heart beats faster when he looks at a woman's picture, will he rate this woman as more attractive than another woman who he thinks does not make his heart beat faster? The answer proved to be an unqualified *yes*. On the 0–100 scale of attractiveness, the subjects gave an average rating of 72 to the pictures that seemed to make their hearts beat faster; to the other pictures they gave a rating of only 54 (14). Thus it appears that at least under some circumstances actual physiological changes are not necessary to produce an emotional state; emotions can occur even if a person merely *thinks* he has been aroused physiologically.

In another experiment, the subjects were men and women who were known to have trouble getting to sleep. They were told that the experiment was a study of how their level of bodily activity, which would be controlled by a pill they were asked to take shortly before going to bed, would affect their dreaming. Actually the pill was what is known in medicine as a placebo—a harmless substance that has no effect on the human body. But half the subjects were told that the pill would arouse them and make them feel as if their minds were racing, the other half that it would relax them and calm down their minds. What the experimenter wanted to discover was what effect, if any, a belief that they were medically aroused or relaxed would have on their ability to get to sleep.

Common sense might predict that the theoretically "aroused" subjects would have more trouble sleeping, while the theoretically "relaxed" would go to sleep more quickly. In actual fact, the results were exactly the opposite—for reasons that you may be able to work out for yourself if you have followed the discussion of emotional interpretations closely. The subjects who thought the placebo had aroused them went to sleep more quickly than usual, presumably because they attributed their keyed-up feelings while lying in bed to the pill rather than to their own emotions. The subjects who thought the placebo had relaxed them stayed awake even longer than they ordinarily did, presumably because they thought they must have been even more emotionally keyed up than usual to remain so tense after taking a pill that was supposed to calm them (15).

In another experiment, subjects were asked to try to solve puzzles while listening to a barrage of loud and unpleasant noises—as part of a study, they were told, of the effect of noise on learning. The experimenters gave them two puzzles and their choice of working on either or both during a three-minute test period. Solving puzzle 1, they were told, would spare them from receiving an electric shock; solving puzzle 2 would bring them a cash reward. Because of the possibility of shock, all subjects showed signs of fear at the beginning of the experiment. But some of them were led to attribute their symptoms of fear—tremors, heart palpitation, and "butterflies in the stomach"—to the noise. The others were told that the noise would merely cause such reactions as ringing of the ears, dizziness,

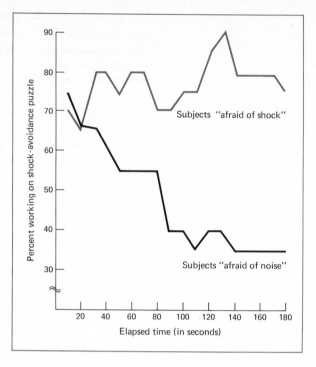

9-5

If you had your choice of trying to solve one puzzle that would spare you from an electrical shock or another puzzle that would bring you the reward of money, which would you choose? The graph lines show what happened when subjects actually faced this situation—and how their choice was influenced by whether they thought their symptoms of fear were caused by the prospect of shock or by noise, as described in the text.

and perhaps dull headache; these subjects presumably knew that their fear symptoms were caused by the prospect of shock.

The real question in the experimenters' minds was how hard the two groups would try either to avoid the shock they thought they would receive if they failed to solve puzzle 1 or to earn some money by solving puzzle 2. (Both puzzles were in fact insoluble.) The answer to the question is shown in Figure 9-5. Of the subjects who recognized that their fears stemmed from the prospect of shock (colored graph line) the majority continued throughout the three minutes to work on the puzzle that would avoid the shock. Of the subjects who attributed their fear to the noise (black line) only a minority continued to work on the shock-avoidance puzzle; when the test period was half over the majority turned their attention to the puzzle that might bring them money (16). Again, interpretation played an important part in emotion and behavior resulting from emotion.

Drugs and Emotions. One interesting but not very well understood aspect of emotions is how they are affected by drugs. In one experiment, volunteers in a prison took LSD without knowing what drug had been administered. A number of them reported experiencing very strong emotions of many kinds, ranging from happiness to anger and fear of loss of control. The emotions occurred without any outside stimulus and for reasons that the subjects were unable to interpret; some of their comments were, "I feel like I'm angry . . . I know that I have no reason to be yet I'm getting angrier by the minute," and "I feel like something funny has happened—everything seems funny, but I don't know why" (17).

The experimenters have speculated that their findings on LSD may contradict the Schachter theory that emotion depends on a cognitive interpretation. However, people who have knowingly taken LSD on a number of different occasions have reported that whether they had a "good trip" or a "bad trip"—that is, pleasant or unpleasant emotions—depended at least in part on the people they were with and the general situation at the time they used the drug. Thus cognitive interpretations seem to be important to those who use LSD in nonlaboratory situations.

individual differences in emotion

Evidence of the wide range of individual differences in capacity for emotion lies all around us. We have friends who go into ecstasy over the receipt of a birthday card and others whom we would not expect to be greatly moved by the gift of a diamond. We have bad-tempered acquaintances who seem to be angry most of the time and good-natured acquaintances who never seem to be angry at all. We know happy people and sad people, brave people and fearful. One person is terrified by a thunderstorm; another is not afraid to fight off and chase a mugger. One student shows signs of tension when he is asked a question in class; another seems to stay calm while addressing a meeting of several hundred.

The individual differences have two sources. Some of them are the result of learning; all of us have had experiences that have conditioned us to react emotionally to particular kinds of stimuli. Other individual differences, however, may depend on characteristics of the glands, the nervous system, and other physical equipment; these differences may be inborn and determined by heredity.

1. glandular differences

One important difference among animals has already been discussed—namely, the fact that the adrenal glands of lions appear to produce large amounts of noradrenalin, while those of animals such as rabbits produce large amounts of adrenalin. In this connection, it has also been found that the adrenal glands of wild rats are much larger than those of rats that have been bred for generations in the laboratory (18).

In human beings, several individual differences have been found in the endocrine glands. Normal thyroid glands have been found to vary from 8 to 50 grams in weight, testes from 10 to 45 grams, ovaries from 2 to 10 grams. The output of human adrenal glands under similar conditions has been found to vary from 7 to 20 grams, of pituitary glands from 250 to 1100 milligrams (19). Although there is no direct evidence, it seems reasonable to suppose that a person with large and active endocrine glands would experience different physiological changes and therefore different emotions from a person with smaller or less active glands.

2. differences in the autonomic nervous system

In our society, generally speaking, the emotion of fear seems to be aroused more easily in women, by stimuli that do not have the same effect on men. Moreover, women are more inclined to behave in a fearful manner. Of themselves, of course, these facts do not necessarily tell us anything about innate differences. Our society teaches women that it is perfectly acceptable for them to become afraid and to act afraid. Men, on the other hand, are not supposed to display the emotion of fear. The apparent differences between men and women, therefore, might be strictly the result of learning and, indeed, might represent the suppression of fear in men rather than its absence.

Some animal experiments, however, indicate that there may in fact be some biological differences in emotional behavior between the sexes. When male and female monkeys are raised in isolation, then placed with other monkeys for the first time, the females tend to act as if they are more afraid of their new companions than do the males. The females often run to a corner of the cage as if to hide or get away; the males generally do not (20). In an experiment with mice, the animals were placed in a cage, a tone was sounded, and a few seconds later an electric shock was administered. Escape from the cage was possible, and records were kept of how quickly the mice learned to get out of the cage when the tone was sounded and thus to escape the shock. Five different breeds of mice were used, and some noticeable differences in speed of learning were found among them. That is to say, one breed learned on the average to escape from the shock considerably more quickly than did another. In each individual breed, however, the female mice learned more quickly than did the males (21).

The experiment with the mice has been interpreted as meaning that the electric shock caused a clearer and stronger perception of unpleasant sensations for the females than for the males. Both this experiment and the observations of the monkeys raised in isolation may mean that the autonomic nervous system of the female has a lower threshold for reaction than does the autonomic nervous system of the male and is inclined to react more quickly, more intensely, and to weaker stimulation.

In human beings, indications of individual differences in the sensitivity of the autonomic nervous system have been provided by experiments with a drug called methacholine. This drug tends to lower the blood pressure but also stimulates the sympathetic nervous system, which has a tendency, as has been noted, to raise the blood pressure. Four quite different reactions to the drug have been observed, presumably indicating differences in the way the sympathetic nervous system responds. Some people show a sharp decrease in blood pressure, with no sign of a return to the previous level after fifteen minutes. Some show a decrease but a return to the previous level after fifteen minutes. Others show only slight changes in blood pressure. In still others the blood pressure rises rather substantially, sometimes after an initial dip. Presumably the sensitivity and activity of the sympathetic system are lowest in the first group, somewhat higher in the second group, still higher in the third group, and highest of all in the fourth (22).

It has also been found that people have characteristic patterns of physiological change in emotional situations. For example, one person may consistently show a rapid pulse, while another may show only a small change in pulse rate but a pronounced increase in skin temperature (23). These varying patterns may also point to individual differences in the activity of the autonomic nervous system.

Considering all the evidence about innate emotional factors, it seems reasonable to assume that people have pronounced constitutional differences in levels of glandular activity and in the sensitivity and activity patterns of their autonomic nervous systems. We might even speculate that there are constitutional differences in the central nervous system, especially in the way the hypothalamus and the limbic system operate.

This line of reasoning has led to a provocative speculation about the processes involved in psychoses (severe forms of mental disturbance). The suggestion has been made that people suffering from psychoses may have some sort of functional disturbances of the nervous structures involved in the physiological reactions to stimuli and that because of these disturbances they may have unusual patterns of physiological change and hence feedback of bodily sensations not generally experienced by other people (24). The person experiencing these sensations must try to interpret them, but the words and concepts he has learned from other people offer him no clues; therefore the interpretations at which he finally arrives may seem completely unintelligible and bizarre by ordinary standards. The strange feelings sometimes experienced by people under the influence of alcohol or a drug such as LSD may be similar examples of bodily sensations, produced by unusual patterns of nervous activity, that defy rational interpretation.

3. emotions and psychosomatic illnesses

Whatever the nature of the individual differences in emotional tendencies, they play a large part in determining how susceptible each of us is to psychosomatic illnesses. It has been known for a long time that psychological stresses are often closely related to such varied physical disabilities as high blood pressure, heart and circulatory diseases, stomach ulcers, arthritis, kidney trouble, and some kinds of asthma. The psychological stresses can be anything that causes intense and prolonged emotion—for example, the frequently mentioned "stress and strain" of modern life that puts all of us under certain pressures caused by competition (for such things as grades in school, acceptances to colleges, and, in the business world, jobs and promotions) as well as by social demands, worries about economic security and war, the struggle to get through traffic jams and reach our appointments on time, and many other similar events.

The manner in which stress affects the body has been dramatically demonstrated by Hans Selye, a biologist at the University of Montreal. Selye has subjected various laboratory animals to many kinds of stress, including exposure to cold and the injection of poisons in doses not quite strong enough to kill. What invariably happens, he found, is that the various glands of the body immediately spring into action, just as in the case of emotion, as the body automatically tries to defend itself. The adrenal glands in particular show some striking changes.

They become enlarged and produce more adrenalin. They also discharge their stored-up supply of steroids, another group of hormones that, as was discussed in Chapter 8, are essential to the body's functions; releasing the steroids causes them to change drastically in color from yellow to brown. Because of this intense activity of the adrenal glands, numerous changes occur in the body. Tissue is broken down to become sugar and provide energy. The amount of salt normally found in the blood stream falls.

In Selye's experiments, animals were subjected to the same high level of stress over a prolonged period. After a few days they seemed to adapt. The adrenal glands returned to normal size, began to renew their supply of stored-up steroids, and changed back to their normal yellow color. The level of salt in the blood rose to normal or even higher. To all intents and purposes, the animals had adjusted to the stress and were perfectly normal; they seemed just like any other animals in the laboratory.

The recovery, however, was only temporary. After several weeks of continued stress the adrenal glands again became enlarged and lost their stores of steroids. The level of salt in the blood fell drastically. The kidneys, as a result of receiving an excess of hormones, underwent some complicated and damaging changes. Eventually the animals died, as if from exhaustion. They had been killed, so to speak, by an excess of the hormones they had produced in their own defense.

Another of Selye's important findings was that even during the period of apparent recovery, the animals were not so normal as they seemed. If a second kind of stress was added in this period, the animals quickly died. One might say that in attempting to adapt to the original stress, they had used their defenses to the maximum and were helpless against a second form of stress (25).

For the sequence of events involved in prolonged stress—the initial shock or alarm, the recovery or resistance period, and at last exhaustion and death—Selye has coined the phrase *general adaptation syndrome*. (To physicians the word *syndrome* means the entire pattern of symptoms and events that characterize the course of a disease.) There are many indications that the general adaptation syndrome that Selye found in animals also occurs in human beings under prolonged stress and that to human beings psychological stress resulting in emotion can be as damaging as any of the physical kinds of stress used in the Selye experiments.

E. the emotion of anxiety

DEFINITION:

ANXIETY

One emotion that deserves special discussion is *anxiety,* which is one of the most powerful of emotions and has far-reaching effects on behavior. Anxiety is *a vague, unpleasant feeling accompanied by a premonition that something undesirable is about to happen.* Anxiety is closely related to the emotion of fear; in fact it is very difficult to draw any sharp dividing line between the two. Generally speaking, fear appears to be a reaction to a specific stimulus and to have a "right now" quality about

it. We see a snake and feel afraid; we know what we are afraid of and recognize that we are afraid right here and now. Anxiety is more vague; its cause is not always apparent. Moreover, as the definition states, it is accompanied by a premonition of something that is about to happen—it is not concerned so much with the here and now as with the future.

1. the physiological basis of anxiety

In physiological terms, anxiety has been found to be accompanied by a number of bodily changes and subsequent sensations. Prominent among them are heart palpitation, a feeling of being out of breath and having trouble breathing, tremors and "shakiness," and tingling sensations of the skin. The palms have a tendency to sweat, producing the galvanic skin reflex. Since anxiety is closely related to fear, one might expect that these physiological changes would depend at least in part on the hormone adrenalin—whose role in the emotion of fear was described on page 309. And this indeed has been the finding of recent studies, although the relation between adrenalin and anxiety is rather complex.

To explain the connection, one must begin with the fact that the carbohydrates in food (starches and sugars) are stored in the liver and other cells of the body in the form of a compound called glycogen. To produce energy, the cells of the body then "burn off" glycogen. One of the by-products of this burning-off process is another substance called lactate—which, as will be made clear in a moment, seems to be of special significance in the emotion of anxiety. When we exercise, our muscles burn off large quantities of glycogen and produce large amounts of lactate; measurement of the level of lactate in the blood stream after strenuous exercise shows a significant rise. The same kind of rise in the lactate level is also produced by the action of adrenalin, whether the adrenalin is secreted naturally by the adrenal glands or injected into the blood stream.

Strong evidence of a connection between lactate and anxiety has been provided by studies at the Washington University School of Medicine. In these experiments, large amounts of lactate were injected into the blood streams of a number of subjects, some of whom were "normal" and some of whom had an unusually strong tendency to suffer from anxiety. The injections of lactate produced at least some of the physiological changes associated with anxiety in all the subjects. Indeed some of the subjects experienced severe attacks of anxiety; this was true of 20 percent of the "normal" subjects and fully 93 percent of those known to be anxiety-prone (26).

Thus the bodily states associated with anxiety may depend on the level of lactate in the blood, which in turn is known to depend at least in part on the secretion of adrenalin. Further evidence of the relation between adrenalin and anxiety comes from experiments with a drug called propranolol, which inhibits adrenalin from raising the level of lactate in the blood stream. Injections of propranolol have been found to prevent or reduce the physiological changes associated with anxiety (26)—a fact that may point to possible relief for people whose tendency to overproduce adrenalin makes them unusually subject to anxiety states.

LACTATE

2. sources of anxiety

From the psychological viewpoint, anxiety is an extremely unpleasant experience and particularly difficult to cope with because of its vagueness. We usually cannot pin down the cause or even the precise nature of what we fear will happen. We can only describe the feeling in the most general terms; we say we are worried, tense, "blue," moody, or "jumpy." The last word, though as vague as the others, is particularly appropriate because the person who is in the grip of anxiety has a lowered threshold for other kinds of emotional responses. He is likely to be quite irritable and quickly moved to anger; on the other hand, he may also overreact to pleasurable stimuli. He tends to have wide swings of mood and his behavior is often unpredictable.

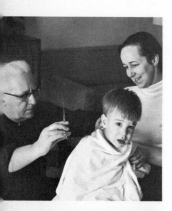

As for the stimuli that tend to set off anxiety, these vary from person to person. Young children tend to become anxious about the possibilities of punishment, loss of a privilege, and physical harm from strange animals, storms, and the dark. The future event that the child fears is in the external world.

Adults, on the other hand, are less often anxious about external events, for they have discovered that lions, storms, and ghosts are hardly likely to hurt them. Their sources of anxiety are not so clearly specified and are often difficult to track down. An adult is likely to say, "I feel uneasy. I don't know why, but I fear something bad is going to happen. It's ridiculous—but I can't help it." Often the unspecified source of their anxiety is one of two things: 1) an inconsistency that they have consciously or unconsciously observed between two different and conflicting beliefs they hold or between their beliefs and their behavior (such as when a person who believes strongly in being nice to everyone performs a hostile act), or 2) feelings of uncertainty, a topic so important that it deserves discussion of its own.

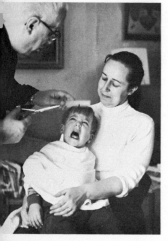

3. anxiety as a result of uncertainty

Numerous studies have shown that anxiety frequently occurs when we are faced with uncertainty—that is, when we do not know exactly where we stand or what to expect next. In one experiment, for example, college men were asked to take part in a study of how pain, in the form of an electric shock administered at the count of twelve, would affect their heart rates. The subjects were divided into three groups. Two of the groups received sample shocks in advance so that they would know what was coming; for one of these groups the shock was mild and for the other it was quite strong. The third group received no indication of what kind of shock to expect.

Measurement of the subjects' heart rates while they were waiting for the experimental shock to be delivered showed only a small increase for those who knew what kind of shock was coming, regardless of whether it was mild or strong. The subjects who did not know what kind of shock to expect, however, showed a pronounced jump in heart rate; by the count of twelve the rate had risen an average of 24 beats a minute (27). The experiment is a clear indication that the unknown produces more anxiety than the known—even when the known, as in the case of the strong shock, is quite unpleasant.

In another experiment, college men were asked to listen to a voice counting to fifteen and were told that at the count of ten they might receive a shock. Whether or not they received the shock, it was explained, depended on the draw of a card from a pack of twenty cards, which was shown to them. For one group of subjects, the deck contained only one "shock" card and nineteen "no-shock" cards—so that they knew their chances of shock were only one in twenty or 5 percent. For the second group the chances were 50 percent, and for the third group the chances were 95 percent.

In this case, common sense suggests that the group with the 50 percent chance of shock would show the most anxiety, while the 5 percent group would feel relatively secure and the 95 percent group would consider themselves almost certain to receive a shock and would be prepared for it. Indeed even the experimenters expected this result. To the experimenters' surprise, however, the 5 percent group showed the most physiological arousal—as clearly indicated by the graph in Figure 9-6—and therefore presumably the most anxiety.

anxiety and uncertainty

9-6

Subjects who had only a 5 percent chance of receiving a shock at the count of ten showed more physiological arousal—hence presumably more anxiety—than subjects who had a 50 percent or a 95 percent chance. For an explanation of this rather surprising result, see the text. The measure of physiological arousal shown here is electrical conductivity of the skin.

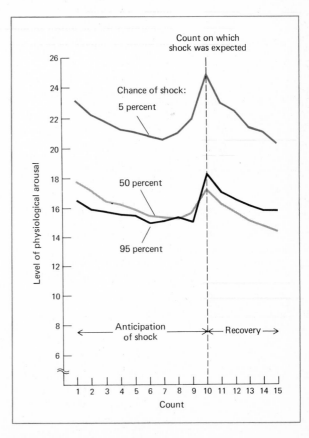

The unexpected result of the experiment is probably explained by the comments of some of the subjects in the 50 percent group, who said they had decided that their chances of getting a shock were high enough to lead them to assume that they would get one—thus reducing their suspense—and merely to hope for a pleasant surprise. In other words, they took much the same attitude as the subjects in the 95 percent group, who were almost certain they would get a shock. The subjects in the 5 percent group, on the other hand, seemed to feel the most uncertainty; their chances of being shocked were so low that they could not resign themselves to the thought, but neither could they dismiss the possibility (28). Because of the uncertainty, they showed the greatest anxiety of all.

4. some effects of anxiety on learning

There is one point about anxiety that deserves special mention because of its particular significance for college students. This is the effect of anxiety on learning, which has been the subject of considerable experimentation. Unfortunately, no experiment on anxiety can be completely satisfactory, because it is extremely difficult to know either how much anxiety a particular person feels or the source of the anxiety. The experimenter usually has to rely on the subject's answers to some sort of questionnaire, and it is almost impossible to devise a questionnaire that will satisfactorily measure all types of anxiety. Much of the experimental work on anxiety has involved the use of scales that attempt to measure the particular kind often called "test anxiety," which centers around the fear of failure at school tasks. On the basis of questionnaires, subjects have been divided as well as possible into groups with "high anxiety" and "low anxiety," and their learning of various tasks has then been studied—with results that, though

anxiety and simple conditioning

9-7

Charted are the results of an experiment in conditioning the eyeblink reflex of two groups of students, one of which had a high level of anxiety and the other a low level of anxiety. Note that on all trials, from the first to the last, conditioning was more rapid for the anxious group. (29)

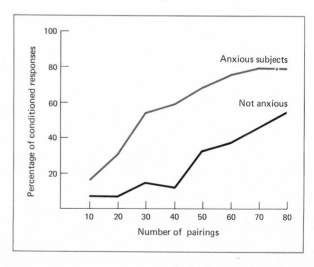

not entirely conclusive because of the limitations just mentioned, are nonetheless interesting.

In one experiment, the learning involved conditioning the eyelid-blinking reflex of college students to a previously neutral stimulus, and the findings were as shown in Figure 9–7. Note how much more quickly the conditioning took place among the "anxious" students than among the "not anxious." In another experiment, however, the results were quite different. In this case the students were asked to find a path through a maze while blindfolded; the maze had ten places where the subjects had their choice of going to either right or left and had to learn which direction was correct. At this task, the "high-anxiety" students learned more slowly than the others (30). One possible explanation for the results of these two experiments appears to be that students with "high anxiety" learn simple tasks more quickly but have trouble with more complicated learning, requiring the making of choices, because their anxiety interferes with intense concentration.

People who are high in test anxiety seem to do particularly badly at learning tasks when someone is watching them; the results of one experiment that demonstrates this fact are shown in Figure 9–8.

anxiety and learning when someone is looking

9-8

The graph lines show the result of an experiment in which college women were divided into two groups, those who scored highest on a scale of test anxiety and those who scored lowest. The women were asked to learn a list of nonsense syllables—some while they thought no one was watching, the others while they were aware that an observer was looking on from behind a one-way mirror. Note that the subjects low in anxiety actually did better when they had an observer, while those high in anxiety did rather badly when they knew they were being watched. (31)

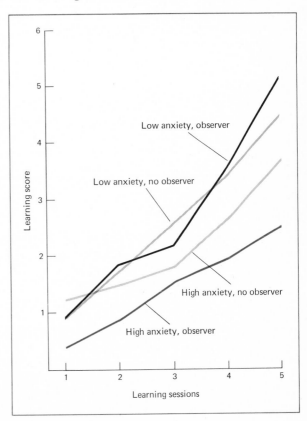

9-9

The bars show the average grades made by "high-anxiety" and "low-anxiety" students of different levels of scholastic ability as indicated by their College Board scores. Note the pronounced differences in the middle ranges of scholastic ability. (32)

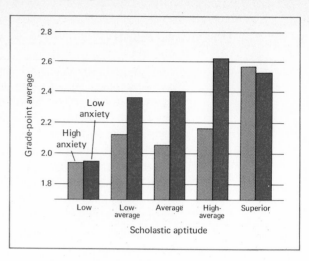

How does anxiety affect actual performance in college? This question was explored by an investigator who selected a group of male students relatively high in anxiety and a group relatively low in anxiety; he then examined their College Board scores, as an indication of their ability, and their actual grades in college. As is shown in Figure 9-9, the students with the lowest levels of scholastic ability made much the same grades regardless of whether they seemed to experience anxiety. So did the students with the highest levels of scholastic ability. But at the in-between levels of ability—where, of course, most students fall—the students who were relatively free from anxiety made significantly better grades than did the anxious students.

In a follow-up study an attempt was made to select "anxious" freshmen who were making low grades and were in danger of flunking out of college. One group of these freshmen took an active part in a counseling program in which they received advice about their problems in college, methods of study, campus life in general, and their relations with their professors—advice that presumably would reduce their anxiety about the college situation. Another group, matched as closely as possible for College Board scores, type of high school attended, and other factors that influence performance in college, did not receive counseling. From midterm to the end of the first semester the counseled group made an average improvement of more than half a grade point. The group that was not counseled improved by less than a tenth of a grade point (33). Anxiety about the college situation would appear to be a frequent—though perhaps correctable—cause of failure in college.

5. anxiety and risk taking

Figure 9-10 illustrates the results of an experiment that offers some clues about the possible relationship between anxiety and the willingness to take risks. Note that the subjects who appeared to be relatively free from test anxiety tended to scorn the "sure thing" in this game; they made very few throws from

326

the close distances at which they were almost certain to succeed but would receive only a low score. They also tended to avoid the high risk of gambling that they could score from the longest distances, which would have given them the highest scores. Subjects who appeared to be relatively high in test anxiety made many more shots from the short distances but also "went for broke" more often by trying from the longest distances.

One might speculate, on the basis of this experiment, that people who are highly anxious about success and failure tend to adopt either a very conservative or a very risky strategy in life situations. They are inclined to settle for the "sure thing" and thus avoid failure that would add to their anxiety, or else they tend to take the kind of chances at which success is such a remote possibility that failure can readily be excused. All of us, certainly, have observed people who do not take many chances in life, settle for jobs that seem beneath their real abilities, yet occasionally take a flier in a gambling casino or in risky investments. Less anxious people, on the other hand, appear to have sufficient confidence to assume

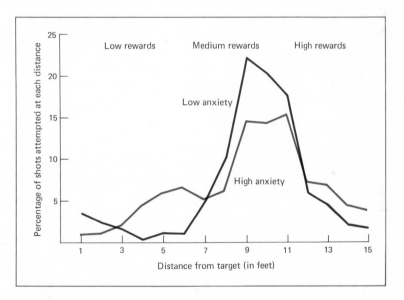

anxiety, conservatism, and "going for broke"

9-10 The curves show the different strategies used by subjects who had been found to be low in test anxiety and others high in test anxiety in a game where they tossed rings at a peg from any distance they chose. For ringing the peg from close distances they received very low scores, from far distances very high scores, and from middle distances middle scores. Note that the low-anxiety subjects chose a strategy of intermediate risks, while the high-anxiety subjects tended to be very conservative or to "go for broke." The two groups of subjects were matched as closely as possible for desire to succeed at the game—that is, for indications of the achievement motive, which will be discussed in Chapter 10. (34)

the middle-range risks that are most likely to lead to success in the long run.

Along similar lines, it has been observed that college students who appear to have a high amount of fear of failure tend to leave examination rooms early (35), as if to avoid the further anxiety of continuing to try on the examination. This strategy, of course, only increases the likelihood of the failure that they find such a disturbing prospect.

summary

1. Emotions involve a wide range of physiological changes—the body may be "stirred up" or "toned down."

2. Some of the changes represent activity by the striped muscles of movement; these include a) muscle tension, b) tremor, c) eye blinking and other nervous movements, d) facial expressions, and e) vocal expressions of emotion.

3. Other changes are controlled by the autonomic nervous system and endocrine glands; these include a) heart rate, b) blood pressure, c) blood circulation, d) composition of the blood, e) activity of the digestive organs, f) metabolic rate, g) breathing, h) salivation, i) sweating, j) gooseflesh and hair standing on end, and k) pupil size.

4. Recent studies indicate that changes in pupil size are often a sensitive measure of emotion; indeed pupil size has been found to increase noticeably even when a person looks at an interesting photograph or engages in mental activity such as trying to remember a telephone number.

5. The physiological changes in emotion were the basis of the *James-Lange theory*, which maintained that the changes were set off by stimuli in the environment, that the changes in turn stimulated sensory nerves inside the organs of the body, and that the messages of these sensory nerves were then perceived as emotion. A striking feature of the theory was its suggestion that we do not tremble and run because we are afraid but instead feel afraid because we are trembling and running.

6. In contrast to the James-Lange theory, the *Cannon-Bard theory* held that stimuli in the environment set off patterns of activity in the brain (notably the hypothalamus) that were relayed simultaneously to the autonomic nervous system, where they triggered the bodily changes of emotion, and to the cerebral cortex, the higher part of the brain, where they resulted in the feelings of emotion.

7. More recent experiments by Schachter have indicated that physiological changes are essential for emotion but that the same pattern of change can result in different emotions in different environmental contexts. This has led to the *cognitive theory* (sometimes called the "juke box" theory), which holds that emotion depends both on physiological changes and on a mental process that interprets the meaning of the changes.

8. Individual differences in emotion appear to be caused both by a) learning, which conditions the individual to react to particular kinds of stimuli, and b) constitutional differences in glandular activity, sensitivity and activity of

the autonomic nervous system, and possibly also characteristics of the central nervous system.

9. Individual differences in emotional tendencies appear to explain the relation between psychological stress and susceptibility to such psychosomatic illnesses as heart disease, high blood pressure, and stomach ulcers.

10. The important emotion of *anxiety* is caused in children chiefly by concern over external events (punishment, physical harm, the dark), in adults chiefly by less specific concerns: inconsistencies between beliefs or between a belief and behavior (as when a person who believes in being nice to everyone commits a hostile act) or feelings of uncertainty (wondering where we stand and what will happen next).

11. People high in anxiety appear to learn faster than people low in anxiety in simple learning situations but more slowly when the learning demands the making of choices. In college, anxiety does not appear to affect the grades of students of lowest or highest learning capacity. Of students of in-between ability, however, those with high anxiety make significantly lower grades than those with low anxiety.

12. Anxiety appears to be related to risk taking. People with high anxiety seem to adopt either a conservative strategy, in which they settle for lower rewards but minimize the chances of failure, or a "go for broke" strategy, in which they take chances with such a remote possibility of success that failure can readily be excused. People with low anxiety appear inclined toward the middle-range risks that usually are the most likely to lead to success in the long run.

recommended reading

Appley, M. H., and Trumbull, R., eds. *Psychological stress: issues in research.* New York: Appleton-Century-Crofts, 1967.

Darwin, C. *The expression of the emotions in man and animals.* New York: Philosophical Library, 1955.

Glass, D. C., ed. *Neurophysiology and emotion.* New York: Rockefeller University Press, 1967.

Goethals, G. W., and Klos, D. S. *Experiencing youth: first-person accounts.* Boston: Little, Brown, 1970.

Lazarus, R. S. *Psychological stress and the coping process.* New York: McGraw-Hill, 1966.

Mandler, G. Emotion. In Brown, R., et al., eds. *New directions in psychology.* New York: Holt, Rinehart and Winston, 1962, pp. 267–343.

Schachter, S. *Emotion, obesity, and crime.* New York: Academic Press, 1971.

CHAPTER 10

drives and motives

Of all the words used by the relatively new science of psychology, perhaps the one that has achieved the quickest and widest popularity is *motives*. It is a word heard almost every day in remarks such as: "I wonder what her motive is?" "I don't trust his motives." "I didn't seem to help the situation, but at least my motives were good."

Now that the word has become so popular, everybody feels free—and competent—to analyze the motives of others. We see a young man who spends as much time as possible around girls and has a date nearly every night, and we say that he is "highly sexed," implying that he has a strong sexual motive. We notice that another young man swears a great deal, even around girls, and we call him "hostile." A young woman is constantly asking her boyfriend for help with her studies, and we label her "dependent." Another young woman studies until late every night, and we call her "ambitious."

Motives operate in a much trickier fashion, however, than is generally supposed. Every one of the judgments in the preceding paragraph could be wrong. The young man who dates every night may not have strong sexual motives but merely a desire to impress his friends with his popularity. The young man who swears may do so not out of hostility but out of a sexual motive; he may think that this kind of behavior makes him seem more masculine and therefore more sexually attractive. The young woman who asks her boyfriend for help with her studies may also have a sexual motive rather than an urge to be "dependent"; she may feel that the appearance of needing help makes her seem more feminine and attractive. The young woman who studies hard may well be the dependent one; she may be not ambitious but merely afraid of losing the approval of her parents if she fails to get good grades.

It is extremely difficult to judge motives from behavior. As a matter of fact, motives may never result in observable behavior. A man who has been eagerly following the developments in space exploration may have a strong motive to go to the moon. Yet the goal is unattainable for him, and he makes no attempt to attain it. On a more commonplace level, many people talk wistfully about going to Europe yet never try to save the money or make the time for the trip.

Though the subject is full of difficulties and confusions, motivation is a key issue in psychology. We are used to thinking in terms of cause and effect. Astronomy tells us *why* the sun rises in the morning and sets at night. Physics tells us *why* a piano sounds different from a saxophone. Chemistry tells us *why* wood burns and iron does not. It is only natural that we should also search for some kind of underlying causes of behavior.

For many centuries the "why" of behavior was attributed to the human soul, which was thought of in part as a force that initiated, organized, and directed the individual's activities. A number of the early psychologists, on the other hand, believed that the explanation lay in inherited instincts. These men were impressed by the inborn and unlearned tendencies of the robin to build the characteristic nest of its species and of the salmon to migrate from river to ocean and back to the river to spawn. Since man is also an animal, they reasoned, he too must behave in accordance with instincts. William James theorized that there were no less than seventeen powerful human instincts: toward imitation, rivalry, pugnacity, sympathy, hunting, fear, acquisitiveness, constructiveness (the urge to build), play, curiosity, sociability, shyness, secretiveness, cleanliness, jealousy, love, and mother love (1).

It is now known, of course, that human beings have few if any instincts. The forces inside the human being that often initiate, direct, and organize behavior are instead called motives. Motives take all the forms mentioned by James as instincts and many others; indeed the list of possible human motives seems almost endless.

One definition of a motive is this: *A motive is a desire for a goal that has acquired value for the individual.* This desire for a goal often leads the person to learn ways of gratifying the motive. The motive to obtain recognition from others can lead a young boy to improve his skill at football; the motive for a romantic relationship may lead a girl to learn how to flatter a young man without his awareness. Thus motives often—though not always—help determine behavior.

The question that the definition of motives leaves unanswered, of course, is how a certain goal comes to acquire value. The answer is not completely known. Most psychologists would agree that goals are determined by a mixture of biological traits—that is to say, characteristics of the human body and nervous system—and learning. There is considerable disagreement, however, as to how these two factors operate and which is more important. Some psychologists believe that human motives derive chiefly from the drives, which are caused by basic physical needs. Others believe that motives are more cognitive—in other words, that they represent a mental process in which we evaluate our possibilities and choose among alternatives. Indeed some psychologists, as will be seen later, believe that the dynamics of the human brain incline men toward what has been called *self-actualization,* or the full realization of one's own potentialities and satisfaction of a thirst for knowledge and beauty.

biological drives

How the drives operate can best be observed among babies who have not yet had time to do any learning. Because of his built-in system of reactions between body and nervous system, the newborn baby behaves in a number of goal-seeking ways. For example, he seeks food, sucks vigorously when it is presented, and cries when he lacks it. He also cries when unable to achieve the goals of warmth and relief from pain. Each of these forms of behavior represents the operation of a drive, which can be defined as a *pattern of brain activity that results from certain kinds of physiological conditions.* These physiological conditions usually occur when the organism is in a state of deprivation (that is, in need of food or water) or of imbalance (such as too warm, too cold, or needing to sleep or to eliminate its waste products). The physiological states trigger special patterns of nervous activity in the brain, especially in the reticular formation (page 284) and the hypothalamus (page 285).

In human beings, the drive pattern usually results in a sensation, such as the feeling of hunger, thirst, or fatigue. It also frequently serves as an energizing force that leads to behavior. When we are hungry, we go to a vending machine for a candy bar or to a restaurant for a meal. When we are thirsty, we go to a water fountain. When we are tired, we go to bed. By so doing, we attain a goal that brings about an end to the physiological condition, stops the pattern of nervous activity, and thus satisfies the drive.

hunger

As the definition of drive implies, the key to our feelings of hunger lies in the brain, rather than in the stomach as popularly supposed. Although common-sense observation tells us that we have hunger pangs and that these pangs come from the stomach—indeed we can often hear our stomachs growling as if demanding food—these are only secondary factors. One experimenter operated on a rat and severed all the sensory nerves leading from the stomach to the brain, yet the rat ate as before (2). In another operation, the entire stomach of a rat was removed, yet the rat continued to show signs of hunger (3). Cases have been reported in which the human stomach had to be removed, without any pronounced effect on the desire for food (4).

What actually happens is that after a period of not eating, the chemical composition of the blood changes; and these changes in the blood stimulate the brain to fire a pattern of nervous impulses that results in our feeling hungry and causes us to seek food. Thus, when blood from a hungry dog is transferred to the veins of a dog that has just eaten, the well-fed dog starts looking for food again (5). Certainly the hypothalamus is in part responsible. When a small portion of the hypothalamus related to the hunger drive is surgically destroyed, an animal loses practically all interest in eating (6). When another small portion is removed, an animal eats constantly and becomes grossly fat (7). Moreover, electrical stimulation of the hypothalamus can cause an animal to start or stop eating. Yet other brain structures also appear to be important. One group of experimenters recently has discovered that a rat that eats in response to electrical stimulation of the hypothalamus will, if no food is present, often turn to other forms of behavior, such as drinking and gnawing (8). Thus nerve patterns in lower parts of the brain connected with the hypothalamus also seem to play a significant role in drives and drive-satisfying behavior.

How the Hunger Drive Is Satisfied. The hunger drive is satisfied not by the mere act of eating but by food itself, which changes the composition of the blood and "turns off" the drive. In one experiment a rat received an injection of milk directly into the stomach if it went to one arm of a T-shaped maze, an injection of salt solution if it went to the other arm. The rat soon learned to prefer the arm in which it received the milk injection (9). In another experiment a tube was attached to the ear of a rabbit so that fluids could be pumped directly into the blood stream. In the rabbit's cage were three plates. If it sat on one plate, salt solution was pumped into the blood stream. On the second plate it received artificially sweetened water with no food value. On the third it received a solution of sugar. After a while the rabbit began spending most of its time on the plate where it received the sugar (10). The drawing in Figure 10-1 illustrates a similar experiment.

Aside from man and the animals he has domesticated, few animals tend to become overly fat. Their hunger drive operates in such a manner as to give them the amount of calories they need to keep their body weight constant. Moreover, they develop hungers for the specific kinds of foods they need. They tend to eat

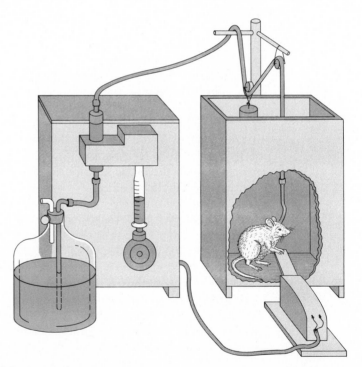

a well-fed rat that never eats

10-1 When the rat presses the bar, a squirt of liquid food is delivered directly to its stomach. The rat never smells, tastes, or swallows the food. Nonetheless, it soon learns to press the bar just often enough to satisfy its hunger and maintain its normal intake of calories. (11)

a balanced diet of carbohydrates, proteins, fats, minerals, and vitamins. If they have been deprived of any of these substances for a period of time, they will eat it in preference to anything else, even if they are otherwise fully satiated with food. These regulatory mechanisms also appear to be related to blood chemistry.

Why Do People Get Fat?   As to why some people become overweight, the obvious reason is that they eat more than the operation of the hunger drive would normally dictate. Their urge to eat is somehow out of kilter. One experiment has shown, for example, that fat people tend to eat when they have the opportunity even if they have already eaten a great deal and would not normally be expected to be hungry, also to eat just as much or even more when they are emotionally upset as when they are calm (12). In another experiment in which clocks were manipulated to make the subjects think that dinner was being served later than usual, fat people ate more than usual but people of normal weight did not (13). Fat people are especially likely to eat a lot when the food tastes particularly good (14). It has also been noted that they tend to be nighttime refrigerator raiders; they often are not very hungry in the morning but have a ravenous urge for food at hours when the average person is finished eating for the day and ready for bed (15).

Thus the experimental evidence provides a picture of the fat person as one who is always hungry, except possibly at breakfast time—or at least whose hunger drive can quickly be triggered by the sight or thought of food, particularly good food, even when a person of normal weight would still be satiated from his last meal.

The reason behind the reason, however, is something of a mystery. One suggestion is that the hunger drive of fat people has somehow been modified through learning so that it is set off not so much by blood chemistry as by external cues such as the sight and smell of food; thus their urge for food is more psychological than physiological (12). Another possibility, however, is that they may have some kind of inborn abnormality that affects the areas of the brain concerned with the hunger drive. This possibility has been supported by a study of babies who were only two to four days old. Some of the babies were already considerably fatter than the others and also showed different eating habits. When offered a bottle containing a formula that had been sweetened and therefore tasted especially good, they ate 28 percent more than usual, while other babies ate only 8 percent more. But when the fat babies were forced to work hard to get food, through a nipple with a hole of unusually small size, they ate 20 percent less than they usually did. Even at that early age, they appeared to be highly responsive to the taste of food but relatively unwilling to work for it (16). The study of the babies seems to indicate that some people are born with some kind of biological tendency to be fat.

thirst

In the case of the thirst drive, the key brain structures appear to be nerve cells that are particularly sensitive to changes in the relative amount of water contained in the cells of the body and in the blood stream.* When the amount of water in the body becomes too low, the nerve cells fire off a pattern of nervous impulses that results in the sensation of thirst and leads the organism to seek liquids. Much as in the case of hunger. The goal of the thirst drive is water, not the act of drinking. When the experiment that was shown in Figure 10-1 is changed so that the animal receives water instead of food directly in the stomach, it soon learns to take in the normal amount of water even though it never drinks.

sleep

The sleep drive is considerably less well understood than the hunger and thirst drives. Certainly it is related in some way to body chemistry, for if the fluid from the brain cavities of a sleepy animal is injected into the brain cavities of a wide-awake animal, the second animal is likely to go right to sleep (18). Moreover, the drive appears to be regulated by a "sleep system" and a "wakefulness system" in the brain. Surgical destruction of one area of the brain causes an animal to remain awake until it dies of exhaustion; destruction of another area causes the animal to sleep almost constantly. However there is as yet no solid knowledge of the exact nature of the chemical changes that stimulate the brain's sleep and wakefulness systems or of what function sleep performs for the organism. Perhaps being awake results in the production by the brain and body of certain chemicals that would be harmful in too large amounts and being asleep permits these chemicals to be eliminated.

Ordinary and Paradoxical Sleep.   One of the peculiar facts about sleep is that it takes two different forms. About 80 percent of sleeping time is spent in what is called *ordinary sleep,* in which the activity of the brain, as can be seen in Figure 10-2, is quite different from its activity during waking hours and the muscles of the body are quite relaxed. The other 20 percent is spent in *paradoxical sleep,* in which the brain's activity becomes very similar to that in the waking state but the muscles become even more relaxed and indeed the sleeper is harder to wake up than during ordinary sleep.

It is in periods of paradoxical sleep that dreaming occurs. The sleeper's eyes dart about as if he is following a series of visual images, and if he is awakened he reports a dream. Thus paradoxical sleep is also known as *REM sleep*—REM stands for the *rapid eye movements* that can be observed during these periods. Paradoxical or REM sleep seems to fulfill some special function. If a sleeper is wakened every time he begins to enter such a period and is thus deprived of this type of sleep, he will make up for it the following night; and if he is deprived for several nights, he becomes irritable and anxious, suffers memory lapses, and has difficulty concentrating (20).

*Strictly speaking, the cells are sensitive to *osmotic pressure*—that is, the relative concentration of chemicals such as salt and sugar in the body fluids (17). But of course osmotic pressure depends chiefly on the amount of fluid in which the chemicals are in solution.

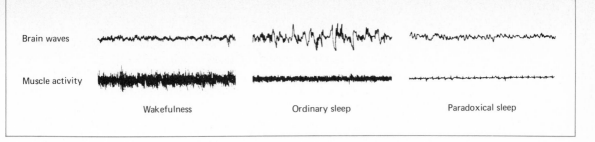

Brain waves			
Muscle activity			
	Wakefulness	Ordinary sleep	Paradoxical sleep

brain and muscle activity during sleep

10-2 The tracings show typical patterns of brain waves and muscle activity during periods of wakefulness, ordinary sleep, and paradoxical or REM sleep. Note that during paradoxical sleep the brain waves resemble the pattern during wakefulness but the muscles are most relaxed of all. (19)

Sleep Rhythms. All of us have a physiological rhythm related to our sleeping habits. During sleep, body temperature reaches its low point of the twenty-four-hour day, and the release of hormones by the glands is at a minimum. Temperature and glandular activity are at their peak when we are widest awake. For some people the peak comes right after waking; for others, considerably later in the day. This accounts for the fact that some of us are "day people," who wake up full of energy, do most of our day's work by noon, and are tired early in the evening, while others of us are "night people," who have a hard time dragging ourselves out of bed, do our best work late in the day, and like to stay up late.

A sudden change in sleeping hours upsets the rhythm and often produces changes in behavior. In this age of jet transportation, people fly to parts of the world where the time is as much as eight hours earlier or later than at home. Recent studies have shown that they usually suffer at first from physical discomfort and reduced physical and mental efficiency—to the point where it is unsafe for a pilot to fly another plane immediately or for a diplomat or a businessman to make a critical decision.

other drives

Four other biological drives deserve brief mention. One is the *temperature drive* that is common to all warm-blooded animals; in human beings its goal is to maintain the body at about 98.6 degrees Fahrenheit. The temperature drive is controlled by cells in a lower part of the brain that are sensitive to temperature changes. When stimulated by increased warmth, they fire off messages that cause perspiration, which cools the body through evaporation, and also send more blood toward the surface of the body, where it loses heat more quickly. When stimulated by cooling, these brain cells induce shivering, the constriction of blood vessels in the skin, and increased activity of the thyroid gland, which in turn leads to increased bodily activity and the production of more heat (18).

The *breathing drive* goes unnoticed under ordinary circumstances, but a man who is drowning or being suffocated will fight as hard for air as he might fight for food when facing starvation. The *elimination drive* gets rid of the body's waste products. The *pain drive* leads to such reflex behavior as pulling the hand away from fire and such learned behavior as swallowing medicine to relieve a headache.

sex as a drive

Among lower animals sex is almost as direct a drive as hunger or thirst. At most times the female sex drive is quiescent, and the female is not sexually attractive to the male of her species. She has regularly recurring periods of heat, however, in which large amounts of hormones are released from her sex glands and trigger a sex control mechanism in the central nervous system. During these periods, which vary in frequency and length from species to species, the female actively seeks sexual contacts and engages in the kind of courtship and copulatory behavior characteristic of the species. A female in heat is usually apparent to the male of the species through various cues such as odors, the sex "calls" of the cat and other animals, and reddening of the sexual skin in monkeys and birds.

For some organisms, sexual behavior is largely unlearned; birds, rats, and other lower animals raised in isolation usually demonstrate normal sexual behavior at the first opportunity. But monkeys raised in isolation do not (21). Among human beings sex can hardly be considered only a biological drive. The desire and ability of the human female to perform the sex act are not significantly dependent on her hormone cycles; nor is her sexual attractiveness to the male. Sex is of course a powerful force in human affairs, but much of this influence derives from its motivational rather than its drive qualities.

drives and incentive objects

The sex drive in animals is a good example of the fact that the drives, though they stem primarily from the brain's reaction to physiological conditions, also depend on events in the environment. That is to say, they can be triggered by stimuli—called *incentive objects*—of which the organism becomes aware through the sense organs. Thus a male rat might show no sign of sex drive until it becomes aware, chiefly through the sense of smell, of the presence of a female in heat. Moreover, a rat that has just satisfied the sex drive through copulation may eagerly approach a second female (22).

Rather similarly, an animal that has eaten its fill of one kind of food may begin eating again if a more preferred kind of food is presented. Thus the indications are that many parts of the brain, including the areas that receive messages from the sense organs, cooperate in producing feelings that accompany the drives and drive-satisfying behavior. (Everyone has had the experience, for example, of suddenly becoming quite hungry because of the smell of hamburgers and onions coming from the open doorway of a restaurant.) One theory is that sensory messages indicating the presence of an incentive object interact with the nerve patterns set up by physiological conditions; in combination the nervous impulses create a *central motive state* that leads the organism to make a *consummatory action*—for example, seeking and eating food (23).

stimulus needs

The biological drives are powerful and dramatic forces. All of them except the sex drive lead to the learning of behavior essential to keeping the organism alive and intact, and the sex drive is essential to the survival of the species. When the drives go unsatisfied, they often result in intense sensations of discomfort and eventually in death. Naturally the biological drives have long been recognized and studied as primary sources for the energizing of behavior. For many years they were considered the only basic and inborn sources, from which all motives were derived.

In recent years, however, more and more evidence has indicated that the basic nature of the organism demands certain other satisfactions. Food, water, sleep, and the other goals that satisfy the biological drives do not seem to be enough. In addition, the organism seems to have inborn tendencies to seek certain kinds of stimulation. Exact understanding of these tendencies is incomplete, and there is not even full agreement as to what they should properly be called. Some investigators believe that they are closely allied to the drives and should bear the same name; these investigators would add to the list of biological drives such others as a curiosity drive, an activity drive, and a manipulation drive. Other investigators, noting that these tendencies seem to spring from the nature of the central nervous system rather than from any other physiological conditions, have called them psychological needs. The term used here, *stimulus needs,* may eventually require revision as more is learned about them. The term has been chosen for two reasons. First, the goal of all these tendencies seems to be some kind of stimulation and particularly change in stimulation. Second, the tendencies do not have the life-and-death urgency of the drives, and their goals are not so specific and clear-cut as goals such as food and water; use of the word *needs* instead of the word *drives* suggests that there are important differences between the two.

There appear to be at least two different kinds of stimulus needs, which deserve individual discussion.

the need for sensory stimulation

This need has already been mentioned, although not by name. In Chapter 7, on perception, the importance of early sensory experience for the development of normal perception was discussed. It was also mentioned that the human baby, when less than two days old, tends to focus his eyes on the apex of a black triangle that is seen against a light background—the exact spot at which the contrast between black and white is the greatest. Thus the baby seems to exhibit an inborn tendency to seek increased *sensory stimulation.*

What happens to adults who are deprived of sensory stimulation has been

10-3

This man is taking part in an experiment designed to show what happens when activity of the human senses is reduced as nearly as possible to zero. The eyeshade permits him to see nothing but a dim haze. The arm casts mask the sense of touch in his hands. The room is soundproofed, and he hears nothing but the constant soft hum of a fan. For what happens to him under these conditions, see the text. (The wires shown at the top of the photo were used to record brain waves.) (24)

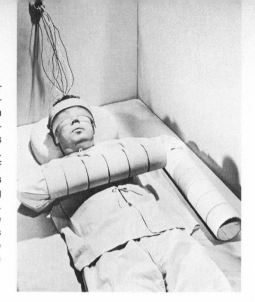

demonstrated in the laboratory, with dramatic results. In one experiment, volunteer subjects were kept in bed as shown in Figure 10-3. In a similar experiment, they were fitted with a sort of diver's helmet and suspended in water held at skin temperature (25). In both cases, the subjects saw nothing but a dim light or no light at all and heard nothing more than a steady low hum; they smelled and tasted nothing, and their sense of touch was masked as much as possible. In other words, activity of their senses was held to almost zero. Rather quickly, it was discovered, many of them found themselves unable to think logically. Their memories became disorganized. Sometimes they felt strangely happy, and at other times they felt anxious or even panicky. Some of them began to develop symptoms that are often associated with severe mental disturbance; for example, they "saw" imaginary sights and "heard" imaginary sounds.

Why a lack of sensory stimulation should have such drastic effects is not completely understood. One possibility is suggested by what has been discovered about the reticular formation of the brain. Nerve impulses from the sense organs pass through the reticular formation on their way to the sensory areas of the cortex, or highest part of the brain, where they result in conscious sensations. As they pass through, they seem to set off other impulses, which are sent by the reticular formation to all parts of the cortex, keeping it in a general state of activity. Without a constant barrage of impulses from the reticular formation, perhaps the cortex cannot function normally. This seems to be a possible explanation of the need for sensory stimulation.

the need for stimulus variability

As was also stated in the chapter on perception, there is something inherently attractive about a *change* of stimulus; this is the most important factor of all in attracting perceptual attention. To this statement it should now be added that organisms appear to display a definite need for *stimulus variability;* given the opportunity, they show an innate preference for a change in stimulus and tend

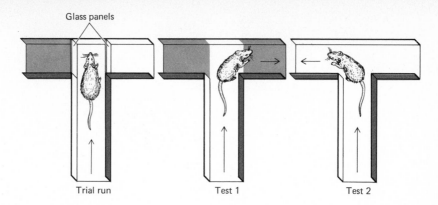

a response to change

10-4 In the trial run a rat enters the T-maze at the bottom and is stopped by the glass panels, at a point where it can see that the left arm is dark and the right arm is white. In test 1 the glass panels are removed and both arms are dark; the rat shows a strong tendency to enter the arm that was formerly white. If the trial run is followed by test 2, the rat shows a strong tendency to enter the arm that was formerly dark. As is explained in the text, this behavior is dictated by a preference for a change in stimulus. (26)

to seek it out. This has been demonstrated in the experiment shown in Figure 10-4. Even in this simple T-maze the rat shows a strong tendency to go to the arm that represents a change of stimulus—the dark arm that was originally white or the white arm that was originally dark.

The results of the experiment with the rat and the T-maze fit in with many other observations of animal and human behavior. If rats have a choice between two mazes, one where food is always found in the same place in the final alley and the other where they have to search for the food after reaching the final alley, they generally choose the one where they have to search (27). Monkeys will learn to open a window, as in Figure 10-5, for the reward of seeing what is happening

the curious monkey

10-5

The monkey, a prisoner in a dimly lit box, learns to push open the window solely for the privilege of watching a toy train in operation for thirty seconds. (28)

10-6

Do the latches unlock anything? No. Does the monkey know this? Yes. Then why does it work so hard to open them? For the answer, see the text.

on the other side (28). Presented with the hooks and latches shown in Figure 10-6, a monkey will work hard to open them even though it has discovered that doing so leads nowhere. Human babies seem irresistibly attracted to rattles, toys hanging over the crib, and their own fingers. Adults gladly pay for the kind of stimulus change represented by a juke-box record or the lights flashing in a pinball game.

It may turn out that there are such things as activity and manipulation drives, as some investigators have speculated, and that curiosity is also a drive in its own right. It seems more probable, however, that all these forms of behavior are undertaken as a result of the need for stimulus variability. Such a need has an obviously useful role for the organism. Every stimulus change represents a new source of information about the environment, and information about the environment is essential to successful adjustment and at times even survival. An organism with an inborn need for stimulus variability has a biological advantage over an organism without it.

One aspect of stimulus variability that deserves special mention is *stimulus complexity*. A very young baby, to whom a toy rattle represents a strange and complicated stimulus, will play with it for a long time. An older infant will put it aside more quickly, and a schoolchild will not play with it at all. To the schoolchild a game of tag is endlessly fascinating; the college student will settle for nothing less than football. To satisfy the organism's needs, the stimulus must have a certain amount of complexity—a factor that is closely related to variability. On the other hand, a stimulus that is too complex is not attractive. A child is more attracted to a nursery rhyme than to a Shakespeare sonnet.

342

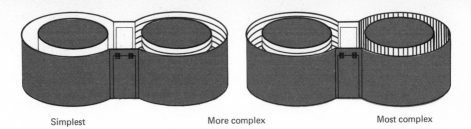

Simplest   More complex   Most complex

a test of complexity needs

10-7 The two mazes, shaped like figure eights, were designed to test the preferences of rats for levels of stimulus complexity. The animals enter through the swinging doors. In the maze at the left the animal has a choice of spending its time in a loop with plain white walls or a loop with walls striped horizontally in black and white. In the maze at the right the animal has a choice between a loop with horizontal stripes and a loop with vertical stripes. The white loop is the simplest of the three stimuli. The loop with vertical stripes provides the most rapid changes from black to white, as the animal runs through it, and is therefore the most complicated of the three. Question: Where did rats introduced into these mazes spend the most time? For the answer, see the text. (27)

One important experiment in stimulus complexity is shown in Figure 10-7. When rats were placed in the maze shown at the left, some spent most of their time in the loop with plain white walls, others in the horizontally striped loop. When rats were placed in the maze shown at the right, some spent most of their time in the horizontally striped loop and some in the vertically striped loop. These results seem to indicate that various individuals have different levels of stimulus complexity with which they are most "comfortable" and for which they show a preference.

After the initial preferences of the rats had been noted, the rats spent several sessions a day in the mazes, for a number of days. It was found that some of them changed their preferences. If so—and this was the most significant finding of the experiment—they always moved from a less complex stimulus to a more complex stimulus, never in the other direction.

The results of the experiments with the loops and with the T-maze that was shown in Figure 10-4 have led to the formulation of an important new psychological idea called the *theory of choice.** The theory holds that every stimulus object has a certain complexity value, which is also its information value. Moreover, every individual organism has his own *ideal level* of complexity—that is, the level for which he has a preference. The individual will seek out objects of his ideal level of complexity, will choose them from among other objects, will work for them, and will learn what he has to do to obtain them. He will also explore objects of a somewhat higher complexity called *pacer stimuli*. As he masters

---

*The term was coined by William N. Dember, the psychologist who directed the experimental work.

the new level of complexity of the pacer stimuli, his own ideal level rises, and he is now ready to deal with new pacers and again raise his own ideal level. Thus the need for stimulus variability provides a basis and reinforcement for increasingly complicated kinds of learning.

motives

As the preceding paragraph shows, behavior undertaken to satisfy stimulus needs is molded and modified by learning. Similarly, the consummatory behavior set into motion by the biological drives is often affected by learning. For example, the organism has to learn how to find the food that is the goal of the hunger drive; indeed baby mammals, after being fed their mothers' milk in the early days of life, must learn that solid foods can be a substitute and also how to eat solid foods. But both the stimulus needs and the biological drives are in themselves innate and unlearned; they are inborn characteristics of the organism's nervous system.

Motives, on the other hand, appear to depend more on learning than on any innate factors. True, they may in the last analysis be derived from some of the inherited characteristics of human physiology and the human nervous system. For example, some psychologists now believe that the interrelated motives called affiliation and dependency stem from an inborn tendency—a theory that will be discussed in the chapter on development (pages 533-34). And some scientists believe that the motive of hostility, which leads to the type of behavior called aggression, has a hereditary base and is therefore an inevitable tendency of the organism (29). In general, however, the motives of the adult human being appear to be chiefly the result of learning; it might be said that they are essentially cognitive rather than biological.

Hence there is general acceptance of the definition of motive that was presented at the beginning of the chapter: a motive is a desire for a goal that has acquired value for the individual. Each of us learns, through life experiences, to value certain goals above others. Even in the same family, one brother may exhibit a strong desire to be dependent on other people, another brother to be hostile, a sister to achieve in school and in a career. Certainly motives vary considerably from culture to culture. A desire for the achievement of material success is a motive frequently found among people in the United States, but material success has little appeal to the leisure-loving people of the South Seas islands—or to many young Americans who have rejected the prevailing cultural pattern.

Moreover, motives may exist as desires or wishes that never become implemented by behavior—a fact that will be discussed in detail later in the chapter. Thus some psychologists have concluded that perhaps the best approach to understanding motives is through the study of mental processes such as dreams (30) and daydreams, where the individual's desires can be observed in their pure form. One study of daydreams, for example, has produced some interesting findings on the differences in motives between men and women in the United

States. In line with the popular belief that men grow up with different goals, it was found that significantly more university men than women had daydreams that indicated hostility ("I see myself getting revenge in a clever way on a teacher or supervisor"), a desire to be a hero ("While rowing with friends the boat capsizes and I manage to save the one who cannot swim"), and sexual motives. Similarly, women showed more passivity ("I sometimes imagine myself lying on my back in a large field of grass and just gazing into the blue sky") and tendencies to value affiliation and physical attraction. But there was no significant difference in the number of daydreams related to achievement or vocation, and women actually reported significantly more daydreams about planning for the future; moreover, their wishes for the future were more practical than those of the men (31). The study would appear to indicate that our culture creates more differences in behavior between men and women than actual differences in motives.

Since the number of goals that we can learn to desire is almost infinite, it is impossible to list all the motives that an individual may acquire. It is useful, however, to list some of the more common motives on which psychologists have accumulated experimental knowledge.

affiliation and dependency

The source of the motive for affiliation is a matter of some dispute. Some psychologists, as has been said, regard it as originating in an actual physiological tendency. Others believe that it results from the fact that a small baby is totally dependent on his mother for the satisfactions of all his drives, including hunger and relief from pain. At any rate, almost every normal person grows up with motives for attachment to his parents, affiliation with other people, and dependency on others. The motives differ in strength, of course, among different individuals. Some people are close to their parents and extremely sociable—"joiners," who are always eager to be in a group. Others prefer to spend much of their time alone. Dependency is more common among women than among men, probably because our society frowns on dependent behavior in men but considers a certain amount of it to be appropriate, "feminine," and rather attractive in women. Yet men also often tend to take their problems to the teacher or the boss, to rely on columnists and television commentators to interpret the world's events, and to give enthusiastic allegiance to political leaders who have strong personalities.

One indication of how the affiliation motive can affect performance comes from a study illustrated in Figure 10-8. As the caption explains, students who rated high in affiliation motive were found to make better grades in university classes where their fellow students and instructors provided a warm and friendly atmosphere than in classes where the atmosphere was more impersonal. The psychologists who made the study found that the tendency was considerably stronger among university men than among women, for whom the results were sometimes inconsistent.

Behavior stemming from the affiliation motive has been found to be especially likely to occur in situations that arouse anxiety. You will perhaps recall

10-8

The bars show the grades made by students who were either high or low in affiliation motive in two kinds of classes—1) "warm" classes, where students were friendly to one another and the instructor took a personal interest in students and called them by name; and 2) other classes, where these evidences of warmth and acceptance were lacking. Note that the students high in affiliation motive did much better in the "warm" classes, whereas students low in affiliation motive did better in classes where there was less personal warmth. (32)

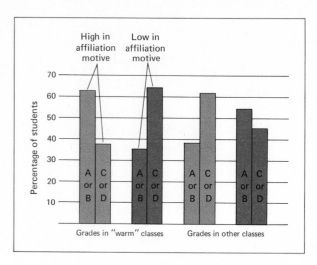

the experiment described on page 22 in which college women made anxious by the prospect of receiving an electric shock showed a much greater tendency to prefer to wait in the company of others rather than alone. Apparently there is considerable truth to the old adage that "misery loves company"; in anxiety-provoking situations people seem to turn to others for both company and comfort.

It is interesting to note that a high degree of affiliation motive is much more likely to be found among first-born children (or only children) than among those

the affiliation motive and order of birth

10-9

The bars show the results of a study of the relationship between being a first-born child (or an only child) and the affiliation motive. Subjects ranging in age from eleven to sixty-two were divided on the basis of tests into those high or low in affiliation motive. A very high percentage of first-born subjects fell into the high group. Of subjects who were born second or later in the family, only a minority proved high in affiliation motive. Note that first-born women were slightly more likely than first-born men to rate high in affiliation motive—but women who were not first-born were considerably less likely than men to do so. (33)

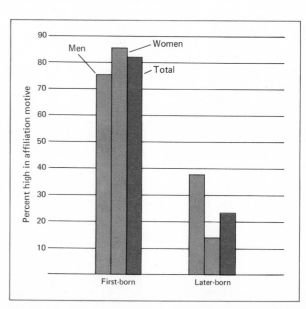

born later. One study that demonstrates this fact is shown in Figure 10-9. A possible explanation is that mothers appear to treat a first-born child differently from later children; they are more physically protective and tend to interfere more with the child's activities and to be more extreme with both praise and criticism, often in a rather inconsistent fashion (34). Another result of this kind of treatment is represented by the fact that first-borns have been found less likely to engage in dangerous contact sports, such as football and rugby, than in less dangerous sports, such as baseball (35).

achievement

The motive for achievement is the desire to perform well and to succeed. Studies of people rated high in achievement motive have shown that their mothers usually demanded considerable independence; these individuals were expected very early in life to go to bed by themselves, to entertain themselves, and later to earn their own spending money and choose their own clothes. Moreover, they were rewarded for these accomplishments with warm displays of physical affection. The mothers of those rated low in achievement motive did not demand the same kind of independence until much later. The striking difference in the kind of training received by people high and low in achievement motive is illustrated in Figure 10-10.

People high in achievement motive tend to try harder and to attain more success in many kinds of situations. In studies where they have been matched with other people of equal ability but weaker in achievement motive, they have

early training and the achievement motive

10-10

A group of boys was divided into those who tested high and low in achievement motive. Their mothers were then asked at what ages they had demanded that the boys show twenty different kinds of independent behavior, such as staying in the house alone, making their own friends, doing well in school without help, and doing well in competition. All mothers agreed that they had made all twenty demands by the time their sons were ten. But the mothers of sons high in achievement motive made about as many demands at the age of two as the mothers of sons low in achievement motive made at the age of four and about as many at the age of five as the other mothers at the age of seven. (36)

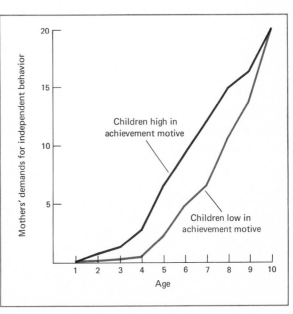

10-11

The bars reflect the sons' occupation levels as compared with their fathers'. Sons whose fathers had lower-middle-level or lower-level jobs were found more likely to rise above the father's level if they were high in achievement motive, more likely to remain at the same level or drop to a lower level if they were low in achievement motive. (41)

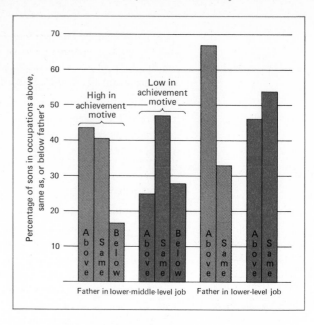

been found to do better on tests of speed at mathematical and verbal tasks (37) and on intellectual problems (38). They also make better grades in high school (39) and college (40). As is shown in Figure 10–11, they are more likely to move upward in society and rise above their family origins.

Individuals who are high in achievement motive tend to be quite realistic about taking risks; they generally avoid tasks in which they are almost sure to succeed but will receive very low rewards and also avoid tasks in which they are almost sure to fail but could gain very high rewards in the remote event of success. This is particularly true of individuals who are high in achievement motive and low in anxiety. (It will be recalled from page 327 that a high level of anxiety inclines people either to be very conservative or to "go for broke.") It has been found that people with a high degree of achievement motive and a low level of anxiety tend to prefer jobs in which they have a reasonable chance of success and can obtain reasonable rewards, while those low in achievement motive and high in anxiety are more inclined either to settle for an easier but low-paying job or to aim for a high-paying job that is probably beyond their capacities (42). A study made in Germany has shown that achievement motive affects even the kinds of risks taken in driving an automobile. Drivers high in achievement motive tended to commit only minor traffic offenses that represented calculated risks, such as illegal parking; drivers low in achievement motive tended to get into trouble either for going too slow or for reckless driving (43).

As might be expected from the different ways in which boys and girls are brought up in our society, men generally score higher on tests of achievement motive than women. First-born children tend to score higher than the later-born, just as they do in strength of affiliation motive. Moreover, first-born children tend to rate high in "autonomy," or the ability to take care of themselves, and if they are male in tendencies to conform to social pressures (44). In addition there are studies indicating that first-borns are more trusting of authority (45).

Few psychologists would go as far as the psychoanalyst Alfred Adler, who once described the first-born child as "a power-hungry conservative" (46)—but there do appear to be some demonstrable differences between the first-born, especially if a male, and his younger brothers and sisters.

hostility

This is a motive that most of us do not like to admit but that all of us possess. Evidence of it first appears in the child at about the age of two. Up to then, all that he has seemed to want from other people is their presence and the stimulation, help, and approval they provide. But at this stage he begins to want something else from them. He wants—at times—to see them display signs of worry, fears of discomfort, actual pain. Later he may hope that misfortune will befall them and that he will have the gratification of knowing about it.

Some scientists, as has been said, consider hostility to represent a biological trait that makes aggressive behavior as inevitable a part of the human condition as fighting over territories is for baboons and other animals. Others, probably a majority, believe that the hostility motive is learned and that it stems from the fact that the child cannot have everything he wants. Some of his desires are bound to be frustrated by the rules of society and by the conflicting desires of other people. He cannot always eat when he wants to. He has to learn to control his drive for elimination except when he is in the bathroom. He cannot have the toy that another child owns and is playing with. His mother cannot spend all her time catering to his whims. Other children, bigger than he, push him around.

The aggression that often results from hostility may take such varied forms as argumentativeness, scorn, sarcasm, physical and mental cruelty, and fighting. Yet, while most people are motivated at some time by hostility, not everyone displays aggression. Boys and men are more inclined to do so than are girls and women, for society approves of a certain amount of aggression in the male but discourages it in the female. Just as dependent behavior is peculiarly a female prerogative in our society, so is aggression largely a male prerogative.

In recent years there has been considerable debate on the question of whether watching aggressive behavior in movies or on television encourages aggression. Some psychologists have taken the view that it does just the opposite—that it has a cathartic effect that tends to purge tendencies toward hostility and therefore to discourage actual aggression (47). Among the experimental evidence that supports this viewpoint is a study of the dreams of boys aged six through eleven. The boys, who were volunteers, slept for two nights in a laboratory, were wakened each time they displayed REM sleep, and were asked to report if they could remember having been dreaming. On one night just before going to bed they watched a baseball film, on the other night a violent scene of an Indian attack on a frontier settlement. Although one might suppose that the violent movie would result in numerous bad dreams, actually the boys had fewer dreams of any kind after watching it—and of the dreams they did have fewer were hostile or otherwise unpleasant (48).

A number of other studies, however, seem to dispute the theory that viewing aggression has a cathartic effect, except perhaps under rather special conditions.

For example, you may recall the photographs in Chapter 2 (page 67) of children attacking a large doll with a hammer after watching a movie of an adult who had done the same thing. In this connection, it is important to note that people are more likely to behave aggressively when they are feeling frustrated or angry, such as when they have been subjected experimentally to situations in which they fail at a task or receive ridicule (49). Some recent evidence indicates that a combination of some kind of angry arousal plus the observation of aggression is especially likely to result in aggressive behavior.

In a study whose results are shown in Figure 10-12, six groups of adolescent youths in a California penal institution volunteered for what they thought was a learning experiment. Three groups were made angry by disparaging remarks from a confederate of the experimenter, while the other three groups were not. All the groups then watched one of three short movies. For all the groups, the first half of the movie was the same—two boys shooting baskets. The last half, however, was different. In one case the boys merely went on to play a friendly game of basketball; this was the film called "neutral" in the figure. In another they got into a fight, in which one boy's angry facial expressions, shouts, and blows were emphasized; this was the "aggression" film. In the third the boys again got into a fight but this time the emphasis was on the beating one boy appeared to be taking and the pain he was supposedly suffering; this was the "pain" film. Afterward the subjects were asked to help in a learning study by giving feedback

aggression, anger, and observation

10-12

The bars show the results of a study of aggressive behavior as measured by the amount of pain six groups of subjects thought they were inflicting on another person. When tested the groups were in different emotional states (angered or not angered) and had just observed different kinds of behavior on film. For a full explanation, see the text. (50)

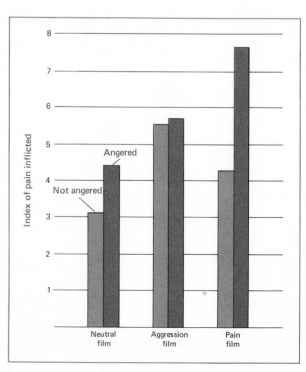

to another person in the form of an electric shock every time he made a mistake. The intensity and duration of the shocks were left to the subjects' own judgment. (Actually no shocks were delivered; the "learner" was again a confederate of the experimenter and only pretended to be suffering pain.) As Figure 10-12 shows, the lowest amount of pain was inflicted by subjects who had not been angered and had watched the neutral film, the highest amount by subjects who were angered and had watched the pain film.

certainty

Quite early in life the child begins to show a desire for the kind of *certainty* represented by his own bed, his own toys, the presence of familiar objects and people in his environment. As he gets a little older, he likes to have rules set for his conduct; he likes the certainty of knowing what he is permitted to do and what he is not permitted to do. The prospect of uncertainty—sleeping in a strange house, being taken care of by a strange baby sitter, going to school for the first time—is likely to upset him.

Adults, too, tend to be motivated toward the known and away from the unknown. For some, such as explorers and astronauts, other motives prove stronger; but, in general, the desire for certainty operates strongly in most of us at most times. We like to feel that we know how our relatives and friends will act toward us, what is likely to happen tomorrow in the classroom or on the job, and where and how we will be living next year. Just as children are often upset by new experiences, adults are often upset by such uncertainties as the possibility of unemployment or failure.

The motive for certainty may be said to take three forms.

1. We like to think that we can predict what will happen next—that is, that future events will be orderly and foreseeable.

2. When unusual events surprise us, we like to try to understand them and relate them in some way to previous experiences.

3. We seek some kind of consistency among the various beliefs that we hold and between our beliefs and our behavior. This aspect of the certainty motive is especially important because of its relation to *living up to standards*.

Living Up to Standards. Every normal person, as he grows up, begins to set certain rules for his own behavior. Through learning what society values and through identification with his parents and other adults, he acquires inner standards of many kinds; he wants—indeed he commands himself—to be such things as attractive, responsible, friendly, skillful, brave, generous, strong, independent, honest, and fair. Boys acquire an inner standard of masculinity, girls of femininity.

Our standards form what is often called our *ego ideal*—our notion of how, if we were as perfect as we would like to be, we would always think and behave. Many of us acquire such high standards that we cannot possibly live up to all of them at all times. In fact some of our standards demand that we suppress other motives, which may be quite powerful at times; they tell us that we should not take food from another person even if we are hungry, that we should be kind even to people toward whom we feel hostile, that we should play fair no matter how much we want to win. As a result, we often have feelings of shame and guilt, over our thoughts if not actually our conduct. In popular terms, our consciences hurt. The pangs of conscience when we fail to meet our standards can be painful indeed. It has been observed that men who have committed crimes frequently

---

PRECONVENTIONAL LEVEL – *TODDLERHOOD 1½ – 6 YRS.*

Child is oriented to
the consequences of his
behavior.

Stage 1. Defers to the power of adults and obeys rules to avoid trouble and punishment.

Stage 2. Seeks to satisfy his own needs by behaving in a manner that will gain rewards and the return of favors.

CONVENTIONAL LEVEL – *CHILDHOOD 6 – 13 YRS.*

Child is oriented to
the expectations of
others and to behaving
in a conventional
fashion.

Stage 3. Wants to be "good" in order to please and help others and thus receive approval.

Stage 4. Wants to "do his duty" by respecting authority (parents, teachers, God) and maintaining the social order for its own sake.

POSTCONVENTIONAL LEVEL – *ADOLESCENCE 13 – 18 YRS,*

Child becomes oriented
to more abstract moral
values and his own
conscience.

Stage 5. Thinks in terms of the rights of others, the general welfare of the community, and a duty to conform to the laws and standards established by the will of the majority. Behaves in ways he believes would be respected by an impartial observer.

Stage 6. Considers not only the actual laws and rules of society but also his own self-chosen standards of justice and respect for human dignity. Behaves in a way that will avoid condemnation by his own conscience.

---

a stage theory of moral development

10-13 Summarized in the table are the six stages in the development of moral judgments found by Kohlberg. For the ages at which American children appear to progress from one stage to the next, see Figure 10–14. (51)

behave in such a way that they are almost sure to be caught and convicted; apparently they prefer punishment by imprisonment to the kind of self-punishment that results from a serious failure to live up to one's own standards.

Standards and Moral Judgments. Many of our inner standards take the form of judgments as to what is right and what is wrong—in other words, they constitute the moral and ethical principles by which we guide (or try to guide) our conduct. The manner in which moral judgments develop has been studied extensively by Lawrence Kohlberg, through the questioning of boys seven years old and up. Kohlberg presented his subjects with a number of hypothetical situations involving moral questions like these: If a man's wife is dying for lack of an expensive drug that he cannot afford, should he steal the drug? If a patient who is fatally ill and in great pain begs for a mercy killing, should the physician agree? By analyzing the answers and particularly the reasoning by which his subjects reached their answers, Kohlberg determined that moral judgments develop through a series of six stages, as shown in Figure 10-13. Children in the two stages of what he calls the preconventional level base their ideas of right and wrong largely on their own self-interest; they are concerned chiefly with avoiding punishment and gaining rewards. Later, in the two stages of what he calls the conventional level, they become concerned about the approval of other people; and finally, in the two stages of the postconventional level, they become concerned with abstract moral values and the dictates of their own consciences.

In other words, the child's reasons for being "good" progress from sheer self-interest to a concern for the approval of others and finally to a concern for the approval of his own conscience. How the pattern of moral judgments changes with age is shown in Figure 10-14. Apparently the stage-by-stage development

stages of moral development by age

10-14

Among seven-year-olds, almost all moral judgments are made at the preconventional level (Kohlberg's stages 1 and 2). By the age of ten, more than half of moral judgments are still made at this level but judgments at the conventional level (stages 3 and 4) are increasing rapidly. By thirteen, judgments at the preconventional level have dropped to a rather small minority, judgments at the conventional level predominate, and judgments at the postconventional level (stages 5 and 6) are beginning to become important. (52)

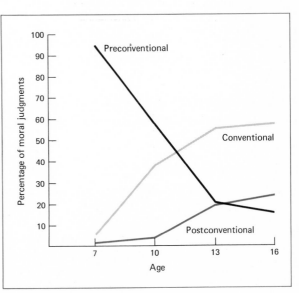

takes place in other societies besides our own; Kohlberg has found a similar pattern among children in Mexico and Taiwan (53).

Cognitive Dissonance. A final word on the motive for certainty can best be introduced by citing a rather strange and amusing fact of human behavior. As you may have noticed from your own experience, a student who drives a hundred miles and sits through a blizzard to watch a football game in which his team is beaten 42-0 is likely to insist afterward that the drive was pleasant, the weather not especially bad, and the game much closer than the score would indicate. A person who pays too much for a used car that turns out to have a bad engine knock when driven at highway speeds is nonetheless likely to insist that he got a bargain. Are such people merely making excuses and trying to save face? Perhaps—but there is some evidence that they may believe what they say.

Many investigators have concluded that there is a widespread human desire—perhaps a motive in its own right or perhaps just one aspect of the motive for certainty—for what has been called *cognitive consonance*—that is, for being consistent and rational in one's thinking and for preserving agreement and harmony among one's thoughts, beliefs, and behavior. Conversely, there is a desire to avoid *cognitive dissonance,* or lack of consistency and agreement. The following experiments will help clarify the manner in which these two desires operate.

In an experiment by the psychologist who developed the theory of cognitive dissonance, college students were asked to work for a long time at a boring task. They were then divided into three groups. The first, or control, group was asked to rate the task on a scale ranging from "extremely dull and boring" to "extremely interesting and enjoyable." As expected, the control group gave the task a quite negative rating on this scale. The other two groups were placed in a situation designed to produce cognitive dissonance: they were asked to tell other students waiting to take part in the experiment that the task had in fact been extremely interesting and enjoyable. In other words, they were asked to say something that they presumably did not believe. Members of group 2 were paid twenty dollars to do this. Members of group 3 were paid only one dollar each.

The hypothesis in this experiment was that group 2 would consider the twenty-dollar payment a sufficient justification for telling an untruth and therefore would experience only a low degree of cognitive dissonance. The results appear to bear out the hypothesis. When asked later to tell what they really thought of the task by rating it on the scale of "dull and boring" to "interesting and enjoyable," they gave it much the same unfavorable rating as had the control group. The hypothesis also dictated that members of group 3, paid only the nominal sum of one dollar, would experience a high degree of cognitive dissonance, which they would be able to reduce only by deciding that the task was in fact rather interesting. As it turned out, they did give the task a positive rating on the scale; they claimed that it had been almost as "interesting and enjoyable" as they had told the waiting subjects (54).

Another experiment with college students produced results that appear to violate all the rules of common sense but offer considerable support to the theory of cognitive dissonance. This experiment is described in Figure 10-15, and the

		Level of shock while learning		Felt level of pain	
		LIST 2	LIST 3	LIST 2	LIST 3
Subjects who had no choice but to learn list 3	GROUP 1	severe	severe	painful	painful
	GROUP 2	severe	moderate	painful	much less painful
Subjects who volunteered for list 3	GROUP 3 ("low dissonance")	severe	severe	painful	painful
	GROUP 4 ("high dissonance")	severe	severe	painful	less painful

cognitive dissonance and felt pain

10-15 The subjects, after learning one list of words under normal conditions, were subjected to two painful shocks per trial while learning list 2. They were then divided into the four groups listed above. Groups 1 and 2 had no choice but to continue with the experiment and learn list 3. Groups 3 and 4 were told they had fulfilled their obligation and were free to leave but that they could volunteer to learn list 3 if they so chose. The hypothesis of the experiment was that the act of volunteering for a painful experience would produce cognitive dissonance. The dissonance of the volunteers in group 3 was reduced to a low level by the experimenters' explanation that their action was of great service to science and to the space program. No such reassurance was given to the volunteers in group 4, whose dissonance therefore presumably remained high. Note that the members of group 4—presumably in an attempt to reduce the dissonance they experienced—said they felt the pain of the shocks on list 3 as considerably less than on list 2. For further discussion of this experiment, see the text and Figure 10-16. (55)

results are illustrated in Figure 10-16. As Figure 10-15 shows, the experiment compared the amount of pain felt by four groups of students who received electric shocks while studying word lists. Note that the subjects who experienced "high dissonance"—because they had rather foolishly volunteered to learn list 3 and thus continue a painful experiment of whose value they were doubtful—said that the pain of the shocks was substantially reduced from that felt while studying list 2. Presumably they could reduce their cognitive dissonance only by believing that the shocks became less severe.

Figure 10-16 demonstrates that not only the subjective perception of pain by group 4 but also the group's learning performance was affected by the high amount of cognitive dissonance. Members of this group actually performed on list 3 as if the amount of painful shock *had* been reduced. They did just about as well as (in fact slightly, though not significantly, better than) group 2, for whom the amount of shock was in fact reduced. Thus members of group 4, experiencing a high degree of dissonance and presumably attempting to reduce it, not only said the pain was less but behaved as if it actually *were* less. The experiment seems

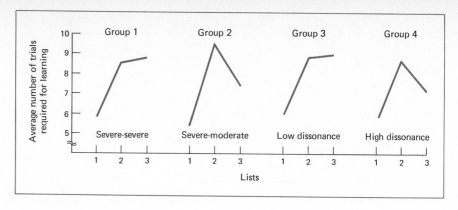

the effect of cognitive dissonance on learning

10-16 The graphs show the number of trials required for learning the three word lists in the experiment that was introduced in Figure 10-15. Note the remarkable similarity of the curves for group 1 and group 3 and for group 2 and group 4. All four groups of subjects performed about equally well on list 1, then were about equally hampered by the severe shocks administered while they were learning list 2, to the extent that they required nearly twice as many trials. On list 3, however, the story was quite different. For what is believed to be the explanation, see the text. (55)

to show that their perception of pain—not just their verbal report—was decreased by their attempt to reduce cognitive dissonance.

These two experiments cast a new light on some factors in human behavior that had heretofore been unexplained. The experiments indicate that human beings are motivated to go to considerable lengths to prove that they are rational and sensible and, if they do something foolish, to find some means of explaining it away—and thus to reduce the dissonance caused by inconsistency.

the theory of self-actualization

Psychologists of different schools take different views of how motives originate and operate. Behaviorists tend to regard motives as learned systems of behavior based largely on the biological drives and the child's early helplessness; the hunger drive becomes transformed through learning into the kind of achievement-seeking behavior that will guarantee an ample supply of food; the child's early dependence leads to many kinds of adult behavior that result in affiliation with friends, groups, husbands or wives, and children. The cognitive psychologists tend to emphasize the mental processes of choosing and planning; they think of the human brain, or parts of it, as acting like an "executive" that analyzes information, weighs alternatives, decides on goals, and formulates plans (sometimes very long-range plans) for achieving the goals.

The humanistic psychologists take a viewpoint that can best be illustrated by describing the *theory of self-actualization* developed by Abraham Maslow. It was Maslow's belief that human beings are innately inclined to seek beauty,

According to Maslow's theory, human motives are arranged in this kind of pyramid. Once the *physiological* motives at the bottom have been satisfied, man is freed to seek the goals of his search for *safety*—and so on up to the top. For the meaning of the self-actualization motive at the apex, see the text. (56)

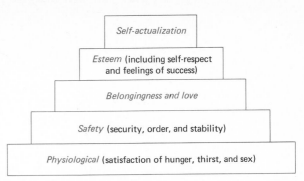

Self-actualization

Esteem (including self-respect and feelings of success)

Belongingness and love

Safety (security, order, and stability)

Physiological (satisfaction of hunger, thirst, and sex)

goodness, truth, and the fullest possible development of their own unique potentialities for perfection and creativity. Human motives, he theorized, exist in the form of the pyramid or hierarchy shown in Figure 10-17. The physiological motives at the bottom of the pyramid are the most urgent; man must satisfy his hunger and thirst drives in particular before he can undertake the search for safety. And only in a safe and stable society can he begin to seek the higher goals to which human nature aspires. Self-actualization, the highest goal of all, represents a sort of all-encompassing self-fulfillment; the self-actualizing person has satisfied his search for such esthetic pleasures as order, symmetry, and beauty; he is in tune with the meaning and mystery of life; he accepts himself and others and the realities of existence; he rejoices in the experience of living; he is spontaneous and creative and has a keen sense of humor; he has made the most of his abilities and has become all that he is capable of becoming (56). This, to Maslow, is the goal toward which all men by their very nature are motivated—although deprivation and unfavorable social pressures may prevent most of them from ever reaching it.

Maslow's view of human nature and human motives must be taken largely on faith; it is not a theory that lends itself to experimental proof or disproof. (Although one study has indicated that high ratings on the qualities Maslow describes as self-actualizing are likely to be accompanied by a high degree of freedom from tendencies to be neurotic (57)—in other words, that self-actualization and what is often called "mental health" tend to go hand in hand.) To many psychologists the theory has the intuitive ring of truth; to others it seems overly optimistic.

motives and behavior

As has been said, motives are related to biological drives, stimulus needs, and perhaps other inborn characteristics of the human organism. Moreover, they are molded by childhood learning experiences that are more or less common to all people in our society. Thus it appears likely that everyone possesses, at least in some degree, each of the motives that have just been mentioned—affiliation, achievement, hostility, and certainty—as well as such related desires as dependency, independence, social approval, living up to standards, and cognitive consonance.

Yet no two of us ever behave exactly alike. Why?

motivational dispositions and aroused motives

One reason is that motives, like the other mediational units acquired or modified through learning, are not always in active awareness. Most of the time our memories lie somewhere in our storehouse of long-term memory, waiting, like our knowledge of the multiplication tables or the telephone number of a friend, to be retrieved at the appropriate time. It follows that motives are not always in operation. At times a college woman may be strongly motivated to get good grades, but this motive is not in her awareness when she is with a young man watching a basketball game. Conversely, the cluster of sexual and social motives that preoccupies her on a date is not in her awareness when she is concentrating on her studies (although it may crop up when she is unsuccessful at concentrating on them).

A distinction must be made between *motivational dispositions,* which represent the sum total of all the motives we have learned, and *aroused motives,* which are those we are thinking about at any given moment. Motivational dispositions are *potential* influences on our thinking and behavior. Aroused motives are *active.* An aroused and active motive is more likely to affect behavior than a motive that is not aroused, although many psychologists believe that a motive can be completely unconscious and still affect behavior.

The concept of unconscious motives, which is perhaps one of the thorniest problems in psychology, was emphasized by Sigmund Freud. It was Freud's belief that people have wishes and desires that they are never aware of but that influence their behavior nonetheless, sometimes to a striking and dramatic degree.

One example of what appears to be an unconscious motive is the phenomenon known as posthypnotic suggestion. The hypnotist tells the subject that after he awakens from his trance he will go and raise a window the first time the hypnotist coughs but will not remember that this instruction has been given to him. The subject comes out of the trance, the hypnotist coughs, and, sure enough, the subject opens a window. If asked why, he is likely to say that the room was getting stuffy or that he felt faint. He has no suspicion that the real reason was simply to comply with the hypnotist's demand.

Other examples appear to be all around us. A mother seems to believe in all sincerity that she has the most generous, affectionate, and even self-sacrificing motives toward her daughter, yet an unprejudiced observer would say that the mother's real motives are to dominate the daughter, keep her from marrying, and have her as a sort of maidservant. A man earnestly denies that he has any hostile motives, yet we can see that in subtle ways he performs many acts of aggression against his wife, his children, and his business associates. A person may feel genuinely motivated to go to the dentist or to keep a date with a friend, yet conveniently "forget" the appointment.

The chief unsolved question is how a desire that is unconscious can actively operate to produce relevant behavior. Perhaps there is no really sharp division between what is conscious and what is unconscious. Although the notion of unconscious motives is puzzling, it appears to be valid, and it indicates that we will often find it as difficult to analyze our own motives as to know the motives that direct the behavior of others.

the principle of functional autonomy

One aspect of motivation and behavior that was found puzzling for many years is illustrated by this frequent real-life occurrence. A young man from a humble background enters the business world and works with almost superhuman energy. By the time he is sixty he is successful and rich. Yet he continues to work as hard as ever. He may work himself into an early grave or, in the attempt to keep enlarging his business, lose everything he has made.

His hard work as a young man is easy to understand. We can assume that he had strong motives for achievement and certainty. But by sixty he is more successful and powerful than he probably had ever hoped, and he has more money than he can possibly spend. Why, then, should he continue to work so hard?

The explanation seems to lie in a principle formulated by Gordon W. Allport, who has termed it *functional autonomy* (58). The principle holds that an activity that is originally a means to an end frequently acquires an independent function of its own and becomes an end in itself. The businessman starts out by working hard to gratify his motives for success and security. But eventually the desire to work hard becomes a motive in its own right. His old motive has been transformed into a new one, which has a self-perpetuating power of its own.

Some other examples have been cited by Allport. A woman does not particularly like or want children; she does not possess the motive to nurture children that is commonly called maternal love. Nonetheless she treats her children well and lovingly because of various other motives centering around the approval of her neighbors and living up to her own standards of how a mother is supposed to behave. Eventually, as she practices devotion to her children, she begins to find that this is a valuable end in itself; the desire to nurture her children acquires functional autonomy. A man who makes custom-built furniture sets himself high standards of workmanship because he believes that this will bring him success and wealth. In later years he finds that this kind of workmanship is actually reducing his income because it takes more time than his customers are willing to pay for, but he continues to do a good job because the desire for craftsmanship has become a motive in itself.

The principle of functional autonomy appears to account for many human activities that seem far removed from the biological drives and stimulus needs and often do not even seem to serve any useful purpose. Desires that have acquired functional autonomy explain why the miser yearns for money he will never spend, the puzzle addict cannot sleep unless he has solved the day's crossword, and the Englishman dresses for dinner (so at least legend has it) even in the jungle.

requirements for behavior

Of all the factors that complicate the relationship between motives and behavior, however, the most important is simply this: even when a motivational disposition is strong and the motive is easily and frequently aroused to the active state, there still may be no effect whatever on behavior. *A motive leads to goal-related behavior only when certain requirements are met.* The requirements can be listed as follows.

1. *Knowledge of how to satisfy the motive.* Before we can set about trying to satisfy a motive, we must have learned the kind of behavior that is likely to result in attaining the goal. Thus a child may have strong motives for affiliation and affection yet not know how to go about obtaining them. Similarly, an adolescent boy may have strong motives for the companionship of girls yet not know how to make himself attractive to girls or ask for a date. An adult may want to earn a lot of money yet lack any skills that have high value in the economic marketplace.

2. *Incentive.* Just as drives interact with the presence of incentive objects to produce consummatory action (page 338), so do motives depend at least in part on the presence of incentives. That is to say, even when we have a motive and have learned the kind of behavior that is likely to gratify it, the motive must be triggered into behavior by something that arouses it. For example, a student goes home at the end of the day with no particular desires at all concerning the evening's activities. A friend calls and suggests they go to an 8 P.M. tryout for parts in a college drama. Going to the tryout is a potential incentive to implement any one of a number of motives—desires for affiliation and achievement, possibly sexual motives. Whether the student will respond eagerly or turn down the invitation will depend in large part on the *incentive value* that trying out for a drama has for him.

The incentive value of any event or object varies considerably from one person to another. Two students may have equally strong motives for achievement, but one student's motive may center around good grades, the other's around political activity. The offer of a dollar to mow a lawn may have sufficient incentive value for one boy but not for another.

3. *Expectation of success.* Even when the first two requirements are met, a motive is not likely to result in any behavior unless a person has a reasonable expectation of success—that is, unless he believes he has a fair chance to reach the goal and thus obtain satisfaction of the motive. Thus even if the student invited to try out for the college play places a high incentive value on getting an acting part, he is likely to turn down the invitation if he believes that he has absolutely no chance of success. Or let us say that the motive aroused to the active state is the desire to call up a girl the student has seen in one of his classes and ask her for a date. He places a high incentive value on the date. But if he is shy and

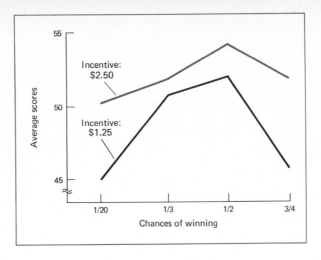

the effect of incentive and chances of success

10-18   The subjects in this experiment were college women who were told they could win a small cash prize in a contest that involved two tasks—one working problems in arithmetic, the other drawing X's inside small circles. Some subjects were offered a $1.25 prize, the others a $2.50 prize. Both groups were divided into four additional groups. One was told that a single prize would be given for the top score among twenty students; in other words, they thought they had one chance in twenty of winning. Others were told that they were in competition with two other students (one chance in three) or with a single other student (one chance in two—or 50-50). A fourth group was told that equal prizes would be given to the top three scorers out of four (three chances in four). Note that the subjects with a chance at a $2.50 prize—in other words, a higher incentive—worked harder than the subjects whose possible prize was only half that amount. In both groups the highest scores were made by those who thought they had a 50-50 chance of winning. (59)

awkward around girls and considers himself unattractive and uninteresting, he may not try to satisfy the motive.

An experiment that explores the role of both chances of success and incentive is illustrated in Figure 10-18. Note how much harder the younger women in this experiment tried to win their "contests" when the prize—the incentive value of winning—was doubled. Note also that the lowest scores were made by the women who believed that they had very little chance of winning. An interesting sidelight is the fact that the women who believed that winning was almost a sure thing also had low scores, particularly when the incentive value of the prize was low. The highest scores of all were made by those who thought they had a 50-50 chance.

4. *Freedom from anxiety.* The manner in which the vague fears and premonitions of anxiety may prevent motives from resulting in behavior can be observed even in very young children. If a child is separated from his mother for a long period of time and becomes intensely anxious over her absence, he may behave very strangely when he has the opportunity to see her again. Although he is

strongly motivated to be reunited with her, he may at first actually avoid her rather than approach her.

Because of the different way the two sexes are brought up in our society, girls and women often have particularly strong anxieties about their hostile motives, and boys and men about the desire for help. Therefore anxiety tends to play a particularly important role in inhibiting aggressive behavior on the part of women and dependent behavior on the part of men.

Sexual motives can generate considerable anxiety in both women and men, sometimes to the point of frigidity and impotence that completely block sexual satisfaction or desire. In an experiment on sexual anxiety, young men were asked what stories a series of pictures suggested to them; although many of the pictures had a strong sexual content, the men tended to ignore this fact in their stories. In fact they were less inclined to read sexual meanings into pictures where it was obviously present—presumably because these pictures aroused anxiety—than into "neutral" pictures. Then they had several drinks and were asked to invent stories for another similar series of pictures. This time—presumably because the alcohol had reduced their anxiety—their responses to pictures with a high sexual content were much more sex-oriented than before, and in some cases they were quite blatantly so (60).

5. *Absence of conflicting motives.* As a student gets ready to eat his evening meal a number of motives may flash into the active state and crowd one after another into his thoughts. The desire to get good grades, representing one aspect of the achievement motive, may suggest that he spend the evening studying. Affiliative and sexual motives may point toward visiting a girlfriend. His inner standards of proper behavior of a son toward his parents may point toward writing a letter home. Obviously he cannot satisfy all these motives. They are in conflict. Only one of them can prevail, and perhaps the conflict will prevent any of them from being translated into behavior. Indeed conflicts among motives are such a complex and important factor in human behavior—and such a strong influence on the human personality—that they deserve a full discussion of their own in the following chapter.

summary
1. *A motive is a desire for a goal that has acquired value for the individual.* The goals are determined by a combination of biological traits and learning.
2. *A biological drive is a pattern of brain activity that results from certain kinds of physiological conditions.* The physiological conditions usually occur when the organism is in a state of deprivation (in need of food or water) or of imbalance (such as too warm, too cold, or needing to sleep).
3. The biological drives are *hunger, thirst, sleep, temperature, breathing, elimination, pain,* and *sex.*
4. An *incentive object* is a stimulus, such as the presence of food, that helps trigger a biological drive.
5. In addition to biological drives, the organism appears to have tendencies to seek certain kinds of stimulation. These tendencies are called *stimulus needs.*

6. Two important forms of stimulus needs are the need for general *sensory stimulation* and the need for *stimulus variability.*

7. Studies of the need for stimulus variability have led to the hypothesis that every stimulus object has a certain complexity value (related to its information value); that each individual organism has its own *ideal level* of complexity; that the organism will seek out stimuli at this level; but that the organism will also explore objects of slightly greater complexity, called *pacer stimuli.* As the organism masters the new level of complexity of these pacer stimuli, its ideal level rises; the organism is then ready to deal with new pacer stimuli and again raise its ideal level.

8. Among important motives are the desires for *affiliation and dependency, achievement, hostility,* and *certainty.*

9. Humanistic psychologists emphasize that human beings are innately inclined to seek beauty, truth, and fullest development of their potentialities. This is called the theory of *self-actualization.*

10. *Motivational dispositions* are the sum total of all the motives that a person has learned; they are *potential* influences on his behavior. *Aroused motives* are those that the person is actually thinking about at the moment; they are *active* influences on behavior.

11. Although the mechanisms are difficult to explain, it is generally believed that human beings may have *unconscious motives,* which influence their behavior even though they are unaware of them.

12. *Functional autonomy* is the term for a principle holding that an activity originally undertaken to implement a motive frequently acquires an independent function of its own and becomes an end in itself.

13. A motive leads to goal-related behavior only when certain requirements are met. These include *knowledge of how to satisfy the motive, incentive, expectation of success, freedom from anxiety,* and *absence of conflicting motives.*

recommended reading

Atkinson, J. W. *An introduction to motivation.* New York: Van Nostrand Reinhold, 1964.

Berkowitz, L., ed. *Roots of aggression.* New York: Atherton Press, 1969.

Bolles, R. C. *Theory of motivation.* New York: Harper & Row, 1967.

Cofer, C. N., and Appley, M. H. *Motivation: theory and research.* New York: Wiley, 1964.

Haber, R. N., ed. *Current research in motivation.* New York: Holt, Rinehart and Winston, 1966.

Kagan, J. *Understanding children: behavior, motives, and thought.* New York: Harcourt Brace Jovanovich, 1971.

McClelland, D. C., and Winter, D. G. *Motivating economic achievement.* New York: Free Press, 1969.

Maslow, A. H., ed. *Motivation and personality,* 2nd ed. New York: Harper & Row, 1970.

Murray, E. J. *Motivation and emotion.* Englewood Cliffs, N.J.: Prentice-Hall, 1964.

The human
personality
is
a richly
varied
fabric.

PART six

Discussion of emotions and motives leads naturally to a consideration of the human personality, for, in large part, each individual's personality depends on the kinds of emotions that life's events tend to arouse in him and on the motives that characteristically influence and guide his behavior. There are people with exuberant personalities who appear to be constantly experiencing the emotion of joy, people with quarrelsome personalities who appear to be constantly experiencing anger, and people with gloomy and frightened personalities who appear to be constantly experiencing anxiety, fear, and guilt. There are "strong personalities" who are highly motivated toward independence and achievement and "weak personalities" who are highly motivated toward dependency and submission.

Personality is made up of many factors—indeed, of all the mediational units that the individual has acquired in his lifetime, including not only his emotions and motives but also his characteristic ways of perceiving the world, thinking about it, solving its problems, and making all the various kinds of adjustments that it requires. Thus many aspects of personality have already been discussed. This section of the book will point out how the threads already mentioned, and some additional ones, are woven into the richly varied fabric of human personality.

Chapter 11 treats frustration of motives and conflicts between motives, both of which play a prominent part in determining personality, and also describes the abnormalities of emotion and behavior to which frustration and conflict sometimes lead. Chapter 12 concerns the various theories of personality that have been developed by psychologists and psychoanalysts and also discusses the treatment of personality disorders.

THE NORMAL AND ABNORMAL PERSONALITY

CHAPTER 11

FRUSTRATION, CONFLICT, AND ABNORMAL BEHAVIOR

S. Virgin Islands St. Croix / St. John / St. Thomas

Students of behavior have sometimes speculated on what life would be like if we human beings were motivated by only one desire at a time, if we had learned exactly the kind of behavior designed to satisfy each motive, and if the world were so arranged that satisfactions for all our motives were there for the taking (1).

It is difficult to imagine such a situation. The closest thing to it, perhaps, exists among some of the nonindustrial societies of the tropical islands, where the climate is so warm that the simplest kinds of shelter and clothing are sufficient and where food can be picked off the nearest tree or scooped out of the ocean. Yet even societies in the midst of the greatest natural abundance are plagued by frustrations and conflicts of one kind or another. Their gods or their social taboos prohibit certain kinds of behavior. They have rules that regulate their eating habits, their expression of hostility, their religious rituals, their social relationships, and their sexual behavior. The rules are often very different from those of our own society and may seem quite lax by comparison. But they are rules nonetheless, and they sometimes prevent satisfaction of the motives of these people, though to us those motives may seem uncomplicated.

Perhaps the frustration of motives is part of the price human beings must pay for the privilege of living together in a society. (No society could survive if its members freely satisfied their acquisitive motives by totally disregarding property rights and satisfied their hostile motives through murder.) Or perhaps man possesses some kind of divine discontent or sheer perversity that makes life in a conflict-free paradise intolerable.

Certainly our own kind of civilization makes frustration and conflicts of motives inevitable. We acquire motives that we cannot possibly satisfy—at least not at all times and in full—and we also acquire motives that are incompatible and thus bound to conflict. The frustration and conflicts give rise to various highly unpleasant emotions, particularly anxiety, which have a profound and sometimes devastating effect on behavior.

frustration

A college basketball tournament provides a good example of frustration in the making. Eight teams and eight coaches are strongly motivated to win the tournament. Forty or more players would all like to be named most valuable player. But only one team can be the champion, and only one man can be most valuable player. All the other teams, coaches, and players are bound to be frustrated. If we watch the losers closely, we will see many kinds of emotional effects. Some of them will display hostility; they will slam the ball or a towel on the floor. Some of them may weep with disappointment. Some will display depression or apathy; they may be "down in the dumps" for days afterward and have a difficult time getting interested in food, studies, and social events. Even those who shrug off the defeat and smilingly congratulate the winners will have some kind of emotional twinges, though they may hide them or quickly get over them.

sources of frustration

The word *frustration* has two different meanings, one based on external events, the other on internal feelings. The external definition is the *blocking of motive satisfaction by an obstacle*. The internal definition of frustration is the *unpleasant feelings that result from the blocking of motive satisfaction by an obstacle*. In either case the key word in the definition is *obstacle*.

Several kinds of obstacles can cause frustration. The environment surrounds us with *physical obstacles*, such as a drought that frustrates a farmer's attempts to produce a good crop, or a broken alarm clock, flat tire, or traffic jam that prevents us from getting to class on time. Our relations with other people create *social obstacles*, such as a refusal by others to give us the affection we desire or social circumstances that frustrate our motive for certainty by raising the threat of economic changes or of war and destruction. All of us are frustrated at times by *personal obstacles;* we may want to be musicians but find that we are tone deaf, or we may aspire to be Olympic champions but lack the necessary skill.

the relative nature of frustration

One interesting aspect of frustration has been demonstrated in an experiment in which children aged two to five were observed in a playroom that was equipped only with "half toys," such as a telephone without a transmitter and an ironing board without an iron. Despite the missing parts, the children played quite happily—until a screen was removed and they saw much better toys in the other half of the room. Then, when a wire barrier was placed between them and the "whole toys," most of them showed signs of extreme frustration (2).

What people find frustrating, as this experiment shows, is a relative matter. "Half toys" are fun to play with if there is nothing better at hand. When better toys lie just beyond reach, the "half toys" are no longer good enough. In adult life a man may be perfectly satisfied with his salary until his best friend gets a raise or with his old used car until his neighbor buys a new convertible. A woman who has never before wished for such possessions may feel frustrated when a friend shows up in a fur coat or moves into a new house. Many people who are quite successful and well liked suffer pangs of frustration because a brother or sister is even more successful and popular.

If a modern American were by some miracle transported to the America of a century ago, he would undoubtedly suffer all kinds of frustrations—from

DEFINITIONS:
1. EXTERNAL FRUSTRA-
TION
2. INTERNAL FRUSTRA-
TION.

OBSTACLES
1. PHYSICAL OBSTACLES
2. SOCIAL OBSTACLES
3. PERSONAL OBSTACLES

lack of central heating in winter and air conditioning in summer, from inability to get quick relief from a toothache, from lack of good lighting to read by at night. Yet the Americans who lived a hundred years ago probably suffered no more frustration than exists today. Among blacks in America, indeed, there is probably more frustration today than there was in the past. Although the civil rights movement and increased economic opportunities have greatly improved the *absolute* level of the black's position in society, they have also served to emphasize the *relative* disadvantages under which he lives and thus have created more intense frustration.

tolerance of frustration

Even in childhood, human beings seem to display rather wide individual differences in the amount of frustration they can tolerate; this has been demonstrated experimentally, as illustrated in Figure 11-1. Apparently the child's

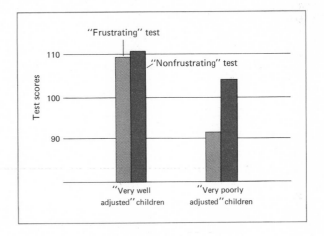

frustration tolerance among children

11-1 An intelligence test was given to two groups of children, one judged to be well adjusted and the other to be poorly adjusted. The test used was the Stanford-Binet, which ordinarily begins with easy items that the child usually gets all correct and progresses to more difficult ones that the child cannot answer. The experiment was designed on the hypothesis that to poorly adjusted children the usual progression might cause frustration and thus lower scores. Therefore the test was given twice—once in the ordinary way (deemed "frustrating") and once by mixing up the easy and difficult questions and returning to an easy one every time the child experienced a failure (deemed "nonfrustrating"). On the average, the well-adjusted children made almost exactly the same scores both times. The poorly adjusted children made substantially higher scores on the "nonfrustrating" test—indicating that their performance on the other test was indeed affected by a lower threshold for frustration. (3)

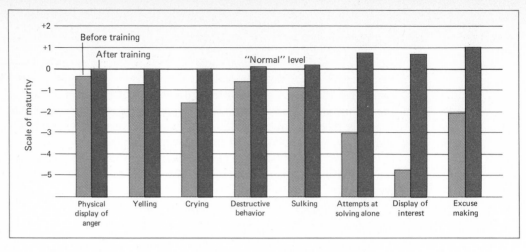

results of training in frustration tolerance

11-2 The height of the bars shows the amount of improvement in various kinds of behavior made by a group of a dozen children who were given special training in an attempt to increase their tolerance of frustration. The shaded bars represent the children's average score on the experimenter's scale of immaturity and maturity before training, the colored bars the average score after training. The children in the experiment were chosen after an initial test in which they demonstrated considerably more frustration when confronted with difficult situations than did other children, whose average scores on the maturity scale are represented by zero. Note that after training the group that originally behaved in an immature fashion actually made better scores on some aspects of behavior than did the more "normal" group. The experimenters trained the children by encouraging them to complete simpler tasks and thus to persist at tasks in expectation of eventual success and by showing them how to attack problems constructively and without the help of adults. (4)

tolerance can be increased to a certain extent through special training, as has been indicated by the experiment described in Figure 11-2.

Among adults, individual differences in frustration tolerance have been dramatically apparent under wartime conditions. Some men break down under the relatively mild frustrations of training camp and display the various symptoms of abnormal behavior that will be discussed later in the chapter. Others are able to withstand the much more severe frustrations of the battlefield and prisoner of war camps. Under more ordinary circumstances, all of us know people who have managed to carry on in normal fashion and even appear relatively cheerful despite serious physical handicaps or tragic disappointments and know others who are reduced to tears or temper tantrums if the breakfast bacon is burned.

conflict

Although the word *conflict* can ordinarily mean many things, ranging from the struggle of two small children over a rubber ball to a world war, for present

372

purposes it has only one meaning. A conflict is the *simultaneous arousal of two or more incompatible motives, resulting in unpleasant emotions.* The emotional factor is an essential part of the definition. The person in conflict experiences uncertainty, hesitation, and the feeling of being "torn" and distressed—elements that are an integral part of conflict and that make conflicts such an unpleasant part of life and a potential threat to normal behavior.

Conflicts fall into two general classes. One class includes conflicts between motives and standards; the other includes conflicts over incompatible goals.

conflicts with internal standards

Our standards, acquired through learning and identification with our childhood heroes, comprise our pattern of how we feel we should behave. When a motive urges us toward behavior that is incompatible with our standards, we have a conflict that often results in intense anxiety. The growing child, for example, may be motivated by hostility and the desire for independence to strike out in some manner against his parents. But these motives conflict with his desire to live up to standards that tell him he must be an obedient child who respects his parents, and the conflict causes him to experience shame or guilt. An adolescent or adult often experiences similar conflicts and anxieties over what would happen to his image in society or to his own self-respect if he struck out angrily against a teacher or boss.

Until the last few decades, sexuality was a motive that often conflicted with standards and generated intense anxiety. But society today takes a more permissive attitude toward sexual behavior; we are surrounded by books, movies, and television shows (all of which have an effect on standards) that seem to define sexual expression as desirable rather than shameful. In today's society, a motive that frequently troubles men is the desire to be dependent, which conflicts with the masculine standard calling for independent and even aggressive behavior. A motive that frequently troubles women is the desire to be dominant (for example, to assume leadership in the business or professional world), which conflicts with the feminine standard calling for dependent and submissive behavior.

conflicts over external goals

The other class of conflicts occurs when two motives for different and incompatible external goals are aroused at the same time. Most students experience frequent conflicts between the desire to get passing grades and the desire for affiliation and approval (as represented by socializing with one's friends). Many times during a school year these two motives conflict acutely and painfully. For example, it is the night before an examination. The motive to get good grades creates a strong pull toward locking oneself in one's room and studying. But friends call and suggest going to the movies or a party. Various motives for acceptance and affection now pull strongly in the opposite direction. Only one of the two motives can be satisfied. An agonizing decision must be made.

To complicate the situation, the decision will arouse anxieties no matter which way the student turns. If he decides to study, he feels anxious about the loss of the goal of being with his friends and also about the possibility that their regard for him may be lowered and that they may be inclined to reject him. If he decides to go with his friends, he feels anxious over the possibility of doing poorly on the examination and perhaps also over rejection by his teachers and his parents.

In life after college the same kind of conflict often occurs between the motive for success and wealth and the motive to be with one's family. Should the young inventor spend the evening in his laboratory (and risk loss of affection from his wife and children) or spend the evening with his family (and risk failure as an inventor)?

Life is full of conflicts over pairs of goals that cannot both be attained. Shall I marry now (and lose my chance for other social experiences with the opposite sex) or wait (and risk losing the person I think I love)? Shall I try for a high-paying but difficult job (and risk failure) or settle for a more modest job (and give up the idea of being rich)? Shall I spend everything I earn (and risk my future security) or save some of it (and miss out on things I want to buy now)? Shall I live in city or country? Shall I have a small family or a large one? The list of conflicts could be expanded almost indefinitely.

achievement versus affiliation

Two motives of special interest in this connection are the desires for achievement and for affiliation, both of which may be quite strong in the same individual. Sometimes the two motives work together toward the same end, as when satisfying the achievement motive by doing well in a class will also gain the approval of a well-liked teacher and thus satisfy the affiliation motive as well. Often, however, the two motives are in conflict. For example, a student may want to make a good grade yet fear losing the friendship of his classmates if he does better than they do. Thus in one study of high school boys it was found that those strongly motivated toward both achievement and affiliation tended to do better if told that their performances would be posted on a bulletin board under secret code numbers than if told the results would be posted by name (5). In another study, university men high in both achievement and affiliation motives did better on a task when working alone than when working in direct competition with another man; they did not, however, show any significant decline in performance when competing against a woman (6). Presumably they were influenced by the popular belief that winning a contest against another male is likely to arouse his resentment, whereas winning against a woman arouses her admiration.

The Motive "to Avoid Success." Along similar lines, there has been some interesting research in recent years on what has been called the *motive to avoid success,* which has been found to be especially frequent among women in our society and presumably is based on a belief that a successful woman runs the risk of being considered "pushy" and unfeminine and therefore of being rejected. The strength of this motive has been found to increase from childhood into young adulthood, presumably because of increased knowledge of society's expectations and prejudices. Thus one investigator has found evidence of a pronounced motive to avoid success among 47 percent of girls in the seventh grade, 60 percent of the women in the freshman class at a large Midwestern university, 86 percent of women students in a top-level law school, and, again, 86 percent of the women in a group of highly efficient secretaries (7).

The motive to avoid success (and therefore society's criticism) is of course in direct conflict with the achievement motive, in a manner that often produces unfortunate results. In a study at one college where women students are chosen for exceptional success in high school and apparently high level of achievement motive in regard to college studies and future life, the investigator found that most of the incoming freshmen were ambitious to have distinguished careers, often in such difficult and traditionally masculine fields as medicine and law. By the time they were juniors, however, about 90 percent of those high in the motive to avoid success had changed their plans in a much more modest direction; they had switched to the study of more "feminine" subjects such as the fine arts and many of them had decided to become teachers or housewives. Although they apparently had resolved their conflict by choosing the motive to avoid success over the achievement motive as far as their actual behavior was concerned, the investigator found that this solution "did not occur without a price—a price paid in feelings of frustration, hostility, aggression, bitterness, and confusion." Although men may suffer from the same conflict and resolve it in a similarly unsatisfactory way, they are less likely to do so. Among college men, the investigator found a strong motive to avoid success in only 9 percent.

approach and avoidance conflicts

One useful way to categorize the various conflicts over goals—of special value because it provides a start toward further explanation of the effects of conflict—is based on the fact that some motives incline us to *approach* a desirable goal (as does the motive for achievement), while others make us seek the *avoidance* of something unpleasant (as does the motive to avoid success). Most conflicts between motives, it has been suggested, fall into one of three categories: 1) *approach-approach,* 2) *avoidance-avoidance,* or 3) *approach-avoidance* (8).

In an *approach-approach conflict* the aroused motives have as their objectives two desirable goals, both of which we want to approach. However, we cannot approach both goals at once, and attaining one of them means giving up the other. We cannot simultaneously satisfy the motive to watch the late movie on television and the motive to get a good night's sleep. We cannot simultaneously satisfy the motive to spend our money on a new tennis racket and the motive to spend it on a coat. The conflict in an approach-approach situation arises from the fact that attaining one desirable goal means giving up another desirable goal. We are torn between alternatives, each of which would be thoroughly pleasant except for our disappointment over losing the other.

In an *avoidance-avoidance conflict* there is simultaneous arousal of motives to avoid alternatives, both of which are *un*pleasant. For example, you are too keyed up over tomorrow's examination to get to sleep. You would like to avoid the unpleasantness of tossing and turning in bed. But you would also like to avoid the grogginess you will suffer tomorrow if you take a sleeping pill.

In an *approach-avoidance conflict* we have mixed feelings about a single goal that has both desirable aspects (that make us want to approach it) and undesirable aspects (that make us want to avoid it). In the laboratory an approach-avoidance conflict can be set up by teaching an animal that if it goes to a certain spot in a maze it will receive food, but it will also receive an electric shock. In real-life situations we may want to go swimming with our friends but know that the water is much too cold for comfort. We may want to follow the school team to an out-of-town game but dislike the idea of driving so far.

Sometimes we are torn between two goals that both have their good points and their bad. This is true in the case of the student undecided between studying and going out with his friends. He wants to approach the goal of study because it will satisfy his achievement motive, and at the same time he wants to avoid it because it arouses anxiety over rejection by his friends. He wants to approach the goal of socializing with his friends because it satisfies his affiliation motive, but he wants to avoid it because it arouses anxiety over the next day's examination. The situation involves a *double approach-avoidance conflict*. Since any decision between two goals is likely to result in a certain amount of regret or anxiety over giving up the one that we decide against, most conflicts are double approach-avoidance.

GRADIENTS OF
APPROACH & AVOIDANCE

Gradients of Approach and Avoidance.   Caught in an approach-avoidance conflict—single or double—what is a person likely to do? It has been established that he will exhibit what is called a *gradient of approach* toward his goal (or toward each of his two goals in a double conflict). In other words, the strength of his inclination to approach a desirable goal will vary in accordance with certain factors. He also will exhibit a *gradient of avoidance*, or changing strength of inclination to avoid an unpleasant goal.

The two gradients have been demonstrated and plotted for certain kinds of animal behavior, as shown in Figure 11-3. Note that the gradient of approach, though it rises as the goal is neared, does not rise very fast; it is not very steep. The gradient of avoidance, however, is much higher at and near the goal than farther away; this gradient is extremely steep. The lines demonstrate two general principles of the tendencies to approach a desirable goal and avoid an undesirable goal:

GENERAL
PRINCIPLES

1. The gradients of approach and avoidance reach their highest level near the goal.
2. The gradient of avoidance is steeper than the gradient of approach.

In the right-hand graph in Figure 11-3, the gradients of approach and avoidance are shown together. In this situation one would expect an animal placed in the alley at point A to have a greater tendency to approach than to retreat from a goal that is simultaneously desirable and undesirable; one would expect it to move toward the goal until it reached the point at which the gradient of

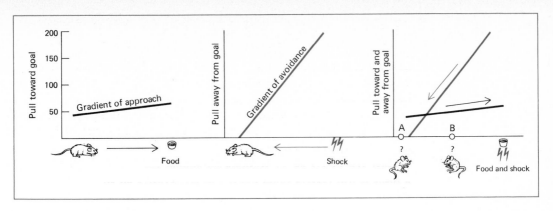

approach and avoidance

11-3 The graphs illustrate the results of an experiment on the tendencies of rats to approach a desirable goal or avoid an unpleasant goal. The animals were placed in a harness attached to a sort of leash, so that measurements could be made of how hard they would pull against an attempt to restrain them. In the part of the experiment illustrated in the graph at left, they ran down a narrow alley toward a goal at which they expected to find food. Note that the pull against the harness—measuring the gradient of approach—becomes gradually stronger as they near the goal. In the part illustrated at center, they had learned to expect not food but an electric shock at the goal; they were placed in the alley near the goal and permitted to run away. Note how much harder they pulled when near the undesirable goal than after they had got some distance away—in other words, how steep the gradient of avoidance is. In the graph at right, the two gradients are both shown, as a theoretical picture of what the situation might be if the animals had received both food and shock at the goal line. Note where the two gradient lines intersect. If an animal that expected both food and shock at the goal were placed at point A to the left of the intersection, what would it be likely to do? If placed at point B, what would it do? For the answer, see the text. (9)

approach and gradient of avoidance intersect and are equal. Similarly, one would expect an animal placed in the alley at point B to move away from the goal until it reached the point at which the gradients are equal, then to stop and hesitate. The experimental evidence suggests that this does indeed happen. It is theoretically possible to predict which direction an animal caught in this approach-avoidance conflict will take and where it will stop (10).

Other Influences on Approach and Avoidance. On the basis of Figure 11-3 and the principles of the gradients of approach and avoidance, the factors that influence decisions in situations of conflict can now be summarized. Note as you go through the following list how similar these factors are to those discussed on pages 360–62 as helping to determine whether a motive will result in behavior.

1. *Distance in space from goal.* In the case of the student torn between going out with his friends and studying for an examination, we can presume that the pull toward joining his friends may well prevail if the friends are physically present. If the student is in his room with his books when the invitation comes,

he may be pulled more strongly toward study. But if the idea of studying arouses strong inclinations toward avoidance, the closer he gets to his books the more likely he will be to pull away from them and join his friends.

2. *Distance in time from goal.* If the student's conflict occurs a full week before the examination, the pull toward study is hardly likely to prevail against the pull toward his friends. But if the decision has to be made the night before the test, the student is likely to resolve the conflict by studying, because the goal of doing well on the examination is so close in time.

3. *Strength of motive.* The importance of motive strength was demonstrated experimentally in the same study that is illustrated in Figure 11-3. If the rat was not very hungry—in other words, if its drive to obtain food was relatively weak—the entire line representing the gradient of approach declined. When the rat was very hungry, the gradient of approach rose.

4. *Incentive value of the goal.* The kind of incentive that arouses the motive also plays a part. An animal will pull harder against a harness to try to reach a preferred kind of food than food that appears less attractive; similarly, it will try harder to avoid a strong shock than a weak shock. The student torn between study and friends will be influenced by the particular incentive value of a good grade in the course and the activities suggested by his friends. Indeed it has been shown that students in general work harder in courses that they consider relevant to their future plans than in courses that seem to have no bearing on their lives (11).

5. *Expectancy of goal attainment.* The final factor that influences the decision in case of conflict is expectancy of goal attainment. For the student the pull toward his friends will depend in part on how successfully he believes he can satisfy his motives for socializing by going out with them; his pull toward studying will depend in part on how much chance he thinks he has of doing well on the examination.

INFLUENCES ON
APPROACH & AVOIDANCE

1. DISTANCE IN SPACE
2. DISTANCE IN TIME
3. STRENGTH OF MOTIVE
4. INCENTIVE VALUE
5. EXPECTANCY OF
   ATTAINMENT

effects of frustration and conflict

By definition, frustrations and conflicts are unpleasant; they result in anxiety and other disagreeable emotions. To escape from the distress, we try in various ways to relieve the frustration or resolve the conflict. Thus many forms of behavior—some of which, unfortunately, can result in even greater distress—are set into motion. For each individual, the manner in which he more or less typically reacts in situations of frustration and conflict constitutes an important part of his personality.

Many of the effects of frustration and conflict appear to be universal; they have been observed in many different kinds of societies. However, there are significant differences in the kinds of reactions that are approved in various societies and are therefore most common. Moreover, even in the same society, there are many dramatic individual differences. Among the most important is the degree of anxiety that the individual suffers. Some people are made extremely anxious and even panicky and will go to great lengths to relieve their distress;

others are less drastically affected. Other differences include the kinds of feelings and behavior that accompany the anxiety, among which are the following.

anger and aggression

When frustrated by some obstacle, both men and other organisms often fight back. They attack the obstacle—whether this be a physical barrier, a person, or society as a whole. The hungry animal, barred from getting at food by a door, will try to gnaw through the wood. The child, frustrated by another child who takes his toy, often gets angry and attacks with his fists. The adult, frustrated by high taxes, writes an angry letter to the editor of his newspaper. Thus *aggression*, displayed in different forms and strengths by different people, is one possible result of frustration.

Direct Aggression. In the experiment with the "half toys" many of the children made a direct assault on the wire barrier that separated them from the better toys that they wanted. This is a good example of direct aggression, which is focused on the obstacle that causes the frustration. Other examples would be the child's striking the other child who has taken his toy and the adult's organizing a political fight against the taxes that frustrate him. Direct aggression may be a rather futile outlet for the emotions aroused by frustration, like angrily kicking at a tire that has gone flat, or it may be a form of operant behavior that attempts to get rid of the obstacle and relieve the frustration (see Figure 11-4). It is often learned through the imitation of other people, as was mentioned on page 67.

different reactions to frustration

11-4   Even thirteen-month-olds show pronounced differences in reactions to frustration. When the boy is separated by a fence from his mother and toys, he displays active behavior by first trying to climb the fence, then trying to squeeze around it. The girl, in the same situation, bursts into helpless tears.

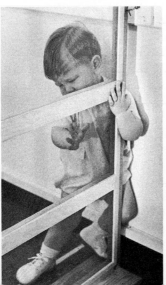
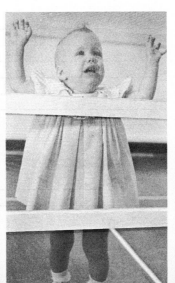

Displaced Aggression.   In some cases, a direct attack on the obstacle is impossible. But aggression is likely to result anyway and to take some rather strange outlets, as was demonstrated by the following experiment. A group of young boys was organized into two handicraft clubs. One was directed by an adult leader who behaved in a friendly and democratic way, taking the boys into his confidence and letting them help make the group decisions. The leader of the other group deliberately ran it with an iron hand, giving the boys no voice in the proceedings and instead issuing arbitrary orders and presumably arousing considerable frustration. The behavior of the two groups was then observed after the leaders had left the room. The outstanding feature was that the boys who had been frustrated by their iron-handed leader began to release their pent-up aggression by directing it toward the members of the group who were least able to stand up and fight back (12).

This kind of *displaced aggression*—aroused by a source of frustration or conflict that cannot be attacked directly and instead is taken out on an innocent bystander—is very common. The man angry at a demanding and powerful boss goes home and behaves aggressively toward his wife and children; in everyday language, he uses them as scapegoats. The child angry at his parents takes out his aggression on a smaller child or on a pet. Scapegoating accounts for a great deal of the prejudice displayed against minority groups or the people of other nations. The prime example occurred in Germany when Hitler made the Jews scapegoats, blaming them for all the frustrations and conflicts that the nation suffered in a time of economic stagnation and political tension.

depression and apathy

Another important reaction to frustration and conflict, found in different degrees among different people, is *depression.* The psychoanalysts, whose theories will be discussed in the next chapter, believe that depression represents a turning inward of anger; the depressed person is one who in effect has made himself his own scapegoat and accuses himself of being stupid, ungrateful, and unlovable—a frame of mind that leads him eventually to feel totally unable to cope with the problems that the world presents. Other psychologists believe that depression usually results from an inability to live up to an overly rigid set of inner standards of behavior. And of course it may at times result from grief over the loss of a loved one—whether through death or rejection. Whatever its cause, extreme depression may lead to an *apathy* so severe that the victim lives his days in what is commonly called "a blue funk"—so sad and listless that he seems to lose all interest in what happens to him and has a difficult time finding the energy for the ordinary chores of life.

withdrawal and fantasy

Some individuals, when beset by frustrations and conflicts, exhibit the kind of behavior called *withdrawal;* they try to avoid close contacts with other people and any kind of goal-seeking behavior that may pose the threat of causing further anxiety. We say of such people that they have "retreated into a shell" or that they have "quit trying." Rather than making an attempt to cope with frustrations and conflicts, the withdrawn person prefers to escape from them by narrowing the horizons of his life—sometimes in the most drastic and self-limiting kinds of ways.

A common form of withdrawal is *fantasy,* in which the person tries to spend as much time as possible not in the real world of obstacles and conflicts but in a make-believe world of daydreams in which he imagines that he is surrounded by love and success. Reading is often a withdrawal into the world of fantasy; the shy and physically weak young man identifies with the hero in a science fiction story; the shy and physically unattractive young woman imagines that she is the glamorous heroine of a romantic novel. For some people, drugs are attractive as a retreat into a world of fantasy.

vacillation

It is in the kinds of feelings and behavior that result from the anxiety produced by frustration and conflict—in tendencies toward anger and aggression, depression and apathy, and withdrawal—that people of different societies and within the same society show the greatest differences. There are several forms of behavior produced by conflict that deserve special mention. One of them is *vacillation*—the tendency to be drawn first toward one possible resolution of a conflict, then toward another. The student torn between studying and going out with his friends may change his mind several times; at one moment he may lean strongly toward studying, at the next moment toward going out. In an extreme case of vacillation he may take so long making up his mind that he has very little time left for either of the possibilities.

In an experiment on vacillation, children were shown two attractive toys and a clock that was set into motion by pressing either of two bars, one under each of the toys. The children were told to select the toy they wanted by pressing one of the bars. The clock would then run for a full minute, after which the toy they had selected would be theirs. At any time before the minute was up, however, they could change their minds and choose the other toy by pressing the other bar. Many children changed their minds at least once and often several times (13). They usually waited until the clock had run for about two-thirds of a minute, at which time anxiety over losing the second toy presumably outweighed their desire to obtain the first toy.

The close relationship between vacillation and anxiety has been demonstrated by the experiment illustrated in Figure 11-5. The beginning parachutists in this study, who continued to vacillate between jumping and not jumping, showed a steady and pronounced increase in physiological signs of anxiety right up to the moment of making the jump. The experienced jumpers presumably felt committed to the jump much sooner; they stopped vacillating and showed no further increase in anxiety.

DEFINITION:
VACILLATION

"Look at it this way—
you're the baby sparrow
and I'm the mamma
sparrow."

Drawing by Peter Arno,
© 1943, 1971, The New Yorker
Magazine, Inc.

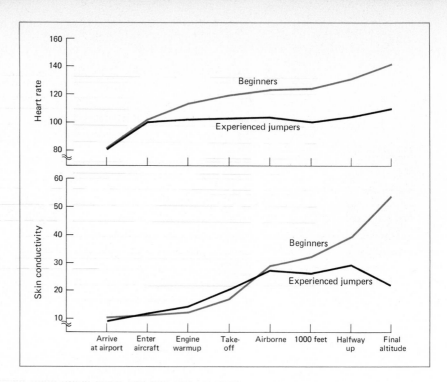

vacillation and anxiety

11-5 As indications of anxiety, records were kept of the heart rate and the electrical conductivity of the skin of parachute jumpers. Note that the heart rate of experienced jumpers increased only until they got into the aircraft, and the skin conductivity only until they were airborne. For the beginning jumpers, heart rate and skin conductivity continued to rise right up to the moment of jumping. One explanation appears to be that the experienced jumpers felt committed to jump as soon as they entered the plane, while the beginners continued to vacillate between jumping and not jumping until the last moment. (14)

regression

One of the most striking findings of the experiment with the "half toys" was that the frustrated children began to behave as if they were, on the average, seventeen months younger than their actual age. This kind of behavior —retreating toward types of activity appropriate to a lower level of maturity— is called *regression*.

DEFINITION: REGRESSION

The first-born child in a family often shows signs of regression when a baby brother or sister arrives; he may go back to such forgotten habits as thumb sucking, or he may want to be fed from a bottle. Frustrated adults may regress to weeping or temper tantrums, or they may try to return to their family homes and the arms of their parents, like the wife who goes home to mother after a quarrel. An extreme case of regression such as is sometimes found among psychotics is illustrated in Figure 11-6.

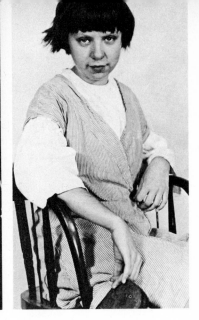

a case of regression

11-6 The girl at left, a seventeen-year-old psychiatric patient, found the old photograph of herself at center, taken when she was five. She then cut her hair and made every other possible attempt to look as she had at five, as shown in the photograph at right. (15)

stereotyped behavior

DEFINITION:
STEREOTYPED
BEHAVIOR

Another reaction to frustration is the tendency to repeat some action over and over again, despite the fact that it appears to serve no useful purpose. This is called *stereotyped behavior.* Among adults it has been observed to a pronounced degree in medical patients who have suffered brain damage that interferes with their speech or motor skills. Frustrated by their disabilities, many such patients keep placing their shoes and other belongings in certain definite places and patterns, and they become upset by any variation in the appearance or arrangement of their rooms or lockers. Many frustrated people have definite stereotyped patterns of conversation—phrases they keep repeating over and over again, whether they are appropriate to the discussion or not.

In a classic experiment on stereotyped behavior, a rat was placed on a stand from which it could jump toward either of two small doorways, one marked with a white circle on a black card, the other marked with a black circle on a white card. If the rat chose correctly, the door opened, and the rat entered a food compartment. If it chose incorrectly, it bumped into a locked doorway and fell into a net. After the rat had learned to discriminate between the white and the black circles, the problem was made insoluble; half the time food was placed behind the white circle and the door behind the black circle was locked, and the other half of the time this procedure was reversed. The rat's attempts to reach the food

383

and to avoid the bump and fall were now frustrated. After a while it simply remained on the stand and refused to jump at all—a reaction resembling apathy. The experimenter then forced the rat to jump by applying a shock, a blast of air, or a prod with a stick. Under these circumstances the animal's behavior became highly stereotyped; it tended to keep jumping time after time to the same doorway, regardless of the marking or whether it was rewarded or was punished by a fall. This stereotyped tendency to jump in the same direction every time persisted for as many as several hundred trials and sometimes continued even when the other doorway was left open so that the food behind it was clearly visible (16).

defense mechanisms

Among the effects of frustration and conflict, as has just been discussed, are such behavioral symptoms as aggression, depression, withdrawal, vacillation, regression, and stereotyped behavior. In addition, frustration and conflict often result in a group of mental or symbolic processes, first described by the psychoanalysts, that are so important that they deserve a section of their own. They are called *defense mechanisms,* and they represent an unconscious attempt to reduce anxiety. All defense mechanisms involve some degree of self-deception and distortion of reality. The processes apparently operate in everyone at times, and in psychotic people they are often seen in extreme and exaggerated form.

rationalization

"That's OK. I wanted some more time to work on my diary anyway."

Perhaps the most common of all defense mechanisms is *rationalization*—which is familiar even to children, though not by its scientific name, through Aesop's fable about the fox, unable to reach the grapes, that consoled itself by deciding that they would have been sour anyway. As the fable implies, rationalization is an attempt to reduce anxiety by deciding that you have not really been frustrated—or that a conflict over goals has not really occurred.

Thus a young woman, frustrated because she was turned down by the college of her choice, manages to convince herself that she did not really want to go to that school anyway; it is too far from home or the student body is too snobbish. A young man, frustrated because he was rejected when he asked for a date, convinces himself that the girl is not very attractive and much less interesting than he had mistakenly supposed.

We also use rationalization at times to conceal from ourselves the fact that we have acted out of motives that conflict with our standards. A mother's real reason for keeping her daughter from dating may be jealousy; she rationalizes by saying that she is acting for the girl's own good. A student may cheat on an examination to avoid the work of studying, but he rationalizes by claiming that everybody cheats. The miser may rationalize his refusal to give money to good causes by claiming that charity weakens the moral fiber of the people who receive it.

projection

The man who claims that everybody is dishonest and the woman who is convinced of the sexual immorality of the younger generation may have reached these conclusions through honest examination of the evidence. On the other hand, they may be exhibiting another common defense mechanism called *projection,* in which the individual foists off or projects onto other people motives or thoughts of his own that cause him anxiety. The man who talks too much about the dishonesty of mankind may very well be concealing his own strong tendencies toward dishonesty. The woman who talks too much about the immorality of young people may be concealing her own strong sexual desires, which cause her considerable anxiety.

In one experimental study of projection, the subjects were college fraternity brothers who lived under the same roof and knew each other well. Each subject was asked to rate his fraternity brothers on a scale that measured four undesirable traits: stinginess, obstinacy, disorderliness, and bashfulness. In the answers the experimenters found general agreement that some members of the fraternity were indeed quite stingy, obstinate, disorderly, or bashful. The subjects were also asked to rate themselves on these traits. These self-ratings showed that some of the men described by their friends as stingy or obstinate freely admitted that they possessed these traits, while others did not. The most significant finding was that the students who were in fact stingy or obstinate, but were unaware of it or unwilling to admit it, were the most inclined to attribute these traits to the others. The student who was generally regarded as stingy but who described himself as generous was likely to rate his friends as possessing a high degree of stinginess (17). Presumably he was relieving his anxiety over possessing this trait by projecting it—by claiming that others, and not he, possessed it.

Projection plays a part in many disagreements in marriage. Many husbands complain that their wives are extravagant, although a disinterested observer can clearly see that it is the husband himself, not the wife, who is wasting money. Wives who are torn by sexual conflicts and urges toward infidelity may falsely accuse their husbands of having affairs. A marriage counselor who hears accusations by husband or wife of bad conduct or improper motives on the part of the other partner always looks for the possibility that the complaints represent projection rather than the truth.

repression

In many cases, people who suffer anxiety over their motives seem simply to banish the motives altogether from their conscious thoughts; they cease to be aware of the motives. This process of pushing down motives (or conflicts) from consciousness into the unconscious is called *repression,* and its effects are frequently observed. A woman who at one time suffered severe conflicts and anxiety over sexual urges may now have repressed her motives to the point where she is not aware of any sexual desires or feelings at all. Many people seem to be entirely unaware that they possess such motives as dependency and hostility. Some cases of *amnesia*, or loss of memory, are believed to be exaggerated forms of repression, although amnesia can also be caused by brain damage.

identification

The term *identification* has already been defined as one of the processes through which the growing child develops his standards. The child comes to think of himself as being almost the same person as his parents and the other figures of authority in his life; he takes into himself their power, their virtues, and their triumphs, and he adopts their standards because he believes that this will help him attain the exalted position that they have attained. The process is often used as a defense mechanism, in one of two ways.

In its simpler form, identification as a defense mechanism represents an attempt by the individual to relieve anxiety over his own conflicts by assuming the virtues of an admired person or group that seems free of such anxiety. Thus a man who is anxious about his lack of courage may identify with an astronaut or a group of mountain climbers so that he can believe that he too possesses their courage. A young woman anxious about her own lack of charm and social skill may identify with a more glamorous and popular roommate.

In a more complex form, an identification is established with a figure of authority who is resented and feared. Thus a young man may defend himself against the anxiety aroused by hostile feelings toward his boss by identifying with the boss; he may imitate the boss's mannerisms, voice the same kind of opinions, and pretend that he possesses the same kind of power. This kind of identification may also be made with a group. Thus young people, anxious about their feelings of envy and hostility toward an in-group, may identify with the group and adopt its standards. A study of prisoners in German concentration camps in the Second World War showed that many of them began to imitate the characteristics of the very guards from whose brutality they were suffering (18).

Identification appears in some cases to be a conscious process; the person seems to be aware of his attempts to make himself similar to a model who possesses characteristics that would reduce his own anxiety. In other cases the whole process is unconscious, and the person is not aware that he is imitating another individual or a group.

reaction formation

DEFINITION: REACTION FORMATION

When a person displays a trait to excess—that is, in an exaggerated form that hardly seems called for by the circumstances—the possibility always exists that he is using the defense mechanism called *reaction formation*. That is to say, he is pretending to himself to possess motives that are the opposite of the real motives that are causing him anxiety. For example, a man appears to be overpolite; he is constantly holding doors open for other people, saying "Yes, sir," and "Yes, ma'am," always smiling, agreeable, and apologetic for his mistakes.

This exaggerated politeness and concern for others may simply be a defense mechanism he has adopted to conceal the fact that he has hostile motives and is made anxious by his hostility. A woman who dresses in a sexually provocative manner and is constantly flirting and telling risqué stories may only be concealing her basic sexual inhibitions and fear of being unattractive.

substitution

The college student who would like to be an athlete but cannot reach this goal because of lack of physical strength or because of his anxiety over competition may turn instead toward the goal of becoming a great painter. The young woman who would like to be the most popular girl on the campus but is unattractive or bashful may turn instead toward the goal of getting the best grades in her class. This defense mechanism is called *substitution*, in which an unobtainable or forbidden goal is replaced by a different goal.

DEFINITION:
SUBSTITUTION

the role of defense mechanisms

In the last analysis, perhaps every person's defense mechanisms are unique. Certainly many investigators would want to add to the list of six that have been mentioned here. Some investigators would use different names for them or perhaps lump some of those mentioned here under the same name. The important thing is that human beings show considerable ingenuity at deluding themselves. In one way or another they persuade themselves that they did not really want the goals from which they have been blocked, that their motives are admirable, that they are living up to their own and society's standards, and that their disappointments are somehow bearable.

Because frustration and conflict are so frequent, all of us use defense mechanisms from time to time. Many of these mechanisms are, of course, irrational. Nonetheless, they often serve a useful purpose. They may help us through crises that would otherwise overwhelm and disable us. If nothing else, they may gain time for us—time in which we can gather the strength, maturity, and knowledge needed to cope more realistically and constructively with our anxieties. It is only in the more extreme cases that the use of defense mechanisms—like the other effects of frustration and conflict mentioned earlier in the chapter—slip over into the realm of abnormal psychology.

DEFENSE
MECHANISMS

. RATIONALIZATION
. PROJECTION
. REPRESSION
. IDENTIFICATION
. REACTION FORMA-
TION
. SUBSTITUTION

normal and abnormal psychology

The dividing line between normal psychological processes and behavior on the one hand and abnormal psychological processes and behavior on the other is difficult to draw. All of us, as has been said, are irrational in our use of defense mechanisms. Moreover, we may be moved to more or less irrational anger and aggression, depression and apathy, withdrawal, vacillation, regression, and stereotyped behavior. At what point does such behavior cease to represent the conduct of a human being who is quite normal (though subject to the usual human frailties) and slip over into the realm of the abnormal? And what is one to say about the fact that a person who behaves normally most of his life and is ordinarily quite successful at his work and in his relations with his fellow workers, his friends, and his family may go through periods when he seems to be behaving abnormally and may even require hospital treatment?

the normal personality

In attempting to define the normal personality, psychologists for many years stressed the word "adjustment." Normal personality traits, it was generally agreed, are those that help the individual adjust to his environment and to the people around him—that is to say, to accept the realities of the physical world and of society and to get along well with his fellow man. This general description of the normal personality is still accepted; but in recent years many psychologists have come to the conclusion that "adjustment" is too passive and negative a word—and that it implies a kind of self-effacing conformity to what others in the society are thinking and doing. Indeed some scholars have decided that "adjustment," if construed as meaning a more or less unquestioning acceptance of some aspects of human society—such as mass killings in warfare and the spending of human resources on military equipment rather than on education and the alleviation of poverty—is itself abnormal (19).

Thus growing numbers of psychologists have come to think less in terms of adjustment than in terms that imply some kind of honest self-awareness, independence, and fulfillment. As was mentioned on pages 356–57, Maslow has suggested the term "self-actualization." Others have suggested that the normal person is one who has a continuing and stable sense of identity (20)—or who possesses the ability and inner freedom to make his own decisions in accordance with his own desires and the realities of the environment rather than because of real or imagined pressure from others (21).

Certainly it is very difficult to define the normal personality, especially in times of rapid social change such as the present; and doubtless there will be continued debate and the formulation of new ideas in forthcoming years. But most psychologists probably would agree on the following points.

NORMAL PERSONALITY

1. Being normal does not mean being perfect. The most normal person encounters frustrations and conflicts, develops a certain amount of anxiety, and does not always cope with his anxiety in a completely successful manner. He can only do his best—which probably means continuing to function more or less successfully despite the inevitable problems of the human condition.

2. Being normal means being realistic. The normal person does not expect perfection, either in himself or in others. He is aware of his own limitations and expects others to have limitations. Since he does not have unduly grandiose expectations, he is not surprised or overly ashamed or angry when he fails or when others fail him.

3. The normal person can "roll with the punch." He may be unhappy at times over disappointments, but he can manage to live with them. He is flexible

and can change his plans; he is confident of his ability to cope with situations as they arise.

4. Similarly, the normal person possesses a certain amount of enthusiasm and spontaneity. He finds things to do in life that give him pleasure, whether these be working productively or watching sunsets. He feels and can display honest affection and is capable of satisfactory relationships with other people.

the abnormal personality

Just as it is difficult to say what is normal, so is it difficult to say what is abnormal. Indeed it is virtually impossible to make any absolute definition of abnormal behavior. Is it abnormal to believe in witches? It was not so considered by the American colonists. Is it abnormal for a young woman to faint from the excitement of attending a dance or the embarrassment of hearing profanity? It was not so considered in Victorian England. Is suicide abnormal? To most Americans, it may seem like the ultimate in abnormality. Yet in the Far East a Buddhist priest who commits suicide as a form of political protest is regarded as exhibiting strength of character rather than abnormality.

One approach to a description of abnormal behavior can be made in statistical terms—that is to say, it is behavior that is rather uncommon and unusual. But in addition, as the preceding paragraph implies, unusual behavior is not generally considered abnormal unless it is regarded as undesirable by the particular society in which it occurs. For example, working eighteen hours a day is probably even more unusual in our society than being addicted to heroin—but the former is generally considered desirable or at least acceptable and is therefore regarded as normal, while heroin addiction is considered undesirable and therefore regarded as abnormal.

What is considered undesirable or "strange" varies from society to society. In our own society, a man who spent much of his day holding conversations with God would certainly be regarded as abnormal, but in rural Brazil such conduct is regarded as perfectly sensible and normal. Our American society generally regards drug addiction and homosexuality as abnormal, but this has not been true of all societies and may be becoming less true of our own.

One quality highly valued by the American culture is happiness—and therefore most Americans, including American psychologists, tend to equate normal personality with happiness. A trait or behavior is considered normal if it leads to personal happiness, at least much of the time, and abnormal if it leads to unhappiness. Thus in the United States a working definition of an abnormal personality trait or type of behavior embraces three points. An abnormal personality trait or type of behavior is 1) statistically unusual, 2) considered strange or undesirable by most people, and 3) a source of unhappiness to the person who possesses or displays it.

ABNORMAL
PERSONALITY

abnormality and stress

Abnormal behavior is closely related to all the forces that are lumped together under the concept of stress. It appears that all human beings, and animals as well, can stand a certain amount of frustration, conflict, and the resultant anxiety. But if the burden becomes too great and exceeds the threshold of what they can endure, they may lapse into abnormality, ranging from the mild to the severe.

It has been known ever since the time of Pavlov that animals can be made to behave abnormally under laboratory conditions that produce frustration and conflict. Pavlov conditioned a dog to discriminate between a circle and an ellipse projected on a screen; the dog learned to salivate to the circle but not to the ellipse. Then the shape of the ellipse was changed gradually so that it became more and more like a circle. Even when the difference in appearance was quite small, the dog still made the discrimination. But when the difference became too small for the dog to perceive and the discrimination became impossible, the dog began to behave strangely. At various times animals placed in this situation became restless, hostile, destructive, and apathetic, and they developed muscle tremors and tics (22).

Many similar experiments have also produced abnormal behavior in laboratory animals. Cats, for example, were taught various means of obtaining food and then, to create a conflict, were given an electric shock or air blast when they performed the act that was rewarded with food. They very quickly—after only one or two repetitions—began to show signs of restlessness, agitation, fear, and panic (23). Among human beings, a common kind of abnormal behavior produced by unusually stressful situations is "battle fatigue," the breakdown sometimes experienced by soldiers who have coped successfully with many difficult problems in civilian life.

influences on abnormal behavior

Some people have a low threshold for stress, others a much higher one. Three kinds of factors appear to determine which people develop the symptoms of abnormal behavior.

Biological Factors. As was mentioned in Chapter 9, there appear to be considerable individual differences in glandular activity, sensitivity of the autonomic nervous system, and, possibly, activity of the brain centers concerned with emotion—all of which may incline one person to be more easily aroused and more intensely emotional than another. Among the possible effects of these individual differences may be unusual patterns of physiological change, which produce sensations that cannot be interpreted by any ordinary standards. Any biological deficiency or abnormality in the emotional apparatus may lower the threshold for stress or cause distorted reactions to stress.

There is strong evidence that hereditary factors can be responsible for tendencies to some of the most severe forms of abnormality, the psychoses that will be discussed later in the chapter. As was stated on page 271, schizophrenia is more common among the close relatives of schizophrenics than among other people. It also has been found that a tendency to manic-depressive psychosis can be inherited (24). There is evidence that tendencies to less extreme forms of abnormality can be inherited as well (25).

Psychological Factors. Regardless of the individual's biological equipment, his psychological experiences play a key role in determining how much stress he is likely to encounter and how much he can endure without lapsing into abnormal behavior. For example, the person who acquires motives for achievement and power that he cannot gratify or whose motives for affiliation and approval are frustrated by the belief that other people dislike him becomes extremely vulnerable. Particularly significant are the person's standards. An event that produces little or no anxiety in a person with relatively low standards of mastery and competence may produce an almost unbearable anxiety in a person with higher standards. Clinical psychologists sometimes are called on to treat people who appear to have suffered a crippling amount of anxiety over violations of standards of sexual behavior, honesty, hostility, or dependency that would seem trivial to most of us.

Cultural Factors. Also important is the kind of culture into which the individual is born—and thus the kinds of social influences to which he is exposed. For example, statistical studies of schizophrenia appear to show that it is most common among people born in the slum or near-slum areas of large cities (26). Perhaps people who are forced to live in that kind of culture experience more frustration and conflict than people at higher levels of society. Or perhaps growing up in a slum environment may reduce a person's tolerance for stress.

Cultural factors also determine in large part the particular kind of abnormal symptoms that a person is likely to display. The culture of middle- and upper-class America has maintained that the individual is personally responsible for what happens to him, and people in this culture who fail to live up to their standards of achievement and virtue are likely to suffer intense feelings of guilt and depression. Americans from less affluent homes are more likely to display symptoms that revolve around feelings of anger, bitterness, and suspicion.

INFLUENCES ON ABNORMAL BEHAVIOR

BIOLOGICAL FACTORS
PSYCHOLOGICAL FACTORS
CULTURAL FACTORS

Thus the chances that any given person will display abnormal behavior—and the particular kind of abnormal behavior to which he is most prone—depend in part on the kind of biological equipment he has inherited, in part on the psychological experiences he has encountered, and in part on the kind of culture in which he finds himself in childhood and adulthood. The three factors work together to make some people behave in what is generally considered a normal fashion—and others in ways considered anywhere from just a bit strange to what psychologists call psychotic, or, in popular terminology, crazy or insane.

psychoneuroses

In a sort of twilight zone between normal behavior and the extreme abnormality of psychosis lie the conditions that are technically known as *psychoneuroses,* usually shortened to *neuroses* in popular usage. In a sense, every psychoneurosis is unique—the product of one person's unique frustrations and conflicts as they affect the tolerance for stress dictated by his own unique biological, psychological, and cultural background. Thus any attempt at classification of the symptoms has to be somewhat arbitrary. One popular and useful classification system, based on the work of Freud and used by many psychotherapists, is as follows (27).

anxiety states

Although anxiety is characteristic of all neuroses, it is a more obvious symptom in some of them than in others. *Anxiety states,* one rather large group of psychoneuroses, include the following.

DEFINITION:
ANXIETY REACTION

Anxiety Reaction.   The outstanding symptom of this anxiety state is a chronic and relatively unfocused feeling of uneasiness and vague fear. The individual feels tense and jumpy, is afraid of other people, doubts his ability to study or work, and sometimes suffers from actual panic. He may experience such physical symptoms as palpitation of the heart, cold sweats, and dizziness. One patient has described his feelings in these terms:

> I feel anxious and fearful most of the time; I keep expecting something to happen but I don't know what. It's not the same all the time. Sometimes I only feel bad—then suddenly for no reason it happens. My heart begins to pound so fast that I feel it's going to pop out. My hands get icy and I get a cold sweat all over my body. My forehead feels like it is covered with sharp needles. I feel like I won't be able to breathe and I begin panting and choking. It's terrible—so terrible. I can go along for a while without too much difficulty and then suddenly without any warning it happens (28).

DEFINITIONS:
1. PHOEBIC REACTION
2. CLAUSTROPHOBIA
3. ACROPHOBIA

Phobic Reaction.   When the anxiety becomes attached to a specific object or event, the patient is said to be suffering from a phobia, or unreasonable fear. Two common phobias are *claustrophobia* (fear of confinement in small places, which makes some people unable to ride in elevators) and *acrophobia* (fear of high places, which affects some people when they have to climb to a top row of a football stadium). But phobic reactions may be attached to any object at all. Some people are thrown into panic by a snake, an ambulance, or even a toy balloon.

obsessive-compulsive reactions

DEFINITIONS:
1. OBSESSIONS
2. COMPULSIONS
3. OBSESSIVE - COM-
   PULSIVE REACTIONS

Obsessions are thoughts that keep cropping up in a persistent and disturbing fashion. Some psychoneurotics are obsessed with the idea that they have heart trouble or that they are going to die by a certain age. A common and mild form of obsession is the feeling of people starting out on a trip that they have left the door unlocked or the stove turned on.

Compulsions are irresistible urges to perform some act over and over again, such as washing one's hands dozens of times a day. The housewife who cannot bear to see a knife or fork out of line at the table and keeps emptying her guests' ash trays is exhibiting mild forms of compulsion.

Obsessive-compulsive reactions seem to represent an attempt to substitute acceptable thoughts or actions for the unacceptable desires that are causing conflict and anxiety.

hysteria

As used to describe psychoneuroses, the word *hysteria* has a different meaning from the usual one. It refers specifically to the following two conditions.

Conversion Reaction. This form of hysteria results in strange and often dramatic physical symptoms that have no organic basis. The patient may suffer paralysis of the arms or legs and even blindness or deafness. He may lose all sensitivity in one part of the body. In one type called glove anesthesia he loses all sensitivity in the hand, as if it were covered by a glove; he cannot feel a pinprick or even a severe cut anywhere from fingertips to wrist.

Dissociative Reactions. In dissociative reactions the patient sets himself apart in some manner from the conflicts that are troubling him. One type of dissociative reaction is *amnesia,* or loss of memory. Another, quite rare, is *multiple personality,* in which the individual seems to be split into two or more different selves that represent sides of his personality that he cannot integrate into a unity. *Sleep walking*, in which a person performs acts while asleep that he cannot remember after he wakes up, is also a dissociative reaction.

Hysteria, obsessive-compulsive reactions, and anxiety states are of course not the only psychoneuroses. There are many others; indeed it might be said that there are as many different kinds of psychoneuroses, some of which defy classification, as there are psychoneurotics. All of them are characterized by high levels of stress and anxiety, lasting over a considerable period of time; but different individuals display the anxiety in different ways. The psychoneuroses may be mild and cause little trouble, or they may be so severe as to verge on the psychotic.

3 TYPES OF
PSYCHONEUROSIS
1. ANXIETY STATES
2. OBSESSIVE - COM-
PULSIVE REACTIONS
3. HYSTERIA

psychoses

Psychosis refers to the extreme forms of mental disturbance that are often known in popular terminology—and also in legal language—as insanity. A psychosis is any form of mental disturbance that is so severe as to make a person incapable of getting along in society. It has been estimated that at any given moment about a million Americans are suffering from mental disorders and that two-thirds of this number are being treated in hospitals, where they occupy about half of all the hospital beds available in the nation (27). It has also been estimated that about one child in ten born today will spend part of his life in a mental hospital (29).

Because of these high figures, many people assume that the "stresses and strains" of modern industrial civilization and city life have greatly increased the amount of mental disturbance, but this does not seem to be true. Although more people are admitted to mental hospitals in the United States today than ever before, much of the increase is due to the fact that more people live to an advanced age and therefore become subject to the kind of brain deterioration that accompanies senility and results in psychosis. Among younger people, there appears to have been little if any change; indeed court records have shown that there were about as many commitments to mental hospitals, in proportion to population, in the relatively rural Massachusetts of the nineteenth century as in the highly industrialized Massachusetts of the present century (29). The same types of mental disturbances found in the United States and other industrialized nations have also been observed in primitive societies throughout the world (30).

a definition of psychosis

In general, the psychotic person appears to display three characteristics.

CHARACTERISTICS
OF PSYCHOSIS

DEFINITIONS:
1. HALLUCINATIONS
2. DELUSIONS

1. His thought processes appear to be different from those of the normal person. His thoughts and statements often seem to be illogical and unrelated to reality. He may have *hallucinations* (imaginary sensations, such as seeing nonexistent animals in the room or feeling bugs crawling under his skin) or *delusions* (false beliefs, such as imagining that he is Napoleon or that he is already dead).

2. He displays inconsistent and inappropriate emotions. He may appear to be more excited than a normal person would be under the same circumstances, or he may seem happy when he should be sad.

3. He is unable to control his thoughts and actions. He may be unable even to dress himself, or he may engage in senseless violence.

DEFINITIONS:
1. SENILE PSYCHOSIS
2. ORGANIC PSYCHOSIS

In some cases, the origin of the symptoms is clearly physiological. In *senile psychosis*, for example, there is actual deterioration of the brain caused by aging or by a succession of what are commonly called strokes, or hemorrhages of blood vessels in the brain. Psychoses can also result from certain diseases, such as untreated syphilis of long standing, from excessive and prolonged use of alcohol and perhaps of other drugs, and, though only rarely, from injuries to the head. Psychoses of these kinds are ordinarily classified as *organic psychoses*.

DEFINITION:
FUNCTIONAL PSYCHOSIS

In other cases, there is no clear-cut physiological explanation. No medical test as yet available shows anything physically wrong with the brain, but it simply does not seem to be functioning normally. These cases therefore have been classified as *functional psychoses*. However, the distinction between organic and functional psychoses no longer seems to be as definite and useful as it once did. The evidence that a tendency toward psychosis can be inherited suggests that there may be some kind of physical basis for most or all psychoses, even though the nature of the physical defects is not yet known. Some psychiatrists now believe that all psychoses are caused by small and subtle chemical imbalances in the brain and someday should be readily controllable through the use of new medications that will restore the proper chemical balance (31).

Even if all psychoses should indeed turn out to have some kind of physical basis, however, there seems to be no doubt that psychological and cultural factors also are important in determining which individuals will manage to overcome the tendency to psychosis and which will actually display psychotic behavior. As is

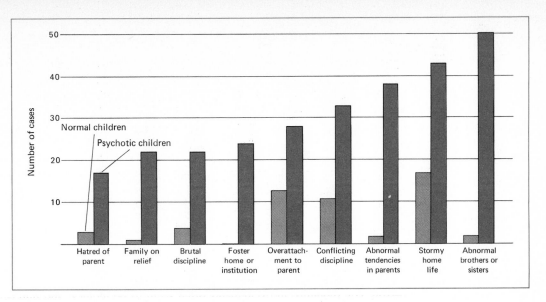

backgrounds of normal and psychotic children

11-7   The bars show some of the more pronounced differences found in
a study of the family backgrounds of a group of psychotic children
as compared with a control group of normal children. Note that the
bars labeled "abnormal tendencies in parents" and "abnormal brothers
or sisters" point to hereditary factors, the others to environmental
factors. (32)

shown in Figure 11-7, the home and family backgrounds of people suffering from
psychosis appear to be less favorable than average in many ways, including many
that have no connection with heredity. The manner in which environment operates
to encourage or discourage psychosis, however, is something of a mystery. Most
people who grow up even in the worst homes do not become psychotic, whereas
many people who come from the most privileged homes (at least homes that appear
on the surface to be the most privileged) do become psychotic. For reasons not
understood, men appear to be more subject to psychosis than women; the ratio
of males to females among first admissions to mental hospitals is about 4 to 3.
Married people are less likely to become psychotic than unmarried people, but
this is probably because people with psychotic tendencies are less likely to get
married in the first place.

the three "functional" psychoses

The psychoses that have traditionally been classified as functional fall
into the following three categories.

Schizophrenia. This is the most common psychosis of all, accounting for
perhaps as many as 25 percent of first admissions to mental hospitals. It is
particularly frequent among young adults in their twenties and is more common
among men than among women. The most striking symptom is a disturbance

An artist who became psychotic painted the cat at left while he was still normal, the others as he became progressively more disturbed.

of thought, displayed in the form of illogical speech, often the invention of new and bizarre words and ideas, and sometimes hallucinations and delusions. Some schizophrenics refuse to talk or answer questions and display little or no emotion. Some act like small children; others sometimes stay frozen in the same rigid positions for long periods of time. The symptoms can be so varied that some investigators believe that schizophrenia is not a single type of disturbance but a number of different types that someday may be classified and treated in quite different ways.

Schizophrenia is notably resistant to any kind of treatment as yet devised, and recovery is usually very slow at best. Therefore many patients remain in hospitals for long periods. There also are many schizophrenics who are not in hospitals, either because they manage to function in some sort of minimal way or because their families take care of them. Many of the men and women on city doorsteps and park benches who appear to the casual observer to be alcoholics are in fact schizophrenics. And there are other schizophrenics sitting in front of television sets sixteen hours a day in homes where they are protected from having to cope with life through their own efforts.

PSYCHOSIS

1. ORGANIC PSYCHOSIS
2. FUNCTIONAL PSYCHOSIS
   SCHIZOPHRENIA
   MANIC-DEPRESSIVE
   PSYCHOSIS
   PARANOIA

Manic-Depressive Psychosis. This psychosis is characterized, as the name indicates, by extremes of mood, sometimes in the form of wild swings from intense excitement to deep melancholy. In the manic phase the patient tends to be talkative, restless, aggressive, boastful, uninhibited, and often destructive. In the depressive phase the patient may become so gloomy and hopeless that he refuses to eat. Some patients swing from the manic to the depressive, while others exhibit only one of the two phases, usually the depressive. Manic-depressive psychosis, particularly the depressive kind, is more common among women than among men. It is most likely to occur in middle adulthood.

Even without treatment, manic-depressive psychosis usually disappears—the manic phase ordinarily in about three months, the depressive phase in about nine. The patient then returns to normal, and about a quarter of all patients do not have a second attack. In other patients the psychosis recurs, often several times.

396

Paranoia. This is the least common of the psychoses; it is indeed quite rare. It is characterized by delusions—sometimes by delusions of grandeur in which the patient believes that he is Napoleon or Christ and sometimes by delusions of persecution in which the patient believes that people are trying to kill him. The delusions of persecution are believed to be an extreme form of projection, in which the patient projects to the rest of the world his own hostile motives.

psychopathic personality

There is one other type of abnormality that differs sharply from the psychoneuroses and psychoses in that it is characterized not by an excess of anxiety but by the absence of anxiety. It is termed *psychopathic personality*, or sometimes *sociopathic personality*. The psychopath (or sociopath) seems to lack a conscience or sense of social responsibility and to have no feeling for other people. On the surface, he may seem quite generous, charming, and candid—but in truth he is selfish, ruthless, and addicted to lying. He has no love for anyone but himself and takes advantage of others without any feelings of guilt (33).

The psychopath is likely to be in and out of trouble all his life, for he does not learn from experience and seems to have no desire to change. The word is mentioned frequently in court cases; the criminal who appears to experience no remorse for even the most cruel kinds of deeds is a good example of the extreme psychopath. The cause of psychopathic personality remains something of a mystery but seems to entail some kind of failure to grow out of a childish insistence on self-gratification and to acquire more mature and responsible ways of behaving.

summary 1. *Frustration* has two meanings: a) the blocking of motive satisfaction by an obstacle and b) the unpleasant feelings that result from the blocking of motive satisfaction. The obstacles that cause frustration may be physical, social, or personal.

2. Some individuals can tolerate relatively large amounts of frustration, whereas others react strongly to relatively small amounts.

3. A *conflict* is the simultaneous arousal of two or more incompatible motives, resulting in unpleasant emotions.

4. Two classes of conflicts are a) conflicts between motives and internal standards (for example, between hostility and standards that prohibit the display of hostility) and b) conflicts over external goals (for example, between the desire to get good grades and the desire to socialize with one's friends).

5. Conflicts over external goals can be a) *approach-approach*, b) *avoidance-avoidance*, or c) *approach-avoidance*.

6. The *gradient of approach* toward a desirable goal becomes higher as the goal is approached. The *gradient of avoidance* of an undesirable goal is higher at and near the goal and is steeper than the gradient of approach.

7. Factors that influence decisions in situations of conflict are a) distance in space from the goal, b) distance in time from the goal, c) strength of the motive, d) incentive value of the goal, and e) expectancy of goal attainment.

8. Among the effects of frustration and conflict are a) anger and aggression, b) depression and apathy, c) withdrawal and fantasy, d) vacillation, e) regression, and f) stereotyped behavior.

9. *Defense mechanisms* are unconscious mental or symbolic processes, involving some degree of self-deception and distortion of reality, that act to reduce the anxiety resulting from frustration and conflict.

10. The defense mechanisms include a) rationalization, b) projection, c) repression, d) identification, e) reaction formation, and f) substitution.

11. *Normal behavior* is defined by many psychologists in terms of honest self-awareness, independence, fulfillment, and a continuing and stable sense of identity.

12. *Abnormal behavior* is defined as behavior that is a) statistically unusual, b) considered strange or undesirable by most people, and c) a source of unhappiness.

13. Abnormal behavior is believed to result from stress beyond a person's threshold for tolerance of stress, which is determined by a) biological factors such as glandular activity and sensitivity of the autonomic nervous system, b) psychological factors, particularly a person's standards and anxiety over failure to meet them, and c) cultural or social factors.

14. *Psychoneuroses* are forms of abnormal behavior that lie between normal behavior and the extreme abnormality of psychosis. They are frequently classified into a) *anxiety states,* including anxiety reaction and phobic reaction, b) *obsessive-compulsive reactions,* and c) *hysteria,* including conversion reaction and dissociative reactions.

15. *Psychosis* is an extreme form of mental disturbance generally characterized by a) disturbances of thought processes, b) inconsistent and inappropriate emotions, and c) inability to control one's thoughts and actions.

16. Psychoses have traditionally been classified as either a) *organic,* those caused by actual damage to the brain, or b) *functional,* those having no apparent connection with any organic disturbance. However, recent evidence that a tendency toward psychosis can be inherited suggests that there may be some kind of physical basis for most or all psychoses—though psychological and cultural factors are important in determining whether the individual will actually become psychotic.

17. Three types of psychosis traditionally classified as functional are a) *schizophrenia,* b) *manic-depressive psychosis,* and c) *paranoia.*

18. Another form of abnormal behavior is *psychopathic personality,* also called *sociopathic personality.* The psychopath (or sociopath) seems to lack a conscience or sense of social responsibility and to have no feeling for other people; unlike other disturbed persons he is free of anxiety.

recommended reading

Allport, G., ed. *Letters from Jenny.* New York: Harcourt Brace Jovanovich, 1965.

Hall, C. S., and Lindzey, G. *Theories of personality*, 2nd ed. New York: Wiley, 1970.

Kaplan, B., ed. *The inner world of mental illness.* New York: Harper & Row, 1964.

Klein, G. S. *Perception, motives, and personality.* New York: Knopf, 1970.

London, P., and Rosenhan, D., eds. *Foundations of abnormal psychology.* New York: Holt, Rinehart and Winston, 1968.

Maddi, S. R. *Personality theories: a comparative analysis.* Homewood, Ill.: Dorsey Press, 1968.

Pervin, L. A. *Personality: theory, assessment, and research.* New York: Wiley, 1970.

APPROACH & AVOIDANCE CONFLICTS

1. APPROACH – APPROACH
2. AVOIDANCE – AVOIDANCE
3. APPROACH – AVOIDANCE

INFLUENCES ON APPROACH AND AVOIDANCE

1. GRADIENTS
2. DISTANCE IN SPACE
3. DISTANCE IN TIME
4. STRENGTH OF MOTIVE
5. INCENTIVE VALUE
6. EXPECTANCY OF ATTAINMENT

EFFECTS OF FRUSTRATION AND CONFLICT

1. ANGER & AGGRESSION
2. DEPRESSION & APATHY
3. WITHDRAWAL & FANTASY
4. VACILLATION
5. REPRESSION
6. STEREOTYPED BEHAVIOR

DEFENSE MECHANISMS

1. RATIONALIZATION
2. PROJECTION
3. REPRESSION
4. IDENTIFICATION
5. REACTION FORMATION
6. SUBSTITUTION

ABNORMAL PSYCHOLOGY

1. PSYCHONEUROSIS
   ANXIETY STATES
   OBSESSIVE – COMPULSIVE REACTIONS
   HYSTERIA
2. PSYCHOSES
   ORGANIC
   FUNCTIONAL
      SCHIZOPHRENIA
      MANIC-DEPRESSIVE PSYCHOSIS
      PARANOIA
3. PSYCHOPATHIC PERSONALITY

PERSONALITY THEORY AND PSYCHOTHERAPY

CHAPTER 12

Sanguine

Choleric

The preceding chapter has already touched on the study of personality—for two critical characteristics of personality are a person's sources of frustration and conflict and his behavior and thought processes when he is frustrated or in conflict. The time has come, however, to take a more sharply focused look: What is personality? What are the ways in which individual personalities differ? What is known about the origins, the structure, and the dynamics of personality? In other words, the discussion must now turn to *personality theory* and to the various types of *psychotherapy,* or attempts to treat abnormal personalities, that are associated with personality theory.

what is personality?

Melancholy

Phlegmatic

Personality is another word that everybody uses but few try to define. It is a concept that has been discussed at least since the time of the ancient Greeks, whose physicians believed there were four types of personalities, each related to different fluids inside the body. The *sanguine* person had a rich flow of blood, which made him happy, warm-hearted, and optimistic. The *choleric* or bad-tempered person had an excess of yellow bile. The *melancholy* person had an excess of black bile, which accounted for his moodiness. The *phlegmatic* person was slowed down and made listless by an excess of phlegm.

The human personality takes far more than four forms, and its origins are extremely complicated. But we might still describe the personalities of some of our acquaintances with the adjectives used by the Greeks. Some people are indeed sanguine, choleric, melancholy, or phlegmatic, at least a good deal of the time—and the tendency to display a particular behavior "a good deal of the time" is part of the modern definition of personality.

DEFINITION :
PERSONALITY

a definition of personality

Personality perhaps can best be defined as the *total pattern of characteristic ways of thinking, feeling, and behaving that constitute the individual's distinctive method of relating to his environment.* There are four key words in the definition, most easily discussed by taking them up in this order: 1) *characteristic,* 2) *distinctive,* 3) *relating,* and 4) *pattern.*

401

CHARACTERISTIC

DISTINCTIVE

RELATING

PATTERN

KEY WORDS OF
"PERSONALITY"
1. CHARACTERISTIC
2. DISTINCTIVE
3. RELATING
4. PATTERN

To qualify as a part of personality, a way of thinking, feeling, or behaving must have some continuity over time and circumstance; it must be *characteristic of the individual*. We do not call a man bad-tempered if he "blows up" only once in ten years. We say that a bad temper is part of his personality only if he displays it many times under different circumstances.

The way of thinking, feeling, or behaving must also be *distinctive*—that is, it must distinguish the individual from other individuals. This eliminates such common American characteristics as eating with a knife and fork, placing adjectives before rather than after nouns, and carrying a driver's license—all of which are more or less the same for every American and do not distinguish one person from others.

Note, however, that a young woman might always wear a ring that is a family heirloom and the only one of its kind in the world; her wearing of the ring would therefore be both characteristic and distinctive. But it would not be considered a part of her personality unless perhaps she attached some deep significance to the ring and acted as if it were an important symbol of personal worth and social acceptance. The word personality is ordinarily attached only to characteristics that play a major part in how the individual goes about *relating* to his environment and especially to the people around him. Moreover, personality characteristics are usually thought of as positive or negative. A positive personality characteristic, such as a friendly manner, helps the individual relate to the people and events around him in a constructive manner. A negative characteristic, such as fear of people, produces anxiety, loneliness, and failure.

There are many kinds of personality characteristics; indeed the English language has at least 4000 words to describe them. Each individual possesses some but not all of them, and his personality is the *pattern*, or sum total, of the characteristics he possesses and displays. Thus one person's pattern of relating to his environment may be such that he is characteristically and distinctively cheerful, outgoing, optimistic, prompt, hard-working, and aggressive. Another person may tend to be depressed, introverted, pessimistic, tardy, lazy, and submissive. Still another may be cheerful but introverted, optimistic but tardy, and hard-working but submissive. A fourth person may be gloomy but extroverted, pessimistic but prompt, and lazy but aggressive. The possible combinations are endless and account for the many varieties of human personality.

the personality hierarchy

One important fact about personality is that like so many other aspects of human behavior, the various possible thoughts, feelings, and responses within a given personality exist in a hierarchy; some are strong and easily and frequently aroused, while others are weaker and less likely to occur. In a social situation, for example, there are many ways that an individual can try to relate to the others in the group; he can be talkative or quiet, friendly or reserved, boastful or modest, bossy or acquiescent, more at ease with men or more at ease with women. One person may characteristically respond by withdrawing into the background, and we say that such a person is shy. Another may characteristically display warmth and try to put the others at their ease; we say that such a person is outgoing. Another may be talkative, boastful, and domineering, and we say that he is aggressive or "pushy." In each of the three individuals, certain responses are strong in the personality hierarchy and easily aroused.

Each person's hierarchy of actions and thoughts has a certain amount of permanence. The shy person behaves shyly under many circumstances, and the aggressive person has a consistent tendency to be boastful and domineering. However, the hierarchy may change considerably according to circumstances. A young person who is aggressive around people his own age may behave rather shyly in the presence of older people. A person who is usually shy may have one close friend with whom he is completely at ease. All of us, no matter how friendly or reserved we may be, are likely to have a strong tendency to make friends if we have been isolated for a long time, such as after an illness or a stretch at a lonely job. On the other hand, we are likely to want some solitude after a round of parties. The businessman who is ordinarily interested in his job and eager to talk about it may shun this kind of conversation when he gets home late at night after a hard day's work.

personality theories

A personality theory is an attempt to organize the great variety of human thinking, feeling, and behavior around some general principles that will help us understand why people are alike in some ways and very different in others. Such a theory attempts to explain which personality characteristics are the most important, the most likely patterns of relationships among characteristics, the way in which these patterns are established, and (at least by implication) the way they can be changed.

Personality theories constitute one of the most complex and difficult of all fields of psychology, and it is impossible to do justice to all of them in an introductory course. In the first place, so many of them have been proposed that they can hardly be counted, much less listed. One reason for the great variety of personality theories is that many of them have grown out of clinical observations of disturbed patients, as performed by many psychologists, psychiatrists, and psychoanalysts* at various times and in various parts of the world, treating patients who came from many different kinds of cultural or social backgrounds and displayed many different kinds of abnormal symptoms. Others have grown out of studies of learning and still others out of studies of individual differences. Thus it is perhaps only natural that the personality theorists, having observed so many different kinds of personality characteristics from different vantage points, should have developed so many varying interpretations.

One important way in which the theorists differ is in the emphasis they

*A psychiatrist is a physician who has gone on to specialize in the treatment of personality disturbances. A psychoanalyst is also usually a physician and has taken special training in psychoanalytic theory, which will be discussed on pages 404-10, and psychoanalytic therapy, discussed on pages 416-17.

place on the three factors—biological, psychological, and cultural—that were mentioned on pages 390-91 as helping determine abnormal symptoms. Some theorists consider biological factors to be most important in determining personality, whether normal or abnormal. Others stress psychological factors, still others cultural or social factors. Thus the theories often seem to be in total contradiction, another fact that adds to the difficulty of trying to summarize or study this complex field. Perhaps the prevailing view among psychologists is that all the theories have something to offer but that none of them is entirely satisfactory. It may be that psychology is only now beginning to accumulate the empirical evidence and the insights that could someday lead to the formulation of a generally acceptable theory of personality.

The three theories chosen for inclusion in this chapter are 1) psychoanalysis, because of the influence it has had on literature, history, and philosophy as well as on psychological thinking, 2) the social learning theory, because it represents a popular and different kind of interpretation, and 3) the self theory proposed by Carl Rogers, because it is one of the outstanding attempts to explain personality in humanistic terms, with emphasis on the idea that man is a creature with a purpose in life. All three theories also have important applications to the practice of psychotherapy, as will be explained later in the chapter.

psychoanalysis

The most famous of all personality theorists, of course, is Sigmund Freud, the founder of *psychoanalysis*. Rather strangely, the school of personality analysis and therapy started by Freud has never grown very large in actual numbers; in recent years there have been only about 2400 Freudian analysts in the United States and about 6000 in the entire world (1). Nonetheless, his ideas have been widely read and debated and have had a profound influence on the views of human personality held not only by many psychologists but also by many people who have never taken a psychology course.

anxiety, repression, and the unconscious

Freud's ideas are very difficult to summarize; the student who hopes to understand them fully must be prepared to do extensive reading of both Freud's own writings and the psychoanalytic textbooks and commentaries that have been written by his followers. The discussion that follows here must of necessity omit many aspects of Freudian theory and confine itself to the ones that have had the most lasting influence.

Some of Freud's most influential ideas concerned concepts so central to the study of psychology that they have already been prominently mentioned. One of them was the role of anxiety. Freud was a pioneer in emphasizing the importance of anxiety, which he believed to be the central problem in mental disturbance. Another was the concept of repression and the other defense mechanisms men-

tioned in Chapter 11. Freud believed that these mechanisms, and especially the process of repression, are frequently used to eliminate from conscious awareness any motive or thought that threatens to cause anxiety. Another influential idea was his concept of the unconscious mind, composed in part of repressed motives and thoughts. Freud was the first to suggest the now widely held theory that the human mind and personality are like an iceberg, with only a small part visible and the great bulk submerged and concealed. All of us, he maintained, have many unconscious motives that we are never aware of but that nonetheless influence our behavior. (An example cited in Chapter 10, where unconscious motives are first discussed, is the case of a man who sincerely believes that he has no hostile motives, yet who in subtle ways performs many acts of aggression against his wife, his children, and his business associates.)

the id

The core of the unconscious, according to Freud, is the *id*, composed of raw, primitive, inborn forces that constantly struggle for gratification. Even the baby in his crib, Freud said, is swayed by two powerful drives. One is what he called the *libido*, embracing sexual urges and such related desires as to be kept warm, well fed, and comfortable. The other is aggression—the urge to fight, dominate, and when necessary destroy.

The id operates on what Freud called the *pleasure principle*, insisting on immediate and total gratification of all its demands. Freud felt, for example, that the baby—though unable to think as yet like a human being and thus more like a little animal—wants to satisfy his libido by possessing completely everything he desires and loves and to satisfy his aggressive urges by destroying everything that gets in his way. As the child grows up, he learns to control the demands of the id, at least in part. But the id remains active and powerful throughout life; it is indeed the sole source of all the psychic energy put to use in behaving and thinking. It is unconscious and we are not aware of its workings, but it continues to struggle for the relief of all its tensions.

the ego

The conscious, logical part of the mind that develops as the child grows up was called by Freud the *ego*—the "real" us, as we like to think of ourselves. In contrast to the id, the ego operates on the *reality principle*; it tries to mediate between the demands of the id and the realities of the environment. Deriving its energies from the id, the ego perceives what is going on in the environment and develops the operational responses (such as finding food) necessary to satisfy the demands of the id. The ego does our logical thinking; it does the best it can to help us lead sane and satisfactory lives. To the extent that the primitive drives of the id can be satisfied without getting us into danger or harm, the ego permits them satisfaction. But when the drives threaten to get us rejected by society or jailed as a thief, the ego represses them or attempts to satisfy them with substitutes that are socially acceptable.

the superego

In the ego's constant struggle to satisfy the demands of the id without permitting the demands to destroy us, it has a strong but troublesome ally in the third part of the mind as conceived by Freud—the *superego*. In a sense the superego is our conscience, our sense of right and wrong. It is partly acquired by adopting the notions of right and wrong that we are taught by society from the earliest years. However, Freud's concept of the superego represents a much stronger and more dynamic notion than the word *conscience* implies. Much like the id, the superego is mostly unconscious, maintaining a far greater influence over our behavior than we realize. It is largely acquired as a result of that famous process that Freud called the *Oedipus complex,* which can be summarized as follows.

OEDIPUS COMPLEX

According to Freud, every child between the ages of about two and a half and six is embroiled in a conflict of mingled affection and resentment toward his parents. The child has learned that the outer world exists and that there are other people in it, and the id's demands for love and affection reach out insatiably toward the person he has been closest to—the mother. Although the child has only the haziest notion of sexual feelings, he wants to possess his mother totally and to take the place of his father with her. But his anger against his father, the rival with whom he must share her, makes him fearful that his father will somehow retaliate. To further complicate the situation, his demands for total love from his mother are of course denied, a fact that also arouses the aggressive drives of the id and makes him want to retaliate against his mother. Thus he becomes overwhelmed with strong feelings of mingled love, anger, and fear toward both parents at once.

This period of storm and stress was named by Freud after the Greek legend in which Oedipus unwittingly killed his father and married his own mother and then, when he discovered what he had done, blinded himself as penance. Girls, according to Freud, go through very similar torments in the period from two and a half to six, except that their libido centers chiefly on their fathers, their aggression chiefly on their mothers.

RESOLUTION OF OEDIPUS COMPLEX

The Oedipus conflict must somehow be resolved; the way this is done, according to Freud, is through identification with the parents. The child resolves his feelings of mingled love and hate for his parents by becoming like them, by convincing himself that he shares their strength and authority and the affection they have for each other. The parents' moral judgments, or what the child conceives to be their moral judgments, become his superego. This helps him hold down the drives of the id, which have caused him such intense discomfort during the Oedipal period. But, forever after, the superego tends to oppose the ego. As his parents once did, the superego punishes him or threatens to punish him for his transgressions. And, since its standards were rigidly set in childhood, its notions of crime and guilt are likely to be completely illogical and unduly harsh.

In their own way the demands of the superego are just as insatiable as the id's blind drives. Its standards of right and wrong and its rules for punishment are far more rigid, relentless, and vengeful than anything in our conscious minds.

Formed at a time when the child was unable to distinguish between a "bad" wish and a "bad" deed, the superego may sternly disapprove of the merest thought of some transgression—the explanation, according to Freud, of the fact that some people who have never actually committed a "bad" deed nonetheless feel guilty all their lives.

superego versus ego versus id

The three parts of the human personality are in frequent conflict. One of the important results of the conflict is anxiety, which is produced in the ego whenever the demands of the id threaten danger or when the superego threatens disapproval or punishment. Anxiety, though unpleasant, is a tool that the ego uses to fight the impulses or thoughts that have aroused it. In one way or another—by using repression and the other defense mechanisms, by turning the mind's attention elsewhere, by gratifying some other impulse of the id—the ego defends itself against the threat from the id or superego and gets rid of the anxiety.

In a sense the conscious ego is engaged in a constant struggle to satisfy the insatiable demands of the unconscious id without incurring the wrath and vengeance of the largely unconscious superego. To the extent that a person's behavior is controlled by the ego, it is sensible and generally satisfying. To the extent that it is governed by the childish passions of the id and the unrelenting demands of the superego, it tends to be foolish, unrewarding, painful, and neurotic.

If the ego is not strong enough to check the id's drives, a person is likely to be a selfish and hot-headed menace to society. But if the id is checked too severely, other problems may arise. Too much repression of the libido can make a person unable to enjoy a normal sex life or to give a normal amount of affection. Too much repression of aggression makes him unable to stand up for himself and to hold his own in the give and take of competition. Too strong a superego may result in vague and unwarranted feelings of guilt and unworthiness, and sometimes in an unconscious need for self-punishment.

the pro and con of Freud

There can be little question that Freud was an important innovator who had a number of extremely useful insights into the human personality. He was the first to recognize the role of the unconscious and the importance of anxiety and defenses as a factor in personality. He also dispelled the myth, widely accepted before his time, that children do not have the sexual urges and hostile impulses that characterize adults.

One criticism of Freud is that he may have overemphasized the role of sexual motivation in personality. In Freud's nineteenth and early twentieth century Vienna, with its strict sexual standards, it is perhaps only natural that many of his neurotic patients should have had conflicts and guilt feelings centering around their sexual desires. In today's Western world, with its more permissive attitudes toward sexual behavior, this kind of conflict and guilt seems to be less frequent. Yet people continue to have personality problems, and the incidence of serious mental disturbance seems to remain about the same as ever. This would indicate that conflicts over sexuality cannot be the sole or perhaps even the most important cause of personality disturbances.

Another frequent criticism of Freud is that many of his ideas about the dynamics of human behavior can be explained more economically without using his concepts of the id, ego, and superego. This will be made clear later when the social learning theory of personality is discussed.

Jung's theory

A number of Freud's disciples broke away from his theories to a greater or lesser degree and established psychoanalytic schools of thought of their own. One of the first of these was Carl Jung, who felt that Freud had overestimated the importance of the sexual drives. To Jung, the instinctive drive called the libido comprised far more than sexual urges; it was an all-encompassing life force that included deep-seated attitudes toward life and death, virtue and sin, and religion. Instead of Freud's id, ego, and superego, Jung emphasized what he called the functions of the personality—modes of viewing the events of the world and making judgments about them. Ideally, he believed, a person would grasp these events with what he called sensation (the evidence of the senses as to what the objects in the world were like at the moment) and also intuition (an understanding of their past and future potential). He would judge objects and events on the basis of both thinking (a more or less coldly logical view) and feeling (an emotional judgment of agreeable or disagreeable, right or wrong). But in most people the function of sensation tends to develop at the expense of intuition or vice versa; the neglected functions are relegated to the unconscious mind and disharmony results.

Jung

It was Jung who invented the words *introvert* and *extrovert*—the former describing a person who tends to live with his own thoughts and to avoid socializing, the latter describing a person whose chief interest is in other people and the events of the world. Both introversion and extroversion, he believed, were necessary for fulfillment of the human personality; unfortunately, one of them tends to develop at the expense of the other. As this brief summary of Jung's ideas indicates, he tended to emphasize the intellectual and spiritual qualities of the human personality, rather than the primitive drives of sex and aggression.

Adler's theory

Another early disciple who rejected Freud's emphasis on sexuality was Alfred Adler. To Adler, who was even more interested in social psychology than Jung, the most important factor in determining a person's motives and therefore his conflicts was the social context in which he grew up.

It was Adler who first used the term *inferiority complex*. One basic influence on human behavior, he believed, is the fact that the baby is born into the world completely helpless, dependent on those around him, and therefore overwhelmed by feelings of inferiority that he must struggle for the rest of his life to relieve. If development is normal, the child acquires such personality traits as courage, independence, and wholesome ambition. If not, he may grow up with feelings

Adler

of inadequacy implied by the term inferiority complex. Or he may overcompensate for his early helplessness and become aggressive and ambitious in the destructive sense.

Adler also suggested that each person develops his own style of life—a certain style of thinking and behaving that makes him unique in the way he attempts to attain his goals. To Adler, this style of life is more important than the particular goals that a person chooses.

current trends in psychoanalysis

In recent years, new generations of psychoanalysts have also added to and in some ways revised Freud's theories—as indeed he himself was constantly doing throughout his lifetime. These so-called *neo-psychoanalysts,* or new psychoanalysts, have tended to move in two major directions.

One group, headed by Heinz Hartmann, has concluded that Freud overstressed the importance of the unconscious demands of the id and superego and neglected the importance of the conscious and rational ego. They have turned their attention to the role of the ego in dealing with reality through such processes as perception, attention, memory, and thinking; they regard the ego as an important force in itself rather than a mere mediator between the id and the superego (2).

Another group of neo-psychoanalysts have turned their attention to cultural and social influences on personality, which were largely neglected by Freud because of the importance he attached to the primitive, biologically determined drives of the id. One prominent member of this group is Erich Fromm, who has suggested that personality problems are caused by conflicts between man's basic needs and the demands of his society. Man, being the kind of creature he is, has lost the kind of unity with nature possessed by other animals. Therefore he has the unique human needs shown in Figure 12-1. But these needs are impossible to satisfy

Fromm

---

1. *Relatedness* This need stems from the fact that man has lost the union with nature that other animals possess; it must be satisfied by human relationships based on productive love (which implies mutual care, responsibility, respect, and understanding).
2. *Transcendence* The need to rise above one's animal nature and to become creative.
3. *Rootedness* The need for a feeling of belonging, best satisfied by brotherliness toward mankind.
4. *Identity* The need to have a sense of personal identity, to be unique. It can be satisfied through creativity or through identification with another person or group.
5. *A Frame of Orientation* The need for a stable and consistent way of perceiving the world and understanding its events.

Fromm's basic human needs

12-1 According to the theory developed by Fromm, these are the five basic human needs—frustration of which causes personality problems. (3)

in our society (or in any other society as yet devised); therefore all of us tend to have frustrations and personality problems. It is society, Fromm has said, that is "sick," and the only lasting solution to personality problems is to create a different kind of society

> in which man relates to man lovingly, in which he is rooted in bonds of brotherliness and solidarity . . . which gives him the possibility of transcending nature by creating rather than by destroying, in which everyone gains a sense of self by experiencing himself as the subject of his powers rather than by conformity (4).

social learning theory

Social learning theory represents a different kind of approach entirely from psychoanalysis—at least from Freud's original formulations of psychoanalysis. It does not accept the idea that human personality is shaped in any important way by biologically determined primitive drives or the Oedipus complex, and it does not accept Freud's notions of the id, ego, and superego. Instead, as its name implies, it holds that most personality traits are the result of learning, particularly the kind of learning that takes place in a social context—or, to put this another way, in interaction with other people.

There are a number of social learning theories, which differ from one another in various respects. However, all regard personality as largely composed of habits—that is to say, of habitual ways of responding to situations. These habits are learned in accordance with the standard principles of learning; they are *learned responses to stimuli in the environment*. Prominent among the originators of social learning theories have been B. F. Skinner, John Dollard and Neal Miller, and more recently Albert Bandura and Richard Walters.

SOCIAL LEARNING THEORISTS

1. B. F. SKINNER
2. JOHN DOLLARD
3. NEAL MILLER
4. ALBERT BANDURA
5. RICHARD WALTERS

the frightened rat

MILLER'S CONDITIONING EXPERIMENT

One simple but impressive experiment devised by Miller is often cited in support of social learning theories. In the course of this experiment a rat is placed in a plain white compartment that contains a bar that can be pressed, like the bar in a Skinner box. There is nothing unusual about the compartment, nothing that would appear in any way frightening. Yet the rat shows signs of fear and immediately presses the bar—which permits it to escape into a black compartment alongside. For some reason the rat fears the white compartment and will work to escape into the black compartment. Why? Does it have an inborn fear? Or some kind of unconscious conflict? The explanation is quite simple. In a previous stage of the experiment the rat received an electric shock in the white compartment, from which it could escape only by learning to press the bar so that it could move to the black compartment. Its apparently neurotic fear of the white compartment is simply the result of learning. It learned to fear the compartment when it was shocked; it still shows fear though the shock is no longer present (5).

This experiment may remind you of the "Albert experiment" described on page 52, in which a baby who had displayed no previous fear of a rat was conditioned to behave fearfully not only toward the rat but also toward other furry objects, such as a rabbit and the face of Santa Claus. Here, too, an observer who saw only the final stage of the experiment might be puzzled by Albert's behavior. In fact Albert had learned to respond with fearful behavior through simple classical conditioning.

the aggressive children

BANDURA &
WALTER'S
OBSERVATION
LEARNING

Bandura and Walters have shown that behavior related to personality characteristics is learned not only through conditioning but also through observation, the method discussed on pages 66-68. One of their experiments, illustrated in Figure 2-12 on page 67, deserves review and elaboration. Children were at play in a room where they could observe an adult. In some cases the adult worked quietly at assembling a sort of tinker toy. In other cases the adult performed some very aggressive actions toward a large doll—kicking it, hitting it with a hammer, and so on. Later the children were subjected to some mild frustration and then were placed in an observation room behind a one-way mirror, where they too could play in any way they chose with a tinker toy or a large doll. Those who had watched aggressive behavior by an adult showed more aggression toward the doll than did those who had watched nonaggressive behavior. The results were the same when the children watched a movie rather than a real-life demonstration of aggression.

the matter of reinforcement

SOCIAL
LEARNING
THEORY

As these experiments indicate, the social learning theories maintain that the wide range of human personality traits, including the abnormal ones, can be explained by the basic principles of learning. The child is born with a certain range of responses, both reflex and operant. Through conditioning and observation these responses become attached to previously neutral stimuli. Through stimulus generalization they may be aroused by many kinds of situations.

The social learning theories place considerable emphasis on reward and punishment—particularly on the kinds of rewards and punishments given by the family and by society. Responses that are reinforced by praise and social reward tend to be repeated and to become habitual; those that are punished by rejection tend to undergo extinction. Dollard and Miller have suggested that the individual moving through his cultural environment is like a complicated version of a rat moving through a T-maze. Only if we know in which arm of the T the rat will be rewarded by food and in which arm it will be punished by a shock can we predict the rat's behavior. To predict an individual's behavior we would have to know which of his responses have been rewarded by society and which have been punished and in what way and to what extent (6). We would also have to know what kinds of models he has observed in the past and has chosen to identify with and to imitate.

learning theories and psychoanalysis

Many of Freud's psychoanalytic concepts are explained by the social learning theorists in much simpler terms than he used. Dollard and Miller agree, for example, that unconscious conflicts are the basis of most severe personality problems. Their explanation, simpler than Freud's, is that most of these conflicts arise in the early years before the child has learned language labels for the stimuli in his environment and for his own visceral drives and reflexes—in other words, at a time when the child, lacking language, does not really have a consciousness. They also believe that many of what Freud calls unconscious desires are wishes that the person represses by the deliberate process of "not thinking" about them, because "not thinking" reduces the anxiety associated with them.

Freud's id, to the learning theorists, is a person's basic biological drives. The superego is a person's learned standards. Anxiety, rather than resulting from conflicts among id, ego, and superego, represents the sensations resulting from a reflex visceral reaction that has become attached, through learning, to many different kinds of environmental situations and to one's thoughts.

Rogers' self theory

There is a large group of hypotheses about personality that are known as *self theories*, the best known of which has been formulated by Carl Rogers. Like Freud, Rogers developed his theories out of his treatment of disturbed people; his first position after receiving his Ph.D. was in the Rochester (New York) Guidance Clinic, and he has continued to spend much of his time in clinical work with patients seeking therapeutic help. Unlike Freud, however, Rogers was trained in psychology rather than in medicine, and the conclusions he has drawn from his observations are different from psychoanalytic theory.

the "phenomenal self"

Rogers' theory centers around the concept of the *phenomenal self*—that is to say, the image of himself that each person perceives in his own unique fashion, based on the evidence of his senses. The phenomenal self does not necessarily correspond to reality: many people who are clearly successful and highly respected nonetheless perceive themselves as unworthy failures. Nor is the phenomenal self necessarily the kind of self the person would like to be, as has been demonstrated by a study inspired by Rogers' theories.

In this study two groups of subjects received packets of cards each of which contained a statement about personality, such as "I am likable," "I am a hard worker," "I am a submissive person." The subjects were asked to sort the cards along a line ranging from those that best described them to those that described them least well. After a record had been made of these sortings the subjects were asked to sort the cards again in a way that best described the kind of person they would like to be.

One group was made up of subjects who were seeking treatment for personality problems. The other was a matched control group of subjects who had not sought therapy and presumably did not consider it necessary. For the experimental group of patients there turned out to be no relation at all between what they considered to be their real selves and the kind of ideal selves they wanted to be. For the control group the relationship was quite high. The logical conclusion was that the patients seeking treatment were dissatisfied with themselves as they saw themselves, while the "normal" subjects were reasonably satisfied—a conclusion borne out by the fact that after treatment the patients showed much more correspondence than before between their real selves and their ideal selves (7).*

self-image and neurosis

The experiment lends support to one important concept in Rogers' theory, which is that personality maladjustments are caused by a person's failure to integrate all his experiences, desires, and feelings into his image of self. This idea can best be explained by an example.

A young boy thinks of himself as being good and as being loved by his parents. However, he also feels hostility toward a younger brother, which he expresses one day by breaking his brother's toys. His parents punish him, and he now faces a crisis in integrating the experience into his image of self. He is forced to change the image in some way. He may decide that he is not a good boy but a bad boy and therefore feel shame and guilt. He may decide that his parents do not love him and therefore feel rejected. Or he may decide to deny that he feels any hostility toward his brother, in which case he sets up a conflict between his true nature and his image of himself.

Each of us, says Rogers, attempts to perceive his experiences and to behave in a way that is consistent with his image of himself. When we are confronted with a new experience or new feelings that seem inconsistent with the image, we can ordinarily take one of two opposite courses.

1. We can recognize the new experience or feelings, perceive them clearly, and somehow integrate them into the image of self. This is a healthy reaction. The boy just mentioned, for example, could under ideal circumstances decide that he does feel hostility toward his brother; this is something he must reckon with, but it does not make him "bad" or mean that he will be totally rejected by his parents and society.

2. We can deny the experience or feelings or perceive them in distorted fashion. Thus the boy may attempt to deny that he feels any hostility toward his brother and maintain that he broke the toys simply in retaliation for his

*The relationships were determined by calculating coefficients of correlation, as will be described in Chapter 13. The correlation between real self and ideal self for the patients was zero, for the control group .58. After treatment the correlation for the patients was .34.

brother's hostility (thus adopting what has been called the defense mechanism of projection).

According to Rogers, the maladjusted person is one who perceives any experience that is not consistent with his self-image as a threat, denies it to consciousness, and thereby sets up an ever widening gulf between his self-image and reality. His image of himself does not match his true feelings and the actual nature of his experiences; he must set up more and more defenses against the truth; and more and more tension results. The well-adjusted person, on the other hand, is one whose image of self is consistent with what he really thinks, feels, does, and experiences; instead of being rigid the self-image is flexible and constantly changes as new experiences occur.

Rogers' theory is an optimistic one; it assumes that human beings are by nature motivated toward a kind of integration and self-fulfillment. In this respect it is reminiscent of Abraham Maslow's ideas about the motive for self-actualization, described on pages 356–57.

psychotherapy

DEFINITION:
PSYCHOTHERAPY

Psychotherapy—the treatment of personality disorders through psychological methods—is in a sense an ancient technique, dating back to the Greek physicians. For example, the Greeks often attempted to treat their disturbed patients by removing them from their families, thus bringing about a change of environment—a method sometimes recommended today. For women suffering from hysteria the Greek physicians suggested marriage—an interesting form of treatment in light of modern discoveries that hysteria is often associated with sexual maladjustments and anxiety.

During the Middle Ages, however, the Greek approach to personality disorders was cast aside, and people suffering from the more intense and obvious forms of personality and mental disorders were punished as witches who were possessed by the devil. Even when the first so-called insane asylums were set up in the sixteenth century they were little more than prisons where the inmates were kept in chains and were "treated," if at all, by being whirled around in harnesses or having holes bored into their heads (see Figure 12-2). It has only been in this century that mental hospitals have become more humane institutions (though of course some of them still leave much to be desired). Today the most advanced psychological and medical techniques are being used in an attempt to help psychotics, and considerable numbers of psychologists and physicians have begun to devote themselves to giving treatment and guidance to the less seriously disturbed.

Just as there are many personality theories, there also are many different kinds of psychotherapy. Followers of Freud practice one kind of technique, the neo-psychoanalysts other kinds. The social learning theories have produced new and quite different techniques, and so has Rogers' self theory. In addition, there are many others; indeed it sometimes would seem that there are almost as many

old "treatments" for the mentally ill

12-2 In the past mental patients were treated by being chained virtually motionless to a wall (left), by being stretched and whirled in harnesses suspended from the ceiling, or by having holes bored in their skulls to release the "evil spirits."

forms of psychotherapy as there are psychotherapists. Each therapist is likely to develop his own methods growing out of his own clinical experiences and the particular problems and needs of the patient, and there is a growing tendency for therapists trained in one method to borrow at times from the methods of other and very different schools of thought.

client-centered therapy

Since Rogers' personality theory has just been discussed, the discussion of psychotherapy can perhaps best begin with the kind of treatment that he developed, which is known as *client-centered therapy.* The central idea in client-centered therapy is for the therapist to display warmth and acceptance toward the patient, thus providing a nonthreatening situation in which the patient is free to explore all his thoughts and feelings, including those that he has been unable to perceive clearly for fear of condemnation by others or by his own conscience. Originally Rogers refrained from expressing any reactions he might have toward the patient's conduct. More recently he has concluded that the therapist should be more "genuine"—that is, should respond to the patient by frankly describing his own feelings. However, the core of client-centered treatment was and is for the therapist to be genuinely sympathetic and understanding—to regard the patient, as Rogers has written, "as a person of unconditional self-worth; of value no matter what his condition, his behavior or his feelings." Indeed the client-centered therapist encourages the patient to clarify and expand on even the most negative aspects of his personality.

415

In the safety of this kind of relationship with an understanding and accepting therapist, the patient is expected gradually to acquire the ability to resolve his conflicts. The process, Rogers has said, takes three steps: 1) the patient begins to experience, understand, and accept feelings and desires (such as sexuality and hostility) that he has previously denied to consciousness; 2) he begins to understand the reasons behind his behavior; and 3) he begins to see ways in which he can undertake more positive forms of behavior. In a word, he learns to be himself.

Many people who hear about client-centered therapy for the first time are struck by the question: If every person were encouraged to be completely himself, would the world not be suddenly filled with aggressive, brawling, murderous, sexually unrestrained, and self-seeking egoists? Rogers says not; he believes that people, if not twisted by conflicts between image of self and true self, tend to grow along wholesome and socially desirable lines.

psychoanalysis

In the classical psychoanalytic treatment developed by Freud the chief tool is *free association.* The patient, lying as relaxed as possible on a couch, is encouraged to speak out every thought that occurs to him—no matter how foolish it may seem, how obscene, or how insulting to the analyst. In this situation, as when drifting off to sleep, conscious control of mental processes is reduced to a minimum, and unconscious forces become more apparent. The analyst has an opportunity to observe when the patient encounters what is called *resistance*—that is, when his thoughts seem to be blocked by anxiety and repressions that indicate unconscious conflicts. He also studies the patient's dreams and any slips of the tongue, which are considered clues to unconscious desires and conflicts.

Another tool that helps the analyst probe the patient's unconscious is the phenomenon called *transference*. This means, to the analysts, that all of us tend to transfer to the people we now know the emotional attitudes that we had as children toward such much-loved and much-hated persons as our parents and our brothers and sisters. In analysis, patients display these emotional reactions toward their analyst; they may at times be overwhelmed by a desire to please him and be praised by him, at other times by resentment and hatred of him.

Through the patient's transferences, free associations, resistances, dreams, and tongue slips, the analyst gradually begins to get a picture of the unconscious problems that represent the patient's real difficulties. He then can interpret the problems and help the patient acquire insights into the unconscious processes and gain control over them. The goal in analysis is to strengthen the ego and give the patient what one analyst has called "freedom from the tyranny of the unconscious" (8).

In its classical form, psychoanalysis is a long process, requiring three to five visits a week for two to five years or more, and therefore very expensive. In recent years, however, many analysts have attempted to shorten the treatment period. While still basing their therapy on the underlying principles developed by Freud (or by one of the neo-psychoanalysts), they have adopted various new and faster techniques for helping their patients achieve, if not full "freedom from the tyranny of the unconscious," at least a working ability to cope with their underlying problems.

behavior therapy

Psychoanalysis tends to regard personality disturbances as a form of long-term illness that can be cured only by seeking its origin; the psychoanalyst resembles a physician who is not so much interested in treating the symptoms of disease, such as a headache or a fever, as in finding out what is causing the symptoms and then treating the underlying illness. A very different approach is taken by *behavior therapy,* a newer method of treatment that has grown out of social learning theories. Behavior therapy does not regard personality disturbances as deep-seated illnesses but as learned forms of thinking, feeling, and especially behaving that can be modified through relearning. It is not concerned with giving the patient insights into any unconscious conflicts; instead it attacks his symptoms directly. It maintains, for example, that a patient who has an unreasonable fear of snakes or a problem that incapacitates him sexually can be taught through various methods to overcome the problem and to substitute more effective forms of behavior.

Behavior therapy has become increasingly popular among clinical psychologists and in recent years has accounted for more studies and research reports than any other kind of psychotherapy (9). As will be seen below, it has produced numerous successes in dealing with various kinds of psychosomatic illnesses, phobias, speech difficulties, sexual problems, and other forms of personality disturbance. When first introduced, it was sharply criticized by the psychoanalysts, who maintained that all it could do was get rid of a specific symptom—for which the patient, since his underlying illness was not relieved, would soon substitute another symptom. (For example, a patient relieved of a fear of snakes might soon develop an even more crippling fear of people.) But numerous follow-up studies of patients who have undergone behavior therapy have shown no proof that symptom substitution actually occurs (10, 11). However, behavior therapy is sometimes combined with other forms of psychotherapy that take a more generalized approach to the patient's personality as a whole; for example, it has been used successfully in combination with client-centered therapy to treat a patient who had a crippling fear of going anywhere alone and an inability to admit to deep-seated feelings of anger and hostility (12).

Since behavior therapy is essentially concerned with relearning, it utilizes many techniques of extinguishing conditioned responses and substituting new responses for old. Among its methods are the following.

Extinction. This method attempts to get rid of a conditioned response that is causing the patient trouble. For example, it was used with spectacular results to treat a nine-month-old baby who had somehow acquired the habit of vomiting shortly after every meal and as a result weighed only twelve pounds and was in danger of starving to death. A nine-month-old baby, of course, cannot be treated by any method of psychotherapy that requires the "talking-out" of problems.

However, the baby responded very rapidly to a form of extinction in which an electrode was attached to his leg and electric shocks were administered whenever he began to vomit, continuing until he stopped. Only a few shocks were needed. The baby soon learned to stop vomiting when the shock was applied, then quit vomiting altogether, except for a few relapses that were quickly ended by further treatment. After a few weeks he was released from the hospital weighing sixteen pounds, which increased to twenty-one pounds in his first month back at home, where he showed no signs of resuming his former behavior (13).

When extinction is achieved by pairing behavior with a disagreeable stimulus, as in this case an electric shock, the technique is called *aversive conditioning*. The patient learns to abandon his troublesome behavior to avoid the unpleasant consequences with which the therapist associates it.

Reinforcement. Another technique used by behavior therapists is providing reinforcement for more effective and desirable kinds of behavior. For example, one group of behavior therapists, dealing with disturbed adolescents who had never learned to talk very well or to sit quietly at a school desk, treated them by withholding breakfast and lunch, then rewarding them with small amounts of food every time they showed any signs of constructive behavior. Given this kind of push toward acceptable behavior—which you will recognize as being a form of operant conditioning and shaping (pages 57-62) with food as the reinforcement—the subjects improved rapidly (14).

In mental hospitals, reinforcement of desirable behavior has been used successfully in the form of what is called a *token economy*. For doing such things as dressing properly, eating in an acceptable manner, and working at useful jobs, patients earn tokens that they can exchange like money for movies, rental of radio or TV sets, cigarettes, candy, and other privileges. Establishment of token economies has produced dramatic changes in patients' behavior and the general atmosphere of the hospital. One example is illustrated in Figure 12-3.

The techniques of reinforcement (to encourage positive behavior) and aversive conditioning (to eliminate undesirable behavior) are often combined. The combination has been found effective in treating many kinds of patients, including men who were sexually incapacitated by sadistic fantasies (16) or by transvestitism (17), which is the desire to dress in the clothing of the other sex.

Desensitization. This is a special technique used in an attempt to eliminate phobias by associating the stimulus that has caused the fear with relaxation rather than with fearful behavior. For example, a subject with an unreasonable fear of snakes would first be made as relaxed as possible, then asked to imagine that he was looking at a snake in a very mildly fear-producing situation, such as from far away. If he was able to imagine this scene without losing his feeling of relaxation, he would then be asked to imagine a slightly more threatening sight of a snake—and so on until he was able to remain relaxed while imagining that he was actually holding a snake. Eventually, if the process is successful, the snake becomes a stimulus that is associated with relaxation and no longer produces fear.

12-3

When a group of forty-four patients in a mental hospital operated under a token economy system, in which desirable behaviors were reinforced with tokens that could be used like money, they worked actively at various jobs helping run the hospital (colored line). When the token economy system was abandoned temporarily and no reinforcement provided, they did very little work (black line). (Adapted from 15. Additional information and related research can be found in *The token economy: a motivational system for therapy and rehabilitation* by T. Ayllon and N. H. Azrin, published by Appleton-Century-Crofts, 1968.)

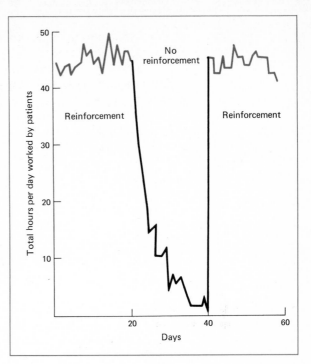

Many kinds of phobias have been treated successfully through desensitization. In one study, the subjects were college students who suffered extreme anxiety when they had to speak in public. After treatment they reported much less anxiety not only about speaking in public but about other kinds of social situations. Two years after treatment their improvement was still quite pronounced. Moreover, their marks in college had improved somewhat. Ninety percent of them either were still in school or had been graduated, whereas 60 percent of an untreated control group of anxious students had dropped out (18).

Observation and Imitation. Another technique used to eliminate phobias is observation or imitation learning, which was discussed on pages 66–68. For example, fear of snakes has been treated successfully by having subjects watch a movie of other people approaching and eventually playing with a snake (see Figure 12-4)—a movie that the subjects could stop and turn back at any time they began to feel fearful. It has also been treated successfully by having the subjects watch live models handle a snake and eventually join the models in playing with the snake. In one experiment, subjects who were fearful of snakes were divided into four groups—a control group that was not treated at all, a group treated through desensitization, another treated by observation of a movie, and the fourth treated through observation and imitation of live models. The results, illustrated in Figure 12-5, showed that observation of live models combined with participation in handling the snake was the most effective treatment (19).

419

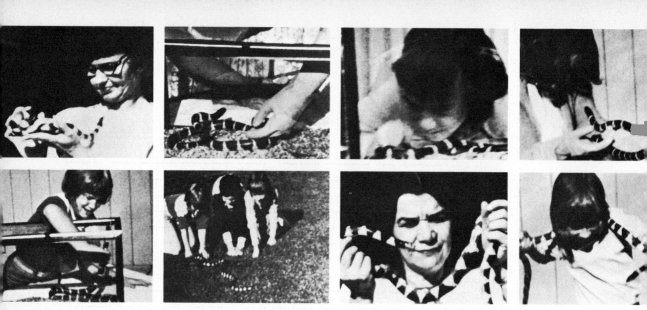

a cure for snake phobia

12-4 These are stills from a movie used successfully by Albert Bandura in the treatment of snake phobia through observation learning, as described in the text.

eliminating snake phobia

12-5

After treatment through behavior therapy, subjects who had been afraid of snakes were able to approach them rather freely. (A score of zero on the approach scale means that the subject was unable even to enter a room in which there was a snake; a perfect score of 29 means that the subject could let a snake crawl over his lap while holding his hands passively at his sides.)

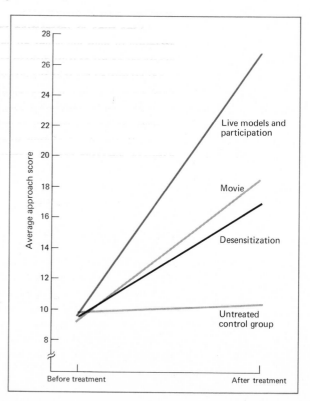

interactional therapies

Behavior therapy seeks to bring about abrupt changes in the individual's own feelings and behavior patterns. Along somewhat similar lines, another group of rather new therapies seeks to bring about changes in the individual's behavior toward other people. These can collectively be called *interactional therapies,* because they concentrate on the individual's interpersonal relations and reactions toward others. Like behavior therapy, they usually make a direct attack on the kind of specific problem that is bothering the patient; they seek change rather than an interpretation of what the problem is and how it originated.

In general, interactional therapists take this attitude toward their patients (or, as both they and the behavior therapists prefer to call them, "clients"): "In your relations with other people, you are now doing this and it is not working. Give it up for a while and try something else instead." Thus male homosexuals have been encouraged to stop associating with other homosexuals and force themselves to seek out the company of women, a new kind of interaction that at least sometimes results in a lasting change to heterosexual behavior (20). Other clients with other problems have been invited to play "games" in which they pretend to act like other people or to behave in extremely selfish or extremely generous ways, thus opening up the possibility of new kinds of interaction they have never tried before (21).

One type of interaction therapy is *family therapy,* in which the therapist attempts to help his client by changing the patterns of behavior that the various members of his family display toward one another. In some cases therapists have made television tapes of the interactions between members of a family; often people who have this kind of opportunity to watch their behavior are helped to see why it is unsuccessful and how it can be improved (22). An even larger-scale approach is represented by *community therapy,* in which the therapist attempts to set up new patterns of interaction to replace existing ones that have caused problems between different groups, between public officials and the citizenry, and so on.

group therapies

Group therapy is the simultaneous treatment of several patients at a time; it has been used by many therapists of various schools of thought, including some psychoanalysts. The method is in part the child of necessity, for there are not enough trained therapists to treat all prospective patients individually. But it also seems to have genuine advantages with some kinds of patients. The group situation may relieve the individual patient's anxieties by demonstrating that there are other people with the same problems, and it also creates a kind of interactional or social give-and-take that is impossible in a face-to-face session between a therapist and a single patient.

In recent years, there has been a great interest in what are called *encounter groups,* in which anywhere from eight to twenty people get together with the goal

interaction in an encounter group

12-6　　A group member learns to trust the others for physical support—perhaps a first step toward trust and openness in other social situations.

of throwing off the masks they usually present in public and airing their true feelings. The emphasis in these groups is on activities, games, and conversation that will help their members interact (see Figure 12-6) with open displays of approval, criticism, affection, and hostility rather than with the restraints and tact that usually inhibit the expression of emotions in ordinary social situations. The assumption behind encounter groups is somewhat like the basic premise of client-centered therapy, namely that the individual will grow in a positive direction if he can free himself from artificial restraints on his attempts to perceive his true self and to interact with others in an honest and open fashion. Indeed Carl Rogers, the founder of client-centered therapy, has led numerous encounter groups.

Encounter groups are usually led by a trained therapist, although sometimes they meet without a leader. The group may meet for several hours a day or evening over a period of time or, as a *marathon group,* for as much as thirty-six hours or more without interruption, except that its individual members drop out occasionally for naps. Whether encounter groups can be considered a form of therapy is a matter of debate. Some psychologists have concluded that they are an effective form of treatment for some kinds of problems, others that they merely provide an opportunity for more or less normal people to enjoy the emotional satisfaction of entering into honest interactions of a kind that are difficult to establish in the real world of social restraints. Some psychologists, indeed, consider them a passing fad and potentially dangerous in that they might trigger acute disturbances in some of the more troubled participants.

Somewhat similar to encounter groups are *T-groups* (short for training groups), also called *sensitivity groups.* It should be pointed out that these various kinds of groups are not so new as many people think. As long ago as 1781, Hans Mesmer, whose name is associated with mesmerism or hypnosis, was leading groups of ten to twenty Parisians in activities rather similar to those found in today's encounter groups, such as holding hands and touching one another (23).

422

how effective is psychotherapy?

At this point it is pertinent to ask: Does psychotherapy work? Which if any of the methods is the most effective?

The scientific method of answering the questions would be to select experimental and control groups—to find, say, fifty disturbed people and have them treated by a client-centered therapist, then send a matched group of fifty other patients to a psychoanalyst, another matched group of fifty to a behavior therapist, and so on, while preventing a matched control group of fifty from having any therapy at all. But this seems almost impossible, for who is to say how disturbed any individual is, and how can we match one disturbed individual with another? For that matter, how can we match the various therapists to make sure they are equally skillful? And how can we measure how much our subjects improve and how long their improvement lasts?

Certainly different therapists, even if they practice the same kind of therapy, vary in the kinds of results they obtain. The most successful of them appear to be those who 1) have strong feelings of liking and warmth toward their patients, 2) have *empathy* toward their patients (that is, can put themselves in the patient's shoes, so to speak, and understand how he thinks and feels), 3) are themselves relatively free of anxieties and other symptoms of disturbance, and 4) have had considerable experience at treating previous patients (24). The patient's own characteristics also play an important part in the outcome of the treatment. For example, it has been found that the patients most likely to profit from psychoanalysis are those whose disturbances are moderate rather than extreme and who are strongly motivated to change, often because they are suffering from acute feelings of discomfort that are of relatively recent origin (25). There are also indications that a patient is more likely to improve if he is suggestible and has faith that the treatment will help him (26).

The problem of evaluating psychotherapy is further complicated by the fact that many people suffering from personality disturbances get over them even if they receive no treatment at all; the passage of time and possibly changing life circumstances restore them to normal. One estimate is that about three-fourths of all people who suffer from neurotic disturbances will recover spontaneously (27). Thus even if a patient shows dramatic improvement after therapy, the question remains as to whether he might have improved just as much without any help.

There appears to be little doubt that behavior therapy is often successful, at least in relieving symptoms such as phobias. As for the other types of therapy, each has its advocates and its critics. Some investigators have concluded that none of them is particularly effective (28). Others maintain that all kinds of psychotherapy have resulted in impressive successes (29). These sharply varying interpretations of the effectiveness of psychotherapy may be inevitable in view of the extreme difficulty of evaluating the success or failure of treatment. Perhaps the majority opinion among psychologists is that there is as yet not enough solid evidence on which to base a judgment (30). Indeed it has been suggested that the research problems are so overwhelming that psychologists and psychiatrists might do better to abandon any attempt at evaluation and instead concentrate on the study of unusually successful therapists and of the life circumstances that result in spontaneous improvement, in search of clues to improving the methods of therapy (31).

medical therapy

*DEFINITION:
CHEMOTHERAPY*

To complete the discussion of treatment of personality disorders, it must be pointed out that the various forms of psychotherapy are often combined with what is called *chemotherapy*—that is, chemical therapy, or treatment with various kinds of medicines that have been discovered to be helpful to many patients. Indeed some psychiatrists rely more on chemotherapy than on psychotherapy. Chemotherapy is also widely practiced in mental hospitals, especially those lacking large enough staffs to offer prolonged psychotherapy to all their patients.

tranquilizers

One widely used group of medicines are the *tranquilizers*, often prescribed for schizophrenics. The tranquilizers have greatly changed the atmosphere of mental hospitals by calming patients who previously were so noisy, hostile, and destructive as to be unmanageable; they have also enabled some patients, if kept on a proper dosage, to return to a more or less normal life. Numerous studies have shown that tranquilizers can reduce or eliminate the schizophrenic's hallucinations and delusions. One investigation found that schizophrenic patients in a mental hospital who received a combination of tranquilizers and psychotherapy over a twenty-month period showed significant improvement in behavior, whereas a control group who received psychotherapy without tranquilizers showed no improvement (32).

Because tranquilizers reduce anxiety, they are also widely prescribed for many people with less serious neurotic symptoms—people who find them helpful in surmounting temporary or chronic stresses in their lives. The tranquilizers apparently are effective because they reduce the sensitivity of the synapses of the brain (that is, the connection points between nerve cells, as was explained on pages 278-79). They apparently do this by reducing the effectiveness of one of the chemicals (noradrenalin) that is produced at some of the synapses (33). In other words, they slow down the excessive nervous activity in the brain that is characteristic of anxiety, hallucinations, and delusions.

psychic energizers

Also important in chemotherapy are the *psychic energizers*, used to relieve depression. The psychic energizers have exactly the opposite effect from the tranquilizers; they increase the effectiveness of noradrenalin as a transmitter of nervous impulses across the synapses, thus speeding up the rate of activity in the brain. There are many kinds of psychic energizers, each working in a slightly different manner and likely to be more helpful for one patient than for another. Recently it has been suggested that they may be most effective when given in a combination that also produces a mild sedative and tranquilizing effect (34), although the reason is not known.

Another method of treating depression is *electroshock therapy,* in which electrodes are fastened to the patient's head and an electric current roughly as strong as household electricity is passed between them for a fraction of a second. The patient goes into a brief convulsion and then is unconscious for a half-hour to an hour. When he wakes up, he is drowsy and confused, but no permanent harm seems to be done to his memory or his learning ability. The treatment, it has been found, produces a long-term increase in the amount of noradrenalin in the brain (35). Thus it operates in much the same way as the psychic energizers, and in many cases it is even more effective. In one study of hospitalized patients treated and observed over a period of several weeks, of those who received electroshock therapy 82 percent were found to have recovered from their depressions and 4 percent to have improved, whereas of those treated with psychic energizers 54 percent recovered and 13 percent improved (36).

other medications

A drug called Dilantin has been effective in controlling *epilepsy,* a mysterious form of brain malfunction that formerly forced many people to live in constant fear of a sudden and crippling seizure or "fit." With a proper daily dosage of Dilantin, most epilepsy sufferers can lead perfectly normal lives and avoid the seizures entirely; many of them eventually grow out of the condition, whatever it is, and can then abandon use of the drug.

Chemotherapy has also been used successfully in the treatment of another strange abnormality, *hyperkinesis,* which is estimated to affect perhaps as many as three million American children under the age of fifteen. The hyperkinetic child, for unknown reasons, is a "jumping jack"—overactive, irritable, and unable to concentrate; he is "hard to handle," given to temper tantrums, and a source of constant disruptions in his school classes, in which he usually does very badly because of the restlessness. For reasons as mysterious as the abnormality itself, hyperkinesis can be controlled in a manner that seems utterly illogical, that is, by giving the child steady doses of stimulant drugs such as the amphetamines. Instead of stimulating the hyperkinetic child, these drugs somehow calm him down to the point where he often shows spectacular improvements in behavior and school performance. For such children the drugs do not cause addiction and can eventually be abandoned as the child grows out of the condition.

the future of chemotherapy

The successes of chemotherapy offer another indication that, as was stated on pages 390–91, most personality disorders seem to have a threefold origin in biological, psychological, and cultural or social factors. Since chemotherapy is a relatively new development, it appears likely that the future will bring many discoveries of new medications that will prove even more effective in attacking the biological roots of the various kinds of personality problems. It may even develop that some disorders are primarily biological, in which case drugs may prove to be a definite cure. The great majority of psychologists, however, believe that most disorders involve functional disturbances as well as biological predispositions and that therefore the individual's thought processes and interpersonal relations have to be examined and changed.

summary 1. *Personality* is the total pattern of characteristic ways of thinking, feeling, and behaving that constitute the individual's distinctive method of relating to his environment.

2. Freud's *psychoanalytic theory* emphasizes three aspects of personality: a) the unconscious *id*, containing the person's instinctive drives toward sexuality (the *libido*) and aggression; b) the conscious *ego*, which is the person's contact with reality; and c) the largely unconscious *superego*, which threatens punishment for transgressions.

3. The superego is acquired in large part as a result of the *Oedipus complex*, a conflict of mingled love and hate toward the parents that every child is assumed to undergo between the ages of two and a half and six. The child resolves the conflict by *identifying* with his parents and adopting what he considers to be their moral judgments, which form his superego.

4. *Anxiety*, another key concept in psychoanalytic theory, is said to be aroused whenever the demands of the id threaten danger or when the superego threatens disapproval or punishment.

5. Among the successors of Freud who have proposed variations of his theories are Jung, who introduced the concepts of *introvert* and *extrovert*; Adler, who introduced the concept of *inferiority complex;* Hartmann, who has emphasized the role of the ego in dealing with reality; and Fromm, who has emphasized the importance of cultural and social influences on personality.

6. *Social learning theory* maintains that personality is composed of habitual ways of responding to stimuli in the environment. It emphasizes the reinforcements and punishments provided by society for certain types of behavior as well as the importance of imitating the behavior of other persons.

7. Rogers' *self theory* centers around the concept of the *phenomenal self*—that is, the image of himself that each person perceives in his own unique fashion.

8. Four influential schools of psychotherapy are a) Rogers' *client-centered therapy*, b) *psychoanalysis*, c) *behavior therapy*, and d) *interactional therapies*.

9. In client-centered therapy the therapist attempts to provide a nonthreatening situation by displaying warmth and acceptance toward the patient; in this permissive atmosphere the patient is free to explore aspects of himself and his experiences that he had previously repressed.

10. Psychoanalysis uses *free association,* study of dreams and slips of the tongue, and *transference* to give the patient insights into his unconscious conflicts.

11. Behavior therapy regards personality disturbances as learned forms of thinking, feeling, and behaving that can be modified through relearning.

12. Interactional therapies emphasize the importance of bringing about changes in the disturbed individual's behavior toward other people.

13. *Group therapy* is the simultaneous treatment of several patients at a time. *Encounter groups, marathon groups,* and *T-groups* are currently popular forms of group therapy.

14. *Medical therapy* is the treatment of personality disturbances through medical methods, including *chemotherapy* (or the use of drugs such as tranquilizers and psychic energizers) and *electroshock* treatment.

recommended reading

Bandura, A. *Principles of behavior modification.* New York: Holt, Rinehart and Winston, 1969.

Bergin, A. E., and Garfield, S. L., eds. *Handbook of psychotherapy and behavior change: an empirical analysis.* New York: Wiley, 1970.

Boszormenyi-Nagy, I., and Framo, J. L. *Intensive family therapy.* New York: Harper & Row, 1965.

Frank, J. D. *Persuasion and healing: a comparative study of psychotherapy.* New York: Schocken, 1963.

Freud, S. *New introductory lectures on psychoanalysis.* Ed. by J. Strachey. New York: Norton, 1965.

Hall, C. S., and Lindzey, G. *Theories of personality,* 2nd ed. New York: Wiley, 1970.

Holland, G. A. *Fundamentals of psychotherapy.* New York: Holt, Rinehart and Winston, 1965.

Jung, C. G. *The basic writings of C. G. Jung.* New York: Random House, 1959.

Levitt, E. E. *The psychology of anxiety.* New York: Bobbs-Merrill, 1967.

Neuringer, C., and Michael, J. L. *Behavior modification in clinical psychology.* New York: Appleton-Century-Crofts, 1970.

Patterson, C. H. *Theories of counseling and psychotherapy.* New York: Harper & Row, 1966.

Pervin, L. A. *Personality: theory, assessment and research.* New York: Wiley, 1970.

Wiggins, G. F., et al. *The psychology of personality.* Reading, Mass.: Addison-Wesley, 1971.

No two
individual
human beings
are ever
exactly alike.

PART SEVEN

All sciences are interested in both general laws and predictions about individual events. Thus chemistry is concerned with the general laws that explain what happens when a large number of molecules of an acid meet a large number of molecules of a metal, and it is also concerned with what happens when specific amounts of two specific substances are put together in a test tube under specific conditions of pressure and heat.

Psychology resembles the other sciences in this respect. It is interested in general laws of learning, thinking, perception, emotions, and motivation—all the psychological processes, common to most organisms, that have been discussed up to this point. As will be seen in this section, it is also concerned with individual differences.

It was Sir Francis Galton who first began collecting proof that no two human beings are ever exactly alike. He studied people's height, weight, hearing, sense of smell, color vision, ability to judge weights, and many other traits and abilities, and he found that all kinds of human characteristics vary over a wide range from small to large, weak to strong, slow to fast.

To establish that differences exist, Galton had to make measurements and analyze his measurements statistically. Thus *measurement,* used to study individual differences, has been an important branch of psychology almost from the beginning.

Chapter 13 discusses general principles of measurement—including the statistical methods used to analyze measurements and to draw inferences from them. Chapter 14, "Measuring Intelligence and Personality," describes the tests that have been devised to measure various kinds of human abilities and characteristics; it also discusses what measurement has disclosed about the nature and distribution of intelligence.

individual differences

CHAPTER 13

MEASUREMENT

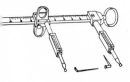

One of the questions that fascinated Sir Francis Galton was whether tall parents had taller than average children. Another was whether successful men tended to have successful sons. Since Galton's time, other investigators have explored many similar questions, such as: Do intelligent parents tend to have children of above-average intelligence? Do strict parents tend to produce children who are more or less aggressive than the children of parents whose discipline is more lenient? Do intelligent people tend to be more or less neurotic than people of less intelligence?

4. why measurement and statistics are important

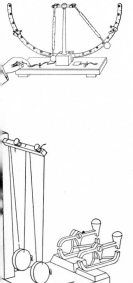

All these are important questions. None of them—as Galton discovered—can be answered satisfactorily without making some kind of measurements and then submitting them to statistical analysis. Both these processes are equally important. We cannot hope to deal with individual differences unless we can measure them. And we cannot understand the meaning of the measurements or the relationships they show among various traits of the organism unless we analyze them in accordance with sound statistical principles.

Thus *measurement* and the *statistical method* of analyzing measurements have been important branches of psychology ever since Galton's time. *Measurement* is defined as the assignment of numbers to traits, events, or objects, according to some kind of orderly system. The *statistical method* refers to the application of mathematical principles to the interpretation of the numbers. Since both processes involve a certain amount of mathematics, they are approached with distaste by some students. However, the mathematics are secondary. The statistical method of analyzing measurements is, above all, what has been called a *way of thinking* (1)—a problem-solving tool that enables us to summarize our knowledge of psychological events, make valid inferences about behavior, and avoid jumping to wrong conclusions, as people who do not understand statistical methods often do.

A person can understand the techniques of measurement and the statistical method and use them to great advantage in analyzing behavior without ever memorizing a single mathematical formula or making a single mathematical computation. On the other hand, the mathematics are interesting in their own

433

right, are not particularly difficult to anyone who has had a high school algebra course, and are an essential tool in almost all types of psychological research. This chapter will talk first about the principles and uses of measurement and statistical analysis, without going into the mathematics any more than is absolutely necessary. A separate section at the end of the chapter will describe the mathematical computations.

1. probability

For an example of how we can profit from thinking in terms of the statistical method, examine Figure 13-1. This illustration tells a great deal about the statistical approach as opposed to the nonstatistical; try to answer the question it poses before you read on to the next paragraph.

Common sense says that the answer to the question in Figure 13-1 is the hand with thirteen spades. When a bridge player gets such a hand, the newspapers are likely to report it as a great rarity. The player is likely to talk about it the rest of his life. And, in all truth, a hand of thirteen spades is extremely rare. It occurs, as a mathematician can quickly calculate, on an average of only once in about 159 billion deals.

However, the other two hands shown in Figure 13-1 are *equally rare.* The rules of statistical probability say that the chance of getting *any* particular combination of thirteen cards is only one in about 159 billion deals. The reason a hand of thirteen spades seems rarer than any other is that bridge players pay attention to it, while lumping all their mediocre hands together as if they were one and the same.

which hand is the rarest?

13-1   These three hands have all been dealt at various times in bridge games. Question: Which hand are you *least* likely to get if you play bridge tonight? For the answer—which casts considerable light on why and how statistics are important—see the text.

Let us think about the hand of thirteen spades in another way. Since it occurs only once in 159 billion deals, is it not a miracle that it should ever occur at all? No, it is not. It has been estimated that there are about 25 million bridge players in the United States. If each of them deals twenty times a week, that makes 26 billion deals a year. The statistical method tells us that we should expect a hand of thirteen spades to be dealt on the average of about once every six years.

2. coincidences

This last fact—that we must expect a hand of thirteen spades to occur with some regularity—explains many occurrences that would otherwise seem baffling. For a simple example, let us say that we go to a party and find ourselves in a group of twenty-three people. Someone at the party remarks, "Tomorrow is my birthday," and someone else says, in surprise, "That's funny; it's my birthday too." Does this seem a strange coincidence? Perhaps. But a mathematician can figure out that in any group ot twenty-three people, the chances are better than even that two of them will have the same birthday.*

Every once in a while the newspapers report that someone shooting dice in Las Vegas made twenty-eight passes (or winning throws) in a row. This seems almost impossible, and in fact the actual mathematical odds are more than 268,000,000 to 1 that it will not happen to anyone who begins throwing the dice. These are very high odds indeed. Yet, considering the large number of people who step up to all the dice tables in Las Vegas, it is inevitable that sooner or later someone will throw the twenty-eight passes.

The laws of probability explain many of the coincidences that seem—to people who do not understand these laws—to represent the working of supernatural powers. A woman in Illinois dreams that her brother in California has died and next morning gets a telephone call reporting that he was killed in an accident. This may sound like an incredible case of some kind of mental telepathy, but the laws of probability offer a much simpler and more reasonable explanation. Most people dream frequently. Dreams of death are by no means rare. In the course of a year millions of people dream of the death of someone in the family. Sooner or later, one of the dreams is bound to coincide with an actual death.

Astrologers and other seers who claim to predict the future also profit from the rules of probability. If an astrologer keeps predicting that a "catastrophe" will occur, he is bound to be right sooner or later, because the world is certain to have some kind of tragedy, from airplane accident to tornado, in any given period. And a prophet who makes his reputation by predicting the death of a

---

*For the benefit of mathematically inclined students it should be explained that the probability of finding two persons in the same room with the same birthday is given by the formula:

$$1 - \frac{365 \times 364 \times 363 \cdots (365 - N + 1)}{365^N}$$

N is the number of people in the room. With twenty-three people the formula gives the probability as 0.507, or slightly better than 50-50.

"world statesman" takes advantage of the fact that there are many world statesmen and that many of them are in an age bracket where death can be expected.

In a world as big as ours, all kinds of coincidences are certain to occur. It would be a statistical miracle if they did not. Statistical analysis enables us to separate cases of sheer coincidence from cases in which some cause may be operating.

→8. problems in measurement

To make a measurement and thus get the data we need for statistical analysis, we must have some kind of scale of numbers. Among such scales used in everyday affairs are length in inches and feet, weight in ounces and pounds, and temperature in degrees Fahrenheit. Without these scales of measurement we could only guess, and our guesses would in some cases be far off. Note the three photographs, for example, in Figure 13-2. Judging from what the people are doing and what they are wearing, we would surely guess that the weather was much warmer when the man and boy were riding bicycles than when the photo was taken of the man in the parka, and probably warmest of all when the children were playing in the surf. Actually all three photographs were made near New York City on the same unseasonably cool August day when the temperature was in the low 70's. Various people reacted to the temperature in quite different ways; some felt that the day was still warm, while others considered it chilly.

what was the temperature?

13-2   Try to guess what the temperature was when each of these three photographs was taken. Then compare your guesses with the correct answers given in the text.

how tall are these young men?

13-3 After studying this picture, how would you describe each of the three young men—as very short, short, average, tall, or very tall? After you have decided on the answers, check them against Figure 13–4 on the next page.

Note also the photograph in Figure 13–3, and estimate the height of the young men as asked in the caption. After you have done so, turn to Figure 13–4. The two photos demonstrate how wrong our judgments of height can be when we lack a scale of measurement.

1. ratio and interval scales

The most satisfactory type of measurement is made on what is called a *ratio scale,* an example of which is the scale of feet and inches. In measuring length we have a true zero point; we can conceive of a mythical point in space that has no length at all. Moreover, all the numbers on the scale fall into perfect ratios. An object that is three feet long is exactly three times as long as a one-foot object, as we can prove by lining up three one-foot rulers and measuring their total length with a yardstick. A man six feet tall is twice as tall as a boy who measures three feet. If we are driving at a steady speed, it takes us five times as long to travel five miles as to travel one mile.

The scale of weight is another ratio scale. An object that weighs two ounces is twice as heavy as an object that weighs one ounce, as can be demonstrated by putting a two-ounce weight on one side of a balance scale and two one-ounce weights on the other side.

Somewhat less satisfactory than a ratio scale, but nonetheless very useful, is an *interval scale,* the best example of which is a thermometer. The intervals on the thermometer are all equal; the liquid inside the tube must expand just as

the young men's actual height

13-4 Here a scale of measurement has been added to the photo shown in Figure 13–3—and we see that the young man at the left is of average height; the young man in the middle is taller than average; and the man at the right is very tall. They looked smaller in Figure 13–3 by comparison with the young woman, who, it can now be seen, is unusually tall for a girl. Thus do scales and numbers provide a far more accurate kind of measurement than is otherwise possible.

far to move from 49 to 50 degrees as from 99 to 100 degrees. However, no ratio is implied by temperature readings; one cannot say that 100 degrees is twice as hot as 50 degrees.

2. ordinal and nominal scales

In psychology, unfortunately, ratio and interval scales are seldom applicable. The major use of ratio scales is in measuring the physical properties of stimuli—for example, the intensity of lights and sounds and the amount of pressure applied against the skin. Interval scales are used in measuring reactions to warmth and cold. In most cases psychology must do the best it can with less satisfactory scales.

Psychology frequently uses *ordinal scales,* which, as the name implies, are scales on which individuals are arranged in order of rank. A good example of an ordinal scale is the scores on a true-false test given as a classroom examination. Let us say that there are 100 questions. One student, and one only, gets all 100 correct; he obviously stands number 1 in the class. The number 2 score is 95 correct, the number 3 score is 94, the number 4 score 90, and so on, down to a score of 25, which is the lowest in the class. Note that the rating of 1 indicates only that this student was ahead of the next highest scorer; it does not say by how much. Indeed the number 1 student got five more answers correct than did the number 2 student, while number 2 had only one more correct answer than number 3. (Teachers often arrange examination results by rank order and arbitrarily give A's to the top 10 percent, B's to the next 20 percent, C's to the next 40, D's to the next 20, and F's to the lowest 10 percent.)

The numbers for intelligence quotient, or I.Q., obtained from intelligence tests constitute an ordinal scale, assigning a number of around 180 or 190 to the highest score made by any person who has ever taken the test and around 10 to 20 to the lowest score. The I.Q. is really nothing more than a measure of what rank order one person occupies among the people who have taken the test. It does not mean that a person who scores 150 is twice as smart as one who scores 75. Moreover, the 5-point difference between a score of 150 and a score of 155 does not represent the same amount of intelligence as does the 5-point difference between 100 and 105. As on all ordinal scales, the differences between I.Q. scores do not have the quality of sameness possessed by the differences on a ratio scale like a ruler or an interval scale like a thermometer.

The simplest of all scales is a *nominal scale,* in which numbers are used to designate different categories. Nominal scales have been used frequently throughout this book in reporting experiments. For example, in the Schachter experiment on reactions to a funny movie (page 312), the subjects who received an injection of adrenalin were called group 1, those who received a tranquilizer group 2, and those who received salt water (the control group) group 3. The numbers given to the groups merely lump some of the subjects together because they are alike in some important respect, with no implication that the number 3 means that this group is in any way larger, smaller, better, or worse than the groups given the numbers 2 and 1. In a study of college students, similarly, the investigator might assign the number 1 to women and the number 2 to men, or he might want to separate students from different schools by assigning number 1 to those from school A, 2 to school B, 3 to school C, 4 to school D, and so on.

→ *3.* is psychological measurement valid?

Since psychology is forced to rely on ordinal and nominal scales rather than the much more sensitive interval and ratio scales, the psychologist is handicapped much as a physicist would be if he had no ratio scale of weights and could say only that something is very heavy, heavy, not so heavy, only slightly heavy, or not heavy at all. (Or as a cook would be if recipes could only recommend a lot of this, a medium amount of that, and a small amount of the other.) This is a continuing problem in the science. Many investigators are trying to devise more adequate scales, and at least modest progress in psychological measurement is being made every year. But any discussion of psychological measurement must contain a warning that the scales on which we must now rely leave a great deal to be desired. We must not overestimate the accuracy of the numbers we use, and we must be cautious about the conclusions that we draw from them.

It should also be pointed out, however, that no form of measurement is completely accurate. Even the measurements used in the physical sciences are subject to error. At what point, for example, does 99 degrees Fahrenheit cease to be 99 degrees and become 100? Or, if we are trying to make finer distinctions, at what point does 99.9 degrees become 100? At what point does a person cease to weigh 120 pounds and begin to weigh 121, and at what point does an automobile cease to travel thirty-five miles an hour and begin to travel thirty-six? (In cooking, how level is a "level teaspoon," and how heaping is a "heaping tablespoon"?) An engineer using the measurements of physical science may feel that he has a reasonably accurate idea of weights, tensile strengths, and possible loads, but he builds the bridge two or three times stronger anyway, to allow for possible errors.

We have to apply psychological measurements with caution—much more caution than is called for in using a yardstick or a thermometer. We must not fall into the error of thinking that our statistical analysis of the measurements is sacred just because it can be put into numbers and mathematical equations. But we have to try to measure psychological traits as best we can if we are to study and understand them. And statistical analysis, used with proper humility, is an invaluable tool in helping us comprehend the meaning of our figures and avoid generalizations that are too sweeping or mathematically false.

→ c. the normal curve of distribution

Closely related to the rules of probability discussed earlier in the chapter is a statistical principle that has particular significance for the study of human behavior, as Galton was the first to notice. This can best be approached through another example taken from outside the field of psychology—an example that you can try for yourself if you like. Put ten coins into a cup, shake them, throw them on a table, and count the number of heads. Do this a number of times, say 100. Your tally will probably be roughly the same as the one shown in Figure 13-5.

What you have come up with is a simple illustration of normal distribution. When you toss ten coins 100 times—a total of 1000 tosses—you can expect 500 heads to come up, an average of five heads per toss. As the tally shows, this number of five heads came up most frequently. The two numbers on either side,

(1) a tally of coin tosses

13-5

Ten coins were shaken in a cup and tossed on a table 100 times. A tally of the number of heads that appeared on each toss is shown here.

Number of heads						
0						
1	/					
2	ⅲ	/				
3	ⅲ	ⅲ				
4	ⅲ	ⅲ	ⅲ	///		
5	ⅲ	ⅲ	ⅲ	ⅲ	ⅲ	//
6	ⅲ	ⅲ	ⅲ	ⅲ	/	
7	ⅲ	ⅲ	/			
8	////					
9	/					
10	/					

(2) the tally in bar form

13-6

Here the results of the coin-tossing experiment, which were shown in tally form in Figure 13-5, have been converted into a bar graph. Note the peak at the center and the rapid falling off toward each extreme.

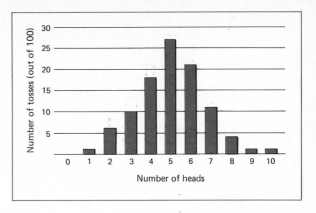

four and six, were close seconds. The numbers farther away from five were increasingly infrequent. Ten came up only once, and zero did not come up at all. (Over a long period, both ten and zero would be expected to come up on an average of once in every 1024 tosses.)

The tally shown in Figure 13-5 can be converted into the bar graph shown in Figure 13-6, which provides a more easily interpreted picture of what happened in the coin tossing. And the bar graph can in turn be shown in the form of a smooth curve. In Figure 13-7 the curve shows what would happen if the coins had been tossed not just 100 times but 1024 and had come out exactly as the law of probability would predict.

(3) a normal curve of distribution

13-7

If the coin-tossing experiment were continued until 1024 tosses had been made, the results would approximate this curve—which is a normal curve of distribution.

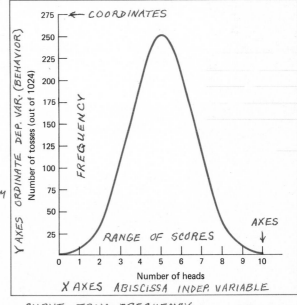

CURVE FROM FREQUENCY
POLYGON

441

3 FORMS OF FREQUENCY
   DISTRIBUTION

1. _TALLY_ OR TABLE

2. _BAR GRAPH_ OR BAR CHART, HISTOGRAM

3. _FREQUENCY POLYGON_: NORMAL
  CURVE OF DISTRIBUTION OR LINE GRAPH
    DISCRIPTIVE STATISTICS
      N. IN GROUP
      AVERAGE MEASUREMENT
      VARIABILITY & STANDARD
          DEVIATION
      PERCENTILES
INFERENTIAL STATISTICS
 | POPULATION & SAMPLE |COMPARING 2 GROUPS |CORRELATION

This is the *normal curve of distribution*, sometimes called the *normal probability curve*, and it is one of the most useful tools in studying individual differences. Note that the curve is shaped like a bell. From its highest point, which is at the average, it declines rather sharply to both left and right, then begins to flatten out. At the extremes, both left and right, it slowly approaches zero.

→ *1.* the curve's meaning

The important thing about the normal curve of distribution is that it provides a picture of the way many events are distributed in the world. The curve in Figure 13-7 resulted from a tally of coin tosses. Galton drew up a normal curve by constructing a device that was something like a pinball machine held up perpendicularly; he poured gunshot into a funnel at the top center, and the round pellets fell past a series of pins to compartments at the bottom. The same sort of device, in more elaborate form, entertained visitors to the New York

a machine that produces the normal curve

13-8

The distribution of the balls in the compartments at the bottom of the machine—a close approximation of the normal curve of distribution—was obtained by chance as they fell from the top past a series of pins that directed most of them to the center, a few to the sides.

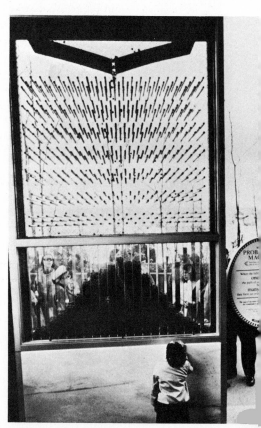

13-9

This curve was constructed by smoothing the data obtained by measuring a group of Englishmen chosen at random some years ago. The average height suggested by the data is 5 feet 7½ inches. Note how few men measured less then 5 feet or more than 6 feet 3 inches. (2) (In the United States today, the average height of men is somewhat greater, but the curve would doubtless take a similar form.)

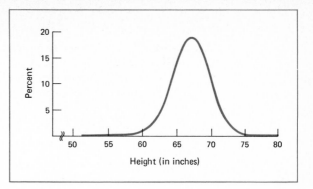

World's Fair of 1964–65, as can be seen in Figure 13-8. Like Galton's invention, it resulted in a chance distribution greatest in the center compartments and falling off to a smaller number in the end compartments.

In human affairs the normal curve applies to many traits. Figure 13-9 shows how men's height falls into the pattern. Figure 13-10 shows how the number of digits that can be remembered after a single presentation is distributed. Similar curves have been found for human weight, mechanical aptitude, and many other characteristics. Intelligence tests are based on the assumption that intelligence is also distributed in this fashion; the tests are then arbitrarily constructed to produce the curve shown in Figure 13-11. The message of the normal curve is that in many measurable traits most people are average or close to it, some are well below or above, and a few are very far below or above. Those who are about average have a lot of company. But some people are as rare in height or in the scores they make on intelligence tests as are twenty-eight passes in a dice game.

distribution of memory span for digits

13-10

The curve shows the distribution of the memory span for digits found in a group of 123 women students. The number of digits is the maximum that the students were able to repeat accurately after hearing them one time only. (3)

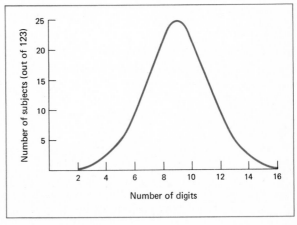

13-11

This curve shows the distribution of intelligence in the United States, as determined by a Stanford-Binet test given to a large standardization group in 1937. A total of 46.5 percent of those measured had intelligence quotients between 90 and 109. Fewer than 1 percent scored below 60 and only 1.33 percent scored 140 or over. (4)

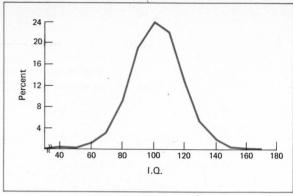

FREQUENCY POLYGON

→ 2. other uses of statistics

The normal curve is the basis for *descriptive statistics,* which provide a quick and convenient method of summarizing the characteristics of any group of people or animals. It is also the basis for *inferential statistics,* which enable us to make reasonably accurate generalizations from measurements. Let us say that we are interested in intelligence. We test 10,000 people. Now we have 10,000 raw scores. To pass along our knowledge of what we have learned about intelligence, we need not quote every one of the 10,000 scores. Through the use of descriptive statistics we can summarize and condense; with a few well-chosen numbers that will be explained in a moment, we can tell another person much of what he needs to know to understand our results. And through the use of inferential statistics we can make some valid generalizations that will probably hold true not just for our 10,000 cases but for the several billion people in the world.

→ D. descriptive statistics

In order to describe the attributes of a group—say, the group of 10,000 people tested for intelligence—we must use three specific numbers. We must compute 1) the number of individuals in the group, 2) the average value (in this case the average I.Q. score), and 3) the variability of the measurements. Let us consider the three in order.

1. number in group

This is simply the total number of subjects in the sample. It is an important number because we can usually draw more confident conclusions from a large sample than from a small sample. If we test only three people for intelligence, we may happen to select three geniuses or three morons. A larger sample is likely to be more representative of the population as a whole.

→ 2. average measurement

MEAN

MEDIAN

MODE

In everyday language, *average* means the sum of all the measurements divided by the number of subjects. For example, six students take an examination containing a hundred true-false questions and get test scores of 70, 74, 74, 76, 80, and 82. What is usually considered the "average" score is 456 divided by 6, or 76. This kind of arithmetic average is a useful measure of central tendency and is technically known as the *mean*.

Another measure of central tendency is the *median*, the halfway point that separates the lower 50 percent of scores from the higher 50 percent. In the example just given the median would be 75, because half the scores fall below 75 and the other half fall above. The median is an especially useful figure when the data include a small number of exceptionally low or exceptionally high measurements. Let us say, for example, that the six scores on the true-false examination were 70, 74, 74, 76, 80, and 100. The one student who scored 100 brings up the mean score quite sharply, to 79. But note that 79 is hardly an "average" score because only two of the six students scored that high. The median score, which remains at 75, is a better description of the data.

A third measure of central tendency is the *mode*—the measurement or score that applies to the greatest number of subjects. In the case of the true-false examination it would be 74, the only score made by as many as two of the students. The mode tells us where the highest point of the curve of distribution will be found.

In a perfectly symmetrical normal curve of distribution, the mean, the median, and the mode are the same. When they are markedly different, it usually means that we are dealing with a *skewed distribution* like those illustrated in Figure 13-12.

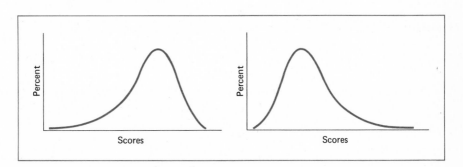

skewed distribution curves

13-12   The curve at the left is said to be negatively skewed. Note that more scores fall below the mode than above it. The curve at the right is positively skewed, with more scores falling above the mode than below it.

NO 3. variability and standard deviation

Some of the examples already shown in the illustrations of this chapter demonstrate that the normal curve of distribution, even when perfectly symmetrical and preserving its characteristic bell shape, may take different forms. Sometimes it is high and narrow. At other times it is shorter and wider. This depends on the *variability* of the measurements, which means the extent to which they differ from one another.

A crude way to describe the variability is simply to give the *range* of measurements—the highest minus the lowest. Another and much more sensitive description is provided by what is called the *standard deviation,* mathematically abbreviated to the initials SD. The standard deviation, which is computed from the data by a formula that will be discussed in the second section of the chapter, is an especially useful tool because it shows quite precisely how many measurements or scores will be found under any part of the curve. As is shown in Figure 13–13, in every normal distribution exactly 34.13 percent of all the measurements lie between the mean and 1 SD above the mean; 13.59 percent lie between 1 SD and 2 SD's above the mean; and 2.14 percent lie between 2 SD's and 3 SD's

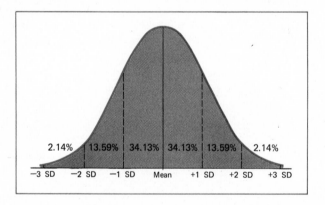

using the SD to analyze data

13-13   In a normal curve of distribution the standard deviation indicates how many measurements or scores will be found at various distances from the mean. As shown here, 34.13 percent of all measurements lie between the mean and 1 SD above the mean. Measurements that are between 1 SD and 2 SD's above the mean make up 13.59 percent of the total, and measurements between 2 SD's and 3 SD's above the mean make up 2.14 percent. The same percentages are found below the mean. Note that the figures do not quite add up to 100 percent. This is because 0.14 percent of measurements are found more than 3 SD's above the mean and another 0.14 percent are found more than 3 SD's below the mean. These various percentages hold for any normal distribution, although the size of the SD is of course quite different from one curve to another.

above the mean. Thus the SD provides an eloquent description of the variability of the measurements.

On the matter of the intelligence quotient, for example, the mean is 100 and the SD is approximately 15. That is to say, an I.Q. one SD above the mean is 115. Armed with this knowledge alone, plus the general statistical rule illustrated in Figure 13–13, we know that human intelligence is distributed according to the following table:

I.Q.	Percentage of people
145 and over	0.14
130–144	2.14
115–129	13.59
100–114	34.13
85–99	34.13
70–84	13.59
55–69	2.14
under 55	0.14

The SD is also used to compute what are called *standard scores,* or *z*-scores, which are often more meaningful than actual scores on a test. The *z*-score tells how many SD's a score is above or below the mean; it is obtained very simply by noting how many points a score is above or below the mean and then dividing by the SD. A *z*-score of 1 is one SD above the mean; a *z*-score of -1.5 is one and a half SD's below the mean.

4, percentiles

DEF: THE PER-CENTAGE OF SCORES WHICH A GIVEN SCORE EQUALS OR EXCEEDS.

There is one other term in descriptive statistics that deserves special discussion. This is *percentile,* which is used not so much to describe the nature of the distribution as to add further meaning to any individual score.

The meaning of percentile can best be explained with an example. Take the case of a college senior who wants to go on to graduate school and is asked to take the Graduate Record Examinations, which are nationally administered aptitude tests often used to screen applicants. He makes a score of 460 on the verbal test and 540 in mathematics. By themselves, these scores do not mean much either to him or to the faculty of the school he wants to attend. But records kept of other people's results on the test provide a means of comparing his scores with those of other college seniors. A score of 460 on the verbal test, the records show, lies on the 40th percentile for men. This means that 40 percent of all senior men who take the test make a lower score and 60 percent make an equal or higher score. The 540 score in math lies on the 66th percentile for men; in other words, 66 percent of senior men make a lower score, and only 34 percent make an equal or higher score. These percentile figures show the student and the school he hopes to attend how his ability compares with that of other prospective graduate students: he is well above average in mathematical ability (only a third of male college seniors make better scores) but below average in verbal aptitude.

Percentile ratings can be made for any kind of measurement, whether or not it falls into a normal distribution. A percentile rating of 1 means that no one had a lower score. A rating of 99—or, to be more exact, 99.999—is the highest. A rating of 50 is exactly in the middle, at the median.

→ E. inferential statistics

When an investigator runs a rat through a maze, he is not really interested in how that particular rat will learn the maze. His primary interest is in discovering a general principle of behavior that says something about the learning process of all rats and, by implication, perhaps about learning processes in general. The investigator who studies the performance of a group of subjects who memorize nonsense syllables or their behavior when they receive an injection of adrenalin and watch a funny movie is not interested in these particular people. His ultimate interest is in learning about the behavior of people in general. This is why *inferential* statistics—which permit us to make valid generalizations from our measurements and to avoid false conclusions—are so important.

→ 1. population and sample

Science is interested in what is called the *population* or sometimes the *universe*—that is to say, all people or all events in a particular category. But we cannot study or measure the entire population. We cannot give an intelligence test, for example, to every human being now on the face of the earth; even if we could, we still would not have reached the entire population, because many people would have died and many new people would have been born in the meantime. We must settle for what is called a *sample*, a rather small group taken from the population.

The rule is that a sample must be *representative* of the population we wish to study. If we wish to make generalizations about intelligence, we cannot use a sample made up entirely of men or a sample made up entirely of women. Both sexes must be represented. If we want to discuss the political attitudes of Americans, we cannot poll merely the Republicans or people who live in big cities or people who belong to one kind of church or one kind of social class. Our sample must be representative of all kinds of Americans.

Ordinarily the sample must also be chosen at *random:* each member of the total population must have an equal chance of being studied. The experimenter who wants to study the emotionality of rats in a laboratory cannot reach into a cage and pull out the first dozen animals that are closest at hand. The very fact that they are close at hand may mean that they are tamer than the others and have a different kind of emotional temperament. To ensure a valid sample, the experimenter might take the first rat, reject the second, take the third, reject the fourth, and so on. The political pollster might interview every tenth voter on the registration lists.

→ 2. control groups

As was pointed out in Chapter 1, the use of a control group is standard experimental procedure. For example, in his experiment with the funny movie, which is discussed in Chapter 9, Schachter wanted to examine the effect of injecting his subjects with adrenalin or a tranquilizer. To make sure the drugs had any effect at all, he had to compare the behavior of his subjects with the behavior of a control group that underwent all the conditions of the experiment except one. The members of the control group had the same kind of needle stuck into their arms and then watched the same movie. The only difference was that the injection they received was a form of salt solution that has no effect on the body rather than adrenalin or a tranquilizer. In experiments on the effect of recitation on learning, the performance of an experimental group that studies part of the time and recites part of the time must be compared to the performance of a control group that attempts to learn the same material under the same conditions (type of room, lighting, noise level, time of day, and so on) but without reciting. In other words, the experimental group must be matched with a control group for which all conditions are the same except for the one experimental variable that is under investigation.

Ideally, every individual in the control group should be identical with a member of the experimental group. But this is of course impossible, because not even identical twins (who are too scarce anyway) are alike in every respect. The investigator must usually rely on a control group that, like the experimental sample, is representative of the population under study and randomly selected. Any individual used in the investigation should have an equal chance of being in the experimental group or the control group.

3. comparing two groups

For an example of how inferential statistics are used to compare two groups, let us imagine an experiment in which we try to determine whether physical health affects the learning ability of high school students. We select an experimental group of sixteen representative, randomly chosen students, who agree to take part in a rigorous health program. We arrange a supervised diet and exercise, give them regular physical examinations, and promptly treat any defects or illnesses. We also select a control group of sixteen similar students, who do not receive any special treatment. At the end of a year, we find that the experimental group has a grade-point mean of 89, with a standard deviation of 3. The control group has a grade-point mean of 85, with a standard deviation of 4. Question: Is this difference of four points between the mean of the experimental group and the mean of the control group significant?

Although four points may sound like a lot, the question is not so easy to answer as it may seem. The reason is that *any* two samples of sixteen people each, taken from the high school population or any other population, are likely to have somewhat different means. Suppose we write the names of all the students in the high school (or in the city) on slips of paper and draw the slips from a hat. The grade-point mean for the first sixteen names we draw may be 85, for the next sixteen names 86, for the next sixteen names 87. If we pull twenty different samples of sixteen students each from the hat, we will find that the means of the samples vary over a fairly wide range. So the question now becomes: Is the difference between the mean score of 89 for the experimental group and the mean score of 85 for the control group larger than a difference we might get accidentally by pulling samples from a hat? In other words, is the difference *statistically significant,* or is it perhaps merely the result of chance?

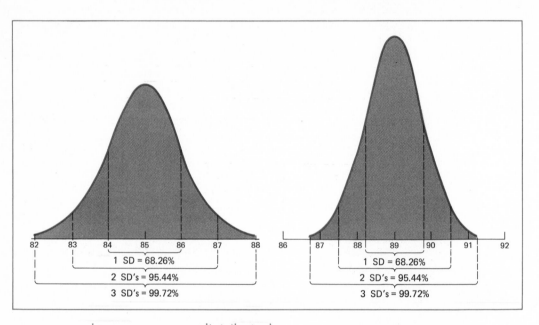

how means are distributed

13-14   These graphs show how the standard error of the mean of a sample is used to infer the true mean that would be found if the entire population could be measured. In the control group of high school students, at left, the mean is 85 and the standard error of the mean is 1.0. Thus we know that the chances are 68.26 percent that the true mean lies between 84 and 86 (1 standard error above or below the mean of our sample), 95.44 percent that the true mean lies between 83 and 87 (2 standard errors above or below), and 99.72 percent that the true mean lies between 82 and 88 (3 standard errors above or below). In the experimental group, at right, the mean is 89 and the standard error of the mean is 0.75. Thus we know that the chances are 68.26 percent that the mean for the entire population under the special conditions of the experiment would have been found between 88.25 and 89.75; the chances are 95.44 percent that the mean would have been found between 87.50 and 90.50; and they are 99.72 percent that the mean would have been found between 86.75 and 91.25. Note how the two graphs utilize the same principle that was illustrated in Figure 13-13.

NO   *Standard Error of the Mean.* Helping answer the question is the fact that the means of randomly chosen samples, like raw measurements or scores themselves, tend to fall into a pattern of normal distribution. From our control group of sixteen with a grade-point mean of 85 and a standard deviation of 4, we can figure out the distribution of all the means we would be likely to get if we continued to pick samples of sixteen students at random, and we find that the curve looks like the one shown on the left in Figure 13–14. We get the curve by using the formula (shown on page 456) for the *standard error of the mean.* For the control group the standard error of the mean comes to 1.0. We can also work out the standard error of the mean for the experimental group, which comes to 0.75.

The standard error of the mean is also known as the standard deviation of the mean, because it can be used just like the standard deviation of the distribution of scores. As is shown in Figure 13–14, we can use the mean and standard error of the mean of the control group to infer the range in which the true mean of the entire high school population must lie. We can also use the figures for the experimental group to infer the range in which the mean would probably have fallen if we had applied the experimental conditions to the entire high school population.

Having drawn these two curves, we can put them together as is shown in Figure 13–15. They show us that the probability is very high that there is a true difference between the grades of students who receive special medical care and the grades of students who do not. The possibility that the difference we found

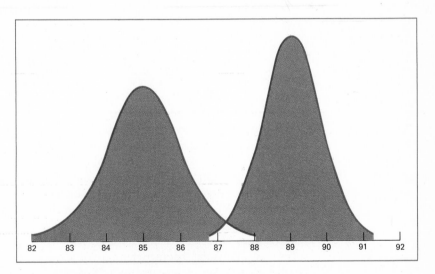

is the difference significant?

13-15   When the curves that were shown in Figure 13–14 are superimposed, they have only the small white area in common. The probability that the difference between the two means is due to chance is represented by this area; the probability that the difference is a real one is represented by the colored areas.

is merely a matter of chance is represented by the small area that lies beneath the extreme right-hand end of the control curve and the extreme left-hand end of the curve for the experimental group.

NO   *Probability and "Significance."* The curves in Figures 13-14 and 13-15 demonstrate the principle that underlies the comparison of two groups through the standard error of the mean. In actual statistical calculation these curves need not be constructed. We can use the two means and the standard error of each mean to work out what is called *the standard error of the difference between two means* (see page 459). This figure can in turn be used to work out the probability that the difference we found was due merely to chance. In the case of the hypothetical experiment we have been describing, the probability comes to less than .01.

It is an arbitrary rule of thumb in experimental work that a difference is considered *statistically significant* only when the probability that it might have been obtained by chance is .05 (5 chances in 100, or 1 chance in 20) or less.

In reports on experiments that can be analyzed with this kind of inferential statistics, the probability figure is always given; you will frequently find the note

$$p \leq .05$$

meaning that the difference would be found by chance only 5 times or less out of 100 and is therefore statistically significant. In virtually all the experiments cited in this book, *p* was .05 or less.

→   *4.* correlation

Galton's question—do successful fathers have more successful sons than other fathers?—is a problem involving another statistical device, called *correlation.* If success on the part of the father is often accompanied by success on the part of the son, then these two events are related to one another in some way. In statistical terms, they are *correlated.* Galton showed that there was indeed a correlation between the two events; other investigators have shown that there are correlations between I.Q. and grades in school, between grades in school and economic success, between a parent's strictness and aggressive behavior in the child, and between many other psychological traits and forms of behavior.

Some correlations are *positive,* meaning that the higher a person measures on scale *X* (for example, I.Q.), the higher he is likely to measure on scale *Y* (for example, grades). *Negative correlations,* in which a high score on scale *X* is likely to be accompanied by a low score on scale *Y,* have also been found. For example, the frequency of premature births has been found to be negatively correlated with social class—meaning that there tends to be less prematurity among upper-income families than lower-income families. Negative correlations also exist between aggressive behavior in children and social class and between test anxiety and school grades.

The relation between the *X*- and *Y*-scales is expressed in mathematical terms by a *correlation coefficient,* calculated in several possible ways as explained on page 459. A correlation coefficient can range from 0 (no correlation at all) to +1 (a perfect positive correlation) or −1 (a perfect negative correlation). But correlations of $+1$ or -1 are very rare. Even such physical traits as height and weight, which would seem to go together in almost perfect proportion, do not reach a correlation of $+1$. Some typical correlations that have been found are:

Between I.Q. and college grades	.50
Between parents' I.Q.'s and child's I.Q.	.49
Between I.Q. and ability at pitch discrimination	.00
Between boys' height at age two and height at age eighteen (5)	.60
Between boys' height at age ten and height at age eighteen (5)	.88

→ *Scatter Plots.* A rough idea of the degree of correlation between two traits can be obtained by plotting each subject's score on scale X against his score on scale Y, as shown in Figure 13-16. A dot is put down for each person at a point that corresponds to both his scores, giving us what is called a *scatter plot.* When the dots are scattered completely at random, we can see that the correlation is 0. If we should run into one of those extremely rare cases where the dots form a straight line, moving diagonally up or down, we know that we are dealing with a correlation of $+1$ or -1. Most scatter diagrams take a form that lies somewhere between. If a fairly narrow oval would enclose most of the dots, the correlation is rather high. If the oval must be fatter to enclose the dots, the correlation is much lower.

The correlation coefficient is a statistical method of expressing the degree of relation with great precision and without going to the trouble of constructing a scatter plot.

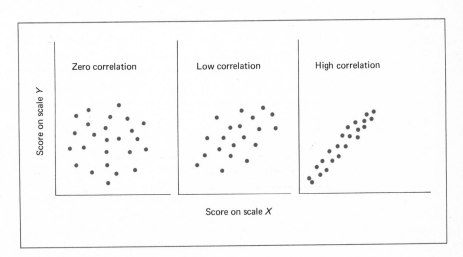

scatter plots of correlations

13-16 These scatter plots were obtained by making a dot for each subject at a point indicating both his score on scale X and his score on scale Y. (6)

→   *Correlation and Prediction.*   One of the chief practical uses of correlation is in predicting. College administrators, for example, know that scores on any standard intelligence test or on a test like the College Boards are correlated with college grades. They can predict, therefore, that a young man or young woman with very high scores will probably get good grades and that a student with very low scores will probably fail. They may decide to limit enrollment, therefore, to students with scores high enough to indicate a reasonable chance of success.

Guidance counselors know that scores on certain kinds of aptitude and interest tests are correlated with success in various kinds of jobs and thus can offer students the prediction that they will probably succeed or fail as computer programers, accountants, auto mechanics, professional musicians, or in whatever other job they may be considering.

It must always be kept in mind, however, that a coefficient of correlation is less accurate in making predictions than it sounds. Only when the correlation is very close to 1, as in the high correlation shown in Figure 13–16, does every subject tend to show a close relationship between score on scale X and score on scale Y. Even in a correlation of .75, which sounds high, there is a considerable amount of scatter, representing subjects who scored relatively low on scale X but relatively high on scale Y, or vice versa. Since most correlations found in psychological studies are lower than .75, we must be quite tentative in making predictions.

→   *Correlation, Cause, and Effect.*   The correlation coefficient is especially useful for measuring relationships between psychological traits that cannot be studied through the preferred method of experimental manipulation, but only through less powerful methods such as naturalistic observation, tests, interviews, and questionnaires. (The advantages and limitations of these methods of investigation were discussed in Chapter 1.) If we want to study the effect of harsh discipline in the home on tendencies to aggression, for example, we cannot deliberately force one group of children to submit to harsh discipline and permit another to grow up under more permissive conditions. We can only try to learn as much as possible about the home backgrounds of children who appear to display various levels of aggression. If we find no correlation between aggressive behavior and strict discipline in the home, we must conclude that the two factors are not related. If we do find a correlation, we are justified in concluding that there may be a connection between the two.

We must be careful, however, not to exaggerate the degree of relationship that is implied even by a rather high numerical value of correlation. And we must also avoid jumping to conclusions about cause and effect. Did the children become aggressive because the parents were strict, or were the parents strict because the children were aggressive? Is it possible that some third factor caused both the parents' strictness and the children's aggression? (For example, it may be that parents who are generally cold and rejecting of their children tend to be strict and that it is the coldness and rejection, rather than the strictness, that make the children aggressive.)

As a reminder of the danger of jumping to false conclusions on the basis of correlations, it is a good idea to keep in mind that there is a very high correlation between the number of permanent teeth that have erupted through the schoolchild's gums and his raw scores on questions answered correctly on any kind of intelligence or aptitude test. But it would be foolish to conclude that his teeth make him smarter or that his scores make more teeth appear. Increased maturity produces both the teeth and the higher scores.

the mathematical computations

As was said earlier, the mathematical knowledge required for statistical analysis is not particularly complicated. One need only be able to manipulate mathematical symbols, the most frequently used of which are explained in Figure 13–17, and to apply the few basic formulas presented in Figure 13–18.

The symbols and formulas are given at the start of this section on computations so that they can be found all in one place for future reference. They may seem rather difficult when shown all together in this fashion, but their application

N	Number of subjects from whom a measurement or score has been obtained
X	The numerical value of an individual score
Y	If each subject is measured on two scales, the numerical value of an individual score on the second scale
Σ	The Greek capital letter sigma, standing for "sum of"
ΣX	The sum of all the individual scores on scale X
M	The mean, which is the sum of the scores divided by the number of subjects
x	A deviation score; that is, the difference between an individual score and the mean for the group of which the individual is a member
y	A deviation score on the second scale, or Y-scale
SD	The standard deviation of the scores
SE_M	The standard error of the mean; also called the standard deviation of the mean
D_M	The difference between two means; for example, the difference between the mean (M) of scale X and the mean of scale Y
SE_{D_M}	The standard error of the difference between two means, used as a measure of whether the difference is significant
p	Probability, expressed in decimals ranging from .00 (no chance) through .50 (50–50 chance) to 1.00 (100 percent chance). A result is considered statistically significant when $p \leq .05$, meaning that there are only 5 chances in 100 (or fewer) that it was obtained by chance.
r	Correlation coefficient obtained by the product-moment method
ρ	Correlation coefficient obtained by the rank-difference method
z	A standard score, expressed in number of SD's above or below the mean
C	Coefficient of contingency; type of correlation used to find relationships between events on a nominal scale

some useful symbols

13–17   These are the mathematical symbols used in the formulas presented in this chapter.

1. For determining the mean:

$$M = \frac{\Sigma X}{N}$$

2. For determining a deviation score:

$$x = X - M$$

3. For determining the standard deviation:

$$SD = \sqrt{\frac{\Sigma x^2}{N - 1}}$$

4. For determining a z-score:

$$z = \frac{x}{SD}$$

5. For determining the standard error of the mean:

$$SE_M = \frac{SD}{\sqrt{N}}$$

6. For determining the difference between two means:

$$D_M = M_1 - M_2$$

7. For determining the standard error of the difference between two means:

$$SE_{D_M} = \sqrt{(SE_{M_1})^2 + (SE_{M_2})^2}$$

8. For determining the critical ratio:

$$\text{Critical ratio} = \frac{D_M}{SE_{D_M}}$$

9. For determining the coefficient of correlation by the product-moment method:

$$r = \frac{\Sigma xy}{(N - 1)SD_x SD_y}$$

(In this formula, SD_x is the standard deviation of the measurements on the X-scale, and SD_y is the standard deviation of the measurements on the Y-scale.)

10. For determining the coefficient of correlation by the rank-difference method:

$$\rho = 1 - \frac{6(\Sigma D^2)}{N(N^2 - 1)}$$

some statistical formulas

13-18 These are some of the formulas most frequently used in statistical analysis. Their use is explained and illustrated in the text and in the following figures.

should be apparent from the examples that will be presented as we go along.

The kind of measurement that an investigator often wants to analyze is illustrated in Figure 13–19. Here seventeen students have taken a psychological test and have made scores ranging from 60 to 97. The raw scores are a jumble of figures, from which we now want to determine the mean, the standard deviation, and the standard error of the mean.

13-19

These raw scores, obtained by seventeen students on a psychological test, will be analyzed statistically in the text.

1.	78	4.	74	7.	92	10.	74	13.	70	16.	82
2.	97	5.	80	8.	72	11.	85	14.	84	17.	78
3.	60	6.	77	9.	79	12.	68	15.	76		

1. the mean

The formula for the mean, as can be seen from Figure 13-18, is

$$M = \frac{\Sigma X}{N}$$

These symbols denote, as can be found in Figure 13-17, that the mean equals the sum of the individual scores divided by the number of subjects.

The way the formula is applied is illustrated in Figure 13-20. The sum of the individual scores, which are shown in column one, is 1326. The number of subjects is 17. Thus the mean is 78.

computing the mean and the SD

13-20

Using the formulas in Figure 13-18, we first compute the mean score (M) for the seventeen students, which comes out to 78. Once we have the mean, we can compute the standard deviation (SD)—starting by obtaining the deviation scores ($x = X - M$), then squaring these scores to get x^2.

TEST SCORES (X)	DEVIATION SCORES (x)	DEVIATION SCORES SQUARED (x^2)
78	0	0
97	+19	361
60	−18	324
74	− 4	16
80	+ 2	4
77	− 1	1
92	+14	196
72	− 6	36
79	+ 1	1
74	− 4	16
85	+ 7	49
68	−10	100
70	− 8	64
84	+ 6	36
76	− 2	4
82	+ 4	16
78	0	0
$\Sigma X = 1326$		$\Sigma x^2 = 1224$

$$M = \frac{\Sigma X}{N} = \frac{1326}{17} = 78$$

$$SD = \sqrt{\frac{\Sigma x^2}{N-1}} = \sqrt{\frac{1224}{16}} = \sqrt{76.5} = 8.75$$

2. the standard deviation

The method of finding the standard deviation is also illustrated in Figure 13-20. The formula for the standard deviation is

$$SD = \sqrt{\frac{\Sigma x^2}{N - 1}}$$

This means that the standard deviation is the square root of the figure we get by dividing the number of subjects minus 1 into the sum of all the deviation scores squared.

The deviation scores shown in column two have been obtained by the formula $x = X - M$—that is, by subtracting the mean, which is 78, from each individual score. These figures in column two have then been squared to give the figures in column three. The sum of the x^2 figures is 1224, and this figure divided by 16 (our $N - 1$) comes to 76.5. The standard deviation is the square root of 76.5, or 8.75.

3. the standard error of the mean

Finding the standard error of the mean for our group is extremely simple. The formula is

$$SE_M = \frac{SD}{\sqrt{N}}$$

We have found that the SD of our sample is 8.75 and our N is 17. The formula yields

$$SE_M = \frac{8.75}{\sqrt{17}} = \frac{8.75}{4.12} = 2.12$$

4. differences between groups

For an example of how the formulas for analyzing differences between groups are applied, let us return to the hypothetical experiment mentioned earlier in the chapter. We had the school grades, you will recall, of an experimental group of sixteen students who took part in a health program; the mean was 89 and the standard deviation was 3. We also had the grades of a control group of sixteen students; the mean for this group was 85 and the standard deviation was 4.

The difference between the two means is easily computed from the formula

$$D_M = M_1 - M_2$$

which means that the difference between the means is the mean of the first group minus the mean of the second group—in this case, 89 minus 85, or 4. To know whether this difference is statistically significant, however, we must calculate the standard error of the difference between the two means. To do so, as Figure 13–18 shows, we must use the fairly complex formula

$$SE_{D_M} = \sqrt{(SE_{M_1})^2 + (SE_{M_2})^2}$$

Our first step is to compute SE_{M_1}, the standard error of the mean of our first or experimental group. We do so as shown earlier, this time with 3 as our standard deviation and 16 as our number of subjects.

$$SE_{M_1} = \frac{SD}{\sqrt{N}} = \frac{3}{\sqrt{16}} = \frac{3}{4} = 0.75$$

We also compute SE_{M_2}, the standard error of the mean of our second or control group, where the standard deviation is 4 and the number of subjects is 16.

$$SE_{M_2} = \frac{SD}{\sqrt{N}} = \frac{4}{\sqrt{16}} = \frac{4}{4} = 1.00$$

Thus SE_{M_1} is 0.75 and SE_{M_2} is 1.00, and the standard error of the difference between the two means is computed as follows:

$$SE_{D_M} = \sqrt{(SE_{M_1})^2 + (SE_{M_2})^2} = \sqrt{(0.75)^2 + (1)^2} = \sqrt{.5625 + 1}$$
$$= \sqrt{1.5625} = 1.25$$

To complete our analysis of the difference between the two groups, we need one more statistical tool—the *critical ratio*. This is given by the formula

$$\text{Critical ratio} = \frac{D_M}{SE_{D_M}}$$

In the case of our hypothetical experiment we have found that D_M is 4 and that SE_{D_M} is 1.25. Thus

$$\text{Critical ratio} = \frac{4}{1.25} = 3.2$$

The critical ratio gives us a measure of the probability that our difference was due merely to chance. For reasons that a mathematically minded student may be able to work out for himself but that need not concern the rest of us, the magic numbers for the critical ratio are 1.96 and 2.57. If the critical ratio is as high as 1.96, then $p \leq .05$, and the difference is considered statistically significant. If the critical ratio is as high as 2.57, then $p \leq .01$, and the difference is considered highly significant. The critical ratio we found for our two groups, 3.2, is well over 2.57; thus we can have some confidence that the difference was not the result of chance.

5. correlation coefficients

There are a number of ways of computing correlation coefficients, depending on the type of data that are being studied. The most frequently used is the *product-moment method*, which obtains a coefficient of correlation designated by the letter r for the relationship between two different numerical test scores. The formula is

$$r = \frac{\Sigma xy}{(N-1)SD_x SD_y}$$

To use the formula we have to determine the amount by which each subject's score on the first test, or scale X, differs from the mean for all scores on scale X—in other words the value for x, the deviation score, which may be plus or

SUBJECT	TEST SCORES X	Y	DEVIATION SCORES x	y	PRODUCT OF DEVIATION SCORES (xy)
1.	60	81	− 12	+ 1	− 12
2.	80	92	+ 8	+12	+ 96
3.	70	76	− 2	− 4	+ 8
4.	65	69	− 7	−11	+ 77
5.	75	88	+ 3	+ 8	+ 24
6.	85	96	+13	+16	+208
7.	60	64	− 12	−16	+192
8.	75	75	+ 3	− 5	− 15
9.	70	77	− 2	− 3	+ 6
10.	80	82	+ 8	+ 2	+ 16
					$\Sigma xy = 600$

$N = 10$
For scale X, $M = 72$, and $SD_x = 8.56$
For scale Y, $M = 80$, and $SD_y = 9.98$

Thus

$$r = \frac{\Sigma xy}{(N-1)SD_x SD_y} = \frac{600}{(10-1) \times 8.56 \times 9.98} = \frac{600}{768.9} = .78$$

computing product-moment correlation

13-21 Note that in the sample of ten, four subjects who scored above the mean on scale X also scored above the mean on scale Y (subjects 2, 5, 6, and 10). Four subjects who scored below the mean on scale X also scored below the mean on scale Y (subjects 3, 4, 7, and 9). Only two subjects (1 and 8) scored above the mean on one test and below the mean on another. Thus multiplying the x-deviations times the y-deviations gives us eight positive products and only two negative products. Σxy, which is the total of the positive products minus the total of the negative products, comes to 600. The correlation coefficient comes to the rather large figure of .78.

The manner in which SD_x and SD_y were computed is not shown, but you can check the figures of 8.56 for SD_x and 9.98 for SD_y by applying the formula for computing a standard deviation as shown in Figure 13–20.

minus. We must also determine the amount by which his score on the second test, or scale Y, differs from the mean for all scores on scale Y—in other words, the value for y, which also may be plus or minus. We then multiply x by y for each subject and add the xy products for all the subjects in the sample. This gives us the top line, or numerator, of the formula. The bottom line, or denominator, is found by multiplying the number of subjects minus 1 $(N - 1)$ by the standard deviation of the scores on the X-scale (SD_x) and then multiplying the product by the standard deviation of the scores on the Y-scale (SD_y). An example is shown in Figure 13-21.

In some cases it is convenient to use the *rank-difference method*, which produces a different coefficient of correlation called ρ (the Greek letter *rho*), which is similar to but not exactly the same as r. The formula is

$$\rho = 1 - \frac{6(\Sigma D^2)}{N(N^2 - 1)}$$

The method of applying the formula is demonstrated in Figure 13-22. Note that

SUBJECT	TEST SCORES X	Y	RANK X	Y	DIFFERENCE IN RANK (D)	DIFFERENCE SQUARED (D^2)
1.	60	81	9.5	5	−4.5	20.25
2.	80	92	2.5	2	−0.5	0.25
3.	70	76	6.5	7	+0.5	0.25
4.	65	69	8.0	9	+1.0	1.00
5.	75	88	4.5	3	−1.5	2.25
6.	85	96	1.0	1	0.0	0.00
7.	60	64	9.5	10	−0.5	0.25
8.	75	75	4.5	8	−3.5	12.25
9.	70	77	6.5	6	−0.5	0.25
10.	80	82	2.5	4	+1.5	2.25
						$\Sigma D^2 = 39.00$

$N = 10$

Thus

$$\rho = 1 - \frac{6(\Sigma D^2)}{N(N^2 - 1)} = 1 - \frac{6(39)}{10(10^2 - 1)} = 1 - \frac{234}{990} = 1 - .24 = .76$$

computing rank-difference correlation

13-22 Here the same scores that were shown in Figure 13-21 have been used to find the rank-difference correlation, ρ, which comes out to .76—very close to the .78 that we found in Figure 13-21 for r. In computing ρ, we disregard the individual scores on scale X and scale Y and use merely the rank of each score as compared to the others on the scale. Note that subjects 2 and 10 are tied for second place on the X-scale. Their rank is therefore considered to be 2.5, halfway between second and third place.

the D in the formula refers to the difference between a subject's rank on scale X—that is, whether he was first, second, third, or so on among all the subjects—and his rank on scale Y. ΣD^2 is found by squaring each subject's difference in rank and adding to get the total for all subjects.

6. contingency

One other frequently used type of correlation is known as the *coefficient of contingency*, symbolized by the letter C. This is used to find relationships between events that can be measured only on what is called a *nominal scale*—where all we can say about them is that they belong to certain groups, to which we can give a name but no meaningful numerical value. For example, we can set up a nominal scale on which all college students taking a humanities course are grouped in class 1, all taking engineering are grouped in class 2, and all taking a preparatory course for one of the professional schools such as law or medicine are grouped in class 3. We might set up another nominal scale on which we designate the students as males or females. If we then want to determine whether there is any relationship between a student's sex and the kind of college course he is likely to take, we use the coefficient of contingency. Its meaning is roughly the same as that of any other coefficient of correlation.

summary 1.   *Measurement* is the assignment of numbers to traits, events, or objects, according to some kind of orderly system.

2.   The *statistical method* is the application of mathematical principles to an analysis and interpretation of the measurements.

3.   The statistical method is of special importance as a *way of thinking* reminding us that events take place in accordance with the laws of probability and that many events that might appear to be remarkable coincidences are bound to happen by chance.

4.   The most satisfactory kind of measurement is made on a *ratio scale,* such as a scale of weight or height, where there is a true zero point and where the number 2 means exactly twice as much as the number 1, 6 means three times as much as 2, and so on. Other scales, in decreasing order of precision, are *interval scales* (such as a thermometer, where each degree represents an equal expansion of the measuring fluid but where 100 degrees cannot be said to be twice as hot as 50 degrees), *ordinal scales* (based on rank order), and *nominal scales* (in which numbers are simply assigned to different categories, as when men are assigned one number and women another).

5.   Events that are distributed by chance, including many human traits, fall into the pattern of the *normal curve of distribution,* which is shaped like a bell. Most such events or traits cluster around the average, and the number declines approaching either the lower or the upper extreme.

6.   *Descriptive statistics* provide a quick and convenient method of summarizing measurements. Important descriptive statistics are:

a. The *number of subjects,* or *N.*

b. Measures of central tendency, including the arithmetic average, or *mean* (total of all scores divided by *N*), *median* (point separating the lower half of scores from the upper half), and *mode* (most frequent score in the group).

c. Index of *variability,* including *range* (obtained by subtracting the lowest score from the highest) and *standard deviation,* symbolized by SD. In a normal distribution, 34.13 percent of the scores lie between the mean and 1 SD above the mean, 13.59 percent between 1 SD and 2 SD's above the mean, and 2.14 percent between 2 SD's and 3 SD's above the mean, while 0.14 percent lie more than 3 SD's above the mean. The same pattern of distribution exists below the mean.

7. *Percentiles* are used to describe the position of an individual score in the total group. A measurement on the 75th percentile is larger than 75 percent of the measurements, or, to put it another way, 25 percent of measurements lie on or above the 75th percentile.

8. *Inferential statistics* are procedures that allow us to make generalizations from measurements. They enable us to infer conclusions about a *population* or *universe,* which is the total of all possible cases in a particular category, by measuring a relatively small *sample.* To permit valid generalization, however, the sample must be *representative.*

9. A set of findings is considered *statistically significant* when the probability that the findings might have been obtained by chance is only 5 in 100 or less; the figure is expressed mathematically as $p \leq .05$.

10. *Correlations* between two measurements—such as scores on two different tests—range from 0 (no relationship) to $+1$ (perfect positive relationship) or -1 (perfect negative relationship).

11. The symbols and formulas used in the statistical analysis described in the chapter are shown in Figures 13–17 and 13–18.

recommended reading

Arkin, H., and Colton, R. R. *Tables for statisticians,* 2nd ed. New York: Barnes & Noble, 1963.

Edwards, A. L. *Experimental design in psychological research,* 3rd ed. New York: Holt, Rinehart and Winston, 1968.

Guilford, J. P. *Fundamental statistics in psychology and education,* 4th ed. New York: McGraw-Hill, 1965.

Hammond, K. R., Householder, J. E., and Castellan, N. J., Jr. *Introduction to the statistical method: foundations and use in the behavioral sciences,* 2nd ed. New York: Knopf, 1970.

Hays, W. L. *Statistics for psychologists.* New York: Holt, Rinehart and Winston, 1963.

McCall, R. B. *Fundamental statistics for psychology.* New York: Harcourt Brace Jovanovich, 1970.

McCollough, C., and Van Atta, L. *Statistical concepts: a program for self-instruction.* New York: McGraw-Hill, 1963.

Siegel, S. *Nonparametric statistics for the behavioral sciences.* New York: McGraw-Hill, 1956.

CHAPTER 14

MEASURING INTELLIGENCE AND PERSONALITY

spect of measurement called *testing* is one area where everybody,
not he ever takes a psychology course, is almost bound to come into
psychology. It is virtually impossible to grow up in the United States
ut sooner or later taking a test that has been devised by a psychologist
n accordance with techniques originally developed by psychologists.
early grades many schools give their pupils some kind of intelligence
ct how well they are likely to perform in their classes. The tests serve
whether they are underachievers who are not living up to their true
r overachievers who are working exceptionally hard and doing better
be expected. In the later grades most pupils take the Iowa or Stanford
t tests, which measure their progress (and the general level of progress
ticular school) against national averages. As part of the requirement
on to many colleges, high school seniors take the Scholastic Aptitude
h are a form of intelligence test.

schoolchild who has trouble adjusting may be asked to take various
rsonality tests that will help identify the nature of his problems. The
o seeks vocational guidance is often asked to take tests for special
uch as mechanics and art, and tests that measure his interests and
. If he goes into the Army, he receives his assignment on the basis
ny's own general intelligence tests and a number of aptitude tests
measure special abilities for work in radio, electronics, mechanical
other fields. When he seeks a job, his prospective employer may test
nce, his specific abilities, and sometimes his personality characteristics.
ng is an important branch of psychology in which many investigators
hard at work for many years. It is the source of much of the data
ith the statistical tools described in the preceding chapter. It has been
seful in the study of human intelligence and has cast considerable light
re of intelligence and the relationship between intelligence and success
r career.

t

ests of human characteristics go back to the beginnings of history.
and literature are full of stories of young men who had to slay dragons
hat they were brave enough to deserve the hand of a princess or had

to answer riddles posed by wise men to prove that they were intelligent enough to become rulers. In the modern world, informal testing continues. A college woman tries out for a campus musical and is asked to read some of the lines and sing a few bars of a song; on the basis of this sample of her talents the judges decide whether she will probably do well in the actual performance. A college man tries out for the basketball team and is kept on the squad or dropped depending on how well he performs some of the skills required in an actual game. Even courtship is a form of informal testing. Most of us choose our future wives or husbands on the basis of what we can observe of their behavior.

Like informal tests, formal psychological tests are forced to rely on a limited sample of behavior, since it is impossible to measure how intelligently a person will perform on every possible kind of task or to observe all the behavior that might reflect his personality. Also like informal tests, they are often used to predict future behavior.

The ways in which formal psychological tests differ from informal methods of assessment can best be explained by describing the four quite strict requirements that they are expected to meet, insofar as it is at all possible. The psychological test should be 1) *objective*, 2) *standardized*, 3) *reliable*, and 4) *valid*.

1. objectivity

The test should provide results that are uncolored by the personal opinions or prejudices of the person who gives and grades the test. In fact the first intelligence test was an attempt to obtain a more objective measure of a child's ability to profit from classes in school than could be provided by the opinion of his teacher, which might be colored by the child's personality, his behavior in class, or his family's position in the community.

Psychological tests are designed so that any qualified person can present them to the subject in the same manner and under the same kind of testing conditions and apply a uniform method of scoring the results; thus the person taking the test should get the same score regardless of who administers the test and who scores it. Ideally, the test should also encourage the subject to give accurate responses, but this is not always possible. On an intelligence test, it is impossible for a person to make a higher score than his own abilities justify, unless he is exceptionally lucky at guessing; he may, however, get a lower score than he should because of anxiety or lack of motivation. On personality tests, the subject may try to put on a good front by giving answers that he believes will result in a "good" score rather than answers that represent the complete truth. Some tests have a built-in system of checks designed to show whether the subject is being honest or giving himself the best of it.

2. standardization

The results of a test are most useful when they can be compared to the scores of other people. Thus tests are standardized whenever possible by administering them to a large and representative sample of the population. The score made by an individual can then be interpreted properly; it can be seen to be average, low, or high.

3. reliability

An analogy can be made between a test and a housewife's oven thermometer. If the thermometer is reliable—that is, if it gives the same reading every time for the same amount of heat—the housewife can count on her roasts and pies to come out cooked as she wants them. But, if the thermometer is damaged and unreliable, it may give a reading of 300 degrees on one occasion and 400 degrees the next, even though the actual temperature is exactly the same; in this case the results of cooking are likely to be somewhat disappointing.

A good test, like a good thermometer, must be reliable; the scores it yields must be consistent. One way of determining the reliability of a test is to compare the same person's score on all the odd-numbered items with his score on all the even-numbered items; these two scores should be similar. Another way is to give a person the same test twice, some time apart; again the scores should be similar.

4. validity

The most important requirement for a test is that it be valid—that is, it must actually measure what it is intended to measure. This is unfortunately the most difficult of the requirements to fill and to explain. Perhaps the best approach is to discuss what is meant by the absence of validity.

Suppose that an investigator wants to develop a test that will predict which college students will make the best teachers in the first three grades of elementary school. On the assumption that the ability to use words is important he devises a test that measures how good college students are at such tasks as defining words, completing sentences, and remembering and repeating the content of paragraphs heard a single time. The test is objective; it is standardized on a large group of subjects; and tests and retests show it to be highly reliable. Thus it meets the first three requirements of a good test. But it is not necessarily valid. It may measure not teaching ability but only the ability to understand and manipulate words.

There are a number of ways to determine the validity of a test. Common sense is one of them; the items in the test must bear a meaningful relationship to the characteristics being measured. (For example, the thought of trying to assess musical ability by asking questions on major-league baseball standings does not "make sense" and must be rejected.) Another way is to observe the behavior of people who have taken the test and determine whether they behave as their test scores predicted. Thus, in the case of the test of teaching ability, the scores of a group of college students might be compared with later ratings of the quality of their teaching. Or, to save time, the test might be given to a group of teachers whose ability was already known. If there proved to be a close relationship between their test scores and their ratings as teachers, this would indicate that the test is valid. If there was no relationship or only a small relationship between the scores

Three of these things are alike in some way. Fill in the answer space beneath the one that is different.

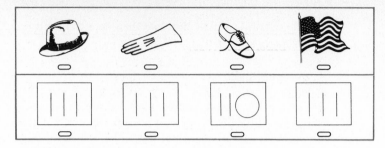

We say: "Boy is to trousers as girl is to what?"

The first two drawings are alike except the second one has a dot inside it. Which drawing goes with the circle in the same way as the first two drawings go together?

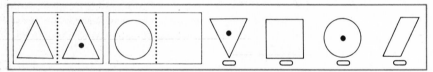

Find the picture that shows two boys running.

Find the circle that has the largest star inside it.

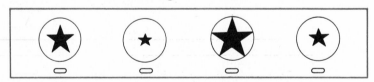

a group intelligence test

14-1   These are sample items for second- and third-graders from the Otis-Lennon Mental Ability Test. At this age level the person administering the test reads the instructions to the children taking the test. In all intelligence tests the sample items demonstrate how the questions should be answered and are not counted in the scoring. The actual items in this test range from about as difficult as the sample items to much more difficult. (1)

and the ratings of teaching ability, the test would have to be rejected as invalid.

Unfortunately, psychology does not yet possess valid tests for many important psychological characteristics. For example, there are no valid tests for anxiety over sexual behavior, tolerance of frustration, or disposition to suicide. The design of such tests is a challenge for psychologists of the future.

types of tests

Before discussing some actual tests, their uses, and what has been learned from them, it will be useful to describe some different types of tests. First, a distinction must be made between a *group test* and an *individual test*. The group test is administered to many people at once; it typically takes the form of printed questions, such as those shown in Figure 14-1, which are answered by making penciled notations. The individual test is given to one person at a time by a trained examiner; in this case the test items can call for a verbal answer or for the subject to perform some kind of task, as illustrated in Figure 14-2. Group tests have made possible the measurement of hundreds of thousands of soldiers and students each year—a job for which there would never be enough time or testers to use the individual method. They have a limitation, however. A low score on a group test may be caused by such factors as temporary ill health, poor vision, and lack of motivation—which would be apparent to a trained examiner administering an individual test.

Another distinction separates *aptitude tests* from *achievement tests*. An aptitude test attempts to measure a person's capacity to learn a new skill. The Scholastic Aptitude Tests are an example; as the name indicates, they measure the student's capacity to learn academic material in college. An achievement test measures how much a person has already learned at the time he takes the test. Thus the Iowa and Stanford achievement tests measure what the student has

an individual intelligence test

14-2

With colored blocks of various patterns, the man is asked to copy a design from the Block Design test, one of the tests that comprise the Wechsler Adult Intelligence Scale. The examiner notes how fast and accurately he can perform this task.

already learned about such subjects as reading and arithmetic and how his present skills in these fields compare with those of students in the same grade in other schools around the nation.

B. intelligence tests

Intelligence tests are perhaps the best known of psychological procedures. Everybody has heard about them and about the I.Q., or intelligence quotient, that they produce. Intelligence tests have been widely used for years by schools, industry, and the military services. The results have been analyzed statistically in various ways, resulting in a considerable body of knowledge on how I.Q. is related to such factors as parents' I.Q., parents' schooling, father's occupation, and the I.Q. of brothers, sisters, and twins. Numerous studies have also been made comparing the I.Q.'s of various nationalities, races, and age groups.

The intelligence test began as a psychologist's answer to a specific and practical problem faced by Paris schools at the beginning of the century. Too many classrooms were crowded, and poor students were holding up the progress of the better ones. The solution, the school authorities decided, was to identify the children who lacked the mental capacity required by the standard curriculum and put these children in a separate school of their own. But how was the identification to be made?

This was a problem, the authorities felt, that could not safely be left to the teachers. There was too much danger that a teacher would show favoritism toward children who had pleasant personalities and would be too harsh on those who were bright enough but tended to be troublemakers. There was also the question of whether a teacher could successfully identify a child who appeared dull but in fact could have done the work had he tried (2). The authorities called in a French psychologist named Alfred Binet, who solved the problem by developing a test that was first published in 1905, has been revised a number of times since, and is still widely used today.

1. the Stanford-Binet test

In the United States one of the best-known current versions of Binet's original test is the 1960 *Stanford-Binet Intelligence Scale.* It is an individual test given by an examiner using the kind of equipment illustrated in Figure 14-3. The child is asked to perform certain tasks with this equipment and to answer questions that test his vocabulary, memory span for sentences and numbers, and reasoning ability. Some of the items used are shown in Figure 14-4.

As can be seen in Figure 14-4, the items are arranged by age levels; six tasks like those shown are listed for age two, six more difficult tasks for age three, and so on. One way of scoring the Stanford-Binet is as follows: The examiner first finds the age level at which the child can perform all six tasks (or answer all the questions) correctly. This provides a basic figure for the child's mental

14-3

These are the "props" used in administering the Stanford-Binet Intelligence Scale to young children.

Two years old	On a large paper doll, points out the hair, mouth, feet, ear, nose, hands, and eyes.
	When shown a tower built of four blocks, builds one like it.
Three years old	When shown a bridge built of three blocks, builds one like it.
	When shown a drawing of a circle, copies it with a pencil.
Four years old	Fills in the missing word when asked, "Brother is a boy; sister is a _____" and "In daytime it is light; at night it is _____."
	Answers correctly when asked, "Why do we have houses?" "Why do we have books?"
Five years old	Defines *ball, hat,* and *stove.*
	When shown a drawing of a square, copies it with a pencil.
Nine years old	Answers correctly when examiner says, "In an old graveyard in Spain they have discovered a small skull which they believe to be that of Christopher Columbus when he was about ten years old. What is foolish about that?"
	Answers correctly when asked, "Tell me the name of a color that rhymes with head." "Tell me a number that rhymes with tree."
Adult	Can describe the difference between laziness and idleness, poverty and misery, character and reputation.
	Answers correctly when asked, "Which direction would you have to face so your right hand would be toward the north?"

items in the Stanford-Binet test

14-4

Above are some of the items for various age levels on the Stanford-Binet Intelligence Scale. (3)

14-5

The curves show the number of children, of chronological ages five through fifteen, who are able to pass three items at different levels of difficulty on the Stanford-Binet Intelligence Scale. For the curve at the left, note that only about 20 percent of six-year-old children can pass the item and only about 40 percent of seven-year-olds. The item is passed, however, by about 60 percent of eight-year-olds, by nearly 80 percent of nine-year-olds, and by more than 90 percent of ten-year-olds. On the basis of data like these, each item is placed at the age level where about 60 percent can pass; these three items will be found in the test form at ages eight, ten, and twelve. (3)

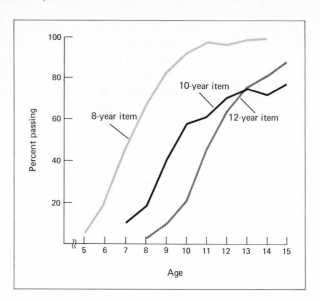

age. The examiner then goes on to the next higher level and continues until he reaches a level where the child cannot pass any of the six items. He then adds up the score, giving credit of two months for each item passed successfully at levels above the basic mental age. For example, a child passes all six items at the six-year-old level, three at the seven-year-old level, one at the eight-year-old level, and none at the nine-year-old level. His final *mental age* (or MA) is determined by crediting him with a basic figure of six years, plus six months for the three questions answered correctly at the seven-year-old level and two months for the single question answered correctly at the eight-year-old level; thus his mental age is six years and eight months.

When a Stanford-Binet test is being constructed, the items are first pretested on a large number of children of different ages. They are then assigned to the various age levels by the method illustrated in Figure 14-5. Each item included in the test at the eight-year level, for example, has been found to be at a level of difficulty where just about 60 percent of all eight-year-old children will pass it and 40 percent will fail. Some children who are younger than eight will also pass the item, and most of those who are older than eight will pass. Note in Figure 14-5 that the particular item illustrated for the eight-year level is passed by a few children as young as five and by nearly 20 percent of six-year-olds. On the other hand, nearly 20 percent of nine-year-olds fail on the item, and a few children fail it even at the ages of eleven, twelve, and thirteen.

2. mental age and I.Q.

The concept of mental age is based on the fact that as children mature they are able to pass more and more of the items on the Stanford-Binet. The test has been designed so that the average child will obtain a mental age corresponding to his actual chronological age. Thus the average seven-year-old child

472

who takes the Stanford-Binet will show a mental age of seven; the average child of seven and a half years will show an MA of seven and a half, and so on. Those who have less intelligence than average as measured by the test will show an MA that is lower than their chronological age; those who have more than the average level of intelligence will show an MA that is higher than their chronological age.

The *intelligence quotient*, or I.Q., is simply the relationship of mental age to chronological age; it is obtained by the formula :

$$I.Q. = \frac{MA}{\text{Chronological age}} \times 100$$

As an example of how the formula is applied, we can consider the mental age of six years and eight months obtained for the child mentioned earlier. For convenience, the mental age is converted into months; six years and eight months equals eighty months. If the child's chronological age is also eighty months, the formula works out as follows.

$$I.Q. = \frac{80}{80} \times 100 = 1 \times 100 = 100$$

If he is only six years old (seventy-two months), his

$$I.Q. = \frac{80}{72} \times 100 = \frac{10}{9} \times 100 = 111$$

If his actual age is eight years (ninety-six months), his

$$I.Q. = \frac{80}{96} \times 100 = \frac{10}{12} \times 100 = 83$$

This is the general principle for computing the I.Q. on the Stanford-Binet. In actual practice, because it is quicker and easier, the I.Q. is usually determined from tables that make it possible to compare the child's raw score with the scores made by other children of the same age. This latter method is also the one used with all other intelligence tests. They are administered to large standardization groups of various ages. The average raw score of the standardization group is then equated with an I.Q. of 100; a raw score that is 1 standard deviation above the group's average usually represents an I.Q. of 115; and a score that is 2 standard deviations above average represents an I.Q. of 130.* This statistical method of computing the I.Q. is valuable because the concept of mental age or of I.Q. based on mental age is not meaningful for adults.

*For students who have not read Chapter 13, it should be explained that the standard deviation is a statistical tool used to describe the distribution of measurements. For our present purposes, the standard deviation is important for two reasons: 1) it provides an accurate method of converting a score on one scale (in this case the raw score on intelligence test items) into a score on another scale (such as I.Q.), and 2) it shows how many individuals in the population will make any particular score. As is explained in greater detail on page 447, about 34 percent of all individuals have an I.Q. between 100 and 114, while 14 percent have an I.Q. between 115 and 129, and 2 percent 130 or over. Similarly, 34 percent fall between 85 and 99, 14 percent between 70 and 84, and 2 percent under 70.

3. the Wechsler tests

Among other widely used individual tests of intelligence are the *Wechsler Adult Intelligence Scale* (called WAIS for short) and the *Wechsler Intelligence Scale for Children* (WISC), to which more recently has been added the *Wechsler Preschool and Primary Scale of Intelligence* (WPPSI). The distinguishing feature of this group of tests is that the items in them are divided into two major categories, verbal and performance. The verbal items measure vocabulary, information, general comprehension, memory span, arithmetic reasoning, and ability to detect similarities between concepts. The performance items measure ability at constructing designs with blocks (as shown in Figure 14-2), completing pictures, arranging pictures, assembling objects, and substituting a set of unfamiliar symbols for digits.

The subject's I.Q. can be calculated for the test as a whole or for the verbal items and the performance items considered separately. This feature is often an advantage in testing people who lack familiarity with or skill in the use of the English language; such people may score much higher on the performance items than on the verbal items.

4. group tests

An example of a group intelligence test has already been illustrated. This is the *Otis-Lennon Mental Ability Test,* shown in Figure 14-1, which is actually a series of five tests of varying difficulty designed to cover the school years from kindergarten to college freshman. A well-known test for children in kindergarten and the first grade is the *Pintner-Cunningham Primary Test,* illustrated in Figure 14-6.

Prospective members of the Army and Navy take the *Armed Forces Qualification Test.* The *Scholastic Aptitude Tests* (SAT) are also group intelligence tests but they have been standardized for high school seniors rather than the population as a whole. The average SAT score is 500, and the standard deviation is 100. Since the seniors who take the test are a rather highly selected group, a score of 500 represents an I.Q. of well over 100.

5. virtues of intelligence tests

All modern intelligence tests are objective and standardized and have a high degree of reliability. A person's I.Q. as given by one of the tests will be similar to his I.Q. as shown by another test or by the same test given after a reasonable interval. Intelligence tests have also proved valid for predicting success in school. In many studies of the relation between I.Q. and school grades, correlations of .40 to .60 have been found* (5). Some forms of school achievement show a higher correlation than others, as is illustrated in Figure 14-7.

*Correlation, which was explained more fully in Chapter 13, is a statistical device for measuring the relation between two different scores, such as I.Q. and school grades. A correlation of 1 indicates a perfect relationship; 0 indicates no relationship; and the figures from .01 to .99 describe low to high levels of relationship.

There are *two* things that belong together in this row. Let's see if we can find them. Put a mark on the fork. Now mark something that belongs with the fork.

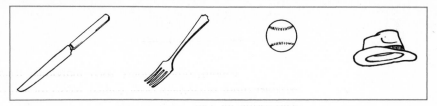

Look at the picture of the rooster. Find what is gone from the rooster and mark it.

the Pintner test

14-6 These are sample items for kindergarten and first-grade pupils from the Pintner-Cunningham Primary Test. (4)

I.Q. and school achievement

14-7

These correlations between I.Q. and achievement in specific school subjects or skills were found in a study that used the Stanford-Binet Scale to measure intelligence. (6)

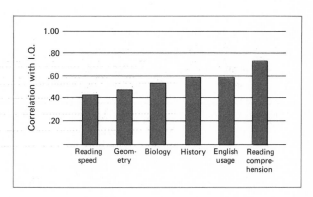

Students who have very low I.Q.'s tend to drop out of school before or immediately after the twelfth grade, leaving a rather highly selected group to go on to college. One study made a generation ago showed that the average I.Q. of college freshmen was 118, of graduates 123, and of those who had obtained the Ph.D. degree 141 (7). Because a larger proportion of young people attend college today, the figures for freshmen and graduates now are probably somewhat lower. At universities with the highest entrance standards, however, the figures are very high.

6. weaknesses of intelligence tests

One weakness of intelligence tests is the impossibility of devising a test of general or basic mental ability that is purely an aptitude test rather than an achievement test. An intelligence test necessarily relies heavily on the individual's current level of achievement—the vocabulary he has acquired, his knowledge of the rules of mathematics, his ability to manipulate numbers and visual symbols. If you study the items from the Stanford-Binet test shown in Figure 14-4, you will note that many of the questions are based on what the subject has learned. To answer them correctly, the two-year-old child must have learned the meaning of hair, mouth, and hands; the four-year-old must have acquired some fairly rich concepts of houses and books; the adult must have learned the points of the compass.

The theoretical difference between intelligence and achievement tests is that the intelligence test attempts, insofar as possible, to measure the subject's ability to use his existing knowledge in a novel way. Thus the two-year-old is asked to apply his knowledge about his own lips and hair to a paper doll; the adult is asked to make a novel spatial orientation based on his knowledge of the compass. Perhaps the best example of the difference between an intelligence test and an achievement test is the Stanford-Binet item at the nine-year level in which the child is asked to point out the absurdity in the statement: "In an old graveyard in Spain they have discovered a small skull which they believe to be that of Christopher Columbus when he was about ten years old." Finding the absurdity is a novel task, but it also requires the child to know that Columbus lived to be an adult and that people do not cast off their skulls as a snake casts off its old skin.

In constructing an intelligence test an attempt is made to base all the items on previously acquired knowledge or skills that everyone has had an equal chance to attain. It is assumed that every two-year-old has had an equal opportunity to learn the meaning of hair, mouth, and hands; every four-year-old knows the words *houses* and *books;* every nine-year-old should know that Columbus discovered America; every adult should have been exposed to information about the points of the compass. No questions should be included that can be answered only by a child who has had specialized training in summer camp about nature study or only by an adult who has taken a course in trigonometry or Spanish.

Nonetheless, there is a strong bias in intelligence tests that favors people who have grown up in environments where they have had an opportunity to acquire the kinds of knowledge and language abilities that are typical of the middle and upper classes and are fostered by a school system largely staffed by middle-class teachers. Thus children from middle- and upper-class homes make higher scores than children from lower-class homes (8). City children tend to make higher scores than children from rural areas (9). Whites make higher average scores than blacks and members of ethnic groups that do not share the typical white middle-class culture (10, 11, 12).

Intelligence tests, it must be remembered, were originally designed to

Analysis of Learning Potential... a fresh approach to measuring school learning ability.

measure the ability to learn the tasks typically taught in school, and this is still what they measure today. Indeed it probably would be more accurate to say that intelligence tests provide an A.Q., or academic quotient, instead of an I.Q., or intelligence quotient. Psychologists are not sure of the degree to which they reflect a basic capacity to think intelligently.

Recently there has been much discussion of revising intelligence tests to remove their weaknesses and biases. For example, a panel of scholars appointed to study the Scholastic Aptitude Tests has recommended that these tests be enlarged and diversified so that they also measure such factors as musical and artistic talent, athletic skills, mechanical skills, the ability to express oneself in nonverbal ways, the ability to adapt to new situations, and many others that are not now taken into account (13).

the nature of intelligence NO pp 477 - 491

Let us put aside all thoughts of intelligence testing and I.Q.'s for a moment and ask a more abstract question: Just what is intelligence? What does the word mean?

Many investigators would agree with the following definition: *Intelligence is the ability to profit from experience, to learn new information, and to adjust to new situations.* But is it a single ability or a combination of several different kinds of ability?

what is intelligence?

One well-known investigation into the nature of intelligence was made by L. L. Thurstone, who gave dozens of different kinds of tests to schoolchildren and decided that intelligence is composed of seven recognizable factors, which he called *primary mental abilities*. The factors are:

1. *Verbal comprehension*—indicated by size of vocabulary, ability to read, and skill at understanding mixed-up sentences and the meaning of proverbs.

2. *Word fluency*—the ability to think of words quickly, as when making rhymes or solving word puzzles.

3. *Number*—the ability to solve arithmetic problems and to manipulate numbers.

4. *Space*—the ability to visualize spatial relationships, as in recognizing a design after it has been placed in a new context.

5. *Associative memory*—the ability to memorize quickly, as in learning a list of paired words.

6. *Perceptual speed*—indicated by the ability to grasp visual details quickly and to observe similarities and differences between designs and pictures.

7. *General reasoning*—skill at the kind of logical thinking that was described in Chapter 5.

Thurstone noted, however, that a person who was above average in any one of these abilities also tended to be above average in the others. He concluded, therefore, that intelligence is composed of the seven primary mental abilities plus some kind of "general factor" that is common to all (14).

Thurstone's "general factor" is a matter of some controversy among psychologists. Newer investigations have shown that when enough tests of widely different kinds of learning and problem solving are devised and given to children, it turns out that some children do much better on some of the tests, others on very different tests—and that the correlations between an individual's scores on various tests often drop so low as to cast doubt on the existence of any "general factor" (15). One group of investigators, headed by J. P. Guilford of the University of Southern California, believes that intelligence is probably made up of 120 different factors; they have devised finely differentiated tests for many of these factors and have found no correlation at all between an individual's scores on many of the tests (16).

I.Q. and heredity

There are many important questions to be asked about intelligence: Is it inherited or determined by environment? Can it be changed? How is it affected by age? What relation does it have to a person's occupation and success? The answers can be presented only with reservations—for, as has just been said, psychologists are not entirely agreed on exactly what intelligence is and there is considerable question as to whether the standard tests really measure intelligence or only measure such aspects of it as apply to schoolwork. Therefore it will be better to discuss the questions in terms of I.Q. (which is what we know the tests measure) rather than in terms of intelligence (which is more difficult to define and measure).

On the question of whether I.Q. is inherited, one must consider the evidence in Figure 14–8, which summarizes some of the correlations that have been found between the I.Q.'s of children, their brothers and sisters, their parents, and other more distant relatives. The correlations indicate that to at least some extent, intelligence as reflected by I.Q. does tend to "run in families." The correlation between the I.Q. of one child and another chosen at random would be zero—but the correlations between a child's I.Q. and the I.Q.'s of his relatives are always positive. Even for such rather distant relatives as cousins, the correlation runs about .30. For identical twins reared in the same home, it can reach .92. This is a very high correlation indeed, especially when it is considered that even the same person's I.Q. ratings, calculated at different times, do not show a perfect correlation. (When the same child takes the Stanford-Binet test at one-year or two-year intervals, the correlation is around .90.)

I.Q. and environment

The correlation shown in Figure 14–8 for identical twins reared apart, however, must be given special attention. Since identical twins inherit exactly the same chromosomes and genes, it must be assumed that they begin life with exactly

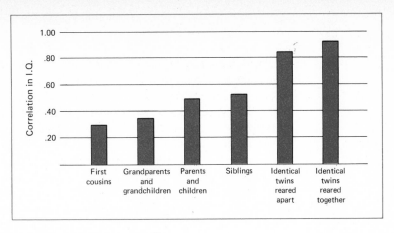

family resemblances in I.Q.

14-8 Studies of members of the same families have shown correlations in I.Q. ranging from about .29 for first cousins to .92 for identical twins reared together. (17, 18)

the same amount of mental capacity except as it may have been altered by such environmental factors before birth as the amount of food and oxygen they received while in the womb. Yet, when for one reason or another they are separated and reared in different homes, the correlation between their I.Q.'s drops to .84. Indeed the I.Q.'s of identical twins who grew up in different home environments often vary by as much as fifteen to twenty-five points.

There is also considerable other evidence that the I.Q. is significantly affected by environment. For example, many studies have shown that a child's I.Q. is correlated with the social class of his parents (19). It has been shown that middle-class mothers tend to spend more time than lower-class mothers in such activities as talking to and playing with their young children and in encouraging them to learn and to solve problems on their own (20)—thus providing exactly the kind of environment that might be expected to result in higher I.Q. ratings. Similarly, the child's I.Q. is correlated with the educational level of his parents; statistically significant correlations, ranging between .32 and .59, have been found for children as young as twenty-seven months to four years (21).

The highest correlations of all between I.Q. and aspects of the environment have been obtained by one investigator who ignored such indirect measures as social class and parents' education and instead made a direct attempt to measure the kind of stimulation provided by the parents. This investigator drew up a scale on which parents were rated on such factors as how much encouragement and help they gave the child in using language and increasing his vocabulary, how much motivation and reward they provided for intellectual accomplishment, and the kinds of opportunities for learning they provided in the home, including personal help, books, and other learning materials. The correlation between the parents' total score on this scale and the child's I.Q. turned out to be .76 (22).

One of the most dramatic examples of the contrasting effects of different kinds of environments was provided by a long-term study of children who began life in the 1930's in an overcrowded, understaffed Iowa orphanage in which they had little opportunity for any kind of intellectual stimulation. Thirteen of the young orphans, with an average I.Q. of only 64 as shown by standard tests, were moved to a less crowded home for retarded teenage girls and women who, despite their own mental handicaps, managed to provide an affectionate and homelike atmosphere for them. Some of the older girls and women served as foster mothers, others as adoring aunts; the attendants in the home provided toys and books; and there was great competition over which of the young children would show the greatest progress in such skills as walking and talking.

Given this kind of personal attention and stimulation, even by "mothers" and "aunts" who were themselves retarded, the children made remarkable advances. After about a year and a half in their new home, their average I.Q. had risen by 28 points to 92 and they were considered suitable for adoption into foster families. A follow-up study thirty years later showed that the children had completed an average of about twelve years of schooling and that all but two, who were women who had married young, had worked successfully at such jobs as office work, school teaching, nursing, vocational counseling, and sales; indeed all of them were living at about the average level of occupation and income for their area of the nation.

The study also followed the careers of twelve other children who, for lack of opportunity to be moved elsewhere, had to remain in the overcrowded and unstimulating environment of the orphanage. These children, as it happened, actually began with a higher average I.Q. than the others, 87. But in the next two years the average declined by 26 points to 61. A follow-up thirty years later showed that they had completed an average of only four years of school, that a third of them were still inmates of an institution, and that only one of them worked at a job above the level of dishwasher or napkin-folder in a cafeteria (23).

effects of deprived environments

All in all, there is considerable evidence that an environment that does not encourage or provide stimulation for the kinds of skills measured by intelligence tests is likely to result in a lower I.Q. score than the developing child would be capable of attaining under different circumstances. Moreover, the longer the child remains in a deprived environment (in terms of these kinds of skills), the lower his I.Q. score is likely to become. For example, Figure 14-9 shows the results of a study of children brought up by mentally retarded mothers. Note that the older the child was—in other words, the longer he had been exposed to the impoverished environment provided by the retarded mother—the lower was the I.Q.

Children who appear to be retarded in early infancy seem to be especially vulnerable to the effects of a deprived atmosphere; a study that points in this direction is illustrated in Figure 14-10. Note that children who appeared to be retarded at eight months had considerably less chance of achieving an I.Q. of at least 80 at the age of four if they grew up in a lower-class home (that is, one less likely to encourage the skills measured by intelligence tests) than if they grew up in a middle-class home. Home environment made no difference in this regard, however, to the children who were most advanced at eight months.

14-9

The bars indicate the average scores on intelligence tests made by the children of mentally retarded mothers. Note that the youngest children proved about normal in intelligence but that the oldest children had an average I.Q. of only about 53. (24)

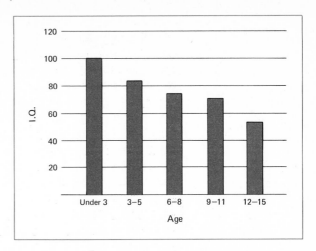

14-10

The bars illustrate the results of a study of more than 3000 children, from families of three different economic and social classes, who were tested for mental and motor skills at the age of eight months and then tested for I.Q. when they reached the age of four. Note the similarity in the height of the colored bars, which shows that infants who scored in the top quarter at eight months were just as likely to have I.Q.'s of 80 or over at age four regardless of the home environment. Children who were retarded at eight months, however, as indicated by the fact that they fell into the lowest quarter of scores on mental and motor tests (shaded bars), proved more vulnerable to the home environment. Only about 88 percent of those from low-class homes showed an I.Q. of 80 or more at four, compared with about 93 percent of those from middle-class homes and 98 percent of those from the high-class homes. (Adapted from 25)

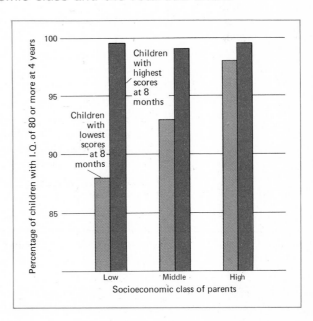

a last word on the heredity-environment issue

The question of whether heredity or environment has the greater effect on I.Q., though it has been the subject of much debate (26, 27), is now regarded by most psychologists as rather meaningless. Mankind's pool of the various genes that may affect performance on an intelligence test is infinitely varied; no two people except identical twins inherit the same pattern. Moreover, no two people including identical twins are ever subject to exactly the same environmental influences every hour of the day and every day of their lives. The prevailing view

481

among psychologists is that in the constant interaction between heredity and environment, heredity probably sets a top and bottom limit on the individual's I.Q. score and that environment then determines where within this range the score will actually fall (28).

As to the possible range of I.Q. scores set by inheritance, opinions vary. One student of the question has suggested that an unusually stimulating environment can raise the I.Q. by ten points and an unusually restrictive environment lower it by ten points, resulting in a total possible range of twenty points (29). Others believe that the range varies from one person to another, that it is smallest for people born with limited capacities, and that it is greatest among those who are potentially very gifted. One investigator has suggested that a person who inherits an unusually favorable pattern of genes may show an I.Q. of well over 150 if he grows up in the most stimulating possible environment or as low as around 65 if his intellectual development is thwarted (30). Whichever estimate is accepted, it is enough to account for all the differences that have been found in average I.Q. scores for different groups and to cast serious doubt on the possibility that any social class, race, or nationality might have any significant superiority in the gene pool that goes to make up the I.Q.

changes in I.Q.

A change to a more favorable environment, as was shown by the study of the Iowa orphans, often produces a substantial rise in I.Q. To be most effective, it appears, the change should take place during the first six or seven years, when the various skills that go to make up adult I.Q. are developing rapidly. The importance of the preschool environment has been recognized by educators who are attempting (for example, in Project Head Start) to improve the school performance of children who come from low-income homes, which do not ordinarily foster the kinds of skills that result in school achievement and high I.Q. scores. It has been found that almost any kind of enrichment of the preschool atmosphere can produce changes; for example, a number of studies of the effect of nursery schooling have shown an average improvement in I.Q. of 5.6 points (31). There is considerable doubt, however, as to whether the increase persists or is only temporary.

One of the most carefully planned and measured attempts at special training for preschool children from impoverished families, plus consultation designed to help their mothers provide a more stimulating environment, has shown mixed results. The children gained in I.Q. while the program was in effect; but by the time they had finished two years of school, they seemed to be losing at least some of their gains. The educators who conducted the study have concluded that programs of the Head Start type, while helpful, cannot adequately change or fully compensate for home environments or schools that do not promote the skills measured by intelligence tests (32).

A Head Start class

Spontaneous Changes. Even children who remain in the homes in which they were born and receive no unusual outside attention often show substantial

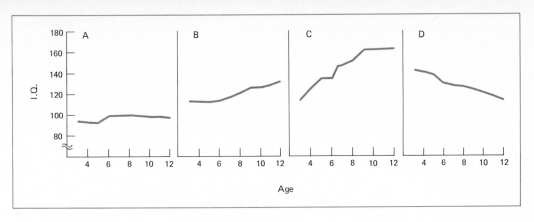

changes in children's I.Q.'s

14-11 When children were tested annually for I.Q., these were some of the curves obtained. About half the children gave nearly straight-line results as in A, showing little change in I.Q. Some showed pronounced improvement as in B (from about 110 to about 130); some showed striking improvement as in C (from about 110 to about 160); and some showed substantial decreases as in D (from about 140 to about 110). (33)

changes in I.Q. over the years. In one study 140 children were tested every year from the ages of two to twelve. For about half of them the I.Q. showed little change—but for the other half there were changes upward or downward that in some cases reached striking proportions. In Figure 14–11, which illustrates some of the individual records from this study, note that one child's I.Q. rose from about 110 to 160, while another's dropped from about 140 to 110.

The children who gained, when compared with those who declined, were found to be more independent, competitive, and aggressive in conversation. They worked harder in school, showed a strong desire to master intellectual problems, and were persistent when faced with difficult tasks. Since these are personality traits that our society encourages in boys—while encouraging girls to be dependent and passive and not to seem smarter than their brothers—it is not surprising that boys were more likely to show increases in I.Q. and that girls were more likely to show decreases.

What conclusions can be drawn from this study? First, it appears obvious that the I.Q. is by no means a constant and unchanging trait like a person's fingerprints. Parents and teachers often take a child's score on an intelligence test too seriously; they give up on the child who has made a low score and expect too much from the child who has made a high score. Second, it appears that intelligence tests as now designed measure achievement motivation as well as ability, for the strength of the child's desire for intellectual achievement seems to be closely related to upward or downward changes in I.Q. Parents who emphasize and reward intellectual accomplishment and independence and who provide a model of intellectual achievement with which the child can identify are the most likely to find their children gaining in I.Q. over the years.

The study raises another interesting question: Can a person improve his I.Q. through a deliberate effort toward better achievement? The answer is not known. But certainly some college students who make rather poor grades as freshmen suddenly begin making much better grades later. It may be that retesting of these students would show an increase in I.Q.

are people getting smarter?

There is no evidence at all that the human species has any greater inborn intellectual capacity today than it had thousands of years ago—but there is some rather impressive evidence that the average level of intelligence, as measured by standard tests, has been rising, at least in the fairly recent years during which measurements have been kept. It appears quite likely that today the average I.Q. of 100 represents a greater knowledge of the concepts and rules measured by the tests than it did in the past.

The best evidence to this effect comes from a comparison of a large group of presumably representative and therefore "average" soldiers of the Second World War, who were tested in the early 1940's, with a similar group of First World War soldiers, tested a little more than twenty years earlier. On the very similar kinds of group intelligence tests given in the two wars, it turned out that the soldier of the early 1940's who scored exactly average, with an I.Q. of 100, would have been way above average with an I.Q. of 115 if he had been competing with the soldiers of twenty years earlier on the test given at that time (34). There is also some evidence that the average I.Q.'s of children rose during the 1930's and 1940's in Scotland (35) and in England (36).

In view of what was said earlier about the effect of environment on I.Q., it is perhaps only to be expected that the average I.Q. score should have risen. In recent years vast numbers of people have moved from the lower classes into the middle and upper. Millions of people have moved from rural areas into cities. Schools have been improved, and the number of students who complete elementary school, high school, and college has greatly increased. Radio and television have exposed children to verbal stimulation and variety. Thus the average young American today may very well possess more of the kinds of abilities measured by intelligence tests than did the average young American of several generations ago. On the other hand, at least part of the difference in test scores may be due to the fact that people today have had more experience taking tests.

I.Q. and age

As has been said, the ability to pass increasingly difficult items on intelligence tests grows rapidly during the years from birth to age seventeen—and particularly in the earliest years of childhood. This fact leads to some interesting questions: At what age does the kind of ability measured by intelligence tests reach its peak? Once the peak is attained, does the ability then decline during middle and old age?

"You let me win, didn't you, Daddy?"

B. Tobey, © 1971 Saturday Review, Inc.

14-12

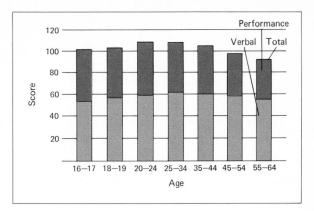

These are the scores made by various age groups on the Wechsler Adult Intelligence Scale. Note that the total score rises through the early twenties, remains fairly steady until thirty-four, then begins to decline rather sharply. Much of the decline after thirty-four, however, is caused by lower scores on the performance part of the test. On the verbal part the plateau lasts through the age of forty-four and the decline after forty-four is relatively slight. (37)

The answers to these questions are not easy to obtain, because they are complicated by the probability, which has just been mentioned, that the average score on intelligence tests has been rising generation by generation in recent years. If one were to administer the same kind of intelligence test to large numbers of people from teenagers to sixty-year-olds, one would naturally expect the younger people to make higher average scores than the older people—and this is indeed what happens.

For example, in standardizing a recent version of the Wechsler Adult Intelligence Scale, the test was administered to representative samples of various age groups from sixteen through sixty-four; and the results were as illustrated in Figure 14-12. Note that the average total score rose through the early twenties, remained more or less on a plateau until thirty-four, then began a fairly sharp and steady decline. However, the age-by-age patterns differed for the two parts of the test, the verbal items and the performance items. Ability at verbal skills, after reaching its peak between twenty-five and thirty-four, remained fairly constant through the age of forty-four and afterward showed only a relatively small decline. Ability on performance items began to decline after the early twenties and at a fairly rapid rate.

What would be the results of a study in which the very same people could be tested over the years, beginning in their teens and continuing into their sixties? Despite the difficulties of making such a study, fortunately one investigator has managed to compare the scores made on a group intelligence test by nearly a hundred men during the First World War, when they were college freshmen averaging nineteen years old, with their scores on the same kind of test taken when they were fifty years old and again when they were sixty-one. The results are illustrated in Figure 14-13.

As the figure shows, scores on the arithmetic items in the test were highest at nineteen and scores on reasoning items highest at sixty-one, while scores on verbal items were substantially higher at fifty than at nineteen but then declined slightly at sixty-one. The total score rose fairly substantially from nineteen to fifty and afterward showed a slight decline. The results are not entirely satisfactory because they are for men only—and for a group that had an above-average I.Q.

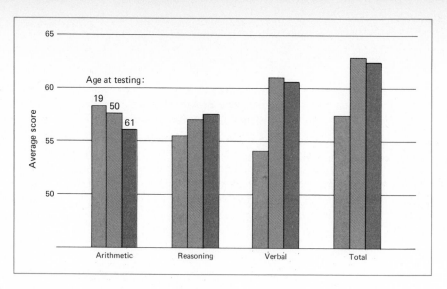

age and intelligence test scores

14-13 The bars show the scores (not I.Q.'s) made on an intelligence test by a group of men first when they were nineteen-year-old college freshmen, again when they were fifty years old, and a third time when they were sixty-one. For a discussion of the results, see the text. (Adapted from 38)

at first testing and presumably led lives more favorable than average to continued intellectual growth. However, they do offer a strong indication that intelligence—at least as measured by present tests—is by no means the monopoly of the young and that there is hardly any cause for despair over what will happen to our mental abilities as we get older.

I.Q. and occupation

The classic study of the relationship between I.Q. and occupation was based on data available from the thousands of men who took the Army's group intelligence test during the Second World War. The results, illustrated in Figure 14-14, show some pronounced differences in the average I.Q. of men in various kinds of jobs, ranging all the way from 93 for miners and 94 for farmhands to around 120 for accountants, lawyers, and engineers. Even more interesting is the large range of I.Q.'s found in every occupation. Some of the miners and farmhands turned out to have I.Q.'s above the average for accountants, lawyers, and engineers.

The study seems to indicate that the various occupations demand a certain minimum level of I.Q. A man who is able to hold a job as a truck driver, for example, might not be able to hold a job as a teacher. In every occupation, however, there are some men with I.Q.'s well above average who presumably could hold their own in even the most demanding professions. One can assume that many of these men lacked the education, opportunity, or motivation to enter higher-level jobs.

Aside from its effect in determining occupational choice, to what extent is I.Q. related to success in life? The evidence is somewhat indirect. One study of college graduates attempted to find the relation between college grades, which as noted earlier are correlated with I.Q., and success as measured by income. In general, A students were found to earn more than B students, and B students more than C and D students; but the differences were smaller than one might expect (40). The differences were greatest among teachers, artists, clergymen, and government workers (all holding jobs where the academic skills measured by intelligence tests are likely to be most useful) and smallest among businessmen (where other skills not measured by present tests may be more important).

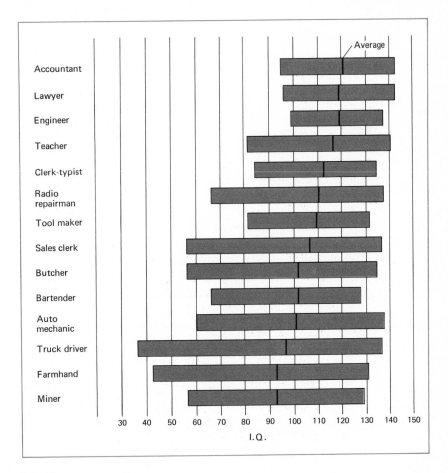

I.Q.'s by occupation

14—14   The bars show the range of I.Q.'s found for men in various occupations in the United States and also the average I.Q. for each occupation. Note that the average I.Q. of accountants was 121, of miners only 93, yet some miners had higher I.Q.'s than some accountants. (39)

Thus a high I.Q. does not guarantee financial success, and a relatively low I.Q. does not seem to doom a person to failure. In some occupations, indeed, a high I.Q. apparently can be a handicap. A study of young women employed in a chocolate factory, for example, found that the most intelligent among them were the most easily bored (41). A study of clerks employed at routine jobs showed that the turnover was highest among the most intelligent (42).

the mentally retarded

People whose I.Q.'s are below 70 are called the *mentally retarded,* who make up 2.28 percent of the population. This is a small percentage, but in a nation like the United States, with a population around 200,000,000, it represents a large number of total cases. There are about 4,560,000 mentally retarded people in the United States, and mental retardation is therefore a widespread and serious problem.

The standard classification of the mentally retarded, from mild to profound, is shown in Figure 14–15, along with a description of their characteristics as infants, children, and adults. Fortunately most cases of mental retardation fall into the "mild" class. These people, though they have trouble in school and often do not get past the sixth-grade level in reading and arithmetic, can usually function adequately as adults; they manage to hold jobs, get along in society, and in general take care of themselves. At the other extreme are the cases of "profound" retardation; these people never learn to do much more than walk and talk a little, and they require care and supervision all their lives.

What causes mental retardation? Some cases stem from specific biological abnormalities. Among these are cases of *Mongolism,* apparently caused by the presence of an extra chromosome (making a total of forty-seven instead of the normal forty-six). The Mongoloid child has many other abnormalities besides mental retardation, including unusual bone structure in the hands, feet, and skull; the condition takes its name from the round face and slant eyes characteristic of its victims. Another form of serious retardation is *cretinism,* caused by an abnormally low level of secretion by the thyroid gland. If detected in time, this type of mental retardation can be prevented by giving the child thyroid substance. Other forms of retardation can be caused by biological abnormalities in metabolism, malnutrition, injury to the brain at birth, and brain damage caused by diseases, such as German measles, suffered by the mother during pregnancy.

There are many other cases, however, where no physical cause is apparent. One cannot be sure whether retardation is due to an undetected illness, a poor and unstimulating environment, or heredity.

Most people who are mentally retarded can profit from special training. Considerable advances in training have been made in recent years, and there are now many state institutions with a good record of preparing the retarded to function in society. A recent follow-up study was made of men and women twenty years after they had left a New York State institution. Some of the reports on these people follow.

Type	Characteristics from birth to adulthood		
	BIRTH THROUGH FIVE	SIX THROUGH TWENTY	TWENTY-ONE AND OVER
MILD (I.Q. 53–69)	Often not noticed as retarded by casual observer but is slower to walk, feed himself, and talk than most children.	Can acquire practical skills and useful reading and arithmetic to a third- to sixth-grade level with special education. Can be guided toward social conformity.	Can usually achieve social and vocational skills adequate to self-maintenance; may need occasional guidance and support when under unusual social or economic stress.
MODERATE (36–52)	Noticeable delays in motor development, especially in speech; responds to training in various self-help activities.	Can learn simple communication, elementary health and safety habits, and simple manual skills; does not progress in functional reading or arithmetic.	Can perform simple tasks under sheltered conditions; participates in simple recreation; travels alone in familiar places; usually incapable of self-maintenance.
SEVERE (20–35)	Marked delay in motor development; little or no communication skill; may respond to training in elementary self-help—for example, self-feeding.	Usually walks barring specific disability; has some understanding of speech and some response; can profit from systematic habit training.	Can conform to daily routines and repetitive activities; needs continuing direction and supervision in protective environment.
PROFOUND (below 20)	Gross retardation; minimal capacity for functioning in sensorimotor areas; needs nursing care.	Obvious delays in all areas of development; shows basic emotional responses; may respond to skillful training in use of legs, hands, and jaws; needs close supervision.	May walk, need nursing care, have primitive speech; usually benefits from regular physical activity; incapable of self-maintenance.

the retarded

14-15 This description of the characteristics of the mentally retarded—of various degrees and at various ages—was drawn up by the U.S. President's Panel on Mental Retardation. (43)

Male, 37 years old, I.Q. 57. Has a license as practical nurse. Has made an "excellent adjustment," owns a car, and is saving money—but is reluctant to marry because he fears his children would be retarded.

Male, 41, I.Q. 51. Has been employed by the same company for twenty years, currently as a tractor driver. Considered "an excellent and loyal" employee. Is married and buying a home.

Female, 52, I.Q. 63. Has been employed as a domestic worker by the same family for twenty years. Does fine handwork, makes her own clothing, and is good at repairing plumbing and wiring.

Female, 41, I.Q. 60. Was pregnant when admitted to institution at fifteen. Afterward worked and managed to support herself and her son. Now happily married and living on a farm; is a good housekeeper. (44)

the mentally gifted

At the opposite extreme from the mentally retarded are the 2.28 percent of the population (again 4,560,000 in all in the United States) who have I.Q.'s over 130. These are the *mentally gifted.* At the very top of the group are the people called *geniuses,* whose I.Q.'s may range up to 190.

A genius is capable of remarkable accomplishments, even early in life. Mozart, who surely would have scored near the very maximum had intelligence tests been invented at the time, began composing music when he was four and wrote a symphony when he was eight. John Stuart Mill, the nineteenth-century economist, read Plato in the original Greek before he was nine. In more recent times Norbert Wiener, the mathematician, graduated from high school at the age of twelve and from college at fifteen.

A classic study of the mentally gifted was begun in 1921 by Lewis M. Terman and continued by him and his associates for many years. He began with 1500 California schoolchildren who had I.Q.'s of 140 or more, and he managed to follow many of them into middle age.

As children, Terman's subjects were superior in many respects besides I.Q. They were above average in height (by about an inch), weight, and appearance. They were better adjusted than average and showed superiority in social activity and leadership.

In later life, not all the gifted children lived up to their early promise. Some of them dropped out of school and wound up in routine occupations; some, even though they went to college, turned out to be vocational misfits and drifters. But these were the exceptions, and their records tended to show problems of emotional and social adjustment and low motivation toward achievement. On the whole the group was outstandingly successful. In large proportion, the gifted went to college, achieved above-average and often brilliant records, and went on to make important contributions in fields ranging from medicine and law to literature and from business administration to government service. Many earned the recognition of a listing in *Who's Who* or *American Men of Science.* The average level of accomplishment was far higher than could be expected of a group chosen at random.

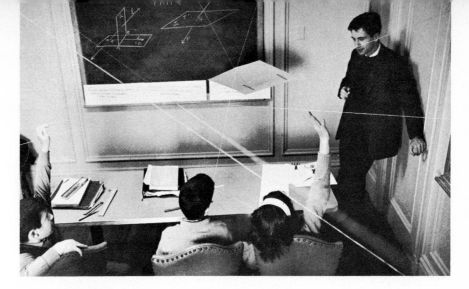

a special project for gifted children

14-16 In a class for the gifted, nine- and ten-year-olds get an early start on the principles of geometry.

The child born with superior mental capacities, however, can meet serious problems. Presumably many such children are born into homes and social environments that do not encourage their development. Indeed the potentially gifted child may in some environments seem to be a know-it-all and come to be resented by his parents, other children, and teachers. If he stays in the same grades as other children his age, he may be bored by the work and become lazy or difficult to discipline; if he skips grades he may have trouble adjusting socially to older children. In some ways the gifted child can benefit from specialized training just as much as the retarded child—as some schools have recognized by providing enriched activities as illustrated in Figure 14–16.

b. other kinds of tests

Although intelligence tests are the most widely used and generally the most valid, there are scores of other kinds of tests, devised for special purposes. Among them, and worthy of special note, are tests of *vocational aptitude, interests,* and *personality.*

1. vocational aptitude

Many tests have been devised in an attempt to measure the skills required for certain kinds of occupations—skills such as mechanical ability, the special kinds of manual dexterity involved in various factory jobs, the motor coordination required for operating complicated machinery, and the speed and accuracy at dealing with details required in clerical jobs.

491

14-17

Using a tweezers, the subject is taking part of the *Crawford Small Parts Dexterity Test.*

14-18

If the pieces shown separately were put together, which of the five figures lettered A through E would they make? These are sample items from the Revised Minnesota Paper Form Board, a paper-and-pencil test of mechanical ability. (45)

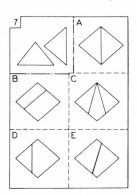 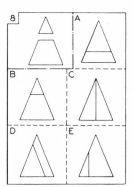

In general, the present tests of vocational aptitude are considerably less satisfactory than intelligence tests in that their correlation with actual success on a job is usually much lower than the correlation between I.Q. and success in school. However, they often offer valuable clues about an individual's pattern of skills, and in the hands of trained counselors they serve as a useful adjunct to vocational guidance.

Some vocational aptitude tests measure actual performance, as does the manual dexterity test illustrated in Figure 14-17. Others, such as those illustrated in Figures 14-18 and 14-19, are written tests.

Follow each numbered line with your eyes to the square at right where it ends and write in its number.

Starting with the circled dot, draw lines between dots to copy the figure at the left.

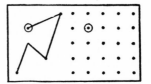

Next to each X, place the number of other blocks that this particular block touches.

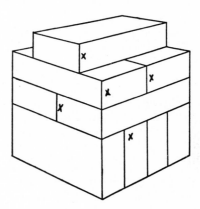

the MacQuarrie test

14-19 Above are sample items from the MacQuarrie Test for Mechanical Ability, another paper-and-pencil test. (46)

One widely used test is in fact a battery of tests measuring several different kinds of vocational ability. It is called the *Differential Aptitude Tests;* sample items are shown in Figure 14-20. As will be seen, it measures eight different kinds of ability, for which scores are calculated separately. The test provides a good indication of the abilities at which the individual is above average and those at which he is below average and thus serves as a general guide to the kind of jobs at which he would be most likely to succeed.

14-20

These sample items illustrate the eight types of vocational ability measured by the Differential Aptitude Tests. (47)

VERBAL REASONING

Each of the fifty sentences in this test has the first word and the last word left out. You are to pick out words that will fill the blanks so that the sentence will be true and sensible.

For each sentence you are to choose from among five pairs of words to fill the blanks. The first word of the pair you choose goes in the blank space at the beginning of the sentence; the second word of the pair goes in the blank at the end of the sentence.

...... is to water as eat is to ......

A. continue —— drive
B. foot —— enemy
C. drink —— food
D. girl —— industry
E. drink —— enemy

NUMERICAL ABILITY

This test consists of forty numerical problems. Next to each problem there are five answers. You are to pick out the correct answer.

Add 13   A 14   Subtract 30   A 15
     12   B 25   20   B 26
              C 16   C 16
              D 59   D 8
              E none of these   E none of these

ABSTRACT REASONING

Each row consists of four figures called Problem Figures and five called Answer Figures. The four Problem Figures make a series. You are to find out which one of the Answer Figures would be the next, or the fifth one in the series. Note that the lines in the Problem Figures are falling down. In the first square the line stands straight up, and as you go from square to square the line falls more and more to the right.

PROBLEM FIGURES   ANSWER FIGURES

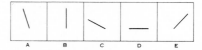

SPACE RELATIONS

This test consists of sixty patterns which can be folded into figures. For each pattern, four figures are shown. You are to decide which *one* of these figures can be made from the pattern shown.

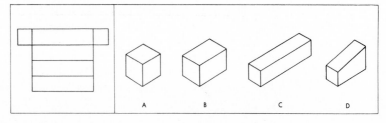

MECHANICAL REASONING

This test consists of a number of pictures and questions about those pictures.

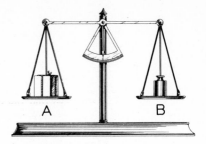

Which weighs more?

(If equal, mark C.)

CLERICAL SPEED AND ACCURACY

This is a test to see how quickly and accurately you can compare letter and number combinations. In each Test Item one of the five is *underlined*. You are to look at the *one* combination that is underlined, find the *same* one after that item number of the separate answer sheet, and fill in the space under it (as has been done here).

TEST ITEMS

V. <u>AB</u> AC AD AE AF

W. aA aB BA Ba <u>Bb</u>

X. A7 7A B7 <u>7B</u> AB

Y. Aa Ba <u>bA</u> BA bB

Z. 3A 3B <u>33</u> B3 BB

SAMPLE OF ANSWER SHEET

	AC	AE	AF	AB	AD
V.				█	
	BA	Ba	Bb	aA	aB
W.		█			
	7B	B7	AB	7A	A7
X.	█				
	Aa	bA	bB	Ba	BA
Y.		█			
	BB	3B	B3	3A	33
Z.					█

LANGUAGE USAGE: SPELLING

This test is composed of a series of words. Some of them are correctly spelled; some are incorrectly spelled. You are to indicate whether each word is spelled right or wrong.

W. man

X. gurl

Y. catt

Z. dog

	R	W
W.	█	
X.		█
Y.		█
Z.	█	

LANGUAGE USAGE: GRAMMAR

This test consists of a series of sentences, each divided into four parts lettered A, B, C, and D. You are to look at each sentence and decide which part has an error in grammar, punctuation, or spelling. If there is no error in a sentence, fill in the space under the letter E.

X. Ain't we / going to / the office / next week?
    A   B   C   D

Y. I went / to a ball / game with / Jimmy.
    A   B   C   D

	A	B	C	D	E
X.	█				
Y.					█

2. interests

In addition to ability there is another important factor to be considered in choosing a vocation. All of us, when we decide on our life's work, must ask: How interesting will the work be to a person like me?

The attempt to provide some kind of scientific answer to this question has resulted in what are called _interest tests_. As the name indicates, interest tests measure the subject's preferences in literature, music, art, science, school subjects, social affairs, kinds of people, and a wide range of activities ranging from butterfly collecting to repairing a clock or making a speech. The subject's pattern of interests can then be compared to the pattern shown by people who are already successfully holding various kinds of jobs.

One widely used interest test is the _Strong Vocational Interest Blank_, which contains about 400 items on which the subject is asked to list his likes, dislikes, and preferences. His scores can be compared to those made by men in around sixty different occupations, ranging from accountant to Y.M.C.A. secretary, and by women in around thirty occupations, including that of housewife. For each occupation that he is considering, the subject receives a score of A to C. A score of A shows a close correspondence between the subject's interests and those of people already in that occupation and is considered an excellent indication that the subject would like the job. A score of C shows a very low correspondence and is considered unfavorable. The in-between scores, from B+ to B−, are considered indecisive.

The _Kuder Preference Record_ is an interest test in which various types of activity are presented in groups of three, as shown in Figure 14–21. The subject is asked to indicate which of the three he likes best and which he likes least. There are several forms of this test. The one that has been used the longest and most widely is the Kuder Preference Record-Vocational, in which the subject's scores are compared with those made by the general population, resulting in a profile on ten separate groups of interests as shown in Figure 14–22. The test has been

P.	Visit an art gallery	○ P ○	
Q.	Browse in a library	○ Q ●	
R.	Visit a museum	● R ○	
S.	Collect autographs	● S ○	
T.	Collect coins.	○ T ○	
U.	Collect butterflies.	○ U ●	

the Kuder test

14-21 In each set of three sample items on the Kuder Preference Record-Vocational the subject has punched a hole in the left-hand column to indicate which type of activity he would most like to engage in (for example, visit a museum) and a hole in the right-hand column to indicate which type he would like least (browse in a library). (48)

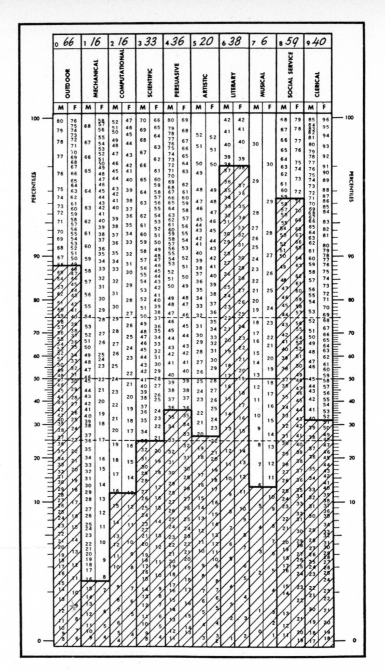

a Kuder preference profile

14-22 As shown by the bars, this subject has an exceptionally high interest in the outdoors (where his score was on the 88th percentile), literary matters (99th percentile), and social service (97th percentile). In all the other seven fields his interest is below average—especially for mechanical matters (below the 2nd percentile), computational (11th percentile), and musical (13th percentile). Presumably he would be considerably happier in charge of library and story activities at a camp for the underprivileged than as an automobile mechanic or accountant. (49)

standardized separately for men and women and for high school, college, and adult groups. The Kuder Preference Record-Personal gives a profile of the subject's preferences in matters called Sociable (being in groups), Practical (dealing with familiar and stable situations), Theoretical (dealing with ideas), Agreeable (avoiding conflicts), and Dominant (directing other people).

3. personality

The search for reliable and valid measures of all the various traits that go to make up personality has been carried on intensively. A test that could accurately measure even a single aspect of personality—for example, degree and type of anxiety—would be an invaluable research tool, opening up almost infinite possibilities for further study. A test that could accurately distinguish between normal and neurotic personalities would enable clinical psychologists to find the people most in need of psychotherapy and to practice preventive psychotherapy on children near the danger line. It would also provide a measure of the effectiveness of various kinds of psychotherapy and perhaps lead to the discovery of new methods. It would make comparisons possible among people who have grown up in different environments and with different kinds of experiences and thus greatly add to the knowledge of developmental psychology. Conceivably, by spotting certain kinds of disturbed personalities it could prevent tragedies like the assassination of the Kennedys and Martin Luther King, Jr.

Thus a great deal of time, energy, and ingenuity has gone into the creation of personality tests. But the goal has been elusive. Although current personality tests are valuable, the ideal kinds of measures have not yet been devised. Personality is a composite of many elements—the product of a tangled and endless web of experiences beginning at birth, continuing throughout life, and unique for each individual—and the difficulties in measuring the elements are staggering.

The personality tests now in use, all of which have some virtues and many limitations, fall into three classes: 1) *objective tests,* 2) *situational tests,* and 3) *projective tests.*

Objective Tests of Personality. The *objective tests* get their name because they are administered and scored according to a standard procedure, and the results are not seriously affected by the opinions or prejudices of the examiner. Like group intelligence tests, they are usually paper-and-pencil tests that have been standardized for large groups of representative subjects.

The *Allport-Vernon-Lindzey Study of Values* is a measure of the subject's concern with six broad fields of human activity and thought—theoretical, economic, aesthetic, social, political, and religious. It is made up of questions like those shown in Figure 14-23, designed to reveal whether the subject values religion above economic matters or literature above sports. One of the interesting findings made with the Study of Values is illustrated in Figure 14-24, which shows the differences in the average scores made by men and by women. Note that men tend to place more value on theoretical, economic, and political matters; women on aesthetic, social, and religious matters.

PART I. In the boxes to the right, rate the two alternative answers 3 and 0 if you agree with one and disagree with the other; if you have only a slight preference for one over the other, rate them 2 and 1, respectively.

EXAMPLE

If you should see the following news items with headlines of equal size in your morning paper, which would you read more attentively? (a) PROTESTANT LEADERS TO CONSULT ON RECONCILIATION; (b) GREAT IMPROVEMENTS IN MARKET CONDITIONS.

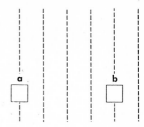

PART II. In the boxes to the right, rate the answers 4, 3, 2, and 1 in order of personal preference, giving 4 to the most attractive and 1 to the least attractive alternative.

EXAMPLE

In your opinion, can a man who works in business all the week best spend Sunday in —
a. trying to educate himself by reading serious books
b. trying to win at golf, or racing
c. going to an orchestral concert
d. hearing a really good sermon

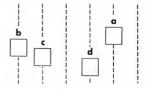

a test of values

14-23 In the Allport-Vernon-Lindzey Study of Values the subject is asked to give numerical values to his preferences among various activities and opinions. (50)

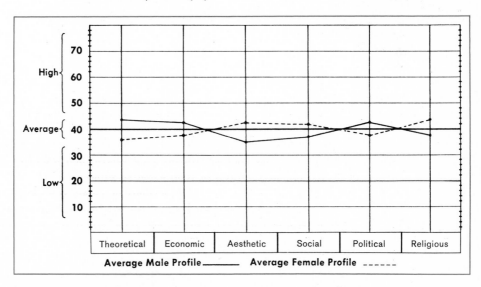

sex differences in values

14-24 On the six types of values measured by the Allport-Vernon-Lindzey Study of Values, these pronounced differences have been found in the average scores of men and of women. (50)

The *Minnesota Multiphasic Personality Inventory,* called MMPI for short, is a widely used test designed to measure many aspects of personality, from introversion and extroversion to tendencies toward schizophrenia and paranoia. The test is composed of nearly 600 statements like those shown in Figure 14–25; the subject is asked to indicate whether the statement is true or untrue of his own behavior and thoughts or to mark "cannot say." The answers are scored on nine or ten different scales for various personality traits and four other scales that measure the subject's attitude toward the test, resulting in personality profiles like those in Figure 14-26. Numerous studies made with the MMPI have indicated that high scores on scales 1, 2, and 3 are often made by neurotics; high scores on scales 6, 7, 8, and 9 by psychotics. A high peak on scale 4 is characteristic of delinquents. As is also true of other tests of personality, the accuracy of the MMPI scores depends on the willingness of the subject to answer truthfully; but one of the scales is designed to detect attempts to falsify answers to achieve favorable ratings.

Situational Tests. In a *situational test,* the examiner observes the behavior of the subject in a situation deliberately created to bring out certain aspects of his personality. For example, the subject might be asked to carry out some difficult mechanical task with the assistance of "helpers" who are in fact stooges and who behave in an uncooperative and insulting fashion (53). Or he may be put through what is called a stress interview, in which the people asking him questions are deliberately hostile and pretend to disbelieve his answers (54).

Unfortunately it is difficult to know whether the situational test actually seems real to the subject and whether his motivation and behavior are the same

---

1. I have certainly had more than my share of things to worry about.
2. I think that I feel more intensely than other people do.
3. I have never done anything dangerous for the thrill of it.
4. I think nearly everyone would tell a lie to keep out of trouble.
5. I am happy most of the time.
6. I tend to be on my guard with people who are somewhat more friendly than I had expected.
7. My mother or father often made me obey even when I thought that it was unreasonable.
8. I feel uneasy indoors.
9. I refuse to play some games because I am not good at them.
10. I find it hard to keep my mind on a task or job.

MMPI items

14-25 The Minnesota Multiphasic Personality Inventory is made up of statements like these, which the subject is asked to score as true, false, or "cannot say." (51)

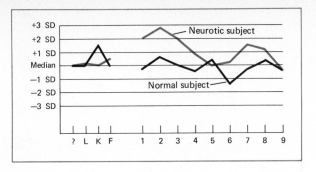

MMPI profiles

14-26 The curves show the profile of scores of two subjects on the Minnesota Multiphasic Personality Inventory (52). The key to the thirteen different scales is as follows:

?   Number of "cannot say" answers.
L   Indicates faking on test in attempt to look good.
K   High score shows attempt to defend self against possible criticism; low score an excessive tendency to reveal defects.
F   Shows carelessness in answering questions.
1   Indicates anxiety over health; hypochondria.
2   Shows feelings of depression, worthlessness, and pessimism.
3   Shows tendency toward psychosomatic ailments.
4   Shows lack of social and moral responsibility.
5   For men, high score shows a tendency to be feminine in interests and emotions; for women, high score indicates an aggressive and masculine attitude.
6   Indicates tendencies toward delusions of persecution.
7   Indicates phobias and compulsions.
8   Indicates bizarre patterns of thought and hallucinations, as in schizophrenia.
9   Indicates tendency to be manic in mood; emotional excitability.

in the test situation as they would be in real life. Moreover, two different observers watching the subject's behavior may reach different conclusions about it. Thus situational tests, though they may give valuable clues to personality traits, do not meet the four ideal test requirements of objectivity, standardization, reliability, and validity. They should be used and interpreted with caution.

Projective Tests. The *projective test* can best be described in connection with Figure 14-27, which shows a picture similar to those presented to the subject in the *Thematic Apperception Test,* called TAT for short. The subject is asked to make up a story about the picture, telling what has led up to the scene, what is happening, and how events will turn out. The theory is that the subject will project some of his own personality traits into the picture and that the story he makes up will reveal something about his attitudes, feelings, motives, and anxieties. For example, there would appear to be a considerable amount of self-revelation in the following story told by one subject about the picture in Figure 14-27.

14-27 What kind of story does this picture tell? What led up to the situation? What is happening? How will events turn out? These are the questions asked about the pictures in the Thematic Apperception Test, to which this drawing is similar. You may want to try making up your own story before reading the discussion and the story made up by one subject, which will be found in the text. (55)

The older woman represents evil and she is trying to persuade the younger one to leave her husband and run off and lead a life of fun and gaiety. The younger one is afraid to do it—afraid of what others will think, afraid she will regret the action. But the older one knows that she wants to leave and so she insists over and over again. I am not sure how it ends. Perhaps the younger woman turns and walks away and ignores the older woman.

The TAT technique has found its most widespread and successful use in measuring the strength of the achievement motive (56). A tendency to invent stories that contain frequent and intense elements of striving and ambition—or that on the contrary show little concern with achievement—appears to be a better measure of this motive than the judgment of people who know the subject well (57) or even the subject's own assessment of his desire to achieve (58). Much of the research that has been done on the origin and operation of the achievement motive has been based on stories told about TAT pictures.

Another well-known example of a projective technique is the *Rorschach Test,* in which the subject is asked to tell what he sees in a series of inkblots like the one illustrated in Figure 14–28. There are ten such blots, some in black and white and some in color, and ordinarily the subject sees twenty to forty different things in them. His answers are scored for a number of different dimensions. For example, a tendency to respond to the blot as a whole is considered to indicate that the subject thinks in terms of abstractions and generalities; a tendency to pick out many minor details that most people ignore may indicate an overconcern for detail.

The *Holtzman Inkblot Test* uses forty-five inkblots, and the subject is asked to make a single response to each. Answers to this test have been standardized for a number of different groups. The scores of a college student, for example,

502

14-28

This is an inkblot like those used in the Rorschach Test. Subjects are asked to examine it and report everything they see. (59)

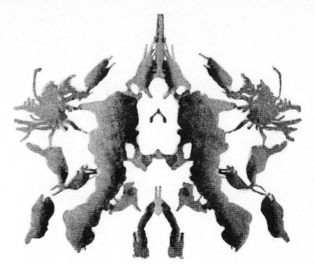

can be compared with those of other students or with those of a group of known schizophrenics. The Holtzman test represents an approach toward a more objective method of scoring projective tests.

Most projective tests require a high degree of skill and experience on the part of the person who gives and interprets them; even trained examiners may reach different conclusions. Aside from the TAT research into the achievement motive, they have been used mostly by clinical psychologists, who often find them a valuable and time-saving supplement to other methods of exploring the problems of patients.

summary 1. A psychological test is a device for measuring a sample of behavior, often in an attempt to predict future behavior.

2. The four requirements of a test are that it be:
   a. *Objective*—meaning that the test can be given and scored in the same manner by any qualified person and that the results will be unaffected by the tester's personal opinions or prejudices.
   b. *Standardized*—based on a large and representative sample so that the individual's score can be interpreted by comparison with the scores of other people.
   c. *Reliable*—yielding similar scores when the same person is tested on different occasions.
   d. *Valid*—found to measure the characteristic that it is supposed to measure.

3. A *group test* can be given to many people at the same time. An *individual test* is given by a trained examiner to one person at a time.

4. An *aptitude test* measures the subject's capacity to learn a new skill. An *achievement test* measures his present level of skill or knowledge.

5. Intelligence tests provide a measure of the subject's *intelligence quotient,* or *I.Q.* The I.Q. is obtained by comparing the individual's raw score on the test with the scores of a standardization group of people his age.

6. All modern intelligence tests have a high degree of reliability and a correlation of around .40 to .60 with grades made in school.

7. Since intelligence tests must rely to a certain extent on the subject's present level of knowledge, they tend to favor people who have grown up in environments where they have had an opportunity to acquire the kinds of knowledge and language abilities typical of the middle and upper classes. Children from upper- and middle-class homes make higher average scores than children from lower-class homes; city children tend to make higher average scores than children from rural areas; and whites make higher average scores than blacks.

8. Intelligence can be defined as *the ability to profit from experience, to learn new information, and to adjust to new situations.*

9. According to Thurstone, intelligence is composed of seven *primary mental abilities* (verbal comprehension, word fluency, number, space, associative memory, perceptual speed, and general reasoning) plus a "general factor." Other investigators believe that intelligence is made up of as many as 120 different factors.

10. Studies of identical twins and foster children have suggested that intelligence is determined partly by heredity and partly by environmental influences. The prevailing view among psychologists is that heredity sets a top and bottom limit on an individual's I.Q. and that environment then determines where within this range the score will actually fall.

11. Even when a child remains in the same home environment, his I.Q. may show spontaneous changes over the years of as much as 50 points, upward or downward. The child's motivation for intellectual achievement seems to be closely related to these changes.

12. The 2.28 percent of the population with an I.Q. below 70 are described as *mentally retarded.* The 2.28 percent with an I.Q. above 130 are described as *mentally gifted.*

13. In addition to intelligence tests, other tests include a) *vocational aptitude tests,* measuring the ability to perform specialized skills required in various kinds of jobs; b) *interest tests,* measuring the individual's interests in and preferences for various kinds of activities; and c) *personality tests.*

14. There are three classes of personality tests:
    a. *Objective tests,* such as the Allport-Vernon-Lindzey Study of Values and the Minnesota Multiphasic Personality Inventory.
    b. *Situational tests,* in which the examiner observes the behavior of the subject in a situation deliberately created to reveal some aspect of his personality.
    c. *Projective tests,* such as the Thematic Apperception Test and the Rorschach Test, in which the subject supposedly inserts or projects aspects of his own personality into the stories he makes up about ambiguous pictures or into the kinds of objects he sees in inkblots.

recommended reading

Anastasi, A. *Psychological testing,* 3rd ed. New York: Macmillan, 1968.

Brim, O. G., et al. *American beliefs and attitudes about intelligence.* New York: Russell Sage Foundation, 1969.

Cronbach, L. J. *Essentials of psychological testing,* 3rd ed. New York: Harper & Row, 1970.

Cronbach, L. J. The interpretation and application of ability tests. In his *Educational psychology,* 2nd ed. New York: Harcourt Brace Jovanovich, 1963, pp. 233-67.

Hoffman, B. *The tyranny of testing.* New York: Macmillan, 1962.

Rosenthal, R., and Jacobson, L. *Pygmalion in the classroom: teacher expectation and pupil's intellectual ability.* New York: Holt, Rinehart and Winston, 1968.

Terman, L. M., and Oden, M. H. *The gifted child grows up.* Stanford, Calif.: Stanford University Press, 1947.

Terman, L. M., and Oden, M. H. *The gifted group at mid-life.* Stanford, Calif.: Stanford University Press, 1959.

Vernon, P. E. *Personality assessment: a critical survey.* London: Tavistock, 1964.

Our knowledge
    of man is incomplete
unless
    we view him as one
        among many—
a member of society,
    constantly interacting
    with other members
        of society...

as child and adult.

PART EIGHT

Previous chapters have been concerned mostly with the *individual*. Now, in the concluding section of this introduction to psychology, it is necessary to describe some of the ways in which the individual's mental processes and behavior are dependent on other people.

As the poet John Donne wrote, "No man is an island." Man does not live in isolation. Even if we know a great deal about how the individual learns, uses language and solves problems, senses and perceives the world, acquires his emotions and motives, and becomes a unique personality, our knowledge of him is still incomplete unless we go on to view him as one man among many—a member of society, constantly interacting with the other members of society.

The final section of the book consists of two chapters. Chapter 15, on developmental psychology, describes the manner in which the child is influenced by many complex interactions with other people—at first his parents, later his teachers and schoolmates. Chapter 16, on social psychology, explains how adult behavior is influenced by other people and by society.

the child, the adult, and society

CHAPTER 15

developmental psychology

More than 300 years ago the poet John Milton wrote:

> The childhood shows the man,
> As morning shows the day.

Today we have ample evidence that Milton was right. Studies of children—especially studies in which the same individuals have been observed from the time they were babies until they were adults—have demonstrated that much of the behavior and many of the personality traits of the adult can be traced to events and influences in childhood, particularly during the first ten years. Note, for example, the following reports written by two different trained observers about the same person, the first when he was a child, the second when he was a young adult.

Peter X., Age 3½

Babyish in appearance . . . . He showed extreme caution and would back away from any situation that smacked of danger. When threatened he would shake his head, clasp his hands, and beg in a frantic tone, "No, no, no." His role with peers was a sedentary, passive, and shrinking one. He stayed out of the swirl of activities of the other children . . . . With the staff of the nursery school he was highly conforming and very dependent. He liked to clean up, liked to wash, liked to take a nap . . . . Whenever he dirtied something, wet himself, or committed what he regarded as a violation, he became very tense and apprehensive, as if he felt that he had been a bad boy.

Peter X., Age 21

He was frail of build and spoke in a soft and high-pitched voice. When interviewed he often meditated for several minutes before answering, and there was a prevailing air of caution and insecurity in his manner. He had decided to teach English at a high school. Although he was primarily interested in teaching at a college, he was afraid to begin there because he doubted his ability . . . . He admired all his high school and college teachers and retained a dependent tie to them. . . . He did not want to marry until he was financially secure, and he had serious doubts about his ability to support a family. He felt tense and uncomfortable when with girls and he preferred not to date. Sexual behavior was still a source of fear. . . . He had few friends and most of his leisure was spent alone. Because he felt tense with strange people, he avoided clubs and social groups. If someone irritated him, he walked away; and he rarely insulted or became sarcastic with anyone. With his parents he was close and conforming, and he enjoyed talking over his problems with them. Fearing a feeling of isolation from his family, he had decided to attend a college close to his home. (1)

The case of Peter X. is extreme, showing an unusually high degree of consistency between the behavior of the child and the behavior of the adult. But it demonstrates what has been established as a general principle. Behavior patterns formed in childhood often determine whether the adult will be dependent or independent, passive or aggressive, shy or friendly, cautious or daring; they also determine his goals, his philosophy of life, his feelings about marriage, and his role as a parent to his children. Moreover, clinical studies of disturbed people and criminals have shown that their problems almost always began in childhood.

DEFINITION:
DEVELOPMENTAL
PSYCHOLOGY

Developmental psychology is the study of the processes by which the child gradually acquires patterns of overt behavior, thinking, problem solving, and perception, as well as the emotions, motives, conflicts, and ways of coping with conflicts that will go to make up his adult personality. For many reasons, developmental psychology is one of the most important and most rapidly growing branches of the science. For one thing, it is virtually impossible to understand adult behavior and the social problems that it often creates without knowing something about developmental psychology. Moreover, developmental psychology points the way to understanding individual children, finding successful methods of rearing them, and handling the difficulties inherent in child rearing. At this particular period in the national history, when there is a strong move toward establishing day-care centers for the children of mothers who are interested in work and careers, developmental psychology offers valuable assistance in the proper operation of such centers. It also offers what is perhaps the best hope for relieving some of the psychological problems that now plague many people in our society—problems such as alcoholism, drug addiction, crime, suicidal depression, and schizophrenia. All these problems when found in established form among adults are difficult to treat and eliminate. The study of development, however, may eventually lead to methods of preventing them or dealing with them more successfully in their early stages.

A. individual differences at birth

To what extent does the baby represent the old idea of the *tabula rasa,* or "blank tablet," upon which anything can be written through learning and experience? Part of the answer has already been presented in various other chapters. The human baby is not imprisoned to any significant degree by inborn patterns of instinctive behavior. Learning will play a crucial role in shaping his behavior, and it will affect not only his thinking but also his emotions, motives, conflicts, and manner of dealing with conflicts. On the other hand, the genes he has inherited determine his basic body build, facial features, eye color, and many other characteristics, including, as was discussed in Chapter 14, the range within which his capacity to learn, or I.Q., can develop.

Developmental psychology has produced many findings that bear on the nature-nurture question. Much of the evidence, you will discover, leans toward the idea of the *tabula rasa;* it indicates strongly that a person's entire life is profoundly influenced by such factors as his earliest contacts with his mother, his first experiences with discipline, identification with his mother and father, and his relations with his teachers and other children in the first five or six years of school. But the study of development has also demonstrated that <u>every child begins life with numerous important characteristics and that there are significant individual differences in many of these inborn characteristics; thus the newborn child is by no means entirely a *tabula rasa.*</u>

the newborn: "a remarkably capable organism"

<u>All normal babies are alike in one respect: they are sensitive from the moment of birth to stimuli in their environments and they respond to these stimuli with a rather wide range of inborn reflex behavior.</u> The newborn baby can feel, hear, smell, and see; indeed a baby only two hours old follows a moving light with his eyes. If the side of the baby's mouth is tickled, he displays the reflex illustrated in Figure 15-1—the "rooting response" that enables him to find food at his mother's breast. If the sole of his foot is gently pricked with a pin, he draws the foot away as shown in Figure 15-2—a reflex that results in escape from pain. He also displays a considerable number of other reflexes, including such protective behavior as closing the eyelids if a bright light is flashed or his eye is gently touched with a piece of cotton. All in all, as one group of psychologists who have studied his behavior have put it, "the newborn is a remarkably capable organism from the moment he begins to breathe" (2).

the newborn's "rooting response"

15-1 When the side of an infant's mouth is tickled (A), his reflex response is to turn his head toward the stimulus (B) and then try to suck the finger (C), as if it were a source of food.

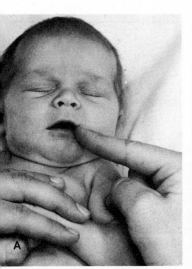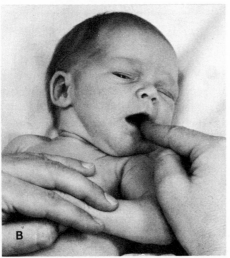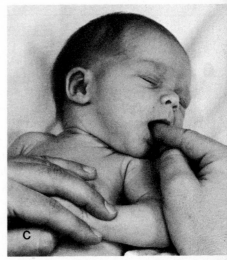

H. Prechtl and D. Beintema

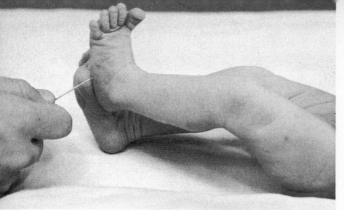
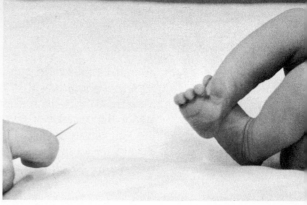

reflex escape from pain   H. Prechtl and D. Beintema

15-2   When the sole of the infant's foot is touched with a pin, his reflex response is to pull the foot away from the offending stimulus.

Very soon, however, it becomes apparent that these "remarkably capable" little creatures, though they all are aware of their environments and can respond, differ in many ways in their sensitivity and reactions to stimuli. Indeed their interactions with their environments seem to be governed by what can be called differences in temperament—and these differences, apparently inborn, tend to persist into later life.

2 level of activity

Even among very young babies, it has been found, some are much more active than others. They move their arms and legs with considerable force, tend to be restless when asleep, suck vigorously when nursing, and appear to have above-average appetites. As they get a little older they tend to make loud noises when they babble, to bang their toys together, and to kick at the sides of their cribs. Other babies are much more placid. Their movements are more gentle; they sleep more quietly and nurse less vigorously; later they babble in a softer voice and make less commotion with their toys (3). In general, boys seem to show a higher level of activity than girls (4).

3. sensory thresholds and adaptation

Some babies respond with muscular reflexes to a very gentle stroking of the skin; others do not respond unless the stroking is fairly firm. Some display what is called a startle reaction to sounds or light flashes of rather low intensity, others only when the intensity is quite high. The threshold for pain also seems to vary; for example, one study showed that newborn girls responded to mild electrical stimulation of the toe more readily than did boys (5).

When a sound loud enough to produce the startle pattern is repeated over a period of time, some babies quickly adapt and stop responding. Other babies have been found to react with the startle pattern even on the thirtieth presentation of the sound (6). Similarly, some babies appear to become "bored" with a stimulus rather quickly and to turn their attention elsewhere.

In one study, infants four months old had an opportunity to watch four

514

different pictures of the human face, projected one after another through four repetitions on a screen above their cribs. Some of the infants attended closely on all sixteen occasions, while others quickly stopped looking, as if they soon got tired of such a repetitive stimulus. The same children were studied again when they were older to observe their behavior while playing with toys. It was found that the children who had patiently attended to all the human faces tended to play for a long time with the same toy, whereas those who had quickly become bored with the faces tended to change from one toy to another. The difference between the two kinds of children, first found at four months in their reaction to the pictures, was apparent in their behavior with toys at eight months and again at twenty-seven months (7).

4. irritability

Another important difference among infants, perhaps related to differences in sensory thresholds, is what for lack of a more precise word may be called irritability. Some babies begin to fret, whine, or cry at the slightest provocation, while others do not show this kind of behavior unless their discomfort or pain is quite intense. Moreover, some babies, once they have begun to fret, seem to work themselves up into what looks like a temper tantrum and soon are bellowing at the top of their lungs. Others may fret for a half-minute or so, then stop, as if they possessed some kind of mechanism that inhibited the buildup of extreme upset (8).

5. differences in temperament

One group of investigators, on the basis of a study of more than 100 children observed from birth to past the age of ten, has concluded that differences in activity level, sensory thresholds and adaptation, irritability, and a number of other characteristics point to the existence of three different patterns of temperament that become apparent as early as the age of two or three months. In the investigators' sample, about 40 percent of the subjects were identified soon after birth as "easy" children—quite regular in their eating and sleeping habits, generally cheerful, and quick to adapt to new schedules, foods, and people. About 15 percent were classed as "slow to warm up"; these children tended to withdraw from their first exposure to a new experience, seemed to be somewhat negative in mood, and displayed a low level of activity. Another 10 percent were classed as "difficult" children; these were quite irregular in sleeping and eating habits, very slow in adjusting to new experiences, quite negative in mood, and given to unusually intense reactions, such as loud laughter, frequent loud crying, and temper tantrums. The remaining 35 percent of subjects showed mixtures of these various traits and did not fall into any general classification (9).

The most pronounced differences found among "easy," "slow to warm up," and "difficult" children are listed in Figure 15-3. A photographic record of the positive response of an "easy" child to an experience with a new kind of food—as contrasted with the negative response of a child with a different temperament—is shown in Figure 15-4. Note that the two children shown responding in such

		CHARACTERISTICS		
Type of child	Regularity (of hunger, sleep, excretion)	Approach or withdrawal (in presence of a new object or person)	Intensity of responses	Mood (pleasant and joyful as contrasted with unpleasant and unfriendly)
"Easy"	Very regular	Active approach	Low or moderate	Positive
"Slow to warm up"	Varies	Partial withdrawal	Low	Slightly negative
"Difficult"	Irregular	Withdrawal	Intense	Negative

three types of childhood temperaments

15-3 The three types of children—"easy," "slow to warm up," and "difficult"—have been found to differ most strikingly in the characteristics listed in the table. As discussed in the text, babies have been found to display these characteristics of temperament as early as the age of two or three months and to retain them into later childhood. (9)

a contrast between three-month-olds

15-4 The top strip of photos shows the eager and positive responses of a three-month-old girl being fed a new kind of cereal for the first time. The bottom strip shows the very different reactions of the girl's younger brother when he was introduced to the same new cereal at the same age. Even at this early age, these babies from the same family displayed far different temperaments.

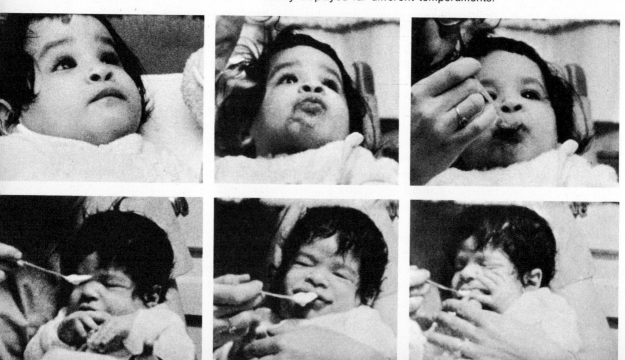

different fashion in Figure 15-4 are sister and brother—a fact that is in keeping with the investigators' finding that differences in temperament among infants do not reflect their parents' personalities or child-rearing methods. The differences appear to be inborn rather than acquired.

6. inborn differences and later life

Follow-up observations of the children who displayed one of the three different types of temperament showed that the differences tended to persist over the years; most of the subjects identified as "easy" children at two or three months were still cheerful and adaptable at the age of ten, while most of the "difficult" children were still irregular in their habits, negative in mood, and intense in their reactions. How they got along in general in later childhood, however, proved to depend as much on their environments as on their inborn traits.

One of the conclusions reached by the investigators was that the three types of children require very different treatment at home and at school. The "easy" child thrives under almost any kind of treatment in early childhood—but, having adapted so well to his home environment, he may have trouble when his school and his schoolmates make a different set of demands. The "slow to warm up" child requires considerable patience; he does best when encouraged to try new experiences but allowed to adapt to them at his own pace; too much pressure tends to heighten his natural inclination to withdraw. The "difficult" child presents a special kind of problem. Because of his irregular habits, his resistance to adjustment, his negative attitude, and his boisterousness, his parents and later his teachers are likely to find him hard to live with. But any attempt to force him into behaving like other children is only likely to make him more negative and difficult than ever. It requires exceptional understanding and tolerance on the part of his parents to bring him around—slowly and gradually—to obeying the rules and getting along with others. Of the "difficult" children in the study, fully 70 percent had required professional attention for behavioral problems by the age of ten; for the "easy" children, the figure was only 18 percent.

What developmental psychology has learned about individual differences present at birth can be of inestimable value to parents, the staffs of day-care centers, and schoolteachers, especially in the early grades. In the past, it was generally assumed that all children were more or less alike—or at least that their behavior *should* be alike. The new findings show that, on the contrary, even the infant in his crib is an individual who requires individual treatment if he is to attain his maximum potential.

B. physical development

Of all the ways in which children develop after birth, the easiest of all to measure is growth in size and in skill at motor performance. Many studies have been made of physical development, and there is a considerable literature from which parents can learn the normal standards for height and weight at all ages from birth on and for the occurrence of such events as smiling, the appearance of the first tooth, crawling, the first step, and the first recognizable word.

⅃ how the body and motor skills develop

The newborn baby grows, as shown in Figure 15-5, from all head and tiny legs to an adult of quite different proportions. His skeleton, which at birth is largely composed of rather soft and pliable cartilage, hardens into bone. His baby teeth appear and later are replaced by permanent teeth. Although he has all the muscle fibers that he will ever have, these fibers grow until they eventually weigh about forty times as much as they weighed at birth. His nerve fibers grow and form additional connections to other fibers, and some of them develop protective sheaths that make them faster and more efficient conductors of nervous impulses. His brain, in particular, gains in size and weight very rapidly during the first two years, then more slowly until he is an adult.

Even in the womb the unborn baby begins to use his muscles; his movements can first be felt in about the twentieth week of pregnancy. After birth his muscles of posture, crawling, and standing develop as shown in Figure 15-6, to the point where he is usually able to walk alone by the age of fifteen months. At first he

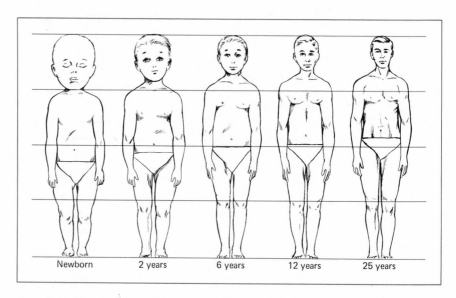

Newborn 2 years 6 years 12 years 25 years

development of body proportions

15-5 The newborn baby has a disproportionately large head and short legs; his head makes up a fourth of his total height, his legs only about a third. From birth to maturity the legs grow the most, to half the total height; and the head grows the least, becoming only about a tenth of the total height. (10)

Fetal posture (Newborn)

Chin up (1 month)

Chest up (2 months)

Reach (3 months)

Sit with help (4 months)

Sit on lap, grasp object (5 months)

Sit in high chair, grasp dangling object (6 months)

Sit alone (7 months)

Stand with help (8 months)

Stand holding furniture (9 months)

Crawl (10 months)

Walk with help (11 months)

Pull up (12 months)

Climb (13 months)

Stand alone (14 months)

Walk alone (15 months)

from birth to first step

15-6 From birth to first step the child goes through a number of stages of gradually increasing motor ability. The ages indicate the average age at which each stage of development occurs. (11)

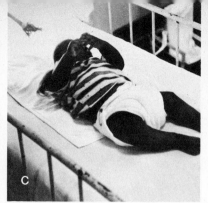
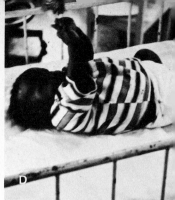

first attempts at reaching

15-7 How soon does the baby develop the desire and ability to grasp a brightly colored, toylike stimulus object held over his crib? The very young baby, typically lying with neck muscles holding his head to one side (A), pays only slight attention to an object (not visible in A and B). Later he occasionally watches his own hand, extended to the side toward which his head is turned (B); at this stage he will glance at an object when it is held on that side but focuses on it for only five to ten seconds at a time and makes no effort to reach it—though about two weeks later he often makes a quick, one-fisted swipe at it. By three to three and one-half months he no longer holds his head to one side and may move his hands in unison; when the object is held directly above him, he clasps his hands together beneath it (C). A little later he begins to raise his clasped hands toward the object (D). This is the final preliminary stage before he actually reaches toward the object with an open hand and attempts to grasp it. (12)

development of grasping ability

15-8

Studies made with a motion picture camera showed this sequence of development in the baby's ability at *prehension*—or grasping. The ages in weeks indicate the average age at which each stage is reached. (13)

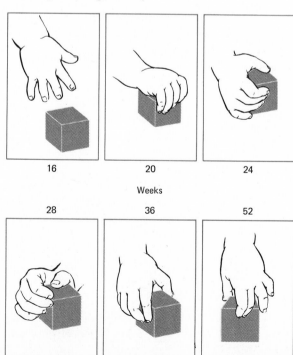

16   20   24

Weeks

28   36   52

cannot reach out and grab objects held in his visual field, but he gradually begins to reach for them as shown in Figure 15-7. His skill at using his hands and fingers increases rapidly as shown in Figure 15-8. The ability to vocalize, which is also partly a motor skill, appears very early; as was explained on pages 159-60, the baby begins to utter some of the <u>basic sounds or phonemes of language in the first few days of life.</u>

2. the role of maturation

The baby's growth and increasing skill at using his muscles are mostly the result of the process called *maturation*—<u>physical changes, taking place after birth, that continue the biological development of the organism from fertilized egg cell to complete adult.</u> To perform such feats as sitting alone and walking, the baby must of course also do some learning, but the learning is impossible until maturation has provided the necessary muscular and nervous structures. Attempts to push a child into performing beyond his level of maturation are futile and can indeed have harmful effects. For example, an attempt was once made to teach a one-year-old baby to ride a tricycle; the attempt was continued every day for seven months. Not only was it a failure, as might have been expected, but afterward, at the normal age for riding a tricycle, the child showed a pronounced lack of interest (14).

How important to the baby is an opportunity to move about, exercise his muscles, and start to learn? The answer is not entirely clear. Certainly there seems to be no lasting impairment of motor development among babies brought up by Indian mothers who carry them about strapped to a board or by Russian mothers who keep them tightly bound in swaddling clothes (see Figure 15-9). Yet when

does swaddling inhibit motor development?

15-9   Russian babies are still bound tightly in swaddling clothes (left), a custom that was also popular at one time in the United States but has long since been abandoned in favor of greater freedom of movement. Yet Russian children appear to walk as soon and as well as any others and may grow up with the motor skills and physical grace of the girls in the Leningrad ballet class shown at right.

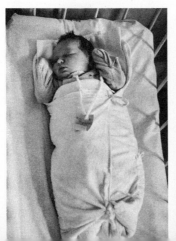

babies remain year after year in restricted environments, such as overcrowded and understaffed orphanages, the results are quite different. Many studies have shown that such children tend to become seriously retarded in motor skills and also mental development (15).

c. development of perception and language

In the early weeks of life the baby clearly exhibits some inborn perceptual tendencies that determine what he will look at or listen to. From the beginning, he is strongly attracted to contrast; as was mentioned on page 235, he tends to focus on the apex of a black triangle seen against a white background. He also seems to show a preference for visual stimuli with a certain amount of pattern and complexity, as has been demonstrated by the experiment illustrated in Figure 15-10. And he tends to look at moving objects, such as hands and bottles that cross his field of vision, rather than at stationary ones. These inborn tendencies, it should be noted, help him to distinguish objects in his environment; and when he begins moving about, they help him to avoid collisions with these objects (17). In a word, the inborn tendencies are extremely useful.

Learning, however, begins very quickly to influence the baby's perceptions. One of the best-known examples is the way he soon begins to smile when he sees a human face—an event that consistently takes place at about four months among babies in many kinds of homes and cultures (18). Presumably the baby

a baby's perceptual preferences

15-10

The three ovals were shown to babies two at a time, in all possible pairings, for a period of two minutes. The bars show how many seconds babies of each age spent looking at each of the three. At all ages the real face and the scrambled face appeared to be considerably more "interesting" to the babies than the simpler oval with the black patch. (16)

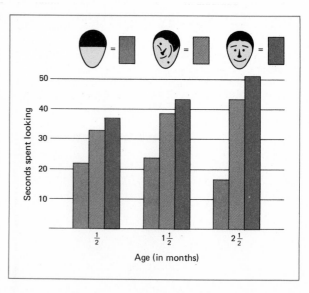

has acquired some sort of mediational unit that represents the human face and he smiles because he recognizes that he is looking at a face, much as an adult laughs at the punch line of a joke. His skill at recognition has developed to the point where he is actively organizing and "making sense" out of his sensory experiences.

f. perceiving details

The cards shown in Figure 15-11 were used in an experiment that demonstrates how the ability to perceive details—and thus to make finer and finer discriminations among stimuli—increases with age. The experiment tested the ability of subjects to recognize the test card shown at the top and to distinguish it from all the other cards, which look rather similar to it but are different in various ways. Children aged six to eight made numerous mistakes at the beginning

an experiment in perception of details

15-11

These are the cards used in the experiment described in the text. Note that each card is different—in the number of coils, the direction of the coils (clockwise or counterclockwise), or the width of the design. Four examples of each of the seventeen cards were included in a deck that totaled sixty-eight cards. The cards were shown to subjects one at a time in random order, and the subjects were asked to speak up each time they saw a card exactly like the one at the top. For a discussion of how age was found to affect the ability to recognize the test card, see the text. (Adapted from *Principles of perceptual learning and development* by Eleanor J. Gibson. Copyright © 1969 by Meredith Corporation. By permission of Appleton-Century-Crofts, Educational Division, Meredith Corporation.)

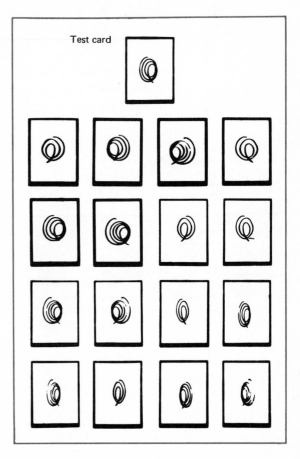

of a series of trials with the cards and only a few of them ever learned to recognize the test card with perfect accuracy. Children aged about nine to twelve did much better, and adults did very well from the beginning (19).

The experiment indicates that stimuli differing only in small details tend to be perceived by young children as very much alike; the young child has not yet learned to pay attention to fine details and to make perceptual discriminations based on them. Older children have developed a much greater ability at perceiving detail, and adults are quite adept at it.

2. scanning

One reason that children improve with age in their ability to perceive detail is that they become more efficient at scanning the environment. They begin to know what to look for and how to go about it; they develop a more effective strategy for seeking important information and ignoring the irrelevant. One might say that their attention becomes more selective, more systematic, and more orderly.

These differences are apparent in their eye movements, as shown in Figure 15–12. Asked to look at and try to remember an unfamiliar design, the three-year-old does not yet know how to extract a maximum of information; he tends to keep his eyes fixed on a single spot for a rather long time and never gets around to concentrating on all the details. By the time the child is six, however, he scans the design with rapid and quite extensive eye movements, paying particular attention to the contour line that determines its shape.

EYE MOVEMENTS:

The design to be scanned   Three-year-old   Six-year-old

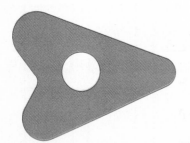
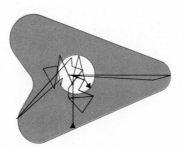
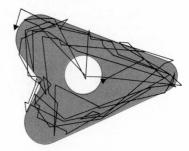

age differences in perceptual scanning

15-12 When children were asked to try to remember the design at the left, a typical three-year-old scanned the design with the rather simple eye movements shown at center, a typical six-year-old with the much more complex and efficient eye movements at the right. (Adapted from 20)

3. the whole versus its parts

At one time, developmental psychologists were in considerable disagreement as to whether children first learn to perceive the parts of a stimulus, such as the eyes and teeth of the mother's face, or the whole of the stimulus, such as the face itself. It is now generally accepted, however, that the two kinds of learning take place at the same time. That is to say, <u>the child seems to develop an ability to attend to and discriminate among more and more details, but at the same time to become more efficient at organizing details into meaningful patterns. He learns that the human face is made up of eyes and teeth but also acquires a notion of the face as a whole, as is shown by the smile he exhibits when he recognizes a face.</u>

<u>One of the most striking aspects of perceptual development is that as the child grows older he requires less and less information to recognize a pattern.</u> Looking at the drawing shown in the margin, the four-year-old is unlikely to perceive the dashes as a rabbit; the child of seven or eight recognizes the rabbit at once. By that age he has become extremely efficient at scanning a stimulus, attending to the distinctive features, extracting information, and comparing the information with his previous perceptual experiences (1).

4. the influence of language on perception

<u>One of the strongest influences on the child's perceptions is his increasing use of language, which helps him in making discriminations and in organizing sensory experiences into patterns.</u> Suppose that a one-year-old sees this figure:

$$\Longrightarrow$$

We can assume that he can translate the stimulus into only some kind of meaningless image. But the six-year-old is likely to perceive the same figure in a way that has been influenced by his language; he may say, "It looks like a finger" or "It looks like a pencil." If we show him the figure, then take it away and ask him to draw it—or ask him to find it in a group of figures that all look a little bit like it—he may make an error indicating that he perceived the figure as resembling a finger or pencil.

<u>With increasing use of language and the increasing development of perceptual expectations based on past experience, the child's interpretation of the world changes rapidly.</u> Let us say that the visual stimulus is a brown and white cow standing in a field of daisies next to a white wooden fence. To the child of one, it can be assumed, the scene is perceived merely as a pattern of figure and ground, with no one figure element outstanding. An older child perceives the scene quite differently. A child who has learned the words *daisy* and *fence* but not the word

cow may concentrate on the objects that have a name and ignore the animal. An older child who has learned the word *cow* may concentrate his attention on the animal but not notice any details such as its color. A boy who has learned to be afraid of being bitten may perceive the cow's mouth. A girl who once tore a dress on a sharp picket fence may notice whether the fence does or does not have pointed stakes.

5. skill at language

The ability to deal with language is composed of two separate processes—*comprehension,* or understanding words, and *expression,* or speaking them. These are different processes and seem to be controlled by different areas of the brain (21). For the growing baby, comprehension is the first of the skills to develop. As is shown in Figure 15-13, there are indications that the child can recognize meaningful speech as early as eight months of age, and a few months later he shows signs of understanding simple requests and commands. One study has shown that the average child can understand 3 words at the age of one year, 22 words at eighteen months, 272 words at two, and 2000 words by the age of five (23).

Expression starts later but also develops rapidly, as is indicated by the differences in speech of a two-year-old and a three-year-old shown in Figure 15-14. By the age of four the average child is constructing sentences that are quite accurate grammatically. By eight his pronunciation of words is virtually as good as an adult's. By age ten his grammar has also reached the adult level. It is interesting to note that the average American child's skill at using language has apparently increased in recent decades, as indicated by the studies summarized

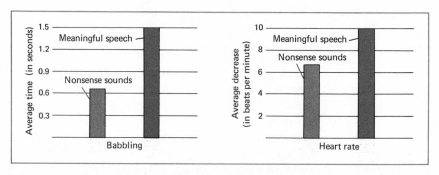

reaction of the eight-month-old to language

15-13 As early as the age of eight months, children appear able to distinguish between speech and nonsense sounds. After a meaningful paragraph had been read to eight-month-olds, they responded with twice as much babbling of their own as when nonsense words were read to them. They also showed a greater decrease in rate of heartbeat, which is a measure of the interest an infant pays to a stimulus. (22)

Two-year-old girl	Three-year-old girl
The rug	Hey, I found Captain Kangaroo
The pretty rug	Mummy?
Table	Can I have this?
Dish	What shall I fix with this?
Doggy tired	What did you found?
The book fall down	Won't it be fun to play with these?
Want hankie	I show you how to play animals
Other side	Hey, this is my dollie
Oh, other side	And then now I will line all mine up like this

in language, what a difference a year makes

15-14 These were the verbatim comments of two young girls, both of whom were playing with toys in the presence of their mothers and other adults. Note the much greater language skill of the three-year-old, including the ability to ask questions.

are today's children better at language?

15-15

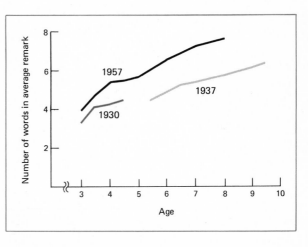

The average number of words used by children in a single remark or sentence was found to be higher in a 1957 study than in earlier studies reported in 1930 and in 1937. The 1957 study included children of ages three, three and one-half, four, four and one-half, five, six, seven, and eight. The 1930 study was of children aged eighteen to fifty-four months, observed at six-month intervals, and the 1937 study was of children aged five and one-half to nine and one-half. Note that the 1957 children seemed to show superior language ability at all ages covered by the studies. (Data for 1957, 24; for 1930, 25; for 1937, 26)

in Figure 15-15. One explanation seems to be that <u>radio and television have provided increased language stimulation.</u>

<u>The effect of environment on the development of language skill appears to be considerable.</u> As is shown in Figure 15-16, babies brought up in orphanages have been found to lag behind other children both in the number of phonemes they speak and the frequency with which they speak at all. As is shown in Figure 15-17, children brought up in middle-class homes, where presumably their mothers talk to them frequently and thus encourage vocal responses, appear to develop language skills faster than children brought up in working-class homes.

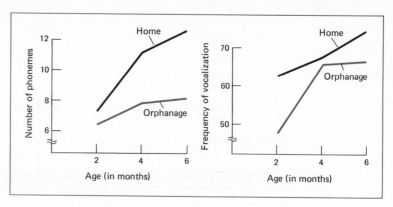

language development in homes and in orphanages

15-16 Children aged two to six months who have been reared in their own homes have been found to utter a higher average number of phonemes than do children of the same age in orphanages, as shown in the graph at left. They also vocalize more frequently, as shown at right. (27)

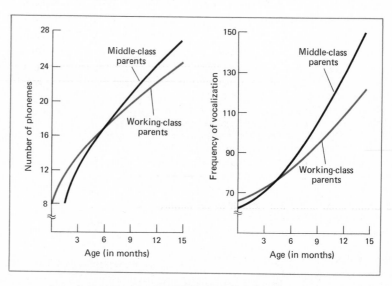

language development in middle- and working-class homes

15-17 Children of middle-class parents have been found to utter a somewhat higher average number of phonemes than children of working-class parents, as shown in the graph at left. The difference begins to appear at about six months and gradually becomes larger. The middle-class children also vocalize with considerably more frequency, as shown at right. (28)

D. intellectual development

The child's increased skill at perception and at using language forms part of the foundation for his intellectual development—that is, for his growing ability to think and solve problems. He begins to acquire concepts, such as the concept of animal for four-legged living creatures. His concepts begin to become more complex; for example, the concept of animal may originally include only dogs and cats but later be expanded to include other creatures as well. At the same time his concepts also become more precise and differentiated; he begins to break down the general concept of animals into subcategories such as pets and nonpets, tame and wild.

The manner in which children increasingly use concepts as a strategy for coding new information into long-term memory—and later retrieving it—has been demonstrated by a study in which the experimenters used a set of twenty-four pictures that fell into four categories of six pictures each. One category was means of transportation, in which the pictures showed an automobile, bicycle, boat, bus, train, and truck; the other categories were animals, furniture, and clothing. The pictures were spread out on a table in a random arrangement, and the subjects, who were children from the first through the sixth grades, were told that they would have three minutes to study them, during which time they could move them around or do anything else that might help them remember what they had seen. They were not told about the categories. The question, answered in Figure 15–18, was whether the children would try to rearrange the pictures into categories

development of use of concepts

15-18

The graph lines show the results of an experiment, described in the text, in which children tried to remember objects they had seen in pictures that could be organized in categories determined by the concepts of means of transportation, animals, furniture, and clothing. The black line demonstrates the tendency to organize the pictures into categories, from zero among first-graders to a rather high level among sixth-graders. The colored line demonstrates a similar increase in the tendency to recall the objects in chunks dictated by the concepts. (29)

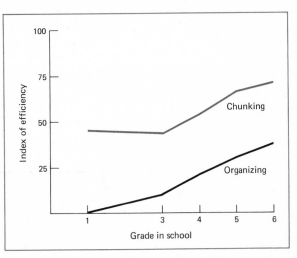

as an aid to memory—also whether they would tend to recall them in chunks determined by the concepts of means of transportation, animals, furniture, and clothing.

As illustrated by the graph in Figure 15–18, none of the first-graders and only a few of the third-graders rearranged the pictures by category. Starting with the fourth-graders, however, there was a rapidly increasing tendency to use concepts as a strategy for memorizing the pictures and to recall the objects in chunks. Other studies have shown that the increasing ability to use concepts in memorizing is correlated with improvement in solving various kinds of problems (30, 31).

1. Piaget's theory of intellectual development

KEY PROCESSES
OF PIAGET'S THEORY

1. ASSIMILATION
2. ACCOMMODATION

The most influential student of intellectual development is the Swiss psychologist Jean Piaget, who has spent a half-century observing the behavior of his own and other children as they grew from infancy through adolescence. Piaget has concluded that mental growth is basically an increased ability to adapt to new situations and that this growth takes place because of two key processes that he calls *assimilation* and *accommodation*. Assimilation is the process of incorporating a new stimulus into one's existing cognitive view of the world; accommodation is changing one's cognitive view and behavior when new information dictates such a change. As a simple example, let us say that to the toys with which a child is familiar we add a new one, a magnet. His initial impulse will be to assimilate the new toy into his existing knowledge of other toys; he may try to bang it like a hammer, throw it like a ball, or blow it like a horn. But once he learns that the magnet has a new and unprecedented quality—the power to attract metal—he accommodates his view of toys to include this previously unfamiliar fact; he now behaves on the revised assumption that some toys are not designed to bang, throw, or make noise with but to attract metal.

There is always tension, Piaget has concluded, between assimilation (which in essence represents the use of old ideas to meet new situations) and accommodation (which in essence is a change of old ideas to meet new situations). And it is the resolution of this tension that results in intellectual growth. Piaget believes that the growth takes place in a series of stages, in each of which the child thinks and behaves in quite different fashion from before; he maintains that the child grows intellectually not so much like a leaf, which simply gets larger every day, as like a caterpillar that is eventually transformed into a butterfly. The various stages and the approximate ages at which they occur have been charted by Piaget as follows (32).

a. Sensorimotor Stage (Birth to Age Two).   At this stage the child has not yet learned to use symbols and language to label the objects and events in his environment; he is dependent on the raw evidence of his senses and bodily actions. He knows the world in terms of his sensory impressions and his motor activities.

By the age of four to six months the child has started to operate on his environment; he will repeatedly kick at a toy that hangs over his crib, apparently to make it swing and thus produce a change of stimulus that he finds "interesting."

By ten months he acts as if he knows that objects are permanent and do not disappear. For example, if an experimenter shows him a toy and then hides it behind two pillows side by side in the crib, the child will look behind one of the pillows; if the toy is not there, he will then look behind the other.

b. Preoperational Stage (Two to Seven). In this stage, the ability to use symbols begins to dominate the development of intellectual ability. As the child's use of language increases, he begins to attach new meanings to the stimuli in his environment and to use one stimulus to stand as a symbol for another. A girl may behave toward a doll as if it were a real child, and a boy may play with a stick as if it were a gun.

By the age of four the child's concepts have become more elaborate, but they are still based largely on the evidence of his senses. He can learn, for example, to select the middle-sized of three rubber balls. He attains what Piaget has called an *intuitive understanding* that the middle-sized ball is bigger than the small one but smaller than the big one. But if three balls of very different size from the original three are then shown to him, he must learn to make the selection all over again (33). The child of this age is still fooled by the puzzle illustrated in Figure 15-19. Apparently the height of the jar is such an outstanding characteristic that he cannot help equating height with the number of beans the jar contains.

c. Stage of Concrete Operations (Seven to Eleven). This stage begins when the child becomes aware that the number of beans does not change in the experiment illustrated in Figure 15-19. He has learned the important principle of *conservation*—that is, the fact that such qualities as mass, number, weight, and volume remain constant regardless of changes in appearance. If asked why the tall jar and the short jar contain an equal amount, he may say, "Well, this one is taller, but this one is fatter." A little later in the stage of concrete operations he may make the even more sophisticated statement, "If you poured the beans back from the tall jar into the other jar, then it would be the same." Thus the child in the stage of concrete operations shows an ability to reason logically about objects and to apply rules. But as Piaget's name for this stage implies, he seems

a preschool puzzle

15-19 The four-year-old child points to both of the squat jars to acknowledge that they contain an equal number of beans. But when the beans are poured from one of these jars into a tall, thin jar, he says that the tall jar then contains more beans. Not until he is around seven years old will he state that the number of beans remains the same.

to be able to reason only about concrete objects that are actually in front of him; he has yet to learn to deal with rules in the abstract.

Stage of Formal Operations (*Beginning at About Eleven or Twelve*). In this final stage of development the child is released from dependence on the actual presence of concrete objects. He can close his eyes and solve problems such as the one about the jar and the beans through the manipulation of symbols and the rules he has learned about how the world operates. In other words, he is now capable of thinking in the abstract like an adult; he can solve problems by breaking them down into their essential elements and bringing many hypothetical solutions to bear.

There are of course individual differences in the ages at which children attain the various stages described by Piaget. There is evidence, however, that the progression of stages holds true in general for children of different nationalities, regardless of what kind of education they have had (34). There is also evidence that it is impossible to hurry a child from one stage to another by trying to teach him the reasoning skills appropriate to a more advanced period (35). It appears that the child can understand only experiences and pieces of information that match the vocabulary, facts, and rules he has already acquired or that are just a bit in advance of his existing information. If a new experience or idea has no readily apparent connection with what he already knows, he is not likely to learn much if anything about it and may not even pay attention to it.

STAGES OF PIAGET

1. SENSORIMOTOR STAGE
    (0 - 2 YRS.)

2. PREOPERATIONAL STAGE
    (2 - 7 YRS.)
    INTUITIVE UNDER-
    STANDING

3. STAGE OF CONCRETE
    OPERATIONS (7-11 YRS.)
    CONSERVATION

4. STAGE OF FORMAL
    OPERATIONS (11 OR
    12 YRS. —)

E. personality development—the caretaker period: birth to eighteen months

The chapter has now discussed physical development, the development of perception and language, and intellectual development. The big topic still remaining, of course, is the development of personality—a many-sided subject that will take up the rest of the chapter. The subject can best be discussed by following the development of the child from birth to the age of about ten, by which time many personality traits have become established in a way that is likely to remain more or less constant into adult life.

Much psychological thinking about the very earliest development of personality traits stems from a much-discussed series of experiments by Harry F. Harlow, who took baby monkeys from their own mothers and placed them with doll-like objects that he called "surrogate mothers." As is shown in Figure 15-20, Harlow gave his baby monkeys two such surrogate mothers. One was made of wire, with a bottle and nipple from which the monkey received milk. The other was made of sponge rubber and terrycloth; it was an object to which the baby monkey could cling.

As the photographs show, the baby monkeys had a strong tendency to prefer the terrycloth doll to the wire doll; indeed they clung to the terrycloth mother

baby monkey and "surrogate mothers"

15-20 The baby monkey has been taken from its own mother and placed with two "surrogate mothers." Note how it clings to the terrycloth mother, even when feeding from the wire mother and especially when exploring a new and unfamiliar object that has been placed in the cage.

even when feeding from the other. Note particularly that when a new object was placed in the cage, they clung to the terrycloth mother while making their first hesitant and tentative attempts to discover what this strange and at first frightening object might be (36). Obviously there was something about the terrycloth surrogate that provided the baby monkey with what in human terms would be called comfort, protection, and a kind of secure base from which new aspects of the environment could be explored.

There is some question as to why the baby monkey should have preferred the terrycloth mother. Harlow concluded that the terrycloth mother met a need of the baby by providing what he has called *tactual comfort*—sensations of warmth and softness. Another possible explanation is that the baby monkey is born with a strong grasp reflex and tends to cling to any object that provides an opportunity to exercise the reflex. Among wild monkeys, it has been observed, the babies cling to the long hair of their mothers' bodies for a number of months after birth (37). At any rate, Harlow's experiments, observations of monkeys in the wild and in zoos, and studies of human infants have led a growing number of psychologists to conclude that the babies of at least the higher species of animals are born with a tendency toward what has been called *attachment*—that is, a close tie with another organism (or, in the case of Harlow's experiment, an object that somehow satisfies the tendency to develop an attachment). Under ordinary circumstances, the attachment occurs between the infant and his caretaker, usually his mother, and plays an important part in his early development.

1. the theory of attachment

The theory of attachment is quite new, and the psychologists who have proposed it are not yet agreed as to whether to call it a form of stimulus need, a motive in its own right, a built-in pattern of reflex behavior, or something that

533

results from a combination of inborn reflexes. They are in general agreement, however, that the human baby inherits a strong tendency to become attached to another person, usually the mother, and that this tendency is shown by (or perhaps results from) such behavior as rooting, sucking, babbling, smiling, and crying. All these behaviors are directed toward stimuli that can only be provided by another human being; it is the mother, ordinarily, who gives the baby the food that is the object of the rooting and sucking reflexes, responds to his babbling, induces his smiles, and relieves his crying (38).

In terms of survival of the species, the theory that babies are born with a tendency toward attachment takes on considerable plausibility. The tendency induces the baby to seek proximity and contact with the mother, to call to her for food and relief from pain; it leads him to actively seek her protection during the long period of helplessness when he could not survive without it. Moreover, the baby's active approach to his mother reinforces her own efforts to be as protective and nurturing as possible.

An Alternate Explanation of the Mother-Child Relationship. Although it is clearly established that babies seek a close relationship with the mother and that this relationship is of vital importance in early personality development, not all psychologists agree that the relationship stems from an inborn tendency to become attached. There is still some support for what was formerly the generally accepted view that the relationship is the result of learning through reinforcement.

The older viewpoint maintains that every baby, except in rare cases of abnormality, must in the nature of things suffer highly unpleasant sensations from time to time as a result of his biological drives. He suffers from the pangs of hunger, the discomfort of thirst, unpleasant sensations of heat and cold, and pain caused by pinpricks, bumps, and colic. Also, in the nature of things, he is unable to relieve any of these unpleasant sensations through his own efforts. What he does, as a reflex response, is to cry. Crying ordinarily brings the mother, who relieves the discomfort and provides the pleasurable sensations of feeding, handling, and fondling.

Thus the normal baby soon learns that crying is an effective way to obtain help; he also learns that the presence of the mother means pleasure and the relief of pain. The mother acquires "reward value"—which, to those who prefer to think in terms of learning, explains why he becomes attached to her.

2. attachment and exploration

Regardless of whether the baby's attachment to his mother represents an inborn tendency or a learned appreciation of her "reward value," it is the strongest influence on the baby's development during the first eighteen months. For one thing, as has been said, it helps him find protection and nurturance. Moreover, it is closely related to another factor that is essential to his survival— that is, exploration of the world around him.

If the tendency to become attached prevailed completely during early infancy, it has been pointed out, the baby would never learn to adapt to his environment;

he would never outgrow his dependency on his caretaker. To become self-sufficient, he must also begin to satisfy his need for stimulus change (pages 340–44) by venturing away from his mother's protection, exploring his environment, encountering new objects and new experiences, and learning how to cope with them.

The photograph on page 533 of the baby monkey cautiously examining a new object while clinging to its surrogate mother has already provided one indication of how attachment and exploration work hand in hand. Among wild monkeys, it has been observed, the baby and its real mother seem almost to work as a team in this respect. At first the baby clings constantly to the mother. Later it ventures off a short distance to explore its environment and play with other young monkeys—but always with one eye on the mother, so to speak, as a haven to which it can scurry back at the first sign of danger. At the same time, the mother keeps an anxious watch on the baby, ready to haul it back if it starts getting in trouble. With increasing age the baby becomes more and more daring and the mother more and more permissive (39).

Human babies also seem to gather courage for exploration from their attachment to their mothers. In one experiment, babies just under a year old were placed in a strange room that contained a chair piled high with and surrounded by toys. When baby and mother were in the room together, the baby actively looked at the toys, approached them, and touched them. All this exploratory behavior dropped off, however, if a stranger was present or if the mother left the room (38).

3, the beginnings of anxiety

The same experiment also produced results that point to another important phase of development in the first eighteen months—namely, the first appearance of behavioral signs of anxiety. When the babies were left in the room alone or with a stranger, many of them began to cry, to make a search for the mother, or both. They were exhibiting *separation anxiety,* which first appears among American babies around the age of ten or eleven months.

A possible explanation of separation anxiety is the fact that the disappearance of the mother—which is unexpected—creates uncertainty and elicits the motive for certainty, which, as was discussed in Chapter 10, is one of the strongest of all human motives. The baby cannot understand or explain the mother's disappearance; therefore it makes him anxious. In an experiment that supports this conclusion, it was found that babies rarely cried if their mothers left them by way of a familiar exit, such as the door from the child's bedroom to the other parts of the home. Presumably this was an everyday event that the babies had assimilated into their experience. But they did cry if their mothers disappeared in an unusual way—for example, behind the door of a closet (40).

Young babies also exhibit *stranger anxiety;* in fact this type of anxiety appears a little earlier in life. If the mother shows her face above the crib, the child of seven or eight months will usually smile. But if the face is that of a stranger, the baby may show anxiety by turning away and perhaps crying. Again, the

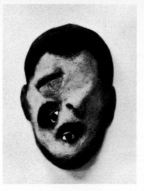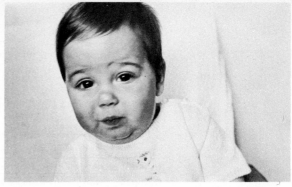

perceptual distortion and anxiety

15-21 Violation of perceptual expectations makes the baby of about eight months express anxiety when he sees the distorted mask at left. At an earlier period, before he learned what the human face is supposed to look like, he might have smiled at the mask.

explanation may be that the appearance of the stranger's face is an event that generates uncertainty. The baby has acquired some sort of mental representation or perceptual expectation of the familiar face, which is violated by the different face. Indeed the behavioral evidences of stranger anxiety can sometimes be produced by showing the baby a distorted mask of the human face, as is illustrated in Figure 15-21.

Among babies reared in impersonal institutions, where many faces appear over the crib at various times and the baby does not become accustomed to one particular face, stranger anxiety is less common. Thus stranger anxiety appears to be the inevitable result of close attachment to a caretaker; and it tends to disprove the popular belief that any anxiety must, of necessity, spring from some kind of unfavorable environment and indicate psychological disturbance. Although anxieties are among the most unpleasant of emotions and the source of many behavioral problems, at least some of them appear to be an unavoidable result of growing up, even in the warmest and happiest kind of family. Indeed experiencing anxiety and having support and help in learning how to cope with it may be among the most useful aspects of the caretaker period.

4. the nurtured child and the neglected child

Out of a close and warm relationship with a nurturing caretaker, the baby develops many traits that begin to mold his personality in a favorable direction. The caretaker provides a safe base from which to explore the environment and assistance in coping with anxiety. Moreover, by making the child's first experiences with another human being pleasant and rewarding, she encourages his development into a social being who will grow up with attitudes of trust and affection for other people.

The child who is neglected in this period grows up under severe handicaps. Even the monkeys raised by surrogate mothers, when they grew up, turned out to have many symptoms of maladjustment; they were unfriendly, aggressive, and sexually incompetent (41). Among human babies, many lasting effects of neglect

536

have been observed (42). One investigator made a study of children who had spent the first three years of their lives in the impersonal atmosphere of an orphanage, then had gone to foster homes. He followed their subsequent development and compared them with a control group of children of the same age and sex who had been brought up from the start in foster homes, where presumably they had received considerably more personal care than was possible in an institution. Spending the early years of life in an orphanage apparently left a permanent mark on the children. Compared with the control group, they were noticeably more aggressive; they showed strong tendencies to have temper tantrums, to kick and hit other children, and to lie, steal, and destroy property. They were more dependent on adults than the control group and tended to demand attention and ask for unnecessary help. They were also more easily distracted and less self-controlled. They tended to be emotionally cold, isolated, and incapable of forming affectionate personal relationships (43).

F. the first social demands: eighteen months through three years

The second period of the child's life, roughly from eighteen months through three years, marks his first important experience with the demands of society. When he leaves the crib and begins walking about the house, he finds innumerable objects that look to him like toys provided for his own special benefit but in fact are expensive and fragile pieces of household equipment—or, like knives and electric light cords, are dangerous. For the first time, therefore, he encounters discipline; he discovers that he can no longer do whatever he pleases. The rules of the home say that he must not destroy valuable property and must not explore dangerous situations. At the same time he encounters a rule of society that says that the elimination drive must be relieved only in the bathroom; he undergoes that much-discussed process called toilet training.

His horizons widen; he leaves the self-centered environment of the crib and takes his place in the world of people, property, and property rights. Sometimes smoothly, sometimes with stormy difficulties that leave lasting blemishes on his personality, he begins to learn to become a disciplined member of society.

1. punishment and anxiety

In toilet training the child must learn *not* to do something—in this case, not to respond immediately to the sensations that call for relief of the elimination drive. He must also learn *not* to respond to such external stimuli as the cupboard full of dishes that he would like to explore and the lamp that he would like to smash on the floor. In other words, he is learning in this period to *inhibit* forms of behavior that would ordinarily be the natural response to internal or external stimuli.

He learns partly through reinforcement in the form of reward. When he is successful in using the toilet, he is usually rewarded with praise and fondling. When he refrains from playing with a vase after being told "No," he sometimes receives the same kind of reward. But, since he is learning inhibition, he also learns through punishment and anxiety. He is punished, physically or verbally, when he soils his pants, breaks something, or gets into a cupboard where he does not belong. As a result of the punishment he acquires a twofold anxiety over committing the acts. He becomes anxious over the prospect of punishment and also, especially if his mother has high reward value, over losing her affection and regard. His anxiety and uncertainty (over loss of the caretaker) now help him become a social being. The same stimuli that urge him to an act of elimination or to explore or destroy now arouse sufficient anxiety to inhibit what had previously been a natural kind of behavior. The closer his ties with his mother and the greater her reward value, the more readily does this kind of learning take place—particularly if she serves as a good model who helps him acquire a knowledge of social demands through observation learning as well as through reward and punishment.

2. exploring and destroying

It is by exploring the world that the child comes into contact with new stimuli and learns the nature of his environment. It is by handling objects— and sometimes, unfortunately, destroying them—that he learns how to operate on the environment. He discovers that he can roam about in the world and in many cases rearrange it; he can reach for objects he wants; he can move them. He learns that he himself can satisfy many of his desires, without depending on anyone else. By reaching into the cookie jar he can satisfy his hunger drive. By crawling under the coat that a visitor has thrown on the sofa he can find warmth. By knocking down a tower of blocks (or by pulling down a tablecloth) he can satisfy his need for stimulus change.

Parents who want to help their child develop along the most favorable lines face a problem at this period. The child must definitely learn to avoid danger; he must not carry his explorations to the point of risking electrical shocks, burns, or a fall from a window. He must also learn to curb his inclinations to let exploration turn into destruction. But there is a point at which the attempt to preserve the child's safety and make him a nondestructive member of society can begin to thwart his opportunities for normal development.

Some mothers are overprotective; they try to keep the child "tied to their apron strings" and object to any activity he attempts to undertake on his own. Others are too concerned with neatness and order; they scold or punish the child every time he makes the slightest mess, gets the least bit dirty, or merely touches a newly waxed tabletop. When disciplined by an overprotective or overly neat mother, the child can acquire a crippling amount of anxiety. His fear of punishment or disapproval may generalize to any new object or new activity. He may therefore grow up with strong inhibitions against trying anything at all that is novel or challenging, including attempts to make adjustments to other people.

The mother who is somewhat more permissive during this difficult period, on the other hand, sets the stage for spontaneous, self-reliant, and effective behavior. Though she must stop the child at times, she does not do so except

"Someone ought to stop us before we get hurt."

when absolutely necessary. When he tries something new that is constructive, such as trying to draw pictures or ride a tricycle, she encourages and rewards him. Thus he learns that only some kinds of exploratory behavior are forbidden, not all, and that in fact many kinds are considered "good." He discovers that curiosity and new attempts to operate on the environment are approved, and he develops independence and self-confidence.

G. the preschool years: four and five

The preschool child uses language and concepts; he is beginning to roam outside the home and play with other children; he may go to nursery school or kindergarten. The years of four and five witness some important changes. The child develops his first feelings of guilt, representing the workings of that rather strange mechanism called conscience. He learns that the world is divided into males and females, for whom society decrees quite different roles; the boy begins to take on characteristics that are appropriate to the male, and the girl takes on characteristics appropriate to the female.

One important reinforcement for the preschool child's learning continues to be provided by his parents in the form of praise and other rewards. He also molds his behavior in order to avoid disapproval or punishment and anxiety over the possibility of these two unpleasant events. However, a new factor now enters. This is the period in which he begins to identify with his parents and to try to imitate them.

1. identification

The nature of the process of *identification* is a matter of controversy. To the psychoanalysts it is a complex process that involves the Oedipus complex and the superego, as was explained on pages 406–07. To many psychologists it has a somewhat different meaning—mostly that the child comes to feel that he and his parents share a vital bond of similarity. He bears the same family name; he may be told that he looks like them; he tends to duplicate their emotions and attitudes. He considers himself in deep and important ways to be like his parents, and he tries to imitate their behavior so that he can share vicariously in their strengths, virtues, skills, and triumphs.

Children with intelligent parents often come to think of themselves as intelligent. A boy whose father holds a job requiring physical strength usually begins to think of himself as being strong, and a girl with an attractive mother thinks of herself as being attractive. Unfortunately, children identify with their parents' faults as well as with their virtues, and it is not unusual for children to become aware of considerable criticism of their parents. They may be able to see for themselves that their father is unable to hold a job and is the object of ridicule in the community or that their mother drinks too much and is unwelcome in the houses of her neighbors. They may hear criticism of their parents from relatives, or their mother, having divorced their father, may tell them bitter stories

15-22

A study of the home backgrounds of delinquent boys, as compared with a matched control group of non-delinquent boys, found that considerably more of the delinquents had lost a parent through death, divorce, or other causes—particularly when they were very young. (44)

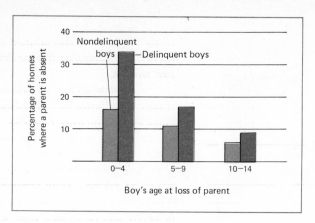

about his conduct. Under these circumstances many children develop the belief that they too are unworthy, unlovable, hateful, stupid, lazy, or mean. Many children treated in guidance clinics for psychological problems have a background of identification with a "bad" parent.

As is shown in Figure 15-22, it has been found that a substantial number of delinquent boys come from homes in which a parent had died or was absent for other reasons. There are many ways in which the death of a parent or divorce can adversely affect the child's development, but certainly one possibility is that they interfere with the normal process of identification.

2. conscience

One of the roles of parents is to provide discipline by being good models, setting standards, prohibiting certain acts, and, when necessary, dealing out punishment. Through reward and punishment and identification with the parents the child begins in the preschool years to develop what is generally called a conscience. The child of two who spills his milk experiences anxiety over the possibility of punishment or disapproval. The child of four experiences a different kind of anxiety; he feels *guilt*. His own conscience provides the disapproval.

Conscience and feelings of guilt develop in connection with the motive to live up to standards. Apparently the child first attempts to behave in accordance with what other people expect of him. Then he internalizes these expectations and turns them into his own standards. One of his early standards concerns toilet habits. At the start of toilet training he feels afraid when he has an accident, because he expects disapproval or punishment. Later he himself sets the standards and feels shame or guilt. Other early standards depend largely on the family situation and the type of conduct that is approved or disapproved by the parents; they may concern aggression, displays of anger, dependent behavior, crying, or sexual play.

3. sex typing

Every society engages in *sex typing*. That is to say, it assigns different roles to men and women; they are expected to have different duties, attitudes, and standing in the community (45). The roles are not always the same as in

our modern Western civilization. In some societies, for example, men do most of the housework and women do most of the gainful labor. But whatever the particular customs of the society, men are expected to act like men and women like women.

Children appear to become aware of this fact very early in life. When children are shown pictures of various objects concerned with play—such as dolls, guns, kitchen utensils, cowboys, and Indians—and asked which they prefer, there are differences between boys and girls even at the age of three and quite pronounced differences at the ages of four and five (46).

The preschool boy seems to be asking, "How masculine am I?" and the girl to be asking, "How feminine am I?" Children of four and five are already developing the notions, which will come into full flower later, that women should be pretty and preferably slim, while men should be tall and strong; that women should be passive, nonaggressive, and submissive toward men, while men should be active, aggressive, and dominant. Their feelings of how well they measure up to these ideals begin to play an increasing part in their evaluation of themselves and their roles in society.

H. the child and his peers: six to ten

When the child starts school, an entirely new dimension enters his life. Up to this point his chief social contacts and sources of learning have been his parents and his brothers and sisters. Now he comes into intimate contact with his own peer group—boys and girls of the same age with whom he shares the experiences of school and play. He also comes under the influence of his teachers. He encounters new sources of uncertainty, notably over his competence at school tasks and at skills admired by his peers. Although the home is still an important factor in his development, other factors begin to play an increasing role.

1. the child in school

Entering school usually represents the child's first separation from the mother for a large part of the day. Now there is a new adult whose discipline he must conform to and whose acceptance he must court. Ordinarily the teacher is a woman, like the mother, and the child's behavior toward the mother is readily generalized toward her. Boys who are identifying with their fathers and rebelling against their mothers, however, often have trouble in the early grades. They may be less fearful of rejection by the teacher and therefore more reluctant to accept her influence. They typically get lower marks and cause more disciplinary problems than do girls.

The teacher usually plays a dual role in the child's development. In the first place, she teaches the intellectual skills considered appropriate in our culture. In the second place, and perhaps even more important to personality development, she tries to encourage intellectual mastery. It is in the early years of school that the child acquires internal standards of intellectual mastery and begins to feel anxiety if he does not live up to these standards. By the age of ten, largely because of the school experience, many children have developed a pronounced fear of failure. The desire to avoid the anxiety attached to failure can become one of the strongest of motives.

2. the influence of peers

To the child of six to ten his peers take on a particular importance for three reasons.

1. *Evaluation.* It is by comparing himself with his classmates that the child judges his own value. By school age he has lost his original faith in the wisdom of adults; he seems to sense that his parents are either too full of praise for his virtues or too critical of his faults. He gets a more realistic reading, he seems to feel, from his relations with other children. For one thing, he can make a direct comparison; he can determine his rank among his classmates on such attributes as intelligence, strength, and skills of various kinds. For another thing, the opinion his classmates hold of him seems more objective, honest, and easily interpreted than his parents' opinion. He can see for himself whether other children his own age regard him as competent and likable or foolish and unpleasant.

2. *Assignment of role.* It appears to be a characteristic of human society, at least in our own kind of civilization, that every group has a leader, a "closest adviser" to the leader, and a scapegoat on whom the group takes out its aggressions. Often there are also an intellectual giant (or wise man) and a court jester (or clown), sometimes a rebel and a psychopath. These roles, into which individuals naturally gravitate or are pushed by others, are found in groups of children as well as of adults. Once a child has achieved or been assigned a role in his group, he usually takes it seriously, receives some kind of satisfaction from it, and begins to take on more and more of the appropriate traits. The leader of the boys in the first grade, for example, is likely to develop many of the techniques of skilled leadership, while the class clown develops an increasingly buffoonlike personality.

3. *Rebellion.* Most schoolchildren, particularly boys, are to some degree rebellious against the adult world—especially against its restrictions on the display of hostility and its demands for cleanliness, order, and quiet. In the society of his peers the growing child finds a place where he can express his hostilities, make a mess, be noisy, and do all the other things that the adult world forbids—and receive the admiration of his classmates rather than disapproval.

In a sense, children often function for one another as psychotherapists. They help one another toward an objective evaluation of their own talents and position in society. The peer group gives each child a role to play and provides models that the child can identify with and imitate. It provides an outlet for feelings, such as hostility, on which the adult world frowns. Thus it is not at all surprising that between six and ten the child begins to learn more from his peer group than from anyone else.

It is interesting to note, however, that the rebelliousness against adult

"Yesterday I received a threatening letter from someone called 'The Fang'; he uses your handwriting."

standards that is fostered by the peer group in the United States is not characteristic of all cultures. This fact has been demonstrated in an ingenious experiment in which American and Russian children were asked to respond to a questionnaire about how they would behave if some of their friends urged them to perform such acts as going to a movie disapproved by their parents, running away after accidentally breaking a window, stealing fruit from an orchard, or taking advantage of finding the questions and answers for a school examination. Some of the children were told that no one would see their answers to the questionnaire except the experimenters, others that their parents would see the answers, and still others that their classmates would see the answers.

In every case, the American children proved far more inclined than the Russian children to perform the forbidden acts. But an even more striking finding was this: when the Russian children believed that their peers would see their answers, they were less willing to admit to an inclination toward forbidden acts than when they thought that no one would see their answers. In other words, the influence of their peers acted as a restraint. For American children, the finding was the opposite; when they believed that their peers would see their answers, they were *more* inclined toward forbidden or rebellious behavior (47). In the Soviet Union, it would appear, the peer group serves to help enforce compliance with adult standards; in the United States, it serves to foster rebelliousness.

3. dominance and submission

One personality characteristic that becomes partially set by the end of the early school years is the child's tendency to be dominant or submissive in his relations with other people. The child of ten who actively makes suggestions to the group, tries to influence and persuade others, and resists pressure to make him conform is likely to remain dominant in his social relations for the rest of his life. The child, especially the girl, who is quiet and readily follows the lead of others is likely to remain passive and submissive.

The tendency to be dominant or submissive is partly learned in the home, but it is also a function of group acceptance. The child who believes he has characteristics that are admired by the group is likely to develop self-confidence and to be dominant; the child who does not consider himself admired by the group is likely to develop feelings of inferiority and to be submissive. The child's physical attributes are important. The large, strong boy and the attractive girl are more likely to be dominant, the small boy and the unattractive girl to be submissive. Other factors are identification with a dominant or submissive parent and also the kind of control exercised by the parents. Permissive parents tend to influence their children in the direction of being dominant, while parents who restrict their children's activities tend to influence them in the direction of being submissive.

4. motives and standards

Another change that occurs in the early school years concerns the relative importance of motives and standards. The desire to live up to standards gradually begins to take top position in the hierarchy. For example, a four-year-old girl values her mother's kiss for its own sake; she has a motive to obtain signs of affection. By the time she is eight she is likely to have developed a standard that in effect says, "I should be valued by my parents." Her desire to live up to this standard of being valued is more general than her earlier motives for physical affection and more difficult to satisfy.

Four important standards that begin to take form in the early school years are these:

1. Being valued by parents and peers.
2. Mastery of physical and mental skills.
3. Behavior appropriate to sex typing—particularly strength, independence, and athletic skills among boys; social skills and inhibition of aggression among girls.
4. Cognitive consonance between thoughts and behavior. (The child wants to behave rationally and sensibly and in a way that confirms his self-concept and his identification with his parents and other heroes.)

5, anxieties and defenses

Because of the rapid development of standards, children in the early grades of school tend to develop new anxieties connected with meeting these standards. They acquire anxieties and feelings of guilt about a wide variety of activities, especially those connected with achievement, sex typing, dependence, independence, aggression, submission, and sexual behavior. They also begin to show pronounced preferences for the various defenses against anxiety; some develop a tendency toward withdrawal, denial, or the other defense mechanisms that were discussed on pages 384–87.

Children who are unsuccessful at coping with their anxieties in this period begin to display many of the symptoms of neurosis that are found in adults. These

same stimulus, different response

15-23 The two young daughters of an astronaut exhibit very different reactions while watching their father on a space-walk broadcast over television. The girl at right stifles a yawn—while her older sister casts a reproachful glance.

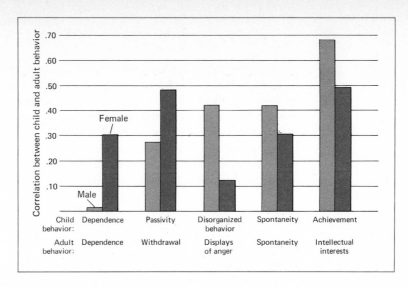

how child foreshadows adult

15-24 The bars show the correlations between the behavior of boys and girls and their behavior later, as young adults. The children rated for dependence, passivity, and disorganized behavior were aged six to ten; those rated for spontaneity and achievement were ten to fourteen. (48)

include unreasonable fears, which often result in nightmares; stereotyped behavior, such as ritualistic hand washing, obsessions, and tics; and psychosomatic ailments, such as headaches, asthma, vomiting, skin disturbances, and even ulcers.

By the time the child is ten he is a vastly different organism from the helpless baby in the crib. He has grown physically and is capable of performing a wide variety of motor skills. He has mastered the language and acquired an almost staggering number of concepts, facts, and premises. His personality has developed in a host of directions; and individual differences in personality among children of this age are readily apparent to anyone who watches their behavior—as can be seen in Figure 15-23.

Many of the personality traits that the child has acquired will be carried through adolescence and into adult life, as indicated by the correlations illustrated in Figure 15-24. The trend of his physical development and the pattern of his mental processes have also been established. <u>Thus the child's personality, physique, and thinking at ten offer a reasonably accurate preview of what he will be like as an adult and an indication of the kind of role he is likely to play in society.</u>

summary 1. *Developmental psychology* studies the processes by which the child acquires his patterns of overt behavior, thinking, problem solving, and perception, and the emotions, motives, conflicts, and ways of coping with conflicts that will go to make up his adult personality.

2. Babies appear to differ at birth not only in capacity for physical development but also in a) level of activity, b) sensory thresholds and adaptation, c) irritability, and d) temperament. On the matter of temperament, about 40 percent appear to be "easy" children, 15 percent "slow to warm up," and 10 percent "difficult"; the others are mixed types.

3. The baby's physical development, including the acquisition of such skills as walking and talking, depends largely on the process of *maturation*—physical changes, taking place after birth, that continue the biological growth of the organism from fertilized egg cell to complete adult.

4. The development of skill at perception and language, though also influenced by maturation, appears to depend largely on learning.

5. The child's skill at perception improves partly because he becomes more efficient at scanning the environment; he begins to know what to look for and how to go about it. One of the strongest influences on the child's perceptions is his increasing use of language, which helps him in making discriminations and in organizing sensory experiences into patterns.

6. Language ability is composed of two separate processes—*comprehension* (understanding words) and *expression* (speaking them)—which seem to be controlled by different areas of the brain. Comprehension is the first of the skills to develop. The average child can understand 3 words at the age of one, 22 words at eighteen months, 272 words at two, and 2000 words at five.

7. Ability at expression or speaking words also develops rapidly. By the age of four the average child is constructing sentences that are quite accurate grammatically.

8. Intellectual development proceeds in an orderly and predictable fashion, partly through maturation and partly through learning, especially the learning of concepts.

9. According to Piaget, intellectual development is basically an increased ability to adapt to new situations. The key processes in development are *assimilation* (the process of incorporating a new stimulus into one's existing cognitive view of the world) and *accommodation* (the process of changing one's cognitive view and behavior when new information dictates such a change).

10. Piaget has charted intellectual development through the following stages: a) the *sensorimotor stage* (birth to age two), b) the *preoperational stage* (two to seven), c) the *stage of concrete operations* (seven to eleven), and d) the *stage of formal operations* (beginning at about eleven or twelve).

11. Personality development begins with the *caretaker period* (birth to eighteen months), when healthy development is characterized by attachment to and a close relationship with the mother, resulting in, among other things, the appearance of *stranger anxiety* and *separation anxiety*. A child neglected during this period grows up under severe psychological handicaps.

12. The period from eighteen months through three years is characterized by the *first social demands* on the child, asking him to conform to discipline and to undergo toilet training. Too much discipline or protection during

this period may instill a crippling amount of anxiety and create lifelong inhibitions against trying anything novel or challenging.

13. The *preschool years*, four and five, are characterized by identification with the parents; the development of standards, feelings of guilt, and a conscience; and the first notions of sex typing and conduct appropriate to males and females.

14. From six to ten, the child comes under the strong influence of his *peers*, that is, of other children. His peers provide a) evaluation, b) a role, and c) an opportunity for rebellion against the restraints of the adult world. The child is also influenced during this period by his teachers, who help him acquire intellectual skills and foster the motive for intellectual mastery.

15. During the ages six to ten, the child usually develops lasting tendencies to seek or fear intellectual mastery, to be dominant or submissive, to have a pattern of standards, to experience anxiety over failure to meet these standards, and to show pronounced preferences for the various defenses against anxiety. Many of these personality traits will be carried through adolescence and into adult life.

recommended reading

Bowlby, J. *Attachment*. New York: Basic Books, 1969.

Elkind, D. *Children and adolescents: interpretive essays on Jean Piaget*. New York: Oxford University Press, 1970.

Elkind, D. *A sympathetic understanding of the child six to sixteen*. Boston: Allyn and Bacon, 1971.

Kagan, J. *Understanding children: behavior, motives, and thought*. New York: Harcourt Brace Jovanovich, 1971.

Lavatelli, C. S., and Stendler, F., eds. *Readings in child behavior and development*, 3rd ed. New York: Harcourt Brace Jovanovich, 1972.

Mussen, P. H., ed. *Carmichael's manual of child psychology*, 3rd ed., 2 vols. New York: Wiley, 1970.

Mussen, P. H., Conger, J. J., and Kagan, J. *Child development and personality*, 3rd ed. New York: Harper & Row, 1969.

Piaget, J., and Inhelder, B. *The psychology of the child*. New York: Basic Books, 1969.

CHAPTER 16

social psychology

DEFINITION:
SOCIAL PSYCHOLOGY

The scene is a street corner where a neon sign brightly spells out the command: WAIT. Several hundred pedestrians approach the corner. Almost all of them wait until the signal changes; only 1 percent violate the command. Then, while pedestrians are waiting at the corner, a rather untidy young man in denim shirt, patched trousers, and scuffed shoes joins the group and proceeds to cross against the light. How many will follow him? How many would follow a young man neatly dressed in a suit?

This series of events took place in a well-known experiment on the effect of social influence. The young man in the denim shirt was a graduate student, and the well-dressed young man was the same student on a different occasion. As it turned out, 4 percent of pedestrians followed him through the "wait" signal when he wore the shabby clothes, 14 percent when he was dressed neatly (1).

This is only one of many experiments that have demonstrated the importance of social stimuli to human behavior. To a very considerable extent, all of us behave as we see the people around us behave or as we believe they expect us to behave. Our thinking is also molded in large part by the people around us. To a greater degree than most of us ever realize, we are the products of our social environments. We develop from child to adult, as was shown in the preceding chapter, not in a vacuum but in close interaction with our parents, families, teachers, and schoolmates. Our actions and mental life as adults are still shaped by others. Hence the importance of *social psychology,* which *studies the manner in which man "thinks, feels, and behaves in social situations"* (2). To put this more broadly, social psychology is the study of how people influence and are influenced by other people. For our behavior is at the same time a stimulus and a response to the behavior of other people—what we do helps determine what they do, but at the same time what we do is partly determined by what they are doing or what they seem to expect us to do (3).

man as a member of society

Unlike some animals, man does not prowl the world alone or with no company save that of a mate. Man is a social animal. Ever since he appeared on the face of the earth he seems to have lived in some kind of community, probably starting with the ancient cave communities. The most primitive people still left in the undeveloped parts of today's world are banded together in some kind of mutual living arrangement. As was seen in the preceding chapter, the human baby cannot develop normally without close contacts with other human beings. Similarly the human adult appears to need the company and cooperation of other human beings if he is to survive.

Society is the name applied to any organized group of people, large or small. The people living in a group of thatched huts in Africa make up a society; so do the people living in a small Midwestern town or in New York City. The United States itself is a society. Or one may speak of the entire Western world as a society.

DEFINITION:
SOCIETY

learning society's ways:
the socialization process and norms

Almost from the moment of birth, a child born in the United States begins to learn the ways of his own society. He learns the English language; he learns how American adults (his parents) speak, behave toward one another, and express or conceal their emotions; he learns how children are expected to treat parents and one another. Later he learns what people in society believe, what they value, and the customs and laws that dictate a whole host of activities, from courting a mate to conducting a business transaction.

This process is called *socialization;* it is the process by which the child is integrated into the society through exposure to the actions and opinions of older members of the society. In many ways, the child becomes a creature of his society (4), molded by its customs and rules. Thus a child born in the United States grows up into a far different person from the child born into a different kind of society. For example, children in complex societies such as the United States, which have considerable specialization of occupations and a wide range of social classes of differing wealth and power, tend to seek attention, recognition, and dominance; they are primarily concerned with their own interests and fortunes. On the other hand, children in simpler societies such as the Philippines tend to offer support and help to others; they appear to be more altruistic (5). In contrast to the United States, there are some societies in which women and not men do all the work, while the men devote themselves to ceremony and self-adornment (6). There are places where two friends would never dream of competing against each other, as in games or athletic contests (7).

One of the important aspects of the socialization process is the acquisition of what are called *norms*—a sociological term for the standards and expectations shared by the members of a society. Every society has a large number of norms regulating almost all kinds of behavior. Some relate to relatively minor matters such as courtesy and dress, and these vary widely from one society to another. In the United States, for example, all of us are expected to behave in accordance with such norms as driving on the right side of the road, eating with a knife and a fork, dressing (usually) in men's trousers and women's dresses, and being on time for classes or business appointments. The norms in England call for driving on the left side of the road; in the Orient for eating with chopsticks; in some

DEFINITION:
SOCIALIZATION

countries for dressing in robes and turbans; in many Latin countries for disregarding clocks and appointment times.

Other norms set standards of behavior regarded by the members of a society as absolutely essential to the welfare of the individual and the group—and therefore often considered unquestionable, inviolable, and even sacred. Such are the norms that prohibit murder, robbery, and cannibalism, that regulate sexual behavior and marriage, and that define the obligations of parents to children and of children to parents. Even these may vary from society to society; cannibalism has been an accepted practice in parts of the world, and in some places it is considered proper for a man to have many wives. But, in general, most societies have rather similar norms governing extremely disruptive forms of behavior such as murder and rape.

socialization and subcultures

Up to this point, the discussion has treated the United States society as if it were a single and unified entity with a set of norms accepted by all its citizens. It must now be pointed out, however, that this is not really true. Within our society there exist many *subcultures,* or ways of life that differ from one another in many rather important respects. This is true partly because the nation has been settled over the years by people from many different parts of the world bringing with them their own particular customs, values, and norms. For example, Americans show such varied ethnic patterns as those illustrated in Figure 16-1, as well as observe many different kinds of religious practices.

Moreover, the child is socialized into different patterns of behavior if he

DEFINITION:
SUBCULTURE

United States subcultures

16-1 Among the ethnic and religious groups that observe different cultural patterns in the United States are the Puerto Rican (right), Amish, Italian, and Chinese (below).

is born in a rural area than if he is born in a small city and into still other patterns if he is born in a large city. He may grow up into membership in subcultures as varied as the hippie community, the world of music, the academic community, the business community, and the scientific community. As can be seen from the many sharp differences revealed in public opinion polls, the United States is a nation of many subcultures holding far different attitudes on religion, politics, militarism, sexual behavior, the use of drugs, and life styles in general.

the importance of social class

DEFINING SOCIAL CLASSES

One important factor in determining how the child will be socialized is the social class of the home in which he is born. In general, social classes can be defined and differentiated in terms of the degree to which their members have power or access to power in the society and believe that they enjoy control over their own and their children's lives. In the United States, this sense of power and control usually depends mostly on education and income; and there are substantial differences between middle-class families in which parents have a college education and an income of $10,000 a year or more and lower-class families in which the parents have not finished high school and have an income of less than $5000 a year. The child born in a lower-class ghetto and the child born in a middle-class suburb both learn to speak English, but they learn to speak it in very different ways. Many students of language believe that English as spoken in the ghetto is actually more direct and expressive than English as spoken by the middle class (8)—but it can be a handicap in schools staffed by middle-class teachers or in middle-class jobs. Many kinds of norms, values, and attitudes also vary with the level of income and education of the home and the neighborhood.

As is shown in Figure 16–2, mothers who may roughly be called middle class tend to be more permissive toward their children than mothers with less education and income. Partly for this reason, and partly because of the different kinds of models and incentives that the environment provides, children from the middle and upper classes show a greater amount of achievement motivation than do children from the lower classes. This fact, illustrated in Figure 16–3, may help account for the greater frequency with which middle-class children move up the social scale or, to use a phrase coined by the sociologists, demonstrate *upward mobility*.

DEFINITION: UPWARD MOBILITY

Members of the upper classes tend to be more conservative in their political and economic beliefs; typically, a majority of the upper classes have voted Republican, whereas the lower classes have produced strong Democratic majorities (11). Sexual behavior varies. The Kinsey studies showed, for example, that intercourse before marriage has been relatively common but masturbation less common among young men of the lower classes, whereas the opposite has been true among young men of the upper classes. Sexual foreplay was found to be more prolonged and varied among the upper classes, more simple and direct among the lower classes (12). Members of different classes also tend to have different tastes in food, entertainment, and sports, as well as different norms regulating many kinds of social conduct.

	Percentage of parents rated "high"	
	MIDDLE CLASS	WORKING CLASS
Severity of toilet training	15	26
Use of physical punishment	17	33
Use of ridicule	31	47
Stress on child's doing well at school	35	50
Pressure for neatness and order	43	57
Father's insistence on immediate obedience	53	67
Permissiveness for aggression toward parents	19	7
Sex permissiveness	53	22

class differences in rearing children

Mothers in a New England metropolitan area were interviewed on the ways they had reared their children from birth to the age of five, and ratings were made. Note that a higher percentage of working-class mothers than middle-class mothers were rated "high" on the six items related to strictness and a lower percentage on the two items involving permissiveness. (9)

social class and achievement motive

16-3

A study of high school sophomores in Connecticut found large differences in achievement motive between boys from the lowest and lower classes and boys from the middle and upper classes. Note that those from the middle class had the highest scores of all. (10)

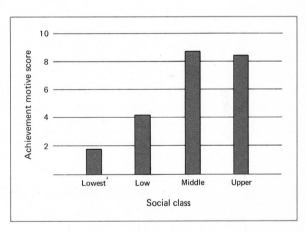

Problems Caused by "Upward Mobility." The United States has always prided itself on being a nation where any worthy young person could improve his station in life. There is considerable evidence that the opportunities for upward mobility depend less on our political ideals than on a more pragmatic factor, the need that scientific and industrial development has created for ever increasing numbers of skilled people (13). At any rate, it is certainly true that many Americans in every recent generation have surpassed their parents in education, job level, income, and the other factors that help determine social class.

The idea of an open-end society where each person is free to find his own level, as dictated by his own abilities and motives, is an attractive one. It must be pointed out, however, that the differences among social classes that have just been discussed can pose some serious psychological problems for the person who moves up the social-class ladder. At each step of the way his old norms no longer suffice, and he is likely to be highly self-conscious and uncomfortable until he has got rid of them and learned the standards of behavior appropriate to his new situation. He may never feel entirely at ease in the company of people who have spent a lifetime developing the customs and attitudes of the class into which he has moved.

One study, made in New Haven, Connecticut, compared the upper class in New Haven with those who had recently moved up from the lower levels. The latter were found in many cases to show "conspicuous consumption," insecurity, and family instability, which often led to broken homes and divorce (14).

position and role

DEFINITION:

POSITION OR STATUS
IN SOCIETY

As society is organized, each of us at any given moment occupies a particular place or niche, giving us more or less prestige among our fellow men. Social psychologists call this our *position* or *status* in society. Position is determined by many factors, including age, place in the family (mother, father, daughter, son), occupation, and membership in groups (a college class, circle of friends, or religious organization).

As we go through life, our position or status changes. We progress from child to adolescent to adult; we find new occupations; we join new groups. At each stage of life, indeed, we occupy several different positions. For example, within the family a woman may be wife to her husband at the breakfast table, then mother to her children until they go off to school, then, on a visit to her own mother, a daughter again. She may have a job in which she has little or much responsibility and respect from her fellow workers. She may lead a troop of Girl Scouts, where she is the oldest person present, and be a member of a garden club, where she is the youngest. In the garden club she may be considered a follower, but she may also belong to the PTA and be its acknowledged leader.

From a person in a given position, society expects a certain kind of behavior; the person is expected to play what social psychologists call the *role* appropriate to that position. The word *role* is taken from the theater; it implies that just as a role written by a playwright is supposed to be played much the same way regardless of who the actor is, so a role in society is supposed to be played in much the same way regardless of the individual. Society decrees that a college student—*any* college student—take a certain number of courses, get a certain level of grades, refrain from cheating on examinations, and maintain a certain standard of personal conduct. It decrees that an instructor—*any* instructor—be an expert in his field, firm but fair with students, and respectable in private life.

Perhaps the best demonstration of the meaning of position or status and its relation to role comes from an ingenious experiment in which a recording was made of what sounded like one end of a telephone conversation. From the conversation it appeared that the speaker was talking to a college instructor, whose words, at the other end, could not be heard. The speaker, it appeared, was about to visit the dean of the college department, to discuss the instructor's skill as a teacher. In the recorded conversation he told the instructor what he was going to say to the dean, beginning with the words, "I'm afraid your teaching hasn't been . . . ."

The recording was played to two groups of subjects, who were then asked to give their impressions of the speaker. One group was told that he was a college student; this group found his comments to the instructor quite critical and described him as "egotistical," "ambitious," and "aggressive." The other group was told that the speaker was the chairman of the college department; this group found his comments to the instructor rather gentle, perhaps even wishy-washy, and described him as at best "compassionate" and at worst "hesitant" or "indecisive" (15).

The subjects had decided, in effect, that a person in the position of student should not behave toward an instructor as the speaker on the recording was behaving; to play the role in this manner was arrogant and disrespectful. For a person in the position of department chairman, on the other hand, to speak in such a manner was just the opposite; the chairman's proper role was to be more firm and decisive. The experiment is eloquent proof of the fact that in each position we hold, society expects us to play the role associated with that position. We are under constant pressure to play the role properly; we receive acceptance and praise if we do and we are punished in various ways if we do not. Thus each role has its own set of norms, to which any person playing the role is expected to conform.

role strain

It is not always easy to obey the norms and meet the expectations of our fellow men, and therefore all of us suffer from time to time from *role strain.* Even in a rather simple two-person relationship, we may not know exactly where we stand or what kind of role we are expected to play; to the social psychologist, a lovers' quarrel is often an attempt to learn more about each other's expectations and thus to clarify the role each is expected to fill (16).

Role strain is particularly likely to occur when we move from one position to another. For example, many of the problems of adolescence represent role strain resulting from the transition from the position of child to the position of adult. The child's role is to be sexless, submissive, and without any particular responsibilities; the adult's role is to be just the opposite (17).

Role strain also frequently occurs because we occupy several different positions at once. For example, the role strains likely to plague the college freshman have been summarized by Roger Brown, a social psychologist, in a description of the situation illustrated in Figure 16-4. In the position of son in his family, the student's role as defined by his parents is to dress, behave, and hold opinions dictated by their norms and to visit them on weekends. In his position as college freshman, his role as defined by the faculty and the upper-classmen may call for him to dress quite differently, behave in a different fashion,

ROLE STRAIN

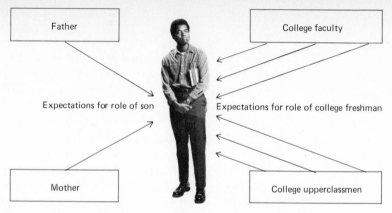

Father		College faculty
Expectations for role of son		Expectations for role of college freshman
Mother		College upperclassmen

a college freshman's role strains

16-4 Charted here are some of the role strains that may beset a college student. This person occupies two important roles; he is a son, for whom his mother and father have set role expectations, and he is also a college freshman, who feels the pressure of expectations from both the faculty and the upperclassmen. His attempts to play the role of college freshman are further complicated, as indicated by the multiple arrows, by the fact that individual faculty members and upperclassmen do not seem to agree on what they expect from him. For a full explanation, see the text. (18)

hold other opinions, and spend his weekends studying (or attending football games or parties). Moreover, while the expectations of his parents are probably quite clear-cut, those of the people among whom he finds himself on the campus may be vague and contradictory. Some members of the faculty may expect him to study very hard, while others are less demanding. Some may give him good grades only if he memorizes their opinions, others only if he shows independence of thought. Some upperclassmen may reject him unless he plays the role of a studious intellectual, others unless he scorns good grades and spends most of his time socializing. He may find many contradictory expectations about cheating, style of dress, dating behavior, drinking, political orientation, religious views, and other matters. His discomfort may be further intensified by the fact that he went to a small high school, where he made good grades, was senior class president, and enjoyed a position of leadership, while now, in the larger college, he makes only average grades, is not regarded as a leader, and feels that he is held in rather low esteem.

role and personality

Some roles permit a considerable amount of leeway. The college student, for example, is free within limits to wear expensive clothes or cheap clothes, to join whatever political or social organizations he favors, to spend his spare time reading or shooting pool.

The same thing is true of most roles in life, although the rigidity of the norms varies from role to role. The college professor generally must live up to more rigid standards and expectations than the student. A physician usually faces

556

more rigorous demands than a professor, and a Jesuit priest more inflexible demands than a physician. The role of mother generally involves more fixed expectations than the role of father.

To the extent that a role permits leeway, the manner in which an individual fills it depends on his own personality. Hence some physicians are quiet and detached, while others are emotional and sympathetic. Some mothers are strict, others permissive. On the other hand, the roles we take in life also affect our personalities. The college freshman arriving on the campus may at first consciously try to imitate the mannerisms of the upperclassmen and at the same time behave as the faculty seems to expect. After a time the conscious imitation is likely to become a way of life; the student actually becomes the kind of person he at first merely pretended to be. Thus every role leaves its mark on a person. Indeed it has been suggested that personality is in large part an integration of the various roles that the individual has played—an interesting and provocative sidelight to the social learning theory of personality (pages 410–12).

attraction to others

Among the questions that have intrigued many social psychologists are these: Why are we more or less instantly attracted to some people and neutral or even antagonistic to others? Is there really such a thing as "love at first sight"—or for that matter hate at first sight? Why do some people "grow on us" as we get to know them better, and others disappoint our original expectations? Is it true, as some old adages have it, that "like attracts like" and that "birds of a feather flock together"? Or is there more truth to the conflicting adage that says "opposites attract"?

These are questions on which social psychology has accumulated considerable evidence over the years, in its study of what is known by the technical term *interpersonal attraction*. It has been found that many factors influence the manner in which we are attracted to other people or repelled by them, often in such complex ways that there is a certain amount of truth in all the old adages, even those that appear to be totally contradictory.

how like attracts like

One of the most important of all the factors, generally speaking, is whether we perceive the other person's attitudes, interests, and personality to be similar to our own. This fact can readily be observed in real-life situations and has also been demonstrated experimentally. At one large university, a psychologist arranged to operate a sort of men's dormitory in which he assigned roommates on an experimental basis. Some roommates were put together because interviews and questionnaires had shown that they were very similar in attitudes, interests, and tastes. Others were put together because they had been found quite different from each other. Having once assigned roommates, the experimenter let nature

take its course and interfered no further in the students' lives. He found that roommates who were very much alike usually liked each other and became good friends, while those who were dissimilar usually did not like each other and did not become friends (19).

Of special importance in the process of like attracting like are *attitudes,* the deep-seated patterns of belief, emotion, and behavioral tendencies that will be discussed in a section of their own later in the chapter. In one experiment, a psychologist measured the attitudes of college students on a variety of issues, such as the strength of their attachment to the Republican or Democratic party. He then showed them what he said were responses to attitude questionnaires by other students they had never met. The supposed answers of these supposed "strangers" had been carefully designed so that the stranger sometimes seemed to have no attitudes at all in common with the subject, in some cases seemed to be in total agreement on all attitudes, and in other cases fell somewhere in between, agreeing with some of the subject's attitudes and disagreeing with others. The subjects were asked to rate these various strangers on a scale ranging from not at all attractive to very attractive. As is shown in Figure 16-5, the attractiveness ratings turned out to bear an almost perfect straight-line relationship to the number of attitudes the subjects believed were held in common (20). The experiment indicates how strongly we tend to be attracted to people who share our attitudes; though we may still be attracted to a person who has similar attitudes on politics and religion but disagrees with us about civil rights, the more attitudes we hold in common the greater is the degree of attraction.

Similarities in interests and traits also enhance attraction. Many college friendships, as can readily be observed, are based on a mutual interest in athletics, music, or the study of art or the drama. And people also form friendships on the basis of similarities in such traits as intelligence and sense of humor.

the more shared attitudes, the greater the attraction

16-5

The independent variable was how subjects would rate a "stranger" on a scale ranging from 2 (not at all attractive) to 14 (very attractive). The dependent variable was the percentage of attitudes that the subject believed he and the "stranger" held in common. Note that the curve is almost a straight line, indicating an almost perfect correlation. (20)

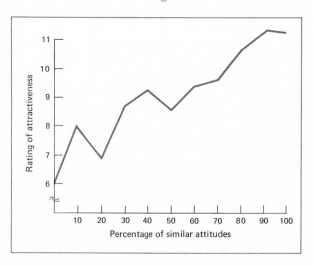

Attraction Between Opposites.   Although it is generally true that like attracts like, it is also occasionally true that opposites attract. As social psychologists put it, people sometimes seek the company of people whose personalities do not match but *complement* their own. This can be seen at times in marriages; an aggressive, boastful, talkative man may be paired with a self-effacing, modest, quiet wife, or a prominent career woman may be paired with a man who has very little ambition and dedicates himself to helping her. The phenomenon is difficult to study experimentally and is not completely understood, but it does occur—presumably because each of the two "opposites" has a need that the other helps satisfy.

finding similarities where none exist

All in all, the tendency for like to attract like is so strong—and the urge toward affiliation and companionship so compelling—that we often believe people are more similar to us than they really are. This is particularly true of people we like. For example, in one experiment fraternity men were asked to make a self-rating of their own traits of various kinds, then to name the fellow members they liked best and least and to rate these men for the same traits. When subject A liked subject B, he showed a strong tendency to rate subject B as having traits considerably more similar to his own than subject B's self-rating showed (21). It has also been found that husbands and wives—especially when happily married—believe they are more similar to each other than they in fact are (22).

This tendency to think that other people resemble us is very reminiscent of the defense mechanism called projection (pages 384–85). It also results at least in part from the fact that other people behave around us in a way that is dictated at least partly by our own behavior; they act more similar to us than they really are. One experiment has shown that subjects who are in the company of people who act egotistical and boastful tend to behave in a rather egotistical and boastful manner themselves, whereas in the presence of people who seem humble and self-effacing they tend to behave in a modest fashion (23). This sort of behavior may at times represent a deliberate attempt to ingratiate oneself and thus receive acceptance, but often it appears to be something that one does naturally and honestly, without any intent to deceive.

the effect of familiarity

One well-established fact in the field of interpersonal attraction is that, contrary to the old adage, familiarity does *not* breed contempt. All other things being equal, the more familiar we are with another person—the more chance we have to get used to him—the more likely we are to be attracted to him. In one experiment, for example, two subjects who did not know each other sat across from each other without talking. Some of them met in this manner on three occasions, others six times, others twelve times. Afterward they were asked how much they liked each other. The more often they had seen the other, the greater was the mutual attraction (24). Indeed the same thing is true even of photographs

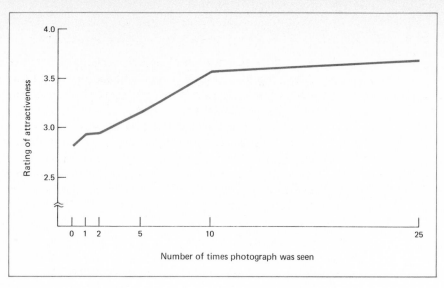

16-6 The amount of attraction felt toward a person seen in a photograph rises sharply with the number of times the photograph has been seen. (25)

of people. In another study, photographs of faces were shown to the subjects, some just once, others as many as twenty-five times. Then the photographs were shown again, along with some never seen before, and the subjects were asked if they thought they would like the person. As is illustrated in Figure 16-6, the amount of attraction they felt toward the person in the photograph was closely related to how often they had seen his picture (25).

Indeed it appears that even the prospect of becoming familiar with another person can make him more attractive. When strangers are introduced in the laboratory, it has been found that they are more attracted to each other if told that they will work together in the future than if they believe they may never meet again (26). Similarly, we tend to like those who live nearest to us. A number of studies have shown that people are likely to be most friendly with those who live right next door to them in a college dormitory, an apartment building, or a suburban group of houses (27).

the importance of first impressions

When we meet a stranger, our first impressions often have a lasting effect on how attractive he seems. In one experiment, subjects first saw a stranger—actually an accomplice of the experimenter—in a laboratory waiting room, in the presence of the experimenter's secretary. In some cases, the accomplice was extremely impolite, belligerent, and demanding toward the secretary. In other cases, the accomplice was polite and pleasant. Later the subjects again met the accomplice-stranger on three to twelve other occasions. As would be expected from what is known about the effect of familiarity, they liked the "pleasant"

560

stranger better when they saw him twelve times than when they saw him only three times. But increased contact did not change their ratings of the "unpleasant" stranger (28). <u>In other words, the effect of the bad first impression outweighed the effect of familiarity.</u>

Another effect of first impressions was demonstrated in an experiment in which subjects watched and listened to a person answering the items on an intelligence test. The person taking the test, an accomplice of the experimenters, followed three different patterns in his answers. In front of some subjects, he answered the first questions very accurately, then began making mistakes. In front of other subjects, he performed evenly and moderately well throughout. Still other subjects observed him do badly on the early questions, then improve his performance later on. When the subjects were asked to rate him on intelligence, he was given the highest marks by those who had observed him answer well at first and then become less accurate as the test went on—in other words, by those whose first impression of him had been most favorable (29).

The fact that first impressions are important is often called the *halo effect*— <u>which means that our general impressions of another person are strongly colored by any one thing, good or bad, that we initially learn about him.</u> Perhaps the most striking demonstration of the halo effect comes from an experiment in which students reporting for class were informed that they would have a substitute instructor that day. To prepare them for the substitute (so they were told), slips bearing a written description of him were passed around. Half the slips described the substitute as "a rather cold person, industrious, critical, practical, and determined." The other half said "a rather warm person, industrious, critical, practical, and determined." The changing of only one word—*cold* to *warm*—had some interesting effects. The students who had received slips calling the substitute "warm" took more part in the classroom discussion that day than did the others. Afterward, asked their impressions, they described the substitute in much more favorable terms than did the students who had been told he was "cold." Figure 16-7 shows some of the differences in the students' ratings of the substitute (30).

DEFINITION: HALO EFFECT

what a difference a word makes

16-7

These are some of the ratings of a substitute instructor made by a class of students—half of whom had been told he was a "warm" person and half of whom had been told he was "cold." Note how the single word *cold* led students to judge him as also irritable, humorless, and so on—characteristics that the students who expected him to be "warm" were much less likely to find.

Characteristics on which substitute was rated	Substitute instructor believed to be	
	"Warm"	"Cold"
Irritable	9.4	12.0
Humorless	8.3	11.7
Ruthless	8.6	11.0
Unsociable	5.6	10.4
Self-centered	6.3	9.6
Formal	6.3	9.6
Unpopular	4.0	7.4

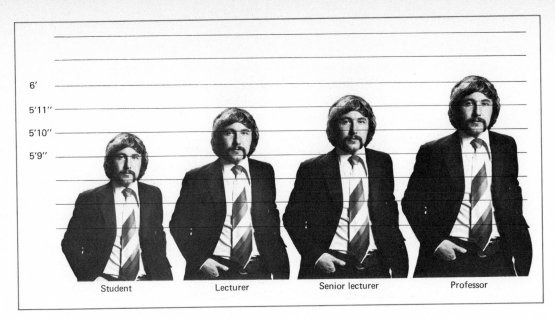

16-8

Estimates of his height, as was discovered in an experiment described in the text, depend on how important he is believed to be by the people making the estimate. The more important he is, the taller he seems to be in the eyes of his beholders.

Somewhat similar to the halo effect and the matter of first impressions is the fact that we tend to judge people and behave toward them in ways dictated at least in part by how important or wealthy we think they are. In one rather amusing experiment, investigators drove several different kinds of automobiles through the streets and tried to arrange as many instances as possible when they would have to stop at a red light and another car would stop behind. When the light turned green, the investigators did not move but instead waited to see how much time would elapse before the driver behind honked at them. When they were in a shiny new luxury automobile, the driver behind waited much longer than when they were in an old and inexpensive car (31). In a similar experiment, a stranger was introduced to a number of college classes—sometimes as a student, sometimes as a lecturer, and sometimes as a full professor. After he departed, the students in the classes were asked to estimate his height. As is shown in Figure 16-8, when he was introduced as a student the average estimate was 5 feet 10 inches; when he was introduced as a professor the average estimate was slightly over 6 feet (32).

liking those who like us

It seems only logical to assume that we tend to be attracted to other people who seem to be attracted to us, and this assumption has been borne out by a number of experimental studies (33). It also has been found that we tend to like people who help gratify our needs and wishes or in whose company we have achieved satisfactions (34), as can be observed by the general air of camaraderie on a winning athletic team. It has been found too that we tend to like people who have a good opinion of us (35).

There is some evidence, however, that attraction based on the fact that another person has a good opinion of us may operate in a manner contrary to the general rules about first impressions. In one experiment, subjects held a series of brief interviews with a person they believed was another subject but was in fact an accomplice of the experimenter. After each interview, they overheard a conversation in which the accomplice gave the experimenter his impressions of them. As would be expected, the subjects were attracted to the accomplice if he consistently expressed a good opinion after each interview. But they were even more attracted if he was critical of them after the early interviews and gradually came around to a favorable opinion (36). Apparently there is a special kind of satisfaction—and thus a strong tendency toward attraction—in obtaining the good opinion of a person who was at first critical.

attitudes

DEFINITION:
ATTITUDE

The word *attitude* has been used several times in this chapter, and the time has now come to define it and elaborate on its importance in social psychology. The definition is this: *an attitude is an organized and enduring set of beliefs and feelings toward some kind of object or situation and a predisposition to behave toward it in a particular way*. For example, a person's attitude toward religion would include a number of beliefs about the existence of a higher power, emotional feelings of awe and humility connected with these beliefs, and a behavioral tendency to go to church, to repond favorably to ministers, and to respond unfavorably toward immoral or atheistic actions. A favorable attitude toward civil rights would include a set of beliefs about the equality of men, positive emotional reactions to signs of progress by minority groups and a dislike of prejudiced comments or actions, and a tendency to vote for candidates who favor equality. A negative attitude toward women's liberation would include a belief that woman's place is in the home, feelings of attraction to passive women and distaste for militant women, and a tendency to seek out a dependent woman rather than a career woman as a wife.

It is chiefly the emotional component of an attitude that distinguishes it from a mere *belief* or *opinion*. A belief that the world is round has no emotional flavor. It is merely the cognitive acceptance of what is presumed to be a matter of fact. The person who holds this belief is neither for nor against roundness—and in the unlikely event that science should suddenly discover that the world is shaped like a football, he would not hesitate to change his opinion. An attitude, because of its emotional overtones—because we are strongly for or against whatever it is that the attitude concerns—is much more resistant to change. Since attitudes are so enduring, and since they influence so much of our behavior toward our fellow men, they are perhaps the central issue in social psychology.

the sources of attitudes

Attitudes are of course learned—and learned in interaction with other people. We acquire many of them by being exposed to the attitudes of our parents, imitating them, and being rewarded for expressing similar attitudes and behaving in accordance with them. Consistent similarities have been found between the attitudes of parents and children toward political and economic affairs and religion (37). Thus one nationwide survey of high school seniors showed that 76 percent of them favored the same political party as their parents, provided that both parents agreed (38). Other studies have shown that parents often are the first source of children's negative attitudes toward minority groups (39).

On the road from childhood to adulthood we also acquire many attitudes from our peer groups; the kinds of companions we find in school play a crucial role in shaping the attitudes we carry into adulthood. For college students, the freshman year is often especially influential in this respect (2). Up to that time, many students have lived in relatively homogeneous environments; then suddenly they find themselves in the company of many different kinds of teachers and fellow students holding attitudes they had not previously encountered. A student from a religious and politically conservative background may find himself exposed to new attitudes of religious skepticism and political liberalism. A student whose family and friends have scoffed at literature and art may find himself around people who greatly admire them.

The college years often produce pronounced changes in attitudes and a certain amount of estrangement between students and their parents—an aspect of the "generation gap" discussed on pages 31–32. For example, the number of college students who prefer the same political party as their fathers drops to between 50 and 60 percent (40). Moreover, attitudes developed as a result of the college experience tend to persist throughout life. One well-known study of this phenomenon began in the late 1930's in a women's college attended largely by students from wealthy and conservative backgrounds but staffed by a faculty that some people would call extremely "liberal" and others would call "radical." By the time students at this college reached their senior year, it was found, some remained quite conservative but most showed pronounced changes toward a liberal attitude. A follow-up twenty years later showed that they continued to hold the same attitudes they had held as seniors (41).

shifts in public opinion

Public opinion surveys and other studies have shown rather marked shifts over the years in the general climate of attitudes in the United States on political and social issues. For example, more people today favor birth control and abortion than in the past; and many more people have strong attitudes about the need for control of pollution of the environment. Prevailing attitudes toward ethnic groups have changed. A survey of Princeton University students made in

Trait	Percent checking trait 1933	Percent checking trait 1967	Trait	Percent checking trait 1933	Percent checking trait 1967
Americans			**Irish**		
Industrious	48	23	Pugnacious	45	13
Intelligent	47	20	Witty	38	7
Materialistic	33	67	Honest	32	17
Progressive	27	17	Nationalistic	21	41
Germans			**Jews**		
Scientific	78	47	Shrewd	79	30
Stolid	44	9	Mercenary	49	15
Methodical	31	21	Grasping	34	17
Efficient	16	46	Intelligent	29	37
Italians			**Blacks**		
Artistic	53	30	Superstitious	84	13
Impulsive	44	28	Lazy	75	26
Musical	32	9	Ignorant	38	11
Imaginative	30	7	Religious	24	8
Revengeful	17	0			

changed attitudes toward ethnic groups

16-9 How do university students characterize Americans in general, members of other nationalities, and particular ethnic groups? As the figures show, their attitudes have changed considerably since 1933.

1933 showed a strong tendency to think about members of ethnic groups in terms of what were then popular stereotypes—Germans as scientific-minded, stolid, and methodical; Italians as artistic and impulsive; blacks as superstitious and lazy. A similar survey in 1967 showed that these notions had faded and had been replaced by attitudes that, though still perhaps stereotyped, were considerably more thoughtful and realistic (42). Some of the differences between the 1933 and 1967 results are shown in Figure 16-9.

Another study of college students has disclosed a different kind of shift in attitudes that may have an important bearing on future political and social developments. This study, begun in 1964, has shown a consistent and statistically significant increase over the years in the number of introductory psychology students, mostly freshmen, who agree with such statements as "Hypocrisy is on the increase in our society," "This country has a dark future unless we can attract better people into politics," "The United Nations will never be an effective force in keeping world peace," and "Most people would be horrified if they knew how much news the public hears and sees is distorted" (43). In other words, college students appear to be growing less trusting of their fellow man and social institutions and less hopeful about the future.

One of the most interesting shifts in public opinion has been a change in the attitude of blacks toward blacks. In a 1947 study of black children, four dolls were shown—two of them black, two of them white. The children then received instructions such as "Give me the doll that looks bad," "Give me the doll that is a nice doll," and "Give me the doll that you want to play with." It was found that the children had a strong tendency to prefer the white dolls and reject the black dolls (44). The study indicated that black children had developed a low opinion of their own race and was one of the reasons cited by the Supreme Court for its 1954 decision ordering desegregation of schools. When the study was repeated recently, however, it was found that black children now prefer black dolls (45).

the search for consistency

As the shifts in public opinion demonstrate, attitudes do sometimes change. They can be changed by new information that affects the beliefs on which they are partially based (for example, by the discovery that not all people of German descent are stolid and methodical). They can be changed by events that affect the emotional component of the attitude (for example, as when a man who has regarded women as second-class citizens finds himself in love with a woman who is an ardent advocate of women's liberation). They can be changed by new kinds of behavior. (This has been particularly noticeable in recent years in the attitudes of whites toward blacks and blacks toward whites. Among both whites and blacks, integration is most favored by those who have attended school or worked with members of the other race, and it is least favored by those who have had no interracial contacts (46).)

One approach to attitude change that has attracted many social psychologists and resulted in much experimentation and theorizing centers around the idea of a *search for consistency*. The idea is based on the motive for certainty, which was discussed on pages 351-56. This motive, it would appear, inclines a person to seek consistency among his beliefs, that is, the cognitive elements of his attitudes, his feelings, and his behavior. When inconsistencies occur, he is strongly motivated to restore harmony by changing his beliefs, feelings, behavior, or all three—and thus changing his attitude.

There are many theoretical approaches to the search for consistency, prominently including the theory of cognitive dissonance discussed in connection with the motive for certainty. In general, followers of the theory of cognitive dissonance believe that ordinarily a change in behavior precedes and brings about a change in attitude, rather than vice versa. There is considerable experimental evidence to support this idea. For example, one study traced changes in the attitudes of factory workers who were members of a strong labor union. In the course of time, some of the workers were elected union stewards, in which case their attitudes became much more firmly pro-union than before. Others were promoted to foreman, in which case their attitudes became markedly pro-management. But when the factory fell on hard times and some of the foremen were demoted to rank-and-file jobs, they again became pro-union (47). The study, of course, also offers additional evidence that attitudes are strongly influenced by

SEARCH FOR
CONSISTENCY

COGNITIVE
DISSONANCE

family and peers. To at least a certain extent, attitudes represent a form of conformity to social pressures (48), a topic that will be discussed later in the chapter.

the effect of emotion

Although a change in behavior may often trigger a change in attitude, there are also cases in which the emotional or cognitive elements of the attitude change first and changes in behavior follow. One dramatic demonstration of this fact was an experiment in which college women underwent a deeply emotional experience related to cigarette smoking. The women, all heavy smokers, were asked to act out a scene in which the experimenter pretended to be a physician and they his patients. Each subject, visiting the "doctor," got bad news about a persistent cough from which she had been suffering; her X-rays had shown lung cancer; immediate surgery was required; before the operation she and the doctor would have to discuss the difficulty, pain, and risk. The experimenter attempted to keep the scene as realistic as possible and to involve each subject emotionally to the greatest possible degree. As a result of the experience, almost all the women quit or drastically cut down on smoking—and a follow-up eighteen months later showed that they continued to show a significant change in their smoking habits (49).

influencing attitudes and opinions

The manner in which attitudes change is an area of social psychology that interests a great many people, for deliberate attempts to alter attitudes and opinions are common in our society. The politician wants people to develop favorable attitudes and opinions toward him and his party. The advertising man and the salesman want to create favorable opinion toward the products they are selling. Many organizations are attempting to find support for—that is, to develop favorable attitudes toward—kindness to animals, conservation, and various kinds of political programs. Even religious leaders and educators are in a sense attempting to influence attitudes and opinions, in the direction of the particular theology, philosophy, values, and moral code to which they adhere. On the world scene, democracy and Communism are often said to be in "a battle for men's minds."

In general, the findings of social psychology do not offer much hope to those who seek to mold the attitudes of large numbers of people in a relatively short period of time. As has been said, attitudes do sometimes change, and under certain laboratory conditions an experimenter can change them rather markedly. The process is much easier in the laboratory, however, than in real-life situations (50).

Studies of what are called *persuasive communications*, or the transmission of information and appeals to emotion in an attempt to change attitudes, have shown that they operate under many handicaps. For one thing, they do not necessarily even reach very many people. A presidential candidate who makes a speech on nationwide television may reach as many as perhaps ten million people directly and several million more through newspaper accounts of his speech—yet

PERSUASIVE COMMUNICATIONS

even these figures, though they may seem high at first glance, represent only a fraction of the seventy million or more people who vote in a presidential election. A religious leader or educator who makes a speech or writes a book reaches a much smaller audience.

Moreover, the kind of audience that any appeal for attitude change reaches is determined largely by a factor called *selective exposure.* By and large, persuasive communications reach people who are already persuaded. The audience that turns out for a Democratic political rally is overwhelmingly composed of Democrats; the Methodist minister's audience is composed almost entirely of Methodists who already agree with him; the people who read magazines favoring the conservation of natural resources are people already interested in conservation. This does not necessarily mean that people deliberately seek out support for their own attitudes and avoid anything that might shake their attitudes. Studies have shown that under some circumstances they do seem to try to control the flow of information to avoid any communications that might challenge their attitudes and thus create cognitive dissonance (51, 52). Under other circumstances, however, they seem to prefer information disagreeing with their own attitudes, as if seeking to check their beliefs (53). Selective exposure is chiefly the result of the fact that people naturally tend to associate with other people and to read or listen to communications that they find interesting, in other words, people and communications they already agree with and therefore find believable.

Perhaps the most concerted effort to change attitudes in our society is represented by a presidential campaign, in which many millions of dollars are spent over a period of several months on all kinds of persuasive communications ranging from doorbell ringing to television speeches and commercials and from billboards to giant campaign rallies. Yet the evidence is that all this effort produces very little attitude change. Many surveys have shown that most voters have their minds made up on the day the candidates are nominated. The number who switch preference has been found to be no more than one in ten (54).

how we resist change

Even when a persuasive communication designed to produce an attitude change actually reaches a person who holds an opposing attitude, it does not necessarily produce any change. All of us may have a tendency to seek consistency among the beliefs, feelings, and behavior that make up our attitudes, but we also have some very effective ways of resisting any changes in our attitudes. Indeed some psychologists are less impressed by the search for consistency than by the amount of inconsistency we somehow manage to tolerate (55).

For example, in a mayoralty election a voter plans to cast his ballot for Candidate Smith, who is running for reelection. Now he reads an extremely persuasive newspaper editorial that describes in detail how Mayor Smith has failed to solve a number of pressing city problems and in fact has accepted graft to permit gambling and inferior performance on city construction contracts. Instead of changing his attitude toward Mayor Smith, he may do any one of several things. He may convince himself that the newspaper is simply prejudiced against the mayor—in other words, that the source of the communication is unreliable. He may engage in a sort of mental debate with the editorial in which he disproves its allegations, at least to his own satisfaction. Or he may put the whole editorial right out of his mind—that is, simply refuse to think about it. Indeed our ingenuity at finding ways of maintaining our attitudes despite strong opposing arguments seems almost boundless.

the effectiveness of persuasive communications

Some persuasive communications, it has been found, are more likely to succeed than others. One of the most important factors is the source of the communication; if it comes from a source of high prestige and credibility—in other words, from a person or organization we respect and trust—we are more likely to be persuaded. Figure 16-10, for example, shows the results of an experiment in which two groups of subjects read exactly the same communications; the

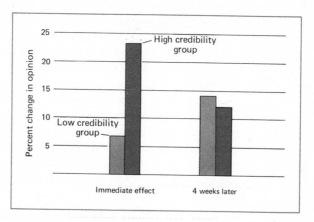

credibility and opinion change

16-10   All the subjects in this experiment read exactly the same messages arguing for a particular point of view on various current events. Subjects in the "high credibility" group were told that the messages came from sources such as *Fortune* magazine. Subjects in the "low credibility" group were told that the messages came from sources such as a Hollywood gossip columnist. Tests of the subjects' attitudes and opinions immediately afterward showed that the messages had a much greater influence when they were believed to come from respectable and reliable sources. The lasting effect of the messages, however, as determined by tests four weeks later, was about the same for both groups. The explanation seems to be that subjects in the low credibility group had forgotten the source of the messages but remembered and were influenced by their content. This is known as a *sleeper effect.* (56)

SLEEPER EFFECT

subjects who were led to believe that the messages came from a source of high credibility showed much greater attitude changes than those who were led to believe the messages were from a source of low credibility. Note, however, that the figure also indicates that arguments from a source of low credibility may influence a listener once he has forgotten where they came from—a phenomenon known as the *sleeper effect*.

There are other factors that also influence the effectiveness of a communication, though they seem to be less important and not to operate under all circumstances. In general, it appears that a speaker who presents only his own side of a controversial question is less likely to win over people from the opposite side than the speaker who presents a "fair" argument, admitting that the other side has its points (57). Arguments that appeal to the listener's motives often tend to be successful, and so do appeals to emotions (58). Arousing fear can be particularly effective at times, as was shown by the experiment with the women who acted out the role of patients suffering from lung cancer. But sometimes the arousal of fear may backfire (59)—presumably because it increases the listener's tendency simply to forget the whole matter.

the communication and the listener

The personality of the listener plays a part in determining whether a communication will be effective, although in ways that are not very well understood. Some people appear to be more easily persuaded than others; experiments have shown that a subject who tends to change his attitudes under one set of circumstances and in response to one kind of communication is also likely to change under different circumstances and in response to different kinds of communications (60). In general, people who have low self-esteem are more easily persuaded than people with high self-esteem (61), and people who are anxious about social acceptance are more easily persuaded than those who are not anxious (62).

Recent research has indicated that a person is more likely to change an attitude if he thinks he has learned it than if he thinks it is something intrinsic to him—that is, an attitude that he possesses because it is a part of human nature or at least of his own inborn dispositions. In one experiment, university students were asked whether they thought it was likely that the next five years might change their attitudes about some of their personality characteristics (such as whether they regarded themselves as trusting, curious, and so on) and toward various social issues (such as capital punishment and legalization of marijuana). If they considered the attitude to be largely the result of their learning experiences (as a majority did for being trusting or favoring legalization of marijuana), they were significantly more likely to expect change than if they regarded the attitude as something innate (as a majority did for the trait of curiosity or opposition to capital punishment) (63). The experiment suggests that the popular but incorrect belief that many aspects of human nature are inherited discourages attitude change, while psychological discoveries about the importance of the environment and learning encourage change. As a simple example, a young man who believes that he was born to be a delinquent is less likely to respond to appeals to change his behavior than a young man who can be convinced that his delinquency is the result of environmental influences.

group dynamics

Throughout literary history, authors have been fascinated by the conduct of people in groups, and countless novels have been written about people who find themselves thrown together by a long trip or a shipwreck or some nuclear disaster of the future. The novels are based on one of the central facts of social psychology—that in any group, some kind of social structure will be formed very quickly.

Human groups seem to form and organize themselves as naturally and spontaneously as crystals in a solution of chemicals or mold formations on a piece of bread. Almost automatically, someone in the group rises to top status and becomes the acknowledged leader. There will be coleaders and subleaders, perhaps, and followers of decreasing status, down to the lowliest. There may be a court jester who amuses the group and a scapegoat whom the others pick on.

DEFINITION: GROUP DYNAMICS

The forces that operate in a group to produce leaders and to bring about other alignments, decisions, and activities are called *group dynamics*. The study of group dynamics is one of the most fascinating subfields of social psychology, though it is often frustrating to investigators because there are many kinds of groups, made up of many different kinds of individuals, operating under different circumstances, and seeking different goals.

communication within the group

One generality about groups that can be made with some confidence is that their structure and dynamics depend in large part on the communications system among their members; what happens in the group is largely determined by who talks to whom and how much. Moreover, the pattern of communication within groups seems to follow a general rule: unless there is some kind of artificial restraint, one person in the group does a great deal of talking, one does very little,

"Eureka! Pass it on!"

Drawing by Ed Fisher,
© 1970, The New Yorker Magazine, Inc.

16-11

In every group, one person does more talking than anyone else. In the study of groups of four to eight illustrated here, the No. 1 talker was always responsible for about 40 percent of the communication within the group—almost as much as all the others put together.

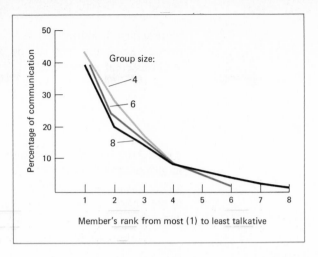

and the others fall somewhere in between. Figure 16-11 shows how this fact has been demonstrated by observing the behavior of groups of four to eight people. Note that in every case the person who was most communicative did almost exactly 40 percent of the talking—while the others, whether they numbered three, five, or seven, split the remaining 60 percent among them. In the groups of six and eight, the least communicative member did almost no talking at all (64).

Almost always, the most talkative member of the group is also its leader. This is because leadership can be defined in terms of influence; the leader is the person who has the most influence on the decisions and behavior of other members of the group. And of course the person who talks the most is naturally the one who sets the subject matter and tone of the group's discussions, makes the most suggestions about decisions and activities, and, if the situation calls for it, issues orders.

So close is the relationship between communication and leadership that it is possible, by artificially controlling the lines of communication within a group, to make it extremely likely that a certain individual will become the leader, regardless of his own personal characteristics. This fact is demonstrated in Figure 16-12, which shows the results of a study of three kinds of communications networks in five-member groups. Note that the person who was in the most central position in the network was the most likely to become the acknowledged leader.

In another experiment, university students who did not know one another were placed in four-man discussion groups. During the first discussion period, the experimenter let nature take its course. In each group, as the general rule would predict, one person did most of the talking and afterward was rated high for leadership by the others. Also in each group, one or two students did little talking and were rated low on leadership. During the next discussion period, however, the experimenter controlled the amount of talking done by each student by manipulating lights on a panel visible only to that particular student; he flashed a green light to encourage the student to talk or a red light to discourage him from speaking further. The lights were manipulated to encourage a student who had been uncommunicative during the first session and to discourage the three

572

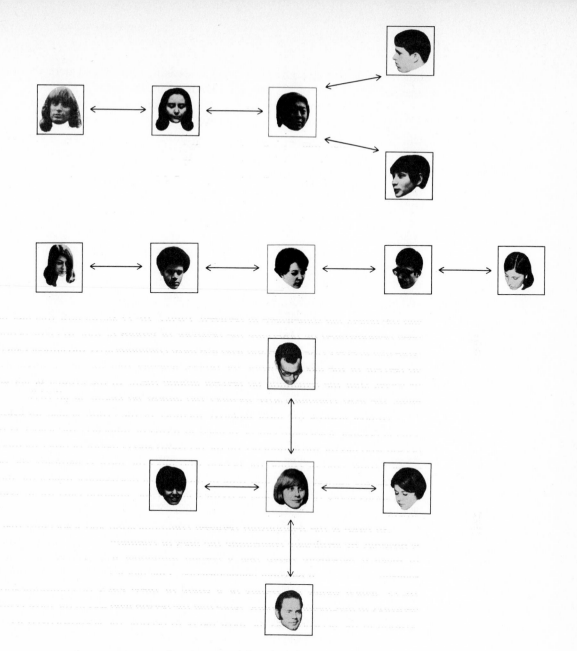

communication and leadership

16-12 In an experiment, groups of five members each were organized into three types of communications networks as shown in the diagrams. Each member was permitted to speak only to the other member or members with whom he was connected by lines and arrows. The person who occupied the most central position in the network, indicated by color, was most often considered the leader—65 percent of the time in the kind of network shown at the top, 67 percent of the time at center, and 100 percent of the time in the highly centralized network at the bottom. (65)

others. As the formerly quiet student began speaking up more and more, the others changed their rating of his leadership ability from low to high (66).

The experiment might indicate that a person can take over leadership of a group simply by making a deliberate effort to talk a lot—but this is true only within limits. The person who tries to dominate the conversation in a group is soon silenced by the other members unless his comments make good sense and contribute something to the group's activities. Leadership cannot be established through mere babbling.

characteristics of leaders

One study has indicated that three factors may be of special importance in determining leaders: 1) amount of activity in the group, including of course communication; 2) ability to perform the task with which the group is concerned; and 3) personal likability. Many people rank low on all three characteristics; these people do not become leaders and indeed may be scorned and turned into scapegoats. Some are high in activity but low in ability and not well liked (for example, the person who tries to talk a lot but says very little); these people are often considered nuisances.

The person who seems to rise to leadership most frequently rates very high in activity and ability but is not the best-liked person in the group; this kind of leader has been called a "task specialist" because the group looks up to him to get the job done. Another kind of person who may become a leader is the one who is best-liked by the group but rates lower in activity and ability; this kind of person has been called a "social specialist" because he is adept at keeping the group happy. Often a "task specialist" and a "social specialist" team up to operate a sort of dual leadership (67). Thus a hard-driving and able but not very popular administrator may have a righthand man who takes care of his problems in human relationships, while an extremely popular but less technically capable leader may have a righthand man who does most of the real work.

There is no evidence for the old popular theory that some people are "born leaders" who would rise to the top under any circumstances. Quite on the contrary, the evidence shows that the selection of a leader depends not only on the personality of the individual but also on the particular nature and needs of the group—including especially the nature of the task the group is trying to perform (68).

the effectiveness of groups

Since so many tasks are performed and decisions made by groups in our society, the effectiveness of groups has also been studied extensively. Some of the pertinent questions are these: Are groups better than individuals at problem solving? Do they generate more ideas? Do they exercise a restraining effect on their members and thus avoid error and dangerous risk taking, or do they encourage the opposite?

It has been known for a long time that an individual studying or working alone behaves in quite different fashion from an individual who is in the company of others, even if they are not talking to one another. For example, in one experiment college students were asked to learn lists of word pairs, in some cases when they were alone and in some cases when they were in the presence of two other subjects. If the list was easy to learn, they did somewhat better when they were in company—but if the list was difficult, they did much worse than when they were alone (69). One reason seems to be that the presence of other people arouses the competitive urge, which improves performance on easy tasks but gets in the way on more difficult tasks. Also, of course, the presence of others introduces distractions; most students find that even though they may enjoy the atmosphere of a college library, they really can study more efficiently in their own rooms.

As the experiment on learning the word lists would suggest, a number of studies have shown that, in general, groups are less efficient than individuals at problem solving and many other kinds of tasks (70). Even at producing new ideas, the group appears less efficient. A few years ago, there was a widespread trend in industry toward a technique known as "brainstorming," in which a group was brought together and asked to cooperate in coming up with as many new ideas as possible, without any fear of discouragement or criticism from other members and in an atmosphere that put a premium on producing the wildest possible flights of imagination. It was believed that members of the group would stimulate each other into feats of creativity that would be impossible for an individual working alone. Experimental evidence has shown, however, that individuals thinking in solitude generally produce more ideas and more unique and creative ideas than the same number of people trying to think as a group (71).

Nonetheless, there are times when a group is more efficient than the individual. This is particularly true of heterogeneous groups whose members possess a wide range of different skills and points of view that can be brought to bear on the task or problem. Heterogeneous groups have been found generally more effective than homogeneous groups; indeed groups containing both men and women seem to be more effective than groups composed only of men (72). However, the group does better if its members, though different in other respects, share similar goals and have a strong attraction toward one another and toward the group itself (73). The effectiveness of the group also depends, of course, on the nature of its goals and the task it faces.

groups and "risky shift"

DEFINITION:

RISKY SHIFT

One aspect of group behavior studied extensively in recent years is called the *risky shift*—the tendency of people to be more willing to undertake risks in decisions made in groups than in decisions made individually. In a typical study of risky shift, subjects were first asked individually to specify the greatest amount of risk taking they would find acceptable in a real-life situation—for example, getting married after a counselor has warned that the partners may be incompatible and that the marriage may not succeed or taking a higher-paid job with a company that may be on the verge of failure. Would they go ahead with the marriage or job if there were just one chance in ten of success? Or would they demand better odds, say five chances in ten or even nine in ten? After making their individual decisions, the subjects were brought together in a group and asked to discuss the problem and agree on a unanimous group decision. On a wide range of problems, subjects have been found to be willing to accept greater risks as members of a group than they were willing to accept by themselves (74).

The reasons for the risky shift are not completely understood. It does not seem to depend on how much the individuals who are inclined to risk taking talk in the group or how persuasive they seem (75). It may, however, result at least in part from the fact that being in a group reduces feelings of personal responsibility, and it may thus be related to the phenomenon of bystander apathy discussed on pages 36–39.

At any rate, risky shift has some important implications for events in society. Most business decisions, such as whether to build a new plant and how much to spend on it, are reached in committee. So are most governmental decisions, including such extremely important ones as how much to spend on the military establishment, how to deal with other governments, and how much risk of war to take in situations of international crisis. It should also be noted that the risky shift is probably related to behavior in mobs, which often engage in acts of violence and cruelty that their members might never even think of as individuals.

conformity

From what has just been said about groups and leaders—and from what was said earlier in the chapter about how each society and each subculture socializes the child into acceptance of its own norms and assigns positions that carry definite role expectations—it should come as no surprise to find the word *conformity* listed among the concerns of social psychology. Conformity is defined as the *yielding by an individual to pressures from the group in which he finds himself*. It is a prominent aspect of social behavior and has been the subject of considerable research.

DEFINITION:
CONFORMITY

the Asch experiment

One of the classic experiments on conformity was performed in the 1950's at Swarthmore College by Solomon Asch. It utilized the method illustrated in Figure 16-13, in which one actual subject, who thought that he was taking part in a study of perceptual discrimination, sat at a table with a group of confederates of the experimenter. The experimenter showed pairs of white cards with black lines of varying length, such as the lines shown in their relative sizes in Figures 16-14 and 16-15, and asked the group which of the lines in Figure 16-15 matched the test line.

For what the experimenter claimed were reasons of convenience, the people sitting around the table were asked to call out their judgments in order, beginning

a group studies the lines

16-13 One of Asch's groups begins its task in "perceptual discrimination." The subject is student 6. All the other students are in league with the experimenter.

with the student at the experimenter's left. The subject was always placed near the other end so that he would hear the judgments of several confederates before making his own. Sometimes the confederates gave the right answer, but on some trials they deliberately called out the wrong answer. On these trials 37 percent of the answers given by the subjects were also incorrect. In other words, the subjects conformed with the group's wrong judgment 37 percent of the time.

Some of the subjects conformed on all trials; others on some but not all; and some remained independent and did not conform at any time. <u>Even the subjects who showed independence, however, experienced various kinds of conflict and anxiety,</u> as is readily apparent from the photographs of the subject in Figure 16-16. Some of their comments later were: "Despite everything, there was a lurking fear that in some way I did not understand I might be wrong." "At times I had the feeling, to heck with it, I'll go along with the rest." "I felt disturbed, puzzled, separated, like an outcast from the rest." <u>Thus the urge to conform—to go along with the group—was strong even among the most independent subjects.</u>

a test line

16-14

This was the relative size of one of the lines shown to subjects in the Asch experiment. They were asked which of the lines in Figure 16-15 matched it.

which line matches?

16-15 Which of these three lines, the subjects in the Asch experiment were asked, matches the line shown in Figure 16-14? In one of the trials the experimenter's confederates insisted unanimously that it was line 1—the one that is in fact least like the test line. (76)

an "independent" subject—shaken but unyielding

16-16 In the top photo, number 6 is making his first independent judgment at variance with the group's otherwise unanimous but incorrect verdict. In the other photos his puzzlement and concern seem to increase, until, preserving his independence despite the pressure, he announces (bottom), "I have to call them as I see them."

the Milgram experiment

Another dramatic experiment on conformity—in many ways a frightening experiment—was performed by Stanley Milgram at Yale. Like many persons interested in human nature, Milgram found himself haunted by the events in Hitler's Germany, where a great many ordinary sorts of people, presumably with ordinary social backgrounds and moral standards, took part directly or passively in a program that resulted in the mass execution of millions of European Jews. How, Milgram wondered, could such a thing happen? What in the human personality or in the structure of society could account for the willingness of so many people to take part in or at least go along with a slaughter of such magnitude?

In search of clues, Milgram devised the following experiment. Eighty men of various ages and occupational backgrounds were chosen as subjects and asked to take part in what they were told was an important experiment in learning. Each subject was assigned to a group of four people, the other three of whom, unknown to him, were Milgram's assistants. One of the assistants was the "learner" in the make-believe experiment; he was assigned a laboratory task to learn. The other two assistants and the subject were the "teachers," given the job of instructing the learner by punishing him with an electric shock when he made an error. The subject was put at controls that regulated the amount of shock, from mild to extremely intense and painful. Actually no electricity was hooked up to the controls and no learning took place; the learner deliberately made mistakes and only pretended to feel a shock when punished.

The purpose of the experiment was to learn to what levels the subjects would raise the amount of electric shock. Forty of the subjects were considered a control group and were not placed under group pressure. The other forty were urged by the other members of the team to raise the amount of electricity higher and higher, on the ground that this was essential to the experiment. The results were startling. Of the forty subjects in the control group, thirty-four stopped at shock levels listed as "slight" (15 to 60 volts) or "moderate" (75 to 120 volts); only six went on to levels higher than 120 volts. For the experimental subjects, urged on by their fellow "teachers," the results were exactly the opposite. Only six stopped at or before 120 volts; the other thirty-four went on, even though the "learner" at first shouted that the shocks were becoming painful and later began to groan and finally scream in pain. Seven of the forty experimental subjects, indeed, went all the way up to what they thought was the maximum they could deliver—a highly dangerous shock of 450 volts. Many of the experimental subjects showed signs of doubt and distress, yet they went along anyway with the other members of their group (77).

conformity and obedience

In a similar experiment, Milgram investigated the effect not of conformity to a group but of the somewhat similar phenomenon of obedience to a single figure of authority. In this case each subject was placed in the company not of two supposed fellow subjects but of the experimenter himself. He was

16-17

On command of an experimenter whom they did not really have to obey for any particular reason, all subjects administered shocks as high as what they believed was 300 volts; 65 percent of them (twenty-six of forty) went all the way to 450 volts.

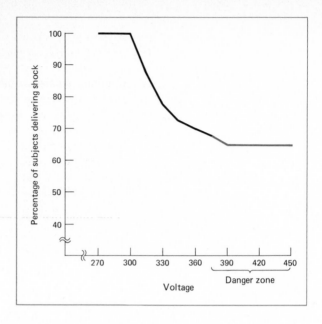

instructed to move to a higher level of shock each time the supposed learner made a mistake. If he showed any signs of hesitation about increasing the voltage, the experimenter urged him on with remarks such as "It is absolutely essential that you continue" and "You have no other choice; you *must* go on."

Under these conditions, the results were even more striking. As is shown in Figure 16-17, all the subjects went as high as what they thought was 300 volts. At that point, the "learner" began pounding on the wall of the room to indicate distress and a few subjects dropped out. But twenty-seven of the forty subjects continued on into what was labeled the zone of DANGER: SEVERE SHOCK— and twenty-six went all the way to 450 volts (78). As Milgram has pointed out, the experimenter had no real power to enforce his demands and the subjects had nothing to lose by disobeying him, yet they showed a remarkable amount of obedience. The Milgram experiments indeed reveal some disturbing aspects of the strength of man's tendencies to conformity and obedience.

why do we conform?

The question, of course, is why people should have such tendencies. It is a question on which we can only speculate. Perhaps the forces that attract us to other people and make us members of groups are so strong that often we would rather conform than run the risk of appearing strange and being rejected. Perhaps we come to realize that a certain amount of conformity is essential to society—that there are many circumstances in which it would be "maladaptive and destructive" to behave differently from others (2), and that in general the mutual expectations of the members of society have to be met if society is to operate smoothly. On the matter of obedience, perhaps we never entirely get over the experience of being a child who has no choice but to obey his parents' commands or suffer the consequences.

Not all people, of course, conform under all circumstances. Indeed, some have the opposite tendency toward being rebels and displaying *counterconformity;* if the people around them are for something, they almost automatically tend to be against it. Others tend to display *independence;* they make up their own minds and behave in accordance with their own wishes and standards. But the factors that make for conformity, counterconformity, and independence are not well understood. They will probably be one of the important areas of social psychology's research in the future.

COUNTER CONFORMITY

INDEPENDENCE

group factors in conformity

One thing that has been found to affect the tendency of an individual to conform is the nature of the group he is in. Among the important characteristics of the group are the following.

1. *Unanimity* within the group appears to be the most important factor of all. If we are in a group where everybody agrees, we are under much stronger pressure to conform than if even one person expresses disagreement. This was shown dramatically in a variation of the Asch experiment in which the subjects were white students, some friendly toward blacks and some prejudiced against them, who were placed in a group of confederates that included one black student. When the confederates were unanimous in the incorrect answers they gave, the subjects showed a strong tendency to conform. But when the black confederate broke the unanimity of the group by giving the correct answer, the subjects were much less likely to conform, even if they were prejudiced against blacks (79).

2. *Credibility* of the group plays a part in conformity just as credibility of the source of a persuasive communication plays a part in attitude change. An individual is most likely to conform if he has confidence in the group and regards its members as having high status and expert knowledge.

3. *Size* of the group is also important, though in ways that are not quite clear. Asch found that the tendency to conform was not very high in a group of two; increased when the subject found himself in a group of three, with two opposed to him; and was still greater in a group of four or five. Increasing the size above five did not appear to have much effect. Other experimenters, however, have found that the influence of the group increases with size even above the figure of four or five (80)—suggesting that possibly the more members there are in the group the greater is its power to produce conformity.

A sidelight on the importance of the size of the group comes from another experiment performed by Milgram and his associates, this time in a rather light-hearted vein. The experiment was addressed to these questions: If you were walking along a crowded city street and saw someone staring up at a building, would you be likely to look up too? Might you even stop to see what was going on? Would you be more inclined to stop and look if there were two people staring at the building? Fifteen people?

To answer the questions, it was arranged for confederates of the experimenters to pretend to be part of the crowd on a busy New York City street. At a signal from a sixth-floor window across the street, they stopped and stared at

16-18

When one man on a New York City street stopped to stare up at something that seemed to be going on in a building across the street, 4 percent of passers-by also stopped to look up. When fifteen people were staring at the building, 40 percent of passers-by stopped to see what was happening. An even larger number of passers-by looked up but kept on walking.

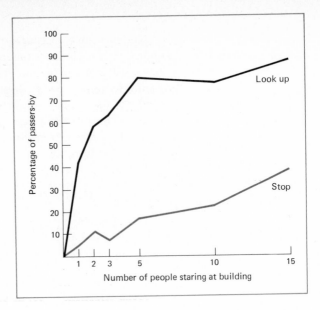

the window for a full minute, while a motion picture camera made a record of how many people joined them. The results are shown in Figure 16-18. Regardless of whether one person or more were staring at the window, more passers-by looked up but kept on walking than stopped. But the number of confederates gazing at the window had a pronounced effect. The larger the group, the more passers-by were induced to stop and join them (81).

individual factors in conformity

As for the factors that make one individual more or less likely to conform than another, these are not well understood. Until recently it was generally believed that women had a greater tendency to conform than men, but this belief was based on experiments that apparently contained a sex bias; the subjects were tested on matters of judgment and opinion that were of more interest and concern to men than to women—and the women were willing to conform because they had no particular stake in the matters. In a recent study that tested subjects on issues of special interest and concern to women, it was found that women conformed not more but less than men (82)—an indication that there may be no real sex differences in the tendency to conform.

Like concern about the matters under consideration, confidence in one's own judgment appears to be an important factor. For example, it has been found that an individual is more likely to conform to the group's judgment on difficult questions where the answer is in doubt than on easy questions where he can be fairly sure of the answer (83). For this reason people with high levels of intelligence and self-esteem are less likely to conform than people of lower intelligence and self-regard.

There is some evidence that the person who can be described as strongly conformity-prone in a wide range of situations tends to have a characteristic kind

582

of personality. In general he is less intelligent and more rigid than the more independent person. He is likely to have feelings of inferiority and anxiety, to be inhibited in the expression of emotions, and to have a low tolerance of stress. His attitudes tend to be conventional and traditionally moralistic (13). Thus he has many of the characteristics of what has been called the "authoritarian personality"—the kind of individual who tends to prefer authoritarian rather than democratic methods in government, crime control, business, and even personal and family relations (84). Yet conformity is by no means confined to any single kind of person; it is a process to which all of us are more or less subject—sometimes in ways that help society function more smoothly, sometimes in highly destructive ways.

summary 1. *Social psychology* is the study of how man "thinks, feels, and behaves in social situations"—or, in broader terms, of how people influence and are influenced by other people.

2. *Socialization* is the process by which the child is taught the ways of his society and is integrated into the society through exposure to its customs and rules.

3. *Norms* are the standards and expectations shared by the members of a society. They regulate many types of behavior, including courtesy and dress, marriage and child rearing, and conduct considered disruptive.

4. The various social classes in the United States socialize their children in different ways, to observe different norms and have different interests and attitudes.

5. The particular place or niche that a person occupies in society is called his *position* or *status*.

6. The kind of behavior society expects from a person in a particular position or status is called his *role*. The individual is often placed under *role strain* because he simultaneously occupies several different positions in which he is expected to play incompatible roles.

7. Study of *interpersonal attraction* has shown that people tend to like people who are similar in interests, attitudes, and personality; who are familiar and live or work nearby; and who reciprocate the feeling of liking.

8. The *halo effect* is the psychological term for the fact that our general impressions of another person are strongly colored by any one thing, good or bad, that we initially learn about him—a fact that makes first impressions particularly important.

9. An *attitude* is an organized and enduring set of beliefs and feelings toward some kind of object or situation and a predisposition to behave toward it in a particular way. Thus an attitude contains a cognitive factor, an emotional factor, and a behavioral factor.

10. Although attitudes are durable, they do sometimes change. One reason is the *search for consistency*—which means that people usually seek harmony among their beliefs, feelings, and behavior. When inconsistencies occur, the

individual is motivated to restore harmony by changing one or all of these three components of an attitude.

11. Deliberate attempts to change attitudes are called *persuasive communications.* Some factors that seem to influence the effectiveness of persuasive communications are the following:

    a. Persuasive communications are most effective when they come from a source of high prestige and credibility.

    b. A "fair" argument presenting both sides of the question is generally more effective than a one-sided argument.

    c. Arguments that appeal to the listener's motives and emotions are often effective.

12. The forces that operate in a group to produce leaders and to bring about other alignments, decisions, and activities are called *group dynamics.*

13. What happens in a group is largely determined by its communications system—that is, by who talks to whom and how much.

14. Three factors of special importance in determining leaders are a) amount of activity in the group, including communication; b) ability to perform the task with which the group is concerned; and c) personal likability.

15. It has been found that people are generally more willing to undertake risks in decisions made in groups than in decisions made individually. This is called the *risky shift* phenomenon.

16. *Conformity* is the yielding by an individual to pressures from the group in which he finds himself.

17. Factors that encourage conformity are a) unanimity within the group, b) the credibility of the group, and c) the size of the group. (The more members the group has, at least up to a point, the more conformity it induces.)

recommended reading

Bem, D. J. *Beliefs, attitudes, and human affairs.* Belmont, Calif.: Brooks-Cole, 1970.

Berscheid, E., and Walster, E. C. *Interpersonal attraction.* Reading, Mass.: Addison-Wesley, 1969.

Brown, R. *Social psychology.* New York: Free Press, 1965.

Buckhout, R., ed. *Toward social change: a handbook for those who will.* New York: Harper & Row, 1971.

Freedman, J. L., Carlsmith, J. M., and Sears, D. O. *Social psychology.* Englewood Cliffs, N.J.: Prentice-Hall, 1970.

Goffman, E. *The presentation of self in everyday life.* Garden City, N.Y.: Doubleday, 1959.

Homans, G. C. *Social behavior: its elementary forms.* New York: Harcourt Brace Jovanovich, 1961.

Jones, E. E., and Gerard, H. B. *Foundations of social psychology.* New York: Wiley, 1967.

Steiner, I. D., and Fishbein, M., eds. *Current studies in social psychology.* New York: Holt, Rinehart and Winston, 1965.

Zimbardo, P. G., and Ebbesen, E. B. *Influencing attitudes and changing behavior.* Reading, Mass.: Addison-Wesley, 1969.

GLOSSARY

abnormal behavior Behavior that is statistically unusual, considered strange or undesirable by most people, and a source of unhappiness to the person who displays it.

abnormal psychology The branch of psychology that studies mental and emotional disturbances and their treatment.

abscissa The horizontal axis of a graph, along which the independent variable is usually plotted.

absolute threshold The minimum amount of stimulus energy to which a receptor will respond 50 percent of the time.

accommodation The process of changing one's cognitive view when new information dictates such a change; one of the processes emphasized in Piaget's theory of intellectual development.

acetylcholine A chemical produced at a synapse when a nervous impulse reaches the end of the axon. Acetylcholine causes the dendrite of the second neuron to fire.

achievement test A test that measures the individual's present level of skill or knowledge. (*Compare* **aptitude test.**)

acuity A scientific term for sharpness of vision.

adaptation The tendency of the sensory apparatus to adjust to any steady and continued level of stimulation and to stop responding.

addiction Physiological or psychological dependence on regular use of a drug.

adrenal cortex The outer part of an *adrenal gland.*

adrenal glands A pair of endocrine glands, lying atop the kidneys. Each consists of two parts: an *adrenal medulla,* which produces the stimulants adrenalin and noradrenalin, and an *adrenal cortex,* which produces steroids essential to life.

adrenal medulla The inner part of an *adrenal gland.*

adrenalin (*also called* **epinephrine**) A hormone, secreted by the adrenal medulla, that affects the rate of heartbeat, raises the blood pressure, and causes the liver to release increased quantities of sugar into the blood to provide additional energy. Adrenalin is associated with the bodily states in fear or "flight" situations.

aerial perspective A clue to distance perception; refers to the fact that distant objects appear less distinct and less brilliant in color than nearby objects, because they are seen through air that is usually somewhat hazy.

affect A term used to describe the feelings that accompany emotional states of the organism; it refers specifically to feelings rather than to patterns of nervous discharge, physiological changes, or the behavior that may result from emotion.

afferent neuron A neuron that carries impulses from the sense organs toward the central nervous system.

afterimage The visual phenomenon produced by withdrawal of a stimulus. Withdrawal is followed briefly by a positive afterimage, then by a negative afterimage.

aggression A type of behavior arising from hostile motives; it takes such forms as argumentativeness, scorn, sarcasm, physical and mental cruelty, and fighting.

agoraphobia Abnormal fear of being in open spaces.

algorithm A formal rule for solving mathematical problems, thus an important tool in logical thinking. (*Compare* **heuristic.**)

alpha waves A pattern of regular waves of 7–10 cycles per second characteristically found when the brain is "at rest."

ambivalence Mingled feelings of like and dislike toward a person or situation.

amnesia Loss of memory. It may be caused by physical injury, or it may be a defense mechanism—an exaggerated form of repression.

amphetamine Any of a group of drugs that excite the central nervous system; of value in the treatment of hyperkinesis but often abused by users who seek to combat fatigue or get "kicks." Also known as "meth," "bennies," "speed," or pep pills.

amplitude The characteristic of a sound wave that determines the loudness we hear.

anal stage One of the stages of psychological development according to Freud; the stage at which the child is preoccupied with sensations from the anal area.

anthropology A behavioral science that is chiefly concerned with the study of societies or large cultural groups.

anxiety An emotion characterized by a vague fear or premonition that something undesirable is about to happen; a frequent result of conflicts among motives and a prominent factor in abnormal behavior.

anxiety reaction A psychoneurosis in which the individual often describes himself as "chronically uneasy" for reasons he cannot explain; the anxiety is the outstanding symptom.

anxiety state One rather large group of psychoneuroses, in all of which anxiety is a prominent symptom. The group includes *anxiety reaction* and *phobic reaction.*

apathy A feeling of indifference in which the individual may seem to lose all interest in what happens to him; a result of frustration.

aphasia The loss of ability to speak or to understand speech.

apparent motion The perception of motion in stimuli that, though they change, do not actually move, as in *stroboscopic motion* or the *phi phenomenon.* (*Compare* **illusory motion.**)

applied psychology The application of psychological knowledge and principles to practical situations in school, industry, social situations, and treatment of abnormal behavior.

approach-approach conflict A conflict in which the aroused motives have two incompatible goals, both of which are desirable.

approach-avoidance conflict A conflict in which the individual has a single goal with both desirable and undesirable aspects, causing mixed feelings.

aptitude A capacity to learn or to perform, such as mechanical or musical aptitude; an inborn ability that exists and can be measured even though the individual has had no special training to develop his skills (such as at mechanical or musical tasks).

aptitude test A test that measures the individual's *capacity* to perform, not his present level of skill or knowledge. (*Compare* **achievement test.**)

aroused motive A motive the individual is actually thinking about at the moment; an active influence on behavior. (*Compare* **motivational disposition.**)

assimilation The process of incorporating a new stimulus into one's existing cognitive view; one of the processes emphasized in Piaget's theory of intellectual development.

asthenic reaction An anxiety state in which the individual is chronically tired, listless, and unable to concentrate or work efficiently. At one time the condition was called neurasthenia.

astigmatism A defect of vision caused by irregularities in the shape of the cornea or lens.

attachment *See* **theory of attachment.**

attachment unit A unit of innate or previously learned behavior, overt or covert, to which a new stimulus can become attached.

attention The process of focusing perception on a single stimulus or limited range of stimuli.

attitude An organized and enduring set of beliefs and feelings toward some kind of object or situation and a predisposition to behave toward it in a particular way.

authoritarian personality The combination of traits that has been found common among people who prefer an authoritarian as opposed to a democratic society; the traits include rigidly conventional standards of behavior and obedience and prejudice against minority groups.

autistic A term used to describe disturbed individuals whose thoughts are extremely self-centered and unrelated to reality.

autokinetic illusion The illusion of self-generated movement that a stationary object, such as a point of light seen in an otherwise dark room, sometimes creates.

autonomic nervous system A complicated nerve network that connects the central nervous system with the glands and the smooth muscles of the body organs.

aversive conditioning A type of behavior therapy that attempts to associate a behavioral symptom with pain and punishment rather than with pleasure and reward.

avoidance-avoidance conflict A conflict in which there is simultaneous arousal of motives to avoid alternatives, both of which are undesirable.

axon The fiber of the neuron that has end branches that transmit messages to other neurons or to muscles and glands; the "sending" portion of the neuron.

balance theory A theory maintaining that, when a person holds two conflicting attitudes, he (1) stops thinking about the problem, (2) changes one of the attitudes, or (3) redefines the meaning of one of the attitudes.

basilar membrane A piece of tissue dividing the cochlea more or less in half for its entire length; the organ of Corti, containing the hearing receptors, lies on this membrane.

behavior The activities of an organism, both overt, or observable (such as motor behavior), and covert, or hidden (such as thinking).

behavior therapy A type of psychotherapy that concentrates on eliminating the symptoms of abnormal behavior, which are regarded as learned responses, through new forms of learning.

behaviorism A school of thought maintaining that psychologists should concentrate on the study of overt behavior rather than of "mental life" or consciousness.

benzedrine ("bennies") One of the amphetamines.

binocular vision A clue to distance perception; refers to the fact that the two eyes, being about $2\frac{1}{2}$ inches apart, receive slightly different images of any seen object.

biological drive A pattern of brain activity that results from certain kinds of physiological conditions—usually when the organism is in a state of deprivation or imbalance.

blind spot The point at which the optic nerve exits from the eyeball, creating a small and mostly insensitive gap in the retina.

brain stem A group of brain structures, including the cerebellum, pons, reticular formation, and medulla, on which the forebrain rests.

breathing drive A biological drive aroused by physiological requirements for oxygen.

brightness One dimension of the visual stimulus; dependent on intensity.

brightness constancy The tendency to perceive objects to be of consistent brightness regardless of the amount of light they actually reflect under different conditions of illumination.

bystander apathy The tendency of people, especially under crowded conditions, to ignore others who need help or situations that call for action.

CAI *See* **computer-assisted instruction.**

Cannon-Bard theory of emotion A neurological theory holding that stimuli in the environment set off patterns of activity in the hypothalamus and thalamus; these patterns are then relayed both to the autonomic nervous system, where they trigger the bodily changes of emotion, and to the cerebral cortex, where they result in the feelings of emotion.

caretaker period The period between birth and eighteen months, during which the child's personality development depends mostly on his close relationship with his mother or caretaker.

cell body (of a neuron) The portion of a neuron containing its genes, as opposed to the fiber portion of the neuron.

central motive state A state of the organism produced by an interaction between a biological drive and an incentive object.

central nervous system The spinal cord and the brain. (*Compare* **peripheral nervous system.**)

cerebellum The portion of the brain stem that controls body balance and helps coordinate bodily movements.

cerebral cortex The highest part of the brain, the surface of the cerebrum; a dense and highly interconnected mass of neurons and their cell bodies.

cerebrotonic temperament A type of temperament ascribed by William Sheldon to the ectomorphic body type; characterized by mental overintensity, secretiveness, emotional restraint, fear of society, and love of privacy.

cerebrum The large brain mass of which the cerebral cortex is the surface. It is divided into two separate halves called the left hemisphere and the right hemisphere.

character disorder (*also called* **personality disorder**) A type of emotional disorder characterized by failure to acquire mature and efficient ways of coping with the problems of adult life.

chemotherapy The treatment of emotional disorders with drugs (or chemicals).

chromosome The mechanism of human heredity. There are twenty-three pairs of the tiny structures, forty-six in all, found in the fertilized egg cell and repeated through the process of division in every cell of the body.

chunking A term used to describe the coding of information into long-term memory in tightly bound associations, especially those dictated by logical rules.

ciliary muscles The muscles that control the shape of the lens of the eye.

clairvoyance The supposed ability to perceive something that is not apparent to the sense organs; a form of extrasensory perception.

classical conditioning A type of learning process through which a response becomes attached to a conditioned (or previously neutral) stimulus. (*Compare* **operant conditioning.**)

claustrophobia Abnormal fear of being in enclosed places, such as elevators.

client A term used, in preference to "patient," by clinical psychologists to refer to the people they treat.

client-centered therapy A type of psychotherapy, developed by Rogers, in which the therapist displays warmth and acceptance toward the patient, or client, thus providing a nonthreatening situation in which the patient is freed to explore all his thoughts and feelings.

clinical psychologist A psychologist who practices psychotherapy or diagnoses abnormal symptoms.

clinical psychology The branch of applied psychology concerned with the application of psychological knowledge to the treatment of personality problems and mental disorders.

cochlea A bony structure of the inner ear shaped like a snail's shell; contains the receptors for hearing.

cognitive consonance Consistency and agreement among one's beliefs, feelings, and behavior.

cognitive dissonance Lack of consistency and agreement among one's beliefs, feelings, and behavior. The desire to relieve cognitive dissonance is believed to be an important human motive.

cognitive psychology A school of thought maintaining that the mind does not merely react to stimuli but actively processes the information it receives into new forms and categories.

cognitive theory of emotion The theory that an emotion is the cognitive interpretation of a change in level and quality of internal sensations in a particular context.

color blindness A visual defect involving deficiency in color discrimination.

color constancy The tendency to perceive a familiar object as of constant color, regardless of changes in illumination that alter its actual stimulus properties.

communication A general term for exchanges of information and feelings between two (or more) people. For its special meaning in social psychology, *see* **persuasive communications.**

community therapy A type of interactional therapy in which the therapist attempts to change conflicts and patterns of behavior through alteration of behavior in the community.

comparative psychology The study of processes common to several animal species, including man.

complementary hues Two hues that, when added one to the other, yield gray.

complexity The characteristic of a sound wave that determines the timbre we hear; caused by the number and strength of the overtones.

compulsion An irresistible urge to perform some act over and over again.

computer-assisted instruction (CAI) A method of programed instruction in which a computer is used as a teaching machine.

concept A symbol that stands for a common characteristic or relationship shared by objects or events that are otherwise different.

concept hierarchy An arrangement of the associations that make up concepts; the very strong ones at the top are likely to be thought of immediately, and the weakest ones at the bottom are less likely to come to mind.

conceptual intelligence The term used by Piaget to describe the developmental process after the age of two, in which the child increasingly uses concepts to organize the evidence of his senses and to engage in ever more complex thinking and problem solving.

concrete operations The term applied by Piaget to the stage of intellectual development (ages seven to eleven) when the child can reason logically about concrete objects that he sees but has yet to learn to deal with rules in the abstract.

conditioned operant Behavior learned through operant conditioning; a type of behavior with which the organism "operates" on its environment to obtain a desired result.

conditioned response A response that has become attached through learning to a conditioned (or previously neutral) stimulus; an example is the salivation by Pavlov's dog to the sound of the metronome.

conditioned stimulus In classical conditioning, a previously neutral stimulus (such as a sound) that through pairing with an unconditioned stimulus (such as food) acquires the ability to set off a response (such as salivation).

conditioning A learning process in which behavior becomes attached to new stimuli. (*See* **classical conditioning, operant conditioning.**)

cones One of the two types of receptors for vision located in the retina. The cones are receptors for color and are also sensitive to differences in light intensity resulting in sensations of black, white, and gray.

conflict The simultaneous arousal of two or more incompatible motives, resulting in unpleasant emotions.

conformity The yielding by an individual to pressures from another person or, more usually, from a group.

connecting neuron A neuron that is stimulated by another neuron and passes its message along to a third neuron.

connotation The implied meaning of a word. Although *landlord* means only a person who rents property, to most people the word connotes stinginess.

conservation The principle that such qualities as mass, weight, and volume remain constant regardless of changes in appearance; learned by the child during Piaget's stage of concrete operations.

consummatory action Behavior undertaken by an organism to satisfy a drive or motive.

control group A group used for comparison with an experimental group. The two groups must be alike in composition and must be observed under the same circumstances except for the one variable that is manipulated in the case of the experimental group. (*Compare* **experimental group.**)

conversion reaction A form of hysteria characterized by physical symptoms that have no organic basis.

cornea The transparent bulge in the outer layer of the eyeball through which light waves enter.

corpus callosum A large nerve tract that connects the left and right hemispheres of the cerebrum and enables the two hemispheres to cooperate and share in duties.

correlation The degree of relationship between two different factors; measured statistically by the correlation coefficient.

correlation coefficient A statistic that describes in numbers ranging from -1 to $+1$ the degree of relationship between two different factors.

cortisol One of the steroids produced by the adrenal cortex.

counseling psychologist One who practices counseling psychology.

counseling psychology The branch of psychology that concentrates on vocational guidance, assistance with marital problems, and advice in other situations regarded as less serious or deepseated than the behavioral problems usually treated by clinical psychologists.

counterconformity The tendency to be opposed to anything suggested by group pressure, regardless of its merits.

covert behavior Hidden processes (such as thoughts) that take place inside the organism and cannot be seen by an observer.

creative thinking A highly imaginative and rather rare form of directed thinking in which the individual discovers new relationships and solutions to problems and may produce an invention or an artistic creation.

cretinism A biological form of mental retardation caused by an abnormally low level of secretion by the thyroid gland.

critical ratio A measure of the degree of difference between two groups.

culture The ways of a given society, including its norms, customs, beliefs, values, and ideals.

curve of forgetting A graph plotting the course of forgetting.

decibel A measure of the amplitude of sound.

deep structure A term used by linguists to describe the *meaning* that a person who constructs an utterance such as a sentence intends to convey. (*Compare* **surface structure.**)

defense mechanism A process, generally believed to be unconscious, in which the individual tries to convince himself that a frustration or conflict and the resulting anxiety do not exist or have no importance.

delusion A false belief, such as imagining that one is already dead.

dendrite The part of the neuron, usually branched, that has the special function of being sensitive to stimuli and firing off a nervous impulse; the "receiving" portion of the neuron.

denial A defense mechanism, closely related to repression, in which the individual simply denies the existence of the events that have aroused his anxiety.

dependent variable A change in behavior that results from changes in the conditions that affect the organism—that is, from changes in an *independent variable.*

depression The feeling of sadness and sometimes total apathy, often due to guilt or the inability to cope with one's problems; a result of frustration or conflict or possibly influenced by chemical imbalances in the brain.

descriptive statistics A quick and convenient method of summarizing measurements. Important figures in descriptive statistics are the number of subjects (or *N*); measures of central tendency, including the mean, median, and mode; and measurements of variability, including range and standard deviation.

desensitization An attempt to eliminate phobias by associating the stimulus that has caused the fear with relaxation rather than with fearful behavior; a technique used in behavior therapy.

developmental psychology The study of the processes by which the newborn baby acquires his patterns of overt behavior, thinking, and problem solving and the motives, emotions, conflicts, and ways of coping with conflicts that will go to make up his adult personality.

dexedrine One of the amphetamines.

didactic learning (*also called* **learning through exposition**) A method of instruction in which the teacher explains a concept and then cites examples. (*Compare* **discovery learning.**)

difference threshold (*also called* **just noticeable difference** *or* **j.n.d.**) The smallest difference in intensity or quality of stimulation to which a sensory receptor will respond 50 percent of the time.

Dilantin A drug that has been used successfully in controlling epilepsy.

direct aggression Aggressive behavior focused directly on the obstacle that has caused frustration.

directed thinking A process in which we try to forge a chain of associations that will reach a definite goal. The most important form of directed thinking is *problem solving.*

discovery learning A method of instruction in which the teacher presents examples of a concept and lets the student discover the concept for himself. (*Compare* **didactic learning.**)

displaced aggression Aggressive behavior directed against an "innocent bystander" because the cause of frustration or conflict cannot itself be attacked.

dissociative reaction A form of hysteria in which the individual undergoes some form of loss of contact with reality; he dissociates himself in some manner from the conflicts that are troubling him. Three forms are amnesia, multiple personality, and sleep walking.

dissonance theory A theory maintaining that inconsistencies among one's beliefs, feelings, and behavior create a state of cognitive dissonance that the individual then tries to relieve, often by changing his attitude.

distributed practice A series of relatively short learning periods. (*Compare* **massed practice.**)

dizygotic twins *See* **fraternal twins.**

DNA (deoxyribonucleic acid) The complex chemical of which genes are composed.

dominant gene A gene, such as the one for brown eyes, that always prevails over a *recessive gene,* such as the one for blue eyes.

double approach-avoidance conflict A conflict aroused by motives toward two goals that both have their good points and their bad.

double blind An experimental technique in which neither the subjects nor the experimenter knows which subjects are in the control group and which are in the experimental group.

"downers" In the parlance of drug users, any drug that has a calming or sedative effect.

drive *See* **biological drive.**

drug abuse The use of drugs, especially heroin but also psychedelic drugs and others, without medical indication and to excess.

ductless gland *See* **endocrine gland.**

eardrum A membrane between the outer part of the auditory canal and the middle ear.

ectomorph One of three basic types of body build described by Sheldon; the ectomorph is characterized by a skin area and nervous system that are large in proportion to his size.

EEG *See* **electroencephalograph.**

efferent neuron A neuron that carries impulses from the central nervous system toward the muscles or glands.

ego According to Freud's psychoanalytic theory of personality, the conscious, logical part of the mind that develops as a person grows up and that is his operational contact with reality.

ego ideal The sum total of a person's standards; his notion of how, if he were as perfect as he would like to be, he would always think and behave.

ego theory One of the neo-psychoanalytic theories, stressing the importance of the ego rather than of the id.

eidetic imagery The ability, possessed by a minority of people, to "see" an image that is an exact copy of the original sensory experience.

electroencephalograph (EEG) A delicate instrument that measures the electrical activity of the brain.

electroshock A medical method of treating behavior disorders, especially depression, by passing an electric current through the patient's brain.

elimination drive A biological drive aroused by physiological requirements to get rid of the body's waste products.

emotion A word used in four different ways: (1) by physiologists to describe various changes inside the body; (2) by neurologists to describe patterns of nervous activity; (3) by those interested in behavior to describe such actions as weeping or laughing, and (4) to describe the subjective feelings (also called *affects*) that bear such names as fear, anger, and so on.

emotional state The condition of the organism during emotion, characterized by patterns of activity in the central nervous system and autonomic nervous system and by changes in glandular activity, heart rate, blood pressure, breathing, and activity of the visceral organs.

empathy Understanding another person by putting oneself in that person's shoes and sharing his thoughts and feelings.

empirical Based on controlled experiments and on observations made with the greatest possible precision and objectivity.

empiricists Those who accept the theory that behavior is determined more by learning and experience than by inborn factors.

encounter group A group of people who meet, usually under the leadership of a psychotherapist, with the goal of throwing off the masks they usually present in public and airing their true feelings.

endocrine gland (*also called* **ductless gland**) A gland that discharges chemical substances known as *hormones* directly into the blood stream, which then carries them to all parts of the body, resulting in many kinds of physiological changes.

endomorph One of three basic types of body build described by Sheldon; the endomorph is characterized by a strong digestive system and tends to be round in build, with relatively weak bones and muscles.

engram Some kind of lasting trace or impression formed in living protoplasm by a stimulus; a deliberately vague term often used to describe the learning connection or memory trace.

epilepsy A form of brain malfunction that produces sudden mental blackouts and sometimes seizures or "fits."

epinephrine *See* **adrenalin.**

ESP *See* **extrasensory perception.**

Eustachian tube A passage between the middle ear and the air chambers of the mouth and nose; it keeps the pressure on both sides of the eardrum constant.

existential psychology A school of thought that emphasizes man's freedom and responsibility for his own existence and experiences.

expectancy wave A type of brain wave that occurs when a person is in a state of expectancy, as when awaiting a stimulus he knows is coming.

experiment A scientific method in which the experimenter makes a careful and rigidly controlled study of cause and effect, by manipulating an independent variable (or condition affecting the subject) and observing its effect on a dependent variable (or the subject's behavior in response to changes in the independent variable).

experimental group A group of subjects whose behavior is observed while the experimenter manipulates an independent variable. (*Compare* **control group.**)

extinction The disappearance of a conditioned response (or other learned behavior) when reinforcement is withdrawn.

extrasensory perception (ESP) Any of several various forms of supposed ability to perceive stimuli through some means other than the sense organs.

extrinsic motivation Motivation that comes from the outside, established artificially and created by rewards that have no real connection with the learning situation. (*Compare* **intrinsic motivation.**)

extrovert An individual who dislikes solitude and prefers the company of other people.

factor analysis A statistical method used to discover the major factor or factors that are measured by a large number of tests or observations; for example, a battery of mental tests usually reveal a verbal ability factor.

family therapy A type of interactional therapy in which the therapist attempts to change the patterns of behavior that various members of a family display toward one another.

fantasy Images; daydreams.

feedback In learning, knowledge obtained by the learner of how well he is progressing.

figure-ground In perception, the tendency to see an object as a figure set off from a neutral ground.

forebrain The top part of the brain mass, including the cerebrum, corpus callosum, thalamus, and hypothalamus.

formal operations The term applied by Piaget to the stage of intellectual development (beginning at about age eleven or twelve) at which the child becomes capable of thinking in the abstract.

fovea The most sensitive part of the retina; contains only cones, which are packed together more tightly than anywhere else in the retina.

fraternal twins (*also called* **dizygotic twins**) Twins who develop from separate eggs and do not inherit the same genes. (*Compare* **identical twins.**)

free association A tool of psychoanalysis in which the patient, lying as relaxed as possible on a couch, is encouraged to let his mind wander where it will and to speak out every thought that occurs to him.

free operant Random, purposeless action, such as the movements of a baby in his crib.

frequency The characteristic of a sound wave determining the tone or pitch that we hear; measured in number of cycles per second.

frustration (1) the blocking of motive satisfaction by an obstacle; (2) the various unpleasant feelings that result from the blocking of motive satisfaction.

functional psychology A school of psychology, associated with James, that emphasized the functions rather than the structure of mental processes.

functional autonomy A principle holding that an activity that is originally a means to an end frequently acquires an independent function of its own and becomes an end in itself.

functional fixedness The tendency to think of an object in terms of its usual functions, not other possible functions; a common barrier to problem solving.

functional psychosis A psychosis having no apparent connection with any organic disturbance. (*Compare* **organic psychosis.**)

galvanic skin reflex (GSR) A change in the electrical conductivity of the skin caused by activity of the sweat glands.

gamma phenomenon The apparent motion of a light when it gets brighter (and seems to draw closer) or dimmer (and seems to move away).

ganglion (*plural:* ganglia) A mass of nerve cells and synapses forming complex and multiple connections.

gene A tiny substance that is a molecule of *DNA*. The genes, grouped together into chromosomes, direct the growth of cells into specific parts of the body and account for inherited individual differences.

general adaptation syndrome A phrase coined by Selye for the sequence of events involved in prolonged stress; the initial shock or alarm, the recovery or resistance period, and at last exhaustion and death.

generation gap Differences in attitudes and behavior between young people and older people.

genital stage One of Freud's stages of psychological development; the final stage, at which the person is able to enter into a heterosexual relationship.

genotype The characteristics of an organism that depend on its genetic inheritance and will be passed along to its offspring. (*Compare* phenotype.)

gestalt psychology A school of psychology that emphasizes the importance of looking at the whole rather than at its parts—for example, in studies of perception and thinking patterns.

goal An object or event toward which a biological drive, stimulus need, or motive is directed.

gradient of approach The changing strength of the desire to approach a goal, dependent on such factors as distance from the goal.

gradient of avoidance The changing strength of the desire to avoid an unpleasant goal, dependent on such factors as distance from the goal.

gradient of texture A clue to distance perception; refers to the fact that nearby objects are seen more sharply and therefore appear "grainier" in texture than more distant objects.

"grass" Slang for marijuana.

group dynamics The forces that operate in a group to produce leaders and to bring about other alignments, activities, and decisions.

group test A psychological test that can be given to many individuals at the same time.

group therapy A type of psychotherapy in which several patients are treated simultaneously.

GSR *See* galvanic skin reflex.

hallucination An imaginary sensation, such as seeing nonexistent animals in the room or feeling bugs crawling under the skin.

halo effect The fact that our general impressions of another person are strongly colored by any one thing, good or bad, that we initially learn about him.

hashish ("hash") A concentrated extract of the active substances of the marijuana plant.

Hering theory (of vision) A theory holding that color vision is attributable to two types of cones with double action, one responsible for red and green, the other for blue and yellow. The Hering theory is now considered incorrect as to the nature of the cones but correct as to the type of nervous impulses sent from the eye.

heroin An opium derivative that creates unusually pleasant feelings; highly addictive.

heterosexuality Sexual attraction to members of the opposite sex.

heuristic A type of thinking that attempts to solve problems less through the application of formal rules than by the use of analogies, rules of thumb, and educated guesses. (*Compare* algorithm.)

hippocampus A part of the brain that appears essential to the transfer of information from short-term memory to long-term memory.

homeostasis An internal environment in which such bodily states as blood circulation, blood chemistry, breathing, digestion, temperature, and so on are kept at optimal levels for survival of the living organism.

homosexuality Sexual attraction to members of the same sex.

hormones Substances produced by the endocrine glands and secreted into the blood stream; complicated chemicals that trigger and control many kinds of bodily activities and behavior.

hue The proper scientific term for what is commonly called color; determined by the length of the light wave.

human engineering A branch of applied psychology concerned with the design of equipment and machinery to fit the size, strength, and capabilities of the people who will use it.

humanistic psychology A school of thought especially interested in the qualities that distinguish human beings from other animals—such as desires for dignity, self-worth, and *self-actualization*.

hunger drive A biological drive caused by deprivation of food.

hyperkinesis A mental abnormality that makes children overactive, irritable, unable to concentrate, and "hard to handle."

hypnosis The act of inducing the hypnotic state, in which the subject is in a sort of dreamlike trance and highly susceptible to suggestions from the hypnotist; sometimes used in psychotherapy.

hypochondriacal reaction An anxiety state in which the individual tends to excuse his failures on the grounds of an imaginary physical illness.

hypothalamus The portion of the forebrain that serves as a sort of mediator between the brain and the body, helping control metabolism, sleep, hunger, thirst, body temperature, and sexual behavior, and that is also concerned with emotions.

hypothesis A theory, especially as to how a problem might be solved.

hysteria A form of psychoneurosis; includes *conversion reaction* and *dissociative reactions*.

id According to Freud's psychoanalytic theory of personality, the unconscious part of the human personality comprising the individual's primitive instinctive forces toward sexuality (the *libido*) and aggression.

identical twins (*also called* monozygotic twins) Twins who develop from the same egg and thus inherit the same genes. (*Compare* fraternal twins.)

identification (1) A process in which the child tries to imitate the behavior of his parents or "heroes" so that he can share vicariously in their strengths and triumphs. (2) In psychoanalytic theory, the process through which the child resolves the Oedipus complex by absorbing his parents into himself. (3) As a defense mechanism, the process through which the individual identifies with another person, or more often with a group, in order to reduce his own conflicts and anxieties.

illusion A perception that is a false interpretation of the actual stimuli.

illusory motion The perception of motion in an unchanging stimulus, such as in the *autokinetic illusion*. (*Compare* apparent motion.)

image The recollection of a sensory experience.

imitation *See* **learning through observation.**

imprinting A rapid form of learning occurring during a critical period early in the organism's life—as when young ducks learn to follow a moving object, usually the mother.

incentive object (*also called* **incentive stimulus**) A stimulus that arouses a drive or motive.

incidental learning (*also called* **latent learning**) Learning that takes place casually, almost as if by accident, then lies latent until reinforcement is provided.

incremental learning Learning that takes place in a series of steps, in which the amount of learning increases, sometimes quickly and sometimes slowly, until the learning is complete. (*Compare* **one-trial learning.**)

independence As used in social psychology, the tendency to make up one's own mind and decide on one's own behavior and thinking regardless of society's norms and pressures.

independent variable A condition, affecting an experimental subject, that is controlled and varied by the experimenter, thus producing changes in the subject's behavior, called the *dependent variable.*

individual difference Any difference—as in physical size or strength, intelligence, sensory threshold, perceptions, emotions, personality, and so on—between the individual organism and other members of his species.

individual test A psychological test that is given by a trained examiner to one person at a time.

industrial psychology A branch of applied psychology, embracing the use of psychological knowledge in setting working hours and rest periods, improving relations between employer and employees, and so on.

inferential statistics Statistics that are used to make generalizations from measurements.

inferiority complex A concept introduced by Adler to describe the condition of a person who for some reason has been unable to develop feelings of adequacy, independence, courage, and wholesome ambition.

inhibit To suppress behavior; for example, the child in toilet training must learn to inhibit his tendency to eliminate whereever and whenever the elimination drive occurs.

inhibition The suppression of behavior; also frequently used to describe emotional and psychoneurotic barriers to action—such as an inhibition against competitive or sexual activity.

inner ear The portion of the ear inward from the oval window; contains the cochlea, vestibule, and semicircular canals.

insight (1) In problem solving, the sudden "flash of inspiration" that results in a successful solution (*compare* **trial and error learning**). (2) In psychotherapy, the discovery by the patient of psychological processes that have caused his difficulties.

instinct An elaborate and inborn pattern of activity, occurring automatically and without prior learning in response to certain stimuli in the environment.

insulin A hormone, secreted by the pancreas, that burns up blood sugar to provide energy.

intellectualization A defense mechanism in which the individual tries to explain away anxiety by intellectually analyzing the situations that produce the unpleasant feelings and making them a matter of theory rather than of action.

intelligence The ability to profit from experience, to learn new pieces of information, and to adjust to new situations.

intelligence quotient (I.Q.) A numerical value assigned to an individual as a result of intelligence testing. The average intelligence quotient is set at 100.

intelligence test A test measuring the various factors that make up the capacity called intelligence. It measures chiefly the individual's ability to use his acquired knowledge in a novel way.

interactional therapies Types of psychotherapy that concentrate on changing the individual's behavior toward other people.

interest test A test measuring the individual's interest or lack of interest in various kinds of amusements, literature, music, art, science, school subjects, social activities, kinds of people, and so on.

interference Failures of memory caused by the effect of old learning on new or new learning on old.

intermittent reinforcement *See* **partial reinforcement.**

interpersonal attraction A person's tendencies to like other people, largely determined by such factors as similarities in attitudes, interests, and personality.

interposition A clue to distance perception; refers to the fact that nearby objects interpose themselves between our eyes and more distant objects.

interval scale A scale (for example, a thermometer) on which the intervals are equal but no ratio between the intervals is implied.

interview A scientific method in which the investigator obtains information through careful and objective questioning of the subject.

intrinsic motivation Motivation that comes from inside the individual. It is an integral part of the learning situation; the individual seeks to learn not for any external reward, but for the joy of knowing. (*Compare* **extrinsic motivation.**)

introspection Inward examination of a "mental life" or mental process that nobody but its possessor can see in operation.

introvert A person who tends to be preoccupied with his own thoughts and activities and to avoid social contact.

intuitive thought The term applied by Piaget to the stage of intellectual development (ages four to six) when the child is developing concepts that become more and more elaborate but are still based largely on the evidence of his senses.

I.Q. *See* **intelligence quotient.**

iris A circular arrangement of muscles that contract and expand to make the pupil of the eye smaller in bright light and larger in dim light.

James-Lange theory of emotion A physiological theory holding that stimuli in the environment set off physiological changes in the individual, that the changes in turn stimulate sensory nerves inside the body, and that the messages of these sensory nerves are then perceived as emotion.

"joint" A marijuana cigarette.

just noticeable difference (j.n.d.) *See* **difference threshold.**

latent learning *See* **incidental learning.**

learned helplessness A condition in which the organism has been subjected to punishment over which it has no control, leading to an impairment of the ability to learn or use old habits.

learning The process by which overt behavior and covert behavior become altered or attached to new stimuli.

learning by imitation *See* **learning through observation.**

learning curve A graph plotting the course of learning. In a learning curve of decreasing returns, progress is quite rapid at first; then the curve starts to level off. In a learning curve of equal returns, progress takes place at a steady rate, with each new trial producing an equal amount of improvement. In a learning curve of increasing returns, very slow progress in early trials is followed by rapid progress in later trials.

learning plateau A period in which early progress in learning appears to have stopped and improvement is at a standstill; the plateau is followed by a new period of progress.

learning sets Attitudes and strategies acquired in one learning situation and carried over to similar situations; "learning how to learn."

learning through exposition *See* didactic learning.

learning through modeling *See* learning through observation.

learning through observation (*also called* **learning through modeling, learning by imitation**) A type of learning in which the behavior of another organism is observed and imitated.

lens A transparent structure of the eye that changes shape to focus images sharply on the retina.

libido According to Freud's psychoanalytic theory of personality, a basic instinctual force in the individual, embracing sexual urges and such related desires as to be kept warm, well-fed, and happy.

lie detector A device designed to reveal whether a subject is telling the truth by measuring physiological changes, usually in heart rate, blood pressure, breathing, and galvanic skin reflex.

limbic system A set of interconnected pathways in the brain, including the hypothalamus, some primitive parts of the cerebrum that have to do with the sense of smell, eating, and emotion, and other structures.

limen *See* threshold.

linear perspective A clue to distance perception; refers to the fact that parallel lines seem to draw closer together as they recede into the distance.

location constancy The tendency to perceive objects as being in their rightful and accustomed place and remaining there even when we move and their images therefore move across our eyes.

logical thinking An objective and disciplined form of thinking in which facts are carefully examined and conclusions consistent with the facts are reached.

long-term memory The permanent storehouse from which information can be retrieved under the proper circumstances.

loudness The hearing sensation determined by the amplitude of the sound wave.

LSD (lysergic acid diethylamide) A psychedelic drug.

management of learning An attempt—often made by educators and by people desirous of learning—to arrange the most favorable possible conditions for learning to take place.

manic-depressive psychosis A functional psychosis characterized by extremes of mood, often by wild swings from intense excitement to deep melancholy.

marathon group A type of encounter group that meets for a single continuous session, often lasting thirty-six hours or more.

marijuana The dried leaves and flowers of the hemp plant; a drug that affects different users in different ways, often interfering with short-term memory and concentration and producing feelings of elation.

masochism Obtaining sexual pleasure from suffering pain or other maltreatment. (*Compare* sadism.)

massed practice A single, long learning session. (*Compare* distributed practice.)

maturation The physical changes, taking place after birth, that continue the biological development of the organism from fertilized egg cell to complete adult.

mean A measure of central tendency obtained by dividing the sum of all the measurements by the number of subjects measured.

measurement The assignment of numbers to traits, events, or subjects according to some kind of orderly system.

median A measure of central tendency; the point separating the lower half of measurements from the upper half.

mediated generalization A process in which two stimuli are generalized through the use of language, although they do not possess any physical similarities. An example is the generalization of a small rubber ball and a giant stuffed animal because both are called toys.

mediated transfer A special kind of transfer of learning in which language is the mediating factor.

mediational clustering The association of words and concepts, not through formal rules of logic but through an informal clustering of ideas that are in some way related.

mediational unit One term (the preferred term in this book) for the engram, association, bond, or memory trace formed in learning; a connection between a new stimulus and an innate or previously learned unit of overt or covert behavior.

medulla The connection between the spinal cord and the brain; an important connecting link that is vital to life because it helps regulate heartbeat, blood pressure, and breathing.

memory trace The basis of a theory of remembering, no longer popular, holding that learning left some kind of trace in the nervous system that could be kept active through use but tended to fade away or become distorted through lack of practice.

mental age A person's age as measured by his performance on an intelligence test; a person who scores as well as the average ten-year-old has a mental age of ten regardless of his chronological age.

mentally gifted Having an I.Q. over 130.

mentally retarded Having an I.Q. below 70.

mental telepathy The supposed ability of one person to know what is going on in another person's mind; a form of extrasensory perception.

mesomorph One of three basic types of body build described by Sheldon; the mesomorph is the athletic type, with strong bones and muscles.

metabolism The chemical process in which the body converts food into protoplasm and energy.

methedrine ("meth") One of the amphetamines.

middle ear The portion of the ear between the eardrum and the oval window of the inner ear; contains three bones that aid transmission of sound waves.

mnemonic device A form of memory aid in which memorized symbols give relation to otherwise unrelated material.

mode A measure of central tendency; the measurement at which the greatest number of subjects fall.

modeling *See* learning through observation.

Mongolism A type of mental retardation apparently caused by the presence of an extra chromosome (making a total of forty-seven instead of the normal forty-six in each cell).

monozygotic twins *See* identical twins.

morphemes The smallest meaningful units of language, made by combining *phonemes* into prefixes, words, or suffixes.

motion parallax A term describing the fact that, when we move our heads, near objects move across our field of vision more rapidly than objects that are farther away.

motivation A general term referring to the forces regulating behavior that is undertaken because of drives, needs, or desires and is directed toward goals.

motivational disposition   The possession of a motive; a potential influence on behavior that can at any time be aroused to become an active motive. (*Compare* **aroused motive.**)

motive   A desire for a goal or incentive object that has acquired value for the individual.

motor skill   A coordinated series of movements, such as those required in walking or riding a bicycle.

multiple personality   A type of dissociative reaction in which the individual seems to be split into two or more different selves that represent sides of his personality he cannot integrate into a unity.

muscle   Fibers capable of producing motion by contraction and expansion. Human muscles include *striped muscles* and *smooth muscles.*

muscle tension   Contractions of a muscle; one of the bodily changes often observed in emotion.

myelin sheath   A fatty sheath, white in appearance, that covers many neuron fibers and speeds the transmission of nervous impulses.

nAch   Short for need for achievement, often used by authors of studies of motivation.

nAff   Short for need for affiliation, often used by authors of studies of motivation.

narcissism   Excessive self-love.

nativists   Those who accept the theory that many of the important factors determining behavior are present at birth.

naturalistic observation   A scientific method in which the investigator does not manipulate the situation and cannot control all the variables; he tries to remain unseen or as inconspicuous as possible.

negative transfer   A process in which learning is made more difficult by interference from previous learning. (*Compare* **positive transfer.**)

neo-psychoanalysts   The recent psychoanalytical theorists who have changed Freud's original ideas in various ways; "neo" means new.

nerve   A group of neurons, small or very large in number, traveling together to or from the central nervous system; in appearance, a single large fiber that is in fact made up of many fibers.

nervous impulse   A tiny charge of electricity passing from the dendrite end of the neuron to the end of the axon.

neuron   The individual nerve cell, basic unit of the nervous system.

neurosis   *See* **psychoneurosis.**

neurotic depression   A form of psychoneurosis in which the individual appears to be particularly sensitive to unhappy events; his normal discouragement and grief are complicated and exaggerated by feelings of dejection, hopelessness, and guilt.

nomadism   A form of withdrawal in which the frustrated individual wanders through life without ever putting down roots.

nominal scale   A scale in which numbers are simply assigned to different categories (as when men are called group 1 and women are called group 2).

nonsense syllable   A meaningless syllable, such as XYL or PLAM, used in the study of learning.

nonsocial behavior   Actions that take place when a person is alone.

noradrenalin (*also called* **norepinephrine**)   A hormone, secreted by the adrenal medulla, that produces bodily changes associated with anger or "fight" situations.

norepinephrine   *See* **noradrenalin.**

normal curve of distribution (*also called* **normal probability curve**)   A bell-shaped curve that describes many events in nature; most events cluster around the average, and the number declines approaching either the lower or the upper extreme.

norms   The shared standards and expectations of a social group.

obedience   In social psychology, conformity to a figure of authority.

object constancy   The tendency to perceive objects as constant and unchanging, even under varying conditions of illumination, distance, and position.

objective personality test   A paper-and-pencil test administered and scored according to a standard procedure, giving results that are not affected by the opinions or prejudices of the examiner.

obsession   A thought that keeps cropping up in a persistent and disturbing fashion.

obsessive-compulsive reactions   A group of psychoneuroses characterized by obsessions or compulsions.

Oedipus complex   According to Freud, the conflict of mingled love and hate toward the parents that every child undergoes between the ages of two and a half and six.

olfactory epithelium   The membrane, at the top of the nasal passages leading from the nostrils to the throat, that contains the receptors sensitive to smell.

one-trial learning   Learning that takes place in a single step. (*Compare* **incremental learning.**)

operant avoidance   Behavior, learned through operant conditioning, by which the organism attempts to avoid something unpleasant.

operant behavior   Behavior that is not initially associated with or normally elicited by a specific stimulus. (*Compare* **respondent behavior.**)

operant conditioning   The process by which, through learning, free operant behavior becomes attached to a specific stimulus. (*Compare* **classical conditioning.**)

operant escape   Behavior, learned through operant conditioning, by which the organism seeks to escape something unpleasant.

opium   A drug derived from the poppy plant, most commonly used in the United States in the form of heroin.

oral stage   One of the stages of psychological development according to Freud; the first stage, in which the infant receives pleasure in the area of the mouth from acts such as sucking.

ordinal scale   A scale based on rank order.

ordinary sleep   A state of the organism in which brain activity is different from that in the waking state and the muscles of the body are quite relaxed. (*Compare* **paradoxical sleep.**)

ordinate   The vertical axis of a graph, along which the dependent variable is usually plotted.

organ of Corti   The collection of hair cells, lying on the basilar membrane, that are the receptors for hearing.

organic psychosis   A psychosis caused by actual damage to the brain by disease or injury. (*Compare* **functional psychosis.**)

organism   An individual animal, either human or subhuman.

osmotic pressure   The relative concentration of chemicals, such as salt and sugar, in the body fluids; cells in the brain sensitive to osmotic pressure set off the thirst drive.

oval window   The membrane through which sound waves are transmitted from the bones of the middle ear to the cochlea.

ovaries   Glands that, in addition to producing the female egg cells, secrete hormones that bring about bodily changes known as secondary female sex characteristics.

overlearning The process of continuing to practice at learning after bare mastery has been attained.

overlearning, law of The principle that overlearning increases the length of time the material will be remembered.

overt behavior Observable behavior, such as motor movements, speech, and signs of emotion such as laughing or weeping.

overtones The additional vibrations of a source of sound, at frequencies higher than the fundamental tone it produces; the overtones account for the complexity and timbre of the sound.

pacer stimuli A term, used in the theory of choice, that refers to stimuli of somewhat greater complexity than stimuli at the individual's ideal level of complexity.

pain drive A biological drive aroused by unpleasant or noxious stimulation, usually resulting in behavior designed to escape the stimulus.

pancreas The endocrine gland that secretes insulin.

Papez-MacLean theory of emotion A neurological theory of emotion that emphasizes the role of the *limbic system.*

paradoxical cold A term for the fact that cold receptors in the skin respond to a stimulus of more than 110 degrees Fahrenheit as well as to stimuli that are actually cold.

paradoxical sleep A state of the organism in which the brain's activity is similar to that in the waking state but the muscles are extremely relaxed and the sleeper is difficult to wake; also known as REM sleep because it is accompanied by the rapid eye movements that characterize dreaming. (*Compare* **ordinary sleep.**)

paranoia A functional psychosis characterized by delusions, sometimes of grandeur, sometimes of persecution.

parasympathetic nervous system A division of the autonomic nervous system, composed of scattered ganglia that lie near the glands and muscles they affect. The parasympathetic system is most active in helping maintain heartbeat and digestion under normal circumstances. (*Compare* **sympathetic nervous system.**)

parathyroids A pair of endocrine glands, lying atop the larger thyroid gland, that regulate the balance of calcium and phosphorus in the body, an important factor in maintaining a normal state of excitability of the nervous system.

part method (of learning) A method in which one part of the material is learned at a time, as in memorizing a speech. (*Compare* **whole method.**)

partial reinforcement (*also called* **intermittent reinforcement**) Reinforcement provided on some but not all occasions.

peer group The group of psychological equals to which the individual belongs; among children, based largely on age.

peers For any individual, other people of about the same age and standing in the community; equals.

percentile A statistical term used to describe the position of an individual score in the total group.

perception The process through which we become aware of our environment by organizing and interpreting the evidence of our senses.

perceptual constancy The tendency to perceive a stable and consistent world even though the stimuli that reach the senses are inconsistent and potentially confusing.

perceptual expectation The tendency to perceive what we expect to perceive; a special form of *set.*

performance Overt behavior; used as a measure of learning.

performance test An intelligence test or part of an intelligence test that measures the individual's ability to perform such tasks

as completing pictures, making designs, and assembling objects. (*Compare* **verbal test.**)

peripheral nervous system The outlying nerves of the body and the individual neurons that make up these nerves. (*Compare* **central nervous system.**)

persistence of set In problem solving, the tendency to continue to apply a certain hypothesis because it has worked in other situations, often at the expense of trying different and much more efficient hypotheses.

personality The total pattern of characteristic ways of thinking, feeling, and behaving that constitute the individual's distinctive method of relating to his environment.

personality disorder *See* **character disorder.**

personality test A test designed to measure the various characteristics that make up the individual's personality.

perspective A clue to distance perception; refers to the fact that three-dimensional objects can be delineated on a flat surface, such as the retina of the eye. (*See* **aerial perspective, linear perspective.**)

persuasive communications The transmission of information and appeals to emotion in an attempt to change another person's attitudes.

phallic stage One of the stages of psychological development according to Freud; the stage at which the child invests interest in the pleasure derived from his sex organs.

phenomenal self A concept proposed by Rogers in his theory of personality; one's uniquely perceived self-image, based on the evidence of one's senses but not necessarily corresponding to reality.

phenotype Characteristics displayed by an individual organism that are not necessarily passed along to its offspring—for example, its appearance. (*Compare* **genotype.**)

phi phenomenon Motion produced by a rapid succession of images that are actually stationary; the simplest form of *stroboscopic motion.*

phobic reaction An anxiety state characterized by unreasonable fears.

phonemes The building blocks of language; basic sounds that are combined into *morphemes* and words.

pitch The property of being high or low in tone, determined by the frequency (number of cycles per second) of the sound wave.

pituitary gland The master endocrine gland that secretes hormones controlling growth, causing sexual development at puberty, and also regulating other endocrine glands.

PK *See* **psychokinesis.**

place theory (of hearing) The theory that special parts of the basilar membrane are "tuned" to various pitches and that the response of receptors in each particular place accounts for the sensations of pitch.

play therapy A type of psychotherapy, usually used with children, in which patients express their feelings by drawing pictures, modeling, or handling puppets or other toys.

pleasure principle According to Freud's psychoanalytic theory of personality, the demand of the unconscious id for immediate and total satisfaction of all its demands. (*Compare* **reality principle.**)

pons A structure of neurons connecting the opposite sides of the cerebellum; it helps control breathing and is apparently the origin of the nervous impulses that cause rapid eye movements during dreaming.

population In statistics, the term for all people or all events in a particular category—such as all male college students in the United States.

position The particular place or niche that an individual occupies in society.

positive transfer A process in which learning is made easier by something learned previously. (*Compare* **negative transfer.**)

posthypnotic suggestion A suggestion made during hypnosis, urging the subject to undertake some kind of activity after the hypnotic trance ends.

"pot" Slang for marijuana.

precognition The supposed ability to forecast events; a form of extrasensory perception.

preconceptual thought The term applied by Piaget to the stage of intellectual development (ages two and three) at which the child begins to use language to attach new meanings to the stimuli in his environment and to use one stimulus as a symbol for another.

prehension Grasping ability.

premise Something that we believe to be true about the objects and events in the environment; an important tool in thinking.

preoperational stage The term applied by Piaget to the period (ages two to seven) when the child's ability to use language begins to dominate intellectual development.

primacy In learning, the fact of being near the beginning of a series of items to be learned. (*See* **primacy and recency, law of.**)

primacy and recency, law of The principle that the learner tends to remember best the items that were first in a series (had primacy) or last (had recency).

primary mental abilities According to Thurstone, the seven abilities that make up intelligence. They are verbal comprehension, word fluency, number, space, associative memory, perceptual speed, and general reasoning, plus some kind of "general factor" that is common to all individuals.

primary reinforcement Reinforcement provided by a stimulus that the organism finds inherently rewarding—usually stimuli that satisfy biological drives such as hunger or thirst.

proactive inhibition Interference by something learned in the past with the ability to remember new learning. (*Compare* **retroactive inhibition.**)

problem solving Thinking that is directed toward the solution of a problem; the most common and important kind of *directed thinking.*

programed learning A system of instruction in which the subject matter is broken down into very short steps, mastered one at a time before going on to the next.

progressive part method (of learning) A method of learning, frequently quite efficient, in which the first unit of the whole (such as the first stanza of a poem) is learned, then the second, then these two are combined; then the third unit is learned and combined with the first two; and so on.

projection A defense mechanism in which the individual foists off or projects onto other people motives of his own that cause him anxiety.

projective personality test A test in which the subject is expected to project aspects of his own personality into the stories he makes up about pictures or the objects he sees in inkblots.

protoplasm The basic substance of living tissue, the "stuff of life."

psychedelic drugs Drugs, such as LSD, that often produce hallucinations and a sense of detachment from one's body.

psychiatrist A physician who has had special training in treating behavior disturbances.

psychic energizer Any of a number of drugs used to relieve depression by increasing brain activity.

psychoanalysis A type of psychotherapy developed by Freud, in which the chief tools are free association, study of dreams and slips of the tongue, and transference. Psychoanalysis attempts to give the patient insight into his unconscious conflicts, which he can then control as they come into his awareness.

psychoanalyst A person, usually a physician, who practices psychoanalysis.

psychoanalytic theory of personality A theory originally formulated by Freud that emphasizes three parts of the personality: (1) the unconscious *id,* (2) the conscious *ego,* and (3) the largely unconscious *superego.*

psychodrama A type of psychotherapy in which the patient is encouraged to act out his problems and fantasies in the company of other patients or therapeutic assistants who have been trained in the techniques of psychodrama.

psychokinesis (PK) The supposed ability of some people to influence physical events through exercise of the mind—for example, to make dice turn up as they wish.

psycholinguistics The study of the relationship between psychological processes and the structure and use of language. Among its important concerns are the rules of language and the manner in which they are learned.

psychology The science that systematically studies and attempts to explain observable behavior and its relationship to the unseen mental processes that go on inside the organism and to external events in the environment.

psychoneurosis (*also called* **neurosis**) A form of emotional disturbance characterized by high levels of stress and anxiety over a period of time.

psychopathic personality (*also called* **sociopathic personality**) A behavior disorder characterized by lack of conscience, sense of social responsibility, and feeling for other people; also by selfishness, ruthlessness, and addiction to lying.

psychophysical methods Techniques of measuring how changes in the intensity or quality of a stimulus affect sensation.

psychosexual development The Freudian theory that psychological development goes through oral, anal, phallic, and genital stages.

psychosis The scientific name for the extreme forms of mental disturbances often known as insanity. The mental disturbance is so severe as to make the individual incapable of getting along in society.

psychosomatic illness An illness in which the physical symptoms seem to have mental and emotional causes.

psychotherapy A technique used by clinical psychologists, psychiatrists, and psychoanalysts in which a patient suffering from personality disorder or mental disturbance is treated by the application of psychological knowledge.

pupil The opening in the iris that admits light waves into the eyeball.

questionnaire A scientific method similar to the interview but in which information is obtained through written questions.

random sample A statistical sample that has been obtained by chance methods that avoid any bias.

range A measurement of variability obtained by subtracting the lowest measurement from the highest.

rapid eye movement (REM) Small movements of a sleeper's eyes that occur during paradoxical sleep and dreaming.

muscles of the neck, arms, and legs tense; the head moves forward; and the mouth may open.

statistical method   The application of mathematical principles to a description and analysis of measurements.

status   As used in social psychology, same as *position.*

stereotyped behavior   A tendency to repeat some action over and over again, almost as a ritual; a result of frustration.

steroids   Chemical substances produced by the adrenal cortex and essential for life.

stimulus   Any form of energy capable of exciting the nervous system.

stimulus complexity   The relative level of simplicity or complexity possessed by a sensory stimulus. The organism apparently has stimulus needs for stimuli of a particular level of complexity found the most "comfortable."

stimulus discrimination   The ability, acquired through learning, to make distinctions between stimuli that are similar but not exactly alike.

stimulus generalization   The tendency of an organism that has learned to associate a stimulus with a certain kind of behavior to display this behavior toward stimuli that are similar though not exactly identical to the original stimulus.

stimulus need   The tendency of an organism to seek certain kinds of stimulation. The tendency does not have the life-and-death urgency of a drive, nor is its goal as specific and clear-cut. Examples are the needs for stimulation, stimulus variability, and physical contact (or tactual comfort).

stimulus-response (S-R) psychology   A school of thought that emphasizes study of the stimuli that produce behavioral responses, the rewards and punishments that help establish and maintain these responses, and the modification of behavior through changes in the pattern of rewards and punishments.

stimulus-response (S-R) theories   *See* **social learning theories of personality.**

stimulus variability   Change and variety in stimulation; believed to be one of the organism's inborn stimulus needs.

stranger anxiety   Fear of unfamiliar faces, one of the first forms of anxiety that develops in the child at about eight months.

stress   In psychological terms, a stimulus that threatens to damage the organism.

stress interview   A form of situational personality test in which the subject is asked deliberately hostile questions and the interviewers pretend to disbelieve his answers.

striped muscle   A muscle of motor behavior, over which the individual ordinarily has conscious control.

stroboscopic motion   Motion produced by a rapid succession of images that are actually stationary, as in motion pictures.

structural psychology   A school of psychology, associated with Wundt, that concentrated on the structure or contents of conscious experience, such as sensations, images, and feelings.

subculture   A culture within a culture—that is, the ways of life followed by a group in a society that does not adhere to all the practices of the society as a whole.

sublimation   One form of the defense mechanism of *substitution;* substituting an acceptable goal for a forbidden one.

subliminal   A word used to describe a stimulus of an intensity below the threshold (or limen) of the senses.

substitution   A defense mechanism in which an unobtainable or forbidden goal is replaced by a different goal.

superego   According to Freud's psychoanalytic theory of personality, a largely unconscious part of the individual's personality that threatens punishment for transgressions.

supraliminal   A word used to describe a stimulus of an intensity at or above the threshold, or limen.

surface structure   A term used by linguists to refer to the combination of *sounds* that makes up an utterance such as a sentence. (*Compare* **deep structure.**)

syllogism   A three-step process of logical thinking, consisting of a major premise, a minor premise, and a conclusion that follows inescapably from the first two.

symbol   Anything that stands for something else. The word *water* is a symbol for the colorless fluid we drink; the skull and crossbones is a symbol for poison; mathematics is a collection of symbols.

sympathetic nervous system   A division of the autonomic nervous system, composed of long chains of ganglia lying along both sides of the spinal column. Its final axons secrete chemicals resembling adrenalin and noradrenalin, thus stimulating the glands and smooth muscles of the body and helping prepare the organism for "fight or flight." (*Compare* **parasympathetic nervous system.**)

synapse   The junction point between the axon of one neuron and the dendrite of another neuron.

synaptic knob   A swelling at the end of a dendrite; an important structure in the transmission of messages across the synapse.

syndrome   A medical term meaning the entire pattern of symptoms and events that characterize the course of a disease.

tabula rasa   A "blank tablet"; a phrase used to describe the theory that the mind of a human baby is a "blank tablet" on which anything can be written through learning and experience.

tactual comfort   Physical contact; one of the stimulus needs.

taste buds   The receptors for the sense of taste; found on the tongue, at the back of the mouth, and in the throat.

teaching machine   A device used in programed learning; the machine presents the program one step at a time and asks a question that the learner answers before going on to the next step.

telepathy   *See* **mental telepathy.**

temperature drive   A biological drive aroused by physiological requirements that the body temperature be kept at a constant level (in human beings, around 98.6° Fahrenheit).

test   A measurement of a sample of individual behavior. Ideally, a scientific test should be (1) objective, (2) standardized, (3) reliable, and (4) valid.

testes   Glands that, in addition to producing the male sperm cells, secrete hormones that bring about secondary male sex characteristics, such as the growth of facial hair and change of voice.

T-group   *See* **training group.**

thalamus   The brain's major relay station, connecting the cerebrum with the lower structures of the brain and the spinal cord.

theory   A statement of general principles that explains events observed in the past and predicts what will happen under a given set of circumstances in the future.

theory of attachment   The theory that the human baby inherits a strong tendency to orient toward and consort with a caretaker, usually the mother, because inborn behaviors such as rooting, sucking, babbling, and crying are directed toward another person.

theory of choice   A theory maintaining that every stimulus object has a certain complexity value (related to its information value), that every individual organism has its own ideal level of complexity, that the individual will seek out stimuli of this level, but that the individual will also explore objects of slightly greater complexity, called pacer stimuli.

thinking The covert manipulation of images, symbols, and other mediational units, especially language, concepts, premises, and rules.

thirst drive A biological drive aroused by deprivation of water.

threshold (*also called* **limen**) The minimum amount of stimulation or difference in stimulation to which a sensory receptor will respond 50 percent of the time. (*See* **absolute threshold, difference threshold.**)

thyroid gland An endocrine gland that regulates the rate of metabolism and affects the body's activity level.

tic The involuntary twitching of a muscle.

timbre The quality of a sound, determined by the number and strength of the overtones that contribute to the complexity of the sound wave.

tip of the tongue phenomenon A partially successful attempt at retrieval in which we cannot quite remember a word (for example) but seem to have it almost available or "on the tip of the tongue."

token economy An arbitrary economic system, often used in mental hospitals, in which patients are rewarded for good behavior with tokens that they can exchange like money for various privileges.

training group (*also called* **T-group, sensitivity group**) A kind of encounter group.

tranquilizer A drug that reduces anxiety and often eliminates the hallucinations and delusions of schizophrenics, apparently by slowing down the activity of the brain.

transfer of learning The effect of prior learning on new learning. (*See* **positive transfer, negative transfer.**)

transference A psychoanalytic term for the tendency of the patient to transfer to other people (including the psychoanalyst) the emotional attitudes he felt as a child toward such much loved and hated persons as parents and siblings.

traveling wave theory (**of hearing**) The theory that the basilar membrane responds as a whole to sound waves and that the sensation of pitch results from the fact that some parts of the membrane are activated more than others.

tremor A shaking produced when two sets of muscles work against each other; one of the bodily changes observed in emotion.

trial and error learning A form of learning in which one response after another is tried and rejected as unsuitable, until at last a successful response is made. (*Compare* **insight.**)

truth serum (**sodium amytal**) A narcotic used in medical therapy to induce a period of drowsiness in which the patient is able to recall and discuss experiences that he ordinarily represses.

unconditioned response An automatic, unlearned reaction to a stimulus—such as the salivation of Pavlov's dog to food.

unconditioned stimulus A stimulus that is innately capable of causing a reflex action—such as the food that originally caused Pavlov's dog to respond with salivation.

unconscious motive A motive that the individual is unaware of but that may influence his behavior nonetheless.

undirected thinking A thinking process that takes place spontaneously and with no goal in view.

"uppers" In the parlance of drug users, any drug that produces a lift in mood, such as the amphetamines.

upward mobility The tendency of an individual to surmount the barriers between social classes and advance his station in life.

vacillation The tendency to be drawn first toward one resolution of a conflict, then toward the other; a type of behavior typical in conflict situations.

valid test A test found to measure the characteristic that it attempts to measure.

variability In statistics, the amount of variation found in a group of measurements; described by the range and standard deviation.

variable A condition that is subject to change, especially in an experiment. (*See* **dependent variable, independent variable.**)

verbal test An intelligence test or part of an intelligence test that measures the individual's ability to deal with verbal symbols; it may include items measuring vocabulary, general comprehension, mathematical reasoning, ability to find similarities, and so on. (*Compare* **performance test.**)

vestibule A chamber in the inner ear containing receptors for the sense of equilibrium.

visceral organs The internal organs, such as the stomach, intestines, liver, kidneys, and so on.

viscerotonic temperament A type of temperament ascribed by Sheldon to the endomorphic body type; characterized by relaxed posture, even emotions, love of physical comfort, tolerance, and complacency.

visual purple A light-sensitive substance associated with the rods of the retina; chemical changes in the visual purple, caused by light, make the rods fire.

vocational aptitude test A test that measures the ability to perform specialized skills required in various kinds of jobs.

vocational guidance The technique of helping a person select the right lifetime occupation, often through tests of aptitudes and interests.

Weber's Law The rule that the difference threshold, or just noticeable difference, is a fixed percentage of the original stimulus.

whole method (**of learning**) A method in which the material is learned or memorized as an entire unit rather than part by part. (*Compare* **part method.**)

withdrawal A reaction in which the individual tries to relieve feelings of frustration by withdrawing from the attempt to attain his goals.

X-chromosome One of the two chromosomes that determine sex; an X-X pairing produces a female, an X-Y pairing a male.

Y-chromosome One of the two chromosomes that determine sex. (*See* **X-chromosome.**)

Young-Helmholtz theory (**of vision**) A theory stating that, since the entire range of hues can be produced by combining red, green, and blue, there must be three kinds of cones differentially sensitive to these wave lengths.

REFERENCES ANd ACKNOWLEdGMENTS

chapter one

1. See, for example, Rhine, J. B., and Brier, R. *Parapsychology today*. New York: Citadel Press, 1968.

2. See, for example, Soal, S. G., and Bateman, F. *Modern experiments in telepathy*. New Haven, Conn.: Yale University Press, 1954.

3. James, W. *Principles of psychology*. Vol. I. New York: Dover, 1950.

4. Schachter, S. *Psychology of affiliation*. Stanford, Calif.: Stanford University Press, 1959.

5. Cates, J. Psychology's manpower: report on the 1968 national register of scientific and technical personnel. *American Psychologist*, 1970, **25**, 254–63.

6. Jones, D. R. *Psychologists in mental health: 1966*. Washington, D.C.: National Institute of Mental Health, Public Health Service Publication, No. 1984, 1969.

7. U.S. Bureau of the Census. *Current Population Reports*, Series P-23, No. 34. "Characteristics of American youth: 1970." Series P-20, No. 207. "Educational attainment: March, 1970." Also *U.S. Census of Population: 1940*, Vol. IV. Characteristics by age, Part I, United States summary. Washington, D.C.: U.S. Government Printing Office, 1971, 1970, and 1943.

8. Feldman, K. A., and Newcomb, T. M. *The impact of college on students*. Vol. 1. San Francisco: Jossey-Bass, 1969.

9. Peterson, R. E. The student protest movement: some facts, interpretations, and a plea. In Korten, F. F., Cook, S. W., and Lacey, J. I., eds. *Psychology and the problems of society*. Washington, D.C.: American Psychological Association, 1970, pp. 388–94.

10. Louis Harris and Associates poll commissioned by *Life* magazine. Change yes—upheaval no. *Life*, 1971, **70**, 23–30.

11. Staff of the Office of Research. National norms for entering college freshmen—fall 1970. *American Council on Education Research Reports*, Vol. 5, No. 6, 1971.

12. Nowlis, H. H. Student drug use. In Korten, F. F., Cook, S. W., and Lacey, J. I., eds. *Psychology and the problems of society*. Washington, D.C.: American Psychological Association, 1970, pp. 408–19.

13. Doorenbos, N. J., et al. Cultivation, extraction and analysis of *Cannabis Sativa L.* Paper presented May 20, 1971, at the Conference on Marihuana sponsored by the New York Academy of Sciences. *Annals of the New York Academy of Sciences*, 1971, **191**, 3–14.

14. Hollister, L. E. Marihuana in man: three years later. *Science*, 1971, **172**, 21–29.

15. Clark, L. D., and Nakashima, E. N. Experimental studies of marihuana. *American Journal of Psychiatry*, 1968, **125**, 379–84.

16. Melges, F. T., et al. Marihuana and temporal disintegration. *Science*, 1970, **168**, 1118–20.

17. Bennett, D. E. Marijuana use among college students and street people: "It just brings out what's there." Unpublished undergraduate honors thesis, Radcliffe College, May, 1971.

18. Tylden, E. A case for Cannabis? *British Medical Journal*, 1967, **2**, 556.

19. U.S. Department of Health, Education, and Welfare. *Marihuana and health*. Washington, D.C.: U.S. Government Printing Office, 1971.

20. Soueit, M. I. Hashish consumption in Egypt, with special reference to psychosocial aspects. *Bulletin on Narcotics*, 1967, **19**(2), 1–12.

21. Ball, J. C., Chambers, C. D., and Ball, M. J. The association of marihuana smoking with opiate addiction in the United States. *Journal of Criminal Law, Criminology, and Police Science*, 1968, **59**, 171–82.

22. Yolles, S. F. Statement before the Subcommittee on Alcoholism and Narcotics, Committee on Labor and Public Welfare, United States Senate, August 6, 1969.

23. Gallup poll, released January 16, 1971. Reported in *The New York Times*, January 17, 1971.

24. Kogan, B. A. *Health*. New York: Harcourt Brace Jovanovich, 1970.

25. Steinhilber, R. M., and Hagedorn, A. B. Drug induced behavioral disorders. *GP*, 1967, **35**, 115–16.

26. Kales, A., moderator. Drug dependency. University of California at Los Angeles Interdepartmental Conference. *Annals of Internal Medicine*, 1969, **70**, 591.

27. U.S. Bureau of the Census. *U.S. Census of Population: 1960*. Vol. 1. Characteristics of the population, Part A, Number of inhabitants. Washington, D.C.: U.S. Government Printing Office, 1961. Also *U.S. Census of Population: 1970*. Series PC (VI)-1, United States, Advance Report.

28. Fraser, S., and Zimbardo, P. G. Unpublished research cited in Zimbardo, P. G., The human choice: individuation, reason, and order versus deindividuation, impulse, and chaos. In Arnold, W. J., and Levine, D., eds. *Nebraska symposium on motivation, 1969*, Vol. 17. Lincoln: University of Nebraska Press, 1970, pp. 237–307.

29. Zimbardo, P. G. The human choice: individuation, reason, and order versus deindividuation, impulse, and chaos. In Arnold, W. J., and Levine, D., eds. *Nebraska symposium on motivation, 1969*, Vol. 17. Lincoln: University of Nebraska Press, 1970, pp. 237–307.

30. Altman, D., et al. Trust of the stranger in the city and the small town. Unpublished research, Graduate Center, City University of New York, 1969.

31. Adapted from *The unresponsive bystander: why doesn't he help?* Bibb Latané and John M. Darley. Copyright © 1970 by Meredith Corporation. Used by permission of Appleton-Century-Crofts, Educational Division, Meredith Corporation.

32. Darley, J. M., and Batson, C. D. From Jerusalem to Jericho: a study of situational and dispositional variables in helping behavior. Unpublished study, 1971.

33. Piliavin, I. M., Rodin, J., and Piliavin, J. A. Good Samaritanism: an underground phenomenon? *Journal of Personality and Social Psychology*, 1969, **13**, 289–99.

chapter two

1. Kagan, J. The determinants of attention in the infant. *American Scientist*, 1970, **58**, 298–306.

2. Irwin, O. C. The amount and nature of activities of newborn infants under constant external stimulating conditions during the

first ten days of life. *Genetic Psychology Monographs,* 1930, **8.** Also Wolff, P. H. Observations on newborn infants. *Psychosomatic Medicine,* 1959, **21,** 110–18.

3. Kagan, J. Personality development. In Janis, I. L., ed. *Personality: dynamics, development, and assessment.* New York: Harcourt Brace Jovanovich, 1969, pp. 405–572.

4. Yerkes, R. M., and Morgulis, S. The methods of Pavlov in animal psychology. *Psychological Bulletin,* 1909, **6,** 257–73.

5. Pavlov, I. P. *Conditioned reflexes: an investigation of the physiological activity of the cerebral cortex.* London: Oxford University Press, 1927 [reprinted by Dover, New York, 1960].

6. Watson, J. B., and Rayner, R. Conditioned emotional reactions. *Journal of Experimental Psychology,* 1920, **3,** 1–14.

7. Sawry, W. C., Conger, J. J., and Turrell, R. B. An experimental investigation of the role of psychological factors in the production of gastric ulcers in rats. *Journal of Comparative and Physiological Psychology,* 1956, **457,** 143.

8. Fel'berbaum, I. M. Interoceptive conditioned reflexes from the uterus. *Trud. Inst. Fiziol. Pavlova,* 1952, **1,** 85–92.

9. Skinner, B. F. *The behavior of organisms.* New York: Appleton-Century-Crofts, 1938.

10. Solomon, R. L., Kamin, L. J., and Wynne, L. C. Traumatic avoidance learning: the outcomes of several extinction procedures with dogs. *Journal of Abnormal and Social Psychology,* 1953, **48,** 291–302.

11. Bachrach, A. J., Erwin, W. J., and Mohr, J. P. The control of eating behavior in an anorexic by operant conditioning techniques. In Ullmann, L. P., and Krasner, L., eds. *Case studies in behavior modification.* New York: Holt, Rinehart and Winston, 1965.

12. Miller, N. E., and Carmona, A. Modification of a visceral response, salivation in thirsty dogs, by instrumental training with water reward. *Journal of Comparative and Physiological Psychology,* 1967, **63,** 1–6.

13. Miller, N. E., and DiCara, L. V. Instrumental learning of heart rate changes in curarized rats; shaping and specificity to discriminative stimulus. *Journal of Comparative and Physiological Psychology,* 1967, **63,** 12–19.

14. Miller, N. E., and Banuazizi, A. Instrumental learning by curarized rats of a specific visceral response, intestinal, or cardiac. *Journal of Comparative and Physiological Psychology,* 1968, **65,** 1–7.

15. Miller, N. E. Learning of visceral and glandular responses. *Science,* 1969, **163,** 434–45.

16. Shapiro, D., et al. Effects of feedback and reinforcement on the control of human systolic blood pressure. *Science,* 1969, **163,** 588–90.

17. John, E. R., et al. Observation learning in cats. *Science,* 1968, **159,** 1489–91.

18. Bandura, A., Blanchard, E. B., and Ritter, B. Relative efficacy of desensitization and modeling approaches for inducing behavioral, affective, and attitudinal changes. *Journal of Personality and Social Psychology,* 1969, **13,** 173–99.

19. Solomon, R. L., and Turner, C. H. Discriminative classical conditioning in dogs paralyzed by curare can later control discriminative avoidance response in the normal state. *Psychological Review,* 1962, **69,** 202–19.

20. McGeer, P. L. The chemistry of mind. *American Scientist,* 1971, **59,** 221–29.

21. Babich, F. R., et al. Transfer of a response to naive rats by injection of ribonucleic acid extracted from trained rats. *Science,* 1965, **149,** 656–57. Also McConnell, J. V. Comparative physiology: learning in invertebrates. *Annual Review of Physiology,* 1966, **28,** 107–36.

22. Byrne, W. L., et al. Memory transfer. *Science,* 1966, **153,** 658.

23. Perin, C. T. A quantitative investigation of the delay of reinforcement gradient. *Journal of Experimental Psychology,* 1943, **32,** 37–51.

24. Weinstock, S. Resistance to extinction following partial reinforcement under widely spaced trials. *Journal of Experimental Psychology,* 1954, **47,** 318–23.

25. Neuringer, A. J. Superstitious key pecking after three peck-produced reinforcements. *Journal of the Experimental Analysis of Behavior,* 1970, **13,** 127–34.

26. Fenner, D. H. Key pecking in pigeons maintained by short-interval adventitious schedules of reinforcement. *Proceedings, 77th Annual Convention of the American Psychological Association,* 1969, pp. 831–32.

27. Neuringer, A. J. Animals respond for food in presence of free food. *Science,* 1969, **166,** 399–401.

28. Carder, B., and Berkowitz, K. Rats' preference for earned in comparison with free food. *Science,* 1970, **167,** 1273–74.

29. Tolman, E. C., and Honzik, C. H. Introduction and removal of reward and maze performance in rats. *University of California Publications in Psychology,* 1930, 4, 257–75. Originally published by the University of California Press; reprinted by permission of The Regents of the University of California.

30. See, for example, Sheffield, F. D. Relation between classical conditioning and instrumental learning. In Prokasy, W. F., ed. *Classical conditioning: a symposium.* New York: Appleton-Century-Crofts, 1965, pp. 302–22.

31. Olds, J. Pleasure centers in the brain. *Scientific American,* 1956, **195,** 105–16.

32. Bindra, D. The interrelated mechanisms of reinforcement and motivation, and the nature of their influence on response. In Arnold, W. J., and Levine, D., eds. *Nebraska symposium on motivation, 1969,* Vol. 17. Lincoln: University of Nebraska Press, 1970, pp. 1–33.

chapter three

1. Ebbinghaus, H. *Memory.* New York: Columbia University, Teachers College, 1913 [reprinted by Dover, New York, 1964].

2. Leavitt, H. J., and Scholsberg, H. The retention of verbal and motor skills. *Journal of Experimental Psychology,* 1944, **34,** 404–17.

3. Shepard, R. N. Recognition for words, sentences, and pictures. *Journal of Verbal Learning and Verbal Behavior,* 1967, **6,** 156–63.

4. Luh, C. W. The conditions of retention. *Psychological Monographs,* 1922, **31**(No. 22).

5. Thompson, R. F. *Foundations of physiological psychology.* New York: Harper & Row, 1967.

6. Penfield, W. The interpretive cortex. *Science,* 1959, **129,** 1719–25. Reprinted in Teevan, R. C., and Birney, R. C., eds. *Readings for introductory psychology.* New York: Harcourt Brace Jovanovich, 1965.

7. Carmichael, L., Hogan, H. P., and Walter, A. A. An experimental study of the effect of language on the reproduction of visually perceived form. *Journal of Experimental Psychology,* 1932, **15,** 73–86.

8. Kintsch, W. *Learning, memory and conceptual processes.* New York: Wiley, 1970.

9. Clemes, S. R. Repression and hypnotic amnesia. *Journal of Abnormal and Social Psychology,* 1964, **69,** 62-69.

10. McGeoch, J. A., and McDonald, W. T. Meaningful relation and retroactive inhibition. *American Journal of Psychology,* 1931, **43,** 579-88.

11. Jenkins, J. G., and Dallenbach, K. M. Oblivescence during sleep and waking. *American Journal of Psychology,* 1924, **35,** 605-12.

12. Newman, E. B. Forgetting of meaningful material during sleep and waking. *American Journal of Psychology,* 1939, **52,** 65-71.

13. Adapted from Underwood, B. J. Interference and forgetting. *Psychological Review,* 1957, **64,** Fig. 1, p. 51.

14. Haber, R. N., and Erdelyi, M. H. Emergence and recovery of initially unavailable perceptual material. *Journal of Verbal Learning and Verbal Behavior,* 1967, **6,** 618-28.

15. Adapted from Shiffrin, R. M., and Atkinson, R. C. Storage and retrieval processes in long-term memory. *Psychological Review,* 1969, **76,** 179-93.

16. Sperling, G. The information available in brief visual presentations. *Psychological Monographs,* 1960, **74**(No. 11, Whole no. 498).

17. Shiffrin, R. M., and Atkinson, R. C. Storage and retrieval processes in long-term memory. *Psychological Review,* 1969, **76,** 179-93.

18. Miller, G. A. Language and psychology. In Lenneberg, E. H., ed. *New directions in the study of language.* Cambridge, Mass.: M.I.T. Press, 1964, pp. 89-107.

19. Sperling, G. Successive approximations to a model for short term memory. *Acta Psychologica* (Amsterdam), 1967, **27,** 285-92.

20. Waugh, N. C. Presentation time and free recall. *Journal of Experimental Psychology,* 1967, **73,** 39-44.

21. Shiffrin, R. M. Forgetting: trace erosion or retrieval failure? *Science,* 1970, **168,** 1601-03.

22. Milner, B. The memory defect in bilateral hippocampal lesions. *Psychiatric Research Reports,* 1959, **11,** 43-52.

23. Milner, B. Amnesia following operation on the temporal lobes. In Whitty, C. W. M., and Zangwill, O. L., eds. *Amnesia.* London: Butterworth, 1967.

24. Brown, R., and McNeill, D. The "tip of the tongue" phenomenon. *Journal of Verbal Learning and Verbal Behavior,* 1966, **5,** 325-37.

25. Bower, G. H., and Clark, M. C. Narrative stories as mediators for serial learning. *Psychonomic Science,* 1969, **14,** 181-82.

26. Paivio, A. Mental imagery in associative learning and memory. *Psychological Review,* 1969, **76,** 241-63.

27. Bower, G. H., et al. Hierarchical retrieval schemes in recall of categorized word lists. *Journal of Verbal Learning and Verbal Behavior,* 1969, **8,** 323-43.

28. Tulving, E., and Pearlstone, Z. Availability versus accessibility of information in memory for words. *Journal of Verbal Learning and Verbal Behavior,* 1966, **5,** 381-91.

29. Tulving, E., and Osler, S. Effectiveness of retrieval cues in memory for words. *Journal of Experimental Psychology,* 1968, **77,** 593-601.

30. Tecce, J. J. Contingent negative variation and individual differences. *Archives of General Psychiatry,* 1971, **24,** 1-16.

31. Walter, W. G., et al. Contingent negative variation. *Nature,* 1964, **203,** 380-84.

32. James, W. *Principles of psychology.* Vol. I. New York: Dover, 1950, p. 662.

chapter four

1. Gibson, E., and Walk, R. D. The effect of prolonged exposure to visually presented patterns on learning to discriminate them. *Journal of Comparative and Physiological Psychology,* 1956, **49,** 239-42.

2. Glaze, J. A. The association value of nonsense syllables. *Journal of Genetic Psychology,* 1928, **35**(2), 255-69.

3. McGeoch, J. A. The influence of associative value upon the difficulty of nonsense-syllable lists. *Journal of Genetic Psychology,* 1930, **37,** 421-26.

4. Lyon, D. O. The relation of length of material to time taken for learning and the optimum distribution of time. *Journal of Educational Psychology,* 1914, **5,** 1-9, 85-91, and 155-63.

5. Katona, G. *Organizing and memorizing.* New York: Columbia University Press, 1940.

6. Tyler, R. W. Permanence of learning. *Journal of Higher Education,* IV (April 1933), Table I, p. 204.

7. Waugh, N. C. Presentation time and free recall. *Journal of Experimental Psychology,* 1967, **73,** 39-44.

8. Yates, F. A. *The art of memory.* Chicago: University of Chicago Press, 1966.

9. Bugelski, B. R., Kidd, E., and Segmen, J. Image as a mediator in one-trial paired-associate learning. *Journal of Experimental Psychology,* 1968, **76,** 69-73.

10. Sarason, I. G., and Sarason, B. Effects of motivating instructions and reports of failure on verbal learning. *American Journal of Psychology,* 1957, **70,** 92-96.

11. More, A. J. Delay of feedback and the acquisition and retention of verbal materials in the classroom. *Journal of Educational Psychology,* 1969, **60,** 339-42.

12. Cohen, H. Unpublished study reported in *Behavior Today,* 1970, **1,** 2.

13. Solomon, R. L. Punishment. *American Psychologist,* 1964, **19,** 239-53.

14. Campbell, B. A., and Church, R. M., eds. *Punishment and aversive behavior.* New York: Appleton-Century-Crofts, 1969.

15. Maier, S. F., Seligman, M. E. P., and Solomon, R. L. Pavlovian fear conditioning and learned helplessness: effects on escape and avoidance behavior of (a) the CS-US contingency and (b) the independence of the US and voluntary responding. In Campbell, B. A., and Church, R. M., eds. *Punishment and aversive behavior.* New York: Appleton-Century-Crofts, 1969, pp. 299-342.

16. Munn, N. L., Fernald, L. D., Jr., and Fernald, P. S. *Introduction to psychology,* 2nd ed. Boston: Houghton Mifflin, 1969.

17. Reported in *Behavior Today,* 1970, **1,** 5.

18. Ward, L. B. Reminiscence and rote learning. *Psychological Monographs,* 1937, **49**(No. 220).

19. Pechstein, L. A. Whole vs. part methods in learning nonsensical syllables. *Journal of Educational Psychology,* 1918, **9,** 379-87.

20. Krueger, W. C. F. The effect of overlearning on retention. *Journal of Experimental Psychology,* 1929, **12,** 71-78.

21. Spence, K. W., and Norris, E. B. Eyelid conditioning as a function of the inter-trial interval. *Journal of Experimental Psychology,* 1950, **40,** 716-20.

22. Starch, D. Periods of work in learning. *Journal of Educational Psychology,* 1912, **3,** 209-13.

23. Gates, A. L. Recitation as a factor in memorizing. *Archives of Psychology,* New York, 1917, No. 40. By permission of the Trustees of Columbia University in the City of New York.

24. Robinson, F. P. *Effective study,* rev. ed. New York: Harper & Row, 1961.

25. Thorndike, E. L. Mental discipline in high school studies. *Journal of Educational Psychology,* 1924, **15,** 83–98.

26. Bruce, R. W. Conditions of transfer of training. *Journal of Experimental Psychology,* 1933, **16,** 343–61. Published by the American Psychological Association.

27. Hunter, W. S. Habit interference in the white rat and in human subjects. *Journal of Comparative Psychology,* 1922, **2,** 29–59.

28. Harlow, H. F. The formation of learning sets. *Psychological Review,* 1949, **56,** 51–65.

29. Levinson, B., and Reese, H. W. Patterns of discrimination learning set in preschool children, fifth-graders, college freshmen, and the aged. *Monographs of the Society for Research in Child Development,* 1967, **32**(No. 7), 1–92.

30. See, for example, Silberman, C. E. *Crisis in the classroom: the remaking of American education.* New York: Random House, 1970.

31. Hess, R. D., and Bear, R. M. *Early education.* Chicago: Aldine, 1968.

32. Coleman, J. S. *Equality of educational opportunity.* Washington, D.C.: U.S. Government Printing Office, 1966.

33. See, for example, Coles, R. Like it is in the alley. In Kagan, J., Haith, M. M., and Caldwell, C., eds. *Psychology: adapted readings.* New York: Harcourt Brace Jovanovich, 1971, pp. 368–81.

34. Rosenhan, D. L. Effects of social class and race on responsiveness to approval and disapproval. *Journal of Personality and Social Psychology,* 1966, **4,** 253–59.

35. Sutter, E. G., and Reid, J. B. Learner variables and interpersonal conditions in computer-assisted instruction. *Journal of Educational Psychology,* 1969, **60,** 153–57.

36. Suppes, P., and Morningstar, M. Technological innovations: computer-assisted instruction and compensatory education. In Korten, F. F., et al., eds. *Psychology and the problems of society.* Washington, D.C.: American Psychological Association, 1970, pp. 225–27.

chapter five

1. Kellogg, W. N., and Kellogg, L. A. *The ape and the child.* New York: McGraw-Hill, 1933. Also Hayes, K. *The ape in our house.* New York: Harper & Row, 1951.

2. Gardner, B. T., and Gardner, R. A. Two-way communication with an infant chimpanzee. In Schrier, A. M., and Stollnitz, F., eds. *Behavior of nonhuman primates.* Vol. IV. New York: Academic Press, 1971, pp. 117–84. Also Gardner, R. A., and Gardner, B. T. Teaching sign language to a chimpanzee. *Science,* 1969, **165,** 664–72.

3. Premack, D. The education of S*A*R*A*H. *Psychology Today,* 1970, **4,** 55–58.

4. Von Frisch, W. *Bees: their vision, chemical senses, and language.* Ithaca, N.Y.: Cornell University Press, 1950.

5. Geshwind, N., and Levitsky, W. Human brain: left-right asymmetries in temporal speech region. *Science,* 1968, **161,** 186–87.

6. Lenneberg, E. H. The capacity for language acquisition. In Fodor, J. A., and Katz, J. J., eds. *The structure of language.* Englewood Cliffs, N.J.: Prentice-Hall, 1964, pp. 579–603.

7. Smith, M. E. An investigation of the development of the sentence and the extent of vocabulary in young children. *University of Iowa Studies in Child Welfare,* 1926, 3(5).

8. Lenneberg, E. H. *Biological foundations of language.* New York: Wiley, 1967.

9. Miller, G. A. *Language and communication.* New York: McGraw-Hill, 1951.

10. Davis, K. Extreme social isolation of a child. *American Journal of Sociology,* 1940, **45,** 554–65. Also Davis, K. Final note on a case of extreme social isolation. *American Journal of Sociology,* 1947, **54,** 432–37.

11. Brown, R., and Bellugi, U. Three processes in the child's acquisition of syntax. *Harvard Educational Review,* 1964, **34,** 133–51.

12. Skinner, B. F. *Verbal behavior.* New York: Appleton-Century-Crofts, 1957.

13. Bandura, A. Vicarious processes: a case of no-trial learning. In Berkowitz, L., ed. *Advances in experimental social psychology.* Vol. II. New York: Academic Press, 1965, pp. 1–55.

14. See, for example, Chomsky, N. *Language and mind,* enl. ed. New York: Harcourt Brace Jovanovich, 1972. Also Bellugi, U. Learning the language. *Psychology Today,* 1970, **4,** 33.

15. Foss, D. J. An analysis of learning in a miniature linguistic system. *Journal of Experimental Psychology,* 1968, **76,** 450–59.

16. Nottebohm, F. Ontogeny of bird song. *Science,* 1970, **167,** 950–56.

17. Kagan, J. Attention and psychological change in the young child. *Science,* 1970, **170,** 826–32.

18. Bruner, J. S., Goodnow, J. J., and Austin, G. A. *A study of thinking.* New York: Wiley, 1956.

19. Heidbreder, E. The attainment of concepts: I. Terminology and methodology. *Journal of General Psychology,* 1946, **35**(2), 173–89.

20. Osgood, C. E., and Suci, G. J. Factor analysis of meaning. *Journal of Experimental Psychology,* 1955, **50,** 325–38.

21. Judson, A. J., and Cofer, C. N. Reasoning as an associative process. I. Direction in a simple verbal problem. *Psychological Reports,* 1956, **2,** 469–76.

22. Thorndike, E. L. *Animal intelligence.* New York: Macmillan, 1911.

23. Wason, P. C. Problem solving and reasoning. *Cognitive Psychology,* British Medical Bulletin, 1971, **27.**

24. Maier, N. R. F., and Burke, R. J. Response availability as a factor in the problem-solving performance of males and females. *Journal of Personality and Social Psychology,* 1967, **5,** 304–10.

25. Dryman, I., Birch, H. G., and Korn, S. J. Verbalization and action in the problem-solving of six-year-old children. Unpublished manuscript, 1969.

26. Donaldson, M. *A study of children's thinking.* London: Tavistock, 1963.

27. Luchins, A. S. Mechanization in problem solving: the effect of einstellung. *Psychological Monographs,* 1954, **54**(No. 248). This material also appears in Luchins, A. S., and Luchins, E. H., *Rigidity of behavior,* Eugene: University of Oregon Books, 1959; and in Seltzer, S. M., ed., *Einstelling tests of rigidity,* rev. ed., New York: Craig Colony School and Hospital.

28. Duncker, K. (trans. by Lees, L. S.). On problem-solving. *Psychological Monographs,* 1945, **58**(No. 270).

29. Birch, H. G., and Rabinowitz, H. S. The negative effect of previous experiences on productive thinking. *Journal of Experimental Psychology,* 1951, **41,** 121–25.

30. Mackinnon, D. W. The personality correlates of creativity: a study of American architects. In Nielsen, G. S., ed. *Proceedings*

of the XIV International Congress of Applied Psychology, Copenhagen, 1961. Copenhagen: Munksgaard, 1962, pp. 11–39.

31. From *Modes of thinking in young children* by Michael A. Wallach and Nathan Kogan. Copyright © 1965 by Holt, Rinehart and Winston, Inc. Reprinted by permission of Holt, Rinehart and Winston, Inc.

chapter six

1. Amoore, J. E., Johnston, J. W., Jr., and Rubin, M. The stereochemical theory of odor. *Scientific American,* 1964, **210,** 42–49.

2. Von Skramlik, E. Psychophysiologie der Tastsinne. *Archiv Für die Gesamte Psychologie,* Supp. Vol. 1937, **4** (Parts 1, 2).

3. Champanis, A. *Man-machine engineering.* Belmont, Calif.: Wadsworth, 1965.

4. Champanis, A., Garner, W. R., and Morgan, C. T. *Applied experimental psychology—human factors in engineering design.* New York: Wiley, 1949.

5. Lipscomb, D. M. High intensity sounds in the recreational environment: hazard to young ears. *Clinical Pediatrics,* 1969, **8,** 63–68.

6. From *Hearing and deafness,* revised edition, edited by Hallowell Davis and S. Richard Silverman. Copyright 1947 by Holt, Rinehart and Winston, Inc. Copyright © 1960 by Holt, Rinehart and Winston, Inc. Adapted and reproduced by permission of Holt, Rinehart and Winston, Inc.

7. Békésy, G. v. *Experiments in hearing.* New York: McGraw-Hill, 1960.

8. Wever, E. G. *Theory of hearing.* New York: Wiley, 1949.

9. Bloom, W., and Fawcett, D. W. *A textbook of histology,* 9th ed. Philadelphia: Saunders, 1968.

10. Wald, G. The photochemical basis of rod vision. *Journal of the Optical Society of America,* 1951, **41,** 949–56.

11. Liebman, P. Detection of color-vision pigments by single cell microphotometry—the method and its efficiency. Summarized in Riggs, L. A. Vertebrate color receptors. *Science,* 1965, **147,** 913.

12. De Valois, R. L. Neural processing of visual information. In Russell, R. W., ed. *Frontiers in physiological psychology.* New York: Academic Press, 1966, pp. 51–91.

13. Young, R. W. Visual cells. *Scientific American,* 1970, **223,** 81–91.

14. Polyak, S. I. *The retina.* Chicago: University of Chicago Press, 1941.

15. De Valois, R. L., and Jacobs, G. H. Primate color vision. *Science,* 1968, **162,** 533–40.

16. Riggs, L. A., et al. The disappearance of steadily fixated visual test objects. *Journal of the Optical Society of America,* 1953, **43,** 495–501.

17. Pritchard, R. M. Stabilized images on the retina. *Scientific American,* 1961, **204,** 72–78.

chapter seven

1. Noton, D., and Stark, L. Eye movements and visual perception. *Scientific American,* 1971, **224,** 34–43.

2. Gibson, E. J. *Principles of perceptual learning and development.* New York: Appleton-Century-Crofts, 1969.

3. From *Elements of psychology,* 2nd edition, by David Krech and Richard S. Crutchfield. Copyright © 1958 by David Krech and Richard S. Crutchfield. Copyright © 1969 by Alfred A. Knopf, Inc. Reprinted by permission of Alfred A. Knopf, Inc.

4. Salapatek, P., and Kessen, W. Visual scanning of triangles by the human newborn. *Journal of Experimental Child Psychology,* 1966, **3,** 155–67.

5. Street, R. F. *A gestalt completion test.* New York: Columbia University, Teachers College, 1931.

6. From *Psychology: the science of mental life* by George A. Miller. Copyright © 1962 by George A. Miller. Reprinted by permission of Harper & Row, Publishers. Figure 7-15 is an adaptation of Fig. 12.

7. Bruner, J. S., Postman, L., and Rodrigues, J. Expectation and the perception of color. *American Journal of Psychology,* 1951, **64,** 216–27.

8. Stratton, G. M. Vision without inversion of the retinal image. *Psychological Review,* 1897, **4,** 341–481.

9. Held, R., and Bosson, J. Neo-natal deprivation and adult rearrangement: complementary techniques for analyzing plastic sensory motor coordinations. *Journal of Comparative and Physiological Psychology,* 1961, **54,** 33–37.

10. Gibson, J. J. *The perception of the visual world.* Boston: Houghton Mifflin, 1950.

11. See, for example, Holway, A. H., and Boring, E. G. Determinants of apparent visual size with distance variant. *American Journal of Psychology,* 1941, **54,** 21–37.

12. *Experiments in optical illusion,* by Nelson F. Beeler and Franklin M. Branley. (Artist: Fred H. Lyon.) Copyright 1951 by Thomas Y. Crowell Company, New York, publishers.

13. Gibson, E. J., and Walk, R. D. The "visual cliff." *Scientific American,* 1960, **202,** 64–71.

14. Rock, I., and Victor, J. Vision and touch: an experimentally created conflict between the two senses. *Science,* 1963, **143,** 594–96.

15. Riesen, A. H. Arrested vision. *Scientific American,* 1950, **183,** 16–19.

16. Nissen, H. W., Chow, K. L., and Semmes, J. Effects of restricted opportunity for tactual, kinesthetic, and manipulative experience on the behavior of a chimpanzee. *American Journal of Psychology,* 1951, **64,** 485–507.

17. Cool, S. J. Some effects of early visual environments on adult discrimination in the rat. Unpublished doctoral dissertation, University of Illinois, 1966.

18. White, B. An experimental approach to the effects of experience on early human behavior. In Hill, J. P., ed. *Minnesota Symposium on Child Psychology.* Vol. I. Minneapolis: University of Minnesota Press, 1967, pp. 201–25.

19. Boring, E. G. Apparatus notes: a new ambiguous figure. *American Journal of Psychology,* 1930, **42,** 444–45.

20. Bugelski, B. R., and Alampay, D. A. The role of frequency in developing perceptual sets. *Canadian Journal of Psychology,* 1961, **15,** 205–11.

21. Siipola, E. M. A study of some effects of preparatory set. *Psychological Monographs,* 1935, **46**(No. 210).

22. McClelland, D. C., and Atkinson, J. W. The projective expression of needs. I. The effect of different intensities of the hunger drive on perception. *Journal of Psychology,* 1948, **25,** 205–22.

23. McClelland, D. C., and Liberman, A. M. The effect of need for achievement on recognition of need-related words. *Journal of Personality,* 1949, **18,** 236–51.

24. Postman, L., Bruner, B., and McGinnies, E. Personal values as selective factors in perception. *Journal of Abnormal and Social Psychology,* 1948, **43,** 142–54.

chapter eight

1. Shapiro, J., et al. Isolation of pure *Iac* operon DNA. *Nature* (London), 1969, **224**, 768–74.

2. Jacobs, P. A., et al. Aggressive behaviour, mental subnormality, and the XYY male. *Nature* (London), 1965, **208**, 1351.

3. Jacobs, P. A., et al. Chromosome studies on men in a maximum security hospital. *Annals of Human Genetics* (London), 1968, **31**, 339.

4. Kessler, S., and Moos, R. H. XYY chromosome: premature conclusions. Letter to the editor, *Science,* 1969, **165**, 442.

5. Shah, S. *Report on the XYY chromosomal abnormality.* Washington, D.C.: U.S. Government Printing Office, 1970.

6. Tryon, R. C. Genetic differences in maze learning in rats. *Thirty-ninth Yearbook of the National Society for the Study of Education.* Bloomington, Ill.: Public School Publishing Co., 1949, Part I, pp. 111–19.

7. Hall, C. S. The inheritance of emotionality. *Sigma Xi Quarterly,* 1938, **26**, 17–27.

8. Hirsh, J., and Boudreau, J. C. Studies in experimental behavior genetics. I. The heritability of phototaxis in a population of drosophila melanogaster. *Journal of Comparative and Physiological Psychology,* 1958, **51**, 647–51.

9. Heston, L. L. The genetics of schizophrenic and schizoid disease. *Science,* 1970, **167**, 249–55.

10. Scarr, S. Social introversion-extraversion as a heritable response. *Child Development,* 1969, **40**, 823–32.

11. Evans, C. L. *Starling's principles of human physiology,* 9th ed. Philadelphia: Lea & Febiger, 1945.

12. Pfaffmann, C. Gustatory nerve impulses in rat, cat, and rabbit. *Journal of Neurophysiology,* 1955, **18**, 429–40.

13. Furshpan, E. J., and Potter, D. D. Transmission at the giant motor synapses of the crayfish. *Journal of Physiology* (London), 1959, **145**, 289–325.

14. Eccles, J. C. *The physiology of synapses.* New York: Academic Press, 1964.

15. Lewis, E. R., Zeevi, Y. Y., and Everhart, T. E. Studying neural organization in *Aplysia* with the scanning electron microscope. *Science,* 1969, **165**, 1140–42.

16. Kandel, E. R. Nerve cells and behavior. *Scientific American,* 1970, **223**, 57–68.

17. Bennett, E. L., et al. Chemical and anatomical plasticity of the brain. *Science,* 1964, **146**, 610–19.

18. Hyden, H., and Egyhazi, E. Nuclear RNA changes of nerve cells during a learning experiment in rats. *Publication of the Proceedings of the National Academy of Science,* 1962, **48**, 1366–73.

19. McConnell, J. V., Shigehisa, T., and Salive, H. In Pribram, K. H., and Broadbent, D. E., eds. *Biology of memory.* New York: Academic Press, 1970, pp. 129–59.

20. Golub, A. M., et al. Incubation effects in behavior induction in rats. *Science,* 1970, **168**, 392–95.

21. See, for example, Jacobson, A. L., et al. Differential approach tendencies produced by injection of RNA from trained rats. *Science,* 1965, **150**, 636–37. Also Gross, C. G., and Carey, F. M. Transfer of learned response by RNA injection: failure of attempts to replicate. *Science,* 1965, **150**, 1749.

22. Schapiro, S., and Vukovich, K. R. Early experience effects upon cortical dendrites: a proposed model for development. *Science,* 1970, **167**, 292–94.

23. Miller, N. E. From the brain to behavior. Invited lecture at XII Interamerican Congress of Psychology, Montevideo, Uruguay, March 30 to April 6, 1969.

24. Guillemin, R. Characterization of the hypothalamic hypophysiotropic TSH-releasing factor (TRF) of ovine origin. *Nature* (London), 1970, **226**, 321–25.

25. Wolf-Heidegger, G. *Atlas of systematic human anatomy.* Basel, Switzerland: S. Karger, 1962.

26. Tang, P. C. Localization of the pneumotaxic center in the cat. *American Journal of Physiology,* 1953, **172**, 645–52. Also Wang, S. C., Ngai, S. H., and Frumin, M. J. Organization of central respiratory mechanisms in the brain stem of the cat: genesis of normal respiratory rhythmicity. *American Journal of Physiology,* 1957, **190**, 333–42.

27. Moruzzi, G., and Magoun, H. W. Brain stem reticular formation and activation of the EEG. *Electroencephalography and Clinical Neurophysiology,* 1949, **1**, 455–73.

28. Pribram, K. H. The neurophysiology of remembering. *Scientific American,* 1969, **220**, 73–86.

29. Luria, A. R. The functional organization of the brain. *Scientific American,* 1970, **222**, 66–79.

30. Sperry, R. W. The great cerebral commissure. *Scientific American,* 1964, **210**, 42–52.

31. Nauta, W. J. H. Hypothalamic regulation of sleep in rats: an experimental study. *Journal of Neurophysiology,* 1946, **9**, 285–316.

32. Leibowitz, S. F. Hypothalamic β-adrenergic "satiety" system antagonizes an α-adrenergic "hunger" system in the rat. *Nature,* 1970, **226**, 963–64. Also Leibowitz, S. F. Reciprocal hunger-regulating circuits, involving alpha- and beta-adrenergic receptors located, respectively, in the ventromedial and lateral hypothalamus. *Publication of the Proceedings of the National Academy of Science,* 1970, **67**, 1063–70.

33. Gibbs, F. A., and Gibbs, E. L. *Atlas of electroencephalography.* Reading, Mass.: Addison-Wesley, 1941.

34. Kleitman, N. Patterns of dreaming. *Scientific American,* 1960, **203**, 82–88.

35. Kamiya, J. Operant control of the EEG alpha rhythm and some of its reported effects on consciousness. In Tart, C., ed. *Altered states of consciousness.* New York: Wiley, 1969.

36. Nowlis, D. P., and Kamiya, J. The control of EEG alpha rhythms through auditory feedback and the associated mental activity. *Psychophysiology,* 1970, **6**, 476–84.

37. Hanley, J., et al. Chimpanzee performance data: computer analysis of electroencephalograms. *Nature* (London), 1968, **229**, 879–80.

38. Berkhout, J., Walter, D. O., and Adey, W. R. Alterations of the human electroencephalogram induced by stressful verbal activity. *Electroencephalography and Clinical Neurophysiology,* 1969, **27**, 457–69.

39. Copenhaver, W. M., ed. *Bailey's textbook of histology,* 15th ed. Baltimore: Williams & Wilkins, 1964.

40. Crosby, E., Humphrey, T., and Lauer, E. W. *Comparative anatomy of the nervous system.* New York: Macmillan, 1962. Based on data in Figs. 337 and 339.

chapter nine

1. Lindsley, D. B. Emotion. In Stevens, S. S., ed. *Handbook of experimental psychology.* New York: Wiley, 1951, pp. 473–516.

2. Hess, E. H. Attitude and pupil size. *Scientific American,* 1965, **212**, 46–54.

3. Young, P. T. *Motivation and emotion.* New York: Wiley, 1961. (After Darwin.)

4. James, W. *Principles of psychology.* Vol. II. New York: Dover, 1950.

5. Ax, A. F. The physiological differentiation between fear and anger in humans. *Psychosomatic Medicine,* 1953, **15**, 433–42.

6. Elmadjian, F. Excretion and metabolism of epinephrin. *Pharmacological Reviews,* 1959, **11**, 409–15.

7. Funkenstein, D. H. The physiology of fear and anger. *Scientific American,* 1955, **192**, 74–80.

8. Mandler, G. Emotion. In Brown, R., et al. *New directions in psychology.* New York: Holt, Rinehart and Winston, 1962, pp. 267–343.

9. Lacey, J. I., and Van Lehn, R. Differential emphasis in somatic response to stress. *Psychosomatic Medicine,* 1952, **14**, 73–81. Also Lacey, J. I., Bateman, D. E., and Van Lehn, R. Autonomic response specificity: an experimental study. *Psychosomatic Medicine,* 1953, **15**, 8–21.

10. Bard, P. A. A diencephalic mechanism for the expression of rage with special reference to the sympathetic nervous system. *American Journal of Physiology,* 1928, **84**, 490–515. Also Cannon, W. B. The James-Lange theory of emotions: a critical examination and an alternative theory. *American Journal of Psychology,* 1927, **39**, 106–24.

11. Schachter, S., and Singer, J. E. Cognitive, social and physiological determinants of emotional state. *Psychological Review,* 1962, **69**, 379–99.

12. Schachter, S., and Wheeler, L. Epinephrine, chlorpromazine, and amusement. *Journal of Abnormal and Social Psychology,* 1962, **65**, 121–28.

13. Opler, M. K. Cultural induction of stress. In Appley, M. H., and Trumbull, R., eds. *Psychological stress.* New York: Appleton-Century-Crofts, 1967, pp. 69–75.

14. Valins, S. Cognitive effects of false heart-rate feedback. *Journal of Personality and Social Psychology,* 1966, **4**, 400–08.

15. Storms, M. D., and Nisbett, R. E. Insomnia and the attribution process. *Journal of Personality and Social Psychology,* 1970, **16**, 319–28.

16. Ross, L., Rodin, J., and Zimbardo, P. G. Toward an attribution therapy: the reduction of fear through induced cognitive emotional misattribution. *Journal of Personality and Social Psychology,* 1969, **12**, 279–88.

17. Katz, M. M., Waskow, I. E., and Olsson, J. Characterizing the psychological state produced by LSD. *Journal of Abnormal Psychology,* 1968, **73**, 1–14.

18. Richter, C. P. Rats, man, and the welfare state. *American Psychologist,* 1959, **14**, 18–28.

19. Williams, R. J. *Biochemical individuality.* New York: Wiley, 1956.

20. Harlow, H. Personal communication.

21. Collins, R. L. Inheritance of avoidance conditioning in mice: a diallel study. *Science,* 1964, **143**, 1188–90.

22. Gellhorn, E., and Miller, A. D. Methacholine and noradrenaline tests. *Archives of General Psychiatry,* 1961, **4**, 371–80.

23. Lacey, J. I., and Lacey, B. C. Verification and extension of the principle of autonomic response-stereotypy. *American Journal of Psychology,* 1958, **71**, 50–73.

24. Maher, B. A. *Principles of psychopathology.* New York: McGraw-Hill, 1966.

25. Selye, H. *The stress of life.* New York: McGraw-Hill, 1956.

26. Pitts, F. N., Jr. The biochemistry of anxiety. *Scientific American,* 1969, **220**, 69–75.

27. Elliott, R. Effects of uncertainty about the nature and advent of a noxious stimulus (shock) upon heart rate. *Journal of Personality and Social Psychology,* 1966, **3**, 353–56.

28. Epstein, S., and Roupenian, A. Heart rate and skin conductance during experimentally induced anxiety: the effect of uncertainty about receiving a noxious stimulus. *Journal of Personality and Social Psychology,* 1970, **16**, 20–28.

29. Taylor, J. A. The relationship of anxiety to the conditioned eyelid response. *Journal of Experimental Psychology,* 1951, **41**, 81–92.

30. Farber, I. E., and Spence, W. K. Complex learning and conditioning as a function of anxiety. *Journal of Experimental Psychology,* 1953, **45**, 120–25.

31. Ganzer, V. J. Effects of audience presence and test anxiety on learning and retention in a serial learning situation. *Journal of Personality and Social Psychology,* 1968, **8**, 194–99.

32. Spielberger, C. D. The effects of manifest anxiety on the academic achievement of college students. *Mental Hygiene,* 1962, **46**, 420–26.

33. Spielberger, C. D., Denny, J. P., and Weitz, H. The effects of group counseling on the academic performance of anxious college freshmen. *Journal of Counseling Psychology,* 1962, **9**, 195–204.

34. Atkinson, J. W., et al. The achievement motive, goal setting, and probability preferences. *Journal of Abnormal and Social Psychology,* 1960, **60**, 27–37.

35. Atkinson, J. W., and Litwin, G. H. Achievement motive and test anxiety conceived as motive to approach success and motive to avoid failure. *Journal of Abnormal and Social Psychology,* 1960, **60**, 53–62.

chapter ten

1. James, W. *Principles of psychology.* Vol. II. New York: Dover, 1950.

2. Morgan, C. T., and Morgan, J. D. Studies in hunger. II. The relation of gastric denervation and dietary sugar to the effect of insulin upon food-intake in the rat. *Journal of Genetic Psychology,* 1940, **57**, 153–63.

3. Tsang, Y. C. Hunger motivation in gastrectomized rats. *Journal of Comparative Psychology,* 1938, **26**, 1–17.

4. Wangensteen, O. H., and Carlson, A. J. Hunger sensations in a patient after total gastrectomy. *Proceedings of the Society for Experimental Biology and Medicine,* 1931, **28**, 545–47.

5. Tschukitscheff, I. P. Über den Mechanismus der Hungerbewegungen des Magens. I. Einfluss des "satten" und "Hunger"-Blutes auf die periodische Tätigkeit des Magens. *Archiv Für die Gesamte Physiologie,* 1930, **223**, 251–64.

6. Anand, B. K., and Brobeck, J. R. Hypothalamic control of food intake in rat and cat. *Yale Journal of Biology and Medicine,* 1951, **24**, 123–40.

7. Hetherington, A. W., and Ranson, W. W. Hypothalamic lesions and adiposity in the rat. *Anatomical Record,* 1940, **78**, 149–72.

8. Valenstein, E. S., Cox, V. C., and Kakolewski, J. W. Re-examination of the role of the hypothalamus in motivation. *Psychological Review,* 1970, **77**, 16–31.

9. Miller, N. E., and Kessen, M. L. Reward effects of food via stomach fistula compared with those of food via mouth. *Journal of Comparative and Physiological Psychology,* 1952, **45**, 555–64.

10. Chambers, R. M. Effects of intravenous glucose injections on learning, general activity, and hunger drive. *Journal of*

Comparative and Physiological Psychology, 1956, **49**, 558–64.

11. Epstein, A. N., and Teitelbaum, P. Regulation of food intake in the absence of taste, smell, and other oro-pharyngeal sensations. *Journal of Comparative and Physiological Psychology,* 1962, **55**, 155.

12. Schachter, S., Goldman, R., and Gordon, A. Effects of fear, food deprivation, and obesity on eating. *Journal of Personality and Social Psychology,* 1968, **10**, 91–97.

13. Schachter, S., and Gross, L. P. Manipulated time and eating behavior. *Journal of Personality and Social Psychology,* 1968, **10**, 98–106.

14. Nisbett, R. E. Taste, deprivation, and weight determinants of eating behavior. *Journal of Personality and Social Psychology,* 1968, **10**, 107–16.

15. Stunkard, A. J. Eating patterns and obesity. *Psychiatric Quarterly,* 1959, **33**, 284–95.

16. Nisbett, R. E. Eating behavior and obesity in men and animals. In Reichsman, R., ed. *Hunger and satiety in health and disease.* White Plains, N.Y.: Karger, forthcoming.

17. Stellar, E., and Jordan, H. A. The perception of satiety. In *Perception and its disorders.* Research Publications of the Association for Research in Nervous and Mental Disease. Vol. XLVIII. Baltimore: Williams & Wilkins, 1970, pp. 298–317.

18. Miller, N. E. From the brain to behavior. Invited lecture at XII Interamerican Congress of Psychology, Montevideo, Uruguay, March 30 to April 6, 1969.

19. Courtesy of Dr. William C. Dement.

20. Dement, W. C. The effect of dream deprivation. *Science,* 1960, **131**, 1705–07.

21. Harlow, H. F., and Harlow, M. K. Social deprivation in monkeys. *Scientific American,* 1962, **207**, 136–46.

22. Beach, F. A., and Ransom, T. W. Effects of environmental variation on ejaculatory frequency in male rats. *Journal of Comparative and Physiological Psychology,* 1967, **64**, 384–87.

23. Bindra, D. The interrelated mechanisms of reinforcement and motivation, and the nature of their influence on response. In Arnold, W. J., and Levine, D., eds. *Nebraska symposium on motivation, 1969,* Vol. 17. Lincoln: University of Nebraska Press, 1970, pp. 1–37.

24. Bexton, W. H., Heron, W., and Scott, T. H. Effects of decreased variation in the sensory environment. *Canadian Journal of Psychology,* 1954, **8**, 70–76.

25. Lilly, J. C. Mental effects of reduction of ordinary levels of physical stimuli on intact healthy persons. *Psychiatric Research Reports,* 1956, **5**, 1–9. Reprinted in Teevan, R. C., and Birney, R. C., eds. *Readings for introductory psychology.* New York: Harcourt Brace Jovanovich, 1965, pp. 57–62.

26. Dember, W. N. The new look in motivation. *American Scientist,* 1965, **53**, 409–27.

27. Dember, W. N., Earl, R. W., and Paradise, N. Response by rats to differential stimulus complexity. *Journal of Comparative and Physiological Psychology,* 1957, **50**, 514–18.

28. Butler, R. A. Discrimination learning by Rhesus monkeys to visual-exploration motivation. *Journal of Comparative and Physiological Psychology,* 1953, **46**, 95–98.

29. Lorenz, K. *On aggression.* New York: Harcourt Brace Jovanovich, 1966.

30. See, for example, Foulkes, D., et al. Dreams of the male child: an EEG study. *Journal of Abnormal Psychology,* 1967, **72**, 457–67.

31. Wagman, M. Sex differences in types of daydreams. *Journal of Personality and Social Psychology,* 1967, **7**, 329–32.

32. McKeachie, W. J., et al. Student affiliation motives, teacher warmth, and academic achievement. *Journal of Personality and Social Psychology,* 1966, **4**, 457–61.

33. Dember, W. N. Birth order and need affiliation. *Journal of Abnormal and Social Psychology,* 1964, **68**, 555–57.

34. Hilton, I. Differences in the behavior of mothers toward first- and later-born children. *Journal of Personality and Social Psychology,* 1967, **7**, 282–90.

35. Nisbett, R. E. Birth order and participation in dangerous sports. *Journal of Personality and Social Psychology,* 1968, **8**, 351–53.

36. Winterbottom, M. R. The relation of childhood training in independence to achievement motivation. Unpublished doctoral dissertation, University of Michigan, 1953. Summarized in McClelland, D. C., et al. *The achievement motive.* New York: Appleton-Century-Crofts, 1953. Adapted by permission.

37. Lowell, E. L. The effect of need for achievement on learning and speed of performance. *Journal of Psychology,* 1952, **33**, 31–40.

38. French, E. G., and Thomas, F. H. The relation of achievement to problem-solving effectiveness. *Journal of Abnormal and Social Psychology,* 1958, **56**, 45–48.

39. Sadacca, R., Ricciuti, H. N., and Swanson, E. O. *Content analysis of achievement motivation protocols: a study of scorer agreement.* Princeton, N.J.: Educational Testing Service, 1956.

40. Morgan, H. H. An analysis of certain structured and unstructured test results of achieving and non-achieving high ability college students. Unpublished doctoral dissertation, University of Michigan, 1951.

41. Crockett, H. J. The achievement motive and differential occupational mobility in the United States. *American Sociological Review,* 1962, **27**, 191–204. By permission of the American Sociological Association.

42. Morris, J. L. Propensity for risk taking as a determinant of vocational choice: an extension of the theory of achievement motivation. *Journal of Personality and Social Psychology,* 1966, **3**, 328–35.

43. Hoyos, C. G. Motivationpsychologische Untersuchungen von Kraftfahrern mit dem TAT nach McClelland. *Archiv Für die Gesamte Psychologie,* 1965. Supp. No. 7.

44. Sampson, E. A., and Hancock, F. T. An examination of the relationship between ordinal position, personality, and conformity. *Journal of Personality and Social Psychology,* 1967, **5**, 398–407.

45. Suedfeld, P. Sensory deprivation stress: birth order and instructional set as interacting variables. *Journal of Personality and Social Psychology,* 1969, **11**, 70–74.

46. Adler, A. Characteristics of the first, second, and third child. *Children,* 1928, **3**, 14–52.

47. Dollard, J., et al. *Frustration and aggression.* New Haven, Conn.: Yale University Press, 1939.

48. Foulkes, D., et al. Dreams of the male child: an EEG study. *Journal of Abnormal Psychology,* 1967, **72**, 457–67.

49. See, for example, Berkowitz, L. The frustration-aggression hypothesis revisited. In Berkowitz, L., ed. *Roots of aggression: a re-examination of the frustration-aggression hypothesis.* New York: Atherton Press, 1969.

50. Adapted from Hartmann, D. P. Influence of symbolically modeled instrumental aggression and pain cues on aggressive behavior. *Journal of Personality and Social Psychology,* 1969, **11**, 280–88.

51. Based on Kohlberg, L. Moral and religious education and

the public schools: a developmental view. In Sizer, T., ed. *Religion and public education*. Boston: Houghton-Mifflin, 1967.

52. Kohlberg, L. The development of children's orientations toward a moral order. I. Sequence in the development of moral thought. *Vita Humana*, 1963, **6**, 11-33, S. Karger, Basel.

53. Kohlberg, L., and Kramer, R. Continuities and discontinuities in child and adult moral development. *Human Development*, 1969, **12**, 93-120.

54. Festinger, L., and Carlsmith, J. M. Cognitive consequences of forced compliance. *Journal of Abnormal and Social Psychology*, 1959, **58**, 203-10.

55. Zimbardo, P. G., et al. Control of pain motivation by cognitive dissonance. *Science*, 1966, **151**(14), 217-19. Copyright 1966 by the American Association for the Advancement of Science.

56. Adapted from *Motivation and personality*, 2nd ed. by A. H. Maslow. Copyright 1970 by Harper & Row, Publishers, Incorporated. Used by permission of the publishers.

57. Knapp, R. R. Relationship of a measure of self-actualization to neuroticism and extraversion. *Journal of Consulting Psychology*, 1965, **29**, 168-72.

58. Allport, G. W. *Personality and social encounter*. Boston: Beacon Press, 1960.

59. From *Motives in fantasy, action, and society* by J. W. Atkinson. Copyright © 1958 by Litton Educational Publishing, Inc. Reprinted by permission of Van Nostrand Reinhold Company.

60. Clark, R. A. The projective measurement of experimentally induced levels of sexual motivation. *Journal of Experimental Psychology*, 1952, **44**, 391-99.

chapter eleven

1. Sanford, F. H. *Psychology, a scientific study of man*, 2nd ed. Belmont, Calif.: Wadsworth, 1965.

2. Barker, R. G., Dembo, T., and Lewin, K. Frustration and regression: an experiment with young children. *University of Iowa Studies in Child Welfare*, 1941, **18**(No. 386).

3. Hutt, M. L. "Consecutive" and "adaptive" testing with the revised Stanford-Binet. *Journal of Consulting Psychology*, 1947, **11**, 93-103, Table IV, p. 100.

4. Keister, M. E., and Updegraff, R. A study of children's reactions to failure and an experimental attempt to modify them. *Child Development*, 1937, **8**, 241-48. By permission of the Society for Research in Child Development, Inc.

5. Entin, E. The relationship between strength of motivation and performance on simple and complex tasks. Unpublished doctoral dissertation, University of Michigan, 1968.

6. Horner, M. S. The psychological significance of success: a threat as well as a promise. In Day, H. I., and Berlyne, D., eds. *Intrinsic motivation in education*. Holt, Rinehart and Winston of Canada, forthcoming.

7. Horner, M. S. Follow up studies on the motive to avoid success in women. Symposium Presentation, American Psychological Association, Miami, Florida, September, 1970.

8. Lewin, K. *A dynamic theory of personality*. New York: McGraw-Hill, 1935.

9. Brown, J. S. Gradients of approach and avoidance responses and their relation to motivation. *Journal of Comparative and Physiological Psychology*, 1948, **41**, 450-65.

10. Brown, J. S. The generalization of approach responses as a function of stimulus intensity and strength of motivation.

Journal of Comparative Psychology, 1942, **33**, 209-26. Also Miller, N. E. Liberalization of basic S-R concepts: extensions to conflict behavior, motivation, and social learning. In Koch, S. ed. *Psychology: a study of a science*. Vol. II. New York: McGraw-Hill, 1959.

11. Raynor, J. The relationship between distant future goals and achievement motivation. Unpublished doctoral dissertation, University of Michigan, 1968.

12. Lewin, K., Lippitt, R., and White, R. K. Patterns of aggressive behavior in experimentally created social climates. *Journal of Social Psychology*, 1939, **10**, 271-99.

13. Maher, B., Weinstein, N., and Sylva, K. The determinants of oscillation points in a temporal decision conflict. *Psychonomic Science*, 1964, **1**, 13-14.

14. Fenz, W. D., and Epstein, S. Gradients of physiological arousal in parachutists as a function of an approaching jump. *Psychosomatic Medicine*, 1967, **29**, 33-51.

15. Masserman, J. H. *Principles of dynamic psychiatry*, 2nd ed. Philadelphia: Saunders, 1961.

16. Maier, N. R. F. *Frustration*. New York: McGraw-Hill, 1949.

17. Sears, R. R. Experimental study of projection. I. Attribution of traits. *Journal of Social Psychology*, 1936, **7**, 151-63.

18. Bettelheim, B. Individual and mass behavior in extreme situations. *Journal of Abnormal and Social Psychology*, 1943, **38**, 417-52.

19. See, for example, Laing, R. D. *The divided self.* Baltimore: Penguin, 1960.

20. Erikson, E. H. *Identity, youth, and crisis.* New York: Norton, 1968.

21. Bühler, C. Psychotherapy and the image of man. *Psychotherapy*, 1968, **5**, 89-94.

22. Pavlov, I. P. *Conditioned reflexes: an investigation of the physiological activity of the cerebral cortex.* London: Oxford University Press, 1927 [reprinted by Dover, New York, 1960].

23. Masserman, J. H. *Behavior and neurosis.* Chicago: University of Chicago Press, 1943.

24. Reich, T., Clayton, P. J., and Winokur, G. Family history studies: V. The genetics of mania. *American Journal of Psychiatry*, 1969, **125**, 64-75.

25. Gottesman, I. I. Beyond the fringe—personality and psychopathology. In Glass, D. C., ed. *Genetics.* New York: Rockefeller University Press and Russell Sage Foundation, 1968, pp. 59-68. Also Gottesman, I. I. Double talk for twins' mothers. (Review of A. Scheinfeld's *Twins and supertwins.*) *Contemporary Psychology*, 1968, **13**, 518-20.

26. Hollingshead, A. B., and Redlich, F. C. *Social class and mental illness, a community study.* New York: Wiley, 1958.

27. Coleman, J. C. *Abnormal psychology and modern life*, 3rd ed. Chicago: Scott, Foresman, 1964.

28. Denike, L. D., and Tiber, H. Neurotic behavior. In London, P., and Rosenhan, D., eds. *Foundations of abnormal psychology.* New York: Holt, Rinehart and Winston, 1968, pp. 345-90.

29. Goldhamer, H., and Marshall, A. W. *Psychosis and civilization.* New York: Free Press, 1953.

30. Benedict, P. K., and Jacks, I. Mental illness in primitive societies. *Psychiatry*, 1954, **17**, 389.

31. Kline, N. S. Personal communication, 1970.

32. Yerbury, E. C., and Newell, N. Genetic and environmental factors in psychoses of children. Reprinted from *The American Journal of Psychiatry*, Vol. 100, pp. 599-605, 1944.

33. McCord, W., and McCord, I. *The psychopath: an essay on the criminal mind.* Princeton, N.J.: Van Nostrand, 1964.

chapter twelve

1. Whitman, A. Freudian analysts gather for the first time in Vienna. *The New York Times,* July 26, 1971, **120,** 1-3.

2. See, for example, Hartmann, H. Ego psychology and the problem of adaptation. In Rapaport, D., ed. *Organization and pathology of thought.* New York: Columbia University Press, 1951, pp. 362-93.

3. Based on Chapter 3, The human situation—the key to humanistic psychoanalysis, from *The sane society* by Erich Fromm. Copyright © 1955 by Erich Fromm. Reprinted by permission of Holt, Rinehart and Winston, Inc.

4. Fromm, E. *The sane society.* New York: Holt, Rinehart and Winston, 1955.

5. Miller, N. E. Studies of fear as an acquirable drive. I. Fear as motivation and fear-reduction as reinforcement in the learning of new responses. *Journal of Experimental Psychology,* 1948, **38,** 89-101.

6. Miller, N. E., and Dollard, J. *Social learning and imitation.* New Haven, Conn.: Yale University Press, 1941.

7. Butler, J. M., and Haigh, G. V. Changes in the relation between self-concepts and ideal concepts consequent upon client-centered counseling. In Rogers, C. R., and Dymond, R. F., eds. *Psychotherapy and personality change: coordinated studies in the client-centered approach.* Chicago: University of Chicago Press, 1954, pp. 55-76.

8. Kubie, L. S. *Practical and theoretical aspects of psychoanalysis.* New York: International Universities Press, 1950.

9. Gendlin, E. T., and Rychlak, J. F. Psychotherapeutic processes. *Annual Review of Psychology,* 1970, **21,** 155-90.

10. See, for example, Gelder, M. G. Desensitization and psychotherapy research. *British Journal of Medical Psychology,* 1968, **41,** 39-46.

11. See, for example, Paul, G. L. Two-year follow-up of systematic desensitization in therapy groups. *Journal of Abnormal Psychology,* 1968, **73,** 119-30.

12. Naar, R. Client-centered and behavior therapies: their peaceful coexistence: a case study. *Journal of Abnormal Psychology,* 1970, **76,** 155-60.

13. Lang, P. J., and Melamed, B. G. Avoidance conditioning therapy of an infant with chronic ruminative vomiting. *Journal of Abnormal Psychology,* 1969, **74,** 1-8.

14. Martin, M., et al. Programing behavior change and reintegration into school milieux of extreme adolescent deviates. *Behavior Research and Therapy,* 1968, **6,** 371-83.

15. Ayllon, T., and Azrin, N. H. *The token economy: a motivational system for therapy and rehabilitation.* New York: Appleton-Century-Crofts, 1968.

16. Davison, G. C. Elimination of a sadistic fantasy by a client-controlled counterconditioning technique. *Journal of Abnormal Psychology,* 1968, **73,** 84-90.

17. Marks, I. M. Aversion therapy. *British Journal of Medical Psychology,* 1968, **41,** 47-52.

18. Paul, G. L. Two-year follow-up of systematic desensitization in therapy groups. *Journal of Abnormal Psychology,* 1968, **73,** 119-30.

19. Bandura, A., Blanchard, E. B., and Ritter, B. Relative efficacy of desensitization and modeling approaches for inducing behavioral, affective, and attitudinal changes. *Journal of Personality and Social Psychology,* 1969, **13,** 173-99.

20. See, for example, Lamberd, W. G. The treatment of homosexuality as a monosymptomatic phobia. *American Journal of Psychiatry,* 1969, **126,** 94-100.

21. Zweben, J. E., and Miller, R. L. The systems game: teaching, training, psychotherapy. *Psychotherapy,* 1968, **5,** 73-76.

22. Bernal, M. E., et al. Behavior modification and the brat syndrome. *Journal of Consulting and Clinical Psychology,* 1968, **32,** 447-55.

23. Alexander, F. G., and Selesnick, S. T. *The history of psychiatry.* New York: Harper & Row, 1966.

24. Bergin, A. E. Some implications of psychotherapy research for therapeutic practice. *Journal of Abnormal Psychology,* 1966, **71,** 235-46.

25. Aronson, H., and Weintraub, W. Certain initial variables as predictors of change with classical psychoanalysis. *Journal of Abnormal Psychology,* 1969, **74,** 490-97.

26. See, for example, The therapeutic process in cross-cultural perspective—a symposium. *American Journal of Psychiatry,* 1968, **124,** 58-69.

27. Eysenck, H. J. The effects of psychotherapy: an evaluation. *Journal of Consulting and Clinical Psychology,* 1952, **16,** 319-24.

28. See, for example, Bandura, A. *Principles of behavior modification.* New York: Holt, Rinehart and Winston, 1969.

29. See, for example, Meltzoff, J., and Kornreich, M. It works. *Psychology Today,* 1971, **5,** 57-61.

30. Fiske, D. W., et al. Planning of research on effectiveness of psychotherapy. *American Psychologist,* 1970, **25,** 727-37.

31. Bergin, A. E., and Strupp, H. H. New directions in psychotherapy research. *Journal of Abnormal Psychology,* 1970, **76,** 13-26.

32. Grinspoon, L., Ewalt, J. R., and Shader, R. Psychotherapy and pharmacotherapy in chronic schizophrenia. *American Journal of Psychiatry,* 1968, **124,** 67-74.

33. Miller, N. E. From the brain to behavior. Invited lecture at XII Interamerican Congress of Psychology, Montevideo, Uruguay, March 30 to April 6, 1969.

34. Browne, M. W. A comparison of two drug treatments in depressive illness. *British Journal of Psychiatry,* 1969, **115,** 693-96.

35. Kety, S. S., et al. A sustained effect of electroconvulsive shock on the turnover of norepinephrine in the central nervous system of the rat. *Publication of the Proceedings of the National Academy of Science,* 1967, **58,** 1249-54.

36. Zung, W. W. K. Evaluating treatment methods for depressive disorders. *American Journal of Psychiatry,* May, 1968 supp., **124,** 40-48.

chapter thirteen

1. Hebb, D. O. *A textbook of psychology.* Philadelphia: Saunders, 1958.

2. Bailey, N. T. J. *Statistical methods in biology.* London: English Universities Press, 1959.

3. Garrett, H. *Statistics in psychology and education,* 6th ed. New York: David McKay Company, Inc., 1966. By permission of the publisher.

4. Terman, L. M., and Merrill, M. A. *Stanford-Binet intelligence scale: manual for the third revision, form L-M.* Reprinted by permission of the Houghton Mifflin Company.

5. Tuddenham, R. D., and Snyder, M. M. Physical growth of California boys and girls from birth to eighteen years. *Child Development,* 1954, **1,** 183-364.

6. Ferguson, G. A. *Statistical analysis in psychology and education.* New York: McGraw-Hill, 1959. Copyright © 1959 by McGraw-Hill Book Company.

chapter fourteen

1. Copyright (1967) by Harcourt Brace Jovanovich, Inc. Reproduced by special permission of the publisher.

2. Cronbach, L. J. *Essentials of psychological testing.* New York: Harper, 1949.

3. Terman, M. L., and Merrill, M. A. *Stanford-Binet intelligence scale: manual for the third revision, form L-M.* Reprinted by permission of the Houghton Mifflin Company.

4. Copyright (1964, 1938) by Harcourt Brace Jovanovich, Inc. Reproduced by special permission of the publisher.

5. Tyler, L. E. *The psychology of human differences,* 2nd ed. New York: Appleton-Century-Crofts, 1956.

6. Bond, E. A. *Tenth-grade abilities and achievements.* New York: Columbia University, Teachers College, 1940.

7. Wrenn, C. G. Potential research talent in the sciences based on intelligence quotients of Ph.D.'s. *Educational Record,* 1949, **30,** 5–22.

8. Janke, L. L., and Havighurst, R. J. Relation between ability and social-status in a midwestern community. II. Sixteen-year-old boys and girls. *Journal of Educational Psychology,* 1945, **36,** 499–509.

9. McNemar, Q. *The revision of the Stanford-Binet scale.* Boston: Houghton Mifflin, 1942.

10. Kennedy, W. A., Van de Riet, V., and White, J. C. A normative sample of intelligence and achievement of Negro elementary school children in the southeastern United States. *Monographs of the Society for Research in Child Development,* 1963, **28**(No. 6).

11. Jensen, A. R. How much can we boost I.Q. and scholastic achievement? *Harvard Educational Review,* 1969, **39,** 1–123.

12. Herzog, E., and Lewis, H. Children in poor families. *American Journal of Orthopsychiatry,* 1970, **40,** 375–87.

13. Tiedman, D. V. *Righting the balance: report of Commission on Tests.* 2 vols. New York: College Entrance Examination Board, 1970.

14. Thurstone, L. L., and Thurstone, T. G. Factorial studies of intelligence. *Psychometric Monographs,* Chicago: University of Chicago Press, 1941, No. 2.

15. Stevenson, H. W., Friedrichs, A. G., and Simpson, W. E. Inter-relations and correlates over time in children's learning. *Child Development,* 1970, **41,** 625–37. Also Stevenson, H. W., et al. Inter-relations and correlates in children's learning and problem solving. *Monographs of the Society for Research in Child Development,* 1968, **33**(No. 7, Series no. 123).

16. Guilford, J. P. *The nature of human intelligence.* New York: McGraw-Hill, 1967.

17. Burt, C. The inheritance of mental ability. *American Psychologist,* 1958, **13,** 1–15, Table I.

18. Newman, H. H., Freeman, F. N., and Holzinger, K. J. *Twins: a study of heredity and environment.* Chicago: University of Chicago Press, 1937.

19. See, for example, Kennedy, W. A. A follow up normative study of Negro intelligence and achievement. *Monographs of the Society for Research in Child Development,* 1969, **34**(No. 2).

20. Kagan, J. Inadequate evidence and illogical conclusions. *Harvard Educational Review,* 1969, **39,** 274–77.

21. Pearson, C. Intelligence of Honolulu preschool children in relation to parents' education. *Child Development,* 1969, **40,** 647–50.

22. Wolf, R. M. The identification and measurement of environmental process variables related to intelligence. Unpublished Ph.D. dissertation, University of Chicago, 1963.

23. Skeels, H. M. Adult status of children with contrasting early life experiences: a follow-up study. *Monographs of the Society for Research in Child Development,* 1966, **31**(No. 3).

24. Speer, G. S. The mental development of children of feeble-minded and normal mothers. *Thirty-ninth Yearbook of the National Society for the Study of Education,* Bloomington, Ill.: Public School Publishing Co., 1940, Part II, pp. 309–14.

25. Willerman, L., Broman, S. H., and Fiedler, M. Infant development, preschool IQ, and social class. *Child Development,* 1970, **41,** 69–77.

26. See, for example, Jensen, A. R. How much can we boost I.Q. and scholastic achievement? *Harvard Educational Review,* 1969, **39,** 1–123.

27. For rebuttal to the Jensen argument (above) see, for example, Cronbach, L. J. Heredity, environment, and educational policy. *Harvard Educational Review,* 1969, **39,** 338–47.

28. Gottesman, I. I. Biogenetics of race and class. In Deutsch, M., Katz, I., and Jensen, A. B., eds. *Social class, race, and psychological development.* New York: Holt, Rinehart and Winston, 1968, pp. 25–51.

29. Bloom, B. S. *Stability and change in human characteristics.* New York: Wiley, 1964.

30. Ellis, N. *Handbook of mental deficiency.* New York: McGraw-Hill, 1963.

31. Wellman, B. L. I.Q. changes of preschool and non-school groups during the preschool years: a summary of the literature. *Journal of Psychology,* 1945, **20,** 347–68.

32. Klaus, R. A., and Gray, S. W. The early training project for disadvantaged children: a report after five years. *Monographs of the Society for Research in Child Development,* 1968, **33**(No. 4).

33. Sontag, L. W., Baker, C. T., and Nelson, V. L. Mental growth and personality development: a longitudinal study. *Monographs of the Society for Research in Child Development,* 1958, **23**(No. 2). By permission of the Society for Research in Child Development, Inc.

34. Tuddenham, R. D. Soldier intelligence in world wars I and II. *American Psychologist,* 1948, **3,** 54–56.

35. Maxwell, J. Intelligence, fertility, and the future. *Eugenics Quarterly,* 1954, **1,** 244–74.

36. Cattell, R. B. The fate of national intelligence: test of a thirteen-year prediction. *Eugenics Review,* 1951, **42,** 136–48.

37. Wechsler, D. *Wechsler adult intelligence scale, manual.* New York: Psychological Corp., 1955.

38. Owens, W. A., Jr. Age and mental abilities: a second adult follow-up. *Journal of Educational Psychology,* 1966, **57,** 311–25.

39. Harrell, T. W., and Harrell, M. S. Army general classification test scores for civilian occupations. *Educational & Psychological Measurement,* 1945, **5,** 229–39.

40. Havemann, E., and West, P. S. *They went to college.* New York: Harcourt Brace Jovanovich, 1952.

41. Wyatt, S., and Langdon, J. N. Fatigue and boredom in repetitive work. Industrial Health Research Board. London: Her Majesty's Stationery Office, 1937, No. 77.

42. Ryan, T. A. *Work and effort.* New York: Ronald Press, 1947.

43. U.S. President's Panel on Mental Retardation. *Mental retardation chart book: a national plan for a national problem.* Washington, D.C.: U.S. Dept. of Health, Education, and Welfare, 1963.

44. Wolfson, I. N. Adjustment of institutionalized mildly re-

tarded patients twenty years after return to the community. Unpublished paper presented at the 1966 annual meeting of the American Psychiatric Association, Atlantic City, N.J.

45. Reproduced by permission. Copyright 1941, renewed 1969 by The Psychological Corporation, New York, N.Y. All rights reserved.

46. From *MacQuarrie Test for Mechanical Ability* by T. W. MacQuarrie. Copyright © 1925, 1953 by T. W. MacQuarrie. By permission of the publisher, CTB/McGraw-Hill, Monterey, California.

47. Reproduced by permission. Copyright 1947, © 1961 for Verbal Reasoning, Numerical Ability, Abstract Reasoning, and Clerical Speed and Accuracy. Copyright 1947, © 1961, 1962 for Mechanical Reasoning, Space Relations, Language Usage—Spelling, Language Usage—Grammar. Published by The Psychological Corporation, New York, N.Y. All rights reserved.

48. From *Kuder Preference Record—Vocational*, Form CM, by G. Frederic Kuder. Copyright 1948, G. Frederic Kuder. Reproduced by permission of the publisher, Science Research Associates, Inc.

49. From the *Profile Sheet* for the *Kuder Preference Record—Vocational*, Forms CH, CM. Copyright 1950, G. Frederic Kuder. Reproduced by permission of the publisher, Science Research Associates, Inc.

50. From Allport-Vernon-Lindzey *Study of Values.* Reprinted by permission of Houghton Mifflin Company.

51. Reproduced by permission. Copyright 1943, renewed 1970 by the University of Minnesota. Published by The Psychological Corporation, New York, N.Y. All rights reserved.

52. Gough, H. G. Tests of personality: questionnaires, A. Minnesota Multiphasic Personality Inventory. In Weider, A., ed. *Contributions toward medical psychology.* Vol. II. New York, copyright 1953, the Ronald Press Company.

53. U.S. Office of Strategic Services, Assessment Staff. *Assessment of men: selection of personnel for the office of strategic services.* New York: Holt, Rinehart and Winston, 1948.

54. MacKinnon, D. W. Stress interview. In Jackson, D. N., and Messick, S., eds. *Problems in human assessment.* New York: McGraw-Hill, 1967, pp. 669-76.

55. Reprinted by permission of the publishers from Henry Alexander Murray, *Thematic Apperception Test.* Cambridge, Mass.: Harvard University Press; copyright, 1943, by the President and Fellows of Harvard College.

56. McClelland, D. C., Clark, R. A., and Lowell, E. L. *The achievement motive.* New York: Appleton-Century-Crofts, 1953.

57. French, E. G. Development of a measure of complex motivation. In Atkinson, J. W., ed. *Motives in fantasy, action, and society.* Princeton, N.J.: Van Nostrand, 1958.

58. DeCharms, R. C., et al. Behavioral correlates of directly measured achievement motivation. In McClelland, D. C., ed. *Studies in motivation.* New York: Appleton-Century-Crofts, 1955.

59. From *The Rorschach technique: an introductory manual* by Bruno Klopfer and Helen H. Davidson, © 1962 by Harcourt Brace Jovanovich, Inc., and reproduced with their permission.

chapter fifteen

1. Mussen, P. H., Conger, J. J., and Kagan, J. *Child development and personality,* 2nd ed. New York: Harper & Row, 1963.

2. Mussen, P. H., Conger, J. J., and Kagan, J. *Child development and personality,* 3rd ed. New York: Harper & Row, 1969.

3. Irwin, O. C. The amount and nature of activities of newborn infants under constant external stimulating conditions during the first ten days of life. *Genetic Psychology Monographs,* 1930, **8.**

Also Wolff, P. H. Observations on newborn infants. *Psychosomatic Medicine,* 1959, **21,** 110-18.

4. Knop, C. The dynamics of newly born babies. *Journal of Pediatrics,* 1946, **29,** 721-28. Also Terman, L. M., and Tyler, L. E. Psychological sex differences. In Carmichael, L., ed. *Manual of child psychology,* 2nd ed. New York: Wiley, 1954.

5. Lipsitt, L. P., and Levy, N. Pain threshold in the human neonate. *Child Development,* 1959, **30,** 547-54.

6. Bridger, W. N. Sensory habituation and discrimination in the human neonate. *American Journal of Psychiatry,* 1961, **117,** 991-96.

7. Kagan, J. *Change and continuity in infancy.* New York: Wiley, 1971.

8. Kagan, J. Personality development. In Janis, I. L., ed. *Personality: dynamics, development, and assessment.* New York: Harcourt Brace Jovanovich, 1969.

9. Adapted from Thomas, A., Chess, S., and Birch, H. G. The origin of personality. *Scientific American,* **223,** pages 106-107, bottom of. August, 1970 issue.

10. Adapted from *Morris' Human Anatomy,* 12th ed., edited by Barry J. Anson. Copyright © 1966 by McGraw-Hill, Inc. By permission of McGraw-Hill Book Co.

11. Shirley, M. M. *The first two years, vol. II.* University of Minnesota Press, Minneapolis, © 1933, 1961 University of Minnesota.

12. White, B. L., Castle, P., and Held, R. Observations on the development of visually directed reaching. *Child Development,* 1964, **35,** 349-64.

13. Halverson, H. M. An experimental study of prehension in infants by means of systematic cinema records. *Genetic Psychology Monographs,* 1931, **10,** 107-286.

14. McGraw, M. B. *The neuromuscular maturation of the human infant.* New York: Columbia University Press, 1943.

15. See, for example, Kohen-Raz, R. Mental and motor development of kibbutz, institutionalized, and home-reared infants in Israel. *Child Development,* 1968, **39,** 489-507. Also Paraskevopoulos, J., and Hunt, J. M. Object construction and imitation under differing conditions of rearing. Unpublished manuscript, University of Illinois, January, 1971.

16. Fantz, R. L. The origin of form perception. *Scientific American,* 1961, **204,** 66-72. Copyright © 1961 by Scientific American, Inc. All rights reserved.

17. Gibson, E. J. The development of perception as an adaptive process. *American Scientist,* 1970, **58,** 98-107.

18. See, for example, Gerwitz, J. L. The cause of infant smiling in four child-rearing environments in Israel. In Foss, B. M., ed. *Determinants of infant behavior.* Vol. III. London: Methuen, 1965, pp. 205-60.

19. Gibson, E. J. *Principles of perceptual learning and development.* New York: Appleton-Century-Crofts, 1969.

20. Zinchenko, V. P., van Chzhi-Tsin, and Tarakonov, V. V. The formation and development of perceptual activity. *Soviet Psychology and Psychiatry,* 1963, **2,** 3-12. By permission of International Arts and Sciences Press, Inc. White Plains, New York.

21. Lenneberg, E. H. *Biological foundations of language.* New York: Wiley, 1967.

22. Kagan, J. Unpublished data.

23. Smith, M. E. An investigation of the development of the sentence and the extent of vocabulary in young children. *University of Iowa Studies in Child Welfare,* 1926, 3(5).

24. Templin, Mildred C. *Certain language skills in children,* University of Minnesota Press, Minneapolis, © 1957 University of Minnesota.

25. McCarthy, D. The language development of the preschool child. *Child Welfare Monographs,* Minneapolis: University of Minnesota Press, 1930 (Series No. 4). Copyright 1930 by the University of Minnesota.

26. Davis, E. A. Mean sentence length compared with long and short sentences as a reliable measure of language development. *Child Development,* 1937, **8**, 69–79. By permission of the Society for Research in Child Development, Inc.

27. Brodbeck, A. J., and Irwin, O. C. The speech behavior of children without families. *Child Development,* 1946, **17**, 145–56. By permission of the Society for Research in Child Development, Inc.

28. Irwin, O. C. Infant speech. *Journal of Speech and Hearing Disorders,* 1948, **13**, 224–25 and 320–26.

29. Neimark, E., Slotnick, N. S., and Ulrich, T. The development of memorization strategies. *Developmental Psychology,* 1971, **5**, 427–32.

30. See, for example, Neimark, E., and Lewis, N. Development of logical problem solving: a one-year retest. *Child Development,* 1968, **39**, 527–36.

31. See, for example, Leskow, S., and Smock, C. D. Developmental changes in problem solving strategies: permutation. *Developmental Psychology,* 1970, **2**, 412–22.

32. Piaget, J. *The origins of intelligence in children.* New York: International Universities Press, 1952.

33. Stevenson, H. W., and Bitterman, M. E. The distance effect in the transposition of intermediate size by children. *American Journal of Psychology,* 1955, **68**, 274–79.

34. Goodnow, J. J., and Bethon, G. Piaget's tasks: the effects of schooling and intelligence. *Child Development,* 1966, **37**, 573–82.

35. Brown, R. W. *Social psychology.* New York: Free Press, 1965.

36. Harlow, H. F. The development of affectional patterns in infant monkeys. In Foss, B. M., ed. *Determinants of infant behaviour.* London: Methuen, 1961, pp. 75–97.

37. Southwick, C. H., Beg, M. A., and Siddiqi, M. R. Rhesus monkeys in North India. In De Vore, I., ed. *Primate behavior: field studies of monkeys and apes.* New York: Holt, Rinehart and Winston, 1965, pp. 111–59.

38. Ainsworth, M. D. S., and Bell, S. M. Attachment, exploration, and separation: illustrated by the behavior of one-year-olds in a strange situation. *Child Development,* 1970, **41**, 49–68.

39. Hamburg, D. A. Evolution of emotional responses: evidence from recent research on non-human primates. In Masserman, J., ed. *Science and psychoanalysis.* Vol. 12. New York: Grune & Stratton, 1968, pp. 39–52.

40. Littenberg, R., Tulkin, S., and Kagan, J. Cognitive components of separation anxiety. *Developmental Psychology,* 1971, **4**, 387–88.

41. Harlow, H. F., and Harlow, M. K. Learning to love. *American Scientist,* 1966, **54**, 244–72.

42. Spitz, R. A. Hospitalism: a follow-up report. In Eissler, R. S., et al., eds. *Psychoanalytic study of the child.* Vol. II. New York: International Universities Press, 1946.

43. Goldfarb, W. Effects of early institutional care on adolescent personality: Rorschach data. *American Journal of Orthopsychiatry,* 1944, **14**, 441–47.

44. Bowlby, J. Childhood mourning and its implications for psychiatry. Adapted from the *American Journal of Psychiatry,* Vol. 118, pp. 481–98, 1961. Copyright 1961, the American Psychiatric Association.

45. D'Andrade, R. G. Sex differences and cultural institutions. In Maccoby, E. E., ed. *The development of sex differences.* Stanford, Calif.: Stanford University Press, 1966.

46. Brown, D. G. Sex-role preference in young children. *Psychological Monographs,* 1956, **70**(No. 421), 1–19. Also Fauls, L., and Smith, W. D. Sex-role learning of five-year-olds. *Journal of Genetic Psychology,* 1956, **89**, 105–17. Also Hartup, W. W., and Zook, E. Sex role preferences in three- and four-year-old children. *Journal of Consulting Psychology,* 1960, **24**, 420–26.

47. Bronfenbrenner, U. Reaction to social pressure from adults versus peers among Soviet day school and boarding school pupils in the perspective of an American sample. *Journal of Personality and Social Psychology,* 1970, **15**, 179–89.

48. Kagan, J., and Moss, H. A. *Birth to maturity.* New York: Wiley, 1962.

chapter sixteen

1. Lefkowitz, M., Blake, R. R., and Mouton, J. S. Status factors in pedestrian violation of traffic signals. *Journal of Abnormal and Social Psychology,* 1955, **51**, 704–06.

2. Freedman, J. L., Carlsmith, J. M., and Sears, D. O. *Social psychology.* Englewood Cliffs, N.J.: Prentice-Hall, 1970.

3. Secord, P. F., and Backman, C. W. *Social psychology.* New York: McGraw-Hill, 1964.

4. Benedict, R. *Patterns of culture,* 2nd ed. Boston: Houghton Mifflin, 1959.

5. Whiting, J. W. M., and Whiting, B. B. Children of six cultures: egoism and altruism. Unpublished study.

6. Mead, M. *Sex and temperament.* New York: Morrow, 1935.

7. McGrath, J. W. *Social psychology: a brief introduction.* New York: Holt, Rinehart and Winston, 1964.

8. Labov, W. The logic of nonstandard English. In Williams, F., ed. *Language and poverty.* Chicago: Markham, 1970, pp. 153–89.

9. Adaptation and abridgment of Table XII: 1, p. 426, *Patterns of child rearing* by Robert R. Sears, Eleanor E. Maccoby, Harry Levin. Copyright © 1957 by Harper & Row, Publishers, Inc. Used by permission of the publishers.

10. Rosen, B. C. The achievement syndrome: a psychocultural dimension of social stratification. *American Sociological Review,* 1956, **21**, 203–11. By permission of the American Sociological Association.

11. Lane, R. E. *Political life.* New York: Free Press, 1959.

12. Kinsey, A. C., Pomeroy, W. B., and Martin, C. E. *Sexual behavior in the human male.* Philadelphia: Saunders, 1948.

13. Krech, D., Crutchfield, R. S., and Ballachey, E. L. *Individual in society: a textbook of social psychology.* New York: McGraw-Hill, 1962.

14. Hollingshead, A. B., and Redlich, F. C. *Social class and mental illness.* New York: Wiley, 1958.

15. Abravanel, E. A. A psychological analysis of the concept of role. Unpublished master's thesis, Swarthmore College, 1962.

16. Waller, W., and Hill, R. *The family.* New York: Holt, Rinehart and Winston, 1951.

17. Benedict, R. Continuities and discontinuities in cultural conditioning. *Psychiatry,* 1938, **1**, 161–67.

18. Adapted with permission of the Macmillan Company from *Social psychology* by Roger Brown. Copyright © The Free Press, a Division of the Macmillan Company, 1965.

19. Newcomb, T. M. *The acquaintance process.* New York: Holt, Rinehart and Winston, 1961.

20. Byrne, D. Attitudes and attraction. In Berkowitz, L., ed. *Advances in experimental social psychology.* Vol. IV. New York: Academic Press, 1969.

21. Fiedler, F. E., Warrington, W. G., and Blaisdell, F. J. Unconscious attitudes as correlates of sociometric choice in a social group. *Journal of Abnormal and Social Psychology,* 1952, **47**, 790-96.

22. Preston, M. G., et al. Impressions of personality as a function of marital conflict. *Journal of Abnormal and Social Psychology,* 1952, **47**, 326-36.

23. Gergen, K. J., and Wishnow, B. Others' self-evaluations and interaction anticipation as determinants of self-presentation. *Journal of Personality and Social Psychology,* 1965, **2**, 348-58.

24. Freedman, J. L., Carlsmith, J. M., and Suomi, S. Unpublished study, 1967, cited in Freedman, J. L., Carlsmith, J. M., and Sears, D. O. *Social psychology.* Englewood Cliffs, N.J.: Prentice-Hall, 1970, p. 72.

25. Zajonc, R. B. Attitudinal effects of mere exposure. *Journal of Personality and Social Psychology,* 1968, **8**, 18.

26. Darley, J. M., and Berscheid, E. Increased liking caused by anticipation of social contact. *Human Relations,* 1967, **20**, 29-40.

27. See, for example, Festinger, L., Schachter, S., and Back, K. *Social pressures in informal groups: a study of human factors in housing.* New York: Harper & Row, 1950. Also Whyte, W. H., Jr. *The organization man.* New York: Simon & Schuster, 1956.

28. Freedman, J. L., and Suomi, S. Unpublished study, 1967, cited in Freedman, J. L., Carlsmith, J. M., and Sears, D. O. *Social psychology.* Englewood Cliffs, N.J.: Prentice-Hall, 1970, pp. 72-73.

29. Jones, E. E., et al. Pattern performance and ability attribution: an unexpected primacy effect. *Journal of Personality and Social Psychology,* 1968, **10**, 317-41.

30. Kelley, H. H. The warm-cold variable in the first impressions of persons. *Journal of Personality,* 1950, **18**, 431-39.

31. Doob, A. N., and Gross, A. E. Status of frustrator as an inhibitor of horn-honking responses. *Journal of Social Psychology,* 1968, **76**, 213-18.

32. Wilson, P. R. Perceptual distortion of height as a function of ascribed academic status. *Journal of Social Psychology,* 1968, **74**, 97-102.

33. See, for example, Tagiuri, R. Social preference and its perception. In Tagiuri, R., and Petrullo, L., eds. *Person perception and interpersonal behavior.* Stanford, Calif.: Stanford University Press, 1958, pp. 316-36.

34. See, for example, Sherif, M., et al. *Experimental study of positive and negative intergroup attitudes between experimentally produced groups.* Robbers Cave Study. Norman: University of Oklahoma, 1954. (Multilithed)

35. See, for example, Worchel, P. Self-enhancement and interpersonal attraction. Paper read at American Psychological Association, New York, August, 1961. Also Deutsch, M., and Solomon, L. Reactions to evaluations by others as influenced by self evaluations. *Sociometry,* 1959, **22**, 93-112.

36. Aronson, E., and Linder, D. Gain and loss of esteem as determinants of interpersonal attractiveness. *Journal of Experimental Social Psychology,* 1965, **1**, 156-71.

37. Hirschberg, G., and Gilliland, A. R. Parent-child relationships in attitudes. *Journal of Abnormal and Social Psychology,* 1942, **37**, 125-30.

38. Jennings, M. K., and Niemi, R. G. The transmission of political values from parent to child. *American Political Science Review,* 1968, **62**, 169-84.

39. Horowitz, E. L., and Horowitz, R. E. Development of social attitudes in children. *Sociometry,* 1938, **1**, 301-38.

40. Goldsen, R. K., et al. *What college students think.* Princeton, N.J.: Van Nostrand, 1960.

41. Newcomb, T. M. Persistence and regression of changed attitudes: long range studies. *Journal of Social Issues,* 1963, **19**, 3-14.

42. Karlins, M., Coffman, T. L., and Walters, G. On the fading of social stereotypes: studies in three generations of college students. *Journal of Personality and Social Psychology,* 1969, **13**, 1-16.

43. Hochreich, D. J., and Rotter, J. B. Have college students become less trusting? *Journal of Personality and Social Psychology,* 1970, **15**, 211-14.

44. Clark, K. B., and Clark, M. K. Racial identification and preference in Negro children. In Newcomb, T., and Hartley, E., eds. *Readings in social psychology.* New York: Holt, 1947.

45. Hraba, J., and Grant, G. Black is beautiful: a reexamination of racial preference and identification. *Journal of Personality and Social Psychology,* 1970, **16**, 398-402.

46. Pettigrew, T. F. Racially separate or together? *Journal of Social Issues,* 1969, **25**, 43-69.

47. Lieberman, S. The effects of changes in roles on the attitudes of role occupants. *Human Relations,* 1956, **9**, 385-402.

48. Kelman, H. C. Processes of opinion change. *Public Opinion Quarterly,* 1961, **25**, 57-78.

49. Mann, L., and Janis, I. L. A follow-up study on the long-term effects of emotional role playing. *Journal of Personality and Social Psychology,* 1968, **8**, 339-42.

50. Hovland, C. I. Reconciling conflicting results derived from experimental and survey studies of attitude change. *American Psychologist,* 1959, **14**, 8-17.

51. Festinger, L. *A theory of cognitive dissonance.* Stanford, Calif.: Stanford University Press, 1957.

52. Ehrlich, D., et al. Post-decision exposure to relevant information. *Journal of Abnormal and Social Psychology,* 1957, **54**, 98-102.

53. See, for example, Freedman, J. L. Preference for dissonance information. *Journal of Personality and Social Psychology,* 1965, **2**, 287-89.

54. Benham, T. W. Polling for a presidential candidate: some observations of the 1964 campaign. *Public Opinion Quarterly,* 1965, **29**, 185-99.

55. See, for example, Bem, D. J. *Beliefs, attitudes, and human affairs.* Belmont, Calif.: Brooks/Cole, 1970.

56. Hovland, C. I., and Weiss, W. The influence of source credibility on communication effectiveness. *Public Opinion Quarterly,* 1951, **15**, 635-50.

57. Hovland, C. I., Lumsdaine, A. A., and Sheffield, F. C. *Experiments on mass communication.* Princeton, N.J.: Princeton University Press, 1949.

58. Weiss, W., and Fine, B. J. The effect of induced aggressiveness on opinion change. In Maccoby, E. E., Newcomb, T. M., and Hartley, E. L., eds. *Readings in social psychology,* 3rd ed. New York: Holt, Rinehart and Winston, 1958, pp. 149-55.

59. Janis, I. L., and Feshbach, S. Effects of fear-arousing communications. *Journal of Abnormal and Social Psychology,* 1953, **48**, 78-92.

60. Hovland, C. I., and Janis, I. L., eds. *Personality and*

persuasibility. New Haven, Conn.: Yale University Press, 1959.

61. Cohen, A. R. Some implications of self-esteem for social influence. In Hovland, C. I., and Janis, I. L., eds. *Personality and persuasibility.* New Haven, Conn.: Yale University Press, 1959, pp. 102-20.

62. Sears, D. O. Social anxiety, opinion structure, and opinion change. *Journal of Personality and Social Psychology,* 1967, **7,** 142-51.

63. Levy, L. H., and House, W. C. Perceived origins of beliefs as determinants of expectancy for their change. *Journal of Personality and Social Psychology,* 1970, **14,** 329-34.

64. Stephan, F. F., and Mishler, E. G. The distribution of participation in small groups: an exponential approximation. *American Sociological Review,* 1952, **17,** 598-608.

65. After Leavitt, H. J. Some effects of certain communications patterns on group performance. *Journal of Abnormal and Social Psychology,* 1951, **46,** 38-50.

66. Bavelas, A., et al. Experiments on the alteration of group structure. *Journal of Experimental Social Psychology,* 1965, **1,** 55-70.

67. Bales, R. F. Task roles and social roles in problem-solving groups. In Maccoby, E. E., Newcomb, T. M., and Hartley, E. L., eds. *Readings in social psychology,* 3rd ed. New York: Holt, Rinehart and Winston, 1958, pp. 437-46.

68. See, for example, Carter, L. F., and Nixon, M. An investigation of the relationship between four criteria of leadership ability for three different tasks. *Journal of Psychology,* 1949, **27,** 245-61.

69. Cottrell, N. B., Rittle, R. H., and Wack, D. L. Presence of an audience and list type (competitional or noncompetitional) as joint determinants of paired-associates learning. *Journal of Personality,* 1967, **35,** 217-26.

70. See, for example, Torrance, E. P. Some consequences of power differences on decision-making in permanent and temporary three-man groups. In Hare, A. P., Borgatta, E. F., and Bales, R. F., eds. *Small groups: studies in social interaction.* New York: Knopf, 1955.

71. Taylor, D. W., Berry, P. C., and Block, C. H. Does group participation when using brainstorming facilitate or inhibit creative thinking? *Administrative Science Quarterly,* 1958, **2,** 23-47.

72. Hoffman, L. R., and Maier, N. R. F. Quality and acceptance of problem solutions by members of homogeneous and heterogeneous groups. *Journal of Abnormal and Social Psychology,* 1961, **62,** 401-07.

73. See, for example, Husband, R. W. Cooperative versus solitary problem solution. *Journal of Social Psychology,* 1940, **11,** 405-09.

74. Kogan, N., and Wallach, M. A. Risk taking as a function of the situation, the person, and the group. In Mandler, G., ed. *New directions in psychology.* No. 3. New York: Holt, Rinehart and Winston, 1967.

75. Wallach, M. A., Kogan, N., and Burt, R. B. Can group members recognize the effects of group discussion upon risk taking? *Journal of Experimental Social Psychology,* 1965, **1,** 379-95.

76. Asch, S. E. Studies of independence and submission to group pressure. I. A minority of one against a unanimous majority. *Psychological Monographs,* 1956, **70**(No. 416), Fig. 2, p. 7. Also Asch, S. E. Opinions and social pressure. *Scientific American,* 1955, **193,** 32. Copyright © 1955 by Scientific American, Inc. All rights reserved.

77. Milgram, S. Group pressure and action against a person.

Journal of Abnormal and Social Psychology, 1964, **69,** 137-43.

78. Milgram, S. Behavioral study of obedience. *Journal of Abnormal and Social Psychology,* 1963, **67,** 371-78.

79. Malof, M., and Lott, A. J. Ethnocentrism and the acceptance of Negro support in a group pressure situation. *Journal of Abnormal and Social Psychology,* 1962, **65,** 254-58.

80. Gerard, H. B., Wilhelmy, R. A., and Connolley, E. S. Conformity and group size. *Journal of Personality and Social Psychology,* 1968, **8,** 79-82.

81. Milgram, S., Bickman, L., and Berkowitz, L. Note on the drawing power of crowds of different size. *Journal of Personality and Social Psychology,* 1969, **13,** 79-82.

82. Sistrunk, F., and McDavid, J. W. Sex variable in conforming behavior. *Journal of Personality and Social Psychology,* 1971, **17,** 200-07.

83. Coleman, J. F., Blake, R. R., and Mouton, J. S. Task difficulty and conformity pressures. *Journal of Abnormal and Social Psychology,* 1958, **57,** 120-22.

84. Adorno, T. W., et al. *The authoritarian personality.* New York: Harper & Row, 1950.

picture credits

UPI   1-1A, 1-1B, 1-1F, 2-1F, 2-7 (top right, bottom right), 8-11, 15-23
Bill Mark   1-1D
F. Roy Kemp, FPG   1-1E
Lynn McLaren, Rapho Guillumette   1-2, 1-2a
Harbrace   1-3, 4-6, 5-10, 5-11, 5-12, 6-1, Plate III, 7-16, 13-1, 13-3, 13-4, p. 549
Bob Combs, Rapho Guillumette   p. 14 (top)
Ted Davies   p. 14 (second from top, bottom)
Shelly Rusten   p. 14 (second from bottom), p. 198 (top)
The Bettmann Archive   p. 15 (top), p. 20 (left), p. 52 (left), p. 86 (left), p. 401, p. 408
Brown Brothers   p. 15 (bottom)
Marlis Müller   p. 16, p. 482, p. 541 (top)
Culver Pictures   p. 17, 12-2 (center)
Historical Picture Service   p. 18
The New York Times   p. 19 (top)
Yves deBraine, Black Star   p. 19 (bottom)
Marcia Roltner   p. 20 (top right)
David Linton, courtesy New York University   1-5
Institute for Sex Research, Indiana University, photo by Dellenback p. 27
Maxwell Coplan, dpi   p. 29
Charles Gatewood   p. 30, p. 34 (bottom)
Ira Mandelbaum, Scope Associates   p. 31
Courtesy of Aetna Life & Casualty   1-6
Michael Dobo, College Newsphoto Alliance   p. 34 (top)
Dr. John Darley   1-10
Morris H. Jaffe   p. 47, p. 68, p. 322
U.S. Navy   2-1A
American Museum of Natural History   2-1B
Leonard Lee Rue II from National Audubon Society   2-1C
Information Canada   2-1D
Sabena   2-1E
Will Rapport, Harvard University   2-5
Courtesy of Dr. H. S. Terrace   2-6
Lou Merrim, Monkmeyer Press Photo Service   2-7 (left)
Godsey, Monkmeyer Press Photo Service   2-7 (right center)
Courtesy of Dr. Neal E. Miller   2-10
Dan Bernstein   2-11
Ylla, Rapho Guillumette   p. 66
Courtesy of Dr. Albert Bandura   2-12, 12-4
Yerkes Regional Primate Research Center of Emory University   2-13, 5-6
Wil Blanche, dpi   p. 76 (left)

James Thurber p. 85
Annan Photo Features p. 87 (left)
Lester V. Bergman—Associates, Inc. p. 91 (left)
Drawing by Frolik—Punch, Ben Roth Agency p. 93 (top)
Berenice Abbott p. 93 (bottom)
Courtesy of Dr. R. N. Haber and Dr. M. H. Erdelyi 3-8
James Smith, Photo Trends p. 98
Syd Greenberg, dpi p. 100
David Margolin, Black Star p. 119, 16-1 (top)
Elihu Blotnick, BBM p. 125, p. 221
Roger Malloch, Magnum p. 129 (top)
Eugene Luttenberg, College Newsphoto Alliance p. 129 (bottom)
College Newsphoto Alliance p. 130
Lee Hebner 4-11
Courtesy of Dr. Harry F. Harlow 4-19
Hella Hamid, Rapho Guillumette p. 150 (top)
Manning Studios for Republic Steel p. 150 (center)
Ken Heyman p. 155 (left)
Drs. R. A. Gardner and B. T. Gardner 5-1
Dr. Nicholas Pastore, Queens College, City University of New York 5-2
German Information Center p. 170
Three Lions, Inc. 5-5
Christopher Johnson p. 184 (left), p. 209
Detail of "The Enraged Musician" by William Hogarth p. 193
Victoria Beller p. 198 (bottom)
Photo by Dr. James Maas, Cornell University 6-2, 6-3, 6-11
Owen, Black Star p. 200 (left)
Francis Laping, dpi p. 202 (left)
Gordon Smith, National Audubon Society p. 203
Hewlett-Packard 6-6
Dr. Hugh Linebach 6-10
Courtesy of Dr. Jules H. Masserman, from *Principles of dynamic psychiatry,* 2nd ed. Philadelphia: W. B. Saunders, 1961 Plate I, 11-6
Courtesy of Munsell Color Company Plate II
Photo by Edith Reichmann Plate VI
Bibliothèque de Genève p. 214 (left)
Photo by A. L. Yarbus 6-16
Fred Lyon, Rapho Guillumette p. 222, p. 435, p. 440 (left)
Photo by Jürgen Graaf 7-3
Collection, The Museum of Modern Art, New York, Philip C. Johnson Fund. Emulsion on composition board, 58⅜″ x 58⅞″, 1964 7-4
Library of Congress 7-6
Photo by Marjorie Burren p. 240 (left)
Photo by Jim Theologus 7-14
Courtesy of Penn Central Transportation 7-19
United Nations Photo 7-21
William Vandivert. Prior publication in *Scientific American* 7-22, 16-13, 16-16
Ted Polumbaum 7-23
Detail of "Study: Falling Man" by Trova p. 265
Dr. J. H. Tjio 8-1
Dr. Lorne MacHattie 8-2
Bruce Gilden p. 268, 13-2, p. 557 (bottom), p. 558 (top)
Gilloon Photo Agency 8-6
Trustees of the British Museum p. 283
Arthur Leipzig 8-17
Courtesy of Dr. José M. R. Delgado 8-18

Dr. W. Ross Adey 8-20
National Library of Medicine p. 292
Horst Schafer, Photo Trends p. 303
Courtesy of Lafayette Instrument Co. 9-1
Dr. Eckhard H. Hess. Prior publication in *Scientific American* 9-2
Camera Clix, Inc. 9-3
Detail of "The Hypochondriac" by Thomas Rowlandson. Courtesy of Les Productions de Paris p. 319
Sigrid Owen, dpi p. 321
John Wollcott p. 335 (top)
John Knaggs, BBM p. 335 (bottom)
Janine Niepce, Rapho Guillumette p. 336
Bell Laboratories 10-3
Photos by Fred Sponholz, University of Wisconsin Primate Lab 10-5, 10-6, 15-20
Linda Moser, dpi p. 345
E. B. Henderson, dpi p. 349
Courtesy of the Virgin Islands Government Tourist Office p. 369
Harvey Barad p. 370
Courtesy of Dr. Michael Lewis, from Play behavior in the year-old infant: early sex differences. Paper presented at the Biennial Meeting of the Society for Research in Child Development, New York, March, 1967 11-4
Jerome Hirsch p. 381 (top)
Busino, reprinted from *Look Magazine* p. 384
Trustees of the Guttmann-Maclay Collection p. 396
Wide World Photos p. 409
Pinney, Monkmeyer Press Photo Service p. 413
New York Public Library 12-2 (left)
Museo del Prado 12-2 (right)
Paul Fusco 12-6
International Business Machine, Corp. 13-8
Harcourt Brace Jovanovich, Inc. Test Department p. 465, p. 477
Bernard Vidal, Editorial Photocolor Archives p. 466
Courtesy of The Psychological Corporation 14-2
Courtesy of Houghton-Mifflin Co. 14-3
Joe Consentino 14-16
Courtesy of Vocational Service Center, YMCA 14-17
From H. Prechtl and D. Beintema. *The neurological examination of the full term newborn infant.* Little Club Clinics in Developmental Medicine, No. 12. London: Spastics Society Medical Information Unit and J. B. Lippincott, 1964. By permission (pp. 400-401) 15-1, 15-2
Dr. Edwin Robbins 15-4
Courtesy of Dr. Burton L. White. From White, Burton L., Castle, Peter, and Held, Richard, Observations of the development of visually directed reaching. *Child Development,* 1964, 35, 349-364 (figures 2, 3, 4, and 6 on tip-in between pp. 352-353) 15-7
Ernest Havemann 15-9
Jerome Kagan 15-19, 15-21
Vivienne, dpi p. 535
Drawing by Siggs—Punch, Ben Roth Agency p. 538, p. 575
Marc & Evelyn Bernhiem, Rapho Guillumette p. 541 (bottom)
The Saturday Evening Post © 1949 The Curtis Publishing Co. p. 542
Bill Strode, Black Star 16-1 (bottom left)
Photo Trends 16-1 (bottom center)
Jan Lukas, Rapho Guillumette 16-1 (bottom right)
Berne Greene p. 557 (top)
Curtis Roseman p. 558 (center)